THE DYNAMICS OF POLITI COMMUNICATION

What impact do news and political advertising have on us? How do candidates use media to persuade us as voters? Are we informed adequately about political issues? Do 21st-century political communications measure up to democratic ideals? *The Dynamics of Political Communication: Media and Politics in a Digital Age, Second Edition* explores these issues and guides us through current political communication theories and beliefs by detailing the fluid landscape of political communication and offering us an engaging introduction to the field and a thorough tour of the discipline. Author Richard Perloff examines essential concepts in this arena, such as agenda-setting, agenda-building, framing, political socialization, and issues of bias that are part of campaign news. Designed to provide an understanding and appreciation of the principles involved in political communication along with methods of research and hypothesis testing, each chapter includes materials that challenge us by encouraging reflection on controversial matters.

Inside this second edition you'll find:

- Expanded discussion of conceptual problems, communication complexities, and key issues in the field.
- New examples, concepts, and studies reflecting current political communication scholarship.
- The integration of technology throughout the text, reflecting its pervasive role in the political spectrum.

Accompanied by an updated companion website with resources for students and instructors, *The Dynamics of Political Communication* prepares you to survey the political landscape with a more critical eye, and encourages a greater understanding of the challenges and occurrences presented in this constantly evolving field.

Richard M. Perloff, Professor of Communication, Political Science, and Psychology at Cleveland State University, has a very successful persuasion textbook with Routledge, now in its sixth edition (2017), as well as an earlier scholarly text on political communication (1998). He is well-known for his scholarship on the third-person effect and theoretical integrations of media influences. A Fellow of the Midwest Association of Public Opinion Research, Perloff has been on the faculty at Cleveland State University since 1979 and served as director of the School of Communication from 2004–2011. Taking scholarship to the public arena, he has had many letters to the editor in *The New York Times* and op-ed columns for *The Cleveland Plain Dealer*. He is an inveterate follower of political communication, reading the news each day in a coffee shop following a morning swim.

THE DYNAMICS OF POLITICAL COMMUNICATION

Media and Politics in a Digital Age

Second Edition

Richard M. Perloff

Routledge
Taylor & Francis Group

NEW YORK AND LONDON

Second edition published 2018
by Routledge
711 Third Avenue, New York, NY 10017

and by Routledge
2 Park Square, Milton Park, Abingdon, Oxon OX14 4RN

Routledge is an imprint of the Taylor & Francis Group, an informa business

First edition published by Routledge 2013

Library of Congress Cataloging-in-Publication Data
Names: Perloff, Richard M., author.
Title: The dynamics of political communication : media and politics in a
     digital age / Richard M. Perloff.
Description: Second edition. | New York : Routledge, 2017.
Identifiers: LCCN 2017024427 | ISBN 9781138651647 (hardback) |
     ISBN 9781138651654 (pbk.)
Subjects: LCSH: Communication in politics—United States. | Mass
     media—Political aspects. | Digital media—Political aspects. | Political
     campaigns—United States. | United States—Politics and government.
Classification: LCC JA85.2.U6 P467 2017 | DDC 320.01/4—dc23
LC record available at https://lccn.loc.gov/2017024427

ISBN: 978-1-138-65164-7 (hbk)
ISBN: 978-1-138-65165-4 (pbk)
ISBN: 978-1-315-62442-6 (ebk)

Typeset in Times New Roman
by Apex CoVantage, LLC

Visit the companion website: www.routledge.com/cw/9781138651654

Contents

Acknowledgments

I want to first thank Routledge's conscientious staff who have provided me with support and reinforcing comments as I worked on this second edition. Thanks to Nicole Solano, Routledge's communication publisher, for the warm, gracious support. She has made me feel appreciated, in the tradition of long-time publisher Linda Bathgate. Thanks also to Kristina Ryan, editorial assistant at Routledge, for being on top of details and her reinforcing messages. Thanks are also due to Autumn Spalding for her painstaking and ever-so-patient work on copyediting.

I also appreciate the willingness of my colleagues in the field to indulge me as I sent them sections of this book. Thank you for the excellent scholarship you contribute to the field. I appreciate the comments of Kevin Coe, Michael X. Delli Carpini, James N. Druckman, Frank Esser, Lauren Feldman, David Greenberg, Douglas B. Hindman, Bruce Hardy, Kathleen Jamieson, Kate Kenski, Hoon Lee, Mitchell S. McKinney, Douglas M. McLeod, Matthew C. Nisbet, Pippa Norris, Raymond J. Pingree, Dvahan V. Shah, Jesper Strömbäck, Jennifer Stromer-Galley, Talia Stroud, Emily K. Vraga, and Dannagal Young. Thanks in particular to Bruce I. Newman, William L. Benoit, and Weiwu Zhang for their reinforcing, helpful comments.

Thanks again to Sharon Muskin for her professionalism and beyond-the-call-of-duty conscientiousness in her work on the aesthetics and production of this book, even in the final stages when she was abroad, two continents from home. This book could not have been completed without her painstaking dedication.

Thanks also to Rashelle Baker of the School of Communication for her balanced perspective and engaging sense of humor, always welcome. In addition, I want to thank the students of my political communication classes at Cleveland State—the students too many to mention, but all memorable—for your inspiration, fondness for the material, and compassion for the problems that afflict America.

On a more personal level, I appreciate the inspiration and broad perspectives taught me by my late father, Robert Perloff, who loved politics and would have loved talking about Donald Trump's style and foibles. We miss the chortles that would have accompanied my dad's following the 2016 campaign. Thanks to my mother, Evelyn Perloff, for serving as a role model for what I do, with her working, working, working motif and loving support. Thanks are also due to my in-laws, Selma and Gerald Krevans, for their incisive comments about politics and their New York flair that gives them a particularly canny and witty approach to the political world.

And thank you Michael, for combining wit and wisdom in our many conversations about the political inequities you are on track to redress, Cathy for your indomitable spirit in your prodigious political journalism, and Julie for continued, kind support during the long hours over weeks, months, and a couple of years when this book was written, rewritten, and, in the interlude between contentious elections, finally completed.

Richard M. Perloff
Cleveland

Preface

Americans have many views about politics, some thoughtful, others goony, still others reflecting the divisions that characterize an increasingly fragmented country. They have plenty to say about politics and the media, much of it unfavorable. Opinions are the oxygen of democracy, so that's fine. The problem is getting past our opinions and grasping the larger context in which political communication occurs. During a time when citizens are increasingly distrustful of democratic institutions, dissatisfied with their leaders, and communicating about politics in increasingly visceral ways on social media, it is important that people have a broader appreciation of the democratic foundations of our society and, in particular, a more thoughtful, penetrating understanding of the media and politics, which influence so many aspects of contemporary life.

This book, guided by theory and research, addresses these and a wealth of other issues, providing an introduction to the cross-disciplinary field of political communication. Politics and political communication are nothing if not controversial, as even a momentary recollection of the searing 2016 presidential campaign illustrates. This book navigates the shoals of controversy, invoking theory, research, and normative concepts to illuminate our vibrant, but flawed, political communication system.

The text is designed to introduce students to the main concepts in the field, the focus and distinctive contributions of political communication, crisscrossing issues of political communication processes and effects, and normative perspectives that offer guidance. One must draw limits in discussing political communication. This book is about politics and media in America, with a focus on the presidential election. However, it calls on research from scholars across the world, as well as philosophical concepts that cut across borders.

In writing the book, I tried to keep it current, interesting to read, and lively; at the same time, the emphasis is singularly academic, with a focus on appreciating intricacies of political media processes and effects, core theories, research findings, methodological caveats, and the complex, sometimes distressing conundrums of political media in an increasingly fractious media age. A theme is Pascal's observation that people do not show their "greatness by being at one extremity, but rather by touching both at once." Thus, I take pains to present a panoply of political, theoretical, and philosophical perspectives, while staying grounded in democratic norms of justice, accountability, and civic, deliberative public discourse. I want to debunk common myths, lay out the complex foundations of political communication, illuminate what we know, and call on the nation's historical past to clarify how political media of today depart from, and draw on, the media of decades and centuries past.

The second edition of *The Dynamics of Political Communication* builds on the first, but is, in many ways, a different book, with new concepts, more research, and an intellectual sophistication befitting our scholarly field. The second edition is characterized by these additions and changes:

- Chapter 1, updated with a lively introductory retrospective on the 2016 presidential election, includes an expanded discussion of definitions of political communication, with more discussion of mediatization, enhanced discussion of social media, and an overview of comparative political communication.
- Chapter 2 provides a more comprehensive examination of democracy, deliberative democracy, and corrosive effects of polarization.
- Chapter 3 continues the introduction to the field of political communication, with updates, especially a new section on the zeitgeist of contemporary political communication scholarship.
- Chapters 4 and 5, focusing on political knowledge and socialization, contain an up-to-date review of the strengths and shortcomings of online news effects on citizenship, along with new sections on hyperreality and cultivation.
- Chapter 6 covers both agenda-setting and agenda-building, with a fresh example inaugurating the chapter and new research on online media agenda-building effects prominently discussed.
- Chapter 7 offers greater discussion of conceptual foundations of framing theory. It replaces the hegemonic and indexing sections with a discussion, more appropriate to political communication, of the political psychology of the recent election: Donald Trump's populist framing, why it was effective, and the different underpinnings (economic, cultural, prejudice-based) of his electoral support. The chapter also discusses Hillary Clinton's framing, thus putting the 2016 election in a larger context that transcends a particular election.
- Chapter 8 is devoted to presidential election campaigns past and present. It contains new sections on the history of presidential persuasion, spin, and political marketing. The chapter provides embellished discussion of social media's role in the

presidential campaign, eschewing a "rah-rah" approach and evaluating its functions and dysfunctions.

- Chapter 9, with its focus on political news bias, provides a thorough overview of the contemporary news environment, complete with a discussion of ideological websites, Facebook, fake news, White House denunciation of the press, and flagrant examples of political gender bias, along with journalistic complexities. A new chapter, Chapter 10, is devoted exclusively to press coverage of the presidential election, permitting more discussion of classic storylines, polling (including 2016 polling controversies), and the time-honored lack of coverage of policy issues. Chapter 11, now focusing on the broader nomination campaign in a more cohesive fashion, examines the outsized effects polls had in cable network debates that exerted an unprecedented winnowing effect on the presidential nominations.

- A final section, focused on political persuasion, begins with Chapter 12, which includes a description of macro political science voting models and a much-expanded discussion of selective perception and selective exposure. Beginning with a telling anecdote about psychological selectivity, the section provides an in-depth research-based examination of selective exposure to congenial information in a digital age, looking at supportive research, exceptions to the selectivity rule, and normative implications. A new section follows, examining an important aspect of political persuasion: the content and effects of presidential language. The section profiles Ronald Reagan's rhetoric, discusses presidential language effects on policymaking, and examines presidential language in an age of 140 online characters, for good and for ill.

- Chapter 13 on political advertising, updated with new research and 2016 applications, now includes a discussion of Citizens United and campaign finance, looking at the controversial Supreme Court decision from both liberal and conservative perspectives. Chapter 14 on presidential debates includes content analytic research, consideration of primary election debates, new critical perspectives on classic debates—Kennedy-Nixon and Ford-Carter, and normative implications.

- There is full discussion of the 2016 election—populism, why Trump won, his incendiary frames, Clinton's popular vote victory, the email controversy, and voter anger—but examined through the frameworks of political communication scholarship. Agenda-setting, framing, news storylines, and political advertising are harnessed, conceptually and with a focus on new research, to explain the election, while also placing it in a larger context.

The book is reorganized, with less focus on determinants of non-political news (formerly in Chapter 10) and transfer of material on polling and campaign finance from an omnibus chapter (formerly Chapter 12) to appropriate chapters on these topics in the book. The organization, I think, is more cohesive, with a strong focus on distressing problems, conflicting, paradoxical aspects of political communication, and the need to appreciate contradictions and different ways of viewing political media in America. The chapter conclusions provide integrative summaries focused on these issues.

There are four parts of the book. The first part consists of a broad introductory chapter, with explication of basic definitions, and a philosophically focused second chapter. The second part encompasses Chapters 3–7, and moves from the field of political communication through citizenship and core theories. The third part, Chapters 8 through 11, focuses on communication in the presidential election, taking readers on a historical tour, examining political news bias, polls, storylines, and the nomination process. The fourth part, Chapters 12–14, examines political persuasion, with an examination of persuasion effects, political advertising, and presidential debates. A postscript takes stock of the 2016 election, evaluating it through normative lenses. The postscript describes challenges of democracy in a no-holds-barred online media age and closes on a cautiously optimistic, but sobering, note.

The overall result is a better structured, more scholarly text that, I hope, continues to offer multiple perspectives on political communication in ways readers can appreciate, enjoy, contest, and contemplate.

PART ONE

Foundations

1 Introduction to Political Communication

PROLOGUE

Before the Justice Department appointed a special counsel to investigate connections between President Donald Trump's 2016 presidential campaign and Russian officials, before Trump tried to persuade the FBI director to shut down an investigation of a former national security adviser, and before he fired the FBI director on suspicious grounds, there was unabashed jubilation among his supporters about his ascendance to the presidency. As Trump swiftly sought to dismantle Barack Obama's long-standing policies on the environment, health care, and immigration with his typical bravado and braggadocio, his base felt vindicated, thrilled that change they thought would be muzzled by the Establishment class would finally occur. Yet his unconventional, untrammeled leadership style and statements seemed to repudiate long-standing American values, terrifying his opponents and confirming the worst of their fears about the mercurial president. As the White House was besieged with rumors, accusations, and distractions from its promised policy agenda during the spring of 2017, leading Republicans expressed concerns about Trump's volatile leadership style, typified by his emotive, rapid-fire tweets.

Trump's strategic use of social media during the 2016 campaign rewrote political communication history, with the most unfathomable aspect his stunning Electoral College victory early in the morning of November 9, 2016. No one saw it coming, except maybe his wife, Melania, who confided long before the election, with utter confidence in her prophetic ability, "If you run, you'll win." The pundits, pollsters, even a leader on Donald Trump's staff, who on the night of the election, told a CNN reporter that it would take a miracle for Trump to win, were dubious until the end. A wildly successful, flamboyant billionaire businessman, big-city real estate magnate and reality television star, who during the campaign could speak harshly of other Americans (yet always had the back of White working class voters), lost the popular vote, but won a convincing Electoral College electoral victory on November 8, 2016, becoming the nation's 45th president.

It was an election of firsts: the first woman nominated for the presidency by one of the two major political parties; the first person in American political history to capture the presidency without having served in public office or as a general in the U.S. military; and the first time, in an acerbically negative campaign, that so many adrenalized Twitter posts reached so many citizens.

Politics is full of unexpected events, and 2016 was a freight train carrying combustible containers of ideological fury and frustration, long simmering, that turned politically consequential during the nomination and general election campaigns. It was also a bizarre campaign, characterized by Trump's insults, charges of sexual assault, an FBI investigation of Hillary Clinton, her bitter denunciations of the Republican standard-bearer, a parade of mini-scandals, evidence of Russian meddling in the election, dizzying falsehoods and untruths surrounding the diffusion of fake news—a political funhouse of mirrors "characterized by an erosion of surety, bizarre and inscrutable subplots worthy of an airport bookstore spy thriller" (Fausset, 2017, p. A10). Trump's campaign circumvented the political elites who dominated the nomination and brought to the fore issues like free trade that had been neglected for years. The campaign also stirred the political cauldron of young people, enchanted by Bernie Sanders, the 74-year-old grandfatherly (gruff, but fiery) populist, who challenged Hillary Clinton from the political left, and inspired thousands of supporters across the nation (see Figure 1.1). His adherents demonstrated their enthusiasm for Sanders at large rallies and in social media donations that averaged $27, as Sanders repeatedly emphasized in an effort to highlight the grassroots nature of his liberal support.

Although Clinton's workaday campaign paled in excitement when compared to Sanders's crusade, it was significant in producing the Democratic Party's first nomination of a female presidential candidate, who announced her candidacy in April 2015 with a 2-minute video that described the heartfelt stories of diverse Americans and ended with her declaration that "everyday Americans need a champion. And I want to be that champion." A campaign that began with the resolve to extend her success in 2008 continued through an early campaign visit in 2015 to a Chipotle restaurant in suburban Toledo, where (perhaps because of the dark sunglasses) she went unrecognized, incognito as she ordered a chicken burrito bowl, carrying her own tray. It ricocheted this way and that as she navigated through the shoals of her arguably self-generated and press-magnified tsunami of credibility-eroding news stories about her controversial private email server, soared during a compelling convention acceptance speech, barreled across the country in the fall, with her combative criticism of Donald Trump, tumbled in the wake of a questionable decision of the FBI director to reopen his investigation of her emails, and

Figure 1.1 The 2016 Bernie Sanders campaign captivated many young people, offering a political outlet to express discontent with politics as usual. While Sanders was not an avid user of technology, his supporters were, and they harnessed social media to mobilize voters, building an unlikely groundswell of support, raising issues that transformed the presidential campaign.

Getty Images

culminated on Election Day with the thrill so many women experienced when voting for a woman who could be president, crying with glee, like Amanda Rafferty who on the day of the election told her 9-year-old daughter, Maeve, that "there's nothing in this world you can't do" (Lyall, 2016, p. 3).

About a year and a half earlier, on June 16, 2015, another candidate inspired hopes of a different sort, with Trump's announcement at—where else?—Trump Tower that he was running for president, emphasizing what would become signature lines: "Our country is in serious trouble. We don't have victories anymore." You couldn't ignore him, and the media made sure we didn't, with more press coverage of Trump than any other candidate during the nomination period, raising questions about news judgment in a ratings-starved social media age (Patterson, 2016). There he was, with the boda-cious hair, all-knowing grin, the cocky smile, "the king of zing" (Bruni, 2015, p. 3), "the presidential candidate that reality TV made" (Grossman, 2015). The star of *The*

Apprentice television show was attracting crowds like no other candidate more than a year before the election. He wasn't the first candidate to capitalize on the once-strange, now quotidian, marriage between media and politics. The media-politics symbiosis had been building since Richard Nixon appeared on the television comedy *Laugh-In*. It grew when Ronald Reagan, famous for his movies (including the alliterative *Bedtime for Bonzo*), became the great communicator president; expanded when Bill Clinton belted out a melody on his saxophone on a late-night variety show in 1992, and broadened when Barack Obama ignited social media with an iconic Will.i.am music video and its own social media network, MyBarackObama.com. Now came Trump, the tweeting presidential contender.

He began the campaign with bravado, his message of economic populism attracting tens of thousands to rallies, filling ballrooms, with people shouting "USA! USA! USA! USA!" emphasizing how much they liked his honesty and refusal to utter the politically correct, Washingtonian statement. But over the course of an unconventional campaign dominated by tweets, voluminous news coverage, and fiery primary and general election debates, Trump offended many women and minorities, even threatened to imprison his political rival, an unprecedented promise even in the dirty domain of American politics. But he confounded and surprised experts by winning support from scores of marginalized, dissatisfied voters in battleground states, inspiring with promises of bygone American greatness millions who had been wronged by the system, voters who recognized his flaws, but seemed to believe that he alone, the blue-collar billionaire, might—just might—have the moxie to offer salve to their economic hardship, cultural anxiety, and (in the view of critics) racial animus. He said what he thought, tweeting so controversially his aides pried away his Twitter privileges like a child at the end of the campaign, sniffling strangely during a presidential debate and prowling the stage during the second debate so insistently that it became fodder for a *Saturday Night Live* satire.

"What do you expect?," a political editor asked, with seemingly bemused resignation. "It's politics: Weird things happen all the time" (Somaiya, 2015, p. A14)—although perhaps not this weird. The campaign circus was a constant for 18 months: publicity stunts (Republican Rand Paul made a film of himself cutting up the tax code, and put the scene on his campaign website); Americana political culture (Clinton's gaining the endorsement of 500 sex workers, most from Nevada brothels who proudly proclaimed they were "Hookers 4 Hillary"); pundits prognosticating (frequently incorrectly), along with the inevitable endorsements from celebrities (Kim Kardashian and Kanye West for Clinton, Spike Lee and Miley Cyrus for Sanders, and Dennis Rodman and Mike Tyson for Trump). When the host of the *Today* news program, Matt Lauer, interviewed Trump for a special campaign program on foreign policy, it showcased the "forced marriage of entertainment and news. The host of NBC's morning show interviewed the former star of its reality show 'The Apprentice,' and the whole thing played out as farce" (Poniewozik, 2016). If ever there was a candidate who appreciated the seamy, entertainment-driven nature of contemporary political media, it was Trump. Eschewing the old-style (circa 2012) approach of showcasing issue positions via strategically crafted sound bites, Trump came at the media with a new approach: "Give them a big, messy show with a regular stream of action, and they will come with their cameras and won't turn them off" (Rutenberg, 2016a).

Welcome to 21st-century American politics, an arena in which communication—conversations, advertisements, Fox, Facebook, Snapchat, and all the white-hot, acrimonious political posts—occupies center stage. Candidates still give speeches, of course—plenty of them—but they are pre-planned to get covered in television and, afterwards, candidates pose for the inevitable selfies, where taller candidates can stretch out their long arms like they are selfie sticks. You may catch a candidate at a rally, and it's always exciting, but the mainstay of the campaign is media, the modality by which candidates, journalists, and citizens experience the candidate. Politics is ceaselessly mediated, or Facebooked or Twittered, or whatever social media term you want to place in the past tense. Can you think of a political figure—candidate, elected official, or president—whom you have seen or spoken with in person? For some, the answer is yes—a rally for a favorite candidate they stood in line for hours to see. But for most others, the answer is no.

Isn't what you know, believe, and feel about politicians based on what you have gleaned from the multitude of media? This is one point on which conservatives, liberals, radicals, and even rabid conspiracy theorists agree. The media, broadly defined, are the place in which politics happens, "the center of gravity for the conduct of politics" (Jones, 2010, p. 23). As communication scholars remind us, "politics is carried out today in a multimedia environment that operates 24/7 and includes online and traditional media supplemented by entertainment shows as well as more typical venues such as news and political talk programs" (Kosicki, McLeod, & McLeod, 2011, p. 550).

Nowadays we cannot talk about politics without invoking media, and we cannot understand contemporary media without appreciating the role they play in the political system. A candidate can't mount a credible campaign for office without crafting an image, and an image is conveyed, disseminated, and constructed through the multiplicity of media. Images, alas, can be deceptive and superficial, designed to brand candidates as smart, likable, and with just enough anti-Washington bluster to win over voters who profess to be sick and tired of—the cliché is apt and time-honored—"politics as usual." Presidential candidates are ubiquitous in social media and appear as frequently as they can on news, talk shows, and *Saturday Night Live*. It's all politics, or media-politics, or mediated political realities, terms that seem so interwoven one can't effectively disentangle them.

Political communication, the focus of this book, is a realm commonly viewed as negative, vitriolic, and dominated by powerful interests. And there is much truth to this. But political communication is at the same time a centerpiece of democracy, a critical arena for the diffusion of democratic discourse. This text will help you appreciate what may seem like a distant realm: how media construct our high-adrenaline, ego-driven, and ideologically polarized world of contemporary politics. We are accustomed to viewing politics through our own beliefs and attitudes. This book takes a step back and applies the vistas supplied by social science theories, research, and political philosophy. Our aim is to understand the processes of political communication, mediated communication effects on citizens and elections, and broader philosophical issues, such as whether political persuasion dupes more than it delivers helpful information, and if citizens are adequately informed. We want to criticize political communication when it fails to achieve democratic ideals and celebrate it when it spurs citizens to work collectively to change the status quo.

But let's get something straight at the get-go. When you talk about politics, many people's eyes glaze over. They think about gridlock in Washington and how Congress can't accomplish anything. Or maybe they think about Stephen Colbert, Seth MacFarlane's *Family Guy*, or an uproarious YouTube political video, and crack a smile. But—you know what?—they're wrong. Politics and political communication affect us, whether we like it or not.

If you are digging deeper in your pockets or your purse to pay for college, politics affected you. Your university decided to raise your tuition because they're not getting as much money from the state on account of funding cutbacks that you don't understand but maybe now think you should read up on a little.

If you are nearly done with college and breathe a sigh of relief because you will still be covered on your parents' health insurance until you are 26, politics affected you. Obama's health care legislation enacted that provision, and the health care law was bitterly contested, nothing if not political.

Or perhaps concerned about the senseless death of unarmed African Americans at the hands of police officers, you have tweeted #BlackLivesMatter. Or, on the other end of the political spectrum, you may be angry about allegations that Planned Parenthood made illegal profits from sales of body parts from aborted fetuses to researchers, and contacted your legislator to demand action. Perhaps you posted comments on topics like these, or others running the gamut from immigration to gun control to the Supreme Court decision legalizing gay marriage.

Maybe, just maybe, you are someone who has strong political interests or attitudes on issues like these, channeling your passions to volunteer in election campaigns, or helping create the social media arm of a mayor's community outreach efforts. Or perhaps you are on the other end of the spectrum—cynical, convinced that our politics is full of vitriol and news is hopelessly biased. You find politics as it is practiced in America conniving, cunning, and at times corrupt. In either case, far from being indifferent, you have attitudes toward politics, ideas about current political issues, feelings about candidates running for office, and perhaps a commitment to exercise your right to vote in local and national elections. Politics may not be as foreign as you may have assumed.

With these issues as backdrop, this chapter introduces political communication, beginning with definitions of basic terms—politics and political communication—and moving to a description of the key features of contemporary political communication.

POLITICS

What thoughts cross your mind when someone mentions "politics"? Gridlock? Wheeling and dealing? Talk shows on Fox or MSNBC where the guests talk soberly about "the problems in Washington" and everybody disagrees with everyone else? Endless acrimony from dogmatic Democrats and Republicans? And, doesn't this one-word metaphor for political gamesmanship also come to mind: spin?

Does that cover it?

Notice I didn't say anything positive. That's because for most people, the word "politics" evokes sighs, recriminations, and even disgust. It has been this way for years in America. Distrusting politicians—"them bums"—goes back to the late 19th century, if not before, when Mark Twain called politicians "dust-licking pimps," and cartoonists like Thomas Nast depicted politicians as "vultures and rats" (Grinspan, 2014, p. A19). Although democracy involves a popularly elected government accountable to the public, Americans have historically derided elected officials and even the concept of government (Schutz, 1977). Long before television shows like *Veep* viewed politicians with contempt, *Scandal* lasciviously focused on the political libido, and *House of Cards* dramatically conveyed the lengths to which politicians will go to maintain power, humorists and writers looked disdainfully at America's politicians and the messages they deliver.

And so it is today. "It's just words," voters tell pollsters, when asked to describe their views of politics. One voter lamented that politics involves "such a control of government by the wealthy that whatever happens, it's not working for all the people; it's working for a few of the people" (Greenberg, 2011, p. 6). We say "it's just politics" when we want to deride the actions of elected representatives. But political scientist Samuel Popkin offers a different view, noting that the phrase "it's just politics" is "the saddest phrase in America, as if 'just politics' means that there was no stake" (Morin, 1996, pp. 7–8).

Consider this: One of the greatest presidents of the United States was "one of the most astute professional politicians the country has produced" (Blumenthal, 2012, p. 34). Abraham Lincoln cut deals, gave political favors, and applied canny strategic skills to persuade congressmen to approve the Thirteenth Amendment which abolished slavery from the U.S. Constitution. When one congressional representative indicated he would support the amendment, the president rewarded him by appointing him minister to Denmark. Lincoln recognized that "great change required a thousand small political acts" (Blumenthal, p. 35). The Steven Spielberg movie, *Lincoln*, celebrates Lincoln's moral and political achievements in persuading Congress to pass the Thirteenth Amendment (see Figure 1.2).

Politics calls up negative associations, but it can be harnessed for good, as well as pernicious, outcomes. Without politics, landmark legislation on civil rights, Medicare, the minimum wage, welfare, tax reform, and health care would never have been enacted. Absent political achievements, the U.S. (during George W. Bush's administration) would not have invested in a global AIDS program that gave millions of African AIDS patients life-saving drugs. Without politics, the American public would not have elected Barack Obama the first African American president, viewed by diverse generations of Americans as one of the most consequential political events of their lifetimes (Deane, Duggan, & Morin, 2016).

There are certainly many reasons to lament the state of contemporary politics: Its negativity, incivility, and the ways that political polarization (Jacobson, 2016) and gridlock, caused in part by gerrymandering or politicians' strategic manipulation of districts to favor their own party, have made it impossible for Congress to bridge partisan differences needed to pass legislation on problems like Social Security and Medicare. Groups that run the gamut from the conservative Tea Party to the more radical Occupy Wall Street identify failures in the system, noting that the electoral process has failed to redress economic grievances (Newkirk, 2016).

Figure 1.2 Abraham Lincoln showcased the ways politics could be harnessed for morally positive ends. He used the tools of political persuasion to convince Congress to pass the Thirteenth Amendment that abolished slavery.

iStock

People in Western democracies seem to have lost faith in democratic processes. Four of five Americans say that government, a core element of democracy makes them feel frustrated or angry (Porter, 2016). Many others are frustrated with the role money plays in politics and don't think the political system cares about people like them. A survey of 18- to 29-year-old adults found that close to half agreed with the statement that "politics today are no longer able to meet the challenges our country is facing" (Johnson, 2016, p. A14). Politics, though it has accomplished great things, is at the same time flawed, and imperfect.

What is politics, more broadly and formally? Pulling together different definitions (Lasswell, 1936; Offe, 1984; Wolin, 1996), focusing on their commonalities and the foundational aspects, I suggest that **politics** be defined as the public clash and debate among groups (who have different degrees of power) regarding resources, visions, and policies, with the goal of reaching broad-based decisions that are binding on, and may benefit, the larger collective.

Politics is rife with passion and controversy. It is a unique domain in which power, compromise, and strong values—racial justice, religious-based opposition to abortion, and free speech—make uneasy alliance. Because politics has a multitude of components— quest for power; harnessing storied symbols like the flag; advocating strong, sometimes unpopular positions in the face of public opposition; and brokering agreement among diverse constituents—it can be conflicted, colorful, and full of sound and fury. Politics is the domain where people express their opinions, exercise their will, and try to change society. It can be ineffectual, is rarely pretty, but perhaps wasn't meant to be. It is the arena in which democracy's citizens and representatives clash in public, arguing, and trying to arrive at policies that affect the lives of hundreds of millions of people, who place their trust, frequently reluctantly, in political leaders. Politics, flawed and impactful, is endemic to democracy.

A couple of centuries ago, you could explain American politics without talking much about the media. In the 19th century, political party bosses ran the show. A coercive quid pro quo frequently operated: Bosses gave jobs to immigrant voters and in exchange immigrants gratefully voted the party line. Chomping cigars and spewing smoke into the political air, party leaders played a key role in selecting party nominees. This has changed. The road to the White House winds through CNN, Fox, and *The New York Times*, while at the same time snaking through Twitter, Facebook, and countless blogs.

"Political life in any mass society is impossible without established methods of political communication," Pye (1993) observes (p. 443). As Esser (2013) notes, the major aspects of the political system—socialization of citizens, candidate selection, elections, and governing—are performed to a considerable degree via mediated communication.

At the most basic level, citizens learn about political events from the media, increasingly on their smartphones. Citizens' preferences are widely diffused through media-communicated or media-constructed opinion polls. Candidates must persuade, and leaders must govern by harnessing the media to productive ends. The media offer a common forum by which all this comes together, sometimes helping society move forward, in other cases polarizing and dividing society into camps.

DEFINING POLITICAL COMMUNICATION

Scholars have defined political communication in a variety of ways. To help you appreciate the breadth of this concept in contemporary, I present three definitions, followed by my own integrative view. In the view of academic experts, political communication is:

- The flow of messages and information that gives structure and meaning to the political process (Pye, 1993, p. 442).
- Two sets of institutions—political and media organizations—which are involved in the course of message preparation in much "horizontal" interaction with each other while on a "vertical" axis, they are separately and jointly engaged in disseminating and processing information and ideas to and from the mass citizenry (Blumler, 2014, p. 39).
- The communicative activity of citizens, individual political figures, public and governmental institutions, the media, political campaigns, advocacy groups and social movements (Jamieson & Kenski, 2014; for other definitions, see Denton & Kuypers, 2008; Denton & Woodward, 1998; McNair, 1995; Powell & Cowart, 2003; Smith, 1990).

The definitions emphasize that political communication cuts a large swath across the public landscape, encompassing citizens, the media, campaigns, government, and even social movements. They stress the flow of messages between two different institutions—political and media—that are disseminated to, and processed, by a nation's citizenry. Although politics and media overlap, they are fundamentally different institutions. Politics is about the allocation of resources and decision-making by representatives elected to serve constituents' needs. Media are organizations powered by technologies that intercede between the communicator and message recipients, diffusing opinions through public space and dramatizing political debate (e.g., Marcinkowski & Steiner, 2014). Building on these definitions and scholarship in the field, I define **political communication** as a complex, communicative activity in which language and symbols, employed by leaders, media, citizens, and citizen groups, exert a multitude of effects on individuals and society, as well as on outcomes that bear on the public policy of a nation, state, or community.

COMPONENTS OF POLITICAL COMMUNICATION

There are seven core dimensions of political communication (see Table 1.1). This section will review each of them in detail.

Complex Bridge Between Political and Media Institutions

Political communication is distinctive in that it does not focus solely on media, or on political institutions, but on both. It involves the intersection of two different social institutions, with different philosophical frameworks, organizational imperatives, and societal roles. The American news media are private, for-profit industries, with journalistic traditions, which have grown up with strong norms of openness, distrust of politicians, and First Amendment freedom. Campaign organizations and government institutions are concerned with political issues—winning election and administering public programs. Some scholars argue that the media, with its focus on finding stories that emphasize sometimes trivial conflict between candidates, is particularly unsuited to playing a core role in an electoral system that should emphasize broader issues of interest to the bulk of citizens (Patterson, 1993). Others believe that the out-in-the-open theater of contemporary media politics cultivates a more transparent, democratic political discourse than the Whites-only, closed-door, smoke-filled rooms of yore.

Political communication effects can occur on the **micro level**, affecting individuals' thoughts, candidate assessments, feelings, attitudes, and behavior. Political advertisements and presidential debates work on this level, trying to change attitudes in pursuit of persuasion. Political communication also works on the **macro level**, exerting broad-based effects on public opinion, institutional change, political activism, and public policy. The groundbreaking *Washington Post* coverage of President Nixon's unethical

Table 1.1 Core features of political communication.

1. Complex communicative activity bridging political and media institutions.
2. Emphasizes symbols, language, and diverse constructions of political symbols.
3. Fundamentally a mediated experience.
4. Centered on technology, with online technologies influencing delivery and reception of messages.
5. Revolves around diverse, multifaceted media, with highly charged intersections among entertainment, news, facts, and opinion.
6. Involves interplay among three key players: leaders, media, and citizens.
7. Operates on a worldwide basis, with commonalities across borders, and differences as a function of a country's economic and political structures.

actions during the Watergate scandal of the early 1970s led to macro-level institutional changes, such as the appointment of a special prosecutor, a series of Senate hearings that ultimately paved the way for Nixon's resignation, and campaign finance regulations to stave off political corruption. Political communication also exerts broad cultural effects. As Michael Schudson (1995) notes,

> the news constructs a symbolic world that has a kind of priority, a certification of legitimate importance . . . When the media offer the public an item of news, they confer upon it public legitimacy. They bring it into a common public forum where it can be discussed by a general audience.

(pp. 33, 19)

More broadly, Jay G. Blumler (2015) observes, political communication is a multilevel phenomenon, with effects on individuals and social systems, as well as connections among media organizations, political institutions, and the electorate. It represents a unique confluence of politics and media, "a volatile politics-media axis" (p. 426).

Symbols and Language

Political communication involves a seemingly endless number of messages from different actors. Messages are simultaneously sent, interpreted, tweeted, retweeted, comprehended, miscomprehended, internalized, and received differently, depending on individual biases, institutional objectives, group values, and political objectives.

Political communication is the domain of words, and symbols, with leaders using "language to move people to think and act in ways that they might not otherwise think and act" (Ball, 2011, p. 42). Presidents—Franklin Delano Roosevelt, Ronald Reagan and Barack Obama—have harnessed language to arouse the imagination of Americans, using speech to captivate, symbols to mobilize, and metaphors to galvanize support for their policies (Hart, 1984). FDR's "the only thing we have to fear is fear itself"—heard as families huddled together listening to radio sets during the cold, despairing days of the 1930s Depression—emotionally moved listeners, offering up hope and optimism, activating the collective confidence of a country (Euchner, 1990). Reagan's rhetoric about America as a "shining city on a hill" evoked patriotism, while Obama's eulogies after American tragedies left Americans with a sense of unity and hope, albeit short-lived.

On the other hand, presidents can use words deceptively to maintain power or disguise risky decisions, like President Richard Nixon did with his description of the U.S. military "incursion," rather than "invasion," of Cambodia in 1970. Words can be weapons that maintain elite control. Scholar Murray Edelman (1964, 1971), viewing politics through the lens of symbolic action, articulated ways that leaders construct political action by applying symbols that reify power. He argued that campaigns are essentially political spectacles by which politicians cleverly exploit patriotic symbols and cherished group meanings to promote the interests of the few rather than the many. Trump, harnessing the contemporary social medium, Twitter, connected directly with many Americans through terse, emotional messages his political base found refreshing and devoid of snobbish elite discourse. But critics worried that he was invoking Orwellian speech, using words as "reality control," denying external reality with falsehoods and "alternative facts" that distorted the truth about a host of topics, from the size of his inaugural crowd to voter fraud in elections (Kakutani, 2017).

The language of political communication is laden with symbols. A **symbol** is a form of language in which one entity represents an idea or concept, conveying rich psychological and cultural meaning. Symbols include words like justice, freedom, and equality, as well as the flag, a patriotic object so redolent with symbolism that candidate Barack Obama was pointedly asked why he chose not to wear a flag pin on his lapel during a 2008 Democratic debate in Philadelphia. (After the dust-up, he decided to wear the pin.) In America, elected officials frequently invoke the Founding Fathers, Lincoln, Jefferson, freedom, and equality. The founders of the conservative political group, the Tea Party, harnessed the symbolism of the colonial-inspired political protest, associating their group with the cause of liberty and freedom from government control.

Words convey different meanings to different groups. Symbols are increasingly objects of fractious debate. To conservatives, particularly rural Americans, guns symbolize liberty, freedom from meddlesome government encroachment, even preservation of a way of life in an increasingly alien culture (Hayes, 2016). For liberals, guns represent violence tearing at the fabric of America and senseless devastation of innocents and loved ones. Political messages call up different meanings to different groups, an inevitable source of conflict in democratic societies. Battles for public opinion can be won or lost, depending on the ability of partisan groups to frame their causes with symbols that resonate with the public.

Trump accessed attitudes toward immigration by raising the specter that Mexico was sending rapists and criminals to the U.S. (In fact, the number of Mexicans caught illegally crossing the border has dropped to its lowest level since 1971, and the crime rate of first-generation immigrants is lower than in the overall U.S. population; see Egan, 2015.) However, Trump's appeals resonated symbolically, connecting with time-honored beliefs that citizenship should be granted to those who meet legal requirements under the law, or hostility toward people of different racial and ethnic origins. The debate about terminology reflects this.

Using the word "illegals," "illegal immigrants," or "aliens" brands people as "less than human and undeserving of fair treatment" (Bazelon, 2015, p. 11). "Undocumented immigrant" or "undocumented worker" avoids these perils, but can strike conservatives as politically correct. "Political correctness" itself is a symbol—to conservatives, one that refers to stifling of free speech to promote questionable aims of diversity, while to liberals, it conveys a long-overdue sensitivity to the ways that speech conveys meanings offensive to cultural minorities.

Political symbols can call attention to problems, convey hope, and unify disparate groups. They also can prove divisive, an impact dating back to 1896 presidential election, where rural, indebted backers of free coinage of silver battled the more expert, financially well-heeled supporters of gold during a campaign characterized more by emotional, conspiracy-laced appeals than sound discussion of issues (Williams, 2010). More than a century later, during the 2016 election, candidates' discussion of complex issues, such as free trade, could devolve into symbolic simplifications (workers versus exploitive capitalists; America First versus globalization) rather than helpful clarifications of complex issues.

Mediation and Mediatization

By definition, political media *mediate* between citizens and institutions of government (Iyengar, 2004; Strömbäck & Kaid, 2008). But the media are not neutral, bland go-betweens. They apply their own judgments and rules, in this way transforming politics (Mazzoleni & Schutz, 1999). If there is one concept that captures the media's role in transforming contemporary politics, it is **mediatization**. Mediatization emphasizes not simply that media come between politicians and citizens, but how media have transformed the structural relations of politics in society. As Jesper Strömbäck and Frank Esser (2014) helpfully observe, the mediatization of politics is "a long-term process through which the importance of the media and their spill-over effects on political processes, institutions, organizations and actors have increased" (p. 6).

Mediatization can be viewed as the process by which the media have come to play a central role in politics, influencing institutions, performing strategic functions for political elites (Van Aelst & Walgrave, 2016), imparting information (and misinformation), socializing young citizens into civic society, creating the public spectacle we call politics, and serving as the playing field on which politics occurs (Jones, 2010). People do not experience politics directly, unless they are among the small minority of individuals who canvass for candidates door-to-door, do volunteer work for political advocacy groups, or are members of political elites. As Strömbäck (2008) notes, "The mediated reality becomes more important than the actual reality, in the sense that it is the mediated reality that people have access to and react to" (p. 238).

When we talk about mediatization, we emphasize the ways media have influenced the practice of politics and set basic ground rules. Because of television's focus on image, candidates are judged in terms of appearance and likability, nice attributes, but arguably peripheral to the ability to govern. Candidates must communicate in the argot of the media—short, encapsulated sound bites and brief, clever tweets. Candidates must adapt to "media logic" for covering campaigns, adjusting to the media's focus on conflict, novelty, and even grandstanding (e.g., Altheide & Snow, 1979). The presidential nominating process revolves around the news media. Publicity advances a candidacy, poor primary debate performance or post-debate coverage can impair it, and cable networks sponsor pre-primary debates, deciding who participates based on media-circulated polls, the debates taking on a "Hunger Games aura," raising "the question of whether unaccountable media institutions should determine the roles of accountable politicians" (Blumler, 2014, p. 37). Even non-electoral campaigns, such as for the nomination of a Supreme Court justice, are waged via media, comporting with the logic of diverse media platforms and harnessing the vast armamentarium of contemporary political marketing (Manheim, 2011).

Naturally, there are complications. The political system, guided by an overall political logic, influences media, just as media influence politics. The nomination system has a set of rules that candidates must follow. Their media strategies reflect the timing of the primaries and number of convention delegates at stake. When national crises ensue, government can impose limits on news-gathering, and government institutions manipulate the news that citizens receive. The notion that political media are governed by an overarching homogenous media logic may oversimplify issues today (Esser & Strömbäck, 2014). There may no longer be a singular media logic, but different logics that vary as a function of the interplay of mass and social media, electoral context, and the country in which the campaign occurs (Kunelius & Reunanen, 2016; Schulz, 2014).

Media Technology

Media technology effects on politics date back long before Facebook Live and network news. The popularity of newspapers among elites in early America helped build political parties, paving the way for blistering attacks on candidates from Hamilton to Jackson that makes today's negative campaigning look tame by comparison. The introduction of photojournalism in the mid-19th century gave voters the chance to view candidates for elective office, presaging the rise of image politics. Magazines, from *McClure's* in the early 20th century, which published exposés of corporate abuses, to *Ramparts* in the 1960s, with its no-holes-barred, left-wing exposés of Vietnam-era deceptions that anticipated websites of today (Grimes, 2016), offered platforms for investigative journalism. Radio gave citizens the first aural exposure to distant events, offering a personal connection to world affairs. Television transformed politics by providing graphic, live exposure to tragedies, like assassinations and wars, as well as presidential press conferences and debates, highlighting the role of visual images, suddenly a major player in political campaigns (Flew & Smith, 2015). TV also elevated the importance of news in society, as television became a fixture in American homes, and viewing the half-hour newscast became an accepted family dinner ritual. Journalists, who for years were longer on scruff than flash, became celebrities and their version of news was viewed, for a time, as veridical, objective, and of preeminent importance.

Political communication is now a multimedia game. It is not just 24/7 news on a television screen, but second-by-second updates and posts on smartphone screens, with editors curating content at social media platforms like Snapchat, Twitter, and Facebook (Herrman, 2016). Digital technologies now constitute a "fifth estate," complementing traditional news media (the fourth estate, which historically built on the clergy, nobility, and common people, the first, second and third estates respectively (Dutton & Dubois, 2015).

Media technologies have transformed the communicative actions of leaders, citizens, and the media itself. Long before Twitter's blue bird became part of its branded logo, political leaders used the media to communicate about politics. Ronald Reagan, appreciating the visual format of the television medium, harnessed props, visual devices, and pictures, such as TV cameras panning on magnificent monuments, to access patriotic themes (Jamieson, 1988; see Chapter 8). Contemporary presidents have a variety of interactive media modalities at their disposal that give them more communicative flexibility in reaching particular audiences than in the days when three broadcast networks ruled the roost. However, they must cut through the clutter and capture the attention of people who seamlessly switch from modality to modality, calling on technologies that prize simplicity as much as instantaneity.

Online messaging plays a key role in the presidential election. It is no longer the mass media election, as Thomas Patterson (1980) dubbed it, but the interactive media election, twittered election or "all media all the time" election. Campaigns complement strategies to gain news coverage with a digital cocktail of media technologies to influence voters, harnessing messages that are exquisitely targeted to particular voters' social media profiles (Stromer-Galley, 2014). They also elide journalistic mediation entirely, reaching the public directly by distributing live video of convention speeches to followers across the nation (Shear & Corasaniti, 2016). The game is still power, but the techniques are refined and more personalized, harnessed by politicians, remarked upon by journalists on the ubiquitous Twitter, and discussed by politically minded citizens in their social networks (Jungherr, 2014). Social media has transformed political campaigns, reducing the power of traditional gatekeepers, like mainstream journalists, while increasing the ability of insurgent candidates (think Trump in 2016) to develop a following on Twitter, enabling challengers to build support around issues and personality characteristics.

Online media have also pushed into public view content that would have been hushed up years ago, a function of both digital technologies and the notion the public has a right to know intimate details about politics (Schudson, 2015), a norm that would have shocked the privacy-obsessed Founding Fathers. It is now out there—public, porous, for citizens to peruse, and the content is frequently salacious.

During the vitriolic 2016 campaign, the release of a lewd 2005 video revealed Trump boasting, in tawdry terms, of how he could grope women and get away with "anything" because he is a celebrity. Unlike previous eras, when there was no video or digital recording of lascivious, offensive comments, the information here—Trump's remarks, the voice that spoke them, and the face shown in the video—was indisputably Trump's, giving the revelations instant credibility and political combustibility (Barbaro & Healy, 2016; Burns, Haberman, & Martin, 2016). Trump responded that the video did not reveal his true attitudes toward women because it constituted "locker room talk," an argument that struck feminists as ridiculous, but which voters who embraced his brio accepted, feeling uncomfortable with a media intrusion that occurred long before he entered politics.

There are other cases in which information that years ago would have been hushed up by candidates or a compliant press noisily entered the public fray. During the height of the 2012 campaign, a secretly recorded video of remarks Mitt Romney made at a fund-raiser surfaced. Romney's comments that 47 percent of Americans do not pay income taxes, "believe that they are victims," and do not take "personal responsibility" for their lives sparked controversy. The message spread so quickly and widely that a couple of weeks after he made the statement, 67 percent of registered voters knew that Romney had uttered the words and half reacted negatively (Stromer-Galley, 2014). Years ago, his remarks would have never surfaced. But today anything said anywhere can be a matter of public record, revealed by those with an ax to grind against the candidate, journalists (operating from professional and economic motives), and even Russian cyberagents, who hacked into Democratic National Committee documents, apparently to propel Trump to office.

In a celebrated case that occurred in 2011, a liberal Democratic Congressman, Anthony Weiner, sent lewd photos, including ones that displayed him in his underpants, to women he met over the Internet. He resigned in disgrace when the sordid tale became public. Did the Internet play a helpful role? It facilitated the resignation of a public official who had engaged in creepy behaviors, hardly befitting a member of Congress. Or did the Internet instead bring to the surface information that was none of the public's business to begin with? It all played out in a truth-is-stranger-than-fiction episode in October 2016, when the FBI, exploring allegations that Weiner had (once again) exchanged possibly illicit sexually explicit messages, discovered an email trove that it deemed relevant to its earlier investigation of Hillary Clinton's emails. The reason the emails appeared on Weiner's laptop—and this shows just how strange politics can be—is that he was the estranged husband of a top Clinton aide. As it turned out, the newly discovered emails did not contain any incriminating evidence against Clinton, but they rocked and possibly damaged her candidacy. Even more dramatically, Russian agents apparently hacked Democratic National Committee private emails, and the confidential messages appeared online on a daily basis in the fall of 2016, disrupting the Clinton campaign, a brazen attempt by a foreign power to interfere with a U.S. election (Lipton, Sanger, & Shane, 2016)

In all these cases, online digital media have made possible revelations that would have been kept behind closed doors in years past, a testament to the eviscerated boundaries between private and public and the ways that contemporary technologies have put virtually everything out in the open, for better and sometimes worse. The sordid, sometimes salutary blending of private and public in contemporary life raises questions about whether we are better off when information that would have been hushed up and kept private is now squarely in the public domain, or whether the intrusions on political leaders' private lives are inappropriate, coarsening our public discourse.

Diverse, Multifaceted, Blurred Lines Media

Pundits typically refer to the media as an all-powerful singular term, invoking the powerful aura of other monolithic entities like the Vatican or the Establishment. They utter the phrase, as one word, in a dry, stentorian tone, or they speak it derisively, as when critics talk about the Liberal (or Capitalist) Media. In fact, there are many media and diverse media platforms: newspapers with their online websites, local TV news, talk radio, 24/7 cable TV news programs, blogs, ideologically partisan political websites, and the complex array of citizen-journalist social media videos and posts (Baker & Blaagaard, 2016).

It is misleading to lump all these platforms together under the moniker "media." There are differences among media in terms of their functions, aims, structure, and economic foundations. For many years in political communication, the term "media" was synonymous with "news media," or conventional journalism. This has changed. Social media, online citizen journalist posts, and partisan websites can influence the political agenda, although conventional media organizations—network and cable news, traditional newspapers, and magazines, now with an online presence—still play an important role in presidential elections.

The conventional media used to serve as the sole gatekeepers, deciding which information passed through society's metaphorical gates, making judgments on which "facts" should be published or broadcast. Just deciding what constitutes a fact is a fraught, complex issue. Separating fact from opinion is a daunting task, in some sense impossible. Some news outlets, like CBS, *Politico*, and *The Washington Post* make judgments on what is newsworthy, based on stringent journalistic criteria, doing their best to minimize biases. A former *New York Times* publisher articulated the goal well, noting that "you're not buying news when you buy a newspaper. You're buying judgment" (Haberman, 2012). Of course, no news organization is without some bias, but certain media outlets—and here is where it gets controversial—have more obtrusive opinionated aims, promoting a particular political agenda (e.g., Davis & Owen, 1998). The liberal cable television network MSNBC, the conservative Fox News Channel, and a variety of politicized websites advance ideological viewpoints, allowing political biases to overtly intrude into their presentation of news.

MSNBC, with liberal-sympathizing hosts Rachel Maddow and Chris Matthews, has tilted Democratic in its coverage of the presidential election (Peters, 2012. By the same token, there is empirical evidence that Fox News slants news toward Republicans (Brock et al., 2012). Fox anchors like Sean Hannity (with an audience of 2.5 million) display the patina of journalistic news, with the authoritative anchor television anchor desk, stream of informative graphics, and dressed-up television appearance, but promote a conservative ideological worldview, where "a fact is dismissed as false when it doesn't fit the preferred political narrative" (Rutenberg, 2016b, p. B3). The more extreme right-wing, White nationalist Breitbart News has gone even further, peddling stories that irk even long-time Republicans, such as those that describe how "Birth control makes women unattractive and crazy" (Bromwich, 2016; Flegenheimer, 2016, p. A12). There are also left-wing sites, like U.S. Uncut and Addicting Info, filled with false information and sensationalized stories. It strains credulity to regard such partisan websites that let ideology govern their choice of facts as legitimate journalism that honor the canons of the profession.

It is ironic. Years ago, Americans placed considerable trust in television news. Yet TV news, while it strove to be objective, contained a host of biases on issues from race to the Vietnam War. Nowadays, people assume news is biased, neglecting the instances when responsible journalistic outlets strive to be fair-minded and offer accurate, incisive accounts of politics. On the collective level, we have a more multifaceted media than ever before. Biased media co-exist with professional journalism, and noisy, mean-spirited, prejudiced social media posts co-occur with thoughtful, long-form blogs that dissect complicated issues. The diversity of outlets celebrates libertarian values, but sites that masquerade opinion as fact and deliver up fake news raise troubling issues for democratic decision-making.

Adding another layer of complexity, political communication in an entertainment-saturated society is part of the popular culture, a type of pop art, post–Andy Warhol, in which politicians are characterized, mischaracterized and lampooned on television, as well as on YouTube videos and comedy shows that deliberately convey faux news to pierce popular culture veneers (Baumgartner & Morris, 2006).

Such is today's political landscape, where time-honored boundaries between fact and opinion, and news and entertainment, are hopelessly blurred. Politics and entertainment blend seamlessly, a development that took off in the 1990s, with Bill Clinton belting out his saxophone on Arsenio Hall's television talk show in 1992 and grew with the role played by celebrity supporters (will.i.am for Obama in 2008, Clint Eastwood for Romney in 2012), along with Tina Fey's now-classic imitations of Sarah Palin on *Saturday Night Live* in 2008 (Chadwick, 2013). In 2016, the political entertainment nexus rose to new highs (or dropped to new valleys) "with primaries resembling nothing so much as a reality television show, debates that drew huge audiences in large part for the spectacle, and a traditional news media that provided Trump with unprecedented coverage because of his celebrity status" (Delli Carpini, 2016, p. 20). Politics is not a simple, but endlessly fuzzy and fascinating, category that would be interesting to observe with bemused detachment if it did not exert such significant effects on people's material and symbolic experiences.

Interplay Among Leaders, Media, and Citizens

Leaders and influence agents are the elites of politics. Elites include candidates for office, elected officials, as well as Washington opinion leaders spanning members of the president's Cabinet, policy experts, and chieftains in the vast government bureaucracy. (The word "elite" has itself become a focus of controversy, evoking negative connotations, linked in the popular mind with wealthy, arrogant leaders out of touch with the problems of the working man or woman. It also has positive connotations, when linked with conscientious government specialists or dutiful elected representatives.)

The next player is the media, broadly defined. As noted earlier, this increasingly diverse group includes the conventional news media, bloggers, citizen journalists, a motley crew comprised of eyewitnesses, activists, and innovative observers, partisan promulgators of websites, and the gaggle of political entertainment hosts and comedians who describe politics, broadly defined.

The centerpiece of political communication (at least in theory) is the citizenry. Citizens are a cacophonous combination of the politically engaged and opinionated, along with the indifferent and woefully ignorant. The citizenry includes those whose contact with politics comes only when they vote (or choose not to); citizens who band together in protest marches, as seen in the women who converged on Washington after Trump's inauguration to protest the new president, and the anti-abortion protesters who gathered at the National Mall a week later; and the litany of organized civic groups (pro-gun control versus pro-gun; evangelical Christian and unabashedly atheist, as well as pro- and anti-fur, pro-vegan and virulently pro–red meat).

Political communication involves the flow of messages among these three groups. Political candidates can initiate the process with a statement, policy pronouncement, or criticism of an opponent. The president can dominate political communication, as President George W. Bush did after the tragedy of 9/11, beginning with a moving speech to the nation on September 20, 2001, in which he articulated the threats the nation faced from terrorist groups, while taking pains to show respect for the Muslims in America and throughout the world. Through his rhetoric and actions, Bush rallied the country around a new and unsettling war on terror, influencing the media agenda and citizenry.

Governing elites do not always dominate political communication. Media can instigate the process, as when news about an upstart Democratic candidate named Barack Obama—with his charisma and cri de coeur, "Yes, we can!"—provided a favorable picture of the young Illinois senator (Falk, 2010), helping propel him to victory in the primaries.

The public can also launch or catalyze political communication, as when polls showed that voters were primarily concerned with the economy in the 2008 and 2012 elections. This propelled candidates and the news media to focus attention on the economy. The influence of the public—or an active segment—occurred famously in the 2016 election when angry, agitated Republican and Democratic voters, dissatisfied with their economic fortunes and out-of-touch politicians, upended the established choices by supporting Trump and Sanders (Leland, 2016). In most cases, the voice of the public is delivered through the cold, disembodied channel of public opinion polls, relayed to elected officials, studied, then massaged by candidates in hopes of influencing and manipulating these sentiments for strategic advantage.

There is a democratic basis to this. In order to get elected and reelected, leaders must be responsive to their constituents, implementing policies that the average voter supports (Hurley & Hill, 2010). Polls that show a candidate gaining in the polls can create a bandwagon effect, leading the press to offer more positive coverage (Patterson, 1993). Citizens' role in a democracy is much debated. Do citizens have a larger impact on candidates today than in yesteryear, in view of the lightning-fast, network-organizing influences of social media? Is the citizenry's impact on politics unduly mediated by polls, with pollsters' questions setting an agenda? Do certain individuals, with more money and power, have a greater influence? In most instances, are citizens uninvolved, apathetic, and circumvented, producing what Entman (1989) dolefully calls a "democracy without citizens"? These are serious issues that raise critical problems with contemporary democracy.

An Example

The three political actors—elites, media, and citizens—influence policy complexly, through overlapping concentric circles. To illustrate with an internationalist example, consider the foreign policy crisis that consumed U.S. leaders in the summer and fall of 2014: the rise of the Islamic State, known also as the Islamic State in Iraq and Syria (ISIS). The militant, terrorist group seemed to appear out of nowhere, but actually had long exploited the upheaval wrought by the Syrian civil war to its strategic advantage, seizing control over Syrian territory and then moving into Iraq, taking control of key cities in the besieged country that had been the site of America's controversial, decade-long war that began in 2003. The rise of ISIS took the Obama administration by surprise, with White House elites initially minimizing the threat that the terrorist group's lightning-fast sweep posed to the region, or viewing it as a problem that could be managed routinely (Baker & Schmitt, 2014).

Then came the barbaric, medieval-style beheadings of two American journalists, which were posted on YouTube, available for the world to see, the stories covered heavily in the mainstream U.S. mass media. Now the media took center stage, seizing the agenda, the carefully crafted, grisly video commanding attention, generating conversation, disgusting civilized observers, and eliciting calls for U.S. action. Conservative media outlets like Fox News seized the moment, criticizing Obama's "indecision" on how to react, and promoting the argument that military action was needed to confront the terrorist group.

The public, indifferent to the issue, suddenly became animated, outraged by the barbarism. A majority of Americans regarded the Islamic State as a major threat to U.S. security, and a whopping 70 percent favored airstrikes to pummel the group (Davis & Sussman, 2014). Increasingly attuned to the threat ISIS posed to national security, cognizant of media reports that he had not acted swiftly enough to contain the danger, and unquestionably aware of the public's shift in mood, Obama addressed the nation on the eve of the 13th anniversary of 9/11, promising swift military action to destroy the extremist group. This appeared to mollify critics and shore up public opinion on his behalf. Yet questions remained. Would Obama have acted as swiftly in the absence of the push from media and public, and did he wait too long to take action? Did the Islamic State cleverly manipulate media and American public opinion by releasing its grisly video? Did media frames of ISIS—for example, Obama's failure to take bold action precipitously—overwhelm other ways of looking at the problem? With all these intricacies, the example illustrates the interplay of political communicative influence in contemporary life.

Figure 1.3 shows how the three key political communication agents—political actors or governing elites, media, and the public—partake in a dynamic flow of influence, with

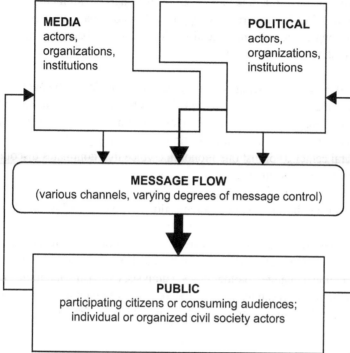

Long-term formal and informal interactions,
creating "patterned" types of relationships over time

Figure 1.3 The flow of political communication

(From Pfetsch & Esser, 2012)

different arrows of causal influence. It can get very complicated. There are different theories as to which player—political leaders, media, or public—is more influential, and when.

Some scholars emphasize elite institutions' capacity to build the agenda in ways that promote and reinforce the powers that be (Herman & Chomsky, 2002). They argue that presidents harness propaganda (a fraught, loaded term) to control media and the public. Certainly, governments—the U.S. when it jailed anti-war critics during World War I, and far worse ruling elites, like North Korea—engage in propagandistic communication. Trump's critics argued that his falsehoods, so-called Orwellian attempts to control information, and White House media-bashing constituted propaganda (e.g., Kakutani, 2017). This is complicated because propaganda involves near or total control over information. Yet the sheer diversity of contemporary media platforms, modalities, and genres makes it high-nigh impossible for one political source or voice to control democratic discourse (Coleman & Freelon, 2015), and Trump's adversaries were quick to pounce on his claims. In addition, propaganda is a value-laden term; critics call disagreeable messages propaganda, while labeling messages they agree with mere "persuasion," or even "the truth"! (In fairness, Trump's supporters did not regard his messages as propaganda, but as long-overdue communication. They viewed Obama's communication on health care as akin to propaganda.)

Other scholars emphasize media power, arguing that media set the agenda and frame issues, influencing the dynamics of strategic battles for public opinion. Still others place an onus on citizens, particularly during close elections, or when economic distress becomes politicized. Political communication is increasingly polycentric, or characterized by several centers, not just one monolithic voice that dominates discourse (Chadwick, 2013; Chadwick, Dennis, & Smith, 2016).

There is consensus that political communication involves a high-stakes battle among groups with varying degrees of power to influence public opinion. Interest coalitions, citizens' action groups, and political leaders seek to mobilize public attitudes, viewing these as an engine by which policy can be influenced. Sometimes the interplay produces meaningful political change, in other cases, paralysis, cynicism, and toxic polarization. Political communication can lead to positive or negative outcomes, as well as mixtures of the two, depending on the democratic and ethical bases of campaigns.

A Global Phenomenon

Political communication transcends America. Political marketing takes place in electoral campaigns across the world, with political advertising and candidate branding a factor in elections in European countries, Israel, and even Russia (Lees-Marshment, 2010; Rose, 2010; Scammell, 2014).

When it comes to elections, mediatization has become coin of the realm, the common currency of elections across the world. Scholars point to four similarities in the roles wielded by media in election campaigns in democracies across the world: (1) Candidates adapt their strategies to fit the news and interactive media technologies; (2) Journalists play an important part in defining and framing political issues; (3) Political marketing and opinion polling are campaign mainstays; and (4) Politics is personalized, with media communicating candidates' personality attributes (frequently, outsized personalities), rather than focusing solely on ideological issues (Esser & Strömbäck, 2012; Swanson & Mancini, 1996).

The same types of evocative advertising strategies guide political consultants in countries separated by thousands of miles and centuries of history. Fear appeals, where ads try to scare voters about the prospects of voting for a candidate or issue, are commonplace. Greek voters, faced with a complex referendum on a financial bailout package in 2015, were treated to an avalanche of doomsday advertisements, with exaggerated claims about the prospects that a vote one way or the other would spell disaster for Greece. "There is no discussion of the real issues," a Greek news media specialist noted (Daley, 2015, p. A4). You could have done a double-take and wondered if you were listening to an American commentator lament political spots during a U.S. national election.

At the same time, there are substantial differences in political media among different countries, as a function of cultural, structural, and economic parameters. As Hallin and Mancini (2004) explain, a political communication system consists of media and political systems, each with a series of defining characteristics. Components of the media system include the development of an autonomous, professional ethos among journalists, and degree of formal connections between the press and political parties (there are few in the U.S. and typically many more in some European countries). Aspects of the political system include whether electoral politics are dominated by two political parties (as in the U.S.) or a number of parties, like in European countries; the degree of power-sharing among diverse political party coalitions, and whether the government intervenes in, or takes a hand-off posture toward, the news media (see Pfetsch & Esser, 2012 for a critical perspective). Media and political system differences can influence the nature of political advertising, candidate debates, and news, such as the average length of sound bites (e.g., Esser, 2008).

The overlap and differences in political media systems, along with their implications for media content and effects, form the foundation of the study of **comparative political communication** (Hallin & Mancini, 2004; Pfetsch & Esser, 2012; Esser & Strömbäck, 2012). While a detailed discussion of comparative issues is beyond the scope of this book, it is worth noting that there is no perfect political/media culture; all have strengths and shortcomings. The adversarial relationship between journalists and candidates in the U.S. advances democracy by encouraging candidate accountability to voters, but can fall short of European approaches in its reluctance to devote time and space to full discussion of issues, particularly those of third party nominees. In some European countries, media provide more public affairs coverage than in the U.S., which can result in higher political knowledge levels than in the U.S. (Pfetsch & Esser, 2012). On the other hand, if news in northern European countries promotes political party interests, it can encourage a subservient attitude toward party leaders. A comparative approach to political communication is important. It reminds us that the American model is one of many, and political communication does not operate in a vacuum. Instead, media must be understood by taking into account such broader contours as the nature of the electoral system, types of media markets, how journalists define professionalism, and the extent of government intervention in the national media system.

CONCLUSIONS

The American presidential election is a P. T. Barnumesque mixture of farce, entertainment, policy issues, big money, partisan politics, and democratic values. It is emblematic of the worst and best in American politics, and a living, breathing, high-flying testament to the central role political communication plays in contemporary political life. After offering a prologue on the tumultuous 2016 election, this chapter explained that political communication is inseparable from politics, and politics is an activity that many disparage, but which influences their lives in subtle, direct, and symbolic ways. Politics, emphasizing the public clash among groups regarding resources and policy visions, aims to reach broad-based consensus on decisions that can benefit the larger community. Politics has produced great achievements, but is also a source of frustration, in view of polarization that impedes legislative progress, and widespread perception that democracy is corrupt or ineffectual.

While you could understand politics a century or more ago without considering media, today that is impossible. Political life in mass society is not possible without the intervention of media, which conveys and constructs the political spectacle. Scholars have defined political communication in different ways, and calling on these definitions, the chapter emphasizes that political communication is: (1) a *complex activity* bridging political and media institutions; (2) the domain of fraught, controversial *symbols* that can divide, but also unify when leaders frame issues persuasively; (3) *a mediated experience*, with conventional and social media defining the terms in which politics is contested; (4) critically influenced by *technology*, particularly digital online media that have eroded the power of conventional gatekeepers; (5) *multifaceted*, blurring boundaries of fact and opinion, as well as news and entertainment; (6) defined by a *dynamic interplay* among leaders, media, and citizens; and (7) *a global phenomenon*, with commonalities across different societies, as well as structural differences.

Amid this all are the basic questions: Is politics advancing democratic aims? Does political communication enhance the public good? What unnerves the populace and ails contemporary media democracies? To grapple with these questions, we need to explore classic philosophical approaches, the focus of the next chapter.

REFERENCES

Altheide, D. L., & Snow, R. P. (1979). *Media logic*. Beverly Hills, CA: Sage.

Baker, M., & Blaagaard, B. B. (2016). Reconceptualizing citizen media: A preliminary charting of a complex domain. In M. Baker & B. B. Blaagaard (Eds.), *Citizen media and public spaces: Diverse expressions of citizenship and dissent* (pp. 1–22). New York: Routledge.

Baker, P., & Schmitt, E. (2014, September 30). Fault is shared in misjudging of ISIS threat. *The New York Times*, A1, A8.

Ball, T. (2011). Manipulation: As old as democracy itself (and sometimes dangerous). In W. Le Cheminant & J.M. Parrish (Eds.), *Manipulating democracy: Democratic theory, political psychology, and mass media* (pp. 41–58). New York: Routledge.

Barbaro, M., & Healy, P. (2016, October 9). Why Republicans broke out in sudden revolt this time. *The New York Times*, 1, 27.

Barnard, A. (2016, August 19). An injured child, symbol of Syrian suffering. *The New York Times*, A1, A9.

Baumgartner, J., & Morris, J.S. (2006). *The Daily Show* effect: Candidate evaluations, efficacy, and American youth. *American Politics Research, 34*, 341–367.

Bazelon, E. (2015, August 23). Status: Unknown. *The New York Times Magazine*.

Blumenthal, S. (2012, October 22). Lincoln plays to win. *Newsweek*, 32–38.

Blumler, J.G. (2014). Mediatization and democracy. In F. Esser & J. Strömbäck (Eds.), *Mediatization of politics: Understanding the transformation of western democracies* (pp. 31–41). London: Palgrave Macmillan.

Blumler, J.G. (2015). Core theories of political communication: Foundational and freshly minted. *Communication Theory, 25*, 426–438.

Brock, D., Rabin-Havt, A., & Media Matters for America (2012). *The Fox effect: How Roger Ailes turned a network into a propaganda machine*. New York: Anchor Books.

Bromwich, M. (2016, August 22). A conservative website with a foot on the pedal. *The New York Times*, B3.

Bruni, F. (2015, August 2). We invited Donald Trump to town. *The New York Times* (Sunday Review), 3.

Burns, A., Haberman, M., & Martin, J. (2016, October 8). Tape reveals trump boast about groping women. *The New York Times*, A1, A12.

Chadwick, A. (2013). *The hybrid media system: Politics and power*. New York: Oxford University Press.

Chadwick, A., Dennis, J., & Smith, A.P. (2016). Politics in the age of hybrid media. In A. Bruns, G. Enli, E. Skogerbø, A.O. Larsson, & C. Christensen (Eds.), *The Routledge companion to social media and politics* (pp. 7–22). New York: Routledge.

Coleman, S., & Freelon, D. (2015). Introduction: conceptualizing digital politics. In S. Coleman & D. Freelon (Eds.), *Handbook of digital politics* (pp. 1–13). Cheltenham: Edward Elgar.

Daley, S. (2015, July 4). Greek voters are battered by a barrage of doomsday ads. *The New York Times*, A4, A8.

Davis, J.H., & Sussman, D. (2014, September 17). Obama faulted in terror fight, new poll finds. *The New York Times*. Retrieved from www.nytimes.com/2014/09/18/us/politics/for-first-time-most-americans-disapprove-of-obamas-handling-of-terrorism. html (Accessed January 31, 2017).

Davis, R., & Owen, D. (1998). *New media and American politics*. New York: Oxford.

Deane, C., Duggan, M., & Morin, R. (2016, December 15). *Americans name the 10 most significant historic events of their lifetimes*. Pew Research Center: U.S. Politics & Policy. Retrieved from www.people-press.org/2016/12/15/americans-name-the-10-most-significant-historic-events-of-their-lifetimes/ (Accessed January 7, 2017).

Delli Carpini, M.X. (2016). The new normal? Campaigns & elections in the contemporary media environment. In D. Lilleker, E. Thorsen, D. Jackson, & A. Veneti (Eds.), *US election analysis 2016: Media, voters and the campaign: Early reflections from leading academics* (p. 20). Poole, England: Centre for the Study of Journalism, Culture and Community.

Denton, R.E., Jr., & Kuypers, J.A. (2008). *Politics and communication in America: Campaigns, media, and governing in the 21st century.* Long Grove, IL: Waveland Press.

Denton, R.E., Jr., & Woodward, G.C. (1998). *Political communication in America* (3rd ed.). Westport, CT: Praeger.

Dutton, W.H., & Dubois, E. (2015). The fifth estate: A rising force of pluralistic accountability. In *Handbook of digital politics* (pp. 51–66). Cheltenham: Edward Elgar.

Edelman, M. (1964). *The symbolic uses of politics.* Urbana: University of Illinois Press.

Edelman, M. (1971). *Politics as symbolic action: Mass arousal and quiescence.* New York: Academic Press.

Egan, T. (2015, July 10). Not like us. *The New York Times.* Retrieved from www.nytimes.com/2015/07/10/opinion/not-like-us.html (Accessed January 31, 2017).

Entman, R.M. (1989). *Democracy without citizens: Media and the decay of American politics.* New York: Oxford University Press.

Esser, F. (2008). Dimensions of political news cultures: Sound bite and image bite news in France, Germany, Great Britain, and the United States. *Press/Politics, 13*, 401–428.

Esser, F. (2013). Mediatization as a challenge: Media logic versus political logic. In H. Kriesi, S. Lavenex, F. Esser, J. Matthes, M. Bühlmann, & D. Bochsler (Eds.), *Democracy in the age of globalization and mediatization.* (pp. 155–176). London: Palgrave Macmillan.

Esser, F., & Strömbäck, J. (2012). Comparing election campaign communication. In F. Esser & T. Hanitzsch (Eds.), *Handbook of comparative communication research* (pp. 308–326). New York: Routledge.

Esser, F., & Strömbäck, J. (2014). A paradigm in the making: Lessons for the future of mediatization research. In F. Esser & J. Strömbäck (Eds.), *Mediatization of politics: Understanding the transformation of western democracies* (pp. 223- 242). London: Palgrave Macmillan.

Euchner, C.C. (1990). Presidential appearances. In *The presidents and the public* (pp. 109–129). Washington, DC: Congressional Quarterly.

Falk, E. (2010). *Women for president: Media bias in nine campaigns* (2nd ed.). Urbana: University of Illinois Press.

Fausset, R. (2017, January 25). Hall of mirrors. *The New York Times,* A10.

Flegenheimer, M. (2016, August 26). Clinton says Trump aids a racist "radical fringe". *The New York Times,* A12.

Flew, T., & Swift, A. (2015). Engaging, persuading, and entertaining citizens: Mediatization and the Australian political public sphere. *Press/Politics, 20*, 108–128.

Greenberg, S.B. (2011, July 31). Why voters tune out Democrats. *The New York Times* (Sunday Review), 1, 6.

Grimes, W. (2016, August 26). Warren Hinckle, editor of Ramparts and voice for radical left, dies at 77. *The New York Times,* B14.

Grinspan, J. (2014, September 13). Don't throw the bums out. *The New York Times,* A19.

Grossman, S. (2015, September 26). Donald Trump, our reality TV candidate. *The New York Times.* Retrieved from www.nytimes.com/2015/09/27/opinion/donald-trump-our-reality . . . (Accessed February 22, 2016).

Haberman, C. (2012, September 30). Publisher who transformed The Times for new era. *The New York Times,* 1, 33–35.

Hallin, D. C., & Mancini, P. (2004). *Comparing media systems: Three models of media and politics*. New York: Cambridge University Press.

Hayes, D. (2016, August 21). Donald Trump takes aim. *The New York Times* (Sunday Review), 1, 7.

Herman, E. S., & Chomsky, N. (2002). *Manufacturing consent: The political economy of the mass media*. New York: Pantheon.

Hurley, P. A., & Hill, K. Q. (2010). In search of representation theory. In J. E. Leighley (Ed.), *The Oxford handbook of American elections and political behavior* (pp. 716–740). New York: Oxford University Press.

Iyengar, S. (2004). Engineering consent: The renaissance of mass communications research in politics. In J. T. Jost, M. R. Banaji, & D. A. Prentice (Eds.), *Perspectivism in social psychology: The yin and yang of scientific progress* (pp. 247–257). Washington, DC: American Psychological Association.

Jamieson, K. H. (1988). *Eloquence in an electronic age: The transformation of political speechmaking*. New York: Oxford University Press.

Jamieson, K. H., & Kenski, K. (2014). Political communication: Then, now, and beyond. In K. Kenski & K. H. Jamieson (Eds.), *The Oxford handbook of political communication*. Retrieved from www.oxford.handbooks.com. (Accessed July 17, 2016).

Johnson, K. (2016, August 19). Seattle's young face a future in scary flux. *The New York Times*, A1, A14.

Jones, J. P. (2010). *Entertaining politics: Satiric television and political engagement* (2nd ed.). Lanham, MD: Rowman & Littlefield.

Jungherr, A. (2014). The logic of political coverage on Twitter: Temporal dynamics and content. *Journal of Communication, 64*, 239–259.

Kakutani, M. (2017, January 28). Why "1984" is a 2017 must-read. *The New York Times*, C17, C23.

Kosicki, G. M., McLeod, D. M., & McLeod, J. M. (2011). Looking back and looking forward: Observations on the role of research methods in the rapidly evolving field of political communication. In E. P. Bucy & R. L. Holbert (Eds.), *The sourcebook for political communication research: Methods, measures, and analytical techniques* (pp. 543–569). New York: Routledge.

Kunelius, R., & Reunanen, E. (2016). Changing power of journalism: The two phases of mediatization. *Communication Theory, 26*, 369–388.

Lasswell, H. (1936). *Politics: Who gets what, when, how*. New York: McGraw-Hill.

Lees-Marshment, J. (2010). Global political marketing. In J. Lees-Marshment, J. Strömbäck, & C. Rudd (Eds.), *Global political marketing* (pp. 1–15). New York: Routledge.

Leland, J. (2016, January 31). They're mad and sure their guy is the one to lead the fight. *The New York Times*, 1, 21.

Lipton, E., Sanger, D. E., & Shane, S. (2016, December 14). Hacking the Democrats. *The New York Times*, A1, A14–A17.

Lyall, S. (2016, November 9). Inspired by history's ghosts, women vote and pay tribute. *The New York Times*, A1, P3.

Manheim, J. B. (2011). *Strategy in information and influence campaigns: How policy advocates, social movements, insurgent groups, corporations, governments, and others get what they want*. New York: Routledge.

Manjoo, F. (2015, May 8). Facebook finds opposing views trickle through. *The New York Times*, A1, B7.

Marcinkowski, F., & Steiner, A. (2014). Mediatization and political autonomy: A systems approach. In F. Esser & J. Strömbäck (Eds.), *Mediatization of politics: Understanding the transformation of western democracies* (pp. 74–89). London: Palgrave Macmillan.

Mazzoleni, G., & Schulz, W. (1999). "Mediatization" of politics: A challenge for democracy? *Political Communication, 16*, 247–262.

McLuhan, M. (1964). *Understanding media: The extensions of man*. New York: McGraw-Hill.

McNair, B. (1995). *An introduction to political communication*. London: Routledge.

Morin, R. (1996, February 5–11). Tuned out, turned off. *The Washington Post National Weekly Edition*, 6–8.

Newkirk, V.R., II. (2016, August 28). One nation, under stress. *The New York Times Book Review*, 14.

Offe, C. (1984). *Contradictions of the welfare state*. Cambridge, MA: MIT Press.

Patterson, T.E. (1980). *The mass media election: How Americans choose their president*. New York: Praeger.

Patterson, T.E. (1993). *Out of order*. New York: Knopf.

Patterson, T.E. (2016, June 13). *Pre-primary news coverage of the 2016 presidential race: Trump's rise, Sanders' emergence, Clinton's struggle*. Harvard Kennedy School Shorenstein Center on Media, Politics and Public Policy. Retrieved from http://shorensteincenter.org/pre-primary-news-coverage-2016-trump-c. . (Accessed August 28, 2016).

Pfetsch, B., & Esser, F. (2012). Comparing political communication. In F. Esser & T. Hanitzsch (Eds.), *Handbook of comparative communication research* (pp. 25–47). New York: Routledge.

Poniewozik, J. (2016, September 8). Matt Lauer loses the war in a battle between the candidates. *The New York Times*. Retrieved from www.nytimes.com/2016/09/09/arts/television/matt-lauer-presidential-election-hillary-clinton-donald-trump.html (Accessed January 30, 2017).

Porter, E. (2016, August 3). The case for more government, not less. *The New York Times*, B1, B5.

Powell, L., & Cowart, J. (2003). *Political campaign communication: Inside and out*. Boston: Allyn and Bacon.

Pye, L.W. (1993). Political communication. In V. Bogdanor (Ed.), *The Blackwell encyclopedia of political science* (2nd ed., pp. 442–445). Cambridge, MA: Blackwell.

Roller, E. (2015, December 29). Donald Trump's unstoppable virality. *The New York Times*, A19.

Rose, J. (2010). The branding of states: The uneasy marriage of marketing to politics. *Journal of Political Marketing, 9*, 254–275.

Rutenberg, J. (2016a, October 9). Donald Trump, the showman, now caught in the klieg lights. *The New York Times*. Retrieved from www.nytimes.com/2016/10/10/business/media/donald-trump-the-showman-now-caught-in-the-klieg-lights.html (Accessed January 30, 2017).

Rutenberg, J. (2016b, August 22). Pundit turns adviser in the service of Trump. *The New York Times*, B1, B3.

Scammell, M. (2014). *Consumer democracy: The marketing of politics*. New York: Cambridge University Press.

Schudson, M. (1995). *The power of news*. Cambridge, MA: Harvard University Press.

Schudson, M. (2015). *The rise of the right to know: Politics and the culture of transparency, 1945–1975*. Cambridge, MA: Belknap Press of Harvard University Press.

Schulz, W. (2014). Mediatization and new media. In F. Esser & J. Strömbäck (Eds.), *Mediatization of politics: Understanding the transformation of western democracies* (pp. 57–73). London: Palgrave Macmillan.

Schutz, C.E. (1977). *Political humor: From Aristophanes to Sam Ervin*. Rutherford, NJ: Fairleigh Dickinson University Press.

Shear, M.D., & Corasaniti, N. (2016, July 25). Live videos, small screens: Campaigns hope voters like what they see. *The New York Times*, A12.

Simon, J. (2015). *The new censorship: Inside the global battle for media freedom*. New York: Columbia University Press.

Somaiya, R. (2015, July 25). Trump's wealth and early poll numbers complicate news media's coverage decisions. *The New York Times*, A14.

Strömbäck, J. (2008). Four phases of mediatization: An analysis of the mediatization of politics. *International Journal of Press/Politics, 13*, 228–246.

Strömbäck, J., & Esser, F. (2014). Mediatization of politics: Towards a theoretical framework. In F. Esser & J. Strömbäck (Eds.), *Mediatization of politics: Understanding the transformation of western democracies* (pp. 3–28). London: Palgrave Macmillan.

Strömbäck, J., & Kaid, L.L. (2008). A framework for comparing election news coverage around the world. In J. Strömbäck & L.L. Kaid (Eds.), *The handbook of election news coverage around the world* (pp. 1–18). New York: Routledge.

Stromer-Galley, J. (2014). *Presidential campaigning in the Internet age*. New York: Oxford University Press.

Swanson, D.L., & Mancini, P. (1996). Patterns of modern electoral campaigning and their consequences. In D.L. Swanson & P. Mancini (Eds.), *Politics, media, and modern democracy: An international study of innovations in electoral campaigning and their consequences* (pp. 247–276). Westport, CT: Praeger.

Van Aelst, P., & Walgrave, S. (2016). Information and arena: The dual function of the news media for political elites. *Journal of Communication, 66*, 496–518.

Williams, R.H. (2010). *Realigning America: McKinley, Bryan, and the remarkable election of 1896*. Lawrence: University Press of Kansas.

Wolfsfeld, G., Segev, E., & Sheafer, T. (2013). Social media and the Arab Spring: Politics comes first. *International Journal of Press/Politics, 18*, 115–137.

Wolin, S.S. (1996). Fugitive democracy. In S. Benhabib (Ed.), *Democracy and difference: Contesting the boundaries of the political* (pp. 31–45). Princeton, NJ: Princeton University Press.

CHAPTER

2

Philosophy, Democracy, and Political Communication

Some argue that the problem with American democracy is there are too many angry voices. Others counter that the voices aren't angry enough. Some believe we need more thoughtful dialogue, others retort that dialogue isn't the problem. It's the money that pollutes the process, contaminating whatever dialogue emerges. Opinions are the oxygen of democracy, and they are to be celebrated and appreciated. But—there is always a "but" when we talk about politics!—we also want to know if opinions like those above are credible, and the degree to which they represent a reasoned evaluation of political communication.

To answer these questions and determine whether our political communication measures up to our ideals, we must begin by asking what we want the system to accomplish. We should examine what constitutes an ideal democratic system and the role communication ought to play in democratic politics. People frequently criticize the role political media play in democratic societies, but how can we come to terms with their criticisms without a working concept of democracy or a notion of the role communication *should* play in the process of self-government? To adequately appreciate contemporary political communication, one should begin with ideals, grappling with great thinkers' visions of how democracy should operate. To do this, we need to turn the clock back, and not just a little, but way back, to the time of ancient Greece, and then proceed chronologically to explore core visions of the democratic state.

Theoretical perspectives on what ought to be are called **normative models**—in this case, ethical frameworks providing prescriptive guidelines for political communication. The sections that follow review normative precepts of classical Greek Democracy, liberal democracy, and deliberative democracy theory. Guided by these philosophical perspectives, I offer a definition of democracy and wrestle with the degree to which the U.S. has been a democratic society. The chapter then outlines four shortcomings of contemporary media-centered democracy, discusses alternative views, and articulates the important role ethics can play in political communication.

NORMATIVE THEORIES OF DEMOCRACY

Classical Direct Democracy

Athenian democracy was distinctive, unique in its time. It also articulated key principles that have guided subsequent democratic theories and underpin contemporary democratic governments.

In ancient Greece, citizens ruled. In the 5th century BC, an assembly with a quorum of 6,000 Athenians met over 40 times each year, discussing, debating, and making policy on taxes, foreign alliances, and declaration of war. Politics was the centerpiece of the polis, or city-state. The classic democratic model embraced liberty and enshrined equality, emphasizing that each citizen was guaranteed the opportunity of "ruling *and* being ruled in turn" (Held, 2006, p. 17). The Greek model presumed that individuals directly participated in everyday legislative and judicial activities. In the Greeks' direct democratic model, citizens were expected to participate in politics. The statesman Pericles put it bluntly: "*We do not say that a man who takes no interest in politics is a man who minds his own business; we say that he has no business here at all*" (Held, 2006, p. 14).

Imagine a politician who uttered those words today. She or he would be called an elitist (as well as a sexist), and would be parodied on YouTube. But, for the ancient Greeks, political participation was endemic to citizenship. The philosopher Aristotle endorsed this view, arguing that human beings were political animals. But he did not mean that people were political in the sense we sometimes use the term today—networking and conniving to gain advantage over others. Aristotle believed that the good life consisted of participation with others on common tasks and deliberating in public to determine just outcomes for the larger community (see Figure 2.1).

Rhetoric (what we now call persuasion) played a central role in Greek society. Intense discussions preceded policy decisions, such as whether to invade a foreign land (Finley, 1973). According to Aristotle, the capacity to formulate reasoned arguments about justice and

Figure 2.1 The Greek philosopher Aristotle championed political communication, arguing that the good life involves active participation with others on common political tasks

Shutterstock

injustice predisposed people to form political communities where such issues could be discussed and solved. Communication presumably helped constitute a political community, defining and shaping the community's identity.

Although civics books traditionally sing the praises of Greek democracy, it has shortcomings and nuanced complexities. The Athenian model enshrined equality, but only allowed male citizens over the age of 20 to participate in politics. Slaves outnumbered free male citizens, but they were precluded from participation. Women had few civic rights and no political rights whatsoever. To paraphrase Orwell (1946), all Athenians were (in theory) equal, but male Athenians were much more equal than others.

Liberal Democracy

There is not one model of liberal democracy, but many. The models have been articulated by some of the most celebrated theorists of democracy, including John Locke, John Stuart Mill, and James Madison. Liberal democratic concepts, which emphasize individual rights and representative government, are the ones that are popularly associated with democracy. However, liberal democracy theorists do not use the term "liberal" in the sense we use it today, as when we refer to liberal Democrats. Theoretically, the term corresponds more closely to "libertarian," emphasizing a system of democracy that preserves individual liberties and disdains government intervention.

Liberal democratic theories evolved in the 17th and 18th centuries as people grew frustrated with the power of absolutist rulers and the many ways that European monarchies stifled individual freedom. Democratic government emerged as a way to protect individuals from oppressive use of political power. Liberal perspectives on democracy emphasize *the natural rights of individuals*—their right to life, liberty, property, and pursuit of happiness, to combine the writings of Locke and Thomas Jefferson. This was exciting and important stuff, the notion that individuals had inalienable rights that government could not sever. Liberal democratic approaches emphasized that an individual should be allowed to follow his (much later, her) own drummer in matters of speech, press, religion, and economics. People needed a sphere of life where despotic monarchs could not intervene. Thus, liberal theories embraced the *private sphere*: for example, private enterprise and private property.

But there was a problem. If people had inalienable rights, what role should government play? How could the need for order, preserved by government, be reconciled with individuals' rights? How could *might* be reconciled with *rights*? (e.g., Held, 2006). It is a quintessential question, still relevant today, and the first liberal democrats developed a series of creative ideas. Noting that society had become too large and cumbersome for all to participate, they recognized that the Athenian notion of direct democracy was impractical for mass society. They advocated representative government, in which citizens elected others to stand in for them and represent their viewpoints on matters of policy. Elections provided a way to ensure that individuals determined government policy, making "public officials the servants rather than the masters of the citizenry" (Katz, 1997, p. 63).

Communication plays a key role in liberal democratic models. With its emphasis on the private market, liberal democracy theorists view politics as a marketplace of ideas, in which a variety of media products—good and bad, accurate and inaccurate—compete for audience attention. Just as different products compete in the economic market, political ideas collide in the intellectual marketplace. In the end, some philosophers argued, truth will win out. Censorship is problematic and unnecessary. John Stuart Mill pinpointed the problems with media censorship, famously noting that

> if the opinion is right, (people) are deprived of the opportunity of exchanging error for truth: if wrong, they lose, what is almost as great a benefit, the clearer perception and livelier impression of truth, produced by its collision with error.
>
> (Mill, 1859/2009, p. 20)

Liberal democracy advocates call for a free, competitive press, in which a thousand flowers—roses and daisies, but also weeds and underbrush—bloom. In the 19th century, theorists embraced the penny press, newspapers that cost a penny and were filled with crime stories, as well as partisan papers that took political positions. Libertarian scholars of the 21st century similarly argue that society needs a no-holes-barred free press, one that includes mainstream media; public, educational television; cable television shows; blogs; and social media, although the latter straddle news and information.

For proponents of liberal democracy theory, arguments, even feisty and aggressive ones, are the coin of the political realm. As theorist Michael Walzer (1983) notes, "Democracy puts a premium on speech, persuasion, rhetorical skill. Ideally, the citizen who makes the most persuasive argument—that is, the argument that actually persuades the largest number of citizens—gets his way" (p. 304). In the private marketplace of ideas that liberal democracy prizes, arguments—uncensored, freewheeling, feisty, and passionately held—are the stuff of democratic communication. The beauty of the marketplace is that it allows diverse viewpoints to be heard and enables advocates to make their best case before the jury of the electorate. Consistent with this view, we do have a great deal of freewheeling disagreement, with eloquent arguments intermingled with angry, venomous posts.

But there is a philosophical problem: In his defense of liberal democratic theory, Walzer conflates the most persuasive argument, the one that convinces the most citizens, with the normatively and ethically *best* argument. He seems to assume that the argument that convinces the most people is also the best, in an ethical sense. But arguments can be persuasive because they scare people or raise the specter that unrealistically negative events will transpire if a candidate from the opposing party takes office. Just because an argument is persuasive does not mean it is worthy of moral approval. What's more, all arguments are not equal. In a nation where money buys access (Schlozman, Verba, & Brady, 2012) and fewer than 400 super-wealthy families raised almost half of the money in the early phases of the 2016 presidential campaign (Confessore, Cohen, & Yourish, 2015), the arguments that carry the greatest weight with most people may be those formulated and delivered by the wealthiest few.

To liberal democrats, these are fair criticisms of democracy, but pale in comparison to the greater good of freewheeling, unfettered speech. Noting that "people are able and willing to put aside their social biases," liberal theorists emphasize that "the best way to guarantee truth in the public sphere is free, open, and unchecked debate in which both error and truth have equal access" (Christians, Glasser, McQuail, Nordenstreng, & White, 2009, p. 49).

Deliberative Democracy

Deliberative democracy theorists, the newest intellectual kids on the democracy block, take issue with liberal democratic theory. What could be wrong with liberal democracy, you may ask? How can one argue with freedom, liberty, and competition among ideas in the political marketplace? Deliberative democracy advocates look at liberal democracy through a different set of lenses, noting that the marketplace metaphor diminishes the deeper role that politics ought to play in the lives of its citizens. Voters are not mere *consumers* choosing among different political brands, but *citizens* whose thoughtful participation in politics serves as the foundation for democratic government. Politics, they emphasize, should not focus simply on protecting the *rights* of individuals, but on discovering ways to enhance the collective *good* of society. They urge "an imaginative rethinking of democracy offering a new kind of participation, one that not only gives citizens more power, but also allows them more opportunities to exercise this power thoughtfully" (Held, 2006, p. 235).

The cornerstone is the concept of deliberation. Unlike conversations or dialogue, deliberation focuses on tackling a shared social or political problem with the goal of coming up with solutions. It involves disagreements among people, assessments of the merits of different arguments, willingness to revise opinions in light of ideas put forth by other discussants, and participation in the hard work of devising a solution that is workable and pleasing to all or most parties (Chambers, 2003; Stromer-Galley, 2007).

Based on these distinctions, political communication scholar Jennifer Stromer-Galley (2007) helpfully defines **deliberation** as "a process whereby groups of people, often ordinary citizens, engage in reasoned opinion expression on a social or political issue in an attempt to identify solutions to a common problem and to evaluate those solutions" (p. 3). Democratic deliberation requires that participants obtain information about the problem and establish a process that ensures a fair, egalitarian process of communication (Gastil, 2008). The key to building a strong democracy is deliberation—discussion, debate, and conversation about political issues. Deliberation, theorists argue, rejuvenates democracy by helping citizens appreciate the connection between government and their everyday concerns, encouraging participation in elections and community activities. On a broader level, deliberation helps citizens view the public sphere as a vital arena in which they can contribute (Jacobs, Cook, & Delli Carpini, 2009).

Deliberative democracy theories parallel other contemporary perspectives that emphasize the importance of the **public sphere**, as opposed to the private sector, and call for more citizen participation in politics (Barber, 1984; Habermas, 1996). The public sphere is an interpersonal or virtual domain that emerges in the space between the private domain of our individual lives and the sphere of government (Ward, 2015). The public sphere is the amorphous arena—frequently online—where people talk, argue (sometimes angrily and harshly), but ideally in a thoughtful fashion. Nowadays, with the plethora of diverse online political sites, there is not just one public sphere, mediated by the conventional press, but many different spheres, varying in the content of political discourse, with networks crisscrossing, overlapping, and dissolving when an issue has reached its zenith in the larger national debate (Baker & Blaagaard, 2016; Bruns & Highfield, 2016). Deliberative democrats celebrate public spheres, but emphasize that these domains should prize thoughtful, public discussions rather than affect-based, knee-jerk, mean-spirited discussions. Lamenting the *quality* of contemporary democracy, deliberative democracy theorists argue that our politics needs a cognitive revamping. A vigorous democracy requires that citizens (a) engage in broad, reflective consideration of political issues; (b) take into account a variety of perspectives that extend beyond their own material self-interest; and (c) articulate sound arguments that can be competently justified in group settings and will ultimately influence public policy (Cohen, 1998; Gastil, 2008; Gutmann & Thompson, 1996; Offe & Preuss, 1991).

Without reflective thinking, theorists note, our politics is nothing more than a shrill blast of noise, a loud cacophony of selfish interests competing futilely on the public stage. Deliberative democracy advocates argue that we should have more civil and respectful public dialogues, such as community forums that can help set agendas and shape municipal policy. They lament that democracy has come to marketing appeals to consumers, rather than thoughtfully directing messages to citizens for reflective discussion.

"The very transformation of publics into exclusive target audiences is a blow to the democratic ideal of publics as inclusive deliberative bodies," two scholars exclaim (Bennett & Manheim, 2001, p. 280). Deliberative democratic supporters urge that journalists cut back on horse race reporting that focuses on election polls and consultants' strategies. Instead, deliberation proponents have recommended that journalists embrace public journalism, a movement born in the 1990s that emphasized ways reporters could reconnect with the larger communities in which they work, elevating concerns of the public over those of political elites (Rosen & Merritt, 1994).

When it comes to the Internet, deliberative democrats applaud websites like www.patch.com that offer citizens opportunities to discuss community problems. They embrace e-democracy programs, such as online public forums and collective dialogues on conservative and liberal blogs, in which online members contribute ideas, others respond, and people can revise ideas in light of the thread of discussion (Perlmutter, 2008). They are more critical of social media posts that lead to long vitriolic harangues. In their attitudes toward communication and other topics, deliberative democrats hark back to the classical theorists of ancient Greece, arguing that a good life is lived in the context of a vibrant civic community that embraces citizenship (Finley, 1983).

Complexities

There is an enormous scholarly literature on deliberation, and it has examined the quality of communication in deliberative discussions, effects of deliberation on democratic outcomes, and the influences of different deliberative formats on knowledge and attitudes (Jacobs et al., 2009; Myers & Mendelberg, 2013). It may sound like deliberation about political issues is a good thing, a cure-all, because who can oppose the idea of people coming together to reach agreement about conflicting solutions to social problems? Indeed, there is evidence that exposure to disagreement in political discussions bolsters knowledge, contributes to people's ability to offer reasons why others might disagree with their perspective, and enhances sophistication of political beliefs (Price, Cappella, & Nir, 2002; Gastil & Dillard, 1999). But there are downsides.

Deliberation can exacerbate conflict between people on different sides of the issue, unleashed when they hear strident comments from partisans from the rival camp. Deliberative political discussions sometimes intensify preexisting attitudes, perhaps leading individuals to cling more defensively to what they already believe (Wojcieszak & Price, 2010). Deliberative groups can also favor the dominant groups in society—men, rather than women, Whites rather than people of color, members of mainstream, rather than minority, religious groups (Sanders, 1997). Deliberation, while good in theory, is hard to achieve in a society as large, diversified, and fragmented as the U.S. Prying people from their political comfort zones is hard. There are plenty of political discussions online, but deliberation that prizes reflective consideration of different perspectives is rare.

Practical problems also emerge. How can citizens' deliberations possibly influence policy in a country governed by elected representatives of the people? How can communicators encourage online deliberation rather than the partisan, venomous, sometimes obscene posts in response to comments that take a dissonant point view? (see Goidel, Kirzinger, & Xenos, 2011; Hibbing & Theiss-Morse, 2002). And, of course, libertarians would argue that deliberative democracy's emphasis on civic, rule-based discussions unnecessarily restricts the unabashed expression of divergent perspectives.

These are not easy questions. Political communication in a democracy is full of trade-offs. Liberal democracy ethos celebrates individuals' *rights* to put forth a range of rhetorical arguments, but assigns less importance to the public *good*: a civil, unprejudiced, and respectful communicative sphere. Deliberative democracy prizes a public good ideally achieved by robust debate, but minimizes the rough-and-tumble downsides of debates: polarization of attitudes and the hurt feelings that result from rancorous discussion of white-hot political issues.

In its most mature, integrative form, deliberative democracy's emphasis on vibrant citizenship is tempered by recognition that, even with spirited, open discussions, citizens of different political positions will not agree on contemporary issues. Faith-based conservatives will not see eye to eye with secular liberals. Big government Democrats will disagree with pro-business Republicans. For deliberative democratic theorists, moral and political disagreements are okay, part of the warp and woof of democracy, provided they are discussed respectfully, based on sound reasons, and with appreciation for the ways different principles underlie divergent political viewpoints. As Gutmann and Thompson (1996) note, "While acknowledging that we are destined to disagree, deliberative democracy also affirms that we are capable of deciding our common destiny on mutually acceptable terms" (p. 361). For deliberative democrats, the means are more important than the ends.

Defining Democracy

Each of the three perspectives celebrates democracy, focusing on different elements. Classical Greek democracy prizes citizen participation, liberal democracy emphasizes individual rights, while deliberative democracy highlights the importance of thoughtful discussion of public issues (see Table 2.1).

By braiding the different strands of these approaches, we can appreciate the core characteristics of democratic government. The term democracy is a commonplace, an

Table 2.1 Three normative perspectives on democracy.

Classical Greek Direct Democracy

Principles
- Direct citizen participation
- Equality
- Citizen obligation to society

Communication emphasis
- Well-crafted rhetorical arguments

Shortcoming
- Impractical in mass society

Liberal Democracy

Principles
- Natural rights of individuals
- Representative government
- Private marketplace of ideas

Communication emphasis
- Free expression, no-holds-barred press

Shortcoming
- Treats citizenship as a private commodity rather than public good

Deliberative Democracy

Principles
- Reasoned public deliberation about issues
- Civil discourse
- Collective dialogue that influences policy

Communication emphasis
- Forums/articles that encourage reflection

Shortcoming
- Is difficult in practice to get partisan citizens to deliberate, rather than argue with one another

everyday platitude, a term advocates throw into a conversation when they want to bolster their side, like a child who says that a popular classmate supports her idea. But democracy is a multifaceted term, defined differently over the years and subject to much scholarly discussion. By integrating the work of scholars, one gains insights into core aspects of the concept. **Democracy** has seven core characteristics: (1) the right of all adult citizens to vote and run for office; (2) free, fair elections involving more than one political party; (3) individual liberty and freedom of expression, including for those who oppose the party in power; (4) protection of human rights, notably those of minorities, or those out of step with the majority; (5) freedom of news media to challenge the powers that be; (6) a civil society characterized by the right to form associations, such as parties and interest groups, that attempt to shape the agenda and influence public policy; and (7) to the extent possible in a large complex society, a culture of public communication that provides opportunities for reasoned public deliberation (Coleman & Blumler, 2009; Dahl, 1989; Kriesi, 2013; *The Economist*, 2013). (We might add an eighth characteristic, after the 2016 campaign when Trump suggested he might not honor the results of the election: acceptance of the legitimacy of the electoral process, a critical precondition for peaceful transfer of power.) Nations clearly differ on these characteristics, and democracy can be viewed as lying along a continuum.

Intriguingly, this typology yields a disturbing conclusion. Using these attributes as a yardstick, it is patently clear that the United States—for all the rhetoric and textbook socialization—did not fully qualify as a democratic society throughout much of the 19th and 20th centuries. We like to think of the American Revolution as blazing new paths for democratic government, and the revolution did achieve important social and political goals (Wood, 1991). But during the 19th century, when slavery deprived Blacks of their freedom and dignity, forcing them to endure unimaginable physical and emotional cruelty, the U.S. was not a democratic society. African Americans could not vote or run for office. When these barriers were lifted, but Jim Crow laws restricted voting and barred Blacks from elective office (among other horrific restrictions), elections remained neither free nor fair. When immigrant groups were treated with prejudice and could not contest the party in power, liberty and individual freedom hardly reigned.

Thanks to civil rights protests and sweeping legal and institutional changes over the past 50 years, the situation changed. The U.S. has traditionally been among the approximately 15 percent of the countries in the world that are regarded as a full democracy (*The Economist*, 2013). Yet in the wake of declining trust of government and elected public officials, a prominent study downgraded the U.S. slightly, but to a sufficient degree that it dropped to the second tier category of a "flawed democracy" (*The Economist*, 2017). More broadly, although the majority of the people in the world choose their governments freely, there is variability in the degree to which these countries can be viewed as full democracies (Kriesi, 2013). Indeed, some countries, such as those in Latin America and Eastern Europe, are defective democracies, lacking some of the core democratic characteristics, like free and fair elections. Still other countries, more than 30 percent, have virtually no democratic characteristics: They are authoritarian regimes.

American democracy, despite its significant strides over the years, remains imperfect, with some laws on the books that require voters to show they have photo identification before they can receive a ballot, and others that eliminate the opportunity to register and vote on the same day. The laws are controversial, with defenders (including a majority of the Supreme Court) and detractors. Importantly, these laws disproportionately affect lower-income and minority citizens, the most vulnerable members of society. By preventing people from registering and voting at the same time, a virtual necessity for poorer Americans who move a lot and find it difficult to regularly update their voting information, the laws in some states can reduce turnout among lower-income citizens. By accepting some types of photo IDs at the polls, like gun permits (held primarily by Whites), but not others (employee or state school IDs), Texas may be inadvertently or deliberately preventing minorities from voting (Rutenberg, 2015). To some critics, the laws reflect the continuation of the nation's visceral legacy of White racism (Coates, 2015). Others note that America's decentralized, local, and partisan election procedures lead to voting irregularities and an uneven record of electoral integrity across different states (Norris, 2016).

Democracy is a "moving target" (Kriesi, 2013), a work in progress, in theory the best of all political systems, but, in reality, a far-from-perfect form of government—an ideal toward which governments strive. Democratic government cannot prevent people—voters who constitute the electorate—from electing a dictator, demagogue, or leader who tramples on human rights. Government faces dangers when "norms of partisan restraint" erode, as they have in recent years when the congressional fili-buster, once rarely employed, becomes a routine mechanism to obstruct legislation, and one party's activists contend that their opponent is not a legitimate candidate or (in the case of strident opponents of Hillary Clinton) believe she should be jailed (Levitsky & Ziblatt, 2016, p. 5).

All is not bleak. Over the long haul, scholars note, democratic governments contain a number of safeguards and time-honored institutional mechanisms, notably a strong constitution with checks and balances to prevent a demagogue from holding onto the reins of power. Viewing the issue broadly, Czech human rights activist and philosopher Václav Havel eloquently stated in an address to the U.S. Congress:

> As long as people are people, democracy, in the full sense of the word, will always be no more than an ideal. One may approach it as one would the horizon in ways that may be better or worse, but it can never be fully attained. In this sense, you, too, are merely approaching democracy.
>
> (Dionne, 1991, epigram)

POLITICAL COMMUNICATION: A CRITICAL APPROACH

It is noteworthy that across the many centuries in which political philosophers have articulated normative perspectives on democracy, communication has emerged as an important feature (see Table 2.1).

To the ancient Greeks, vigorous debate and the formulation of cogent rhetorical arguments were core elements of direct democracy. In the view of liberal democracy advocates, free and open access to diverse media is the best way to guarantee truth and advocate different political ideas. For deliberative democrats, thoughtful reasoned dialogue builds the civic culture and "commitment to citizenship" that sustains democratic life (Christians et al., 2009, p. 102). Theorists of all three approaches would agree that you cannot have a vibrant democracy without thriving communication. "Free communication among the people," as James Madison noted, is an essential part of democratic self-government, the "only effectual guardian of every other right" (Sunstein, 2002, p. 155). The converse is also true, as Madison observed. A democracy that fails to provide critical information to its citizens, he suggested, "is but a prologue to a farce or a tragedy; or, perhaps both."

In our own times, scholars echo these sentiments. "Political communication is a precondition of democracy, and democracy depends heavily on the infrastructure of the media system," Frank Esser (2013, p. 155) observes. But here is the paradox: As the number of democracies has increased over the several decades (Strömbäck & Esser, 2014), expanding the reach and influence of electoral communication, a dysfunctional set of communicative consequences have resulted, what Pippa Norris (2011) calls "democratic deficits." Political communication is increasingly scandal- and personality-driven. Market-dominated, poll-driven politics have replaced the person-to-person, press-the-flesh, face-to-face politics of yore. Media discussions have become increasingly caustic. Citizens are increasingly dissatisfied with political leaders, in some cases preferring non-politicians to those with experience in the political arena. Voter turnout and trust in political institutions has plummeted (Norris, 2011). During the 2016 election, faced with non-stop negative campaigning, just 46 percent of likely voters indicated they were very enthusiastic about casting a vote, a drop of 16 percent from 2012 (Stolberg, 2016). More than 8 in 10 voters indicated they were disgusted with the presidential campaign (Martin, Sussman, & Thee-Brenan, 2016). All this raises the question of how political reality measures up to democratic ideals. In the view of many contemporary critics, it does not measure up well.

Critics identify four key shortcomings in contemporary American democracy that represent departures from normative ideals.

1. Citizens Are Neither Able Nor Motivated to Partake in Politics

Philosophers from Plato onward have lamented that individuals lack the cognitive competence and motivation to partake in democratic government. Such is the case in America today.

"Vast numbers of Americans are ignorant," one scholar observed, and "not merely of the specialized details of government . . . but of the most elementary political facts—information so basic as to challenge the central tenet of democratic government itself" (see Delli Carpini & Keeter, 1990, p. 23). There is evidence to corroborate this claim. Only about a fourth of the American public can name all three branches of government, but two-thirds could name a TV judge on the *American Idol* television program (Annenberg Policy Center, 2016; Breyer, 2010)! Americans are more ignorant of international affairs than are citizens in other industrialized Western democracies (Iyengar & Hahn, 2011). The competence problem is compounded by a motivational deficit. Just over half of Americans vote in high-profile national elections, compared to three-fourths of their counterparts in Britain and Germany. Nearly 8 in 10 French voters cast ballots in the contentious April 2017 election (Bilefsky, 2017). Voter turnout in the United States remains near the bottom of all democratic societies (Martinez, 2010).

How can one place the United States among the pantheon of the world's democracies when its voters know so little and participate so infrequently? Apathy extends beyond the U.S. On the eve of a critical referendum focused on whether Britain should remain in the European Union, fraught with economic ramifications for the country, many young British voters were more immersed in the frivolities of summer than in casting a vote. Typifying some politically indifferent young Brits, Jennifer Burnett was more intrigued by the British Soap Awards, particularly the teenager soap opera, "Hollyoaks." While she was uncertain about the Brexit vote, she harbored more definite attitudes toward the soap opera. "I know exactly who I'm going to vote for," she said, enthusiastically raising a plastic champagne glass. "Vote 'Hollyoaks,'" she exclaimed, gleefully showcasing the disparity between her motivation to follow a soap opera and lack of interest in a critical national election (de Freytas-Tamura, 2016, p. 1).

2. Politics Is Awash in Greenbacks

Contrary to democratic ideals, all citizens do not have equal access to the political process. Those with more money—millionaires and billionaires—exert an outsized effect on politics. Partly as a result of a controversial 2010 Supreme Court decision, spending by independent political groups has grown exponentially over the past seven years. Major donations are frequently kept secret and donations are slipped through tax-exempt groups that can hide the names of donors who doled out the cash. Organizations with patriotic-sounding names like Alliance for a Free Society spend millions of dollars promoting issue positions, disguising the fact that they are front organizations for groups that stand to benefit financially from the positions they embrace (Confessore & Willis, 2014). This is dishonest and deceptive, and runs counter to democratic norms of transparency.

The name of the game is lobbying, paying to play, advocacy for companies large and small. Those who have more money have greater access to power. As Baumgartner and his colleagues (2009) concluded, "defenders of the status quo usually win in Washington" (p. 239). "Of the billions of dollars spent annually on lobbying in Washington, 72 percent comes from organizations representing business interests, and no more than 2 percent from organizations representing the vast majority below the very top," Schlozman, Verba, and Brady noted (2012, p. 2). For example, the cigarette industry was concerned that a Food and Drug Administration ruling that imposed regulations on potentially hazardous e-cigarettes would cut into tobacco company profits. To fight the rule, America's largest tobacco company enlisted high-powered, politically connected lobbyists, as well as former and current members of Congress to fight the ruling. In one case, the tobacco company literally ventriloquized the words: A member of Congress sympathetic to the tobacco industry introduced a counter-measure that was taken verbatim from the draft of a proposal written by Big Tobacco (Lipton, 2016).

The major party candidates for the 2016 election fit right in. Both were millionaires many times over. One candidate (Trump) argued for tax breaks that would help real estate moguls, reducing his taxes enormously (Stewart, 2016). The other (Clinton) felt "most at ease around millionaires, within the gilded bubble," seemingly willing to bend her positions to fit the wealthy (Chozick & Martin, 2016, p. 8). The continuing influence of powerful moneyed elites disturbs American citizens and is likely a reason why many voters distrust the democratic process.

3. Our Politics Is More Polarized Than Ever

Congress has become dysfunctional, the House of Representatives increasingly dominated by ideologically extreme members of each party who eschew compromise. Democratic and Republican senators threaten to block or filibuster qualified nominees for public office, notably justices for the Supreme Court. It was not always this way. During the 1960s, in particular, and even through the '90s, members of different parties worked together, sometimes compromising so that important bills could pass. Nowadays, partisanship—thanks to gerrymandering of districts, take-no-prisoners interest groups, and election of candidates beholden to them—has increased party polarization, as well as strident conflict between congressional Democrats and Republicans (Kimball & Gross, 2007).

The number of "swing districts" that are up for grabs has declined dramatically over the years. Only about 1 in 5 congressional seats is actually competitive. The majority of elections are taken-for-granted victories by the party that has majority control of the congressional district (Cook, 2013; Wasserman, 2013). The number of moderates in the House—members who broker compromises between the two parties—has sharply declined from 344 of 435 (79 percent) in 1982 to 137 of 435 (31 percent) in 2002 to—are you ready?—4 (0.009 percent) in 2013, and is probably equal to or less than that today (see These two charts, 2014). Party polarization impedes the ability of lawmakers to build bridges to get legislation passed on issues ranging from immigration to Social Security. Gridlock, not consensus building, becomes the byword.

Similar trends have occurred in the American electorate, although less so, and there is debate about the extent of polarization and exactly what this means (Fiorina, 2005). Polarization seems to occur primarily among strong political partisans. Partisans have become more ideologically and affectively polarized in recent years, disliking each other more than ever (Lelkes, 2016). Democratic and Republican voters are more divided along partisan lines and harbor more negative views of the opposing party than in previous years (see Political polarization in the American public, 2014; Jacobson, 2016). Media coverage, with its focus on high-profile partisan combatants, can increase perceptions of polarization; when media depict a divided citizenry, perceptions of polarization increase (Levendusky & Malhotra, 2016a). Selectively tuning in to news information they agree with or that algorithmically reaches their news feed, partisans become more convinced their side is right and may be less exposed to evidence that questions their view. But this runs counter to the canons of deliberative democracy. In contemporary democracy we want voters to deliberate, to think, to consider the other side. We want citizens to listen as well as lambast, to contemplate as well as criticize, to search for nuance as well as negation.

4. Contrary to Deliberative Democratic Ideals, Contemporary Political Communication Is Unrelentingly Negative, Simplistic, and Superficial

Political journalist Joe Klein (2006) spoke for large numbers of Americans when he lamented that "I am fed up with the insulting welter of sterilized, speechifying insipid photo ops, and idiotic advertising that passes for public discourse these days" (p. 13). Jeffrey M. Berry and Sarah Sobieraj (2014) describe contemporary political communication as "the outrage industry." Diana C. Mutz (2015) refers to it as "in your face" media politics. More than 8 in 10 Americans said that the 2016 campaign, with its rampant attack politics, left them feeling disgusted about the state of American politics (Martin et al., 2016).

To wit: Keith Olbermann, a liberal television commentator formerly of MSNBC, peered into the television camera, addressing then President George W. Bush and called him a "fascist." "You, sir," he continued, "have no place in a government of the people, by the people, for the people." Conservative TV talk show host Glenn Beck called Obama a racist, "a guy who has a deep-seated hatred for white people or the white culture." He also likened former Vice President Al Gore's environmental talks at schools to Nazi indoctrination propaganda (Berry & Sobieraj, 2014, pp. 51, 53). In other cases, verbal vitriol has come from candidates. Trump mocked his opponents, belittled women and a disabled reporter, and charged that a judge could not preside fairly over a civil lawsuit involving Trump University because of his Mexican heritage. His opponents returned the venom. Republican candidate Marco Rubio, a Florida senator, paraphrasing a 1980s public service announcement, tweeted that "Friends don't let friends vote for con artists" and suggested Trump had urinated in his pants (Babaro, Haberman, & Parker, 2016)! During the general election campaign, verbal aggression intensified, with Clinton saying in no uncertain terms that Trump was "temperamentally unfit" to be president. She later went so far as to even lambast voters who backed him, famously claiming that one could place half of Trump's supporters into "the basket of deplorables." As these examples show, political media can be the instigator and transmitter of verbal aggression.

Critics also lament that the media focus more on scandals and candidates' personalities than on serious political arguments, offering airtime to polarizing arguments between liberals and conservatives on cable TV talk shows (see Figure 2.2). "Punditry has replaced reporting as journalism's highest calling," political writer Mark Leibovich (2013) laments, noting that it is "accompanied by a mad dash of 'self-branding,' to borrow a term that had now fully infested the city: everyone now hell-bent on branding themselves in the marketplace, like Cheetos" (p. 8). Political manipulation, angry cacophonous talk, and the perception that reporters and public leaders are all part of the same power-absorbed "chattering class"—the Beltway Establishment—can leave people feeling dispirited or cynical. "All they do is fight between each other and don't get anything done," remarked John Miller, an independent voter from Iowa. Kenneth Haynes, who hails from Louisiana, shared a similar opinion when he arrived to vote in the 2014 midterm elections. "They're always calling each other the bad guy when they're all the bad guy," he said. Christi Miller from Hot Springs, Arkansas, went further. "There's no such thing as a good politician, I'm sorry," she said. "They're running for office for money and power" (Nagourney, 2014, p. P9). It isn't just politicians; the Internet and social media is full of anger and venom, as partisans on both sides stream invectives.

But just when you think politics in America can't get any worse, you are reminded that politics is blood sport in other countries too. Take Brazil, where a corruption scandal and clash over whether to impeach the Brazilian president transformed family members, friends, and even subway passengers into enemies. Rallies turned into shouting matches, a former city councilor got in the middle of a brawl that left him with a bloody lip, and children even were enlisted as representatives for one side or the other. It got so bad that a 22-year-old Brazilian saleswoman, clad in a red tank top (red was the color linked with the president's controversial political party), got elbowed on her way to

Figure 2.2 While cable television talk shows on Fox and MSNBC draw large audiences, they also feature polarizing discussions that can turn off many Americans from politics. Here, Fox News talk show host Sean Hannity, who supported Trump during the 2016 campaign, talks politics with one-time Trump campaign manager Corey Lewandowski. In a parallel fashion, over at MSNBC, liberal talk show hosts like Rachel Maddow frequently discuss political issues with liberal commentators who bash conservatives and right-wing ideas.

Getty Images

work by passengers in a crowded subway car who called her a name. "Red happens to be my favorite color," she said adamantly, "and I'm not going to stop wearing it" (Jacobs, 2016a, p. A6). "People compare the legislature to the *House of Cards*, one expert said, "but I disagree. *House of Cards* is actually more believable" (Jacobs, 2016b, p. 11).

Perspectives

Concerned by these problems, critics argue that American politics is in jeopardy. They maintain that our system is in crisis. The arguments are cogent and the issues critics raise are disturbing.

Is there another point of view? There is. You can raise questions about each of the criticisms. A theme of this book is that multiple perspectives shed light on complex issues.

Thus, there are alternative views of the criticisms noted above, glimpsed by viewing them through different lenses. In response to the first lamentation about citizens' lack of knowledge, one might ask whether voters can forget some of the civics they learned in high school, yet still be capable of evaluating the fitness of politicians for public office. Many voters knew the basics of Trump's and Clinton's positions on the issues, while also having well-developed opinions about their personal attributes. Second, one can challenge familiar arguments about money in politics, invoking the First Amendment to argue that political groups should be free to spend as much as they wish in elections. Or one could observe that Bernie Sanders mounted a serious challenge to the Democratic front-runner in 2016 without relying on big money or super PAC donations. Third, although national politics is deeply polarized, political polarization can be less problematic at the state and county government levels, as well as local communities, where people with different viewpoints compromise and work together. What's more, due to "red state versus blue state" media depictions, people perceive the public to be more ideologically divided than it actually is (Levendusky & Malhotra, 2016b).

Fourth, attacks, criticism, and even virulent negative appeals have long been part of politics, dating back to the days when Federalists lambasted Jefferson, calling him the anti-Christ and a demagogue. Political attacks can serve a function for the system by calling attention to long-dormant problems that require a harsh, public airing.

Who is right? Who's wrong? The answers are neither easy nor simple. Some of the problems that face the U.S. are endemic to democracy. Democracy is an imperfect form of government. It depends on citizens to make decisions, and citizens have pet peeves and biases. It relies on elected officials to put aside self-interest and work for the common good, but politicians are ambitious. Democracy requires that different departments of government to work together, but the Constitution disperses power among different branches of government, impeding efforts to find common solutions (see Box 2.1). Democratic society depends on media to relay critical facts and opinions, but in a capitalist and partisan society, the media can be influenced by the lure of profit to favor the most salacious views and devote the most airtime to partisans who speak with the loudest voices.

Yet for all its flaws, democracy remains, as Winston Churchill famously said, the worst form of government, except for all the others. Democracy's aims are noble. It prizes "the human desire to be free and to live under the only form of government consistent with that desire—representative government installed with the consent of the people" (Cohen, 2016, p. A23). Democracy's advocates highlight its strengths by emphasizing that democracy grants all citizens an inherent, equal right to self-determination. They emphasize that democracy is more likely than other forms of government to maximize the collective good, as well as to offer citizens opportunities to fulfill their human potential by working for the public welfare (Delli Carpini & Keeter, 1996).

Ultimately, democracy depends upon its ability to crystallize the relationship between two core elements: the government and the citizens it governs (Mandelbaum, 2007, p. 104). Communication, as theorists from Madison to contemporary scholars note, plays a central role by connecting the leaders who govern with the citizens they govern. Communication cannot, alas, change economic or political structures, but it allows for dialogue among different core participants, providing the fuel that fosters democratic decision-making and enhancing the tolerance on which democracy depends. Communication provides an avenue to promote leaders' accountability to citizens. It diffuses ideas and information that can grow the seeds of political change. Yet all this presumes that communication is grounded in decency and ethics.

Ethics in Political Communication

Here's the rub: What exactly does an ethical political communication perspective mean? After all, many people would not utter politics and ethics in the same breath, figuring they don't have much to do with each other, believing that politics is nothing if unethical. With lobbying, political opportunism, cronyism, and rampant reports of politicians who will do whatever it takes to amass power or resources, it may be high-nigh impossible to practice ethical politics.

This view has a long history. It is frequently traced to the writer, Niccolò Machiavelli, who famously penned *The Prince* in the 16th century, arguing that political rulers should be concerned only with acquiring and maintaining power, focused on doing whatever is politically expedient (Stanford Encyclopedia of Philosophy, 2014). Machiavelli said that winning power requires more than being morally upright or good; rulers need to inspire fear, not affection in the masses (Coleman & Wu, 2015; Nederman, 2009). He is frequently viewed as counseling against practicing common virtues of mercy and justice, propounding instead the view that political leaders should do what is needed to maintain power. But Machiavelli's writings were complex, and others view his advice to rules as more descriptive than normative, exposing, rather than endorsing, the strategies rulers must employ to hold onto power. They emphasize that his insightful appreciation of politics as the quest for power ushered in a new perspective on the science of politics, forming the foundation for modern political science (e.g., Mansfield, 1981; Viroli, 1990).

In either case, contemporary scholars of political communication do not view politics in amoral terms—as devoid of morality or ethical precepts. Instead, they strive to articulate an ethics of politics that fits the contemporary age. Scholars from different perspectives and research traditions prioritize different attributes and view the inevitable trade-offs through different philosophical lenses. But academic observers agree that there are certain core cornerstones of an ethically based system of political communication. An ethos of political communication unquestionably requires that communicators—leaders, journalists, and citizens—respect the free flow of information, even when it offends conventional views; respect the dignity of each participant; treat people as free, autonomous agents that are capable of making rational choices; present information without prejudice, fairly, and accurately; listen in an open-minded fashion to the other side, changing opinions when facts and circumstances warrant; display compassion and empathy; present a diversity of perspectives to enlarge and crystallize political discussions; and provide the types of communicative forums that encourage innovation and change.

Obviously, we have a long way to go. Our politics does not come close to reaching these ideals and perhaps never will. Politics involves fundamental disagreements about values and allocation of resources. It is a clash of personal ambition with the public good. It will never be pretty, as civil as we wish, or some hands-clasped journey where adversaries sing "Kumbaya!" Sometimes problems require forceful change, intervention by caring leaders, and a feisty press to set the agenda of important national problems. But process is important. An ethical political communication values adherence to the rule of law, norms that govern institutions, respect for adversaries in interpersonal and social media conversations, a vibrant civic society, and abiding appreciation for the value of media-relayed criticism of an imperfect status quo.

BOX 2.1 HOW WE GOT HERE

During the steamy summer of 1787, the framers of the American Constitution labored over language and debated principles in Philadelphia. There was much curiosity about what these men of reputation and privilege had accomplished behind closed doors. A large crowd formed, gathering outside the building where they met. One of those milling about the crowd cornered Benjamin Franklin as he left the meeting, asking Franklin, "What have you given us?"

"A republic, if you can keep it," he groused.

I love his quote. It gives me goose bumps every time I read it. *A republic, if you can keep it.* Franklin was making two important points. First, he emphasized that the new United States of America was not a direct democracy, where each citizen participated directly in political affairs. The delegates who drafted the Constitution recognized that the country was too large to permit citizens to

Continued

partake in each decision (as had occurred to some degree in ancient Athens). In addition, the Founding Fathers did not want a direct democracy. They did not trust the masses, fearing they would be overtaken by their passions and let emotion interfere with reason. However, although the new government did not give citizens direct rule, it was democratic in that it enshrined popular consent. It enabled citizens to choose the individuals who would represent them.

The second noteworthy aspect of Franklin's comment was his emphasis on duty. He was at pains to suggest that everyone had an obligation to work for the public good and do their civic utmost to ensure that a political experiment over which much blood had been shed could survive.

Meeting in Philadelphia in the hot summer of 1787, the delegates at the Constitutional Convention accomplished a great deal. They created "a wholly new written constitution, creating a true national government unlike any that had existed before. That document is today the world's oldest written national constitution" (Wilson & Dilulio, 2001, p. 24). With the politically savvy crafting of a constitution that expanded the powers of the federal government, they transformed a loose confederation of strong-willed states into a nation that would become the United States of America, "a nation-size republic, indeed the largest republic ever established" (Ellis, 2015, p. xiii).

The Constitution had strengths and shortcomings. A strength was the Bill of Rights, a gift and American invention. The Bill of Rights, the first 10 amendments to the Constitution, includes freedom of religion, speech, press, and assembly (the First Amendment); right to bear arms (the now controversial Second Amendment); no unreasonable searches or seizures (Fourth Amendment), prohibition against a person testifying against himself or herself (Fifth Amendment); and right to a speedy, public impartial trial with defense counsel (Sixth Amendment).

A shortcoming was race. Although slavery continued apace in the new United States, subjugating one people to the whims and powers of another, the Constitution said nothing about this. Its silence was deafening. In fact, the Constitution sanctioned slavery, determining apportionment of seats in the new House of Representatives by counting all free persons and three-fifths of "all other persons," namely slaves. Many of the signers of the Declaration and Constitution owned slaves, yet they did nothing to halt its continuance.

There were other noteworthy aspects of the founding legal document. Concerned that power could be vested in one group and that a majority of citizens would selfishly act to the detriment of others, the framers decided that safeguards were needed. Of course, as Madison famously said, "if men were angels, no government would be necessary." But men (and women) were not angels. Thus, "ambition must be made to counteract ambition," he observed.

The framers insisted on **separation of powers**, whereby power is constitutionally shared by three branches of government: the executive (i.e., the president), legislative (Congress), and judicial (Supreme Court). This involves the elegantly articulated **checks and balances** among the three branches. For example, Congress can act as a check on the president by refusing to approve a bill the president favors. The president can serve as a check on Congress by refusing to sign—or vetoing—a bill it has passed. The Supreme Court can perform a check on the president by declaring the president's actions to be unconstitutional and it can check Congress by ruling that a law is unconstitutional (Wilson & Dilulio, 2001).

The strength of checks and balances is that it restrains one branch of government and allows powers to be dispersed among a pluralism of groups. As James Madison noted in Federalist 10, one cannot always assume that elected officials will be "enlightened statesmen" (Gerson, 2016, p. A18). Thus, liberals worried about the powers wielded by Donald Trump (and conservatives fearful of the Obama presidency) could find solace knowing that the president's ability to wreak havoc is constitutionally constrained by powers vested in other branches of government. The drawback of the American system is gridlock: each branch checks the other, blocks the other's actions, and nothing gets accomplished.

This is a problem we face today. Congress and the White House can't agree on how to reform entitlements like Social Security or Medicare, and nothing gets done.

Nevertheless, the Constitution remains a vital document, providing legal guidance on political dilemmas, some of which the framers anticipated, many others raising questions they could have never expected. Whatever its flaws, it offers the nation a civilized, frequently elegant, way to reconcile conflict. When President Donald Trump, convinced of the merits of his action, took steps to quash federal investigation of ties between his 2016 election campaign and Russian officials, going so far as to try to convince the FBI director to shut down an inquiry into his former national security adviser's suspicious activities, checks and balances kicked in. The Justice Department appointed a well-respected former FBI director to serve as special counsel, investigating Russian influences on the Trump campaign, with broad investigatory powers and independence from political influence. Whatever the flaws of the American political system, the special counsel role, as well as similar procedures, derived from the Founders' insistence on checks on abuse of political power, attests to the wisdom of the nation's founding generation.

CONCLUSIONS

People have a multitude of opinions about politics. In a democracy, we would not have it any other way. But opinions can differ in quality and substance. In order to assess the quality of these opinions—to separate out the philosophical wheat from the chaff—it is instructive to review normative philosophies of democracy. Truth be told, there is not one theory of democracy, but many, with each offering different perspectives on the proper role of citizens, government, and communication.

The classical Greek model emphasizes direct citizen participation in politics and citizens' obligation to contribute to the common good of the community. Liberal democratic theories stress individual liberty, politics as a marketplace of ideas, in which truth emerges in its collision with falsehood, and a feisty no-holds-barred press that challenges government. The deliberative democracy model, arguing that the liberal marketplace metaphor diminishes the deeper role politics ought to play in public life, highlights the importance of thoughtful consideration of political ideas and communication that seeks to encourage collective deliberation on community problems. Deliberative democracy has philosophical virtues, but it can be high-nigh impossible to induce partisans of different stripes to consider the other point of view. In addition, there can be circumstances in which a political wrong is so striking that protest, not reflective consideration, is the most appropriate response.

Building off these and other perspectives, theorists have articulated core aspects of democracy, including the right of all citizens to vote, free and fair elections, individual liberty, a press that challenges government, and a civil society, with opportunities to form associations and interest groups that enrich and challenge the status quo. Thriving, open political communication is a cornerstone of a vibrant democracy. Even as it has emerged as a fully democratic society (after years of exclusion of minority groups), American democracy remains fraught with conundrums and shortcomings. Critics argue that in the U.S., citizens are neither able nor motivated to participate in politics, politics is awash in money, the country is increasingly and problematically polarized, and political discourse is negative and simplistic, hardly a paragon of deliberative thought. From a deliberative perspective, these criticisms can be the grist for robust discussion, but they do highlight the imperfections and trade-offs of political communication in a wide-open media democracy. Despite their different prescriptions for democratic communication, theorists embrace the need for ethically based communication, a respect for process, and free expression of a multitude of ideas.

But these are just that: ideals. As the human rights activist Vaclav Havel reminded us, democracy is always an ideal glimmering in the distance. "One may approach it as one would the horizon in ways that may be better or worse, but it can never be fully attained," he noted (Dionne, 1991, epigram). In the best of times, citizens try to improve the quality of their democracy and political communication. Their efforts frequently fall short, however, stymied by a host of problems: ambition, greed, intolerant, intransigent attitudes, and institutional roadblocks. Democratic, enlightened political communication remains a work in progress, an elusive green light of a goal citizens ceaselessly pursue.

REFERENCES

Baker, M., & Blaagaard, B.B. (2016). Reconceptualizing citizen media: A preliminary charting of a complex domain. In M. Baker & B.B. Blaagaard (Eds.), *Citizen media and public spaces: Diverse expressions of citizenship and dissent* (pp. 1–22). New York: Routledge.

Barbaro, M., Haberman, M., & Parker, A. (2016, February 27). Rubio fires back with crude remarks. *The New York Times*, A1, A10.

Barber, B. (1984). *Strong democracy: Participatory politics for a new age*. Berkeley: University of California Press.

Baumgartner, F.R., Berry, J.M., Hojnacki, M., Kimball, D.C., & Leech, B.L. (2009). *Lobbying and policy change: Who wins, who loses, and why?* Chicago: University of Chicago Press.

Bennett, W.L., & Manheim, J.B. (2001). The big spin. Strategic communication and the transformation of pluralist democracy. In W.L. Bennett & R.M. Entman (Eds.), *Mediated politics: Communication in the future of democracy* (pp. 279–298). Cambridge: Cambridge University Press.

Berry, J.M., & Sobieraj, S. (2014). *The outrage industry: Political opinion media and the new incivility*. New York: Oxford University Press.

Bilefsky, D. (2017, May 1). French polls got it right, but how? *The New York Times*, A10.

Breyer, S. (2010). *Making our democracy work: A judge's view*. New York: Knopf.

Bruns, A., & Highfield, T. (2016). Is Habermas on Twitter? Social media and the public sphere. In A. Bruns, G. Enli, E. Skogerbø, A.O. Larsson, & C. Christensen (Eds.), *The Routledge companion to social media and politics* (pp. 56–73). New York: Routledge.

Chambers, S. (2003). Deliberative democratic theory. *Annual Review of Political Science, 6*, 307–326.

Chozick, A., & Martin, J. (2016, September 4). For Clinton campaign trail winds to wealthy enclaves. *The New York Times*, 1, 8.

Christians, C.G., Glasser, T.L., McQuail, D., Nordenstreng, K., & White, R.A. (2009). *Normative theories of the media: Journalism in democratic societies*. Urbana: University of Illinois Press.

Coates, T-N. (2015). *Between the world and me*. New York: Spiegel & Grau.

Cohen, R. (2016, September 20). The age of distrust. *The New York Times*, A23.

Coleman, R., & Wu, H.D. (2015). *Image and emotion in voter decisions: The affect agenda*. Lanham, MD: Lexington Books.

Coleman, S., & Blumler, J.G. (2009). *The Internet and democratic citizenship: Theory, practice and policy*. New York: Cambridge University Press.

Confessore, N., Cohen, S., & Yourish, K. (2015, August 2). A wealthy few lead in giving to campaigns. *The New York Times*, 1, 13.

Confessore, N., & Willis, D. (2014, November 3). Hidden donors spend heavily on attack ads. *The New York Times*, A1, A16.

Cook, C. (2013, February 19). Death of the swing seat. *The Cook Political Report*. Retrieved from http://cookpolitical.com/story/5442 (Accessed July 20, 2016).

Dahl, R.A. (1989). *Democracy and its critics*. New Haven, CT: Yale University Press.

de Freytas-Tamura, K. (2016, June 12). Young Britons favor staying in E.U. but aren't big on voting. *The New York Times*, 1, 8.

Delli Carpini, M.X. & Keeter, S. (1996). *What Americans know about politics and why it matters*. New Haven, CT: Yale University Press.

Dionne, E.J., Jr. (1991). *Why Americans hate politics*. New York: Simon & Schuster.

The Economist. (2013). Democracy index 2012: Democracy at a standstill. Retrieved from pages. eiu.com/rs/eiu2/images/Democracy-Index-2012.pdf (Accessed February 3, 2017).

The Economist (2017, January 25). Declining trust in government is denting democracy. Retrieved from www.economist.com/blogs/graphicdetail/2017/01/daily-chart-20 (Accessed February 9, 2017).

Ellis, J.J. (2015). *The quartet: Orchestrating the second American revolution, 1783–1789*. New York: Knopf.

Esser, F. (2013). Mediatization as a challenge: Media logic versus political logic. In H. Kriesi, S. Lavenex, F. Esser, J. Matthes, M. Bühlmann, & D. Bochsler (Eds.), *Democracy in the age of globalization and mediatization* (pp. 155–176). London: Palgrave Macmillan.

Finley, M.I. (1973). *Democracy ancient and modern*. New Brunswick, NJ: Rutgers University Press.

Fiorina, M., Abrams, S.J., & Pope, J.C. (2005). *Culture war? The myth of a polarized America*. New York: Pearson Longman.

Gastil, J. (2008). *Political communication and deliberation*. Thousand Oaks, CA: Sage.

Gastil, J., & Dillard, J.P. (1999). Increasing political sophistication through public deliberation. *Political Communication, 16*, 3–23.

Gerson, M. (2016, November 10). America has institutions to tame a populist. *The Plain Dealer*, A18.

Goidel, K., Kirzinger, A., & Xenos, M. (2011). Too much talk, not enough action? Political expression in a digital age. In K. Goidel (Ed.), *Political polling in the digital age: The challenge of measuring and understanding public opinion* (pp. 99–114). Baton Rouge: Louisiana State University Press.

Gutmann, A., & Thompson, D. (1996). *Democracy and disagreement*. Cambridge: Belknap Press.

Habermas, J. (1996). *Between facts and norms: Contributions to a discourse theory of law and democracy*. Cambridge, MA: MIT Press.

Held, D. (2006). *Models of democracy* (3rd ed.). Stanford, CA: Stanford University Press.

Hibbing, J.R., & Theiss-Morse, E. (2002). *Stealth democracy: Americans' beliefs about how government should work.* Cambridge: Cambridge University Press.

Iyengar, S., & Hahn, K.S. (2011). The political economy of mass media: Implications for informed citizenship. In W. Le Cheminant & J.M. Parrish (Eds.), *Manipulating democracy: Democratic theory, political psychology, and mass media* (pp. 209–228). New York: Routledge.

Jacobs, A. (2016a, April 16). Leader's fate strains the ties, binding Brazil. *The New York Times,* A1, A6.

Jacobs, A. (2016b, May 15). Brazil's graft-prone Congress, a circus that has its own clown. *The New York Times,* 1, 11.

Jacobs, L.R., Cook, F.L., & Delli Carpini, M.X. (2009). *Talking together: Public deliberation and political participation in America.* Chicago: University of Chicago Press.

Jacobson, G.C. (2016). Polarization, gridlock, and presidential campaign politics in 2016. *The Annals of the American Academy of Political and Social Science,* 226–246.

Katz, R.S. (1997). *Democracy and elections.* New York: Oxford University Press.

Kimball, D.C., & Gross, C.A. (2007). The growing polarization of American voters. In J.C. Green & D.J. Coffeey (Eds.), *The state of the parties: The changing role of contemporary politics* (pp. 265–276). Lanham, MD: Rowman & Littlefield.

Klein, J. (2006). *Politics lost: How American democracy was trivialized by people who think you're stupid.* New York: Doubleday.

Kriesi, H. (2013). Democracy as a moving target. In H. Kriesi, S. Lavenex, F. Esser, J. Matthes, M. Bühlmann, & D. Bochsler (Eds.), *Democracy in the age of globalization and mediatization* (pp. 19–43). New York: Palgrave Macmillan.

Leibovich, M. (2013). *This town: Two parties and a funeral—plus plenty of valet parking!—in America's gilded capital.* New York: Penguin Group.

Lelkes, Y. (2016). Mass polarization: Manifestations and measurements. *Public Opinion Quarterly, 80,* 392–410.

Levendusky, M., & Malhotra, N. (2016a). Does media coverage of partisan polarization affect political attitudes? *Political Communication, 33,* 283–301.

Levendusky, M.S., & Malhotra, N. (2016b). (Mis)perceptions of partisan polarization in the American public. *Public Opinion Quarterly, 80,* 378–391.

Levitsky, S., & Ziblatt, D. (2016, December 18). Is our democracy in danger? *The New York Times* (Sunday Review), 5.

Lipton, E. (2016, September 3). Tobacco lobby tries to shield e-cigarettes. *The New York Times,* A1, A11.

Mandelbaum, M. (2007). *Democracy's good name: The rise and risks of the world's most popular form of government.* New York: Public Affairs.

Mansfield, H.C., Jr. (1981). Machiavelli's political science. *American Political Science Review, 75,* 293–305.

Martin, J., Sussman, D., & Thee-Brenan, M. (2016, November 4). In poll, voters express disgust in U.S. politics. *The New York Times,* A1, A16.

Martinez, M.D. (2010). Why is American turnout so low, and why should we care? In J.E. Leighley (Ed.), *The Oxford handbook of American elections and political behavior* (pp. 107–124). New York: Oxford University Press.

Mill, J.S. (1859/2009). *On liberty and other essays*. New York: Kaplan.

Mutz, D.C. (2015). *In-your-face politics: The consequences of uncivil media*. Princeton, NJ: Princeton University Press.

Myers, C.D., & Mendelberg, T. (2013). Political deliberation. In L. Huddy, D.O. Sears, & J.S. Levy (Eds.), *The Oxford handbook of political psychology* (pp. 699–734). New York: Oxford University Press.

Nagourney, A. (2014, November 5). To voters, Washington is biggest loser. *The New York Times*, P1, P9.

Nederman, C. (2009). *Machiavelli: A beginner's guide*. Oxford: Oneworld.

Norris, P. (2011). *Democratic deficit: Critical citizens revisited*. New York: Cambridge University Press.

Norris, P. (2016, September 28). *Why American elections are flawed (and how to fix them)*. Harvard Kennedy School Working Paper No. RWP16–038. Retrieved from https://ssrn.com/abstract=2844793. (Accessed January 5, 2017).

Offe, C., & Preuss, U.K. (1991). Democratic institutions and moral resources. In D. Held (Ed.), *Political theory today* (pp. 143–171). Stanford, CA: Stanford University Press.

Orwell, G. (1946). *Animal farm*. New York: Harcourt, Brace.

Perlmutter, D.D. (2008). *Blogwars*. New York: Oxford University Press.

Political polarization in the American public. (2014, June 12). Pew Research Center: U.S. politics & policy. Retrieved from www.people-press.org/2014/06/12/political-polariza tion-in-the-american-public/ (Accessed September 6, 2016).

Price, V., Cappella, J.N., & Nir, L. (2002). Does disagreement contribute to more deliberative opinion? *Political Communication, 19*, 95–112.

Rosen, J., & Merritt, D., Jr. (1994). *Public journalism: Theory and practice*. Dayton, OH: Kettering Foundation.

Rutenberg, J. (2015, December 20). Block the vote. *The New York Times Magazine*, 30–37, 57.

Sanders, L.M. (1997). Against deliberation. *Political Theory, 25*, 347–376.

Schlozman, K.L., Verba, S., & Brady, H.E. (2012, November 11). Sunday dialogue: Giving all citizens a voice. *The New York Times* (Sunday Review), 2.

Stanford Encyclopedia of Philosophy. (2014). *Niccolò Machiavelli*. Retrieved from http://plato.stanford.edu/entries/machiavelli

Stewart, J.B. (2016, September 2). Tax cuts for Americans like Trump. *The New York Times*, B1, B4.

Stolberg, S.G. (2016, October 15). The place to gauge how turned off the voters are. *The New York Times*, A10, A15.

Strömbäck, J., & Esser, F. (2014). Mediatization of politics: Towards a theoretical framework. In F. Esser & J. Strömbäck (Eds.), *Mediatization of politics: Understanding the transformation of western democracies* (pp. 3–28). London: Palgrave Macmillan.

Stromer-Galley, J. (2007). Measuring deliberation's content: A coding scheme. *Journal of Public Deliberation, 3*, 1–35.

Sunstein, C. (2002). *Republic.com*. Princeton, NJ: Princeton University Press.

The Economist (2011, July 9). The news industry, Special report in *The Economist*, 3–16.

These two charts show the incredible disappearing center in American politics. (2014, April 10). Moyers & Company. Retrieved from billmoyers.com/2014/04/10/these-two-charts-show-the-incredible-disappearing-center-in-american-politics/ (Accessed September 6, 2016).

Viroli, M. (1990). Machiavelli and the republican idea of politics. In G. Bock, Q. Skinner, & M. Viroli (Eds.), *Machiavelli and Republicanism* (pp. 143–171). Cambridge: Cambridge University Press.

Walzer, M. (1983). *Spheres of justice: A defense of pluralism and equality.* New York: Basic Books.

Ward, S.J.A. (2015). *Radical media ethics: A global approach.* Malden, MA: Wiley-Blackwell.

Wasserman, D. (2013, April 4). Introducing the 2014 cook political report partisan voter index. *The Cook Political Report.* Retrieved from http://cookpolitical.com/story/5604 (Accessed July 20, 2016).

Wilson, J.Q., & DiIulio, J.J., Jr. (2001). *American government: Institutions and policies* (8th ed.). Boston: Houghton Mifflin.

Wojcieszak, M., & Price, V. (2010). Bridging the divide or intensifying the conflict? How disagreement affects strong predilections about sexual minorities. *Political Psychology, 31,* 315–339.

Wood, G.S. (1991). *The radicalism of the American Revolution.* New York: Vintage Books.

PART TWO

Political Communication Concepts and Effects

3

The Study of Political Communication

For nearly a century, the debate has raged. Does political communication have massive, "propagandizing" effects on the public? Are its effects more limited, circumscribed by psychological and sociological factors? Do political media effects (especially in an era of congenial social media posts) simply reinforce what people already believe, or do they expand ideological horizons? How strong are political media effects, what approaches should we harness to study them, and which methods reign supreme?

Although the study of political communication is popularly believed to have begun with television, it actually dates back nearly a century. It was Walter Lippmann, the American journalist writing in the 1920s, who eloquently and influentially described the ability of the media to mold the images people carried in their heads about a distant world that was "out of reach, out of sight (and) out of mind." This chapter describes the journey Lippmann helped launch, chronicling the history of political communication research, with its many currents, waves, and oscillating changes. The chapter introduces the concepts and methods that have guided the field, continuities and changes in academic thinking about political communication over the past century, and the surprising conflicts that make the history of political communication so animating.

The history of political communication research is not a placid story of academic scholars gathering facts and dutifully placing each droplet of information into the vessel of knowledge. On the contrary, it is more like a maritime expedition, with competing explorers, armed with different maps and diving equipment. One group amasses findings, only to have these notions questioned by another group of explorers, who, guided by their own maps, probe a different portion of the ocean's depths, uncovering new facts and theories of what constitutes the underlying structure of the sea. All too often we think of the history of an academic discipline as a monotonous description of how naïve thinkers developed ideas that were overturned by their more intelligent, savvy, and contemporary disciples. But this understates the excitement of intellectual discovery. By reviewing the twists and turns in the history of political communication research and describing some of the personal aspects of the scholarly journey, I hope to engage readers, helping them appreciate the intellectually vigorous issues that animate scholars.

The chapter is organized chronologically. The first portion reviews the early, classic scholarship, and the second section looks critically at the early research. In the third section, I integrate classic and contemporary orientations, articulating the scholarly consensus about political communication in the current era. The fourth portion focuses in depth on social science, explicating the social scientific foundations of political communication and major empirical methods.

EARLY HISTORY OF POLITICAL COMMUNICATION SCHOLARSHIP

Lippmann's Insights

Ideas were combusting and crystallizing at a furious pace. The old guard was under siege.

Across Europe and the United States, a new, darker explanation of human behavior was afoot. In France, Gustave Le Bon (1896) gravely warned of the irrational power of a new force in society: the crowd, a barbaric mass, in which emotion overtook reason, placing civilization in jeopardy. Prophetically forecasting the powers of 20th-century media, French scholar Gabriel Tarde argued that modern newspapers could "set off a million tongues," transporting thoughts across vast distances and molding ideas. In a similar fashion, German sociologist Ferdinand Tonnies warned that the newspaper was packaging information like "grocers' goods," marketing and manufacturing public opinion, shaping public sentiments in powerful ways (Ewen, 1996). In America, the sociologist Robert Park echoed these views, expressing pessimism about the power of reason to conquer public opinion formed by a manipulation of catchphrases. Sigmund Freud synthesized these disparate sentiments, arguing that the conformist crowd behavior Le Bon and others had described had its underlying roots in the unconscious, psychodynamic forces of the individual.

Enter Walter Lippmann. Lippmann synthesized these ideas with his knowledge of the prevailing political practices of the time. Graduating from Harvard in 1910, in a class that included the poet T. S. Eliot and radical reporter John Reed (immortalized by Warren Beatty in the movie *Reds* many years later), Lippmann served as founding editor of *The New Republic*, the avant-garde political magazine of the 20th century. He also wrote books that earned the praise of a U.S. president and Supreme Court justice (Steel, 1999; see Figure 3.1).

Lippmann had worked in Europe during World War I, at the behest of the administration of President Woodrow Wilson, trying to harness the powers of propaganda—the word du jour—to assist the U.S. war effort. But after the terrible war, which, in the memorable words of a British foreign secretary, had darkened the lamps of Europe (Tuchman, 1962), Lippmann began to lament the power of government to spin and control information in the service of wartime victory. During World War I the White House took extraordinary steps to manufacture support for the war effort. President Woodrow Wilson appointed publicist George Creel to direct the Committee on Public Information (CPI). The CPI disseminated 100 million pamphlets and posters, sent countless educational materials to schools, and plastered war posters on streetcars and trains. In 1917 Congress passed the Espionage Act, which permitted the government to fine or imprison people who intentionally made false statements with the intent of interfering with military operations. The CPI raised the specter of government control of information, producing a firestorm of controversy.

You could argue that Creel had done the nation a service: By convincing the public of the necessity of war, he had unleashed American power during a time when the nation's military might was needed to save the people of Europe. Or you could contend that Creel's effort was deceptive and manipulative, and when taken in concert with Wilson's application of political censorship, represented a foreboding development in American history. Viewing these issues a century later, one is struck by the continuity between then and now. The same issues have been raised in a host of mass information campaigns, such as those waged during the Vietnam War, the 1990–1991 Persian Gulf conflict, and the controversial 2003 War in Iraq.

Figure 3.1 Walter Lippmann, the journalist and scholar who helped pioneer scholarship on political communication. Lippmann argued that in a political world few experienced directly, media symbols and interpretations influenced public attitudes and opinions. His writings spotlighted the impact of media, but were vulnerable to criticism that they privileged elites at the expense of conscientious members of the public.

Getty Images

Back to Lippmann in the 1920s. After the war, Lippmann became disillusioned by the ways that Creel had used the powers of persuasion and coercion to influence the mass public. He rejected classic liberal democracy concepts, such as the power of rational thought or the ability of the press to relay accurate information. Instead, he concluded that people were prone to psychologically distort information and engage in stereotyping. "We do not first see, and then define, we define first and then see," he said. But there was more. Unlike earlier eras, where individuals lived in small towns and had direct experience with issues of their communities, in the modern world, people were compelled to make decisions about complex problems that they could not directly experience. Living in a world that was "out of reach, out of sight, out of mind," Lippmann (1922) poetically penned, people had to rely on governments and the press for accurate information (p. 18). But—and here was the modern wrinkle—governments could effectively manipulate symbols to *manufacture* consent. The press did not convey deeper truths, Lippmann concluded. Instead, it simply transmitted events, even forcing attention on selected issues. News, he emphasized, was not the same as truth, a theme emphasized by today's press critics, but sometimes in ways that undercut the virtues a free press performs for society.

Writing at the end of the 20th century, Ewen (1996) observed that "one cannot avoid being struck by Lippmann's clairvoyance; the extent to which his analysis of symbols—how they may be employed to sway the public—sounds uncomfortably familiar" (p. 158). Prior to Lippmann and others writing during this period, there was little appreciation of the ways that media images could mold public sentiments. Lippmann grasped that the media would necessarily assume a large role in shaping public opinion in a world where individuals had to rely on indirect experience to make sense of politics.

Some critics have viewed Lippmann as elitist, calling attention to his belief that the public is passive, easily diverted, and incapable of appreciating complex political events (Carey, 1995). These scholars, critical of Lippmann's faith in a class of political experts, have been drawn to Lippmann's contemporary, John Dewey (1927), who placed greater stock in citizens' capacity to understand politics and participate in democratic dialogue (Westbrook, 1991). These criticisms have merit (some more than others). They spotlight Lippmann's biases and are intellectually intriguing (Schudson, 2008). Still, political communication owes a debt to Lippmann: He was a pathbreaking thinker who laid the groundwork for the study of political media by conceptualizing the critical roles that press and public opinion play in American politics, and where they can go astray.

ABCs of Propaganda

The United States was changing, and perceptive observers took note. Chronicling the ways government could exploit mass media, political scientist Harold Lasswell (1927), following in Lippmann's footsteps, described the power communications could exert on the mass soul. Lasswell and others used the term "propaganda" to describe these effects, although today these might be referred to as persuasion or social influence.

In the 1930s, the Institute of Propaganda assembled a list of the "ABC's of propaganda" that included *testimonial*, the ability of a communication to call on the views of a credible spokesperson; *bandwagon*, the persuasive influence exerted by the perception that large numbers of people supported a cause; and *transfer*, the powerful impact that a message could exert if it was associated with a popular image or symbol. The organizers of the Institute feared that these techniques could be used widely and for pernicious purposes.

As it turned out, scholars working in the Institute of Propaganda during the 1930s accurately forecast the future. During the 1930s and 1940s, the world witnessed the exploitation of mass propaganda for more heinous objectives. In addition to brute coercion, Hitler's Nazi Party harnessed mass communication—rhetoric, speech-making, and movies—to seduce the people of a once democratic country, Germany, to adopt a horrific policy of world domination.

The Institute of Propaganda dissolved in the early 1940s. The term propaganda, with its sweeping, heavy, and negative connotations, gave way to less pejorative terms like persuasion and information control. (The term propaganda continues to be fraught, frequently invoked to describe persuasive communications "we" dislike, or, more denotatively, communications under government control.) Importantly, the questions the Institute of Propaganda raised in the 1930s would continue to consume students of political persuasion. For example: Do governments in democratic countries mislead citizenry through the power of mediated political messages? How can the tension between democratic values and elites' ability to manipulate public sentiments be satisfactorily resolved? Do mass media offer citizens the information they need to make informed judgments, or massage people with deceptive political imagery?

These questions would be put on hold in the 1940s as the field of political communication research took a different direction. It moved in a more concrete, pragmatically American path. Intrigued by the effects of radio, researchers examined the social effects of a new medium that conveyed content that ran the gamut from speeches featuring the melodious voice of President Franklin Delano Roosevelt to the dramatization of H. G. Wells's *The War of the Worlds*, a science fiction story that described the invasion of Earth by Martians. In contrast to some of the early propaganda theorists, the new researchers adopted a decidedly empirical approach, one that underscored the complexity of media effects of programs like the now famous *War of the Worlds* telecast. Although the program amazingly led some Americans to believe that Martians were invading our planet, its impact was actually contingent on a host of psychological factors (Cantril, Gaudet, & Herzog, 1940; McDonald, 2004). The radio studies suggested that media effects might just be more complicated than some scholars originally believed, a conclusion that would also find resonance in a pioneering study of political communication in Ohio during a presidential election.

The Pendulum Shifts

Sandusky, Ohio, is a quaint city on Lake Erie's shores. It is more than 400 miles from Washington, D.C., and New York City, the teeming centers of elite influence that housed the powerful purveyors of mass communications. In 1940, Sandusky was a small, quiescent Midwestern community that bore an intriguing characteristic: in every presidential election of the 20th century, it had closely reflected national voting patterns. For this reason it attracted the interest of three political scientists, eager to explore the role communication played in people's voting decisions.

Paul Lazarsfeld and two colleagues from Columbia University made the trip to Sandusky, embarking on a study of the 1940 election that pitted President Franklin D. Roosevelt, a popular incumbent and a Democrat, against Wendell Wilkie, a corporate lawyer and dark horse Republican candidate. Roosevelt won handily, which was not exactly a surprise. But the results that Lazarsfeld, Berelson, and Gaudet (1944) obtained must have been something of a whopper, a balloon-bursting surprise to those who believed in the power of the political communication media. In a scientific study of Sandusky (or more generally Erie County, Ohio) residents' uses of newspapers and radio, their conversations with others, and voting, the researchers reported clear and dramatic effects. They found that media exerted modest influences, clarifying attitudes about the candidates and strengthening vote intentions of those who felt strongly about the election. But they converted only a handful of voters to the other side.

It was not mass media that sent the researchers scurrying to their typewriters. Instead, it was interpersonal communications, or face-to-face conversations. Certain individuals served as **opinion leaders** for others, influencing followers' political views. Ideas seemed to flow from radio and newspapers to these influential leaders; the opinion leaders then scooped them up, distilled them, and conveyed them to the less involved, less active members of the electorate. The researchers dubbed this the **two-step flow**. Thus, media did not impact the mass audience directly, as the propaganda theorists feared. Instead, their influence was itself mediated—watered down, perhaps, but certainly tempered—by these influential leaders. The model looked like this:

Media → Opinion Leaders → Voting Public

It seemed as if the much-ballyhooed media were not all they had been cracked to be. Instead, they were just another factor in the persuasion mix and not nearly as important as interpersonal communication (see also Berelson, Lazarsfeld, & McPhee, 1954).

Influence in Illinois

The Erie County, Ohio, study propelled Lazarsfeld's career. Born in Austria, Lazarsfeld had obtained a Ph.D. in applied mathematics from the University of Vienna. With the political situation in his native Austria disintegrating in the wake of World War II, Lazarsfeld immigrated to the United States and took up a position as a faculty member in sociology at Columbia University. Lazarsfeld was a complex man: a brilliant researcher, but also something of an operator, a bustling entrepreneur to some, a savvy manipulator to others (Morrison, 2006; Simonson, 2006; see also Gitlin, 1978). Building on the now internationally famous findings in the Erie County voting study, he sought to explore new venues, hoping to study the new opinion leader notion as a sociologist, while, doffing his entrepreneurial cap, seeking to attract new streams of money to the university's Bureau of Applied Social Research. He convinced Macfadden Publications, a publisher of American magazines, to underwrite a study of consumer decision-making in the small but representative community of Decatur, Illinois.

Lazarsfeld, for his part, needed money to conduct an in-depth, statistical study of the role communication played in Decatur women's decisions about marketing, fashion, movie-going, and public affairs. He enlisted his graduate student, Elihu Katz, who went on to become an important political communication scholar. Their survey (Katz & Lazarsfeld, 1955) became a milestone in communication research, one of the most cited studies in the social sciences (Lang & Lang, 2006). It made Katz and Lazarsfeld an internationally famous communication dyad. When talking about personal influence, you couldn't say one name without mentioning the other, usually in the same breath. For our purposes, their study's main contributions were that it (a) pioneered a precise scientific technique to examine the flow of influence; (b) suggested that mass media played second fiddle to interpersonal influence; and (c) demonstrated that context mattered (emerging as an opinion leader in the area of fashion did not mean one influenced opinions toward public affairs).

Interesting as these findings were at the time, to some degree they reflected a conservative, pro-social system bias. The Decatur study received some of its funding from a magazine publisher, and the earlier, classic Erie County study had been underwritten by the well-heeled Rockefeller Foundation and *Life*, a mass circulation magazine. The funding may have restricted the scope of the projects, encouraged the researchers to view politics and opinion leadership as marketing phenomena, and implicitly suggested that the larger cultural system, with its social inequities, was not to be questioned (Gitlin, 1978; Weimann, 1994).

These criticisms have merit. Yet they should not blind us to the contributions of the opinion leader concept, pioneered through Katz and Lazarsfeld's study. You might say that a half century before Mark Zuckerberg created Facebook, Katz and Lazarsfeld found social networks matter, influencing consumer and political decisions. What's more, the opinion leader concept enriched and clarified understanding of media effects. To those researchers who believed that the media audience was an undifferentiated mass of clay shaped by an all-powerful mass media, Katz and Lazarsfeld sounded a note of caution, emphasizing that the audience was composed of social networks of opinions leaders and their peers, with interpersonal leaders exerting a persuasive impact on acquaintances and followers. It is a conclusion that is intriguingly relevant to today's era of social media.

During the same period when Katz and Lazarsfeld documented opinion leadership, researchers at Columbia University and the University of Michigan showed that demographic factors like religion, urban versus rural residence, and in particular party identification exerted stable influences on voting behavior. The academic wisdom in this pre-television era came to emphasize the impact that stable individual difference factors exerted on voting behavior. Although media effects might have been uncovered had survey instruments included appropriate measures of media uses, the pendulum shifted to minimize media effects. This came to an intellectual crescendo with a book published in 1960, the iconic beginning of a decade that would change perspectives on political communication.

Joseph Klapper Makes His Statement

So, Joseph Klapper wanted to know, when all is said and done: What *are* the effects of mass media and political communication? Guided by Lazarsfeld, his dissertation adviser, Klapper thought it was high time that someone wrote up a summary statement about this new field of communication research. Now that there had been a considerable number of studies of mass media effects and a new decade—the 1960s—was set to begin, it seemed a propitious moment to put together a book that summarized knowledge of media effects.

Following the tradition blazed by Katz and Lazarsfeld, Klapper (1960) concluded that media influences on society were small to modest. People had acquired strong preexisting attitudes before they came to media. They were members of reference groups, like the family, religious organizations, and labor unions. These groups generally exerted a stronger impact on attitudes than mass media. The media were not the sole or primary agent that influenced political attitudes and behavior. Instead, Klapper emphasized, media worked together with social environmental factors, contributing to or reinforcing the effects these other agents exerted. This became known as the **limited effects model**.

Klapper acknowledged that mass media could strengthen attitudes. But, to Klapper, they did not have the immense effects that many observers seemed to attribute to them. People were not a "tabula rasa" on which media could imprint their message. They brought preexisting group identifications (such as religion) and attitudes (such as liberalism or conservatism) to their encounters with media. Their well-learned beliefs and preexisting biases helped determine how individuals reacted to political media fare, as well as the effects media exerted. For Klapper, the media did not exert the massive impact that so many seemed to assume.

A NEW PERSPECTIVE

Suddenly, things changed.

During the decade in which Klapper published a book describing minimal media effects, something very different was occurring in the supposedly minimally significant mass media. The very different phenomenon was television news. It swept the country by storm, expanding to a half hour, capturing viewers and captivating audiences with vivid, sometimes visceral images. Televised pictures and sounds bombarded Americans in the 1960s. There was a handsome John F. Kennedy challenging the jowl-faced, sweaty Richard Nixon in the first 1960 presidential debate; Southern police clubbing impassioned Black protesters; gut-wrenching scenes of American soldiers battling enemy troops in the rice paddies of Vietnam; angry, long-haired, scruffy college students holding signs, circling around campus buildings, protesting, denouncing a president, or strumming guitars, with a less aggressive mien, singing blissfully of a nonviolent future. These images, TV's ubiquity, and the media's presumptive effects clashed with Klapper's thesis that the media were of little consequence. Intuitively, it seemed, broadcast news exerted a strong impact on Americans' political attitudes, even if no one had yet documented the effects empirically (Lang & Lang, 2006).

There was also this quandary, frequently bandied about: If media were so ineffective, why did advertisers spend so much on commercials for cars like the hot new Mustang? Why were they spending money to promote candidates like Richard Nixon in 1968, whose blatant marketing spawned a book called *The Selling of the President* (McGinniss, 1969) and perhaps a movie, *The Candidate*, with the actor Robert Redford depicting an empty-headed politician who had been sold by vapid TV images? True, the paradox of advertisers spending lavishly on a supposedly ineffective media did not scientifically prove that media advertising had effects, but the question could not be ignored.

A New Set of Questions

"There has to be a problem, this just can't be right, the media obviously have an impact, the limited effects view must be wrong." Ruminations like these no doubt settled in a growing number of researchers' minds as the stormy '60s ended. Political communication researchers began to take another look at the research that purported to show minimal effects. Among those exploring this issue was Jack M. McLeod, a mass communication researcher at the University of Wisconsin.

In 1975, McLeod, Lee B. Becker (who had worked with McLeod as a doctoral student at Wisconsin and was currently a young assistant professor at Syracuse University), and the researcher Maxwell McCombs came upon an intriguing discovery. They pored over Lazarsfeld's Erie County study, with Becker taking the lead in scrutinizing the charts that broke down the sample on the basis of both partisanship and exposure to media that favored Republican and Democratic candidates. Becker and his colleagues came up with a serendipitous but exciting discovery: Lazarsfeld and his colleagues had unwittingly understated the media's effects. Upon closer analysis, it turned out that that nearly half of Republicans with exposure to predominantly *Democratic* media actually voted for the *Democrat*, President Franklin D. Roosevelt. A similar pattern emerged for Democrats: Democratic voters who had exposure to primarily *Republican* newspapers and radio stations were more likely to vote for the *Republican* candidate than those who had primarily Democratic media exposure. The media seemed to have strongly influenced the voting behavior of both Republican and Democratic respondents. Voters still might interpret political media fare in light of their biases (and this could also be evidence of selective exposure; see Chapter 12). Yet the reanalysis suggested that media had greater effects than the early researchers believed (Becker, McCombs, & McLeod, 1975).

Another problem surfaced. Lazarsfeld and his colleagues focused only on voting behavior. Had they looked at factors other than voting—for example, discussion, voters' cognitions, or factors operating on the macro level—media effects might have emerged (Chaffee & Hochheimer, 1985). For example, the Republican candidate, Wendell Wilkie, seemed to come from nowhere to become the Republican candidate. Media surely played some part in this. And then there was this—so obvious a problem in the limited effects model it must have almost embarrassed scholars to mention it: Klapper had based his conclusions on studies that had been conducted before television had become the preeminent medium of political communication. These minimal effect findings could hardly be expected to describe the latter part of the 20th century, an era in which TV had widely diffused throughout society and conveyed so much of the political spectacle.

The limited effects edifice was crumbling, but still standing. In the social sciences, the bottom-line test of a theoretical approach is evidence, and in the early 1970s, the proponents of strong political media effects had yet to amass much evidence. But the facts would not be long in coming.

Influenced by Lippmann's speculations, researchers showed that the media could set the agenda or influence people's perceptions of problems ailing America (McCombs & Shaw, 1972; McLeod, Becker, & Byrnes, 1974). This turned out to be a major revision of the conventional wisdom. Media might not affect what people thought—their basic beliefs—but they powerfully influenced what voters thought about. This turn of a phrase became a mantra in the field. Agenda-setting, as the model became known, offered a different, more optimistic view of media effects, and it became the focal point of a new perspective on political communication (see Chapter 6). At the same time, research on the uses and gratifications of media (Katz, Blumler, & Gurevitch, 1974) emphasized that audience could actively use media, deriving particular gratifications, like knowledge or vote guidance. These gratifications could steer audiences in certain ways, influencing how they used media and impacting how media eventually influenced their attitudes and beliefs.

Emboldened by these new frameworks, research blossomed, changing the received wisdom of the field. Surveys demonstrated that media did not just influence individuals' cognitions, but could affect the dynamics of the larger political system. Thomas E. Patterson (1980), a political scientist who had long argued that media effects in elections were understated, showed that presidential campaigns were organized around the media, from primary elections to news media verdicts on presidential debates. Gladys Lang and Kurt Lang (1983) examined Watergate, the series of events that led to the resignation of President Richard Nixon. They argued that the news media's ubiquitous presence— and the very public impeachment hearings shown on television—encouraged political leaders to hold Nixon accountable for crimes he committed. Kathleen Hall Jamieson (1984) took readers on a colorful tour of American elections from 1840 to 1980. She showed that candidates had long harnessed communication—primarily speeches and campaign appearances—to mold images. Television advertising followed this rhetorical tradition, emerging as a particularly effective modality by which politicians "package the presidency." By 1980, when Ronald Reagan, a former Hollywood actor whose communication skills on the small screen became legendary, was elected president, the academic consensus was that media mattered. Research would come to demonstrate empirically that mediated messages and campaign rhetoric exert key effects on voters by influencing agendas, priming cognitions, and activating attitudes, the latter impact intriguingly suggested by Lazarsfeld back in the 1940s, fusing contemporary and classic research around common themes (Jamieson, 2014).

The effects of media—once questioned, frequently misunderstood, and always changing as a function of the times—became increasingly salient over the ensuing decades, as candidates like George H. W. Bush employed negative advertising in political campaigns; Bill Clinton used clever wording, even prevarication, to persuade the public to accept his controversial, sexual affair–infused candidacy in 1992 and later, to tamp down concerns about his womanizing as president; George W. Bush called on patriotic rhetoric to unify the country after 9/11, as well as deceptive messages to persuade the public to support the war against Iraq in 2002; Barack Obama harnessed new media to gain election in 2008 and a cocktail of social media and Internet platforms to influence public opinion about his controversial health care plan; and Donald J. Trump tweeted his way to the Republican nomination in 2016, energizing supporters, manipulating media to gain a cavalcade of favorable news coverage (Patterson, 2016), and massaging his populist base with a torrent of frequently incendiary attacks on his Democratic opponent. These media effects focus on presidential elections and White House policymaking, the emphasis of political communication research. Research has also examined a host of media and communicative influences on lower-level American elections, as well as on elections in countries with different political and media systems.

Attuned to these different contexts as well as new developments in academic scholarship, political communication researchers proposed a variety of models of media and public opinion that emphasize the more subtle, indirect effects of media on attitudes and behavior. These include agenda-setting, agenda-building, and framing approaches. Researchers also have explored the content of election news, shedding light on the key storylines that emerge in political news, some functional for the system, others less so. They examined the impact of news, political advertising, debates, the rhetoric of presidential address, and galloping technological appeals on attitudes and behaviors.

Over the past several decades, researchers working in different social science disciplines have coalesced, forging a cross-disciplinary field of political communication that examines a multitude of issues that cut across different levels, including psychological processing of political media, content and effects of political news, political marketing of presidential campaigns, interfaces among news, polling, and the presidential nomination, as well as macro effects of political communication on the larger electoral system. Scholars Kate Kenski and Kathleen Hall Jamieson (2014) have pulled together different contexts, genres, processes of meaning construction, complex media effects, and implications for the new communicative landscape in an authoritative handbook of political communication.

Interest in these panoply of issues began with Lippmann; morphed with Dewey; continued through Katz and Lazarsfeld's interpersonal influence research; oscillated in the wake of Klapper's limited effects thesis; rebounded with research on the subtle influences of news; expanded with a focus on institutional intersections among media, public opinion, and politics; and continues apace as scholars explore how political communication has changed for good and for ill in the wake of the social-networked era of 21st-century public life.

PUTTING IT ALL TOGETHER

Let's bring past and present together. What can we conclude from the historical review of political communication research? What do the twists and turns in the intellectual history of American political communication research tell us? What general themes emerge? Threading together Lippmann, Lazarsfeld, Klapper, McLeod, McCombs, Jamieson, and rejuvenated scholarly interest in political media effects, we discover six important themes.

First, Lippmann Was Right: Media Shape Our Images of the World

Lippmann famously suggested that the media form the "pictures in our heads" of the world that lies outside our immediate experiences. His insight was prescient and continues to be true today. We do not experience politics directly. Instead, citizens necessarily rely on the media (and now the Internet) to learn what is happening in Washington, D.C., and in far-off war zones like Kabul, Afghanistan. The media supply us with images that we use to construct beliefs about the political world. This is one reason they are powerful.

Second, Social Networks Matter

Opinion leaders are important. Katz and Lazarsfeld called attention to this in their Decatur study, and it remains true today, ever more so in the era of social media. In our social media–dominated environment, national companies like American Eagle and Hewlett-Packard hire opinion-leading student ambassadors who promote the brands on Facebook, exploiting their social connections to market the product (Singer, 2011). Political conversations occur frequently on social media (Southwell, 2014), often tendentiously, with conversations frequently reinforcing people's views of the political world. In electoral contexts, interpersonal influence and frequency of discussion complexly affect political decisions and participation in politics (Huckfeldt & Sprague, 1995; Eveland & Hively, 2009).

Other research documents that individuals' political networks can moderate media effects. For example, voters who spend time in politically consonant networks, characterized by political agreement among members, feel more strongly about their voting preferences when exposed to candidate ads (Neiheisel & Niebler, 2015). When a real-life Facebook friend posts a news story on Facebook and is perceived as an opinion leader, social media recommendations amplify media trust, inducing people to want to read more news from the particular media platform in the future (Turcotte, York, Irving, Scholl, & Pingree, 2015).

In these ways, a concept advanced in 1955—interpersonal influence—continues to plays a vital role in political communication today, as controversies about whether online political exposure reinforces preexisting biases or offers more salutary electoral effects continue apace.

Third, a Review of the Early Research Shows That It Was Right About Some Things, Wrong About Others, But Got People Thinking

The two-step flow—whereby media influence opinion leaders, who in turn affect others—was an innovative, heuristic concept when it was proposed in 1955. It still operates today. Research published more than a half century after Katz and Lazarsfeld's landmark study found that exposure to a national anti-drug media campaign influenced older siblings, who in turn shaped the beliefs of their younger sisters and brothers (Hornik, 2006). There is evidence suggesting a two-step flow operates in online political marketing. For example, campaigns ask activists—for example, union supporters in Ohio who visited a Big Labor website—to contact less political involved union members from work who might be susceptible to an appeal from a trustworthy, politically similar source (see Duhigg, 2012).

On the other hand, the two-step flow does not always operate. For some issues, there is a one-step flow: from media to public (Bennett & Manheim, 2006). This was a theme in research on **news diffusion**, the idea that exposure to mass communication spreads new information through society. Where do people learn about important events, like who won a presidential election, a candidate's political gaffe, a key Supreme Court decision on health care or gay marriage, or U.S. military action? Facebook? Twitter? Or even television? (e.g., Kaye & Johnson, 2011). Diffusion is complicated. Increasingly, people are learning about important political events through the Internet and increasingly social media apps like WhatsApp, the way that some Turkish adults first learned about the country's 2016 coup. Researchers have studied diffusion over the past decades, assembling a variety of conclusions about how people learn about events of national consequence, such as when news diffuses first from media, when it spreads primarily through interpersonal communication channels, and when followers spread information to leaders (Weimann, 1994). These lines of inquiry were generated by the original research on the two-step flow.

Nowadays, the diffusion concept is out of date and less interesting than before, because people quickly and obviously obtain information instantly from social media apps, Twitter, and a host of online text platforms. At the time it gained currency in the 1960s, diffusion research demonstrated that media effects transcended simple attitude change, the province of psychologically oriented studies, and could branch out to include learning and beliefs about politics. Subsequently, evidence that people learned about national tragedies directly from media, without the intervention of opinion leaders, led to modifications in the two-step flow concept. Nowadays, diffusion questions, while less salient, revolve around the accuracy, completeness, and degree of bias that occurs when people acquire information instantaneously from online media. In these ways, an old concept expands in form and content, offering new applications to the understanding of political communication.

Fourth, Two Different Political Communication Perspectives Can Be Simultaneously True

The media profoundly influence politics. The early work got that right. At the same time, voters harbor strong attitudes. What people bring to media can strongly influence how they use and process media content, and can limit the impact of media on attitudes. As Klapper emphasized, people filter campaign messages through their attitudes, rejecting communications that conflict with their political attitudes and accepting those that congeal with what they believe. Klapper was correct that preexisting biases dampen media effects, but his work underplayed the subtle ways political media influence cognitions (Tessler & Zaller, 2014, as well as exert macro effects on institutions, like the presidential nominations, and the larger political system. What's more, the concepts of strong media effects and powerful preexisting psychological attitudes can interact, as when committed partisans tune in to politically congruent social media posts and the content leads them to feel even more strongly about their preferred candidate.

Fifth, Concerns About Powerful Media Effects Are a Pervasive Theme in American Political Communication

Scholars have detected an interesting continuity in communication research. During the 1930s, critics worried about pernicious influences wielded by radio programs. When comic books came around, fears centered on them. Not to be outdone, television, particularly violence, then, video games, next the Internet and now social media are the repository of concerns about—typically—harmful media effects. As Ellen A. Wartella and her colleagues noted, both academics and the public at large typically *assume* that the new media will exert powerful effects (Wartella, 1996; Wartella & Reeves, 1985). Over time, as the technology diffuses and becomes part of everyday life, a more modest, complex theory takes hold. Scholars change their tune, recognizing that the medium is not as powerful as they once feared, and they qualify their conjectures (Wartella, 1996).

This has stimulated an interesting "meta-debate" among communication researchers. For many years it was widely assumed that early propaganda researchers believed in a simplistic model of media effects that likened the media to a hypodermic needle that injected a message into audiences. But when scholars tried to find the term in the early research of the 20th century, they could find little evidence that the phrase *hypodermic needle* was invoked to describe mass media effects (Chaffee & Hochheimer, 1985; see also Bineham, 1988). Adding another layer to the discussion, Wartella and Stout (2002) reported that some research conducted during the 1930s adopted a more complex and nuanced view of media effects, hardly what one would expect if all the researchers thought of media in simple terms. Other scholars (Lubken, 2008) have even argued that the hypodermic needle notion served the function of a "straw man" for contemporary researchers. It allowed them to pat themselves on the back for coming up with more sophisticated perspective on media, when in fact few scholars actually held a simplistic view in the 1930s and '40s.

Academics aside, there is no question that across different eras, many people have *assumed* the media exert powerful effects. In 1922, Lippmann worried that the powers that be could instill pictures in our heads and manufacture consent. In 2011, a *New York Times* critic, describing video art, remarked on "the degree to which our world, what we take for reality, is formed by recording and image-making machinery." He noted that "our minds organize incoming information into images and narratives that may or may not be true to the facts," adding "we live in a world of scary, reality-determining technologies" (Johnson, 2011, p. C22).

The critic may be correct, but the point is you could have found a similar paragraph in articles writers penned in the 1920s, except they would have worried that movies or radio or propaganda controlled us. This represents a common thread in American political history. "The central paradox of America's constitutional tradition," Hogan (2013) observes, "lies in a persistent tension between our commitment to popular sovereignty and fears that 'the people' might be too easily distracted or manipulated to govern themselves" (p. 10). A conundrum of democracy is that government needs an institutional mechanism to inform and persuade the citizenry. However, the presence of both institutionalized public relations and mass media industries generate fears of abuse, some based in fantasy, others in fact. When is the public justified in fearing manipulation? When are fears about "brainwashing" and massive media effects out of whack with reality? When should critics worry about White House news management and implanting of false information? When do these worries reflect a cynical projection of sinister motives to well-intentioned policies developed by the nation's leaders? These are important questions that thread their way through American political communication.

Sixth, Continued Debate and Dialogue Characterize Current Political Communication Scholarship

There is not a party line, but continuing questions, the mark of a healthy discipline. Do social media facilitate or impede democracy? Do campaigns inform or mislead the electorate? Some scholars are more optimistic about the Internet and social media effects, arguing they can strengthen civic engagement (Boulianne, 2009). Others see a more negative picture, arguing that they merely reinforce existing prejudices (Sunstein, 2001). Some researchers point to the deceptive, manipulative aspects of campaigns, emphasizing their singular ability to cultivate beliefs that align with the powers that be (Le Cheminant & Parrish, 2011). Newer approaches emphasize the multitude of diverse platforms, as well as the ways that social media reaffirm what people believe via the online architecture of social networking sites, characterized by strong personalized connections to a narrow range of (frequently congenial) partisan views (Seaton, 2016). This too has stimulated debate between critics who believe social media promotes new forms of participation, and others who fear it divides and polarizes. Dialogue among proponents of different scholarly frameworks is healthy. It generates vigorous discussion and helps researchers come up with more sophisticated models of political communication.

WHERE WE ARE NOW

Amid all the debate, a new scholarly consensus has emerged. As social media have proliferated, people no longer simultaneously receive the same mass message delivered by television; individuals are more likely to receive news customized to their own political tastes on Facebook; and boundaries between opinion and fact have blurred. The long-held consensus that political media exert simultaneous, homogenizing effects on the mass public has come under scrutiny.

The dominant model used to emphasize that political media had top-down influences, with government and leading political elites using media to promote particular political perspectives. It was never that simple, of course, as there has long been a pluralism of elite viewpoints on most issues in America. However, the media-to-public model, with news as a centerpiece, had considerable support. In contemporary scholarship, the mass mediated model has been supplemented with a "networked public sphere" (Friedland, Hove, & Rojas, 2006). Mainstream media exist online alongside competing platforms and a multitude of online posts. Citizens are no longer exclusively receivers of political messages, but now initiate political conversations with friends, journalists, and leaders, frequently seeking out information that confirms what they already think (Bennett & Iyengar, 2008). What's more, with individuals increasingly living in communication enclaves peopled by those who share their perspective, there are questions about whether citizens gain exposure to a common set of consensually agreed-on facts (like on climate change and terrorism threats), whether they even come into contact with facts that call their ideas into question, and if they are open to viewpoints other than their own.

The change from past to present is a matter of degree, because mainstream media, including broadcast news, are still major sources of information (Holbert, Garrett, & Gleason, 2010). Even young people who get most of their information from the Internet and social media tune in to sites operated by big media like CNN, which gather and disseminate information to a public that sees content streamed rather than just transmitted via television. There is debate about the extent to which people are exposed primarily to information with which they agree, or if they actually have greater access to different viewpoints nowadays, given the sea of information available on the Internet. And there are questions about who has the power. Is it the active online publics that tweet vociferously, give money to candidates with whom they agree, and build movements online, as occurred as palpable voter anger helped solidify support for the conservative Tea Party and the candidacies of Bernie Sanders and Donald Trump in 2016? Or does this understate the ways that government, powerful elites, and corporate interest groups still control and frame major policy issues in this country?

In either case, there is little doubt that a centralized model of mass media news has been replaced by a far more decentralized, less linear approach. People actively seek out content and cluster in online networks that at least sometimes provide a congenial symbolic worldview, in ways that greatly extend the uses and gratifications approach that emphasized an active political audience. We don't speak of media audiences anymore because that diminishes the ways people act on, choose, and, through online media campaigns, influence politics.

Gray areas abound, contexts matter, and normative questions, such as what is good and bad about social media–dominated politics (and what "good" and "bad" mean) are ever more interesting. Political media scholarship provides a way of exploring ideas in systematic ways by articulating theories, teasing out hypotheses, testing predictions, accumulating knowledge, and comparing knowledge to the anchor of normative philosophy. This is the purview of social science research, the theme of the next section.

SOCIAL SCIENCE AND POLITICAL COMMUNICATION

It has come to this: After tossing different topics over in your mind, you decide that an examination of political media bias seems like a pretty good topic for a paper in your political communication class. After all, you think to yourself, "it's a well-known fact the media are biased." It should be an interesting paper, you muse. Almost fun, though that might be stretching it.

Expecting the paper to roll out smoothly, it comes as a surprise when suddenly intriguing questions grab hold of you and won't let go. Questions like: What do we mean by *bias*? Can the news put a candidate in a negative light without showing bias? How do you measure bias anyway? How do you figure out if the candidate is described in a way that is favorable, unfavorable, or neutral?

As it turns out, those are good questions, just the kind that social scientists wrestle with when conducting research (see Chapter 9). Research fundamentally focuses on exploring the unknown and uncovering mysteries. It is about finding answers to questions that puzzle us and trying to figure out if a hunch is correct or an observation that is commonly believed to be true actually is. But research is not a walk in the park. Social science involves a series of logical and empirical steps (Babbie, 2004). The logic concerns development of theories and hypotheses. The empirical refers to the testing of hypotheses through evidence gathered in actual social settings. Social scientists apply scientific methods to try to uncover regularities or patterns in human behavior. This section describes the social science methods that political communication researchers employ to answer interesting questions about politics and media.

Communication and political science scholars strive to develop a body of knowledge of the role political communication plays in society (Holbert & Bucy, 2011). To be sure, the social scientific approach is not the only way to approach the study of politics and media. We can gain insights from investigative articles in the press, film documentaries, and even political novels. But social science offers a dispassionate framework in which researchers ideally set aside personal biases and explore issues through the rigorous realm of hypothesis testing and empirical methodologies.

Social science cannot answer "should" questions. It cannot tell us whether limits should be placed on campaign spending or, alternatively, if a hands-off approach is better for democracy. It cannot say whether presidential debates should be open to third party candidates, if news should be required to devote a certain amount of time to issues or if voting should be compulsory. However, by accumulating research findings, social science *can* provide insights on normative questions like these. For example, if we find that voters are woefully uninformed by current news formats, and learn more from interactive styles of presenting news, this suggests that news platforms might emphasize interactive methods of news presentation. If it turns out that the wealthiest individuals and companies dominate campaign advertising, and their commercials powerfully influence the vote, this would suggest tinkering with campaign finance law or political commercials. If people are more likely to be informed, seek out media, and feel politically efficacious in countries with compulsory voting, this would suggest that the U.S. might want to weigh the pros and cons of requiring the vote.

Research will not direct you to one policy option or another. This involves a careful consideration of values and political philosophy. But, in some cases, research can help. More generally, research expands our knowledge about the effects of political communication in society. It explodes myths or time-honored misconceptions about politics, while building knowledge of political communication processes and effects. These are laudatory pursuits.

Research starts with a theory and hypothesis. To some degree, everyone has theories about politics and media. If you think the media are the primary influence on people's beliefs about politics, you have a theory. If you think the media are irrelevant, and it's our friends who influence us, you have a theory. If you believe that the media bash conservatives, prop up the powers that be, or, alternatively, are increasingly irrelevant to how young people experience politics, you have a theory.

At least, sort of. These are "lay theories" or intuitions about political communication. Truth be told, they are not formal scientific theories unless they contain a well-developed underlying conceptualization and a series of predictions that describe, explain, and predict events. A **theory** is a large, sweeping conceptualization that offers a wide-ranging explanation of a phenomenon and generates concrete hypotheses about when and why specific events will occur. A **hypothesis** is a specific proposition that can be tested through evidence.

Researchers begin with a theory and hypothesis because they provide a potential roadmap to the territory. Starting a research journey without a theory and hypotheses would be like venturing off onto a journey of a foreign land with your eyes closed, or like starting a day's trek through the circuitous pathways of a European city—say, Florence, Italy—with no roadmap, only a desire to see some art. Theories offer a way to interpret the world of human phenomena; hypotheses present a way to empirically determine if these ideas are likely to be true. Together they can help us arrive at a body of factually based knowledge, which in turn can offer insights and build a body of knowledge of political communication effects.

Strictly speaking, research tests a hypothesis derived from a theory. When enough hypotheses from different layers of the theory are supported, we no longer call it a theory, but an established body of knowledge. In the biological sciences, evolution fits into this category. We have much less certainty in the social sciences, but there are areas where hypotheses have been confirmed with enough regularity and sufficient confirming evidence has been obtained that we can speak with confidence about the validity of the knowledge base.

When you are talking with your friends, you can claim that such-and-such is true and people will politely agree. (Or perhaps not, if you have a particularly contentious group of friends!) When you are working in the domain of social scientific studies of political communication, you cannot say something is true unless there is scientific evidence to substantiate it. And that's the beauty of research. It separates the fanciful wheat from the factual chaff. It tells us what is more likely to be true and more likely to be false. In a world where some like trying to deny that there are facts and the Trump White House has put forth Orwellian statements suggesting that falsehoods constitute "alternative facts," a social science discipline that plies theory and methods to discover empirical truths has much to offer society.

Research Methodologies

Methodology is to research as cooking is to the work of a chef. You need creative recipes, but the key to a good meal is how you executive the culinary plans in the kitchen. In the realm of social science, methods put hypotheses to the test. There are a number of research methodologies that are harnessed in political communication studies.

A widely used tool in social science research, **content analysis** is a systematic method to quantitatively examine the characteristics, themes and symbols of a message. Content analyses can tell us if news covers certain candidates more favorably than others, whether female politicians receive different types of news coverage than male politicians, and the themes candidates use in negative ads. Content analysis was an ingenious invention because it offered a fine-grained method to describe the attributes contained in a message. It helped researchers to map the symbolic landscape of a nation's political system. However, an analysis of media content does not indicate that the content has effects. This requires evidence gleaned from experiments and surveys.

Content analysis quantifies—or describes with numbers—components of the content of communications. Content analyses usually examine verbal dimensions of media content, such as words and arguments. But they can also quantify audiovisual images, like how frequently candidates display compassion or toughness in their nonverbal displays, as well as the camera shots the news selects that depict a candidate smiling or frowning

(Grabe & Bucy, 2011). Visual images play an important role in political communication, and content analysis offers a way to carefully document these images.

A challenge in content analysis is determining your unit of analysis. Should you search for bias in each paragraph in a news story? Or should you focus instead on the adjectives reporters use to describe a political figure? In addition, you probably will not want to examine each and every news story, political speech, or website. You will need to sample. But what type of sample should you draw and how? There are criteria researchers employ to help answer these questions.

Content analysis also differentiates between manifest and latent content (Benoit, 2011). Manifest content refers to what is obviously there, right on the surface, like the issues that a politician discusses or sources a reporter quotes. Latent content is the subtle, deeper message that requires more judgment and analysis to ferret out, like the emotion that a candidate expresses or the degree to which news coverage showcases support for the electoral system. Note that a particular content does not demonstrate that the advertisement or news story exerts an impact on voters or the larger political system. This is a question of media effects, the purview of methods that follow.

The hallmark of scientific research, an **experiment** is a controlled study that provides evidence of causation through random assignment of individuals to a treatment or control group. A treatment is a stimulus of interest—for example, an experimental drug in a medical study, and an election news story or segment from a presidential debate in a political communication experiment. A scientific experiment involves at least two conditions: an experimental condition in which the treatment is administered, and a comparison or control group. Random assignment refers to the allocation of individuals to conditions, based on chance factors. Names may be assigned numbers, and numbers are randomly selected from a random numbers table.

Experiments have demonstrated that news influences beliefs about national problems, negative advertisements shape attitudes, and televised political humor can increase cynicism. Although it may seem funny to think about rarefied experiments in the rough-and-tumble world of politics, they are actually extremely useful in helping us say with certainty whether Factor X causes Outcome Y. Political communication is so complicated that it is good to know for certain if a variable can cause an outcome (Arceneaux, 2010).

The strength of experiments is also their weakness. Precisely because they take place in a controlled setting, experiments cannot tell us whether the experimental finding actually occurs in the real world. An experiment may tell us that exposure to a carefully edited fictitious political advertisement makes people more cynical about politics. But does this apply to the real world, where voters already have formed attitudes toward candidate displayed in ads, or in instances where they may scarcely see the commercial in question? Will effects persist over time? Over the past decades, researchers have perfected a number of strategies to increase the realism of experiments, enhancing confidence they can apply the results to real-life political contexts (Iyengar, 2011).

Survey

A primary research strategy in political communication (Holbert & Bucy, 2011), the **survey** is a questionnaire or interview-based study that documents a correlation or relationship between two or more variables in a real-world setting, identifying factors that can best predict a particular outcome. A correlation is a measure of the linkage or relationship between two factors. You undoubtedly have taken many surveys yourself, from course evaluations to Facebook polls.

Surveys play a particularly important role in political communication because they are so flexible. Researchers can ask a variety of questions about different political variables, and unlike super-sensitive topics like prejudice, where people don't always tell the truth, people are usually fairly comfortable answering questions about politics on a questionnaire. A survey can tell us many interesting things, like if Internet use leads to more civic participation, whether television news increases knowledge of candidate issue positions, and the degree to which the impact of news on knowledge depends on your educational level.

A key aspect of surveys is measurement: measuring concepts reliably and validly in a questionnaire. Let's say you are a journalism major and believe that political news has many positive influences, like increasing knowledge of politics and offering voters guidance in making candidate choices. Tired of your friends' cracks that the news is boring and ridiculously superficial, you decide to conduct a survey to demonstrate that your hypothesis (news enhances political knowledge) is supported by evidence. But you first need to empirically assess news media use to differentiate those who follow the news a lot from those who hardly follow it at all. You ask people how much exposure they have to news.

Alas, exposure to political news is a general category. It would be like testing the hypothesis that college increases critical thinking skills by asking students how much exposure they had to college or to college classes. It's not just exposure that could catalyze critical thinking. It is how much attention that students pay to the material, how they process the information, how they link up the class to other goals in their life, and so forth. Applying this to news, it would be better to ask respondents how much attention they pay to news, as well as how they reflect on and process what they see (Hoffman & Young, 2011; Kosicki, McLeod, & McLeod, 2011).

News is also a general category. What type of news? Fox? MSNBC? Politico? An amalgamation of information seen on Facebook? If you ask respondents about their online news use, what exactly do you mean? A newspaper website, a CNN report, or a series of posts on Facebook, which might not be news at all but opinionated statements with supportive videos attached? A decidedly fake news report? You need a clear definition of political news that meets journalistic canons.

Specificity is a cardinal virtue in research, and when it comes to measurement it is best to develop precise, validated measures of news exposure. This is eminently doable, and there is considerable contemporary research to guide instrument development, as Hoffman and Young (2011) note. The payoff is that more fine-tuned measures could help you make a stronger case to your politically apathetic friends that news has a salutary impact on knowledge. Of course, you would also need to develop a scientifically reliable and valid measure of public affairs knowledge. Happily, recent refinements in political communication survey research have enabled researchers to make more specific and precise statements about cognitive and related media effects (e.g., Eveland & Morey, 2011; Hayes, Preacher, & Myers, 2011; Kenski, Gottfried, & Jamieson, 2011).

Certain problems still bedevil researchers who study political media impact. Respondents may indicate on a survey that they learned a candidate's issue position from a presidential debate, believing this is where they gleaned the information. But they may have acquired the information from news of the debate or a conversation with a friend who attended closely to the debate. The survey information would therefore overstate news media effects. The trick is to tease out the particular factor that caused an effect and empirically demonstrate that news exposure is causally related to political knowledge—a complex, but important, issue. There are ways to home in on these issues, and there are several additional research strategies that can help pinpoint communication effects (see Box 3.1).

BOX 3.1 ADDITIONAL POLITICAL COMMUNICATION METHODOLOGIES

More than 40 years ago, when the modern field of political communication was launched (Chaffee, 1975), the discipline lacked the methodology and technology to zoom in on a number of important issues. Over the past decades, the intellectual horizons of the field have expanded, and with this have come a proliferation of new and improved methods (Kosicki et al., 2011). These include:

- Secondary analysis, a technique that allows researchers to reanalyze national data sets with a particular focus or innovative twist (Holbert & Hmielowski, 2011);
- Focus groups, in which a trained leader coordinates a group interview that can yield rich insights on a variety of topics, such as how people talk about politics in everyday life, why many young people do not vote, and reactions to political ads (Jarvis, 2011);
- Multiple strategies to explore communication that occurs in deliberative meetings. This includes systematic analysis of discussion at a school board meeting or town hall forum, as well as post-meeting follow-up interviews with participants (Black, Burkhalter, Gastil, & Stromer-Galley, 2011); and
- Psychophysiological measures of heart rate, facial muscle activation, brain imaging and other bodily arousal that occurs while watching candidate speeches and negative political ads (Bucy & Bradley, 2011).

Complementing these approaches, rhetorical and discourse-focused scholars study political communication with more qualitative methods. Although these lack the precision of scientific techniques, they can illuminate the rich tableau of political communication, as practiced by leaders and activists. Campbell and Jamieson (2008) call on elements of classical political rhetoric in delineating characteristics of presidential inaugural addresses, State of the Union speeches, war rhetoric, and national eulogies. Other scholars have employed discourse analysis to offer insights into communicative practices and sometimes contradictory political beliefs expressed by ordinary people in community gatherings, such as school board meetings (Tracy, 2010).

CONCLUSIONS

This chapter traced the trajectory of political communication research, describing milestones, critical junctures, the current zeitgeist (or consensus about scholarly effects), and research methods used to test hypotheses. Emphasizing that the history of a field of study is not a boring, straight-line summation of facts, the discussion tracked political communication's zigzag path of historical development, from late 19th-century theoretical speculations about media and crowd behavior through Lippmann's path-breaking observations about the power of media to mold public opinion, coupled with criticisms that his elitist focus neglected the role played by citizen dialogue. As the new field took a turn toward propaganda analysis, political media research seemed to upend the assumption of powerful media effects by documenting that the political press exerted only a modest impact on voting, emphasizing instead the role played by interpersonal influence and opinion leadership. Based on research of the 1940s and '50s, researchers concluded that political media had minimal effects. This perspective, epitomized by Klapper's (1960) conclusions, proved controversial, rankling scholars who believed media exerted a preeminent role in politics. With the diffusion of television, apparent influences of political news, widespread popular belief in media impact, and growing scientific evidence of strong political communication influences, Klapper's limited effects model fell by the wayside, supplanted by a model that emphasized the direct, indirect, subtle, micro, and macro ways media influence politics.

Reviewing the history of political communication scholarship, one glimpses twists and turns as well as continuities. As will be discussed throughout this book, political media decidedly influence our pictures of the world, molding ideas, and helping us construct beliefs about politics. Interpersonal influence, an old concept that became passé in the 1970s and '80s as television exerted significant effects (and the field sought to define itself in terms of primordial media impact), has become important again. We live in an era of social networks, where communication that occurs online has accoutrements of old-style interpersonal communication. In an era of social networks and online opinion configurations, socially mediated opinion leadership and information flows can influence political participation, while also reinforcing selective exposure to politically congruent information. Political media exert a wealth of effects, but—packaging old political communication wine in new online bottles—refinements of Klapper's view have some support. Political media intersect with preexisting attitudes, reinforcing attitudes in politically consequential ways.

Over the years, researchers have documented a multitude of political communication effects, such as agenda-setting, framing, and persuasion that results from cognitive processing of electoral messages. These concepts departed from the original social psychological focus of the field, pointing to the ways that mediated communication processes and effects explain the dynamics of political communication. There continue to be lively debates about whether political media exert strong or modest impacts, the extent to which messages inform or mislead the public, and, in a vibrant social media age, the degree to which media are echo chambers mirroring what we already believe, or expose us to divergent points of view, broadening our range of political beliefs.

The chapter emphasized the social scientific underpinnings of political communication and scholars' commitment to accumulating a body of empirical knowledge. Theory, hypotheses, and a host of research methods guide political communication inquiries. Rigorous tests of hypotheses allow us to advance theory and build a body of knowledge of political communication effects. There are always limits, a function of the difficulties of studying ongoing media effects over the course of a campaign, convincingly establishing causality, wrestling with unreliable measures, and grappling with the temptation of overgeneralizing empirical results (Kosicki et al., 2011). Imperfect as methods are, they do yield interesting, scientifically based insights about political communication. And while our research cannot answer "ought" questions, they clarify issues, pinpoint falsehoods, and offer broad insights about the quality of contemporary democracy.

REFERENCES

Arceneaux, K. (2010). The benefits of experimental methods for the study of campaign effects. *Political Communication, 27*, 199–215.

Babbie, E. (2004). *The practice of social research* (10th ed.). Belmont, CA: Thomson/Wadsworth.

Becker, L.B., McCombs, M.E., & McLeod, J.M. (1975). The development of political cognitions. In S.H. Chaffee (Ed.), *Political communication: Strategies for research* (pp. 21–63). Newbury Park, CA: Sage.

Bennett, W.L., & Iyengar, S. (2008). A new era of minimal effects? The changing foundations of political communication. *Journal of Communication, 58*, 707–731.

Bennett, W.L., & Iyengar, S. (2010). The shifting foundations of political communication: Responding to a defense of the media effects paradigm. *Journal of Communication, 60*, 35–39.

Benoit, W.L. (2011). Content analysis in political communication. In E.P. Bucy & R.L. Holbert (Eds.), *The sourcebook for political communication research: Methods, measures, and analytical techniques* (pp. 268–279). New York: Routledge.

Berelson, B., Lazarsfeld, P.F., & McPhee, W.N. (1954). *Voting: A study of opinion formation in a presidential campaign.* Chicago: University of Chicago Press.

Bineham, J.L. (1988). A historical account of the hypodermic model in mass communication. *Communication Monographs, 55*, 230–246.

Black, L.W., Burkhalter, S., Gastil, J., & Stromer-Galley, J. (2011). Methods for analyzing and measuring group deliberation. In E.P. Bucy & R.L. Holbert (Eds.), *The sourcebook for political communication research: Methods, measures, and analytical techniques* (pp. 323–345). New York: Routledge.

Boulianne, S. (2009). Does Internet use affect engagement? A meta-analysis of research. *Political Communication, 26*, 193–211.

Bucy, E.P., & Bradley, S.D. (2011). What the body can tell us about politics: The use of psychophysiological measures in political communication research. In E.P. Bucy & R.L. Holbert (Eds.), *The sourcebook for political communication research: Methods, measures, and analytical techniques* (pp. 525–540). New York: Routledge.

Campbell, K.K., & Jamieson, K.H. (2008). *Presidents creating the presidency: Deeds done in words.* Chicago: University of Chicago Press.

Cantril, H., Gaudet, H., & Herzog, H. (1940). *The invasion from Mars: A study in the psychology of panic.* Princeton, NJ: Princeton University Press.

Carey, J.W. (1995). The press, public opinion, and public discourse. In T.L. Glasser & C.T. Salmon (Eds.), *Public opinion and the communication of consent* (pp. 373–402). New York: Guilford.

Chaffee, S.H. (Ed.). (1975). *Political communication: Issues and strategies for Research.* Beverly Hills, CA: Sage.

Chaffee, S.H., & Hochheimer, J.L. (1985). The beginnings of political communication research in the United States: Origins of the "limited effects" model. In M. Gurevitch & M.R. Levy (Eds.), *Mass communication review yearbook* (Vol. 5, pp. 75–104). Newbury Park, CA: Sage.

Dewey, J. (1927). *The public and its problems*. New York: Holt.

Duhigg, C. (2012, October 14). Campaigns mine personal lives to get out vote. *The New York Times*, 1, 14.

Eveland, W.P., & Hively, M.H. (2009). Political discussion frequency, network size, and "heterogeneity" of discussion as predictors of political knowledge and participation. *Journal of Communication, 59*, 205–224.

Eveland, W.P., Jr., & Morey, A.C. (2011). Challenges and opportunities of panel designs. In E.P. Bucy & R.L. Holbert (Eds.), *The sourcebook for political communication research: Methods, measures, and analytical techniques* (pp. 19–33). New York: Routledge.

Ewen, S. (1996). *PR! A social history of spin*. New York: Basic Books.

Friedland, L.A., Hove, T., & Rojas, H. (2006). The networked public sphere. *Javnost—The Public, 13*(4), 5–26.

Gitlin, T. (1978). Media sociology: The dominant paradigm. *Theory and Society, 6*, 205–253.

Grabe, M.E., & Bucy, E.P. (2011). Image bite analysis of political visuals: Understanding the visual framing process in election news. In E.P. Bucy & R.L. Holbert (Eds.), *The sourcebook for political communication research: Methods, measures, and analytical techniques* (pp. 209–237). New York: Routledge.

Hayes, A.F., Preacher, K.J., & Myers, T.A. (2011). Mediation and the estimation of indirect effects in political communication research. In E.P. Bucy & R.L. Holbert (Eds.), *The sourcebook for political communication research: Methods, measures, and analytical techniques* (pp. 434–465). New York: Routledge.

Hoffman, L.H., & Young, D.G. (2011). Political communication survey research: Challenges, trends, and opportunities. In E.P. Bucy & R.L. Holbert (Eds.), *The sourcebook for political communication research: Methods, measures, and analytical techniques* (pp. 55–77). New York: Routledge.

Hogan, J.M. (2013). Persuasion in the rhetorical tradition. In J.P. Dillard (Ed.), *The persuasion handbook: New directions in theory and research*. Thousand Oaks, CA: Sage.

Holbert, R.L., & Bucy, E.P. (2011). Advancing methods and measurement: Supporting theory and keeping pace with the modern political communication environment. In E.P. Bucy & R.L. Holbert (Eds.), *The sourcebook for political communication research: Methods, measures, and analytical techniques* (pp. 3–15). New York: Routledge.

Holbert, R.L., Garrett, R.K., & Gleason, L.S. (2010). A new era of minimal effects? A response to Bennett and Iyengar. *Journal of Communication, 60*, 15–34.

Holbert, R.L., & Hmielowski, J.D. (2011). Secondary analysis in political communication viewed as a creative act. In E.P. Bucy & R.L. Holbert (Eds.), *The sourcebook for political communication research: Methods, measures, and analytical techniques* (pp. 81–95). New York: Routledge.

Huckfeldt, R., & Sprague, J. (1995). *Citizens, politics, and social communication: Information and influence in an election campaign*. New York: Cambridge University Press.

Iyengar, S. (2011). Experimental designs for political communication research: Using new technology and online participant pools to overcome the problem of generalizability. In E.P. Bucy & R.L. Holbert (Eds.), *The sourcebook for political communication research: Methods, measures, and analytical techniques* (pp. 129–148). New York: Routledge.

Jamieson, K.H. (1984). *Packaging the presidency: A history and criticism of presidential campaign advertising*. New York: Oxford University Press.

Jamieson, K.H. (2014). The five-decade long evolution of the concept of effects in political communication. In K. Kenski & K.H. Jamieson (Eds.), *The Oxford handbook of political communication.* Retrieved from www.oxford.handbooks.com (Accessed July 17, 2016).

Jarvis, S.E. (2011). The use of focus groups in political communication research. In E.P. Bucy & R.L. Holbert (Eds.), *The sourcebook for political communication research: Methods, measures, and analytical techniques* (pp. 283–299). New York: Routledge.

Johnson, K. (2011, August 26). Unfiltered images, turning perceptions upside down. *The New York Times*, C22.

Katz, E., Blumler, J.G., & Gurevitch, M. (1974). Preliminary overview—Utilization of mass communication by the individual. In J.G. Blumler & E. Katz (Eds.), *The uses of mass communications: Current perspectives on gratifications research* (pp. 19–32). Beverly Hills, CA: Sage.

Katz, E., & Lazarsfeld, P.F. (1955). *Personal influence: The part played by people in the flow of mass communications.* Glencoe, IL: Free Press.

Kaye, B.K., & Johnson, T.J. (2011). *The shot heard around the World Wide Web: Who heard what where about Osama bin Laden's death.* Paper presented to annual convention of Midwest Association for Public Opinion Research, Chicago.

Kenski, K., Gottfried, J.A., & Jamieson, K.H. (2011). The rolling cross-section: Design and utility for political research. In E.P. Bucy & R.L. Holbert (Eds.), *The sourcebook for political communication research: Methods, measures, and analytical techniques* (pp. 34–54). New York: Routledge.

Kenski, K., & Jamieson, K.H. (Eds.) (2014). *The Oxford handbook of political communication.* Retrieved from www.oxford.handbooks.com (Accessed April 10, 2017).

Klapper, J.T. (1960). *The effects of mass communication.* New York: Free Press.

Kosicki, G.M., McLeod, D.M., & McLeod, J.M. (2011). Looking back and looking forward: Observations on the role of research methods in the rapidly evolving field of political communication. In E.P. Bucy & R.L. Holbert (Eds.), *The sourcebook for political communication research: Methods, measures, and analytical techniques* (pp. 543–569). New York: Routledge.

Lang, G.E., & Lang, K. (1983). *The battle for public opinion: The president, the press, and the polls during Watergate.* New York: Columbia University Press.

Lang, K., & Lang, G.E. (2006). *Personal Influence* and the new paradigm: Some inadvertent consequences. *Annals of the American Association of Political and Social Science, 608,* 157–178.

Lasswell, H. (1927). *Propaganda technique in the world war.* New York: Knopf.

Lazarsfeld, P.F., Berelson, B., & Gaudet, H. (1944). *The people's choice: How the voter makes up his mind in a presidential campaign.* New York: Columbia University Press.

Le Bon, G. (1896). *The crowd: A study of the popular mind.* London.

Le Cheminant, W., & Parrish, J.M. (2011). Introduction: Manipulating democracy: A reappraisal. In W. Le Cheminant & J.M. Parrish (Eds.), *Manipulating democracy: Democratic theory, political psychology, and mass media* (pp. 1–24). New York: Routledge.

Lippmann, W. (1922). *Public opinion.* New York: Free Press.

Lubken, D. (2008). Remembering the straw man: The travels and adventures of *hypodermic.* In D.W. Park & J. Pooley (Eds.), *The history of media and communication research: Contested memories* (pp. 19–42). New York: Peter Lang.

McCombs, M.E., & Shaw, D.L. (1972). The agenda-setting function of mass media. *Public Opinion Quarterly, 36,* 176–187.

McDonald, D.G. (2004). Twentieth-century media effects research. In J.D.H. Downing, D. McQuail, P. Schlesinger, & E. Wartella (Eds.), *The Sage handbook of media studies* (pp. 183–200). Thousand Oaks, CA: Sage.

McGinniss, J. (1969). *The selling of the president.* New York: Penguin.

McLeod, J.M., Becker, L.B., & Byrnes, J.E. (1974). Another look at the agenda- setting function of the press. *Communication Research, 1,* 131–165.

Morrison, D.E. (2006). The influences influencing *Personal Influence:* Scholarship and entrepreneurship. *Annals of the American Association of Political and Social Science, 608,* 51–75.

Neiheisel, J.R., & Niebler, S. (2015). On the limits of persuasion: Campaign ads and the structure of voters' interpersonal discussion networks. *Political Communication, 32,* 434–452.

Patterson, T.E. (1980). *The mass media election: How Americans choose their president.* New York: Praeger.

Patterson, T.E. (2016, June 13). *Pre-primary news coverage of the 2016 presidential race: Trump's rise, Sanders' emergence, Clinton's struggle.* Harvard Kennedy School Shorenstein Center on Media, Politics and Public Policy. Retrieved from http://shorensteincenter.org/pre-primary-news-coverage- 2016-trump-c. . . (Accessed June 14, 2016).

Schudson, M. (2008). The "Lippmann-Dewey debate" and the invention of Walter Lippmann as an anti-democrat 1986–1996. *International Journal of Communication, 2,* 1–20.

Seaton, J. (2016). The new architecture of communications. *Journalism Studies, 17,* 808–816.

Simonson, P. (2006). Introduction. *Annals of the American Association of Political and Social Science, 608,* 6–24.

Singer, N. (2011, September 11.) On campus, it's one big commercial. *The New York Times* (Sunday Business), 1, 4.

Southwell, B.G. (2014). Two-step flow, diffusion, and the role of social networks in political communication. In K. Kenski & K.H. Jamieson (Eds.), *The Oxford handbook of political communication.* Retrieved from www.oxfordhandbooks.com (Accessed June 7, 2014). New York: Oxford University Press.

Steel, R. (1999). *Walter Lippmann and the American century.* New Brunswick, NJ: Transaction.

Sunstein, C. (2001). *Republic.com.* Princeton, NJ: Princeton University Press.

Tessler, M., & Zaller, J. (2014). The power of political communication. In K. Kenski & K.H. Jamieson (Eds.), *The Oxford handbook of political Communication.* Retrieved from www.oxfordhandbooks.com (Accessed June 7, 2014).

Tracy, K. (2010). *Challenges of ordinary democracy: A case study in deliberation and dissent.* University Park: Pennsylvania State University Press.

Tuchman, B. (1962). *The guns of August.* New York: Palgrave Macmillan.

Turcotte, J., York, C., Irving, J., Scholl, R.M., & Pingree, R.J. (2015). News recommendations from social media opinion leaders: Effects on media trust and information seeking. *Journal of Computer-Mediated Communication, 20,* 520–535.

Wartella, E. (1996). The history reconsidered. In E.E. Dennis & E. Wartella (Eds.), *American communication research—The remembered history* (pp. 169–180). Mahwah, NJ: Lawrence Erlbaum Associates.

Wartella, E., & Reeves, B. (1985). Historical trends in research on children and the media: 1900–1960. *Journal of Communication, 35,* 118–135.

Wartella, E.A., & Stout, P.A. (2002). The evolution of mass media and health persuasion models. In W.D. Crano & M. Burgoon (Eds.), *Mass media and drug prevention: Classic and contemporary theories and research* (pp. 19–34). Mahwah, NJ: Lawrence Erlbaum Associates.

Weimann, G. (1994). *The influentials: People who influence people.* Albany: State University of New York Press.

Westbrook, R.B. (1991). *John Dewey and American democracy.* Ithaca, NY: Cornell University Press.

4 Media and Political Knowledge

Some years back, an amusing YouTube video generated a lot of buzz. An Australian reporter interviewed Americans on the street, asking them ridiculously easy questions about politics, and they answered them all incorrectly. The reporter posed questions to bemused Americans on a city street; some puzzled over questions, while others spouted confidently whatever popped into their minds. The Q&A included this:

Reporter: Name a country that begins with U.
Man 1: Yugoslavia?
Man 2: With U: Utah.
Woman 1: A country that starts with a U? Utopia.
Woman 2: A country? . . .
Reporter: What about this one?
Woman 2: What?
Reporter: United States of America.
Woman 2: [Gasps, recognizing her obvious error.]
Reporter: What is the religion of Israel?
Man 1: Israeli.
Man 2: Muslim.
Man 3: Islamic.
Man 4: Catholic probably.
Reporter: What religion are Buddhist monks?
Man 1: Buddhist monks?
Man 2: Islamic, I don't know.
Reporter: Who won the Vietnam War?
Woman: We did [laughing]. Wait, were we even in the Vietnam War?

Reporter: What is the currency used in the United Kingdom?
Man: Possibly American money?
Woman: Queen Elizabeth's money?

Okay: Some of the people may have been pulling the reporter's leg, and the sample is hardly representative of the public. But consider this:

Several years back, comedian Jimmy Kimmel conducted an on-air experiment about attitudes toward health care, asking people what they thought of Obamacare and the Affordable Care Act, the sweeping health policy passed during the Obama administration. Of course, they are the same! Obamacare is a nickname for—or more pejorative description of—the Affordable Care Act. But interviewees did not know this. They frequently said they disagreed with Obamacare, saying, as one woman did, that there were "a lot of holes in it and it needs to be revamped." She added, though, that the Affordable Health Care Act is better. One man said the Affordable Care Act is more "affordable" than Obamacare, adding that "just the name says it all." Another said the Affordable Care Act is "more American" than the identical Obamacare.

It turns out that the anecdotal results of Kimmel's interviews are supported by empirical evidence. More than 1 in 3 Americans did not know that Obamacare and the Affordable Care Act are the same policies, and nearly 1 in 5 Americans thought Obamacare and the Affordable Act were different health care plans (Dropp & Nyhan, 2017).

These two amusing examples—the YouTube video and Kimmel's interviews—touch on two serious issues in democratic theory: What do Americans know about politics? Does it matter?

These quintessential questions about citizenship in a media age were posed some years back by Michael X. Delli Carpini and Scott Keeter (1996) in a classic book. The answers to both questions are fascinating and may surprise you. Normative democratic theories place a premium on citizen knowledge and competence. You cannot have a functioning democratic society if citizens are ignorant of basic facts of government and cannot grasp the array of problems facing their society. As James Madison famously said, "a popular Government, without popular information, or the means of acquiring it, is but a Prologue to a Farce or a Tragedy; or perhaps both." Echoing these sentiments, political scientists Niemi and Junn (1998) noted more concretely that "for democratic decision making to be meaningful and legitimate, citizens must be capable of understanding what is at stake in politics, what their alternatives are, and what their own positions are" (p. 9). Nowadays, the media are the major vehicles that transmit political information to citizens.

This chapter and the one that follows offer an in-depth examination of citizenship in an age of mediated politics. The present chapter focuses on knowledge and Chapter 5 examines the socialization of political beliefs and attitudes. This chapter is divided into three sections. The first section examines what Americans know about politics, what they don't know, and the reasons why knowledge levels are not as high as they could or should be. The second portion examines the media's impact on knowledge acquisition, guided by different disciplinary perspectives. The third section discusses the ups and downs of political learning in a digital age.

WHAT DO AMERICANS KNOW ABOUT POLITICS?

First, the good news.

In their systematic review of national surveys of political knowledge conducted over the course of a half century, Delli Carpini and Keeter concluded that Americans are modestly informed about politics and have basic knowledge of a number of aspects of government. In this vast, richly diverse country, marked by striking differences in income and education, there is widespread knowledge of the definition of a presidential veto, the length of a presidential term, and the meaning of deregulation. There is also substantial knowledge of key aspects of the U.S. Constitution and civil liberties, such as the fact that the Constitution can be amended, freedom of press is guaranteed by the First Amendment, and citizens have the right to a trial by jury. Most Americans can name at least one position in the U.S. Cabinet and know the number of senators from their state. Ninety-nine percent of Americans can correctly name the U.S. president, compared to just 89 percent of Italians who can name their head of state! Large majorities know America's leaders and policies with which they are associated.

But the ignorance and disparities in knowledge, reported by Delli Carpini and Keeter and others, are well . . . nothing short of breathtaking:

- Just over a fourth of the public can name all three branches of government (executive, legislative, and judicial, in case you forgot); yet two-thirds could name a TV judge on *American Idol* (Annenberg Public Policy Center, 2016; Breyer, 2010).
- Less than half the public can accurately define several concepts that are central to democratic politics, such as *liberal* and *conservative*, or know how presidential delegates are selected.
- Just 35 percent could name both senators from their state. Three-quarters of all Americans do not appreciate the difference between a legislator and a judge (Breyer, 2010).
- More than 4 in 10 do not know that free speech is protected in all media (Delli Carpini & Keeter, 1996).

- Nearly 4 in 10 Americans incorrectly believe that the Constitution gives the president the power to declare war; a little over half recognized that the Constitution gives Congress the power to declare war (Annenberg Public Policy Center, 2016).
- About 25 percent of Americans can identify *more than one* of the five freedoms ensured by the First Amendment (freedom of speech, press, religion, assembly, and petition for redress of grievance). But more than half had no trouble naming two members of *The Simpsons* (Shenkman, 2008).
- Forty-four percent of Americans without health insurance believed Obama's health care law would exert no impact on the quality of health care they receive, even though the law improves the overall quality of health care (Goodnough & Kopicki, 2013).
- Geographical knowledge is staggeringly low. Just over half of the public could locate Central America or France on a map. What's more, only 50 percent of Americans could locate Ohio on a map and 42 percent could accurately locate New Jersey.
- There are widespread inequalities in political knowledge. Educated and wealthier Americans are considerably more knowledgeable than their less educated and poorer counterparts.

Adlai Stevenson, the Democratic presidential candidate of 1952 and 1956, said it best. A supporter once told him, "Governor Stevenson, all thinking people are for you." Stevenson replied, "That's not enough. I need a majority" (Shenkman, 2008, p. 37).

There is a paradox here. We live at a time when we are swamped with information, glutted with facts, and bombarded by political stimuli. Never before has society had so much political information, and never before has it been easier to access information. Yet people are frequently uninformed on political issues, and the Internet is awash in falsehoods and misleading statements of political fact. Democracy requires political knowledge, and it is there for the grasping. But citizens' knowledge does not reach the levels deemed appropriate by political philosophers. Alternatively, is the situation this dire? There are different perspectives on knowledge in contemporary democracy, with some scholars taking a less pessimistic view. Let's examine the issues, beginning with explanations for evidence of low knowledge levels.

WHY DO PEOPLE KNOW SO LITTLE?

Americans' ignorance of basic facts about government is disturbing. Americans know significantly less about political issues, particularly international problems, than citizens from a host of European countries (Aalberg & Curran, 2012). What accounts for the knowledge deficits? Five explanations have been advanced.

One reason is lack of incentive. A key way people make their voices known in democracy is through voting. Yet one person's vote makes virtually no difference in the outcome of an election. From a purely rational perspective, it is not in an individual's self-interest to expend much time soaking up political information when his or her input is of such little consequence.

A second explanation emphasizes the way news is presented. Its focus on facts, figures, and jargon can overwhelm people. News about the economic crisis can contain mind-numbing discussion of *mortgage-backed securities*, *over-leveraging*, or *liquidity shortfall*, concepts that most people do not understand and that are explained poorly, if at all, by journalists. In addition, American television networks devote less time to news during peak hours (7 p.m. to 10 p.m.) than do European broadcasts (Aalberg, van Aelst, & Curran, 2012). Despite the growth of CNN and Fox, there is actually less news provided during prime time in the U.S. than in six European nations. This helps explain why Americans know less about politics than their European counterparts.

A third explanation lies in the expansion in media choices. With a multitude of entertaining cable channels, YouTube, and social media sites, news may be swamped by other channels, lost in the mix. "Those who prefer nonpolitical content can more easily escape the news and therefore pick up less political information than they used to," one scholar observes (Prior, 2005, p. 577). Ironically, as the volume of political information has grown exponentially with the Internet, political knowledge may have declined among the less interested members of the public. When television was the dominant medium, even the more apathetic could not avoid the news. When the television set was on, they watched and may have soaked up some facts. Nowadays, politics may be easier to ignore.

Fourth, leaders deliberately dissemble information, intentionally conveying misleading political facts. Back in the 1990s, some political leaders described Social Security in doomsday terms, talking about the "impending bankruptcy" of the financial program. Policymakers claimed that the program would run out of cash by the 2030s, even though there would actually be enough funds available to pay retirees for another two decades to come. Some politicians may have resorted to hyperbole in an effort to push Congress into acting sooner rather than later. Others may have had more opportunistic motives. Whatever the reason, the political rhetoric did not match the facts. Yet it had demonstrable effects on public knowledge. During the debate about Social Security in 1998 and 1999, as many as a third of Americans incorrectly believed that Social Security would completely run out of money (Jerit & Barabas, 2006). Similarly, many Americans harbored misperceptions about aspects of Obama's Affordable Care Act, about which leaders consistently ventured incorrect claims (Pasek, Sood, & Krosnick, 2015). The rhetorical sleight of hand—politicians calling the Affordable Care

Act "Obamacare," frequently to disparage it—left disturbing residues. Given that over a third of Americans did not know that Obamacare and the Affordable Care Act are the same, they are apt to erroneously believe that repealing Obamacare would not adversely affect popular features of the Affordable Care Act (Dropp & Nyhan, 2017).

A more complicated example is free trade. During the 2016 campaign, Trump and Sanders lambasted global trade agreements, arguing that they had harmed American workers and manufacturing. Trade is complex: While international trade deals have taken a toll on American manufacturing jobs, they also have slashed prices consumers pay and created jobs in broad sectors of the economy. In the past, both Democratic and Republican administrations have embraced global trade agreements. The ensuring conflict—and confusion—sowed doubt, causing just 19 percent of American voters to say that trade with other countries creates more U.S. jobs, a claim that professional economists would contest (Goodman, 2016).

Politicians of both parties, enamored of the possibilities of capturing constituents with clever social media snippets, increasingly offer short, tweet-like quips and visuals, devoid of meaningful political information.

The final explanation for low knowledge levels lies in the increasing disconnect between politics and everyday life. To many Americans, politics has become the province of political professionals—consultants for hire who manage campaigns that people passively watch, a faraway road show that has little to do with their personal lives.

A More Optimistic View

Maybe it's not so bad. Perhaps the criticism of citizens is misplaced, placing unreasonable expectations on contemporary voters. Perhaps people are doing just fine, when all is said and done. Cogent arguments have been advanced for this position.

Scholars acknowledge that in an ideal world, people would closely follow politics and formulate thoughtful perspectives on every issue. But this is unrealistic, given the demands on citizens' time and difficulty of comprehending torturously complex issues. Consequently, people develop cognitive shortcuts or **heuristics** to help them make political decisions. Voters evaluate candidates based on whether short descriptions of candidates' positions are roughly congenial with their own values. They use political party labels as guides, casting a vote for nominees of their preferred party. Voters loosely follow presidential debates, checking to see if their candidate is knowledgeable about the issues and can competently defend positions. They may rely on the views of respected opinion leaders, as expressed in newspaper editorials, on cable TV, or in blogs. People may fall short in their knowledge of basic civics or international issues, but nonetheless remain capable of making reasonable decisions in elections (Sniderman, Brody, & Tetlock, 1991).

In 2012 a majority of Americans could accurately identify the Republican and Democratic Party's positions on raising taxes on the wealthy, increasing gay rights, and restricting abortion (Pew Research Center for the People and the Press, 2012). Although voters in 2016 lacked knowledge of candidate issue specifics, they were familiar with Trump's economic promises and immigration plans (Tavernise, 2016). Women who voted for Trump knew about his temperamental liabilities, even to the point of cringing when they heard him denigrate women, but felt his business braggadocio carried more weight (Chira, 2017). Voters knew about Clinton's long experience and her email scandal, filtering their beliefs through partisan attachments.

Some researchers point out that tests of political knowledge are flawed, requiring people to supply trivial facts that are peripheral to the actual task of citizenship. Questions asking the names of politicians in the news are efficient for researchers, enabling them to score tests quickly, but may unfairly penalize citizens (Graber, 2012). Although fewer than 40 percent of Americans could name the 2016 Republican candidate for vice president (Mike Pence), considerably more voters were likely familiar with the Trump-Pence positions on immigration and building a border wall. Lupia (2016) notes that there has never been any demonstration that the recall questions on these tests constitute "necessary or sufficient conditions for the broader competences or important kinds of knowledge" that citizenship requires (p. 229). He also points out that recall questions can use confusing jargon, pose issues vaguely, and offer little motivation for respondents to answer questions correctly.

Others point out that good citizenship does not require intimate knowledge of every issue covered in the news. Citizens can scan the political environment, looking out for dangers to their personal well-being and the public welfare. They can fulfill their civic duty by simply monitoring the political environment (Schudson, 1998; see also Zaller, 2003).

Some scholars go further, noting that the system can function adequately so long as there is a healthy minority of individuals who closely follow political issues, remain knowledgeable about politics, and partake in activist causes. Everyone does not have to boast top-flight knowledge, so long as some do. According to this view, emphasizing the virtues of elite democracy, politics in industrialized democracies has become so complicated and time-consuming that it requires a class of experts to make high-level political decisions. These experts are elected officials who are accountable to the people through free and fair elections. Political theorist Joseph Schumpeter (1976) bluntly noted that "democracy means only that the people have the opportunity of accepting or refusing the men who are to rule them . . . Now one aspect of this may be expressed by saying that democracy is the rule of the politician" (pp. 284–285).

As you might expect, this elite view of democracy has generated considerable criticism. Leave democracy to the politicians? That's precisely the problem with modern politics, critics charge. Professional politicians are not responsive to the people, but to lobbyists and moneyed interests who finance their campaigns. Advocates of deliberative and participatory democracy argue that even in our mediated age, democracy must be based on the active engagement of citizens in decisions that affect their lives. Fair enough. But how much should people know about politics? What does the good citizen need to know to fulfill civic duty? What facts can the dutiful voter reasonably ignore? There are not hard-and-fast answers to these questions.

MEDIA AND POLITICAL KNOWLEDGE: INFORMATION AND MISINFORMATION

So, how do people acquire information about government and public affairs? What is the source of their knowledge? The mass media and Internet play an important role, offering the raw materials from which citizens construct beliefs about politics. We gain insight on the impact media exert on political knowledge by exploring different perspectives on the issue. The approaches discussed in this section emphasize concepts from the fields of mass communication, psychology, and sociology.

Mass Communication Perspective

A classic mass communication perspective examines the distinctive effects that a particular communication medium exerts on knowledge. Newspapers contain detailed articles with considerable information. Their format allows people to reread articles, which can encourage deeper processing of information. For these and other reasons (such as the higher education level of many newspaper readers), newspaper readership has long been associated with high levels of political knowledge (Becker & Whitney, 1980; Robinson & Levy, 1986). Newspapers were supplanted by television in the middle of the 20th century, as TV became the dominant medium for conveying news to the public. For years there were scholarly debates about the role television news played in political learning. Critics charged that frequently simplistic stories failed to do justice to complex social problems. Defenders retorted that television's dramatic format could helpfully communicate symbols and emotionally arousing events, such as national tragedies; TV could be particularly effective in imparting information to audiences with less formal education, who might resonate with the simpler, more visual format (Grabe, Kamhawi, & Yegiyan, 2009; Graber, 2001; Prior, 2002).

These findings become more nuanced when considered in the context of today's online era. Older research suggests that reading stories online should facilitate cognitive information-holding, while watching TV or viewing dramatic visuals online should impart emotional information, particularly (though not exclusively) among those of lower educational levels. The picture is complicated by the fact that newspaper websites blend traditional long-form articles with visuals and TV-style interviews, while television network sites offer articles that can be read online, as well as graphic visuals. Thus, in the online age it is harder to make a simple distinction between print and television or to argue they are qualitatively different media that exert different influences on knowledge. There may be more cognitive information associated with some online print websites (*The New York Times*) than online broadcast or cable television sites (Fox or local news), though there are bound to be differences across media outlets. Users of information-rich websites are probably more educated, motivated, and capable of processing political information, suggesting that the Web may replicate the greater cognitive benefits associated with print of years past. But it is much more complicated and multifaceted today, as individuals receive information from multiple sites, with sites fusing words and pictures, reading and viewing. Sites vary greatly in their journalistic credibility and commitment to comprehensive reporting of politics.

A more specific, still-relevant mass communication approach is **constructionism**, pioneered by W. Russell Neuman, Marion R. Just, and Ann N. Crigler (Armoudian & Crigler, 2010; Neuman, Just, & Crigler, 1992). Constructionism examines how people construct meaning from media messages. It focuses on how individuals form beliefs and political attitudes from exposure to media. Like the limited effects perspective discussed in Chapter 3, constructionism emphasizes that media rarely have simple, uniform effects on everyone. Unlike the limited effects view, it stipulates that political media can strongly influence cognitions. Constructionism says that effects depend on the interaction among demographic categories, the psychology of the audience member, and content of a particular medium.

Psychological Approach

A psychological viewpoint focuses more directly on the many cognitive and emotional attributes individuals bring to political media. Like constructionism, the psychological view emphasizes that you cannot appreciate the effects of news media on knowledge without understanding how people process or think about news.

A key psychological factor is a **schema**, defined as "a cognitive structure consisting of organized knowledge about situations and individuals that has been abstracted from prior experiences" (Graber, 1988, p. 28). Political communication scholar Doris A. Graber extensively studied the types of political schemas citizens employ in processing the news. She shook up the political communication field by showing that viewers do not just soak up whatever happens to be shown on the nightly news. Instead, processing of news is active, not passive. People don't start with a blank slate. The act of remembering news invariably involves relating the news to what people already know or believe. You might have a schema for politicians, or for issues like gun rights, immigration, or tax cuts; these cognitive structures would serve as filters or information storehouses that influence how you process political information.

Misinformation

News that resonates with viewers' preexisting beliefs is likely to reinforce and strengthen their attitudes. News stories that shake up or conflict with knowledge structures are apt to be rejected. This is why many Americans had trouble accepting the fact that Iraq did *not* possess weapons of mass destruction (WMDs) some years back. The White House, thought by many to be a source of factual information, drummed in the linkage between Iraq and WMDs, arguing that Iraq possessed devastating weapons of mass destruction. The linkage had been repeated for many years by both Democrats and Republicans. As it turned out, there was virtually no evidence that Iraq had WMDs. But this contradicted long-held beliefs and took a long time to sink in. In a related fashion, nearly half of poll respondents mistakenly thought there was clear evidence that Iraq president Saddam Hussein was closely working with the terrorist group al-Qaeda (Kull, Ramsay, & Lewis, 2003). Even as of 2015, some four years after U.S. troops left Iraq, about half of Republicans, and Fox News viewers, said they believed the U.S. had located active WMDs in Iraq (Breitman, 2015). George W. Bush's pronouncements as president and the media's hammering in of the false connection among Iraq, al-Qaeda, and WMD left an imprint on the public, one that did not give way for some time.

Partisans—strong liberals and conservatives—are particularly likely to harbor misperceptions, even in the face of countervailing evidence. People with strong attitudes engage in a biased evaluation of information, discounting facts that don't mesh with their preexisting views (see Chapter 12). Beliefs can be held so tenaciously that even corrections can fail to temper misperceptions, in some cases actually strengthening false beliefs out of dogmatism or sheer spite (Nyhan & Reifler, 2010).

A particularly troubling example was "birther" beliefs, the notion that former President Obama was not born in the United States. Repeatedly asserted by Donald Trump and reinforced by social media sites, information circulated in media and the Internet that questioned Obama's U.S. birthplace in Honolulu and fallaciously claimed his birth certificate was "a fraud" (Barbaro, 2016). Although these claims were continually shown to be incorrect, and Obama released birth certificates in 2008 and 2011, large majorities of Republicans (as late as 2016) doubted Obama's American citizenship (e.g., Clinton & Roush, 2016). While some of these individuals undoubtedly changed their beliefs after Trump acknowledged Obama had been born in the U.S. (as Trump was a high-credibility source to them), others probably clung to their original perceptions. Tenacious adherence to false perceptions—an increasing problem in the wake of reports of fake news (see Chapter 9)—is a fact of political life, attributable to the powerful impact that emotional biases and selective exposure to political information exerts on attitudes.

Sociological Approach

A sociological view emphasizes the influence of broad demographic and social structural factors. Education is a time-honored predictor of knowledge. With more education comes significantly greater knowledge about politics (Delli Carpini & Keeter, 1996; Fraile, 2011). Social class also exerts a major impact on knowledge. Wealthier individuals know more about politics than do their less affluent counterparts. This is not to say that those with little education or income lack knowledge about issues that bear directly on their well-being, or that they lack political opinions. However, at least as judged by standard tests of political knowledge, individuals with lower income and lower education do not fare as well as those with more money and education. Social class enhances knowledge for a couple of reasons. First, people with a college degree are better able to understand and process the news. Second, middle- and upper-middle-class individuals are freed from the strains of poverty, which affords them more time (one might say the luxury) to reflect on political issues.

Research has combined sociological and mass communication perspectives, focusing on intersections between the disciplines. One of the persistent findings in political communication research is that there are **knowledge gaps**, where media exacerbate differences produced by two sociological factors: income and education, called socio-economic status, or SES (see Figure 4.1). According to the knowledge gap hypothesis, people higher in socioeconomic status are, at the outset, more knowledgeable about politics than their lower socioeconomic counterparts. Ideally, publicity, media messages, or an Internet campaign should provide the "have-nots" with more information, leveling the gap. But the knowledge gap hypothesis asserts that the opposite occurs: High-status, well-informed citizens acquire more information and at a faster clip than their low-status, poorly informed counterparts. They benefit from skills in encoding, storing, and retrieving news information (Grabe, Kamhawi, & Yegiyan, 2009). Thus, the knowledge gap widens rather than closes (Gaziano, 1997; Nadeau, Nevitte, Gidengil, & Blais, 2008; Tichenor, Donohue, & Olien, 1970; Grabe, Yegiyan, & Kamhawi, 2008; Bas & Grabe, 2015). The "knowledge-rich get richer," and the less informed fall further behind (e.g., Brundidge & Rice, 2009). This is unfair

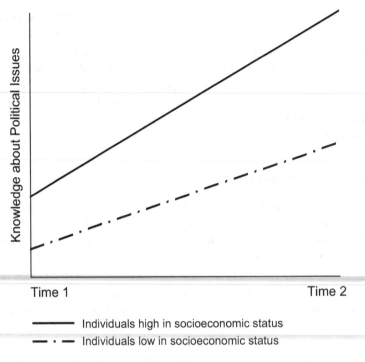

Figure 4.1 Diagram of the knowledge gap in political communication. Knowledge is measured at Time 1, before media publicity of a political issue, and again at Time 2, after the issue has been publicized in the media.

and does not comport with the value that democratic theorists—philosophers, scholars, all of us really—place on equality.

When higher socioeconomic groups benefit more from mediated information on topics spanning climate change, automobile company safety cover-ups, and health care, they can take preventive steps more efficiently and efficaciously than lower SES citizens. When media accentuate knowledge gaps, the system fails the poor, less educated, and marginalized, contributing to their greater disenfranchisement. For example, despite the wide diffusion of the Affordable Care Act, a law that significantly expands health care for the poor, many uninsured Americans had no knowledge of the law, impeding their efforts to get insurance for their families (MacGillis, 2015). Some scholars have suggested that moderately arousing and visual formats might be most conducive to increasing information gain among less educated citizens (Grabe et al., 2008; Grabe et al., 2009). And yet, the democratizing potential of the Internet (and social media) to reduce knowledge gaps remains in doubt, not least because 34 million Americans lack access to high-speed, broadband transmission technologies (Von Drehle, 2017).

It is possible that the instantaneity of information—transmitted on Facebook Live, Twitter's Periscope, or on smartphone apps—may provide such wide, pervasive access to cutting-edge information that we will see a diminution in gaps in factual knowledge rooted in SES differences. Complicating matters, the definition of a fact is often in dispute—especially on controversial issues like climate change, where ideology and partisan media influence how people perceive facts and values. It is intriguingly possible that in today's environment, political ideology might overtake socioeconomic status as the key factor influencing acceptance of newly minted information and internalization of beliefs. "When beliefs become shortcuts for knowledge, all that political elites and media pundits need to communicate to audiences fragmented along partisan lines," notes Douglas B. Hindman (2009), "is what the reference group believes about the issue, regardless of inconsistencies with traditional ideological principles or contrary facts" (p. 793). It's a dark possibility, with some support, and complicating evidence (see Chapter 12), yet another indication of a contemporary political communication paradox: There is more information available and there are more ways to check information's empirical basis, yet there are continued, troubling examples of ignorance or tenacious adherence to beliefs founded on falsehoods.

Putting It Together

What do we take from all this? News media have a variety of effects, some positive, others less so, all explained by social-structural and psychological factors. Research offers five broad conclusions about media and knowledge levels.

First, the Media Play an Instrumental Role in Informing Americans. But They Are Imperfect Informational Vessels

For all their faults, the media provide information that is indispensable to informed citizenship. "Those who follow the news in any medium are more knowledgeable than their peers who do not," observed political communication scholar Steven H. Chaffee (Chaffee & Yang, 1990, p. 138; see also Barabas & Jerit, 2009; Pasek, Kenski, Romer, & Jamieson, 2006). The downside is that the informational diet that citizens consume can be low in analytical content, offering limited context and depth. As a long-time journalist noted,

> people are turning more frequently to skeletal updates they consume quickly on the small screens of their phones and tablets. During many hours of the day, even the news channels are devoting prime-time hours to opinion shows and infotainment about travel, food and sports, [offering] "the news equivalents of those 100-calorie bags of chips and cookies."
>
> (Begleiter, 2015)

The information is out there; news consumers acquire knowledge from attending to news, but the quality of what they learn is a subject of concern and debate.

Second, There Are Issues and Conditions That Facilitate Knowledge Acquisition

When information is clearly presented and personally relevant, people are motivated to process information systematically. Presidential election campaigns, and particularly 2016, tend to involve people because they concern material economic issues, raise highly charged symbolic concerns, and are covered incessantly. This may be why more than 9 in 10 Americans reported they learned campaign information over the course of a week (Gottfried, Barthel, Shearer, & Mitchell, 2016). On the other hand, when information is complex, or elites disagree among themselves, or leaders dissemble, offering misleading, cleverly packaged snippets, political learning is compromised.

Third, We Should Be Suspicious of Simple Statements about the "Powers of Media"

Media are plural, they have different content, and the particular content can determine what people learn. Effects depend on the specific medium, content of the information, the style the program uses to depict an issue, the age and cognitive skills of the news consumer, and gratifications he or she derives from political media.

Fourth, Individuals Bring a Great Deal to the News Media Equation

You cannot talk about media effects in the abstract. What people know—or think they know—influences what they learn from media. People who know a lot about politics and have strong cognitive abilities get more out of the news and process it more thoughtfully than those who know less and have not yet developed strong political cognitive skills. What's more, a voter does not soak up political information like a sponge. Instead, as constructionist scholars emphasize, "people learn through the development of a composite framework, not by remembering disparate facts. Through the 'barrage' of campaign messages, voters extract and compile information to 'construct' candidates" (Armoudian & Crigler, 2010, p. 310). The news influences what people know, but what people already know affects how they integrate information into their worldviews. Individuals with less knowledge or fewer cognitive skills gain information from assorted news media, but are more likely to learn if the format is moderately arousing and favors visuals over turgid presentations of words.

Fifth, Media Effects on Knowledge Are Indirect and Complex. Sociological Factors, Working via Communication and Psychological Processes, Influence Political Knowledge

Figure 4.2 shows how broad demographic and ideological factors (box 1) set psychological and communication forces in motion. Cognitive skills, schemas, and biased beliefs (box 2) are a function of social structural factors. Differential political media use (box 3) results from these factors as well, which in turn leads to surveillance, attention, and elaboration of news (box 4), with elaboration differing as a function of prior levels of information (Eveland, Shah, & Kwak, 2003). This in turn leads to knowledge levels (box 5), which may be adequate in presidential elections, but wanting at other times.

On the other hand, we need to be careful not to be elitist. Poorer individuals can know a great deal about political issues that impinge directly on their well-being, such as how people cheat the welfare system (Vance, 2016), or the ways poverty and race conspire to lead to unjust incarceration of African Americans. And in a social media age, access to information is instantaneous and more readily available to citizens of all economic stripes than in previous times. However, gaps in understanding political issues, abetted by SES, ideology and selective exposure to information on social media, continue apace.

POLITICAL KNOWLEDGE IN THE AGE OF THE INTERNET AND SOCIAL MEDIA

So, you may be thinking, what does all this have to say about the current communication environment, with its multifaceted features: constant updates on news feeds; ceaseless coverage on cable television, with plenty of opinionated talk; plethora of detailed analyses of politics from top newspapers and websites; YouTube videos; and apps on Facebook, Twitter, and all the rest?

Figure 4.2 Political knowledge determinants and processes

In the mid-20th century, television supplanted print as the main source for news. In the early 21st century, Internet and websites began to replace television, and in today's era, social media is beginning to eclipse TV, particularly among young adults. About 62 percent of American adults get news from social media, and 18 percent do so frequently (Gottfried & Shearer, 2016). This represents a 13 percent increase in social media use over a four-year period. Facebook, followed by Twitter, leads the social media pack, although Instagram is particularly popular among young adults. Many social media news users prefer mobile to laptops for news.

Does this mean that the era of television news is over, kaput? Not quite. When we look at how *frequently* Americans get news online, as opposed to just turning to social media for news from time to time, the picture changes (see Figure 4.3). Thirty-eight percent of Americans report they often get their news online (from social media, apps, and websites), while 57 percent often get news from TV, 25 percent from radio, and 20 percent from print. So, TV news remains the dominant platform for news use on a regular basis. Interestingly, 50 percent of 18- to 29-year-olds often get news online, compared to 29 percent of 50- to 64-year-olds. Seventy-two percent of 50- to 64-year-olds and 85 percent of those over 65 often get news from TV, with nearly half of the oldest group turning regularly to print for news (Mitchell, Gottfried, Barthel, & Shearer, 2016). There is some variability in results on news use, depending on how researchers ask the question, for example if they explicitly ask about how *often* adults get news on a particular platform, or ask about social media in general rather than spelling out specific sites.

When research finds that social media or the Internet is a primary source of news and political information, it may appear as if conventional news channels are no longer seen or read. But this is not so. Many people searching for news on the Internet turn to newspaper and television news sites, as well as news assemblers like Google and Yahoo, which also get information from conventional sources. Social media users open apps for *The New York Times*, *The Wall Street Journal*, *Time* magazine, CNN, Fox, and other conventional media news. At the same time, people—typically strong partisans—are increasingly exposed to ideological sites that do not subscribe to journalistic norms of relative fairness and will publish information skewed by a right-wing or left-wing perspective that can be of questionable factual accuracy.

So, what impact does the new communication environment exert on learning from news? There is debate about this. Skeptics argue that the lure of entertainment, from cable television shows to Facebook posts, pull large numbers of young people from attending closely to news. Prior's (2007) work suggests that in the old days, when broadcast news dominated the market, television news could make a dent in the knowledge gap. Under some (though not all) conditions, it could reduce the disparity between the

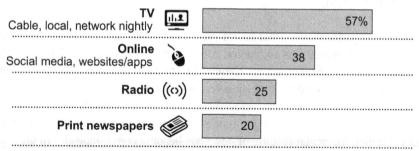

About 4 in 10 American often get news online

% of U.S. adults who <u>often</u> get news on each platform

Platform	%
TV Cable, local, network nightly	57%
Online Social media, websites/apps	38
Radio	25
Print newspapers	20

% of each age group who <u>often</u> get news on each platform

	18–29	30–49	50–64	65+
TV	27%	45%	72%	85%
Online	50	49	29	20
Radio	14	27	29	24
Print newspapers	5	10	23	48

Note: Just 1% said they never got news on any platform (not shown).
Source: Survey conducted Jan. 12-Feb. 8, 2016.
"The Modern News Consumer"

PEW RESEARCH CENTER

Figure 4.3 Where Americans get their news. While about 40 percent of U.S. adults report they often receive news online, an even higher percentage of young Millennial adults indicate they often get news from online outlets. Interestingly, close to 60 percent of adults get news from television.

About 4 in 10 Americans often get their news online.
(From Mitchell et al., 2016)
PEW Research Center

well-informed and the less knowledgeable, and between news junkies and the politi-cally apathetic (Eveland & Scheufele, 2000). With television the only game in town, tens of millions of people were perched before their television sets. But the prolifera-tion of cable channels—as well as all the choices the Internet affords—pulled people away from broadcast television and lured them from the 6:30 p.m. news. In particular, individuals who prefer entertainment to news seem less inclined to follow the news today than during the era when network television dominated the media landscape. As a

result, political knowledge has decreased for a sizable segment of the electorate: entertainment devotees with access to new media. The lure of entertainment cable shows
(and, of course, the Internet) has pulled these viewers away from inadvertent viewing
of news (Prior, 2005).

The more optimistic view is that social media exert salutary effects on information-
holding. Prior's research was conducted before social media (with its 24/7 availability
on mobile phones and quick access to news all the time) became a prominent part of
many people's informational fare. Inadvertent exposure to news media, which bolstered knowledge in the broadcast television age, is also common today, except it takes
place on small mobile screens or computers. Among the American adults who own a
tablet computer, incidental reading of news has become commonplace. An older study
reported that close to 9 in 10 of tablet owners who read long articles over a seven-day
period also read news articles they had not sought out initially (Pew Research Center's Project for Excellence in Journalism, 2011). Intriguingly, nearly 80 percent of
American adults read news when they are on Facebook, even though they sought out
Facebook for other reasons; some 30 percent of Americans watch news videos online
(Mitchell et al., 2013; Murray, 2014). This suggests that, just as inadvertent TV news
viewing enhanced knowledge among TV viewers a couple of generations ago, incidental reading of news on the Internet and social media may increase knowledge in our
own era. Common and widespread sharing of news posts online makes it more difficult
for people to totally ignore the news (Messing & Westwood, 2014).

Others emphasize the virtues of soft news, or stories about public affairs that concern
human interest topics or are the focus of attention on late-night talk shows, daytime talk
programs, entertainment TV newsmagazines, and televised political satire like *Saturday
Night Live* or John Oliver's *Last Week Tonight*. There is evidence that these programs
can pull the young and even less attentive viewers into the fold, offering up political information they find appealing, perhaps enticing them to watch other news media
fare (Baum, 2002, 2003; Feldman & Young, 2008; Xenos & Becker, 2009; Young &
Tisinger, 2006).

On a broader level, those who are optimistic about contemporary news argue that online news use—whether via the broad-based Internet or social networking sites—can
enhance knowledge because it is so easy to access political news online. Indeed, social
networking site use is significantly related to knowledge of campaign issues (Gottfried
et al., 2017). Online use of news can theoretically bolster political efficacy, or the belief
that "people like me" can influence government, because it is much easier to get in
touch with elected officials—and hear back—online than through the slower transmission channels of yore. Consistent with this view, there is evidence that online exposure
to political information is associated with greater political knowledge, interest, efficacy,

and political engagement, expanding the universe of political participation (Boulianne, 2009; Dimitrova, Shehata, Strömbäck, & Nord, 2014; Kenski & Stroud, 2006). Engagement with online media predicts political participation, both offline, such as signing a petition or attending a rally, as well as online, as in sending an email political message, or making an online candidate contribution (Bakker & de Vreese, 2011; Bode, Vraga, Borah, & Shah, 2014; Brundidge, Garrett, Rojas, & de Zúñiga, 2014; de Zúñiga, Jung, & Valenzuela, 2012; de Zúñiga, Molyneux, & Zheng, 2014; Shehata, Ekström, & Olsson, 2016; Zhang, Seltzer, & Bichard, 2013).

This is complicated stuff. The direction of causation can work in different ways. First, media can increase political knowledge, interest, and efficacy. Or, people already knowledgeable, interested, and politically efficacious may gravitate to online news and related apps to reinforce their civic engagement. More complexly, it could work both ways, with the politically knowledgeable and involved gravitating to online media, and media enhancing their participation in online and offline causes (Shehata et al., 2016).

Online news use can influence political participation by providing a reinforcing feeling of interactivity and connection to an online community, which in turn can promote a desire to translate political cognitions into participation (de Zúñiga et al., 2012). Another mechanism by which online media could enhance political capital is through second screening, whereby individuals employ a laptop or smartphone while watching TV to scroll through social media or websites to gain more information, or text about the program they are viewing. By watching, information-searching, and discussing content, second screeners elaborate and reflect on political content more thoughtfully and comprehensively. In one study, second screening, preferred by younger adults, significantly predicted online political participation, suggesting that (at least for the more active news consumers) new technologies can facilitate, not depress, political involvement (de Zúñiga et al., 2015). In a similar fashion, the Moments feature on Twitter, a full-screen phone story conveyed via a sequence of tweets arrayed by Twitter's editors (Manjoo, 2015), might entice young adults ordinarily uninterested in politics to follow political issues more frequently.

Clearly, research suggests that online media, the focus of this discussion, can catalyze political engagement, but we're not sure how strong or long-lasting the effects are. There are also questions about whether people just tune in to online political information that supports their existing sentiments or if the short snippets of information people read in an online era encourage meaningful political deliberation. When people get news from YouTube or Twitter, what exactly are they receiving? Are they getting a comprehensive, fairly even-handed compilation of the panoply of political events, or just snippets, pictures, optics, and snarky stories devoid of context and depth? Can they reliably identify the difference between an opinionated link and a fair-minded news story? And are there downsides if political participation promoted by online media engagement produces self-righteous convictions that "I'm right" and "you're wrong," along with nasty online comments directed at political opponents?

CONCLUSIONS

"A democracy can't be strong if its citizenship is weak," observed political scientist William A. Galston (2011). Others have echoed this sentiment, emphasizing that democracy depends in important ways on the political character of its citizenry and the quality of citizens' opinions and beliefs (see Roberts, 2015). Meaningful democratic decision-making requires that citizens understand basic facts of government and issues that are at stake in elections. National surveys show that most Americans know key aspects of the U.S. Constitution and civil liberties. Happily, they also know the number of senators from their state! But people are woefully ignorant of basic civics and can lack knowledge of candidates' stands on key political issues. This underscores a time-honored paradox of political communication: There is more information available than ever before, yet citizens' knowledge levels do not approach normative ideals (e.g., Neuman, 1986).

There are a number of reasons why Americans lack knowledge of basic facts of government. These include journalists' failure to clearly explain difficult concepts clearly, superficial, glitzy coverage of issues on the news, leaders' tendency to deliberately convey misleading information, and the increasing disconnect between everyday life and politics, as it occurs in the elite corridors of Washington. Do low knowledge levels offer a compelling indictment of the state of political citizenship? There are different views here. Some scholars, with an eye on normative democratic ideals, answer in the affirmative. But a number of theorists make a compelling case that effective citizenship does not require knowledge of arcane government facts. Citizens can fulfill their democratic duties by relying on shortcuts to make political decisions, as well as by scanning the political environment to detect dangers to their personal well-being and the public welfare. Nonetheless, both critics and defenders of the status quo agree that knowledge levels are not as high or as they could or should be, based on normative democratic ideals.

What are the sources of political knowledge? The mass media, Internet, and social media impart voluminous amounts of information, providing the raw materials from which people construct political beliefs. There is abundant evidence that individuals who follow the news are more knowledgeable about politics than their counterparts who do not turn to the news media for political information. At the same time, there are striking inequalities in political knowledge, even in a society like the United States, where media are inescapable. Educated and wealthier Americans are significantly more knowledgeable than their less educated and lower-income peers, at least about national political issues that affect mainstream American society. This can have dysfunctional effects, when lower SES citizens lack knowledge of issues that bear directly on their own lives. Sociological factors influence political knowledge by way of psychological and communication processes, which in turn help explain inequities in knowledge.

Media do not exert uniform effects on knowledge. What people know influences what they learn from media. The ways that individuals process information and construct events affect the ways media influence their cognitions. If you want to devise strategies to increase learning from political news, you need to appreciate how people process news. You go about devising your strategies so they are in sync with individuals' styles of processing political information.

Citizens are increasingly getting news online and from social media, although (contrary to popular opinion) much of the information has been gathered and packaged by conventional media outlets (though increasingly by ideological sites). There are different perspectives on how online news influences knowledge. Some scholars are skeptical, arguing that because individuals are no longer perched before their television sets for the evening news, they are less likely to gain incidental information from the evening news. However, there is considerable evidence for a more optimistic view, indicating that online media and new informational platforms are keeping individuals informed, enhancing online and offline political participation, and expanding the nature of participation beyond that possible in the analog era. These findings "should ease the concerns of cyber-pessimists who feared that Internet would have a negative effect on the efficacy, knowledge, and participation" (Kenski & Stroud, 2006, p. 189).

In the end, as Berkman and Kitch (1986) remind us, "information is the fuel of democracy," an essential ingredient of participation in electoral decision-making. And yet, they note, "without the availability of reliable, objective, and politically diverse information, citizens are without the raw material needed to exercise their political franchise intelligently" (p. 311). Nowadays when voluminous amounts of political information is at people's fingertips (literally with smartphones), the paradox of politics is more salient than ever. More information is available, but the news frequently provides short snippets low on substance and analysis. As profit-making organizations, news media are wary of offering in-depth stories, even if those stories might bring in audiences. It is a time-honored, decades-long critique of news, but in a social media era, when news snippets may be even shorter and sometimes of questionable journalistic validity, the critique is increasingly pertinent. People can be reasonably informed when electoral issues are at stake, but even here, and more so in non-electoral contexts, knowledge levels rarely approach normative standards.

Low knowledge levels can have important effects. Virulently negative attitudes toward government can have their roots in mistaken beliefs, such as grossly exaggerated views of how much money the government spends on foreign aid, or an errant belief by Medicare recipients that they make no use of federal social programs (Krugman, 2017). Skepticism toward big government is reasonable and rooted in classic conservative values. But rejection of government that is steeped in lack of knowledge, even ignorance, can undermine democratic government, leading to support for draconian cutbacks in government programs that violate even conservative precepts. For this reason, some reformers believe that the nation needs to launch a systematic program to educate citizens about government and democratic institutions (Perloff, 2017). They argue that America should upgrade its civics education, emphasizing knowledge of the different branches of government; values of checks, balances, and a robust media; and the normative importance of appreciating views different from one's own. During a social media era when so many adults are tethered to supportive, frequently superficial social media posts, such education could enhance knowledge and increase political tolerance.

REFERENCES

Aalberg, T., & Curran, J. (Eds.) (2012). *How media inform democracy: A comparative approach.* New York: Routledge.

Aalberg, T., van Aelst, P., & Curran, J. (2012). Media systems and the political information environment: A cross-national comparison. In T. Aalberg & J. Curran (Eds.), *How media inform democracy: A comparative approach* (pp. 33–49). New York: Routledge.

Annenberg Public Policy Center. (2016, September 13). *Americans' knowledge of the branches of government is declining.* The Annenberg Public Policy Center of the University of Pennsylvania. Retrieved from www.annenbergfpublicpolicycenter.org/americans-knowledge-of-the-branches-of-government-is-declining/ (Accessed March 28, 2017).

Armoudian, M., & Crigler, A.N. (2010). Constructing the vote: Media effects in a constructionist model. In J.E. Leighley (Ed.), *The Oxford handbook of American elections and political behavior* (pp. 300–325). New York: Oxford University Press.

Bakker, T.P., & de Vreese, C.H. (2011). Good news for the future? Young people, Internet use, and political participation. *Communication Research, 38,* 451–470.

Barabas, J., & Jerit, J. (2009). Estimating the causal effects of media coverage on policy-specific knowledge. *American Journal of Political Science, 53,* 73–89.

Barbaro, M. (2016, September 17). Trump gives up a lie but refuses to repent. *The New York Times,* A1, A10.

Bas, O., & Grabe, M.E. (2015). Emotion-provoking personalization of news: Informing citizens and closing the knowledge gap. *Communication Research, 42,* 159–185.

Baum, M.A. (2002). Sex, lies, and war: How soft news brings foreign policy to the inattentive public. *American Political Science Review, 96,* 91–109.

Baum, M.A. (2003). *Soft news goes to war: Public opinion and American foreign policy in the new media age.* Princeton, NJ: Princeton University Press.

Becker, L. B., & Whitney, D. C. (1980). Effects of media dependencies. *Communication Research,* *7*, 95–120.

Begleiter, R. (2015, October 24). Sunday Dialogue: The media gap. *The New York Times.* Retrieved from www.nytimes.com/2015/10/25/opinion/sunday- dialogue-the-media-gap. html (Accessed February 7, 2017).

Berkman, R., & Kitch, L. W. (1986). *Politics in the media age.* New York: McGraw-Hill.

Bode, L., Vraga, E. K., Borah, P., & Shah, D. V. (2014). A new space for political behavior: Political social networking and its democratic consequences. *Journal of Computer-Mediated Communication, 19*, 414–429.

Boulianne, S. (2009). Does Internet use affect engagement? A meta-analysis of research. *Political Communication, 26*, 193–211.

Breitman, K. (2015, January 7). Poll: Half of republicans still believe WMDs found in Iraq. *Politico.* Retrieved from www.politico.com/story/2015/01/poll-republicans-wmds-iraq—114016 (Accessed September 17, 2016).

Breyer, S. (2010). *Making our democracy work: A judge's view.* New York: Knopf.

Brundidge, J., Garrett, R. K., Rojas, H., & de Zúñiga, H. G. (2014). Political participation and ideological news online: "Differential gains" and differential losses" in a presidential election cycle. *Mass Communication and Society, 17*,464–486.

Brundidge, J., & Rice, R. E. (2009). Political engagement online: Do the information rich get richer and the like-minded more similar? In A. Chadwick & P. N. Howard (Eds.), *Routledge handbook of Internet politics* (pp. 144–156). New York: Routledge.

Chaffee, S. H., & Yang, S-M. (1990). Communication and political socialization. In O. Ichilov (Ed.), *Political socialization, citizenship education, and democracy* (pp. 137–157). New York: Teachers College Press.

Chira, S. (2017, January 15). Women who voted for Donald Trump, in their own words. *The New York Times*, 12.

Clinton, J., & Roush, C. (2016, August 10). *Poll: Persistent partisan divide over "birther" question.* Retrieved from www.nbcnews.com/politics/2016-election/poll-persistent-parisan-divide-over-birther-question-n627446 (Accessed September 17, 2016).

de Zúñiga, H. G., Garcia-Perdomo, V., & McGregor, S. C. (2015). What is second screening? Exploring motivations of second screen use and its effect on online political participation. *Journal of Communication, 65*, 793–815.

de Zúñiga, H. G., Jung, N., & Valenzuela, S. (2012). Social media use for news and individuals' social capital, civic engagement and political participation. *Journal of Computer-Mediated Communication, 17*, 319–336.

de Zúñiga, H. G., Molyneux, L., & Zheng, P. (2014). Social media, political expression, and political participation: Panel analysis of lagged and concurrent relationships. *Journal of Communication, 64*, 612–634.

Delli Carpini, M. X., & Keeter, S. (1996). *What Americans know about politics and why it matters.* New Haven, CT: Yale University Press.

Dimitrova, D. V., Shehata, A., Strömbäck, J., & Nord, L. W. (2014). The effects of digital media on political knowledge and participation in election campaigns: Evidence from panel data. *Communication Research, 41*, 95–118.

Dropp, K., & Nyhan, B. (2017, February 8). Many don't know Obamacare and affordable care act are the same. *The New York Times*, A10.

Eveland, W.P., Jr., & Scheufele, D.A. (2000). Connecting news media use with gaps in knowledge and participation. *Political Communication, 17*, 215–237.

Eveland, W.P., Jr., Shah, D.V., & Kwak, N. (2003). Assessing causality: A panel study of motivations, information processing and learning during campaign 2000. *Communication Research, 30*, 359–386.

Feldman, L., & Young, D.G. (2008). Late-night comedy as a gateway to traditional news: An analysis of time trends in news attention among late-night comedy viewers during the 2004 presidential primaries. *Political Communication, 25*, 401–422.

Fraile, M. (2011). Widening or reducing the knowledge gap? Testing the media effects on political knowledge in Spain (2004–2006). *International Journal of Press/Politics, 16*, 163–184.

Galston, W.A. (2011, November 6). Telling Americans to vote, or else. *The New York Times* (Week in Review), 9.

Gaziano, C. (1997). Forecast 2000: Widening knowledge gaps. *Journalism & Mass Communication Quarterly, 74*, 237–264.

Goodman, P. (2016, September 29). More jobs, but not for everyone. *The New York Times*, A1, B8, B9.

Goodnough, A., & Kopicki, A. (2013, December 19). Uninsured skeptical of health care low in poll. *The New York Times*, A1, A27.

Gottfried, J., Barthel, M., Shearer, E., & Mitchell, A. (2016, February 4). *The 2016 presidential campaign—A news event that's hard to miss.* Pew Research Center: Journalism & Media. Retrieved from www.journalism.org/2016/02/04/the-2016-presidential-campaign-a-news-event-thats-hard-to-miss/ (Accessed September 18, 2016).

Gottfried, J., & Shearer, E. (2016, May 26). *News use across social media platforms 2016.* Pew Research Center: Journalism & Media. Retrieved from www.journalism.org/2016/05/26/news-use-across-social-media . . . (Accessed September 17, 2016).

Gottfried, J., Hardy, B.W., Holbert, R.L., Winneg, K.M., & Jamieson, K.H. (2017). The changing nature of political debate consumption: Social media, multitasking, and knowledge acquisition. *Political Communication, 34*, 172–199.

Grabe, M.E., Kamhawi, R., & Yegiyan, N. (2009). Informing citizens: How people with different levels of education process television, newspaper, and Web news. *Journal of Broadcasting & Electronic Media, 53*, 90–111.

Grabe, M.E., Yegiyan, N., & Kamhawi, R. (2008). Experimental evidence of the knowledge gap: Message arousal, motivation, and time delay. *Human Communication Research, 34*, 550–571.

Graber, D.A. (1988). *Processing the news: How people tame the information tide* (2nd ed.) New York: Longman.

Graber, D.A. (2001). *Processing politics: Learning from television in the Internet age.* Chicago: University of Chicago Press.

Graber, D.A. (2012). Government by the people, for the people—Twenty-first century style. In J. Friedman & S. Friedman (Eds.), *The nature of belief systems reconsidered* (pp. 207–218). New York: Routledge.

Hindman, D.B. (2009). Mass media flow and differential distribution of politically disputed beliefs: The belief gap hypothesis. *Journalism & Mass Communication Quarterly, 86*, 790–808.

Jerit, J., & Barabas, J. (2006). Bankrupt rhetoric: How misleading information affects knowledge about social security. *Public Opinion Quarterly, 70*, 278–303.

Kenski, K., & Stroud, N. J. (2006). Connections between Internet use and political efficacy, knowledge, and participation. *Journal of Broadcasting & Electronic Media, 50*, 173–192.

Krugman, P. (2017, March 17). Conservative fantasies run into reality. *The New York Times*, A25.

Kull, S., Ramsay, C., & Lewis, E. (2003). Misperceptions, the media, and the Iraq war. *Political Science Quarterly, 118*, 569–598.

Lupia, A. (2016). *Uninformed: Why people know so little about politics and what we can do about it*. New York: Oxford University Press.

MacGillis, A. (2015, November 22). Who turned my blue state red? *The New York Times* (Sunday Review), 1, 4.

Manjoo, F. (2015, October 8). A Twitter feature aims to tame the chaos. *The New York Times*, B1, B11.

Messing, S., & Westwood, S. J. (2014). Selective exposure in the age of social media: Endorsements trump partisan source affiliation when selecting news online. *Communication Research, 41*, 1042–1063.

Mitchell, A., Gottfried, J., Barthel, M., & Shearer, E. (2016, July 7). *Pathways to news*. Pew Research Center: Journalism & Media. Retrieved from www.journalism.org/2016/07/07/pathways-to-news/ (Accessed September 17, 2016).

Murray, A. (2014, March 26). Seven reasons for optimism about the news business. *The Wall Street Journal*, A15.

Nadeau, R., Nevitte, N., Gidengil, E., & Blais, A. (2008). Elections campaigns as information campaigns: Who learns what and does it matter? *Political Communication, 25*, 229–248.

Neuman, W. R. (1986). *The paradox of mass politics: Knowledge and opinion in the American electorate*. Cambridge, MA: Harvard University Press.

Neuman, W. R., Just, M. R., & Crigler, A. N. (1992). *Common knowledge: News and the construction of political meaning*. Chicago: University of Chicago Press.

Niemi, R. G., & Junn, J. (1998). *Civic education: What makes students learn*. New Haven, CT: Yale University Press.

Nyhan, B., & Reifler, J. (2010). When corrections fail: The persistence of political misperceptions. *Political Behavior, 32*, 303–330.

Pasek, J., Sood, G., & Krosnick, J. A. (2015). Misinformed about the affordable care act? Leveraging certainty to assess the prevalence of misperceptions. *Journal of Communication, 65*, 660–673.

Perloff, R. M. (2017, April 5). A national civics exam. *The New York Times* (Letter to the Editor), A22.

Pew Research Center's Project for Excellence in Journalism. (2011). *The tablet revolution: How people use tablets and what it means for the future of news*. Retrieved from www.journalism.org/analysis_report/tablet (Accessed February 7, 2017).

Pew Research Center for the People & the Press. (2012). *What the public knows about the political parties*. Retrieved from www.people-press.org/2012/04/11/what-the-public-knows-about. (Accessed February 6, 2017).

Prior, M. (2002). Political knowledge after September 11. *PS: Political Science and Politics, 35*, 523–529.

Prior, M. (2005). News vs. entertainment: How increasing media choice widens gaps in political knowledge and turnout. *American Journal of Political Science, 49*, 577–592.

Prior, M. (2007). *Post-broadcast democracy: How media choice increases inequality in political involvement and polarizes elections.* New York: Cambridge University Press.

Roberts, S. (2015, January 15). Walter Berns, whose ideals fueled neoconservative movement, dies at 95. *The New York Times*, A20.

Robinson, J. P., & Levy, M. R. (1986). *The main source: Learning from television news.* Beverly Hills, CA: Sage.

Schudson, M. (1998). *The good citizen: A history of American civic life.* New York: Martin Kessler Books.

Schumpeter, J. (1976). *Capitalism, socialism and democracy.* London: Allen and Unwin.

Shehata, A., Ekström, M., & Olsson, T. (2016). Developing self-actualizing and dutiful citizens: Testing the AC-DC model using panel data among adolescents. *Communication Research, 43*, 1141–1169.

Shenkman, R. (2008). *Just how stupid are we? Facing the truth about the American voter.* New York: Basic Books.

Sniderman, P. M., Brody, R. A., & Tetlock, P. E. (1991). *Reasoning and choice: Explorations in political psychology.* New York: Cambridge University Press.

Tavernise, S. (2016, November 13). Amid years of decay, Ohioans flipped votes, seeking change. *The New York Times*, 1, 14.

Tichenor, P. J., Donohue, G. A., & Olien, C. N. (1970). Mass media flow and differential growth in knowledge. *Public Opinion Quarterly, 34*, 159–170.

Vance, J. D. (2016). *Hillbilly elegy: A memoir of a family and culture in crisis.* New York: HarperCollins.

Von Drehle, D. (2017, April 10). What it will take to rebuild America. *Time*, 23–27.

Xenos, M. A., & Becker, A. B. (2009). Moments of Zen: Effects of *The Daily Show* on information seeking and political learning. *Political Communication, 26*, 317–332.

Young, D. G., & Tisinger, R. M. (2006). Dispelling late-night myths: News consumption among late-night comedy viewers and the predictors of exposure to various late-night shows. *Press/Politics, 11*, 113–134.

Zaller, J. (2003). A new standard of news quality: Burglar alarms for the monitorial citizen. *Political Communication, 20*, 109–130.

Zhang, W., Seltzer, T., & Bichard, S. L. (2013). Two sides of the coin: Assessing the influence of social network site use during the 2012 U.S. presidential campaign. *Social Science Computer Review, 31*, 542–551.

5 Contemporary Political Socialization

Kate grew up in a liberal Democratic household. Her parents protested against nuclear weapons when they were in high school and later attended rallies that opposed George W. Bush's War in Iraq. Liberals (progressives as they called themselves), they ritualistically listened to the Arlo Guthrie ballad "Alice's Restaurant" each Thanksgiving, the song's endless refrain eliciting eye rolls from Kate in high school. But she came to love the ballad and her parents' commitment to liberal causes, internalizing the values herself. Clearly influenced by her parents' activism, she helped organize a Bernie Sanders chapter on her college campus in 2016, posting blistering blogs berating capitalists, typing furiously on her smartphone at the protest site. Pro-union and critical of anything that smacked of Republican politics, she could not believe it when the university dorm lottery system paired her with Sarah.

The first thing Sarah placed in her room, after unpacking her computer, iPod, and favorite posters, was Ayn Rand's conservative classic, *The Fountainhead*. A member of campus Young Republicans and the local Tea Party branch, she is a libertarian who fervently believes that runaway, out-of-control big government is crushing the American spirit. She credits her activism in conservative causes to her parents' encouraging her to explore politics during family discussions, never minding if she disagreed with their positions. Soon after she arrived at college, she became Facebook friends with Jeremy, a funny, easygoing guy, but whose politics she could not figure.

Jeremy lives down the hall from Kate and Sarah. He is amused by their political passions. Personally, he does not give a hoot about politics. To Jeremy, politicians are cynical and out for themselves. As a child growing up with a single mom, he rarely talked politics. Maybe it was because his mother (loving, but super-feisty) had such strong views she would not brook disagreement. She meant well, but you learned it was best not to take the other point of view. Although he steers clear of politics, he is big on alternative music—and volunteering. It's something he picked up in high school and stuck with him.

These anecdotal descriptions are based on people I have known and may resemble students you have encountered as well. They were created to emphasize that young adults have acquired political attitudes long before they set foot in their first college classroom. How *do* we acquire political attitudes and beliefs? Why are some young adults committed Democrats and others partisan Republicans, while still others are strident supporters of third party candidates? Why do some people participate in politics, yet others shy away? What role do the endless variety of media play in the acquisition of political attitudes? This chapter discusses these issues as it extends the focus on citizenship to political socialization. The first section explores a prominent theme in political socialization research: continuity and change in the development of political attitudes. The second portion describes contemporary approaches to the study of political socialization. The third section summarizes the impact of family and schools on political socialization, while the fourth portion, guided by theory and research, pinpoints the different ways media influence the development of political attitudes.

THEMES IN POLITICAL SOCIALIZATION

Citizenship is not passed through the genes. It is learned. Indeed, as one scholar observed, "democracy's vitality and continuity greatly depend upon transmitting to each young generation the visions of the democratic way of life and the commitment to it" (Ichilov, 1990, p. 1). This is the central premise in the study of **political socialization**, "the way in which a society transmits political orientations—knowledge, attitudes or norms, and values—from generation to generation" (Easton & Dennis, 1973, p. 59).

Political socialization performs a valuable function. It helps a society communicate its political heritage to new generations. We want children to understand the storied history of the United States, both its strengths and shortcomings. We want them to appreciate the importance of First Amendment freedoms, dissent, vibrant civic dialogue, and loyalty to country. Other countries convey their political lineage to young members of society, emphasizing distinctive national norms and values. Democratic societies in particular seek to nurture four virtues in citizens: *knowledge of the political system; loyalty to democratic principles; adherence to traditions like voting*; and *identification with citizenship* (Dahlgren, 2000). In the next sections I will examine how socialization occurs, focusing on the United States, but suggesting implications for other nations, as appropriate.

Two themes weave their way through the socialization of political attitudes: continuity and change.

Continuity refers to the fact that political predispositions that we acquire at a young age tend to persist throughout our lives. Attitudes are formed through early macro and micro level experiences. On the broader, macro level, national events that people experience during their youth shape political attitudes. Events—wars, assassinations, political protests, technological changes, and economic catastrophes—that occur during a "critical period" of late childhood, adolescence, and early adulthood—can leave a lasting imprint on memories, feelings, and political behavior (Schuman & Corning, 2012). World War II loomed as a defining political event for "Greatest Generation" Americans born in the 1920s and 1930s, while Vietnam, civil rights, and gender rights were important for Baby Boomers. For Americans born over the course of the succeeding decades, events like the Reagan presidency, Clinton's impeachment, 9/11, the 2008 financial crisis, and the infusion of social media shaped attitudes and interpretations of subsequent political events. A national online survey of the American public offers specifics.

Survey participants were asked to indicate the 10 historic events that occurred in their lifetimes they believed had the greatest impact on the country. Respondents were divided into four groups: (1) the Millennial generation (born from 1981 to 1998); (2) Generation X (born 1965 to 1980); (3) Baby Boom generation (born 1946 to 1964), and (4) the Silent generation (called this because of their so-called silence, lack of protest, and generalized trust in the wake of tumultuous change, born 1928 to 1945). Across generations, 9/11, the Obama election, and the technological revolution were seen as the most historic three events that exerted the greatest impact on the country. It is noteworthy, that despite growing up in different eras, Americans are unified in their horror about 9/11 and their pride in the election of the first Black president. There were differences among groups, reflecting the ways that critical events of a particular era influence the mind-sets of young people growing up during these political epochs (Deane, Duggan, & Morin, 2016; see Table 5.1). Respondents were asked to name the 10 historic events that occurred in their lifetimes that they thought had the greatest impact on the country. The top five are reprinted here; notice the similarities and differences that emerge as a function of political socialization (from Deane et al., 2016).

Political socialization also occurs on the micro or individual level. On this more molecular, interpersonal individual level, children form political attachments and develop political attitudes based on the views of their parents or influential socialization agents (Shulman & DeAndrea, 2014). Few individuals change party affiliations once they enter middle age (Green et al., 2002). Attitudes toward race and the two political parties remain stable and influential across the life cycle (Sears & Funk, 1999; Sears & Brown, 2013).

Table 5.1 Americans' perceptions of most significant historic events by generational cohort.

Millennials	Generation X
1. 9/11	1. 9/11
2. Obama election	2. Obama election
3. Iraq/Afghanistan wars	3. Fall of Berlin Wall/end of Cold War
4. Gay marriage	4. The tech revolution
5. The tech revolution	5. Iraq/Afghanistan wars
Baby Boomers	**Silent Generation**
1. 9/11	1. 9/11
2. JFK assassination	2. World War II
3. Vietnam War	3. JFK assassination
4. Obama election	4. Vietnam War
5. Moon landing	5. Moon landing

The continuity perspective emphasizes the powerful impact that early socialization experiences exert on subsequent attitudes. Growing up in a household that rewards certain viewpoints or associates these views with strongly held values can bolster these attitudes and increase the likelihood they will be translated into action. "It was once said that the Jesuits could control people's thinking for life if they controlled their education up to the age of five," noted David O. Sears (1990), a proponent of the continuity view.

Social scientific concepts help explain why political attitudes formed at an early age persist over time. First, individuals (like Kate, the liberal college student) acquire considerable information simply through **observational learning**, or modeling respected parental, peer, and media opinion leaders (Bandura, 1971). Children whose parents display a particular political identification are likely to exhibit the same political identification as their parents (Jennings & Niemi, 1968). If your parents are staunch Republicans, particularly if they are active politically, you are likely to be a strong Republican (Clawson & Oxley, 2013). A second reason attitudes persist across the life cycle is, as persuasion theories suggest, attitudes developed based on systematic thinking and reflection can stick with people over the course of many years. The more we think about an issue, the stronger and more elaborated our cognitive beliefs. Third, political attitude stability is facilitated through repetition. Repeated exposure to political information leads to positive attitudes (Grush, McKeough, & Ahlering, 1978). The more people see and hear fellow citizens talking favorably about a candidate, political party, or ethnic group perspective, the more they come to develop a positive attitude toward this issue. Repetition breeds liking and facilitates the development of heuristics favoring the in-group. Fourth, children acquire emotion-packed attitudes via associations. Watching adults solemnly pledge allegiance to the flag, or patriotically sing their country's national anthem in anticipation of a hometown baseball game or European soccer match powerfully links positive feelings to one's country of origin, helping strengthen a favorable attitude toward the country in which one was reared.

There is also evidence that some political attitudes have a genetic basis (Banaji & Heiphetz, 2010; Fazekas & Littvay, 2015). Beliefs about politics are affected by genes, and ideologically based attitudes may be inherited genetically (Alford, Funk, & Hibbing, 2005; Fowler et al., 2011; Hatemi & McDermott, 2011). However, few would suggest that genes are a primary determinant of political attitudes. There remain questions about the strength and degree of their impact. In any case, nature does not operate in isolation of nurture. Whatever influences genes exert on attitudes interact with the environment, and intersections are critical. For example, research on twins indicates that heredity affects how strongly individuals feel about partisan politics, but not whether they *choose* to be liberal or conservative (Settle, Dawes, & Fowler, 2009). Your parents and other socialization agents influence your choice of a political party, and partisan attitudes remain relatively stable over the course of the life cycle. The peer, family, and media environment in which you grow up have persistent influences on political attitudes and behavior.

Complicating matters, change is also part of the political socialization equation. Americans have dramatically changed their views of race, gender roles, and gay marriage over the past half century (e.g., Leonhardt & Parlapiano, 2015). Media portrayals of prejudice, as well as interpersonal communication between members of different cultural groups, have shaken up individuals' assumptions, leading them to reconsider long-held stereotypes. Political attitudes are also in flux, in the wake of increasing skepticism about elected leaders, perhaps even representative democracy itself (Norris, 2011). A life span–development view emphasizes that political socialization does not stop in childhood. Instead, it continues over the course of the life cycle, as people adjust to the procession of new developments on the political stage. In addition, as Zukin and his colleagues note:

> People also change as they grow older because of age-specific experiences. Different stages of the life-cycle bring different politically relevant events, for example, paying income taxes for the first time, choosing a school for a child, or helping an elderly parent deal with Medicare and other health care choices.
>
> (Zukin, Keeter, Andolina, Jenkins, & Delli Carpini, 2006, p. 11)

Continuity and change are the yin and yang of political socialization.

BROAD PERSPECTIVES ON POLITICAL SOCIALIZATION

In 1965 the Los Angeles Dodgers defeated the Minnesota Twins to win the World Series. If you were driving to the game, a gallon of gas would cost 31 cents. You could buy a car for $2,650. Skateboards were big that year. In academia during the same year, a landmark study was published that probed elementary and middle school children's attitudes toward government. The researchers found that children evaluated government very favorably, viewing government as benevolent, protective, and helpful (Easton & Dennis, 1965). Children's positive evaluations of government reflected the insular nature of the times. They showcased a faith in the system to do good things, displaying an admirable, if idealized, view of the country.

You would not find as many children who harbor such uniformly positive attitudes today. On television and social media, kids are exposed to sordid problems of society, the lascivious acts of politicians, and bitter denunciations of politics, politicians, and the opposing party by leaders and partisans alike.

From an academic perspective, the 1965 study of children's attitudes toward government represented a pioneering investigation of political socialization. Scholars began exploring the topic, curious about the political psychology of the '60s protesters, cultural variations in socialization practices, and the role mass communication played in knowledge generation. The first perspective described below offers penetrating insights into why young people today have a more skeptical attitude toward political authority than their counterparts of several generations ago. It assigns central importance to the media of mass communications. The second approach focuses on interpersonal communication dynamics.

Impact of Televised "Backstage" Portrayals

In an intriguing account, Joshua Meyrowitz (1986, 2009) argued that the electronic media, broadly defined, have rearranged our public space, obliterating traditional borderlines between private and public behavior. Years ago, the media covered only the most public of behaviors, avoiding like an electronic plague stories of people engaging in mean-spirited or sexually offensive acts in public. Over the years this has changed, as television exposes—literally it sometimes seems—young viewers to what used to be backstage, backroom behavior. In the political arena, a news media that for years resisted revealing the "backstage" private behaviors of public officials has changed its tune. Eighteenth-century newspaper readers never knew that Thomas Jefferson suffered from rheumatism and migraine headaches. Nineteenth-century news aficionados had no idea that Abraham Lincoln could become depressed. Twentieth-century radio and TV connoisseurs barely knew that Franklin Delano Roosevelt was paralyzed, and had no idea that John F. Kennedy enjoyed multiple affairs (Meyrowitz, 1986).

Over the ensuing decades, the distinction between public and private blurred, as it became increasingly permissible to offer deeper access into the back regions of public officials' lives. The press became increasingly cognizant of politicians' abrogation of the public trust and more motivated to publicize this, in light of norms favoring the public's "right to know" (Schudson, 2015). They were more than happy to cover salacious stories about politicians that could push up ratings as interest in mainstream news waned. Eventually, social media and the Internet placed everything before the public, and the curtains to the backstage of politics were permanently removed.

From the 1970s on, Americans learned that President Jimmy Carter had "looked on a lot of women with lust"; Senator Gary Hart departed the presidential race after revelations that he committed adultery; Bill Clinton had sexual relations with Monica Lewinsky; President George W. Bush overcame alcoholism; Democratic presidential candidate John Edwards impregnated a sycophantic videographer, while his cancer-stricken wife enthusiastically campaigned on his behalf; a once promising New York Congressman, Anthony Weiner, sent lewd photos to women he met over the Internet (see Figure 5.1); the 2016 Democratic National Committee, tied to Hillary Clinton, tried to undermine the campaign of rival Bernie Sanders; and Donald Trump bragged of sexual assault, calling it "locker room talk."

By Meyrowitz's account, these behind-the-scenes portrayals should have left an imprint on children's

Figure 5.1 Salacious revelations of former New York Congressman Anthony Weiner's sending lewd photos to women he met over the Internet in 2011 provide one of many examples of how media blur the public and private, offering children and adolescents backstage information on the lives of public officials. Weiner entered the public fray again in 2016 when emails relevant to the investigation of Hillary Clinton's private email server controversy were discovered on Weiner's computer, surfacing in an unrelated federal examination of Weiner's continued sexting. Political truth is often stranger and more freakish than fiction, all part of the socialization to politics that media sometimes unwittingly provide.

Getty Images

political attitudes. "By revealing previously backstage areas to audiences, television has served as an instrument of demystification. It has led to a decline in the image and prestige of political leaders" (Meyrowitz, 1986, p. 309). These tendencies have increased in recent years, as children have more exposure to political back regions on the Internet and Facebook.

Like all things in political communication, there are at least two normative sides to the story. Meyrowitz's work suggests that children are more cynical about politics than they were a generation ago, an effect he views with consternation. Others counter that a Pollyannaish faith in politics is naïve and dysfunctional. When troubling issues like sexual aggression enter the public fray, as it did in 2016 in the wake of disclosure of Trump's comments, it can be helpful to take the issue from hushed conversations into the open, where its frequency and moral depravity can be acknowledged (Taub, 2016). The same could be said for other issues too, although it could be challenging to discuss civics with seventh graders in the midst of a visceral election campaign (Bosman, 2016). Teachers immersed in the day-to-day business of socializing children about politics have to balance children's exposure to seamy reality with the goal of helping them appreciate that politics can accomplish important objectives.

Interpersonal Communication Dynamics

Other scholars have focused on the role of interpersonal agents in political socialization, adopting a broad, integrative perspective.

University of Colorado researcher Michael McDevitt has articulated a dynamic approach, emphasizing that adolescents can play an active role in family communication about politics. The traditional view is that parents impart their attitudes to children in a top-down manner. McDevitt notes that the direction of influence can go the other way, trickling up from children to parents (McDevitt, 2006; McDevitt & Chaffee, 2002). Teenagers who become animated by politics from exposure to civic programs in schools or discussions with peers can stimulate parents to rethink a political belief. Or they may bring up a perspective gleaned from movies or music that goads parents to defend or forcefully discuss their position on the issue. The result can be a thought-provoking series of reciprocal parent–child discussions that transforms the family political communication dynamic.

Dhavan V. Shah and his colleagues have examined the ways political socialization plays out in today's era, focusing on the notion of communication competence (Shah, McLeod, & Lee, 2009; Shah, Cho, Eveland, & Kwak, 2005; McLeod & Shah, 2009). Communication competence involves an ability to thoughtfully deliberate about political issues, formulate cogent arguments, reflect on information presented in the media, and arrive at a complex understanding of public issues. Children and adolescents ideally develop these deliberative skills through communication with parents and peers, in school civics classes, and through exposure to media educational programs. The skills become the engine that propels participation in civic and political activities. What's more, participation in deliberative classroom tasks, such as teacher-led discussion of political issues and political role-playing, can encourage middle school and high school students to follow politics online, engage in online political messaging, and talk face-to-face about current events with friends. These communication activities in turn increase participation in community service and election campaigns (Lee, Shah, & McLeod, 2013).

This is interesting because it shows that communication underlies the impact that thoughtful issue-oriented discussions in schools (as well as in families and peer groups) exert on democratic deliberation. The results optimistically indicate that, even in a society as fragmented and niche media–focused as ours, institutions can encourage the development of democratic norms. But there is a caveat: Schools and families that don't have the luxury to engage in these activities—either because they are economically impoverished or weighed down by other barriers, like ethnic prejudice or parental dysfunction—cannot even come close to contemplating these tasks. When poverty, prejudice, or family stressors are operative, a thoughtful focus on democracy and civic engagement is unlikely to occur. Not only does social class lead to gaps in knowledge, but also in democratic deliberation.

With these optimistic (and realistic) perspectives in mind, let's now review the effects of three major agents of political socialization: families, schools, and media.

FAMILY COMMUNICATION

What was your dinner-table conversation like growing up? Was there much conversation about politics? Did your parents trash certain politicians? Did they encourage you to say what you thought, even if you disagreed with what they espoused? Were certain topics—entire categories of politics—off-limits? Did you even have conversations with a parent or parents over dinner?

These questions are the centerpiece of a time-honored factor that influences political socialization: family communication patterns. There are two core dimensions of parent–child communication: **socio-oriented** and **concept-oriented communication**. In socio-oriented families, parents emphasize harmony and deference to adults. These parents may have strong, heartfelt views on social issues that they want to impart to their children. They may believe that the best way to rear competent adults is to teach them to defer to their elders. However, socio-oriented parents tend to be intolerant of dissent. Concept-oriented families, by contrast, encourage open exploration of contemporary issues, facilitating an environment in which there is exposure to diverse perspectives. The child or adolescent is encouraged to challenge others' viewpoints (Chaffee, McLeod, & Wackman, 1973).

Children who grow up in homes where parent–child communication is highly concept-oriented, but low in harmony or socio-orientation, are distinctive in a number of ways. They tend to be the most knowledgeable about politics and display the strongest preference for public affairs programs (Chaffee et al., 1973). They are more likely to value exposure to opposing political information and to talk with others with whom they disagree (Borah, Edgerly, & Vraga, 2013). Children reared in homes that encouraged discussion, but did not place a premium on harmony (like Sarah, the conservative college student mentioned earlier), are especially likely to participate in political discussions (Hively & Eveland, 2009). This has a salutary effect. Children reared in homes with considerable political discussion are more likely to participate in civic or political activities as adults than kids who grew up in homes with no political talk. More than a third of young adults who were frequently exposed to political discussions while growing up volunteer regularly, compared to 13 percent reared in homes with no political discussion (Zukin et al., 2006).

Presumably, when parents encourage children to openly explore ideas and challenge others' beliefs, their kids feel motivated to do the same on a larger level. Turned on to ideas and information, they may explore issues in the media, discuss political topics with others, and become active in civic causes. (Had Jeremy's mother, mentioned earlier in the chapter, discussed political issues more thoughtfully, he might have complemented his social volunteering with more political discussion and participation.)

Research on family communication and politics tends to be conducted in middle-class contexts. There is undoubtedly wide variation in family communication styles as a function of class, race, and the nature of the family (two-parent, single-parent, divorced, and so forth). We do not know whether the findings described above would hold in different sub-cultural contexts. Even so, one can readily agree with Chaffee and Yang (1990) that a child-rearing style that emphasizes concept exploration is conducive to democracy. They lament that "a pluralistic democratic society presumes a citizenry tolerant of divergent viewpoints, but most people are not raised in home where such tolerance is practiced, so they do not develop mass-communication habits that are appropriate to sustaining that pluralistic posture" (p. 145).

SCHOOLS

Political philosophers have long argued that education is of central importance in teaching the values of democratic citizenship. If schools do not provide instruction on civics, such as the right of citizens, the importance of dissent, and governmental checks and balances, who will? By the time or slightly before students graduate from high school, they will be able to vote and can enter into military service. Clearly, it is important that young people have a functioning knowledge of democratic principles.

Key inputs come from high school civics and history courses. What impact does civics instruction exert on students' political knowledge? Although research results vary, the findings from an extensive national study offers convincing support for the notion that exposure to a high school civics curriculum significantly increases students' knowledge of American politics and government (Niemi & Junn, 1998). Knowledge is far from perfect, as we have seen, but it is substantially greater than it would be in the absence of civics books and coursework.

This does not mean that everyone is happy with the content of the curriculum. High school civics and history courses have become a battleground in the cultural wars between liberal and conservatives. For much of the 20th century, history textbooks offered a puffed-up view of the American past celebrating conquest of the American West and industrial growth, despite injustices wrought on White blue collar workers, Native Americans and Blacks. In order to correct these errors, textbooks written over the past several decades articulated a different narrative, discussing prejudice and celebrating accomplishments of minorities and women. These books have rankled conservatives, who regard the books as politically correct and an attempt by Baby Boomer historians to rewrite history. Of course, history is always rewritten. There is no objective recitation of past events, for the past is necessarily subject to interpretation, reinterpretation, and revision in light of the present. Still, you do want a pluralistic version of American history, provided that it is steeped in democratic values and based on a consensual view of the facts.

Controversies over the historical content of textbooks are a way that societies come to grips with different interpretations of the past and try to negotiate a common narrative. Indeed, the United States is far from the only country in which controversies over textbooks play out. This issue crosses national boundaries, as can be seen in controversies that have swirled over Israeli, Arab, German, and Japanese textbooks. For example, some Israeli textbooks have celebrated the country's history, described previous wars as justified acts of defense, and frequently portrayed Arabs as violent and treacherous. Palestinian textbooks, for their part, have suggested that the state of Israel should not exist. While Israeli and Palestinian textbooks no longer describe the other side in cruel, dehumanizing terms, they still present the out-group as the enemy and offer glowing descriptions of their side. Research suggests that 87 percent of maps in Israeli texts do not refer to the Palestinian Authority, while 96 percent of maps in Palestinian texts do not mention Israel (Wexler, Adwan, & Bar-Tal,

2013). Teenagers growing up in the Gaza Strip, controlled by the extremist Hamas movement, read texts that falsely claimed that the Jewish Torah is "fabricated" and that Zionism is a racist social movement that seeks to drive out Arabs (Akram & Rudoren, 2013).

It is not just the Middle East. For many years German history books did not mention the Holocaust and barely described the horrific extermination of Jews that occurred in concentration camps. This has changed, as contemporary German textbooks devote considerable coverage to the Holocaust, describing it as one of the darkest periods in human history. In a similar fashion, textbooks used in Japanese high schools have offered a condensed, distorted version of World War II and Japanese war crimes. This aroused the ire of Japanese historians seeking a more truthful version of Japanese history. Thus, controversies over the role American history textbooks play in political socialization should be placed in a larger international context.

MEDIA IMPACT ON POLITICAL SOCIALIZATION

Unlike parents and schools, mass media and the Internet typically do not deliberately seek to shape attitudes and beliefs. Yet they most assuredly exert these effects. Think about it: When you were a child, what was your first exposure to the president? Where did you first hear the words "politician," "candidate," "presidential election," and "negative advertising?" From TV or the Internet, perhaps? Didn't books, television, offbeat websites, and rancorous social media discussions create some of the political pictures in your head? And where, if not from satirical media programs or YouTube snippets, did you learn to laugh at politicians' missteps? The next portions of the chapter explore the dynamics of these issues, extending early research that explored the effects of news on political socialization (Chaffee, Ward, & Tipton, 1970; Conway, Wyckoff, Feldman, & Ahern, 1981) by examining ways entertainment media can subtly influence political attitudes. Discussions focus on three broad concepts: hyperreality, with its fusion of facts and fiction; cultivation; and the time-honored arena of political satire.

Hyperreality, Facts, Fiction, and Entertainment

From Cronkite, the legendary television anchor, to Colbert, the political satirist (Baym, 2010); from the daily newspaper to *The Daily Show*; and from Mike Wallace (longtime *60 Minutes* reporter) to Michael Moore (who needs no introduction), the media have emerged as important agents of political socialization. What's more, many media genres, from nonfiction books to hip-hop music, distributed across multiple platforms, influence political attitudes.

In the old days it was simple. Newspapers, magazines, and broadcast news bestrode the earth, offering up facts and conveying reality, symbolized by the phrase that Walter Cronkite used to close his news broadcast: "And that's the way it is." Novels, movies, and television programs that presented a fictionalized view of politics were available to entertain or enlighten, but were clearly separated from the "factually based" news. Of course, journalists made a series of judgments as to what constituted a fact, and some news reports had a more veridical grounding in facts than others. Nonetheless, the delightfully simple view of news-as-fact and entertainment-as-fiction prevailed. As a result of the vast political, economic, and cultural changes in journalism that occurred over the past 50 years (Schudson & Tifft, 2005), this separation is no longer tenable. And the blurred lines have important implications for contemporary political socialization.

Over the past couple of decades, politics has become increasingly inseparable from popular culture, as television dramas such as *The West Wing, 24, Veep,* and *House of Cards* have attracted mass audiences. *The Simpsons* cultivated a new generation of viewers. *Saturday Night Live* regained its comedic footing, famously in Tina Fey's spoofs of Sarah Palin in 2008, and continuing in 2016 with Kate McKinnon playing Hillary Clinton and Alec Baldwin impersonating Donald Trump. Political satire that dates back to the Greek playwright Aristophanes and Jonathan Swift's *Gulliver's Travels* found a contemporary home in *The Daily Show with Jon Stewart, Last Week Tonight with John Oliver, The Late Show with Stephen Colbert,* and in the laughter of millions of young viewers turned off by the pretenses of network news.

These contemporary changes invite the question of where reality ends and fiction begins in media discussion of national and international events (Williams & Delli Carpini, 2011, p. 116). The list of films that merge fact and fiction date back decades, but let's start with Oliver Stone's *JFK*, with its charge that the CIA, FBI, and Secret Service may have conspired to assassinate Kennedy (a view doubted by experts, but favored by conspiracy theorists). A 1996 political novel with a catchy title, *Primary Colors*, told the story of a charming, loquacious, and philandering Southern governor—a thinly veiled stand-in for President Bill Clinton—famous for his sexual appetites, political gifts, and questionable morality. The novel was fictional, but in the deeper sense in which fiction plumbs the layers of life, it may have conveyed emotional truths about Clinton and the presidency.

Two years later, in 1998, when Clinton was in the midst of revelations of his affair with White House intern Monica Lewinsky, along with controversy over his prevarications, another piece of political fiction—a movie titled *Wag the Dog*—became popular. In the movie, the president, hoping to deflect media attention from a sex scandal less than a couple of weeks before the election, concocts a plan to stage a phony war with Albania, hyped by a war theme song and fake movie footage to dramatize the war. In a bizarre, truth-is-stranger-than-fiction coincidence, Clinton actually ordered the bombing of a Sudanese pharmaceutical factory in August 1998, on the basis of evidence that the factory was manufacturing chemical weapons that could get in the hands of international terrorists. Critics questioned the necessity of the attack, pointing to the eerie similarity between the bombing and the comparable action in the movie, suggesting that Clinton had ordered the attack to distract the media from the Lewinsky scandal (Haas, Christensen, & Haas, 2015). But defenders pointed to evidence that the factory was linked with Osama bin Laden, noting that in any case that White House deliberations focused on serious foreign policy issues, not media-hyped connections between a movie and presidential action (Risen, 1999). But from a political socialization perspective, the movie became part of the popular culture fodder on Clinton, with rich potential for deepening the cynicism of the young.

The list goes on. News about the aftermath of the unspeakable tragedy of 9/11 is viewed in tandem with Michael Moore's vituperatively satirical movie, *Fahrenheit 9/11*, which cast then President George W. Bush in a negative light. Kathryn Bigelow's 2012 film, *Zero Dark Thirty* seamlessly (and selectively) fused fact and fiction to suggest that CIA torture helped lead the agency to Osama bin Laden's secret compound in Pakistan. Critics said there was little evidence to support the claim that torture helped the U.S. find Bin Laden, but filmmaking buffs said this was legitimate artistic license, and, in any case, the movie was about storytelling, not facts, working on a metaphorical instead of a literal level. Similarly, Oliver Stone's 2016 biographical movie, *Snowden*, about the iconic CIA dissident, Edward Snowden, who exposed massive U.S. global surveillance of its citizens, complexly blended fact with fiction. As an example of blending biography and hyperbole, Snowden's boss was named after an antagonist in George Orwell's book about Big Brother, *1984*. The factual accuracy of the movie is open to debate, with some defending it and others suggesting that the movie grossly underplays the notion that Snowden was a spy for Russia or was exploited to benefit Russian interests (Epstein, 2017).

Televised examples that blur fact and fiction abound: the Bush administration's use of the escapades of Jack Bauer on Fox's fictional *24* to defend its enhanced interrogation techniques; HBO's *The Wire*, which offered up insights on how political corruption and the drug trade explained urban violence in Baltimore; and *The Daily Show*'s classic melding of real and faux news (before fake news entered the consciousness in 2016; see Morreale, 2009).

More broadly, the media do not offer up a uniform, literal, reality-based mirror of politics. Instead, they present multiple, conflicting representations of politics in news—a veritable funhouse mirror of representations of politics. Critics have invoked the concept of hyperreality to explain this. **Hyperreality** is defined as:

a postmodern sense of the real that accounts for our loss of certainty in being able to distinguish clearly and hierarchically between reality and its representation, and in being able to distinguish clearly and hierarchically between the modes of its representation.

(Fiske, 1996, p. 62)

Hyperreality is an imaginative and insightful, yet sometimes slippery concept. It emphasizes the ways that traditional distinctions between news and entertainment, fake and real news, fact and opinion, and truth and fiction have become blurred, creating an environment in which mediated political reality assumes more importance than underlying facts (Delli Carpini, 2016). In the arena of media effects, hyperreality highlights the challenges young people face in deciphering reality, distinguishing the real from the authentic and the manufactured from the genuine. It suggests that events deliberately staged for media, like political speeches with crowd-sourced supporters, or slick interviews between TV anchors and candidates, become the essence of political reality itself. The problem is that proponents offer scant evidence to support their hypothesis that young adults are as susceptible to hyperreality effects as they claim. Advocates can overstate the impact of media, underestimate young people's ability to differentiate different platforms, and overemphasize the degree to which there is no reality, when certain media coverage, like portrayals of inequality, economic hardship, and terrorism, are inescapably real. At the same time, the hyperreality concept is rich, calling attention to the murky, shady domain of political reality in an age of blurred lines between media genres.

Cultivation of Politics

Cultivation theory, a classic mass communication perspective, emphasizes that media weave stories and construct narratives that convey a culture's values, ideologies, and underlying socio-political perspectives (Morgan, Shanahan, & Signorielli, 2009, 2012). A society's media system conveys information about society's "winners and losers . . . (and) who gets away with what, when, why, how and against whom" (Gerbner & Gross, 1976, p. 176). By creating a symbolic environment that promotes particular political views of the world, media communicate the political values of society, transmitting and inculcating these viewpoints.

Cultivation theory suggests that the news media's depiction of a candidate (usually male) who wins an election after a bruising, verbally aggressive competition, and entertainment television's portrayal of how politicians exploit power to get their way (think *House of Cards*), cultivate the view that politics is all about power, abuse, and doing whatever it takes to defeat the opposition. There *is* a factual basis to these portrayals ("politics ain't bean-bag," as one writer famously observed; it is a combat sport). At the same time, media depictions offer a cartoon-like view of the political world. They conspicuously neglect the roles pluralistic coalitions that forge compromises, checks and balances, political parties, and fervent adherence to political ideologies play in politics.

Cultivation theory has traditionally argued that television, in particular, exerts a mainstreaming influence, bringing viewers from different social and political perspectives into a common fold. According to **mainstreaming**, exposure to television portrayals of politics overrides the diverse orientations viewers from different demographic groups bring to the small screen, accentuating similarities among the viewing population. TV cultivates in its heavy viewers a common, shared socio-political orientation or consciousness that reflects the images and values that dominate television news and entertainment (Gerbner, Gross, Morgan, & Signorielli, 1984; Morgan et al., 2012). Television theoretically serves as a mechanism of social control, socializing young people to accept the preeminent, mainstream cultural viewpoints in a particular country (Morgan, Leggett, & Shanahan, 1999). Is this still true today?

On the one hand, television entertainment presents a mainstream, homogenized view of the political world that cultivates a moderate, conventional pro-American system political worldview (Gerbner et al., 1984; Hardy, 2012). Older studies found that heavy viewers hold conservative attitudes on minority issues, perhaps because television frequently depicts African Americans in a crime-related narrative and in the physical clutches of police officers (Entman & Rojecki, 2000). In line with mainstreaming, television viewing tends to pull individuals with a more liberal perspective into the dominant, conservative fold (Shanahan & Morgan, 1999). But this viewpoint is complicated by evidence that entertainment programs presenting a more liberal view of the political world cultivate liberal viewpoints.

Over the past couple of decades, television has offered an increasingly multifaceted, less conventional view of politics, shining a light in primetime entertainment and daytime shows on changing mores in American families, as well as the economic and social struggles families experience on a daily basis. Television entertainment programs increasingly have depicted single-parent families and focused on child care problems that demand government intervention. By raising these issues, TV entertainment can encourage viewers to adopt more liberal, pro-government viewpoints. In line with cultivation theory, research shows that heavy TV viewers are especially likely to harbor positive attitudes toward single parenthood and the (once unconventional) notion of bearing children out of wedlock (Morgan et al., 1999). Similarly, there is evidence that exposure to daytime talk shows, with their regular portrayal of structurally induced family stress, is associated with support for government funding of family and social programs, while at the same bolstering mainstreaming (Glynn, Huge, Reineke, Hardy, &

Shanahan, 2007). Thus, television can mainstream both conservative and liberal political viewpoints, encouraging viewers to adopt whichever of these viewpoints is more pervasive on TV at a particular time.

On a theoretical level, cultivation is an ingenious concept, one empirically tested in innovative ways. It is not without problems. Researchers have raised questions about the strength of the effect (Potter, 2014), as well as how one can meaningfully pinpoint a mainstreamed, conventional set of values that consistently appears across the diverse, frequently authority-questioning panorama of contemporary television. And yet cultivation effects have consistently emerged in the U.S. and a host of countries over the years and have emerged after application of rigorous statistical controls (Van den Bulck, 2012; see also Hardy, 2012 for a helpful review of cultivation and politics).

The larger question is whether cultivation theory, with its emphasis on the dominance of *televised* storytelling, is still relevant in an era of fragmented, niche, and personalized social media—a time when TV no longer reaches a mass audience with the same ubiquity and simultaneity of impact as it did in days gone by (Perloff, 2015). Cultivation posited that the media's—notably television's—capacity to tell stories shaped the contours of culture, influencing beliefs and values. But today, when young people are heavy users of multiple social networking sites, sometimes simultaneously, the influence of televised political stories may be diminished or neutralized by competing stories from diverse media platforms. On the other hand, television remains a dominant medium, particularly in the political arena. People still watch lots of TV, view news and political advertisements, and tune in to popular television shows on their mobile devices (Morgan, Shanahan, & Signorielli, 2015). Shows like *Breaking Bad* of some years back, *Homeland*, and *House of Cards*, with their striking political themes, command large audiences.

Given the important role political stories continue to play in culture, transporting and immersing individuals, offering themes consonant with particular societal worldviews, it seems likely we will witness media cultivation effects in the years to come. Mainstreaming is likely to be less impactful and pervasive than in the era when television was the primary source of political information. Yet society depends on its media system to transmit and inculcate basic values.

Increasingly, media can cultivate traditional political worldviews, while also exposing young people to oppositional perspectives through diverse social networking sites that take up alternative positions or mock mainstream culture. Exposure to alternative viewpoints that are critical of conventional social values, such as graphic social media site condemnation of police violence, can override the dominant values received via conventional media. Thus, answers to the questions of political cultivation are more complicated than in years past. Do media still cultivate political attitudes, helping social-ize young people into society? Undoubtedly, yes. Do media mainstream or promote pri-marily conventional political worldviews? Not necessarily. Do media impacts depend on the particular media platform viewers tune in to, with effects less uniform than in years past? Increasingly, yes. Finally, do media content stifle or encourage needed polit-ical change? This important question is hardest to answer. It depends on what one means by change and the yardstick used to establish it. Cultivation tends to answer this ques-tion by concluding that media perpetuate the status quo, but in an age of multifarious media, it is best to adopt a contingent perspective that emphasizes change, as well as conservative continuity. With diverse media telling different political stories, with nar-ratives varying from the conservative to the conspiratorial and White nationalistic to the racially and ethnically diverse, the larger problem is whether American society provides children with a coherent set of political values steeped in the best of American culture.

Satire

In October 2015, Hillary Clinton performed a dead-on impersonation of Donald Trump on *Saturday Night Live* as the 2016 campaign unfolded, and Trump appeared on *SNL* not long after, parodying his famously egotistical style. Comedian Larry David imi-tated the ethnic, no-frills mannerisms of 2016 Democratic presidential candidate Bernie Sanders so well in an *SNL* skit that Sanders introduced himself to a rally of supporters as Larry David. Alec Baldwin's imitations of Donald Trump became legendary, even to the point of propelling the thin-skinned Trump to tweet that the show is "unwatchable" and "totally biased."

Comedy Central has produced a number of political satires, the chief among them *The Daily Show* (originally with Jon Stewart, subsequently with Trevor Noah). *The Daily Show* was a comedic trendsetter that deliberately created a seemingly authentic, but obviously fake, news program to satirize politics, emphasizing how much was actually false in "real" television news (Baym, 2010). Stephen Colbert, who played a character on *The Daily Show* before he spun his parodies of conventional TV news into his own Comedy Central program and *The Late Show*, showed a flair for ironic authenticity (Day, 2011; Young, Holbert, & Jamieson, 2014). He could convey implicit, deadpan agreement with mainstream, sometimes conservative values, though his actual intent was to question these conservative assumptions. In 2012, Colbert expressed seemingly genuine bewilderment at the madcap nature of U.S. campaign finance. He proceeded to create his own political action committee, the irony enhanced when followers, con-veying their own dissatisfaction with campaign finance, helped him raised more than $1 million! Other televised satirical programs have included the ethnically focused *Kay & Peele* and *Master of None*, and the televised political humor of Samantha Bee, Larry Wilmore, Bill Maher, John Oliver, and D. L. Hughley.

What is satire? **Satire**, as you probably know, is a form of humor that employs ridicule to expose human foibles, with its humorous hooks typically directed at the powers that be (Parker, 2015). It is complex, calling on a variety of humorous techniques to parody, frequently to deconstruct power (Bakhtin, 1981). These include slapstick imitations of presidents, buffoonery, fake news shows, and irony. **Irony** is a classic comedic device that uses language to suggest an incongruity between the surface and deeper meanings of an event.

Satire and irony are also vibrantly alive and well outside the U.S., famously and tragically in France, after terrorists slaughtered 12 journalists at the satirical magazine *Charlie Hebdo* in retaliation for its courageous publication of spoofs and cartoons lampooning the Prophet Muhammad. Televised satire and parody are popular across Europe, including Eastern European nations like Hungary and Romania, as well as in countries with authoritarian governments such as Egypt and China (Baym & Jones, 2012; Larmer, 2011).

Russia, under the sober, iron-fisted Prime Minister Vladimir V. Putin, is not immune from satire. Some years back, Putin likened the white ribbons of Russian protesters to, of all things, condoms, inviting ridicule. Within minutes after his comment, cleverly edited photos of a condom pinned to Putin's lapel went viral. With many in Russia tired of Putin's rule and his self-aggrandizing style, satire offered a weapon to defuse anger and organize political opposition. After allegations of widespread ballot box stuffing and vote stealing in a December 2011 Russian parliamentary election spread across the country, a joke gained currency: "The wives of United Russia party members don't fake orgasms. They falsify them" (Yaffa, 2012, p. 4)!

Even in Nigeria, a country where a former military general has governed the country and the militant cult Boko Haram terrorizes millions, satire offers cathartic release. Comedian Ali Baba lamented to an audience of attorneys that the robbers were having great success, striking every car along a potholed-filled road until a former governor of the country drove by. "They looked at him, and said he should drive on," the comedian deadpanned as the audience grew silent. One of the armed robbers asked, "Why? Why did you let that car go?"

"Esprit de corps"—comradeship among brothers—another robber said, drawing a parallel between the thievery of robbers and politicians, eliciting gales of laughter from the audience (Onishi, 2015, p. 1).

Satirists even satirize the global terrorist organization, ISIS, but this can provoke controversy. In Britain, a BBC skit, which recruited millions of views on social media sites, showed a British woman wearing a hijab worried about how her outfit would impress ISIS militants. "It's only three days to the beheading, and I've got no idea what I'm going to wear," she says. Another woman shows off a new suicide vest to other jihadist wives. "What do you think?" she asks. "Ahmed surprised me with it yesterday" (Bilefsky, 2017, p. A8). While some viewed the satire as an appropriate way to belittle ISIS, others felt it was inappropriate to provoke laughs from a group that had performed heinous acts on women.

There is little question that political satire is widely available in contemporary media across the world. The more nettlesome question now becomes: What impact does media satire exert? The research that sheds light on this question was conducted primarily in America, offering interesting findings, although its applications to other countries must be tempered by appreciation of their different cultural norms.

Processes and Effects of Satire

We know young people are exposed to televised satire. A national survey reported that young adults were more likely to obtain campaign information from late-night comedy shows than older individuals, and other research reports consistent exposure to the classic *Daily Show*, as well as *SNL*, among young adults (Young & Tisinger, 2006; Baumgartner & Morris, 2006; see also Chadwick, 2013). In a famous example, Tina Fey's "I can see Russia from my house" parody of Sarah Palin in a skit from September 13, 2008, elicited more than 5.5 million views within four days on NBC's online site alone; about a month later, NBC had streamed Fey's skits 43 million times, and 72 percent of the public reported that they had heard about Fey's comedic portrayal of Palin (Chadwick, 2013), with some believing that Palin had actually uttered the "Russia from my house remark." Given the continued popularity of *Saturday Night Live* political skits, as well as new satires on YouTube, there is every reason to believe that large numbers of young adults continue to watch televised political comedic programs. Indeed, younger adult viewers tend to feel more absorbed in satire than in conventional news, compared with older viewers (Boukes, Boomgaarden, Moorman, & de Vreese, 2015). And the plethora of online satire, from JibJab parodies of presidential candidates to YouTube's *Bad Lip Reading*, can become viral hits.

Just watching satire does not translate to media influence. People bring attitudes acquired from other socialization agents, such as parents, to the viewing of political satire, as a classic study of the 1970s TV program *All in the Family* demonstrated (Vidmar & Rokeach, 1974). Thus, an *SNL* skit lampooning President Trump might elicit laughs from Trump supporters, but will not change their attitudes toward Trump. Liberals and conservatives viewed comedian Stephen Colbert's deadpan satirizing of a conservative pundit through the prism of their political attitudes, assimilating his comedy to their preexisting views. In one study, conservatives took Colbert at his word, presuming that he is a political conservative, just like them. By contrast, liberals thought Colbert was just kidding around, opting not to perceive him as conservative, and seeing him as more liberal, in line with their own attitudes (LaMarre, Landreville, & Beam, 2009; see also Mohammed, 2014).

To appreciate satire's effects more deeply, we need to understand how viewers think about political satire. This requires an exploration of the cognitive mechanisms at work when people watch late-night humor, as Dannagal G. Young (2008a) and Mark Boukes and his colleagues (2015) have emphasized. On the one hand, when young adults are absorbed in a political satire, they can feel psychologically immersed or transported. This absorption in the satirical skit can diminish their motivation or ability to formulate mental arguments with what the satirist has suggested (Boukes et al., 2015; Young, 2008a). Thus, at some level, they are open to persuasion. On the other hand, people can enjoy a satirical skit, finding it funny, yet recognize it's just a joke, thereby discounting the satire as irrelevant to the more serious political attitudes they hold (Nabi, Moyer-Gusé, & Byrne, 2007). No longer absorbed in the humor, but instead scrutinizing the message, perhaps selectively perceiving humor in terms of their prior attitudes, they remain steadfast in their preexisting beliefs, despite the intent of the humorist. Thus, discounting and absorption cancel each other out (Boukes et al., 2015). Interesting, isn't it, how complicated something rip-roaringly funny can be!

Complicating matters further, satire can be ambiguous, ironic, and difficult to decipher. Appreciating, let alone systematically processing humor requires some cognitive ability, and in the case of political satire, it requires political knowledge (LaMarre & Walther, 2013). You can't get the joke about the budget debt or Washington gridlock if you are not familiar with these issues. Satire can be dramaturgically complicated. Satirists combine an appearance of seriousness with deeper ironic disparagement of the status quo, and those unfamiliar with the genre or the satirist may fail to get beyond the superficial to appreciate the satirist's underlying intent (Mohammed, 2014). In a similar fashion, younger adolescents or those at a lower cognitive-developmental stage may not understand satire well enough for the jokes to sink in.

Given that people filter satire through partisan attitudes, it is likely it has a more subtle effect, influencing cognitions rather than affect. Does satire, with its biting attacks on politicians, bolster cynical beliefs about politics?

Before a packed audience at a communication convention, communication scholars Roderick P. Hart and E. Johanna Hartelius proffered exactly this charge. "We accuse

Jon Stewart of political heresy," they said, tongue in cheek but with serious rhetorical overtones. They continued,

> We find his sins against the Church of Democracy to be so heinous that he should be branded an infidel and made to wear sackcloth and ashes for at least two years, during which time he would not be allowed to emcee the Oscars, throw out the first pitch at the Yankees game, or eat at the Time Warner commissary. Our specific charge is that Mr. Stewart has engaged in unbridled political cynicism.
>
> (Hart & Hartelius, 2007, p. 263)

Drawing on rhetorical principles, they argued that Stewart mocked democratic aims by making cynicism appealing. In their view, by cleverly editing public figures' statements so they appear ludicrous, Stewart debased the decent intentions that underlie public leaders' actions.

There is some data indicating that viewing satirical programs of some years back—*The Daily Show with Jon Stewart* and *The Colbert Report*—is associated with cynicism, mistrusting media, and believing the political system is corrupt (Balmas, 2014; Guggenheim, Kwak, & Campbell, 2011; Baumgartner & Morris, 2006; Morris & Baumgardner, 2008). But there is also evidence that political satire has more salutary effects. Satire, after all, contains an implicit idealism, offering up the hope that by humorously identifying the flaws of individual leaders, satirists can help people appreciate the visionary goals of the democratic system that leaders have selfishly or stupidly failed to implement (Schutz, 1977). Thus, satire can enhance knowledge and facilitate deeper thinking about politics (Hardy et al., 2014; Young & Tisinger, 2006; Landreville & LaMarre, 2013). Research by Lindsay H. Hoffman and her colleagues found that satire increased political efficacy or the belief that citizens can influence politics; efficacy in turn enhanced and predicted political participation (Hoffman & Young, 2011; Hoffman & Thomson, 2009; see also Becker, 2014).

So, does satire increase cynicism or enhance efficacy? Does it amplify skepticism or bolster political participation? Both views might be correct, given that one can be cynical about politicians, yet motivated to change the system. A little cynicism could be a good thing if it leads to more questioning of authority.

Another possibility is that satire's impact hinges on other variables or moderators. In an intriguing study, Hoon Lee and Nojin Kwak (2014) reasoned that political satire bolsters political participation by eliciting particular negative emotions, such as anger at, or worry about, government actions depicted in the satirical skit. Feeling angry can motivate individuals to participate in politics to throw the bums out of office and restore decency and common sense. Lee and Kwak found that satire was more likely to produce participation by evoking negative emotions, but primarily among individuals higher in education. "Those with greater skills and resources are more likely to obtain benefits from political satire," Lee and Kwak noted, "because understanding humor itself requires a certain level of expertise" (p. 322). In order for satire to enhance faith in politics, one needs a basic level of political knowledge and expertise.

On a broader level, satire can exert normative benefits (Holbert, 2013), offering a way for society to renew its politics through humor. Satire can educate and entertain (Young, Holbert, & Jamieson, 2014), with entertainment laying the groundwork for political reflection. Political humor can illuminate problems and hypocrisies that are outside the realm of conventional political communication genres, like news and advertising. Endemic to democracy, but not limited to societies with democratic governments, satire socializes the young by helping to unmask the powerful. It disrupts "the herd thinking (and) the herd mood" (Parker, 2015, p. 51) and celebrates the ways free speech reveals political wrongdoing beneath the surface. Despite the appearance of negativity, satire is optimistic. It "weeps, scolds, and ridicules, generally with one major end in view: to plead with man for a return to his moral senses" (Bloom & Bloom, 1979, p. 38; Young, 2008b). In this way, satire opens up pathways for questioning the status quo, enables vicarious "talking back" to authorities, and, by channeling negative emotions into positive energy, can lay the groundwork for political change (Baym & Jones, 2012; Gray, Jones, & Thompson, 2009).

CONCLUSIONS

Societies with diverse electoral and political structures enculturate and socialize citizens, introducing them to their country's foundational political values and norms. Children, adolescents, and young adults are not born with an appreciation for democratic values, and society needs to cultivate these ideals. Ideally, societies should present a pluralism of perspectives on history and values, so young adults can appreciate different viewpoints and make an informed choice about how they want to participate in politics. Countries do not always do this, traditionally favoring the dominant ideological perspective. Even in countries like the U.S., which justly pride themselves on contemporary democratic processes, one can find examples of how textbooks of yore whitewashed the nation's political shortcomings. Across the world, where democracy runs along a continuum, there are variations in the degree to which political socialization is open, transparent, and tolerant.

Political communication plays an important part in political socialization Communication of traditions and norms of citizenship are diffused through family, peer, school, and diverse media portrayals of politics. From a psychological perspective, there are striking continuities and changes in political socialization, as it occurs across the life cycle. Political predispositions acquired at a young age, and through identification with a particular generational cohort, tend to persist throughout the life cycle. Attitudes acquired during one's youth can remain influential during the adult years. Just as there is continuity in political socialization, there is also change. As a result of exposure to media and interpersonal communication, Americans have changed their attitudes toward race, gay marriage, abortion, and big government over the past several decades.

Communication scholars emphasize that contemporary socialization to politics is dynamic, characterized by interaction among different socialization agents and growth in communication competence, a generalized ability that ideally should spur civic engagement. Parents are a major influence on children's political views, with family communication patterns exerting a significant influence on children's interest in politics. Schools also socialize children, through textbooks and the increasing number of programs designed to promote voting, deliberative debate, and civic participation. Of course, there are plenty of criticisms of conventional socialization, ranging from the view that socialization reflects a pro-secular bias to the concern that it affirms a conservative political perspective.

Contemporary media represent portals that introduce young people to a world of politics that is played and constructed electronically, cinematically, and digitally. News, television dramas, movies, and music from heavy metal to rap (Jackson, 2002) introduce young people to the serious and sublime—along with the admirable and absurd— aspects of contemporary politics. Meyrowitz has persuasively argued that electronic media (and the Internet) have profoundly influenced political socialization. By showing the "back regions" of public life and revealing the imperfections, personal shortcomings, and sexual infidelities of political leaders, the media have made it difficult for young people to revere elected officials or believe in the electoral system. Normatively, this has dysfunctions, but it also gives young adults a realistic rather than sugarcoated view of the contemporary political world.

Media news and entertainment are a primary source of information about the political world, which young people experience, as Lippmann (1922) noted, nearly a century ago, as "out of reach, out of sight (and) out of mind." Politics has become increasingly inseparable from popular culture, as fictional films about politics, satire, even fake news, blend seamlessly with more authentic political accounts. Emphasizing the concept of hyperreality, critics have argued that the idea of reality has become fuzzy, blurred in the amalgamation of fact, opinion, news, and fiction, creating an environment in which mediated political reality is of greater importance than the actual day-to-day, rough-and-tumble business of institutional politics. Of course, politics is part mediated reality. Critics are probably correct that the platform-bending, border-crossing nature of political communication confuses and misleads some young adults. On the other hand, horrific events like mass terrorism, and concrete problems like economic recessions, have a way of clarifying the mental picture. Young adults, as digital natives with long experience in differentiating between authentic and staged images on diverse social media platforms, are less gullible than critics assume, though not immune from influence.

Cultivation theory offers rich insights about the ways in which contemporary media cultivate beliefs about the political world, including mainstreaming individuals to adopt the views that dominate on the small television screen. However, today's teenagers and young adults are exposed to a panoply of political portrayals across different media platforms that are more diverse than those their parents and grandparents received via television. Mainstreaming is more complex and multifaceted in today's society, not necessarily inculcating a particular (conservative) political perspective.

Media also shape political attitudes through satire, a favorite technique of political humorists throughout the ages, a strategy that, through criticism of democracy's actors, can ironically celebrate tenets of democratic government. Satire works through different psychological pathways, sometimes increasing cynicism, but more frequently amplifying political efficacy and participation, particularly among those with a more educated, sophisticated view of the political world. It remains a vital part of political communication, providing a mechanism for dissent to push through society's rigid communicative strictures.

Political socialization is a work in progress, with new media genres that socialize young people emerging in our digital culture. Activists have devised innovative websites in an effort to promote civic engagement and political participation. These sites have a mixed record of success (Bachen, Raphael, Lynn, McKee, & Philippi, 2008; Bennett, Wells, & Freelon, 2011; Xenos & Foot, 2008). Many fail to offer interactive learning opportunities to which young people are accustomed. On the other hand, social media can help catalyze offline participation in political activities, as seen in the conservative Tea Party movement and the many groups that have sprung into action to challenge the Trump administration. These developments suggest that dour predictions of the demise of citizenship in a digital era are in need of reexamination. Activism and resistance on the left and right, catalyzed by social media, are alive and well. What is missing amid all the partisan hue and cry is civic socialization that teaches the young how to understand—even appreciate—perspectives that differ from their own and acquire a tolerance for divergent perspectives promoting integrative solutions to the status quo.

REFERENCES

Akram, F., & Rudoren, J. (2013, November 4). To shape young Palestinians, Hamas creates its own textbooks. *The New York Times*, A1, A11.

Alford, J., Funk, C., & Hibbing, J. (2005). Are political orientations genetically transmitted? *American Political Science Review, 99*, 153–167.

Bachen, C., Raphael, C., Lynn, K-M., McKee, K., & Philippi, J. (2008). Civic engagement, pedagogy, and information technology on web sites for youth. *Political Communication, 25*, 290–310.

Bakhtin, M.M. (1981). *The dialogic imagination: Four essays* (Translated by C. Emerson & M. Holquist). Austin: University of Texas Press.

Balmas, M. (2014). When fake news becomes real: Combined exposure to multiple news sources and political attitudes of inefficacy, alienation, and cynicism. *Communication Research, 41*, 430–454.

Banaji, M.R., & Heiphetz, L. (2010). Attitudes. In S.T. Fiske, D.T. Gilbert, & G. Lindzey (Eds.), *Handbook of social psychology* (5th ed., vol. 1, pp. 353–393). New York: Wiley-Blackwell.

Bandura, A. (1971). Analysis of modeling processes. In A. Bandura (Ed.), *Psycho-logical modeling: Conflicting theories* (pp. 1–62). Chicago: Aldine-Atherton.

Baumgartner, J., & Morris, J.S. (2006). *The Daily Show* effect: Candidate evaluations, efficacy, and American youth. *American Politics Research, 34*, 341–367.

Baym, G. (2010). *From Cronkite to Colbert: The evolution of broadcast news*. Boulder, CO: Paradigm.

Baym, G., & Jones, J.P. (2012). News parody in global perspective: Politics, power, and resistance. *Popular Communication: The International Journal of Media and Culture, 10*, 2–13.

Becker, A.B. (2014). Humiliate my enemies or mock my friends? Applying disposition theory of humor to the study of political parody appreciation and attitudes toward candidates. *Human Communication Research, 40*, 137–160.

Bennett, W.L., Wells, C., & Freelon, D. (2011). Communicating civic engagement: Contrasting models of citizenship in the youth web sphere. *Journal of Communication, 61*, 835–856.

Bilefsky, D. (2017, January 6). Can a satire of ISIS be funny? BBC viewers are split. *The New York Times*, A8.

Bloom, E.A., & Bloom, L.D. (1979). *Satire's persuasive voice*. Ithaca, NY: Cornell University Press.

Borah, P., Edgerly, S., & Vraga, E.K. (2013). Hearing and talking to the other side: Antecedents of cross-cutting exposure in adolescents. *Mass Communication & Society, 16*, 391–416.

Bosman, J. (2016, October 18). Teaching seventh graders in a "total mess" of an election season. *The New York Times*. Retrieved from www.nytimes.com/2016/10/19/us/teaching-seventh-graders-in-a . . . (Accessed October 23, 2016).

Boukes, M., Boomgaarden, H.G., Moorman, M., & de Vreese, C.H. (2015). At odds: Laughing and thinking? The appreciation, processing, and persuasiveness of political satire. *Journal of Communication, 65*, 721–744.

Chadwick, A. (2013). *The hybrid media system: Politics and power*. New York: Oxford University Press.

Chaffee, S.H., McLeod, J.M., & Wackman, D. (1973). Family communication patterns and adolescent political participation. In J. Dennis (Ed.), *Socialization to politics: A reader* (pp. 349–364). New York: Wiley-Blackwell.

Chaffee, S. H., Ward, S., & Tipton, L. P. (1970). Mass communication and political socialization. *Journalism Quarterly, 47*, 647–659, 666.

Chaffee, S. H., & Yang, S-M. (1990). Communication and political socialization. In O. Ichilov (Ed.), *Political socialization, citizenship education, and democracy* (pp. 137–157). New York: Teachers College Press.

Clawson, R. A., & Oxley, Z. M. (2013). *Public opinion: Democratic ideals, democratic practice* (2nd ed.). Thousand Oaks, CA: Sage/CQ Press.

Conway, M. M., Wyckoff, M. L., Feldman, E., & Ahern, D. (1981). The news media in children's political socialization. *Public Opinion Quarterly, 45*, 164–178.

Dahlgren, P. (2000). The Internet and the democratization of civic culture. *Political Communication, 17*, 335–340.

Day, A. (2011). *Satire and dissent: Interventions in contemporary political debate.* Bloomington: Indiana University Press.

Deane, C., Duggan, M., & Morin, R. (2016, December 15). *Americans name the 10 most significant historic events of their lifetimes.* Pew Research Center: U.S. Politics & Policy. Retrieved from www.people-press.org/2016/12/15/americans-name-the-10-most-significant-historic-events-of-their-lifetimes/ (Accessed January 7, 2017).

Delli Carpini, M. X. (2016). The new normal? Campaigns & elections in the contemporary media environment. In D. Lilleker, E. Thorsen, D. Jackson, & A. Veneti (Eds.), *US election analysis 2016: Media, voters and the campaign: Early reflections from leading academics* (p. 20). Poole, England: Centre for the Study of Journalism, Culture and Community.

Easton, D., & Dennis, J. (1965). The child's image of government. *The Annals of the American Academy of Political and Social Science, 361*, 40–57.

Easton, D., & Dennis, J. (1973). The child's image of government. In J. Dennis (Ed.), *Socialization to politics: A reader* (pp. 59–81). New York: Wiley-Blackwell.

Entman, R. M., & Rojecki, A. (2000). *The black image in the white mind: Media and race in America.* Chicago: University of Chicago Press.

Epstein, E. J. (2017). *How America lost its secrets: Edward Snowden, the man and the theft.* New York: Knopf.

Fazekas, Z., & Littvay, L. (2015). The importance of context in the genetic transmission of U.S. party identification. *Political Psychology, 36*, 361–377.

Fiske, J. (1996). *Media matters: Everyday culture and political change.* Minneapolis: University of Minnesota Press.

Fowler, J. H., Loewen, P. J., Settle, J., & Dawes, C. T. (2011). Genes, games, and political participation. In P. K. Hatemi & R. McDermott (Eds.), *Man is by nature a political animal: Evolution, biology, and politics* (pp. 207–223). Chicago: University of Chicago Press.

Gates, H. L., Jr. (2016, September 24). Proving Black history matters. *The New York Times*, A21.

Gerbner, G., & Gross, L. (1976). Living with television: The violence profile. *Journal of Communication, 26*, 173–199.

Gerbner, G., Gross, L., Morgan, M., & Signorielli, N. (1984). Political correlates of television viewing. *Public Opinion Quarterly, 48*, 283–300.

Glynn, C. J., Huge, M., Reineke, J. B., Hardy, B. W., & Shanahan, J. (2007). When Oprah intervenes: Political correlates of daytime talk show viewing. *Journal of Broadcasting & Electronic Media, 51*, 228–244.

Gray, J., Jones, J.P., & Thompson, E. (2009). The state of satire, the satire of state. In J. Gray, J.P. Jones, & E. Thompson (Eds.), *Satire TV: Politics and comedy in the post-network era* (pp. 3–36). New York: New York University Press.

Grush, J.E., McKeough, K.L., & Ahlering, R.F. (1978). Extrapolating laboratory exposure research to actual political elections. *Journal of Personality and Social Psychology, 36,* 257–270.

Guggenheim, L., Kwak, N., & Campbell, S.W. (2011). Nontraditional news negativity: The relationship of entertaining political news use to political cynicism and mistrust. *International Journal of Public Opinion Research, 23,* 287–314.

Haas, E., Christensen, T., & Haas, P.J. (2015). *Projecting politics: Political messages in American films* (2nd ed.). New York: Routledge.

Hardy, B.W. (2012). Cultivation of political attitudes in the new media environment. In M. Morgan, J. Shanahan, & N. Signorielli (Eds.), *Living with television now: Advances in cultivation theory and research* (pp. 101–119). New York: Peter Lang.

Hardy, B.W., Gottfried J.A., Winneg, K.M., & Jamieson, K.H. (2014). Stephen Colbert's civic lesson: How Colbert Super PAC taught viewers about campaign finance. *Mass Communication & Society, 17,* 329–353.

Hart, R.P., & Hartelius, E.J. (2007). The political sins of Jon Stewart. *Critical Studies of Mass Communication, 24,* 263–272.

Hatemi, P.K., & McDermott, R. (Eds.) (2011). *Man is by nature a political animal: Evolution, biology, and politics.* Chicago: University of Chicago Press.

Hively, M.H., & Eveland, W.P., Jr. (2009). Contextual antecedents and political consequences of adolescent political discussion, discussion elaboration, and network diversity. *Political Communication, 26,* 30–47.

Hoffman, L.H., & Thomson, T.L. (2009). The effect of television viewing on adolescents' civic participation: Political efficacy as a mediating mechanism. *Journal of Broadcasting & Electronic Media, 53,* 3–21.

Hoffman, L.H., & Young, D.G. (2011). Satire, punch lines, and the nightly news: Untangling media effects on political participation. *Communication Research Reports, 28,* 159–168.

Holbert, R.L. (2013). Developing a normative approach to political satire: An empirical perspective. *International Journal of Communication, 7,* 305–323.

Ichilov, O. (1990). Introduction. In O. Ichilov (Ed.), *Political socialization, citizenship education, and democracy* (pp. 1–8). New York: Teachers College Press.

Jackson, D.J. (2002). *Entertainment & politics: The influence of pop culture on young adult political socialization.* New York: Peter Lang.

Jennings, M.K., & Niemi, R.G. (1968). The transmission of political values from parent to child. *American Political Science Review, 62,* 169–183.

LaMarre, H.L., Landreville, K.D., & Beam, M.A. (2009). The irony of satire: Political ideology and the motivation to see what you want to see in *The Colbert Report. International Journal of Press/Politics, 14,* 212–231.

LaMarre, H.L., & Walther, W. (2013). Ability matters: Testing the differential effects of political news and late-night political comedy on cognitive responses and the role of ability in micro-level opinion formation. *International Journal of Public Opinion Research, 25,* 303–322.

Landreville, K.D., & LaMarre, H.L. (2013). Examining the intertextuality of fictional political comedy and real-world political news. *Media Psychology, 16*, 347–369.

Larmer, B. (2011, October 30). Where an Internet joke is not just a joke. *The New York Times Magazine*, 34–39.

Lee, H., & Kwak, N. (2014). The affect effect of political satire: Sarcastic humor, negative emotions, and political participation. *Mass Communication and Society, 17*, 307–328.

Lee, N-J., Shah, D.V., & McLeod, J.M. (2013). Processes of political socialization: A communication mediation approach to youth civic engagement. *Communication Research, 40*, 669–697.

Leonhardt, D., & Parlapiano, A. (2015, June 30). A march toward acceptance when civil rights is the topic. *The New York Times*, A3.

Lippmann, W. (1922). *Public opinion*. New York: Free Press.

McDevitt, M. (2006). The partisan child: Developmental provocation as a model of political socialization. *International Journal of Public Opinion Research, 18*, 67–88.

McDevitt, M., & Chaffee, S. (2002). From top-down to trickle-up influence: Revisiting assumptions about the family in political socialization. *Political Communication, 19*, 281–301.

McDevitt, M., & Ostrowski, A. (2009). The adolescent unbound: Unintentional influence of curricula and ideological conflict seeking. *Political Communication, 26*, 11–29.

McLeod, J.M., & Shah, D.V. (2009). Communication and political socialization: Challenges and opportunities for research. *Political Communication, 26*, 1–10.

Meyrowitz, J. (1986). *No sense of place: The impact of electronic media on social behavior*. New York: Oxford University Press.

Meyrowitz, J. (2009). Medium theory: An alternative to the dominant paradigm of media effects. In R.L. Nabi & M.B. Oliver (Eds.), *The Sage handbook of media processes and effects* (pp. 517–530). Thousand Oaks, CA: Sage.

Mohammed, S.N. (2014). "It-getting" in the Colbert nation online forum. *Mass Communication and Society, 17*, 173–194.

Morgan, M., Leggett, S., & Shanahan, J. (1999). Television and family values: Was Dan Quayle right? *Mass Communication and Society, 2*, 47–63.

Morgan, M., Shanahan, J., & Signorielli, N. (2009). Growing up with television: Cultivation processes. In J. Bryant & M.B. Oliver (Eds.), *Media effects: Advances in theory and research* (3rd ed., pp. 34–49). New York: Routledge.

Morgan, M., Shanahan, J., & Signorielli, N. (2012). The stories we tell: Cultivation theory and research. In M. Morgan, J. Shanahan, & N. Signorielli (Eds.), *Living with television now: Advances in cultivation theory and research* (pp. 1–14). New York: Peter Lang.

Morgan, M., Shanahan, J., & Signorielli, N. (2015). Yesterday's new cultivation, tomorrow. *Mass Communication and Society, 18*, 674–699.

Morreale, J. (2009). Jon Stewart and *The Daily Show*: I thought you were going to be funny! In J. Gray, J.P. Jones, & E. Thompson (Eds.), *Satire TV: Politics and comedy in the post- network era* (pp. 104–123). New York: New York University Press.

Morris, J.S., & Baumgartner, J.C. (2008). *The Daily Show* and attitudes toward the news media. In J.C. Baumgartner & J.S. Morris (Eds.), *Laughing matters: Humor and American politics in the media age* (pp. 315–331). New York: Routledge.

Nabi, R.L., Moyer-Gusé, E., & Byrne, S. (2007). All joking aside: A serious investigation into the persuasive effect of funny social issue messages. *Communication Monographs, 74*, 29–54.

Niemi, R.G., & Junn, J. (1998). *Civic education: What makes students learn*. New Haven, CT: Yale University Press.

Norris, P. (2011). *Democratic deficit: Critical citizens revisited*. New York: Cambridge University Press.

Onishi, N. (2015, December 6). In a Nigeria in need of laughs, comedians have crowds roaring. *The New York Times*, 1, 16.

Parker, J. (2015, November 8). Is legitimate satire necessarily directed at the powerful? *The New York Times* (Book Review), 51.

Perloff, R.M. (2015). Mass communication research at the crossroads: Definitional issues and theoretical directions for mass and political communication scholarship in an age of online media. *Mass Communication and Society, 18*, 531–556.

Potter, W.J. (2014). A critical analysis of cultivation theory. *Journal of Communication, 64*, 1015–1036.

Risen, J. (1999). To bomb Sudan plant, or not: A year later, debates rankle. *The New York Times*. Retrieved from www.library.cornell.edu/colldev/mideast/sudbous.htm (Accessed February 10, 2017).

Schudson, M. (2015). *The rise of the right to know: Politics and the culture of transparency, 1945–1975*. Cambridge, MA: Belknap Press of Harvard University Press.

Schudson, M., & Tifft, S.E. (2005). American journalism in historical perspective. In G. Overholser & K.H. Jamieson (Eds.), *The press* (pp. 17–47). New York: Oxford University Press.

Schuman, H., & Corning, A. (2012). Generational memory and the critical period: Evidence for national and world events. *Public Opinion Quarterly, 76*, 1–31.

Schutz, C.E. (1977). *Political humor: From Aristophanes to Sam Ervin*. Rutherford, NJ: Fairleigh Dickinson University Press.

Sears, D.O. (1990). Whither political socialization research? The question of persistence. In O. Ichilov (Ed.), *Political socialization, citizenship education, and democracy* (pp. 69–97). New York: Teachers College Press.

Sears, D.O., & Brown, C. (2013). Childhood and adult political development. In L. Huddy, D.O. Sears, & J.S. Levy (Eds.), *The Oxford handbook of political psychology* (2nd ed., pp. 59–95). New York: Oxford University Press.

Sears, D.O., & Funk, C.L. (1999). Evidence of the long-term persistence of adults' political predispositions. *Journal of Politics, 61*, 1–28.

Settle, J.E., Dawes, C.T., & Fowler, J.H. (2009). The heritability of partisan attachment. *Political Research Quarterly, 62*, 601–613.

Shah, D.V., Cho, J., Eveland, W.P., Jr., & Kwak, N. (2005). Information and expression in a digital age: Modeling Internet effects on civic participation. *Communication Research, 32*, 531–565.

Shah, D.V., McLeod, J.M., & Lee, N-J. (2009). Communication competence as a foundation for civic competence: Processes of socialization into citizenship. *Political Communication, 26*, 102–117.

Shanahan, J., & Morgan, M. (1999). *Television and its viewers: Cultivation theory and research*. New York: Cambridge University Press.

Shulman, H.C., & DeAndrea, D.C. (2014). Predicting success: Revisiting assumptions about family political socialization. *Communication Monographs*, *81*, 386–406.

Taub, A. (2016, October 23). Trump recording narrows national divide on sexual assault. *The New York Times*, 4.

Van den Bulck, J. (2012). International cultivation. In M. Morgan, J. Shanahan, & N. Signorielli (Eds.), *Living with television now: Advances in cultivation theory and research* (pp. 237–260). New York: Peter Lang.

Vidmar, N., & Rokeach, M. (1974). Archie Bunker's bigotry: A study in selective perception and exposure. *Journal of Communication*, *24*, 36–47.

Wexler, B.E., Adwan, S., & Bar-Tal, D. (2013, March 7). Trying to bridge the Mideast divide. *The New York Times* (Letter to the Editor), A22.

Williams, B.W., & Delli Carpini, M.X. (2011). *After broadcast news: Media regimes, democracy, and the new information environment*. New York: Cambridge University Press.

Xenos, M., & Foot, K. (2008). Not your father's Internet: The generation gap in online politics. In W.L. Bennett (Ed.), *Civic life online: Learning how digital media can engage youth* (pp. 51–70). Cambridge, MA: MIT Press.

Yaffa, J. (2012, February 26). The Kremlin's not laughing now. *The New York Times* (Sunday Review), 4.

Young, D.G. (2008a). The privileged role of the late night-joke: Exploring humor's role in disrupting argument scrutiny. *Media Psychology*, *11*, 119–142.

Young, D.G. (2008b). *The Daily Show* as the new journalism: In their own words. In J.C. Baumgartner & J.S. Morris (Eds.), *Laughing matters: Humor and American politics in the media age* (pp. 241–259). New York: Routledge.

Young, D.G., Holbert, R.L., & Jamieson, K.H. (2014). Successful practices for the strategic use of political parody and satire: Lessons from the P6 Symposium and 2012 election campaign. *American Behavioral Scientist*, *58*, 1111–1130.

Young, D.G., & Tisinger, R.M. (2006). Dispelling late-night myths: News consumption among late-night comedy viewers and the predictors of exposure to various late-night shows. *Press/Politics*, *11*, 113–134.

Zukin, C., Keeter, S., Andolina, M., Jenkins, K., & Delli Carpini, M.X. (2006). *A new engagement? Political participation, civic life, and the changing American citizen*. New York: Oxford University Press.

6 Setting and Building the Agenda

Trade has bubbled to the surface from time to time in American politics, famously in 1992, when candidate Ross Perot bemoaned the "giant sucking sound" that, he claimed, would be emitted as the controversial North American Free Trade Agreement vacuumed up American jobs. Since then, global trade deals have been relatively quiescent, dormant, a generally accepted economic fact of life.

Until 2016.

During the campaign, Trump excoriated global trade deals, arguing that the North American Free Trade Agreement (NAFTA) devastated manufacturing. On the left, Bernie Sanders promulgated a similar message, lashing out at trade deals like NAFTA and the Trans-Pacific Partnership (TPP), calling them disastrous, and arguing vociferously that U.S. trade policies benefit corporate America. Their jeremiads resonated with millions of working class Americans, suffering financially and feeling marginalized from elite discussions. Even economic research showed up on the national stage when an MIT study that showed Chinese trade had wiped out nearly one million U.S. manufacturing jobs from 1999 to 2011 received national publicity (Autor, Dorn, & Hanson, 2016). News coverage radiated out, noting "trade deals promised prosperity but delivered anxiety" (e.g., Goodman, 2016, p. A1). Influential media and political commentators discussed the issue. By the time of the Republican and Democratic conventions in the summer of 2016, trade was so toxic that the latest trade deal, the Trans-Pacific Partnership negotiated by a liberal Democratic president ostensibly sympathetic with labor interests, was viewed as a non-starter by both parties. In contrast to both parties' traditional embrace of free trade, neither party endorsed the TPP.

Despite the fact that the pros and cons of trade are not new, the issue became a hot topic of coverage in 2016, when it caught fire after Trump and Sanders railed against trade, capturing the attention of working class Whites understandably frustrated by job loss and government indifference to their plight. As candidates discussed it, voters reacted, and media discussed the ins and outs of the trade conundrum, free trade became a salient issue in the national election conversation, an example of how media set the agenda or influence the issues on the cusp of public debate.

Trade is complex. Free trade is a canon of economic thought; both liberal and conservative economists embrace the values of free trade. Trade brings winners and losers. For all the hue and cry about NAFTA, economists see a more nuanced picture, arguing it raised incomes in the U.S., saving the jobs of many American autoworkers, while also shedding thousands of manufacturing jobs (Irwin, 2016a; Porter, 2016). Trade is not the only, nor necessarily the most important, reason for the decline in American manufacturing jobs in the industrial heartlands. Other causes are automation and companies moving jobs to other parts of the country to save costs. Trade deals are inordinately complex, exerting a multitude of positive effects on U.S. industries, like computers and information technology, lowering prices, and creating jobs, but also eliminating employment in the manufacturing sector, an important area of the economy, yet one that today accounts for only 8.5 percent of jobs (Irwin, 2016b). Trade deals are an easy, symbolically rich, understandable target of worker—and populist—angst (see Chapter 7). They captured the public agenda and were frequently framed in negative terms, as more about corporate greed than American jobs, even though this is one of many ways of looking at the problem.

Agenda-setting and framing, the foundation of the next two chapters, are core concepts in political communication and election research. This chapter on agenda-setting is divided into six sections, reflecting the voluminous research on this topic. The first and second sections define agenda-setting and discuss social scientific research that explores its impact. The third portion examines consequences of agenda-setting, viewed through the lens of an intriguing concept called priming. In the fourth section, I examine electoral implications of agenda-setting and priming. The fifth and sixth sections examine the building of policy agendas and implications for a social media age. As you read this, keep in mind that agenda-setting has traditionally referred to the press, the news media, or conventional journalism. Because this is the focus of research, and still a mainstay of the concept, discussions will revolve around news media effects. However, as examined later in the chapter, agendas are set and built online and by social media, intersecting with traditional media in a number of ways.

WHAT WE KNOW ABOUT AGENDA-SETTING

A linchpin of agenda-setting is the term, agenda. An **agenda** is defined as an issue or event that is perceived at a particular point in time as high in social or political importance (Rogers & Dearing, 1988). Agendas are important. Groups that control a nation's agenda own the keys to the corridors of power. As the political scientist E. E. Schattschneider (1960) famously said, "the definition of the alternatives is the supreme instrument of power" (p. 68). There are a multitude of problems that afflict individuals and social systems, and governments cannot work on them all at once. Democratic societies must decide which problems to shelve, which ones to tackle, and how to formulate policies to address the problems they have chosen. "Every social system must have an agenda if it is to prioritize the problems facing it, so that it can decide where to start work. Such prioritization is necessary for a community and for a society," James W. Dearing and Everett M. Rogers (1996) explained (p. 1).

This is where the media come into the picture, as Walter Lippmann noted presciently in 1922. Lippmann was among the first to call attention to the power of the press to create pictures in people's minds. He recognized that the world had changed with the growth of cities, the advent of mass media, and the exploitation of government information control that could shape political sentiments. He emphasized that citizens could only deal with a secondhand political reality conveyed by media (redolent of Plato's Allegory of the Cave, where the shadows projected on a wall constituted prisoners' only reality). Lipmann argued that the burgeoning news media serve as our window on the distant political world, shaping political beliefs.

Some years later, during the television news era, political commentators offered even stronger pronouncements about media effects. Journalist Theodore White observed that "the power of the press in America is a primordial one. It sets the agenda of public discussion . . . It determines what people will talk and think about" (White, 1973, p. 327). Political scientist Bernard Cohen (1963) noted that

> the press is significantly more than a purveyor of information and opinion. It may not be successful much of the time in telling people *what to think*, but it is stunningly successful in telling its readers *what to think about*.
>
> (p. 13, italics added)

Cohen's pithy statement is the most famous description of agenda-setting in the academic literature. Just about every major article or book on the subject quotes it. His observation highlighted the subtle but powerful effects that media could exert on public opinion. It also directed attention away from the popular belief that political communication swayed attitudes and voting behavior. Instead, it emphasized that media exerted effects in another arena, one traditionally overlooked: the simple, but politically consequential, perception of what constitutes society's most important problems. By simply emphasizing certain problems rather than others, the media can significantly influence public opinion, and, as we will see, policy.

Agenda-setting is defined as "a process through which the mass media communicate the relative importance of various issues and events to the public" (Rogers & Dearing, 1988, p. 555). By allocating space or time to certain issues, the news media increase their **salience** or perceived importance. As David H. Weaver (1984) notes, "Concentration by the media over time on relatively few issues leads to the public perceiving these issues as more salient or more important than other issues" (p. 682). Historically, by shining the beam of their searchlight on social inequities, the press has done considerable good, exposing political corruption, spotlighting fraudulent business practices, and revealing abuses that cause physical harm (see Box 6.1).

Not every political media effect is agenda-setting. News can impart information, increase knowledge, intensify opposition to candidates, and elicit positive affect without influencing the political agenda. Agenda-setting refers specifically to the tendency of mediated news to elevate the importance people attribute to a political issue. As we will see, agenda-setting sheds light on a host of intriguing and consequential events in the world of politics. It offers an explanation—one among many—of how a little-known governor from Arkansas named Bill Clinton was elected president in 1992—and why his wife did not capture the White House in 2016. It explains how climate change ascended in the policy hierarchy, capturing policymakers' attention and perhaps global action. And, turning the concept on its head, it suggests why few Americans thought about or worried about terrorism until 9/11.

But before we can say with certainty that these effects are attributable to agenda-setting, there must be evidence that the media actually set the agenda. You may say that it is obvious that the media set the agenda, based on these examples or your own intuitions. But how do you know the examples accurately represent the political universe or your intuitions are correct? We turn to social science to determine the truth of hunches and assumptions.

BOX 6.1 MUCKRAKING AS AGENDA-SETTING

A reporter did not popularize the classic image of the investigative journalist. Neither did an editor. Instead, President Theodore Roosevelt coined the term, describing investigative writers as men with the "muck-rake." Intriguingly, Roosevelt used the term in a pejorative manner, criticizing journalists for focusing on negative rather than lofty aspects of society. However, reporters came to view the term "muckraker" positively, emphasizing the ways that journalistic investigations could call attention to social problems in need of improvement.

Continued

In the early 1900s, investigative journalists and writers were a new and courageous breed, uncovering political corruption and business abuse for the new mass medium of their era, magazines like *McClure's*. Lincoln Steffens exposed urban political corruption in a series called "The Shame of the Cities." Ida Tarbell, a crusading female journalist, revealed how Standard Oil bullied rival businesses and railroad companies that threatened their interests. Ida B. Wells, a stunningly courageous African American reporter, documented the decades-long horrors of lynchings in the South. These and other exposés called attention to social problems festering under the polite surface of American society, creating an agenda for reform.

By the late 20th century, when Bob Woodward and Carl Bernstein broke the Watergate story, investigative reporting had become accepted—indeed revered—in American journalism. But few were prepared for the consequences unleashed in 1972 when these two rookie *Washington Post* reporters painstakingly revealed the break-in at the Democratic National Committee Headquarters at the Watergate Hotel in Washington, D.C., connected the Watergate burglary to the Nixon White House, showed how Nixon campaign funds had been involved in the break-in, and documented that political sabotage had played a key role in Nixon's reelection campaign. The stories set in motion a series of incredible developments that led to a trial of the Watergate burglars, televised hearings by a Senate committee, evidence of a White House cover-up, a House impeachment vote, and Nixon's resignation. Contrary to popular mythology, *The Washington Post* investigations did not cause Nixon to resign. Few other media picked up on the Watergate story in 1972, either because it seemed too unbelievable or too risky to cover. But the drip-drip of *Post* coverage helped build the agenda that led inexorably to Nixon's resignation.

Investigative journalists are a rare breed, motivated by a combination of moral zeal (Ettema & Glaser, 1998) and raw ambition. Their articles spotlight social inequities and business abuses, helping to set the agenda, subsequently sparking public discussion and, in some cases, prodding government to correct the problem. The annual Pulitzer Prize in Investigative Journalism recognizes journalistic achievements. For example:

● Sarah Ryley was awarded a 2017 Pulitzer Prize for hard-hitting stories in *The New York Daily News* and *ProPublica* that dramatically documented how the New York City police evict hundreds of poor people from their homes based on an obscure legal procedure.

- In 2016, two reporters from *The Tampa Bay Times* and a journalist from *The Sarasota Herald-Tribune* won a collaborative Pulitzer for revealing a pattern of violence and neglect in Florida's mental hospitals that was the fault of callous state officials.

- *New York Times* reporter Eric Lipton won the 2015 Pulitzer Prize for exposing insidious corporate lobbying inside the offices of state attorneys general across America.

- In 2012, Sara Ganim and *The Harrisburg Patriot-News* staff won a Pulitzer Prize for pathbreaking coverage of the Penn State child sexual abuse scandal involving former football coach Jerry Sandusky.

- In 2008, *The Chicago Tribune* staff was awarded the Pulitzer for exposing inadequate, shoddy government regulation of toys and car seats, leading to a major recall of the products and action by Congress.

- *The Boston Globe* won the Pulitzer Prize in 2003 for its hard-hitting investigative coverage of sexual abuse by Roman Catholic priests (fictionalized in the 2016 Oscar-winning Best Picture, *Spotlight*). The series galvanized public opinion, led to increased legal scrutiny of abusive priests, and produced institutional changes in church practices.

- In 1987, John Woestendiek of *The Philadelphia Inquirer* received a Pulitzer for prison beat reporting that proved that a man convicted of murder was innocent of the crime.

It is important to note that Pulitzer Prize–winning investigative reporting does not always or inevitably lead to policy changes spurred by the wrongdoing reporters have uncovered. One of Eric Lipton's prize-winning stories persuasively documented how Oklahoma Attorney General Scott Pruitt shamelessly colluded with oil companies who had lobbied on his behalf. Two years after the stories ran, Trump nominated Pruitt to head the Environmental Protection Agency and the Senate confirmed his choice. Not surprisingly, though perhaps disappointingly, political factors play an important part in determining whether and when investigative stories lead to public policy changes. This issue is taken up later in the chapter.

Do the Data Support Agenda-Setting?

To demonstrate that media set the agenda, researchers need to do three things. First, they must show that there is a relationship between the media agenda—news stories appearing prominently in the media—and the public agenda, the issues people perceive to be the most important in the community or nation. Second, they must show that the operates for different issues and in different contexts. Third, researchers need to establish that the media *cause* changes in citizens' ranking of most important problems. To make the case for agenda-setting, researchers conduct content analyses, surveys, and experiments.

The first study—the one that is frequently cited even today, more than 40 years after its publication—was conducted by Maxwell E. McCombs and Donald L. Shaw, then young professors of journalism at the University of North Carolina. McCombs and Shaw explored the perceptions of undecided voters in Chapel Hill, North Carolina during the 1968 election. The researchers asked voters to indicate the issues that most concerned them, the ones that they believed "government *should* concentrate on doing something about." The researchers' content analyzed news stories, editorials, and broadcast segments in the media available to Chapel Hill residents, looking to see which issues the news emphasized. McCombs and Shaw (1972) discovered a near-perfect correlation between the ranking of issues on the media agenda, as verified by the content analysis, and citizens' issue rankings on questionnaires. The more the media played up an issue, the more important the issue was to voters.

Talk about a study that set the agenda for the field! Research testing the agenda-setting hypothesis followed, like an avalanche, in the wake of McCombs and Shaw's suggestive evidence of media effects. Empirical research substantiated the researchers' findings.

Numerous studies conducted at a single point in time reported a significant correlation between the media and public agendas. Longitudinal research, conducted over different time points, also revealed a strong relationship between the media agenda and public opinion. For example, Winter and Eyal reported back in 1981 that there was a strong relationship between news coverage of civil rights and the percentage of Americans who named civil rights as the most important problem facing the U.S. over a 23-year period.

Agenda-setting effects have been emerged for numerous issues, including energy, drugs, crime, and foreign affairs, What is more, effects have been obtained across the world, in studies conducted in Argentina, Britain, Germany, and Spain (McCombs, 2014). More than 425 studies of agenda-setting have been conducted. The hypothesis holds up strongly in the bulk of the research, as documented by a statistical analysis of 90 empirical studies (Wanta & Ghanem, 2007).

Evidence for Causation

So far the evidence shows that there is a strong relationship between the media and public agendas. But it does not conclusively demonstrate that the media exert a *causal* impact on the public agenda. As discussed in Chapter 3, one way to establish causation is to conduct experimental research. Shanto Iyengar and Donald R. Kinder (1987, 2010) employed just this strategy, publishing a series of now classic experiments that demonstrated the impact that television news exerted on perceptions of the most important problems facing the nation.

In one key study, the researchers asked their participants to evaluate the importance of a series of national problems. Over the course of a week, individuals viewed television newscasts that had been edited so they focused heavily on one particular problem. One group watched a week's worth of news that emphasized nuclear arms control. Another group viewed news focusing on civil rights, and a third saw news on unemployment. Participants subsequently indicated their beliefs about the importance of national problems.

As agenda-setting predicted, individuals perceived the targeted problem to be more important after viewing the newscasts than prior to viewing the news (see Table 6.1). The results made it abundantly clear that sustained exposure to the news can exert a causal impact on beliefs about the importance of national problems.

Does this mean that the media's choice of top items influences the priorities of each and every newspaper reader, blog scrutinizer, or viewer of television news? No, it does not.

Consider evidence that physical exercise is associated with health and well-being. This indicates that the more you exercise, the better your overall health. However, this does not mean that physical exertion will have an identical effect on the heart rate of each person who exercises frequently each week. Circumstances matter. Amount and type of exercise, time spent exercising, the genetic makeup of the individual, the person's overall health, and the juncture in the individual's life when he or she began exercising influence the strength of the relationship. It is the same with agenda-setting. "Agenda-setting does not operate *everywhere*, on *everyone*, and *always*" Rogers and Dearing explain (1988, p. 569).

Table 6.1 Experimental evidence for agenda-setting.

	Importance rating of problem		
	Pre-experiment	Post-experimental change	
Arms control	76	82	6
Civil rights	64	69	5
Unemployment	75	82	7

(From Iyengar & Kinder, 2010)

You can think of issues the media could cover until the cows come home that would fail to influence the public agenda. Even if the media provided round-the-clock coverage of prejudice against left-handed individuals, it is unlikely this would register as a problem with the public (Iyengar & Kinder, 2010). News coverage during wartime that tried to convince the public that the nation faced no foreign threat would be doomed to failure. When the media direct attention to an "implausible problem," one that flies in the face of common sense, their efforts are not likely to bear fruit (Iyengar & Kinder, 2010). What's more, when news describes a problem that seems unbelievable to the public, contradicting their political beliefs or long-held expectations, it will not break through their prototypes. For example, despite scrupulous *Washington Post* stories on Watergate in 1972 (and coverage on network news), the issue did not resonate with voters during the 1972 Nixon-McGovern election. Disbelieving what turned out to be true—high-level political operatives engaged in political sabotage against their opponents in a gambit linked to the White House—few voters regarded honesty in government as a major campaign issue (Lang & Lang, 1983; McLeod, Becker, & Byrnes, 1974).

Of course, there are always exceptions to principles of political communication effects. In general, across many situations, there is convincing evidence that media set the agenda. But *how* does it work psychologically? How do media agenda penetrate and influence viewers' minds? A first explanation emphasizes accessibility of information. A great deal of media coverage of an issue (say, terrorism) can *access* the issue, or bring it quickly to mind. When people are considering problems facing the country, the ones media frequently cover spring initially to mind. In addition, media coverage can cue a *heuristic* or decision-making rule (Pingree & Stoycheff, 2013; Pingree, Quenette, Tchernev, & Dickinson, 2013). I may observe that news has focused a lot on the national debt, recognize that journalists know more about politics than I do, and reason that if they think it's an important problem, it probably is. Alternatively, if I am personally concerned about an issue, like opioid dependence, I may begin to read lot of the news stories on my news feed and conclude, based on processing facts in the stories, that this is a pretty serious problem facing the country as a whole (Bulkow, Urban, & Schweiger, 2013). The first explanation of agenda-setting emphasizes top-of-the-head or short-circuited processing, while the second focuses on systematic processing of the media agenda. The first process is more likely to hold when we are not particularly concerned about an issue, while the second operates when the issue affects us personally or symbolically.

Agenda-Setting Wrinkles: Power of Context

After reading about agenda-setting, you might assume the media just set the agenda and suggest what the most important issues are, period. It does not work this way. Scientific research emphasizes that effects of media do not occur in a vacuum, but, as Klapper emphasized more than a half century ago, effects depend on the nature of the individual and social forces. When media effects depend on other factors, we emphasize that these factors **moderate** or help determine when media are influential and when they are less important. This is actually quite interesting, because it pinpoints the conditions under which media are effective and when they are not, illuminating agenda-setting effects. Here are some of the key conditions that moderate agenda-setting effects. They are diverse, interesting, and tell us lots about issues in the news today.

News Play

Stories that lead off network newscasts have a stronger influence on public perceptions than more ordinary stories (Iyengar & Kinder, 2010). Lead stories are influential partly because viewers assume network news is credible, inducing them to accept journalists' judgments that the first or second story is the most important. Lead stories also appear early—before people leave the room to get something to eat or text a friend. Transplanting these findings to contemporary media, one presumes that the stories that top the list of trending stories on a social media page would exert stronger agenda-setting effects than less prominent stories.

Nature of the Issue

Agenda-setting depends on the particular issue or event (Rogers & Dearing, 1988). A rapid-onset issue involves critical, cataclysmic events like terrorism, which occur immediately. These leap instantly or quickly to the top of the nation's agenda, as occurred in the wake of terrorist attacks on Paris and San Bernardino, California, in 2015 (Martin & Sussman, 2015). Slow-onset issues have a gradual, less immediate trajectory, and these topics, such as climate change, can take longer to reach the agenda, because the problem is harder to visualize, effects are not immediate, and coverage is spottier. This is interesting because, according to some climate change experts, it took far too long for the media to place it at the apex of the public agenda. This may have stemmed from foot-dragging by public officials or widely publicized (and politicized) doubts that climate change was for real, when, as the 2015 international climate accord emphasized, it is a pressing global crisis.

A related issue is obtrusiveness, or the extent of direct experience people have with the issue, the degree to which it impinges directly on their personal lives. On the one hand, the less direct experience individuals have with an issue, the more they will depend on news and come to accept the media agenda (Zucker, 1978; Mutz, 1998). When the issue is far off, does not impinge directly on us and is unobtrusive; the media are the ones that bring the matter to us and shape our thinking.

The other side of the coin is when issues are obtrusive, impinging on us directly. In these cases, we do not need the media to tell us the topic is important. The media might have less agenda-setting impact for obtrusive issues, like unemployment, when you are out of a job, or a trade deal that bears directly on the livelihood of manufacturing workers. Unemployment would already be on your mind, and you aren't likely to be more con-vinced by reading about the plight of displaced workers from a different region of the country. On the other hand, people who are unemployed may tune in to coverage of the jobless rate, think a lot about it, relate the coverage to their own life, and end up feeling all the more strongly and deeply that the problem affects the country as well.

There are not simple answers to these questions. Some people might be more affected by issue obtrusiveness than others, as a function of their need for political orientation and uncertainty (Kim, 2014; Matthes, 2006; McCombs & Reynolds, 2009). Moderating effects of issue obtrusiveness also depend on the degree to which people see a similarity between their own obtrusive problem (say, unemployment) and the people shown strug-gling with joblessness in media portrayals.

Partisan Media

This is a new twist on classical agenda-setting. In the very old days, the mainstream media all focused on many of the same issues. This has changed. Nowadays, in an era of partisan media, Fox News will focus on issues that appeal to conservatives. Working in concert with Republican politicians some years back, Fox sought to set a politicized agenda on issues such as the "birther" question, raised ceaselessly by Donald Trump; the network suggested (incorrectly) that Obama had not been born in the U.S., while also pushing other issues, like Hillary Clinton's role in the 2012 terrorist attack on the U.S. diplomatic compound in Benghazi, Libya, which killed four Americans (Corasaniti, 2016). MSNBC, for its part, tilts toward liberals' concerns. The same dynamic plays out in websites, blogs, and social media.

Back in 2004, when the Iraq war and terrorism were major issues, partisan cable outlets covered the issues differently. Research indicates the agenda-setting effects were consequential. Conservative media outlets—Fox News and like-minded radio shows—emphasized the evils of terrorism, while liberal outlets like MSNBC gave more attention to problems in how the Bush administration conducted the Iraq War. Thus, conservative Republicans who relied on conservative media were more likely than others to believe that terrorism was the number one problem facing the U.S. But individuals who used liberal media were less inclined to view terrorism as the most important problem (Stroud, 2011; see also Johnson & Wanta, 1995). Thus, in an era of fragmented media, news can strengthen beliefs people already hold about which issues are most important.

Partisan agenda-setting can be a good thing if it allows for a variety of different agendas to take hold, reducing the ability of a handful of media outlets to set a homogeneous agenda. Diverse viewpoints celebrate the spirit of democracy. Where partisan agenda-setting becomes problematic is when it serves, as research suggests, to merely reinforce what people already believe, whereby media become echo chambers mirroring and strengthening perceptions of important issues rather than exposing individuals to different political agendas. Ironically, the old-style broadcast media, so lamented by scholars as fostering a single-minded, even hegemonic view, had a salutary feature. It offered a common agenda on which citizens could draw, strengthening communal bonds and national linkages which shore up commitment to a common heritage. But in an era of niche media, full of partisan websites, if "like-minded media use encourages Republicans and Democrats to perceive different issues as important, it may become difficult to bring citizens together to solve the nation's problems" (Stroud, 2013, p. 15).

CONSEQUENCES OF AGENDA-SETTING: THE POWER OF PRIMING

What difference does it make if the media set the agenda? True, the effect is interesting because it demonstrates a subtle and pervasive media influence. However, agenda-setting takes on more importance if it can be shown that it affects other aspects of the political system, such as voting behavior and policymaking. In their theoretical account of news impact, Iyengar and Kinder (2010) articulated an explanation of how agenda-setting can influence voting behavior. It is a five-step process that begins with what people cannot do.

First, individuals can't pay close attention to all or even most of what happens in the political world. "To do so would breed paralysis," the scholars noted (Iyengar & Kinder, 2010, p. 64). Second, rather than carefully analyzing all issues, people rely on the most accessible information, or stuff that comes immediately to mind. Thus, when evaluating the president, Americans do not draw on everything they know about the chief executive's policies, ideological positions, personal traits, achievements, and political mishaps. Instead, people call on a small sample of their knowledge—a snapshot that comes immediately to mind, or is accessible, at the time they must decide how to cast their vote.

Third, the media powerfully determine which issues come to mind. Problems that receive a great deal of news coverage are the ones people invariably mention when asked to name the most important problems facing the country. This, of course, is agenda-setting. Fourth, once the media set the agenda, they can **prime** voters. "By calling attention to some matters while ignoring others," Iyengar and Kinder observe, "television news influences the standards by which governments, presidents, policies, and candidates for public office are judged" (2010, p. 63). Fifth, priming can influence the way people cast their votes.

Priming is a psychological concept that describes the way a prior stimulus influences reactions to a subsequent message. It stipulates that concepts are connected to related ideas in memory by what are called associative pathways. When one idea is piqued or aroused by a message, it activates related concepts, producing a chain reaction.

Political communication research calls on this concept, suggesting that the media agenda prime other realms of political thought. **Priming** specifically refers to the impact of the media agenda on the criteria voters employ to evaluate candidates for public office.

In theory, it works this way: The issues that the media happen to be covering at a particular time are communicated to voters. Voters—some more than others—then decide these are the most important issues facing the country. With these issues at the top of their political mind-sets, people call on these issues and decide to evaluate the president or presidential candidates based on their performance in handling these particular problems. Schematically, in its most basic form, the model looks like this:

Media agenda → Voters' agenda → Priming → Voting

Importantly, there are a variety of factors that determine whether priming leads to voting in a particular election, including the individual's party affiliation. The model offers a pure, simple illustration of the hypothesized pathways.

Researchers have tested priming in a number of studies. In their research, Iyengar and Kinder randomly assigned research participants to one of three experimental treatments. Over a week's time, one group of individuals watched newscasts that focused on unemployment. A second group viewed news that emphasized arms control. In a third condition, individuals watched newscasts with a strong focus on civil rights. According to priming, participants who viewed stories on a particular issue should accord more weight to the president's performance on the targeted issue when assessing the chief executive's overall performance. This is indeed what happened. Individuals who viewed unemployment stories gave more weight to the president's performance on unemployment after watching the news than they did before. Similarly, participants who viewed news emphasizing arms control and civil rights placed more weight on these issues when assessing the president's performance.

Other studies, including more real-world investigations, have also supported and enhanced knowledge of priming (Domke, 2001; Kim, 2005; Krosnick & Kinder, 1990; McGraw & Ling, 2003; Moy, Xenos, & Hess, 2005; Pan & Kosicki, 1997; Valentino,

1999). Like agenda-setting, media priming has emerged in contexts outside the U.S., for example in Israel, Switzerland, and South Korea (Balmas & Sheafer, 2010; Sheafer, 2007; Kühne, Schemer, Matthes, & Wirth, 2011; Kim, Han, & Scheule, 2010). Clearly, the media can exert strong effects on political agendas and priming. Pointing to research evidence for priming, some scholars argue that the media have a tremendous capacity to influence political thought. Iyengar and Kinder speak of its "insidious" effect.

Priming Revisited

Are citizens hapless victims, manipulated by media marionettes? Do journalists, talk show hosts, and activist bloggers implant the criteria people use to select their nation's leaders? Some scholars have raised concerns about media power. By covering an issue a great deal, the media make the issue more accessible to voters. Almost without thinking, voters call up issues—and political standards—acquired from casual exposure to political communications. Does this mean media exert a primordial impact on political cognitions?

Other researchers have questioned this notion (Althaus & Kim, 2006; Eveland & Seo, 2007). They have suggested that the media can temporarily access an issue or place it at the forefront of consciousness. However, this still may not cause voters to alter the criteria they employ to evaluate a political leader, particularly if they have strong attitudes about the candidate or election. Accessibility may be a necessary, but not sufficient, condition for priming to operate. Media coverage can influence subsequent evaluations if the news springs to voters' minds, but only if they regard the issue as applicable or relevant to the judgment they have been asked to make (Althaus & Kim, 2006; Roskos-Ewoldsen et al., 2009; see also Price & Tewksbury, 1997). Just because media heavily cover an issue does not mean the issue will exert a priming effect. Voters appear to be less susceptible to conventional media manipulation than critics fear (Miller & Krosnick, 2000). However, like-minded media posts that prime agendas voters already believe to be important might strengthen voting intentions, although we don't know how pervasive these effects actually are.

ELECTORAL IMPLICATIONS

Agenda-setting and priming take on particular importance in elections. By focusing attention on certain political issues, rather than others, media can access, prime, and influence the weight voters attach to these topics when casting their vote.

Evidence from the 1992 election showed how candidates harnessed agenda-setting and priming to their advantage. With the nation's economy sagging and middle-class families feeling the brunt of a recession, voters viewed economic issues and unemployment as the nation's top problems. Democratic consultant James Carville famously brandished a sign, "The Economy, Stupid" in Clinton's headquarters in Little Rock, Arkansas, to underscore the point, lest anyone forget. His blunt statement became the mantra of Clinton's campaign. Clinton reinforced this message, building his agenda around the economy, with one of his ads asking voters to recall how the incumbent president, George H. W. Bush, had promised in 1988 that they would be better off four years from now. Reminding voters that family health care costs had risen nearly $2,000 in four years, the announcer asked, "Well, it's four years later. How're you doing?"

Clinton's ads helped set an economic agenda. They primed voters by suggesting that a candidate's ability to improve the economy was the most important factor to consider when deciding who to vote for. Voters with high exposure to advertising were more likely than those with low exposure to base their vote decision at least in part on the economy. They were also more inclined to believe that Clinton possessed the ability to improve the economy (West, 2010). This does not prove that ads (or news coverage of ads) caused the apparent priming effect. Other scenarios are also possible, such as that those who based their vote on the economy and thought Clinton had the right economic stuff gravitated more to political ads. It is also possible, and perhaps more likely, that ads strengthened a growing media-instigated, poll-reinforced perception that the economy was an important factor to consider in the vote, and that Clinton was a better steward than his Republican opponent.

Sixteen years later, in 2008, candidates, media, and voters again converged on the economy in the wake of the financial crisis, the collapse of a major securities company, and the largest single-day drop in the Dow Jones Industrial average since September 11, 2001. Most voters regarded the economy as the most important issue facing the country and cited it as the key factor influencing their vote decision. With the agenda set, the stage was set for priming. The Democrats seized the opportunity, recognizing that the public blamed the party in power (the Republicans) for economic woes and typically regard Democrats as more capable than Republicans of resolving economic problems (Kinder, 2003). Barack Obama sought to prime economic issues, encouraging voters to regard a candidate's performance in the economic sphere as a key factor in their voting choice.

Obama argued that his policies would do more than John McCain's to restore economic solvency. Criticizing McCain for stating that "the fundamentals of the economy are sound," when obviously they weren't, Obama contended that his opponent was ill-suited to managing America's financial problems. Obama's strategy seems to have worked. Voters expressed greater confidence in his ability to make the right decisions on the economy (Toner & Nagourney, 2008). Sixty percent of voters said the economy was the most important issue facing the country, and most of them voted for Obama (Calmes & Thee, 2008).

Agenda-Setting and Priming in 2016

Both agenda-setting and priming factors played key roles in the 2016 election. Although we can't be sure exactly what the influences were, as research is just beginning to pinpoint their effects, one can speculate about their influences, based on theory and the empirical literature.

On the eve of the Republican primaries in 2016, news of terrorism sadly intervened, exerting apparent agenda-setting and priming effects. Savage terrorist attacks in Paris and San Bernardino, California in late 2015 put Americans on edge, evoking more worries about terrorism than at any time since the weeks following 9/11. Television news, online news sites, and social media posts covered the aftermath and victims of Paris and San Bernardino, leaving a residual of emotional and cognitive effects. A December 2015 New York Times/CBS News poll revealed that nearly 1 in 5 Americans viewed terrorism as the most important problem facing the nation, compared to just 4 percent in early November (Martin & Sussman, 2015). Eighty-three percent of voters said they viewed a major terrorist attack in the U.S. in the near future as somewhat or very likely (Kakutani, 2016), The new media-set agenda redounded with political implications; polls showed that more than 4 in 10 Republican primary voters regarded strong leadership as the most important quality in a presidential candidate. These voters strongly favored Trump, who said he would "bomb the shit" out of ISIS's oil operations, his strong verbal statements and demeanor giving them confidence that he could handle terrorism (Martin & Sussman, 2016).

One of the puzzles in suggestive findings like these—they are poll results that only suggest a causal impact of media on agenda-setting and priming—is that they don't explain the dynamics of probable media influences. Was it news coverage, candidate pronouncements on terrorism, primeval citizen concerns instigated by the horror of recent events, or voters' complex constructions based on what they saw and heard? Agenda-setting is silent on how this occurs, an issue that must be unraveled through systematic research.

From a political strategy perspective, what matters is candidates' ability to control and prime their preferred agenda, a goal that is often thwarted by agendas favored by other politicians, news media, and social media. When Sanders and Trump spoke in 2015 of a dysfunctional political system rigged by the powers that be—with Sanders arguing from a liberal-progressive perspective and Trump from a populist vantage point—their agendas caught fire. The media wrapped this around the "angry voter" narrative

(Leland, 2016), because the "angry at the political system" storyline was filled with drama (which journalists like) and tapped into a bona fide phenomenon.

During the general election campaign, Clinton and Trump sought to prime issues they thought would work to their advantage. One fall election poll showed a majority of voters perceived Clinton had the temperament for the presidency and would do a better job handling foreign policy, while believing Trump could bring about real change and was better at handling the economy (Healy & Sussman, 2016). Clinton's speeches that criticized Trump's temperament and emphasized her "steady" (a word highlighted in one of her ads) foreign policy leadership could have primed these traits, accessing them as voters contemplated which factors to weigh in voting for the president. Trump, for his part, emphasized immigration and terrorism as major problems, and a majority of voters who thought these were the most important issues supported him (Peters, Thee-Brenan, & Sussman, 2016). Trump's immigration-focused tweets (Oates, 2016) could have primed this issue for sympathetic and undecided voters, nudging them into perceiving that immigration—and a candidate's forceful stand on the issue—were important criteria in judging the presidential candidates.

The ubiquitous news coverage of Clinton's email scandal (see Chapter 10) probably primed this issue for some undecided voters. With 35 percent of stories covering Clinton's emails from June 2016 through Election Day (Vavreck, 2016), the coverage might have convinced voters who had doubts about Clinton's veracity that a candidate's use of private email for occasionally classified purposes represented a red-flag problem, a reasonable standard to which a potential president should he held. The email story may have exerted a double whammy of priming effects for late-deciding voters, influenced by FBI Director James Comey's revelation in late October that his agency was examining new emails that were pertinent to Clinton's use of a private email server. The fact that the FBI was reopening the case could have primed the issue, convincing some voters that the email scandal was an all-the-more important criteria in casting their vote. Although Comey recanted about a week later, saying he had found no new incriminating evidence, his decision—praised by those who liked his transparency, criticized by others who felt his intervention into an election was entirely inappropriate—may not have attenuated the priming effects of earlier email stories. This was the view propounded by frustrated Clinton supporters after the election, and it remains interesting, but empirically unproven as yet.

POLITICAL AGENDA-BUILDING

Agenda-setting takes us only so far. Evidence that media set the agenda does not tell us what happens once the agenda is set. It does not explain the ways news intersects with policymaking and whether news influences policy, legislation, or laws to address problems media highlight. To appreciate these issues, we need to focus on the broader, macro issue of agenda-building, or how media work within the white-hot corridors of power politics, where agendas are an instrument of power, influence, and intrigue. Several concepts underlie the subsequent discussion. **Agenda-building** is defined as "a process through which the policy agendas of political elites are influenced by a variety of factors, including media agendas and public agendas" (Rogers & Dearing, 1988, p. 555). The **public agenda** consists of the issues the general public views as most important at a particular time. The **policy agenda** refers to the issues that top the priority lists of political leaders.

The Big Picture

National leaders face a dizzying array of problems. They cannot focus their resources on all issues simultaneously. They must select among issues, concentrating energies on certain social problems and letting others fall by the wayside. Issues compete for attention, and their proponents—well-heeled lobbyists, activists, and passionate ideologues—must persuade policymakers to devote time and money to their issue rather than someone else's. As David Protess and his colleagues (1991) observed:

> It is no easy matter for social problems to get on policymakers' agendas and produce corrective actions. The number of problems that policymakers might address is virtually infinite . . . Policymakers must decide which problems will receive priority attention.
>
> (pp. 238–239)

Deciding that something is a problem is itself an important—and political—act. If an issue is not defined as a problem by the media or political elites, it cannot move through the series of stages necessary for a problem to be contemplated, considered, discussed, and ameliorated. There are countless national problems, but a policymaker's agenda can only accommodate a handful at a given time. There is not a one-to-one relationship between the importance or breadth of the problem and its emergence on the media agenda. Epic tragedies like the extermination of Jews during World War II (Lipstadt, 1986), institutional racism during the early 20th century, and the spread of AIDS (Kinsella, 1988) were not covered because they raised uncomfortable truths that threatened elites' belief systems and did not mesh with conventional journalistic news-gathering routines.

Some media investigations have helped build agendas that have reached policymakers' attention. These include Vietnam in the 1960s, where the media gradually placed the issue of U.S. military deaths in Vietnam on the front burner (see Hallin, 1986);

Watergate, where media coverage of increasingly jaw-dropping corruption by the Nixon White House inflamed public opinion and influenced policymakers, causing Nixon to resign from office (Lang & Lang, 1983); the spread of crack cocaine in the 1980s; the Monica Lewinsky scandal that engulfed Bill Clinton's presidency, where media coverage coupled with a special prosecutor's investigation led to the impeachment of President Clinton, but not his ouster from office; terrorism after 9/11; and government overreach in widespread surveillance of private citizens.

When media—and increasingly we are talking about a rich mashup of conventional news, specialized website stories, and activist social media—direct their journalistic searchlights on an issue, a policy agenda can diffuse throughout society, leading to policy change. News effects are complex (Dearing & Rogers, 1996; Gonzenbach, 1996). The media can influence the public agenda, which in turn influences policymaking. In the classic case, news stories rouse the public into action, propelling them to influence elites. Investigative news stories about political corruption or a sorely neglected societal problem unleash public anger, through a journalism of outrage (Protess et al., 1991). The public communicates its dissatisfaction to policymakers via polls or social media messages, like tweets to political officials or a fusillade of angry social media posts.

In other cases, media directly influence policymakers, with effects unmediated by public opinion. In these cases, journalists' reporting congeals with agendas leaders are already working on, and in some cases journalists and policymakers work in tandem. Some years back, *The Philadelphia Inquirer* ran a series headlined "Kidney Patients vs. the Bottom Line." The stories showcased how federally funded kidney dialysis treatment centers placed profits over care of victims of kidney failure, documenting how clinics reused dialysis equipment to cut costs and the federal government failed to adequately police its own treatment centers (Protess et al., 1991). Although the hard-hitting stories had only a modest impact on public opinion, they significantly influenced policymakers. Two weeks after the series broke, the Pennsylvania Board of Medicine launched an investigation of a clinic profiled in the articles. Four months later, a bill was introduced in Congress that recommended imposition of stiff penalties on clinics providing substandard care.

For agenda-building to occur, the news must work in concert with other powerful social forces. News is a necessary but not a sufficient condition for policy change. Students sometimes conflate media with power, assuming that just because an issue is covered in The Media (the capital letters reflecting the media's omnipotence), the Force is with media, and policies will be changed. But the media are one of a number of actors on the public stage, and they work with other institutions, sometimes producing change, in other cases informing the public but failing to make a dent in an entrenched political establishment.

A Complicated Process

Agenda-building plays an important role in democracy because it provides a pathway by which media and political institutions can sow the seeds for social change. Scholars have explored how and when agendas are built, focusing on when certain issues become matters of policy concern, occupy policymakers' attention, and produce meaningful change. Political scientists have emphasized that effective agenda-building requires that an issue needs to be "independently and similarly articulated by several different groups or notables both within and outside of government at about the same time" (Cook & Skogan, 1991, p. 192). There must be a suitable or "ripe" issue climate for an issue to rise to the top of the policy agenda and action to be taken. Policymakers and journalists must *(1) recognize that a problem exists, (2) have available a variety of solutions, and (3) find themselves in a ripe social or political climate to act on the problem* (Cook & Skogan, 1991; Protess et al., 1991; Kingdon, 2011).

First, the media play a role in bringing a problem to public attention, as they have in the case of countless issues—environmental pollution, health care, racial injustice, and outcries against abortion—that were viewed as aspects of modern life until media coverage transformed them to *problems* in need of corrective action. But attention is not sufficient.

For media, public, and policy agendas to trigger policy change, a second hurdle must be crossed: Policymakers must have viable solutions and there must be more unity than divisiveness among policymakers. One reason why health care reform occurred under Obama and not Clinton, despite mighty efforts to change health care during the Clinton years, is because there was more policy consensus on how to ameliorate health care when Obama was president, greater agreement among health care interest groups on how to proceed, more effective consensus-based politicking by the Obama team, and less conflicted media coverage about health care in Obama's first term than when Clinton tackled the fractious issue in 1993 (Kingdon, 2011). Media coverage of deficiencies in American health care over decades probably helped set the agenda, a necessary condition for media agenda-building, but it took years of concerted efforts on the policy front for an issue to move from the stage of problem attention to legislative implementation.

The third condition necessary for policy action is a ripe political climate, an opinion climate built over time by activists, news coverage, policymakers, and public attitudes. The political timing must be right for policy change. On the other hand, if credible counter-voices or opponents mount a challenge, persuasively arguing that the problem is less serious than assumed, bureaucrats and policymakers fail to pursue the issue, and media attention declines, the issue can fall off the policy agenda. For action to be taken, there must be a confluence of positive forces operating simultaneously, with active, concerted policy deliberations and media attention. We can appreciate this more concretely by considering the case of international action on climate change.

Environmental concerns—first about pesticides and later global warming—were discussed in the media as early as 1962, with Rachel Carson's *Silent Spring*, later in the 1970s in the wake of the Earth Day movement, subsequently through news on scientific consensus about climate change, and dramatically in Al Gore's 2006 movie, *An Inconvenient Truth*. This transformed the environmental issue into a problem. But policy action did not materialize because leaders could not agree on solutions. Some politicians doubted global warming is serious or caused by humans, believed concerted actions extracted too high an economic price, bowed to pressure from anti-environmental business groups, and argued that the federal government had no right to meddle in what they viewed as a private sector issue. The problem rose and fell from the policy agenda over the years. But by 2015, there was enough agreement on problem definition and solutions, as well as public support for environmental change, that the climate—so to speak—was ripe for change.

By 2015, years of activism by environmental groups, sustained media coverage, changes in public attitudes, and geopolitical developments created a ripe issue climate paving the way for a pathbreaking international climate control accord signed by 195 nations. Why did this happen after years of infighting within and between nations? There was increasing recognition that global warming was not a far-off problem, but a threat with immediate, devastating consequences, palpably experienced in recent droughts, heat waves, and floods. Dramatic policy actions by the U.S. and China to curb greenhouse gases convinced each country and the global community that the world's superpowers were willing to act on the problem, and that solutions were possible (Davenport, 2015). Global policymakers felt a collective pressure to act. In this case, diverse political streams converged, producing a ripe issue climate for policy action.

On other fractious issues, like public school funding, immigration, and gun violence, there are sharp differences in perceptions and framing of the problem, political schisms, and powerful interest groups that impede collective efforts to build a collective, bipartisan agenda around reforms. Elite interests diverge, and media reflect and cultivate these differences of opinion. Reaching the top of the media agenda is a necessary condition for political change, but not a sufficient one.

There is debate among scholars as to how democratic agenda-building is. Some argue that the system is exploited by wealthy individuals and corporations that can hire lobbyists to persuade policymakers to place their issue at the forefront of their agendas. Others point to the ability of grassroots groups like the radical Occupy Wall Street and the conservative Tea Party to commandeer media attention, solicit public support, and push policymakers to contemplate or push policy change. While change can and does occur, there is little doubt that agenda-setting and agenda-building are frequently skewed to favor the rich and powerful, as seen in the case of indifference to the problems faced by poor, primarily Black residents of Flint, Michigan, in 2014. The city's decision to switch Flint's source of drinking water from Lake Huron to the Flint River to cut costs led to water contamination, rashes, sickness, and possible lead poisoning, which can have devastating effects on pregnant women and children. Although community representatives complained, their concerns were disregarded, and the issue did not make it onto the national agenda for a couple of years, when national political leaders and the news seized on the story (Eligon, 2016). By then the health damage—some likely to be irreversible—had been done. "There is little doubt," *The New York Times* editorialized, "that an affluent, predominantly white community . . . would never face such a public health catastrophe, and if it had, the state government would have rushed in to help" (Depraved indifference toward Flint, 2016, p. A22).

AGENDAS IN THE DIGITAL AGE

Let's switch gears to examine the ways agenda-setting and agenda-building are changing the contemporary digital environment. McCombs and Shaw developed the agenda-setting model during a time when mass media had enormous impact. Journalists were the primary gatekeepers; they decided, based on journalistic conventions, whether and what information would reach the public. Back in the day, media could present a fairly consistent and uniform agenda at any particular time (Metzger, 2009). But these assumptions are no longer tenable. People no longer rely exclusively on the conventional media for information. They turn to online news and social media sites. The media's ability to convey a singular agenda to hundreds of millions of Americans has slipped.

Over the past decade, studies have explored agenda-setting in a world of interactive media (Johnson, 2014; Meraz, 2014; Tran, 2014). Research has examined changes in **intermedia agenda-setting**, or the ways that particular media outlets (e.g., *The New York Times*, *The Washington Post*, *Time* magazine, CBS News, but also blogs and partisan sites) set the agenda for other media and the news in general.

It is important to clarify the terms of discussion. People sometimes assume online media means new media. That is not true. Much online news is gathered and produced by mainstream news organizations, but is packaged for online platforms. When people follow *The New York Times*, CNN, Fox, or MSNBC online, the news they see or read is frequently the same as, similar to, or complementary to that appearing in the conventional format. Popular news websites frequently cover on the same issues as conventional print and broadcast news (Maier, 2010). News aggregators like Google News rely on automatic computer algorithms rather than human decision-making to select news items for display. But Google scans thousands of major news sites to determine which items to display. These are typically conventional news outlets, like *The New York Times*, *The Washington Post*, Reuters, BBC, and Voice of America. Thus, choices made by gatekeepers at established media outlets continue to influence the agenda of Google and other online aggregators.

Even with all these changes, agenda-setting continues apace nearly a half century after it was originally posed. As Eli Skogerbø and his colleagues (2016) note, "the agenda-setting hypothesis seems to remain robust and productive in an online environment" (p. 106). Let's now review the knowledge base about agenda-setting in today's era. Here is what we know.

Conventional Journalists No Longer Dictate the Media Agenda

Blogs have famously pushed the mainstream media to cover stories they ignored or minimized. Celebrated cases include blog revelations of CBS's well-meaning but flawed reporting of a 2004 exposé that then President George W. Bush had pulled strings to enlist in the Texas Air National Guard rather than face possible deployment to Vietnam, as well as revelations on Facebook and Twitter in 2015 that NBC anchor Brian Williams had distorted his record as a war correspondent in Iraq, information that diffused to the mainstream media and resulted in Williams's suspension from NBC News (Somaiya, 2015). Research finds that blogs can set the agenda for mainstream media, creating a buzz that journalists follow and report (Meraz, 2011a; Messner & DiStaso, 2008; Schiffer, 2006; Sweetser, Golan, & Wanta, 2008). In this way, online media have yanked some of the power from conventional media, redistributing the flow of influence by giving citizen-generated content a way to reach readers' and journalists' attention. Blogs can help test the waters, making controversial stories more palatable, in this way giving traditional journalists "permission" to cover more controversial content.

At the same time, social networking sites play a role in political marketing (see Chapter 8), giving candidates a new way to highlight issues they hope will diffuse widely, ideally building their agenda (Conway, Kenski, & Wang, 2015). Twitter has provided political elites with a new channel by which to set and control the agenda, although there are cross-national differences. Political leaders' tweets are cited frequently in the American news media (Wallsten, 2015), while British newspapers have cited non-elite sources more than political leaders (Skogerbø et al., 2016).

It is a two-way street. Just as blogs and social media set the agenda for conventional media, conventional media influence the agenda of the blogosphere and Twitter (Conway et al., 2015; Tran, 2014). In some instances, political reporters and bloggers follow and respond to each group's coverage, leading to bidirectional, reciprocal agenda-setting (Wallsten, 2007). And in other cases, agendas diverge, with social media focusing on social issues like abortion and same-sex marriage, blogs covering foreign affairs, and traditional media covering events with a heavy dose of official sources (Neuman, Guggenheim, Jang, & Bae, 2014). Tweets can also feed partisan media, reinforcing a political agenda, as when Trump's tweets about immigration and a Muslim ban likely intensified the partisan agenda of his followers that redounded to influence Republicans running for elective office in 2016. What emerges is less a case of online media slavishly parroting conventional media than parallel universes—conventional media and partisan social media—each with its own set of concerns, at least on controversial political issues.

Social Media Can Play Different Roles in Setting and Building Agendas

Social media can exert at least three different agenda-building effects. First, they can provide a pathway by which partisan agendas are constructed, as online messages reinforce salient beliefs and diffuse among like-minded others (Vargo, Guo, McCombs, & Shaw, 2014). Second, social media can exert influence via opinion leaders in a networked two-step flow (Messing & Westwood, 2014). Issues covered by social media (like the Brian Williams falsifications and the horrific 2012 Steubenville, Ohio high school rape) are picked up by mainstream journalists, who report on them in widely viewed conventional media stories. This coverage can influence public priorities, even priming the public and policymakers when they think about politics or make voting decisions.

Third, social media can exert a more direct role in agenda-building. You could argue that a ripple of a short-term agenda-setting effect occurred entirely online in the case of the popular deluge of Twitter, Tumblr, and Facebook to protest a decision by America's leading breast cancer advocacy organization to end most of its financing of Planned Parenthood in February 2012. A day after the protest was reported widely across the mainstream media, the organization reversed its position and restored its partnership with Planned Parenthood. In another case, Internet activists worked with Anonymous to demand that Canadian authorities prosecute a 2011 rape case, perhaps contributing to the prime minister's call for indictments (Bazelon, 2014). Either solely because of the activists' online investigations (which can produce tsunamis of tweets to political leaders) or in combination with mainstream media coverage, the issue seemed to have emerged as an important agenda item (Perloff, 2014).

Don't Count Out the Mainstream Media. But They're One Among a Variety of Influence Agents

Elite newspapers like *The New York Times* and *The Washington Post* still set the agenda for other media outlets. When they break a story, other news media follow suit, conveying their stories and sometimes sending their own reporters to cover the latest developments. Even in an era of blogs and social media, conventional media continue to set the agenda of many blog networks, which react to mainstream news stories, putting their own spin on events. Conventional mainstream media also exert a hefty influence on the public agenda or public opinion (Shehata & Strömbäck, 2013). Mainstream media's coverage of Hillary Clinton's email scandal placed the issue on the public agenda, influencing the trajectory of campaign discourse. Subsequent conventional news coverage of Trump's chaotic beginning and missteps as president seems to have left an imprint on public opinion, even causing his supporters to focus on Russian interference in the 2016 election (though framing it differently than opponents; see Chapter 7).

Thus, mainstream news and an increasing number of partisan blogs, tweets, and social media sites straddle the colossus of online media (Meraz, 2011b). Conventional media still matter, probably more for issues on which there is ideological consensus, like terrorism. Mainstream media attention is typically essential for issues to reach the agenda of elite policymakers, though much less than in years past. Online information-seeking now affects perceptions of the importance of national problems (Lee, Kim, & Scheufele, 2016).

Are these changes good or bad? That's a tough question, and the answer is shaped by your perspective. As agenda control was wrested from East Coast media hegemons—elite newspapers, magazines, and television networks—to a panoply of online platforms, sometimes coordinated by diverse ideological organizations and activist bloggers, social influence is diffused across a wider number of political groups and citizens. The expansion of voices enriches democracy. Citizens have more control; they no longer must take their cues exclusively from elites. The downside is that agenda-building blogs and partisan media can contain and spread inaccurate, even false information. And when people just get information from one social media outlet, with a plethora of posts on one side, partisan agenda-setting and fragmentation can intensify.

Increasingly, partisan media are playing an outsized role in political agenda-building. In the 2016 election, a fiery, feisty conservative media network, centered on the website, Breitbart News (see Chapter 9), harnessed social media to drive a right-wing agenda (Benkler et al., 2017). Led by the oppositional Breitbart website, with stories focused on immigration and Clinton's emails, many false, the conservative, mediated ecosystem drove Republican conversations and built a virulently anti-Clinton, pro-Trump agenda that appealed to supporters' biases, forcing its way into mainstream media coverage. Is this bad for democracy? In some ways, yes, if one emphasizes the importance of truth and protection of civil rights, neither of which are priorities for Breitbart; on the other hand, to the degree that such partisan agenda-building allowed a highly engaged conservative minority to actively participate in the election, it exerted a democratizing influence (Hylton, 2017).

There is one other quandary in play. We have gone full circle from the days when a handful of elite White male gatekeepers controlled the flow of information, frequently with class and cultural prejudice, to an era when individuals, sometimes informed, sometimes less so, frequently biased, can influence the news agenda. As Pariser (2011) notes:

> Now, the *Huffington Post* can put an article on its front page and know within minutes whether it's trending viral; it if it is, the editors can kick it by promoting it more heavily . . . At Yahoo's popular *Upshot* news blog, a team of editors mine the data produced by streams of search queries to see what terms people are interested in, in real time. Then they produce articles responsive to these queries.
>
> (pp. 70–71)

Reddit has gone further. Articles that do not receive consistent voices of approval drop off its pages. A particular individual's page consists of stories favored by the group of registered users, and those which the person likes. The agenda is set by the group and is exquisitely tailored to fit users' preferences. Facebook's algorithm emphasizes "likes" and the ability to easily offer comments (Tufekci, 2016). The old model has been supplanted (though not totally replaced) by a communicative system that gives more power to users, but also to social media companies, via their algorithmic formulas. This raises policy questions.

On the one hand, blogs and a panoply of websites give grassroots groups, previously relegated to the margins, increased ability to influence the public agenda. But the criteria for agenda-setting on a site can be social popularity, viral trending, and algorithms based on users' interests and preexisting political sentiments (Goel, 2015) rather than journalistically based standards. Happily, media gatekeeping decisions are based less on the predispositions of East Coast elite journalists. On the other hand, decisions may be based more on algorithmic popularity or interests congenial with the user than on matters of legitimate, salient policy significance. Have we made progress?

CONCLUSIONS

The Media Set the Agenda

This is the most famous of all political media effects, one that is well-known in political and journalistic circles. It is among the most well-documented political communication effects. Agenda-setting is sometimes believed to be synonymous with any and all media influence. It is not. Agenda-setting has a precise meaning. It is the process through which media communicate the importance of specific issues to the public. It occurs when concentrated media coverage of a problem causes the public to believe this is more salient than other problems. By defining a problem as important, media can profoundly influence public opinion and, under some conditions, policymaking. This is the fundamental insight of agenda-setting theory.

There is abundant evidence that the media help set the agenda. Evidence comes from cross-sectional and longitudinal surveys, experiments, and a variety of studies conducted in different countries across the world. It is in some sense a truism that an issue cannot be regarded as important unless stories about it appear in the media and on the Internet. But simply because an issue appears in the media does not logically lead to the conclusion that it will increase in perceived importance as a result of media coverage. Yet concentrated media coverage of an issue frequently increases its perceived importance

Agenda-setting has consequences. One is priming, which occurs when the media agenda primes or influences the standards voters use to judge a president or political leader. By calling attention to certain issues and not others, news can affect the criteria voters invoke to judge candidates for office. Although media priming effects occur, they are more likely to emerge when voters regard the criteria as applicable or relevant to the decision at hand. Priming and agenda-setting have intriguing implications for the conduct of political campaigns. Candidates try to harness conventional and social media to emphasize an issue central to their campaigns, and use advertising (as well as other messages) to prime these topics. Thus, the media, broadly defined, are an instrument by which politicians hope to influence voters. Candidates do not always succeed. The news must pick up on their issues, and the topics must resonate with voters. Candidate agendas vie with conventional news media agendas, as well as those on blogs and partisan media sites, for influence on the richly symbolic political stage. Partisan media have become an important factor in agenda-setting and priming during presidential election years. Their capacity to raise issues that conventional media ignore counts as a major plus, but their tendency to exclude dissonant agendas or play fast and loose with facts are compelling cons.

The media do not exist in a vacuum. Media agenda-setting operates in the context of a larger culture, society, and political environment. Deciding that something is a problem is itself an important—and political—activity. If an issue is not identified as a problem by the media or political elites, it cannot move through the series of stages necessary for the problem to be contemplated, considered, discussed, and hopefully solved. These broader questions are the purview of agenda-building, which examines the intersection among media agendas, public agendas, and policymaking. Agenda-building is the process by which media and public opinion influence the policymaking agenda of political elites. There are complex relationships among the media, public, and policy agendas, with media influencing policymakers' agenda directly, and indirectly via public opinion.

Media agenda-setting is a part—a substantial one, to be sure, but not the only component—of the larger policymaking process. It is never a sufficient condition for the implementation of a change in policy; media can cover an issue until the cows come home, but unless there is a ripe climate, receptive policymakers, and feasible proposals, no action will be taken. Agenda-building is, at its core, a political process.

It is important to emphasize that an issue does not remain on the agenda forever. It stays on the shelf for only so long. The Occupy Wall Street issue, which garnered so much attention in the fall of 2011, dropped off the radar screen by March 2012, recruiting virtually no coverage (Schmidt, 2012). With substantially fewer people participating in the protest and the story bereft of novel, newsworthy aspects, journalists lost interest. This is typical. After a story dominates the national agenda for a time, it inevitably slips out of view. Other problems come up. The media lose interest. The public becomes enamored by the issue du jour. Policymakers consider new legislative proposals. The shelf life for a problem that is in need of improvement is short, and if action is not taken when the time is ripe, change may not occur for years, if at all.

Agenda-building is a complicated process. Although it is frequently assumed that media investigative stories mobilize the public into demanding action from their leaders, organized alliances between policymakers and journalists (as well as partisan social media activists) also provide a vehicle by which policy agendas are constructed. There is no guarantee a particular agenda will produce change, or that the presence of a problem will produce policy action. Change is the exception, not the rule. Policy change does occur, but requires the recognition on the part of policymakers and journalists that a problem exists, plausible solutions are available, and there is a ripe social climate for change.

In a digital age, conventional media have less impact on agenda-building than they did when the broadcast networks ruled the roost. Blogs and social media play important roles, on some issues more than others. Agendas can diverge, with social media, blogs, and traditional media sometimes favoring different issues. Conventional media still matters, of course. Much of the content that appears on websites and social media apps is gathered by major news organizations, and their investigative stories can diffuse rapidly online, influencing agendas of blogs and social networking sites. Mainstream media coverage is usually a necessary condition for public opinion and policy change (Shehata & Strömbäck, 2013), but the plethora of online media are helping build niche agendas that can influence policy choices of legislators in highly partisan, gerrymandered electoral districts.

The struggle in agenda-building is to control the direction the country takes and to shape a policy agenda. It is a high-stakes battle. While many lament that "political games" must be played, the fact is that these are endemic to democracy. Democratic societies must determine which problems to prioritize, which to put on the back burner, and how to reach consensus on public policy questions. The emergence of blogs and alternative media outlets offer hope that citizens unconnected with powerful lobbies, but concerned about social and economic issues, can exert a greater impact on the process. But change is hard. Interests collide. Entrenched forces try to block innovation. Thus when change occurs, through media and political agenda-building, it is appropriate to recognize the efforts so many individuals and groups expended on a solution and the sweeping positive effects democratically produced change can exert.

And yet, a hard-edged caveat needs to be mentioned. For all the changes in communication and politics, America and other Western democracies still struggle (endlessly, it seems) with intractable political problems—economic malaise, inequality, and the asymmetrical power of terrorist groups over superpower nations. Solutions continue to elude us, and consensus over how to solve national problems is bogged down in legislative gridlock. Different agendas compete for policy attention over an increasing number of electronic and online platforms. Despite all we know and breathtaking advances in political communication technologies, democracies continue to struggle to find solutions to the problems that ail their citizens. Progress is fitful, and solutions are the exception, not the rule.

REFERENCES

Althaus, S.L., & Kim, Y.M. (2006). Priming effects in complex information environments: Reassessing the impact of news discourse on presidential approval. *Journal of Politics, 68,* 960–976.

Autor, D.H., Dorn, D., & Hanson, G.H. (2016, January). *The China shock: Learning from labor market adjustment to large changes in trade.* NBER Working Paper No. 21906. Retrieved from www.nber.org/papers/w21906 (Accessed October 3, 2016).

Balmas, M., & Sheafer, T. (2010). Candidate image in election campaigns: Attribute agenda setting, affective priming, and voting intentions. *International Journal of Public Opinion Research, 22,* 204–229.

Bazelon, E. (2014, January 19). The online avengers. *The New York Times Magazine,* 28–33, 38–40.

Benkler, Y., Faris, R., Roberts, H., & Zuckerman, E. (2017, March 3). Study: Breitbart-led right-wing media ecosystem altered broader media agenda. *Columbia Journalism Review.* Online: https://www.cjr.org/analysis/breitbart-media-trump-harvard-study.php. (Accessed August 21, 2017).

Bloom, J., Fausset, R., & McPhate, M. (2016, July 18). Attack on officers jolts a nation on edge. *The New York Times,* A1, A18.

Bulkow, K., Urban, J., & Schweiger, W. (2013). The duality of agenda-setting: The role of information processing. *International Journal of Public Opinion Research, 25*, 43–63.

Calmes, J., & Thee, M. (2008, November 5). Poll finds Obama built broader base than past nominees. *The New York Times*, A1, P5.

Carson, R. (1962). *Silent spring*. Boston: Houghton Mifflin.

Cohen, B.C. (1963). *The press and foreign policy*. Princeton, NJ: Princeton University Press.

Conway, B.A., Kenski, K., & Wang, D. (2015). The rise of Twitter in the political campaign: Searching for intermedia agenda-setting effects in the presidential primary. *Journal of Computer-Mediated Communication, 20*, 363–380.

Cook, F.L., & Skogan, W.G. (1991). Convergent and divergent voice models of the rise and fall of policy issues. In M.E. McCombs & D.L. Protess (Eds.), *Setting the agenda: Readings on media, public opinion, and policymaking* (pp. 189–206). Hillsdale, NJ: Erlbaum Associates.

Corasaniti, N. (2016, July 23). Fox's impact, absent Ailes. *The New York Times*, B1, B2.

Davenport, C. (2015, December 13). A climate deal, 6 fateful years in the making. *The New York Times*. Retrieved from www.nytimes.com/2015/12/14/world/europe/a-climate-deal-6-fateful-years-in-the-making.html (Accessed December 21, 2015).

Dearing, J.W., & Rogers, E.M. (1996). *Agenda-setting*. Thousand Oaks, CA: Sage.

Depraved indifference toward Flint. (2016, January 22). (Editorial). *The New York Times*, A22.

Domke, D. (2001). Racial cues and political ideology: An examination of associative priming. *Communication Research, 28*, 772–801.

Eligon, J. (2016, January 22). A question of environmental racism in Flint. *The New York Times*, A1, A16.

Ettema, J.S., & Glaser, T.L. (1998). *Custodians of conscience: Investigative journalism and public virtue*. New York: Columbia University Press.

Eveland, W.P., Jr., & Seo, M. (2007). News and politics. In D.R. Roskos-Ewoldsen & J.L. Monahan (Eds.), *Communication and social cognition: Theories and methods* (pp. 293–318). Mahwah, NJ: Erlbaum Associates.

Goel, V. (2015, June 24). Instagram to offer millions of current events photos. *The New York Times*, B3.

Gonzenbach, W.J. (1996). *The media, the president, and public opinion: A longitudinal analysis of the drug issue, 1984–1991*. Mahwah, NJ: Erlbaum Associates.

Goodman, P.S. (2016, September 29). More jobs, but not for everyone. *The New York Times*, A1, B8–B9.

Hallin, D.C. (1986). *The "uncensored war": The media and Vietnam*. New York: Oxford University Press.

Healy, P., & Sussman, D. (2016, September 15). Voters' view of a Donald Trump presidency: Big risks and rewards. *The New York Times*. Retrieved from www.nytimes.com/2016/09/16/us/politics/hillary-clinton-donald-trump-poll.html (Accessed October 19, 2016).

Hylton, W.S. (2017, August 20). The megaphone. *The New York Times Magazine*, 30–35, 49, 51, 53.

Irwin, N. (2016a, October 4). No painless way to undo Nafta, and few rewards for the trouble. *The New York Times*, A1, A14.

Irwin, N. (2016b, June 28. Donald Trump's economic nostalgia. *The New York Times*. Retrieved from www.nytimes.com/2016/06/29/upshot/donald-trumps-economc-nostalgia.html (Accessed October 3, 2016).

Iyengar, S., & Kinder, D.R. (1987). *News that matters: Television and American opinion*. Chicago: University of Chicago Press.

Iyengar, S., & Kinder, D.R. (2010). *News that matters: Television and American opinion* (Updated ed.). Chicago: University of Chicago Press.

Johnson, T.J. (Ed.). (2014). *Agenda setting in a 2.0 world: New agendas in communication, a tribute to Maxwell McCombs*. New York: Routledge.

Johnson, T.J., Wanta, W., Byrd, J.T., & Lee, C. (1995). Exploring FDR's relationship with the press: A historical agenda-setting study. *Political Communication, 12*, 157–172.

Kakutani, M. (2016, January 26). Portraits of the terrorists next door. *The New York Times*, C1, C4.

Kim, S-H., Han, M., & Scheufele, D.A. (2010). Think about him this way: Priming, news media, and South Koreans' evaluation of the president. *International Journal of Public Opinion Research, 22*, 299–319.

Kim, Y.M. (2005). Use and disuse of contextual primes in dynamic news environments. *Journal of Communication, 55*, 737–755.

Kim, Y.M. (2014). Contingent factors of agenda-setting effects: How need for orientation, issue obtrusiveness, and message tone influence issue salience and attitude strength. In T.J. Johnson (Ed.), *Agenda setting in a 2.0 world: New agendas in communication, A tribute to Maxwell McCombs* (pp. 65–81). New York: Routledge.

Kinder, D.R. (2003). Communication and politics in the age of information. In D.O. Sears, L. Huddy, & R. Jervis (Eds.), *Oxford handbook of political psychology* (pp. 357–393). New York: Oxford University Press.

Kingdon, J.W. (2011). *Agendas, alternatives, and public policies*. (Updated 2nd ed.). Boston: Longman.

Kinsella, J. (1988). *Covering the plague: AIDS and the American media*. New Brunswick, NJ: Rutgers University Press.

Krosnick, J.A., & Kinder, D.R. (1990). Altering the foundations of support for the president through priming. *American Political Science Review, 84*, 497–512.

Kühne, R., Schemer, C., Matthes, J., & Wirth, W. (2011). Affective priming in political campaigns: How campaign-induced emotions prime political opinions. *International Journal of Public Opinion Research, 23*, 485–507.

Lang, G.E., & Lang, K. (1983). *The battle for public opinion: The president, the press, and the polls during Watergate*. New York: Columbia University Press.

Lee, B., Kim, J., & Scheufele, D.A. (2016). Agenda setting in the Internet age: The reciprocity between online searches and issue salience. *Communication Monographs, 28*, 440–455.

Lippmann, W. (1922). *Public opinion*. New York: Free Press.

Lipstadt, D.E. (1986). *Beyond belief: The American press and the coming of the Holocaust 1933–1945*. New York: Free Press.

Madhani, A. (2012, December 27). Tighter gun laws favored in poll. *USA Today*, A1.

Maier, S. (2010). All the news fit to post? Comparing news content on the Web to newspapers, television, and radio. *Journalism & Mass Communication Quarterly, 87*, 548–562.

Martin, J., & Sussman, D. (2015, December 11). Poll has Trump gaining ground on terror fear. *The New York Times*, A1, A17.

Matthes, J. (2006). The need for orientation towards news media: Revising and validating a classic concept. *International Journal of Public Opinion Research, 18*, 422–444.

McCombs, M. (2014). *Setting the agenda: The mass media and public opinion* (2nd ed.). Cambridge: Polity Press.

McCombs, M., & Reynolds, A. (2009). How the news shapes our civic agenda. In J. Bryant & M.B. Oliver (Eds.), *Media effects: Advances in theory and research* (3rd ed., pp. 1–16). New York: Routledge.

McCombs, M.E., & Shaw, D.L. (1972). The agenda-setting function of mass media. *Public Opinion Quarterly, 36*, 176–187.

McGraw, K.M., & Ling, C. (2003). Media priming of presidential and group evaluations. *Political Communication, 20*, 23–40.

McLeod, J.M., Becker, L.B., & Byrnes, J.E. (1974). Another look at the agenda-setting function of the press. *Communication Research, 1*, 131–165.

Meraz, S. (2011a). Using time series analysis to measure intermedia agenda-setting influence in traditional media and political blog networks. *Journalism & Mass Communication Quarterly, 88*, 176–194.

Meraz, S. (2011b). The fight for "how to think": Traditional media, social networks, and issue interpretation. *Journalism: Theory, Practice, and Criticism, 12*, 107–127.

Meraz, S. (2014). Media agenda setting in a competitive and hostile environment: The role of sources in setting versus supporting topical discussant agendas in the Tea Party Patriots' Facebook group. In T.J. Johnson (Ed.), *Agenda setting in a 2.0 world: New agendas in communication, a tribute to Maxwell McCombs* (pp. 1–27). New York: Routledge.

Messing, S., & Westwood, S.J. (2014). Selective exposure in the age of social media: Endorsements trump partisan source affiliation when selecting news online. *Communication Research, 41*, 1042–1063.

Messner, M., & DiStaso, M.W. (2008). The source cycle: How traditional media and weblogs use each other as sources. *Journalism Studies, 9*, 447–463.

Metzger, M.J. (2009). The study of media effects in the era of Internet communication. In R.L. Nabi & M.B. Oliver (Eds.), *The Sage handbook of media processes and effects* (pp. 561–576). Thousand Oaks, CA: Sage.

Miller, J.M., & Krosnick, J.A. (2000). News media impact on the ingredients of presidential evaluations: Politically knowledgeable citizens are guided by a trusted source. *American Journal of Political Science, 44*, 295–309.

Moy, P., Xenos, M.A., & Hess, V.K. (2005). Priming effects of late-night comedy. *International Journal of Public Opinion Research, 18*, 198–210.

Mutz, D.C. (1998). *Impersonal influence: How perceptions of mass collectives affect political attitudes*. New York: Cambridge University Press.

Neuman, W.R., Guggenheim, L., Jang, S.M., & Bae, S.Y. (2014). The dynamics of public attention: Agenda-setting theory meets big data. *Journal of Communication, 64*, 193–214.

Oates, S. (2016). Trump, media, and the "oxygen of publicity." In D. Lilleker, E. Thorsen, D. Jackson, & A. Veneti (Eds.), *US election analysis 2016: Media, voters and the campaign: Early reflections from leading academics* (pp. 22–23). Poole, England: Centre for the Study of Journalism, Culture and Community.

Pan, Z., & Kosicki, G.M. (1997). Priming and media impact on the evaluations of the president's performance. *Communication Research, 24*, 3–30.

Pariser, E. (2011). *The filter bubble: What the Internet is hiding from you*. New York: Penguin Press.

Perloff, R.M. (2014). Mass communication research at the crossroads: Definitional issues and theoretical directions for mass and political communication scholarship in an age of online media. *Mass Communication and Society, 18*, 531–556.

Peters, J.W., Thee-Brenan, M., & Sussman, D. (2016, November 9). Exit polls confirm stark divisions along racial, gender and economic lines. *The New York Times*, P6.

Pingree, R.J., Quenette, A.M., Tchernev, J.M., & Dickinson, T. (2013). Effects of media criticism on gatekeeping trust and implications for agenda setting. *Journal of Communication, 63*, 351–372.

Pingree, R.J., & Stoycheff, E. (2013). Differentiating cueing from reasoning in agenda-setting effects. *Journal of Communication, 63*, 852–872.

Porter, E. (2016, March 29). Nafta may have saved many autoworkers' jobs. *The New York Times*. Retrieved from www.nytimes.com/2016/03/30/ business/economy/nafta-may-have-saved-many-autoworkers-jobs.html (Accessed October 3, 2016).

Price, V., & Tewksbury, D. (1997). News values and public opinion: A theoretical account of media priming and framing. In G.A. Barnett & F.J. Boster (Eds.), *Progress in communication sciences: Advances in persuasion* (vol. 13, pp. 173–212). Greenwich, CT: Ablex.

Protess, D.L., Cook, F.L., Doppelt, J.C., Ettema, J.S., Gordon, M.T., Leff, D.R., & Miller, P. (1991). *The journalism of outrage: Investigative reporting and agenda building in America*. New York: Guilford Press.

Rogers, E.M., & Dearing, J.W. (1988). Agenda-setting research: Where has it been? Where is it going? In J. Anderson (Ed.), *Communication yearbook 11* (pp. 555–594). Newbury Park, CA: Sage.

Roskos-Ewoldsen, D.R., Roskos-Ewoldsen, B., & Dillman Carpentier, F. (2009). Media priming: An updated synthesis. In J. Bryant & M.B. Oliver (Eds.), *Media effects: Advances in theory and research* (3rd ed., pp. 74–93). New York: Routledge.

Schattschneider, E.E. (1960). *The semisovereign people: A realist's view of democracy in America*. New York: Holt, Rinehart & Winston.

Schiffer, A.J. (2006). Blogswarms and press norms: News coverage of the Downing Street memo controversy. *Journalism & Mass Communication Quarterly, 83*, 494–510.

Schmidt, M.S. (2012, April 1). For occupy movement, a challenge to recapture momentum. *The New York Times*, 19.

Semetko, H.A., & Mandelli, A. (1997). Setting the agenda for cross-national research: Bringing values into the concept. In M. McCombs, D.L. Shaw, & D. Weaver (Eds.), *Communication and democracy: Exploring the intellectual frontiers in agenda-setting theory* (pp. 195–207). Mahwah, NJ: Erlbaum.

Sheafer, T. (2007). How to evaluate it: The role of story-evaluative tone in agenda-setting and priming. *Journal of Communication, 57*, 21–39.

Shehata, A., & Strömbäck, J. (2013). Not (yet) a new era of minimal effects: A study of agenda setting at the aggregate and individual levels. *International Journal of Press/Politics, 18*, 234–255.

Shoemaker, P.J., & Reese, S.D. (2014). *Mediating the message in the 21st century: A media sociology perspective*. New York: Routledge.

Skogerbø, E., Bruns, A., Quodling, A., & Ingebretsen, T. (2016). Agenda-setting revisited: Social media and sourcing in mainstream journalism. In A. Bruns, G. Enli, E. Skogerbø, A.O. Larsson, & C. Christensen (Eds.), *The Routledge companion to social media and politics* (pp. 104–120). New York: Routledge.

Somaiya, R. (2015, June 22). Social media keep the facts checkable. *The New York Times*, B3.

Stroud, N.J. (2011). *Niche news: The politics of news choice*. New York: Oxford University Press.

Stroud, N.J. (2013). The American media system today: Is the public fragmenting? In T.N. Ridout (Ed.), *New directions in media and politics* (pp. 6–23). New York: Routledge.

Sweetser, K.D., Golan, G.J., & Wanta, W. (2008). Intermedia agenda setting in television, advertising, and blogs during the 2004 election. *Mass Communication and Society*, *11*, 197–216.

Toner, R., & Nagourney, A. (2008, September 18). McCain seen as less likely to bring change, poll finds. *The New York Times*, A1, A22.

Tran, H. (2014). Online agenda setting: A new frontier for theory development. In T.J. Johnson (Ed.), *Agenda setting in a 2.0 world: New agendas in communication, A tribute to Maxwell McCombs* (pp. 205–229). New York: Routledge.

Tufekci, Z. (2016, May 19). The real bias built in at Facebook. *The New York Times*, A23.

Valentino, R.A. (1999). Crime news and the priming of racial attitudes during evaluations of the president. *Public Opinion Quarterly*, *63*, 293–300.

Vargo, C.J., Guo, L., McCombs, M., & Shaw, D.L. (2014). Network issue agendas on Twitter during the 2012 U.S. presidential election. *Journal of Communication*, *64*, 296–316.

Vavreck, L. (2016, November 25). Candidates fed a focus on character over policy. *The New York Times*, A16.

Wallsten, K. (2007). Agenda setting and the blogosphere: An analysis of the relationship between mainstream media and political blogs. *Review of Policy Research*, *24*, 567–587.

Wallsten, K. (2015). Non-elite Twitter sources rarely cited in coverage. *Newspaper Research Journal*, *36*, 24–41.

Wanta, W., & Ghanem, S. (2007). Effects of agenda-setting. In R.W. Preiss, B.M. Gayle, N. Burrell, M. Allen, & J. Bryant (Eds.), *Mass media effects research: Advances through meta-analysis* (pp. 37–51). Mahwah, NJ: Erlbaum.

Weaver, D.H. (1984). Media agenda-setting and public opinion: Is there a link? In R.N. Bostrom (Ed.), *Communication yearbook 8* (pp. 680–691). Beverly Hills, CA: Sage.

West, D.M. (2010). *Air wars: Television advertising in election campaigns, 1952–2008*. Washington, DC: CQ Press.

White, T. (1973). *The making of the president, 1972*. New York: Bantam.

Wines, M., & Cohen, S. (2015, April 30). Police killings rise slightly, though increased focus may suggest otherwise. *The New York Times*. Retrieved from www.nytimes.com/2015/05/01/us/no-sharp-rise-rise-seen-in-police-killings-though-increased-focus-n (Accessed December 19, 2015).

Winter, J., & Eyal, C. (1981). Agenda-setting for the civil rights issue. *Public Opinion Quarterly*, *45*, 376–383.

Zucker, H.G. (1978). The variable nature of news media influence. In B.D. Ruben (Ed.), *Communication yearbook 2* (pp. 225–240). New Brunswick, NJ: Transaction Books.

7 Framing

He threw down the gauntlet, decried the status quo and gave voters a new explanation.

For years political leaders defended, rationalized, or mildly criticized American capitalism, arguing that it was the necessary order of economic life, a free enterprise system that offered countless rags-to-riches paths to advancement, or one that needed to be merely tweaked to ameliorate problems. Capitalism, politicians readily acknowledged, is an economic system with pluses, as well as serious minuses, but reforming its salient shortcomings lay beyond their mortal capabilities. Bernie Sanders saw things differently.

During his 2016 campaign for the Democratic nomination, the liberal, earnest, Vermont senator with the aging hippie visage, who pronounced "huge" without the "h," articulated a different frame. He lambasted gaps in economic inequality in America, arguing that the U.S. has more inequality of income than any other developed nation on Earth, emphasizing that the gap between the super-rich and everyone else has grown distressingly wider, with the top one-tenth of 1 percent of the population owning nearly as much wealth in America as the bottom 90 percent. Time and again, he excoriated the ways wealthy corporations evaded taxes and condemned Wall Street greed that came at the expense of Main Street unemployment. Lacing his attacks with a moral rectitude (but not arrogance), Sanders framed the problems in America as centering around corporate avarice, trade deals that benefited big companies but led to the loss of millions of manufacturing-related jobs, and a corrupt campaign finance system. His proposals, though not always economically or politically feasible, were sweeping. Increase the minimum wage. Make tuition free at the nation's public colleges. Break up massive financial institutions. Reform campaign finance.

His vision—rooted in old-style democratic socialism, fervently applied to the present milieu—thrilled young adults, with their white Bernie-emblazoned wigs and iPhones featuring his picture on their screens. He had inspired an army of young, digitally connected volunteers who were excited by his political ideals, engaged by his unvarnished political message (Chozick & Alcinder, 2016). His success in reframing politics—and doing so passionately and earnestly—served up a campaign surprise to the vaunted Hillary Clinton candidacy, propelling him to victory in 23 nomination campaign contests, giving him more than 1,800 of the 2,382 delegates needed to clinch the nomination.

His success in mobilizing so many disaffected Democrats speaks to the power of the *frame*. Broader battles for public opinion and policy change can be viewed as a competition among different political frameworks, a combative struggle to see which frame will capture the greatest popular support. Framing has generated considerable research over the past decades (D'Angelo & Kuypers, 2010), and for good reason. It cuts to the core of the meanings people attach to political communication, pinpoints the impact that symbols exert on political behavior, and sheds light on the role that language, messages, and psychological constructions play in the pursuit of power. This chapter takes a broad look at framing, its social scientific bases, general applications, and implications for presidential campaigns.

The first section introduces core features of framing, beginning with a definition of the concept, an explanation of how it differs from related terms, and prominent examples of framing in action. The second section defines key frames and reviews what we know about framing effects—when and why they work. In the third section, I discuss the interplay of frames and message strategies in recent presidential elections, invoking framing to explain surprising and unexpected results.

DEFINING FRAMING

To appreciate framing, it is helpful to differentiate it from its forerunner in the study of political communication effects on cognition—the big dog of political communication, the concept discussed in Chapter 6: agenda-setting. Both concepts elide the classical psychological examination of media effects on attitudes, or how media change people's feelings and evaluations about political issues. Instead, their focus is more subtle, how political media influence cognitions about politics. However, framing differs from agenda-setting in several respects.

Agenda-setting examines the salience of issues—their brute importance in voters' minds. While agenda-setting extended previous research by illuminating how political media could exert significant effects without necessarily changing voters' attitudes, it neglected the rich ways that people construct the political world, as well as the many strategies that leaders employ to define a problem in a particular fashion (Takeshita, 2006). As Gerald M. Kosicki (1993) pithily put it, agenda-setting research frequently "strips away almost everything worth knowing about how the media cover an issue and leaves only the shell of the *topic*" (p. 112).

When it comes to policy debates that dominate mainstream media or bounce around social media, there is no question that the political agenda matters. But more than agenda-setting is going on. What makes for a colorful and consequential political debate is how different political actors describe the debate, the metaphors they use, and the spin they put on the issues at stake. Agenda-setting examines "*whether* we think about an issue." Framing explores "*how* we think about it" (Scheufele & Tewskbury, 2007, p. 14). Framing also assigns more importance to causal reasoning and the very different ways people explain the same problem (Maher, 2001; Pan & Kosicki, 1993). What's more, agenda-setting and priming work in part by accessing, as when the media call to mind certain political ideas. Framing works through resonance—the degree to which news coverage resonates with individuals' preexisting beliefs about the problem.

Agenda-setting examines *the particular story* the media select, stipulating that more coverage of the story bolsters perceptions of issue importance and priming of political standards. Framing is less concerned with the particular issues the media decide to cover than on "the particular ways those issues are presented" (Price & Tewskbury, 1997, p. 184). Framing suggests the *applicability* of certain ways of thinking about the problem, calling attention to certain values and not others (Hertog & McLeod, 2001; Scheufele & Tewksbury, 2007). This can be powerful stuff.

Poverty did not catch anyone's attention when it was framed as part of the natural order of things, an unfortunate byproduct of survival of the fittest. This is the way the issue was implicitly framed in the first decades of the 20th century. When activists framed poverty as a social problem with human consequences, one that warranted government action, the media, the public, and policymakers took notice. On the other side of the political ledger, in the 1970s and 1980s, conservatives, arguing that federal government programs reduced individual initiative, reframed government as part of the problem rather than a solution, changing the discourse and policy parameters over the course of decades.

While most scholars view framing as distinct from agenda-setting, some prefer to think of framing, agenda-setting, and priming as spokes within a larger conceptual wheel. Some agenda-setting scholars view framing as a second level of agenda-setting, one that extends the media's impact on political saliences to a consideration of the attributes of the particular political issue (Maher, 2001; McCombs & Ghanem, 2001). This raises a nit-picky (though interesting) academic issue—the precise specification of a concept. The drawback of viewing framing as part of agenda-setting is that it muddies the waters. It places two somewhat different concepts under the same roof, in the process obscuring their differences and understating the richness of framing (Maher, 2001; Scheufele, 2000; Scheufele & Iyengar, 2014; Takeshita, 2006). The scholarly consensus today is: Viva la difference. Let agenda-setting be agenda-setting, with all its implications for problem importance, and framing focus on its emphasis on problem definition.

So, what is meant by framing? Given the complexity of the term, it is best to start simply, with the English language. We can view a frame as a noun. A picture frame encloses the picture. The frame of a house is the foundation that provides essential support. Frame is also a verb. You can frame a response, frame a policy, or frame an innocent man. Framing is a present participle, too. A trendy California store promotes its business by noting that it does needlework framing, antique photo framing, and even sports jersey framing.

What all these different grammatical forms have in common is they denote the ways that an entity defines and structures subordinate physical or verbal objects. In the social sciences, where framing has been invoked to explain a variety of phenomena, a **frame** is defined as a primary organizing theme or narrative that gives meaning to, and connects, a series of events (Gamson & Modiglini, 1987; see also Kuypers, 2006; Nisbet, 2010; Reese, 2007; Schaffner & Sellers, 2010). Political communication scholars have a more precise definition. They define **framing** as:

> selecting and highlighting some facets of events or issues, and making connections among them so as to promote a particular interpretation, evaluation, and/or solution.
> (Entman, 2004, p. 5)

News media frames work by drawing a connection between ideas in our heads. As Matthew C. Nisbet (2010) notes:

> Media frames work by connecting the mental dots for the public. They suggest a connection between two concepts, issues, or things, such that after exposure to the framed message, audiences accept or are at least aware of the connections.
> (p. 47)

Frames, like social beliefs, contain different attributes. According to Entman, fully developed frames are composed of different elements, with four core characteristics: (1) problem definition; (2) hypothesized cause; (3) moral evaluation, and (4) proposed remedy. All this is abstract, but, as we will see, frames call on a host of colorful, strongly held beliefs. You can appreciate this by reviewing an older, but sadly still relevant frame for 9/11 and the war on terrorism (see Figure 7.1).

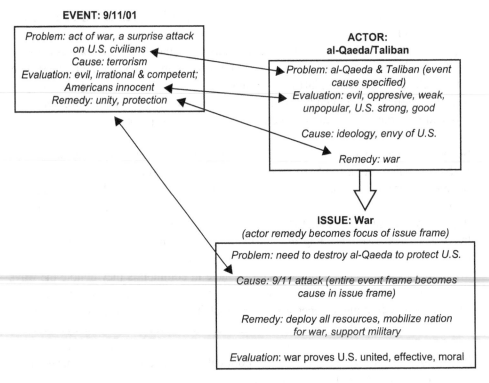

EVENT: 9/11/01

Problem: act of war, a surprise attack on U.S. civilians
Cause: terrorism
Evaluation: evil, irrational & competent; Americans innocent
Remedy: unity, protection

ACTOR:
al-Qaeda/Taliban

Problem: al-Qaeda & Taliban (event cause specified)
Evaluation: evil, oppresive, weak, unpopular, U.S. strong, good
Cause: ideology, envy of U.S.
Remedy: war

ISSUE: War
(actor remedy becomes focus of issue frame)

Problem: need to destroy al-Qaeda to protect U.S.
Cause: 9/11 attack (entire event frame becomes cause in issue frame)
Remedy: deploy all resources, mobilize nation for war, support military
Evaluation: war proves U.S. united, effective, moral

Figure 7.1 Frame for 9/11 and War on Terrorism.

(Adapted from Entman, 2004)

The figure shows that a frame can have different components: an event, actor, and issue. Each contains sub-components: a perceived problem, cause, evaluation, and remedy. While this diagram offers only broad contours, it suggests the different dimensions that frames contain.

Framing operates at different levels. Politicians harness frames in an effort to advance a particular definition of a problem, hoping this will coalesce supporters around a piece of legislation or appeal to voters during an election campaign. Journalists use frames when they employ broad themes to structure factual details. Citizens interpret political issues in terms of broad principles that help them structure and organize the political world. The relationships among elite, media, and citizens' frames are complex, just as the relationships among these actors' different agendas are complicated.

Framing is at the heart of political discourse. As Donald R. Kinder (2007) notes:

The issues taken up by government and the events that animate political life are always subject to alternative interpretation; they can always be read in more than one way . . . Frames (or something very much like frames) should be ubiquitous in political communication. Frames suggest how politics should be thought about, thereby encouraging citizens to understand events and issues in particular ways. By defining what the essential issue is and suggesting how to think about it, frames imply what, if anything, should be done.

(p. 158)

And that is the essence of politics.

If you are looking for a simple, contemporary term to describe "frames," think of "spin." If you want a broader synonym, think "perspective."

Offering a more scholarly approach, communication researchers David Tewksbury and Dietram A. Scheufele (2009) point out that frames are the rhetorical devices that make linkages among concepts. Information provides the starting point, but frames connect the dots and build critical associations, inviting citizens to view the issue in particular ways. "Frames link issues to particular beliefs that carry with them concepts for interpreting the origins, implications, and treatment of the issue," they observe (p. 20). Frames emphasize certain aspects of politics, while excluding other facets, encouraging individuals to interpret issues in different ways (Borah, 2011).

If you think about some of the most important—and contentious—issues on the political tableau, you readily see frames in action. For example:

Immigration is a political lighting rod and touchstone of framing controversy. Different frames generate different emotional responses in the U.S. and Europe (Lecheler, Bos, & Vliegenthart, 2015). Immigration burst into the frame wars in 2016 when Donald Trump branded Mexican immigrants as dangerous and promised to build a wall to keep them out. He framed the freighted immigration problem as a problem of drugs, crime, and national security, with a focus on barring Muslims from the U.S., a frame that gained resonance after the December, 2015 San Bernardino, California, terrorist attack, in which one of the terrorists, a Pakistani woman, immigrated to the U.S., eluding authorities.

By contrast, as president, Obama framed the issue around compassion and the American Dream when he announced policies to stop deporting illegal immigrants who came to the U.S. as children. (At the same, more surreptitiously, Obama deported millions of illegal immigrants during his time in office.) Trump's emphasis on undesired illegal immigrants actually dates back to the 1920s, when "illegals" were accused of stealing jobs from Americans and later became associated with the prejudiced label, "wetback." Using the word "illegal immigrants" or "aliens" condemns these individuals, treating them as "less than human and undeserving of fair treatment" (Bazelon, 2015, p. 11). Thus, liberals have preferred the term "undocumented immigrant" or "undocumented worker," though these can strike conservatives as politically correct. The issue can be so politically sensitive that the adroit conservative consultant Frank Luntz cautioned that it was prudent to "always refer to people crossing the border illegally as 'illegal immigrants'—NOT as 'illegals'" (Bazelon, p. 11). However, Trump adopted a blunter, more pejorative—and some would say more transparent—frame.

Birth control has been the site of some of the most contentious framing wars. In 2012, the Obama administration touched off a firestorm when it announced new regulations that required employers to provide coverage for contraception in health care plans they offer to their employees. Framing the issue around women's access to health care and the medical benefits that contraceptives offer women, the administration believed it had a strong philosophical case. Not so, said many Catholic bishops. Adopting a freedom-of-religion frame, they argued that the rules violated their First Amendment rights, requiring them to pay for birth control, a practice they strenuously oppose on religious grounds. In response, the Obama administration modified its proposal. The new plan, which also earned the ire of Catholic bishops, ultimately became official policy, though not before comedian Stephen Colbert joked that "a woman's health decisions are a private matter between her priest and her husband!"

Climate change has been a hotbed of framing, a battle between liberals and conservatives that illustrates the inseparability of frames and politics. Liberals, pointing to incontrovertible evidence of global warming, have framed the issue in terms of impending environmental disaster, a matter of urgency for the planet. Conservatives have focused on economic costs, framing climate change as a recipe for job loss, although environmentalists take issue with this, counter-framing climate change as an opportunity to grow innovative jobs for the economy. More cynically, Republican consultant Frank Luntz argued that climate change should be viewed as "scientifically uncertain," calling on the views of the minority of scientists who dispute global warming (Nisbet, 2010). In the wake of the landmark international agreement, signed in Paris in 2015, which commits countries to reducing greenhouse gas emissions, it is more difficult to adopt the latter frame, although Republican candidates in the 2016 election dismissed the importance of climate change. "There has never been a moment when the climate is not changing," Republican Marco Rubio opined, arguing that human activity is not responsible for climate change, despite abundant evidence to the contrary (Edwards, 2015). Scott Pruitt, director of the Environmental Protection Agency, has framed global warming as a matter of debate, although scientists regard it as a foreboding fact.

Elections. Framing is a key to winning elections, with candidates choosing frames that reflect their ideology, yet will also capture votes. In 2016, Republicans framed the election in part as a referendum on Obama's "failed" policies, while Democrats framed it around continuing the successful policies Obama had executed. The news media also selects frames, frequently framing the election as a strategic game rather than a serious clash of issues (Cappella & Jamieson, 1997; see Chapter 10). News also frames certain political issues as scandals, while choosing to avoid the "scandal" frame in other cases (see Box 7.1). Social media can offer a panoply of alternative frames. For example, social media framed Edward Snowden, who leaked massive amounts of classified information to call attention to government surveillance, as a hero, allied with other whistle-blowers. However, British news, following official source condemnation of Snowden, portrayed him as a traitor, linked with national security issues (Qin, 2015).

As these examples indicate, frames are wellsprings of controversy, with divergent frames tapping into different problem definitions. In elections, frames are the focus of debate. Elections can be won or lost, based on the cogency and resonance of the frames candidates select.

BOX 7.1 WHAT'S A SCANDAL? IT'S ALL IN THE FRAME

This is a story of two Republican presidents who engaged in two ethically problematic actions that led to two national outpourings of anger and dismay. But there was only one scandal.

The first president in our story is Ronald Reagan. During his second term, Reagan presided over a strange, controversial deal. The United States secretly sold weapons to Iran in order to facilitate the release of American hostages, held by a terrorist group that had ties to the Iranian government. The decision violated U.S. policy that forbade selling weapons to Iran. Even more strangely, the Reagan administration funneled a portion of the money from the arms sale to a cadre of rebels thousands of miles away in Central America, who were fighting what Reagan regarded as "the good fight" against a Communist regime. This too violated U.S. policy, as well as a congressional amendment—and was conducted so secretly that few in the Washington power elite knew what was going on. The revelations rocked the nation's capital, ricocheted across the country, and led to congressional and public outcry, along with the formation of a presidential commission to uncover the truth. A national scandal ensued (see Figure 7.2).

Continued

Figure 7.2 President Ronald Reagan speaks with the news media during congressional hearings on the Iran-Contra affair in 1987. A scandal erupted in the case of Iran-Contra, but not for another Republican president (George W. Bush), whose decision-making prior to the Iraq War also raised troubling moral and political issues. A difference lies in the way the issues were framed, highlighting the political and journalistic factors necessary for a series of misdeeds to be characterized as a scandal.

Getty Images

The second president in our story is George W. Bush. In 2002 and early 2003, in the tragic wake of 9/11, the Bush administration embarked on a full-throated national campaign to make the case that Iraq had weapons of mass destruction (WMDs) that could launch a second, even more serious, attack on the U.S. It turned out that Iraq did not possess WMDs. What's more, the Bush administration may have known this from the get-go, but opted to use WMDs as a galvanizing argument to propel forward the case for war. The American public bought the argument, and Congress authorized the use of military force against Iraq in 2002, to some degree based on a false set of facts. The Iraq War had devastating human consequences: More than 4,000 Americans and well over 100,000 Iraqis lost their lives. Critics condemn as scandalous the Bush administration's deliberate distortion of facts about WMDs, as well as its authorization of torture in Iraq in violation of the Geneva Convention (Entman, 2012). But no scandal developed. Why? What does this tell us about more recent scandals?

Entman, in a book aptly titled *Scandal and Silence*, proposes a framework to help answer this question. He argues that scandals are not objective events calibrated to the actual existence of moral wrongdoing. Instead, they are socially constructed by journalists and other participants in the political communication process. A critical factor is how reporters frame the events. An avalanche of media coverage that frames public officials' misdeeds as scandalous can create the political momentum necessary to hold elected officials accountable for their actions. But—and this is the important point—journalists cannot do this on their own. News is not created out of whole cloth, but emerges from a web of relationships between journalists and public officials, formal events, and legitimizing public activities. To build and frame an agenda, reporters require cooperation from government institutions that hold hearings, form commissions, and otherwise begin a formal process of remedial action. This legitimates news stories and allows journalists to frame misdeeds as scandals.

Government took official actions in the wake of Iran-Contra. A presidential commission was appointed, members of Congress actively spoke out, and leaders of the opposition party publicly denounced Reagan's actions. This allowed journalists to frame Iran-Contra as a scandal. None of this happened in the case of the WMDs and Iraq. Initially, there was much less finger-pointing and there were no formal investigations that journalists could cover and harness to frame a series of stories. Leaders from both parties had long believed Iraq had WMDs, so it was dissonant for them to change their minds on a dime. Democrats were sensitive to being seen as "soft" or "weak" on defense. Consequently, Congress did not demand that a presidential commission be formed to examine the Bush administration's conduct. Thus, there was little elite disagreement to which stories could be indexed. In addition, Bush's actions did not explicitly violate established policies, as was the case with Iran-Contra. Finally the public, still reeling from the tragic aftershocks of 9/11, was inclined to accept the White House's version of the facts.

Frames help us understand why there was a scandal in the case of Iran-Contra, but not for WMDs and the Iraq war. (Conservatives would take issue with this analysis, arguing that the scandal metaphor is inappropriate. Given the president's sovereign duty to protect the citizens of the U.S., he had reason

Continued

to fear another attack on U.S. soil in view of the accumulation of considerable evidence, mistaken as it turned out, that Iraq had WMDs. Furthermore, conservatives would contend that the Iraq war achieved important benefits, such as neutralizing a U.S. enemy and producing a more democratic Iraqi government. To conservative activists, what was scandalous perhaps was Bill Clinton's refusal to aggressively pursue al-Qaeda during his term. But this too illustrates that scandals are socially defined, with frames playing an important role.)

What do you think? Can you think of other misconduct that did not become a scandal, but should have? What about the 2008 financial crisis, which had grave implications for the U.S. economy and global repercussions, and was abetted by government decisions and Wall Street greed? Yet although the Treasury, the Federal Reserve, and Wall Street bore responsibility, no one was held accountable, and no scandal developed. As Entman notes, "The more powerful the individuals and interests implicated by the allegations, then—all else being equal—the less, not more, likely they are to spark a major scandal," (2012, p. 8).

The email scandal involving Hillary Clinton fits this narrative, but is distinctive because of the different ways the scandal was constructed and the many questions that were raised (see discussion later in the chapter). Was the Clinton email issue a legitimate scandal because her use of a private email server threatened national security, or because, according to the FBI director, she did not seem to be entirely truthful about sending classified emails? Was it a scandal created by the Republicans to malign her, much ado about nothing, a non-scandal blown out of proportion by the media, her opponents, and many (though not all) voters, who had come to view her use of a private email server as another manifestation of her lack of transparency? And from whence did the perception of her lack of transparency, her lack of trustworthiness, spring? Rampant media coverage over the years? Her own unartful comments and actions? Her questionable moral judgments in the cases of her email server and failure to distance herself as Secretary of State from the Clinton Foundation? Gender biases that would never have plagued a male candidate? All of the above? A scandal is not an objective quantity, but depends on its social construction. The way it is complexly constructed can redound with significant political implications—and, in the case of Clinton, this poses gnawing "What might have beens?" had the scandal not occurred or been constructed in different ways.

SOCIAL SCIENTIFIC UNDERPINNINGS

Theory and Research

Psychological research offers a theoretical basis for political framing effects. The psychologists Amos Tversky and Daniel Kahneman theorized that frames guide processing of different choices and direct individuals to define problems in subtly different ways (Kahneman, 2011). In a classic study on framing surgical options, they found that research participants were significantly more likely to favor surgery if informed that 95 of 100 patients *survived* the surgical procedure rather than if 5 of 100 *died* from it (Kahneman & Tversky, 1984). The mortality was exactly the same in both cases. What differed was the frame. This study, based on the psychology of perceived gains and losses, started the ball rolling on framing, leading to voluminous research documenting its influence on different outcomes.

Frames are complex because they operate at so many different levels of analysis. Even when examined on the narrow individual, psychological level, they are multifaceted because they can call on broad thematic constructs ranging from language to ideology to rhetoric. The most basic frame is the **equivalence frame**, in which identical information is framed differently through adroit use of logically equivalent but differently phrased information. For example, highlighting 6 percent unemployment, rather than 94 percent employment, would call attention to the downside rather than the upside of the economy. However, in the complex world of politics, issues do not always neatly present themselves in terms of logically identical features.

Emphasis frames highlight different message features and are more common in political communication. These frames do not necessarily present identical information. Instead, some frames emphasize certain considerations, while other frames call attention to alternative aspects of the problems (de Vreese, 2010; Druckman, 2001a). Thus, terrorism can be framed in terms of national security, violations of civil liberties, or a problem overshadowed by more pressing domestic concerns. Emphasis frames complicate matters, muddying the waters, by encompassing more than just the equivalence-based mode of verbal or linguistic presentation (Scheufele & Iyengar, 2014). If everything in political persuasion is a frame, then the term becomes unwieldy.

All this makes framing research interesting, but sometimes abstruse and hard to unravel. The increasing number of conceptualizations and operational measures of frames (e.g., Coleman, 2010) have made framing an exciting area of cross-disciplinary research, but also an area fraught with ambiguities, an issue of concern to precision-focused social science research (Cacciatore, Scheufele, & Iyengar, 2016).

There is a silver lining. Despite their different academic perspectives, scholars of different intellectual stripes agree that framing plays a key role in the battles of political communication, exerting subtle, sometimes potent effects on public opinion and policy. In an interesting article, Christian Burgers and his colleagues (2016) integrated framing with theory on conceptual metaphors. They argued that **figurative frames** contain metaphors, hyperbole, and irony, as well as key conceptual content about political issues. Figurative frames call on Lakoff and Johnson's (1980) idea of conceptual metaphors, famously illustrated with conservatives' sleight of semantic hand in proposing the frame "tax relief." The expression "tax relief" reflects the assumption that taxation constitutes a "burden" or weight that presses down on citizens, rather than a benefit (taxes fund schools and roads). Given the embedded conceptual implication (taxes are a burden), the logical (seemingly inescapable) conclusion is that people need "tax relief," a political position congenial with conservative philosophy. Figurative frames derive from broad conceptual metaphors, shaping public dialogue that can challenge established political constructions.

Some scholars worry that framing gives political leaders immense power to mold public opinion. By simply choosing one slant rather than another and adroitly spinning the issue with focus group-tested words, elites can manipulate political opinions (Brewer, 2001). Critics lament that in the real world of political marketing, consultants play word games, trying to figure out if voters will respond more favorably to reductions in taxes when they are described not as *tax cuts* but as *tax relief* (Lakoff, 2004). Republicans derisively framed Obama's health reform legislation *Obamacare*, hoping that the creation of a neologism would invoke the specter of government health care run amok, where patients are mere puppets in a health care system steered by the president. Democrats, for their part, like to frame educational programs designed to help underrepresented groups disadvantaged by society as *affirmative action*. Opponents prefer the term *reverse discrimination*.

It is not just a frame game—it's a name game as well. One political writer emphasized the role language plays in framing:

> Call it what you will—enhanced interrogation or torture, collateral damage or civilian deaths, pro-life or anti-reproductive rights, global warming or climate change, homosexual marriage or marriage equality, assault rifles or "semi-automatic small-caliber sporting rifles with plastic accessories"—it's all the same.
>
> (Hertzberg, 2013, p. 23)

Hertzberg underscores the impact that not-so-subtle changes in language can exert on politics. While critics worry that national leaders can manipulate language to mislead the public, political activists more optimistically point out that frames on issues ranging from abortion to global warming can be a potent way to influence public attitudes, offering new ways to view contemporary problems. Frames can be harnessed for positive and negative ends, but as with all political persuasion, involve verbal sleights of hand that promote the persuader's view of the issue. These can both educate and mislead.

This raises an empirical question: Do frames influence political attitudes? We cannot know for sure until research examines framing effects. Frames have been studied in classic experiments, where research participants are randomly assigned to read different frames and indicate their opinions on the issue. If participants change opinions in accord with the frame, framing effects have occurred. These studies, which have focused on emphasis frames, have found that beliefs can be altered merely by varying the frame, or the way the story is told.

In one study, Druckman (2001b) informed research participants that the Ku Klux Klan had asked for a permit to hold a rally on campus. For one group, the request was framed in term of the right of a racist group to exercise its right to free speech. For another group, the emphasis was public safety and violence that might result. Individuals who read a *New York Times* article emphasizing free speech expressed more tolerance toward the rally than those who read a public safety article.

Nelson and Oxley (1999) examined framing through a similar experimental paradigm. A mock newspaper story offered two frames of a land development controversy in south Florida. The information was the same, but the slants differed dramatically. An economically framed article claimed that the project would create thousands of construction jobs, noting that creating jobs "is more important than protecting frogs and snakes." The environmentally framed article stressed how regional wetlands would be harmed by the development, arguing that "we shouldn't sacrifice planet Earth's diversity for the sake of yet another hotel" (Nelson and Oxley, 1999, p. 1062). Participants who read the economic frame held a more positive opinion toward the development than those in the environmental framing condition. Individuals who read the environmental frame were less likely to believe that the project would exert a positive environmental impact.

Other emphasis framing research has focused on news frames, in particular, a comparison of effects of episodic versus thematically framed news. In a series of classic field experiments, Iyengar (1991) framed poverty in terms of either heartfelt anecdotes, or episodic frames, or more general thematic explanations. In one episodic frame that focused on a single poignant episode, individuals viewed a news report describing two homeless Black adolescents living on New York City streets or a homeless White couple forced to live in their car in San Diego. The focus was on the personal plights of these individuals. A thematically framed story juxtaposed a description of national increases in poverty with discussion of reductions in federal social programs. Participants who viewed the episodic story attributed poverty to individualistic factors, blaming poverty on character and education. Those who watched the thematically framed story attributed poverty to societal conditions. The implication is that news, with its dramatic focus on frequently sad stories involving particular individuals, can lead citizens to view politics as a non-stop, chaotic cacophony of unrelated terrible events that have no overarching explanation. Moreover, as Iyengar found, the episodic emphasis causes people to blame individuals for problems, rather than seeing them as a function of larger economic, social, and political forces. A systemic view of problems is consonant with a liberal philosophy, while attributing social problems to individuals tends to be aligned with conservative views.

The findings from these older studies nicely establish cause and effect, but as is the case with laboratory experiments, they do not take into account real-world complexities. Framing experiments may be conducted on college students, who do not reflect the population of citizens, with their preexisting attitudes, strongly held frames, and pressing economic needs. The experiments typically do not expose research participants to competing frames—as when people come into contact with dueling, opposing frames on issues like immigration, or hear different frames in political debates. In an effort to increase the breadth and validity of framing research, scholars have embarked on more in-depth, externally valid studies in recent years, offering more generalizable insights about the impact of political frames (Brewer & Gross, 2010).

How and When Do Frames Work?

How do frames influence political beliefs? Which cognitive processes mediate framing effects? Three interpretations have been advanced to answer these questions. The first process is accessibility, discussed in the previous chapter, the notion that frames access particular attributes, making certain ideas more accessible. A second view highlights belief importance, whereby political frames make some considerations appear more relevant than others, giving them more weight in an individual's decision-making, perhaps also rendering these attributes more applicable (Nelson, Clawson, & Oxley, 1997; Price & Tewksbury, 1997). A third interpretation emphasizes belief change, suggesting that frames offer new arguments on behalf of a political viewpoint.

Researchers who emphasize accessibility view framing as akin to priming, suggesting that political opinions are superficial, tilting with the political wind, susceptible to manipulation by "top-of-the-head" cues (Perloff, 2013). Those who advance the other interpretations, notably belief importance, emphasize that framing can be more mindful, rendering individuals less susceptible to media persuasion, and requiring the deployment of more thoughtful or at least more compelling political messages.

When do frames exert the greatest impact on beliefs and policy outcomes? A psychological approach to the "when" question emphasizes the beliefs individuals bring to the framing process. Political media frames are filtered through citizens' motivations, ideology, knowledge, and values. People bring a storehouse of knowledge and strong opinions, founded on previous frames, to the media experience. Constructionist research reviewed in Chapter 4 reminds us that citizens are not blank slates when it comes to framing. Instead, they have a rich repertoire of views about politics, some highly developed, others more carelessly put together, but views that, in either case, influence their evaluation of political appeals. For example, Sanders's framing of the economy in terms of inequality resonated with progressives, while Trump's anti-immigration, populist frame congealed with many White working class voters who felt marginalized and disenfranchised. They, therefore, were receptive to Trump's pro-American, nativist rhetoric.

Just as media cannot create agendas out of whole cloth, they also cannot implant frames in audience members' minds. Media framing effects intersect with the values individuals bring to the media, in some cases inducing complex thinking (McLeod & Shah, 2015; Shah, Kwak, Schmierbach, & Zubric, 2004). As these examples illustrate, framing effects are more likely when frames are consistent or resonate with individuals' core values, connecting psychologically with political cognitions (Boyle et al., 2006; Brewer, 2001; Edy & Meirick, 2007; Keum et al., 2005; Nisbet, Hart, Myers, & Ellithorpe, 2013; Shen & Edwards, 2005; Shah, McLeod, Gotlieb, & Lee, 2009; Wagner & Gruszczynski, 2016).

Frames are particularly impactful when they congeal with deep-seated political values. Research indicates that political conservatives tend to endorse values of group loyalty and patriotism, while liberals embrace values like fairness and equality. Thus, group loyalty and patriotism frames should be maximally effective on conservatives, while fairness and equality appeals should be most influential with liberals. Willer and Feinberg (2015, p. 9) found that conservatives were more likely to support gay marriage if gay rights were framed in terms of patriotism ("same-sex couples are proud and patriotic Americans" who "contribute to the American economy and society" than if the message emphasized fairness). By contrast, liberals were more likely to support increased military spending (a position they might initially oppose) if the message highlighted fairness—"through the military, the disadvantaged can achieve equal standing and overcome the challenges of poverty and inequality"—than if the message emphasized patriotism and loyalty (Feinberg & Willer, 2015, p. 1671).

Frames do not operate in a vacuum. While experiments have examined framing effects in isolation, in the real world frames operate in a volatile political environment characterized by competition among frames (Chong & Druckman, 2007a). In elections, candidates frame the same issues—immigration, terrorism, the economy—very differently, employing a host of emphasis frames. When presidents try to convince the public to support a policy—from health care reform to military interventions—they are faced with opposition from leaders with markedly different frames. Context influences framing effect in a host of complex and politically consequential ways (Druckman, 2004). Ideally, as deliberative democratic theory would suggest, competition among frames should stimulate deliberation and encourage more thoughtful processing. This rarely happens. Usually, people stubbornly resist different frames, selectively perceiving frames in light of their biases and perhaps also the intensity of the partisan environment (Klar, Robison, & Druckman, 2013).

Contemporary elections do not promote a polite, by-the-book academic discourse in which frames are discussed, compared, and evaluated based on arguments and evidence. Instead, candidates hurl frames like grenades in a battle ("More immigration means more terrorism!" "If you oppose immigration, you're prejudiced!"). Candidates employ emotional appeals in ads and increasingly tweets. In many instances, macro factors play a key role. The side with the most money and resources is likely to be more effective than its counterparts in persuading citizens to adopt a particular frame (Chong & Druckman, 2007b). And framing battles can lead to polarization, rather than attitude change, on white-hot political and international issues.

Douglas M. McLeod and Dhavan V. Shah (2015) documented this in a series of experiments. Breaking down the episodic versus thematic frame into cleaner categories, they examined the impact of individual versus collective frames on the issue of national security and civil liberties. For example, an individually framed story on anti-terrorism legislation emphasized that the Arab-American Solidarity Front member Youssef Hazim "is concerned his situation may worsen if the new legislation is passed," while the collective-framed story stressed that Arab-American Solidary Front "members are concerned their situation may worsen if the new legislation is passed" (p. 92). Intriguingly, individually framed stories on a host of topics exerted striking polarizing effects. Individuals sympathetic with civil liberties became even more concerned about defending political activists' freedom and privacy, while those more concerned with national security were less likely to favor extending democratic rights when the story was framed around a particular individual. Individually framed stories were processed more quickly and more likely to evoke stereotypes and extreme judgments than group-framed stories.

Thus, the journalistic practice of framing a story around a particular extreme, committed individual, in the interest of engaging and drawing in audience members, may unwittingly lead to greater polarization of opinions. Americans differ in their attitudes, with some hewing closer to national security and others favoring civil liberties. McLeod and Shah counsel that, in the interest of enhancing political tolerance, "the press should make an effort to focus less on individuals and more on the collective implications when covering these conflicts" (p. 142). You can see how news (economically driven by high ratings and Internet clicks) that cynically spotlights the background of terrorists (or extremist activists) can inflame and polarize, causing individuals on both sides to feel more passionately about their side rather than inducing greater deliberation about the issues we collectively face.

In some cases, though, journalists have harnessed frames in ways that exert positive systemic effects, showcasing the ways frames can instigate social change in a process of frame-building. Consider capital punishment.

For years, capital punishment was framed around such categories such as "an eye for an eye" (you take someone's life, you deserve to be killed), and the pros and cons of deterrence—whether the death penalty does or does not deter crime. In the 1980s and '90s, a new frame diffused: *the innocence frame*, the notion, buttressed by facts, that as a result of prosecutorial misconduct, fabrication of evidence and wrongful convictions, many innocent people had been executed. As journalistic investigations, buttressed by legal research, began to home in on spectacular cases of innocent people being put to death, more news stories framed capital punishment around the innocence frame, and it began to dominate other frames, garnering media attention (Baumgartner, De Boef, & Boydstun, 2008).

Importantly, the gradual building of the innocence frame seems to have reduced public support for capital punishment, as well as perhaps contributing to a dramatic decrease in the number of death sentences over the past two decades (see America and its fellow executioners, 2016). Heartrending stories of the execution of innocent people, coupled with hard-nosed journalistic evidence, appealed to public compassion and the normative requirement that justice be based on fairness to all. At the same time, other forces operated on the macro front. DNA evidence became a more accepted forensic technique, lending credibility to the claim that wrongful death row convictions stem from structural problems in the judicial system. In a complementary fashion, concerns about racial disparities in death sentences also increased.

Thus, paralleling the agenda-building process, frames are more likely to influence policy when journalists and policymakers recognize that a problem exists, and public and elite forces converge toward acceptance of a new way of viewing the problem. It is important to emphasize that news media exposes ushered in a new way of framing capital punishment, showcasing how frames can produce change on the micro and macro levels.

ELECTORAL IMPLICATIONS: THE CASE OF 2016

"Campaigns," Kinder (2003) observed, "are not so much debates over a common set of issues as they are struggles to define what the election is about" (p. 365). Think of it this way: There is consensus in difficult economic times that economic factors are among the most important problems ailing the country. Framing emphasizes that, given that everybody agrees with this assessment, agenda-setting is not sufficient to explain voting behavior. What matters is how candidates and media frame the economy—how they talk about it, what they choose to emphasize, and whether, for example, they suggest that the problem can be fixed by tax cuts, improved by a monetary focus on lowering interest rates, building the infrastructure to create a massive infusion of jobs, or through a radical, if sometimes simplified, Sanders-style critique centering on how policies have favored the upper 1 percent at the expense of the middle class.

Campaigns represent a battle among different value-based frames as they vie for public and elite attention (Bystrom & Banwart, 2014). The three actors in the political process—candidates, journalists (de Vreese, 2010), and citizens—can share or diverge in the way they frame electoral issues, with plenty of framing variation within each group. These frameworks can be in sync, as in those rare instances during a national emergency when all three groups speak with roughly the same voice, but are usually in conflict, increasingly bouncing off one another in the non-symmetrical domain of cyberspace. Let's take the classic example of Watergate. The White House framed the break-in at the Democratic National Committee at the Watergate Hotel by high-level Republican Party operatives as a trivial "third-rate burglary attempt." *The Washington Post*, the newspaper that did critical investigative reporting, framed it as a threat to democracy, while many Americans, doubting that government would concoct such a scheme, viewed it as a caper, or an event with little relevance to central political issues. In the end, media frames, augmented by those of congressional leaders, carried the day, influencing public opinion and propelling Nixon to resign from office.

2016 Frames: Populism, Trump, and Clinton

Political Psychology of Trump's Frames

Trump framed issues metaphorically, calling on issues as symbols to represent broader concepts. A *New York Times* analysis of Trump's speeches and comments, in the wake of extremist and terrorist attacks in Colorado and San Bernardino in 2015, found that he employed a drumbeat of divisive language, violent images, and mentions of "you" and "we." He stoked concerns about "them"—the generalized other, such as illegal immigrants and Syrian migrants who, he said, threatened the American identity (Healy & Haberman, 2015). His muscular language and stern but seemingly authentic "Trust me,

I know folks" rhetoric resonated with conservative members of his base, though it horrified liberals. We can better appreciate this by examining how Trump's frames congealed with conservative and liberal values.

Conservatives, whose pessimistic perspective on human nature leads them to stress people's selfishness and capacity for evil, believe society cannot function in the absence of authority and strong group ties. Conservatives attach importance to loyalty to the in-group and authority, or what Lakoff (2016) calls "the strict father," where "father knows best . . . and that, in a well-ordered world, there should be (and traditionally has been) a moral hierarchy in which those who have traditionally dominated *should* dominate (see Lakoff, 1996; Haidt, 2012; Graham, Haidt, & Nosek, 2009). Trump's authoritative, take-no-prisoners and law-and-order frame appealed to conservatives who sincerely value authority and loyalty (Ekins & Haidt, 2016). Liberals, who place more value on compassion, saw in Trump's law-and-order frame subtexts of coded racial prejudice. They sensed that Trump was calling, Nixon-style, on fear of crime as a "convenient proxy for race" (Zeitz, 2016).

In framing terms, conservatives typically construct their political views around the conceptual metaphor of the state as a strict father, where morality reflects strength and group loyalty; liberals prefer a different conceptual metaphor: the state as nurturing parent, with morality based on compassion and secular fairness. A framing analysis offers a non-judgmental way of appreciating why Trump's frames appealed so strongly to conservatives but unnerved liberals.

A core Trump frame was classic, time-honored **populism**. Populism dates back to the late 1800s, when there was widespread anger at moneyed elites, corporate exploitation, and businesses that were believed to be robbing working people blind (Kazin, 1995; Perloff, 2016). Populist leaders championed the cause of wage-earners in cities and rural areas, calling for a shorter work day and state control of exploitative railroads. They subsequently succeeded, through a complex of political forces, in gaining better working conditions under FDR's administration. The term "populism" has a checkered history; it has been linked with working class grievances and support for authoritarian, prejudiced political figures like Joseph McCarthy and George Wallace. In the main, populism contrasts the storied (if stereotyped) decency of ordinary people, notably the working class, with the corrupt, dishonest, moneyed elites (as in "Crooked Hillary"). It reflects resentment of authorities, such as corporations, political parties, the media, and the scientific establishment; places faith in authoritarian leaders who espouse the will of ordinary people; and values patriotic, nationalistic, nativist sentiments ("America First") over global, cosmopolitan, and classical liberal viewpoints (Inglehart & Norris, 2016). Media have long played a critical role in framing populist movements in the U.S. and abroad, laying their groundwork, telling their stories, and implicitly ceding control to charismatic leaders, who have sometimes manipulated news coverage to their advantage (Waisbord, 2003; Laurence, 2003; Stewart, Mazzoleni, & Horsfield, 2003).

Populism reemerged in 2016 in the wake of gaping inequality between the rich and poor, hopes sundered by unemployment, and increasing resentment of the "haves." Sanders tapped into this on an ideological level, avoiding prejudiced rhetoric. Trump accessed White working class concerns more emotionally, with his intense language and frames that blamed workers' problems on thoughtless leadership, global trade deals, and illegal immigration. Although the economy has rebounded since the financial crisis of 2008, broad sectors that were once centers of manufacturing in Pennsylvania, Ohio, Kentucky, and other states have lagged behind (Appelbaum, Cohen, & Healy, 2016). Job losses have devastated a number of class communities, causing a host of social ills—community disintegration, drug use, and family strife. Many White working class voters felt drawn to Trump because he promised a brighter economic future.

People base their vote not only on pocketbook considerations—assessments of which candidate will bring back jobs to their communities—but on symbolic attachments, derived from psychological identifications with larger social groups (Sears & Funk, 1999). Like candidates before him, Trump called on symbolic frames to build his constituency.

By framing his message in blunt, unparsed, poll-oblivious speech, Trump, the scion of a wealthy real-estate developer and billionaire member of New York's elite, became the unlikely champion of (primarily White) blue-collar Americans. He was the candidate who thrilled overflow crowds with his denunciation of political correctness, connecting with voters from working class communities "where courage, country and cussedness are core values" (Cohen, 2016, p. 6; see Figure 7.3). When Trump lambasted political elites, framing criticism around time-honored populist critiques of career politicians' indifference, he became a tribune for the Republicans' base of blue-collar Whites, who viewed immigration and trade as symbolic signature issues, felt party leaders were indifferent to their problems, looked on Washington as "a gilded city of lobbyists, contractors and lawmakers" (Confessore, 2016, p. A12), and found it cathartic to blame others for a nexus of elite-inflicted and culturally reinforced decay.

Trump harnessed a complementary "somebody is taking everything you are used to and you had" frame (Cohen, 2016, p. 6) that packed symbols, beliefs, and time-honored resentments into a cohesive populist framework. It and his other frames served as condensational symbols (Edelman, 1964) that distilled into a simple symbolic framework a multitude of emotions, hopes, recollections of previous glories, and remembrances of perceived and real indignities. In a similar fashion, "Make America Great Again" called up patriotic emotions while also evoking the perception that America wasn't

Figure 7.3 Trump's frames emphasizing the economic woes of the working class, promises to restore a past founded on America's greatness, and mix of symbolic, sometimes racially freighted, appeals resonated with many working class Americans, particularly men who felt marginalized by the new global order.

Getty Images

particularly good or great, along with a host of humiliations, materially and vicariously experienced, some projections of anger at the seemingly ill-gotten gains of other ethnic groups—all told, an assortment of dreams, desires, and understandable, if sometimes untenable, expectations of what leaders could realistically deliver in the wake of a tsunami of economic and cultural changes that had transformed society from what it had been when were young.

The facts frequently did not comport with Trump's claims. Much of what he said about the negative consequences of trade deals and immigration were not true, or were base simplifications contradicted by other facts (Goodman, 2016; Reich, 2010; Egan, 2015; Krugman, 2016). Sadly, politics is not about the literal accuracy of facts. Politics is about symbols, identifications, and grievances, real or perceived. And on a broader level, Trump's frame resonated with many White working class workers because it captured an emotional truth: America's elites, trying to harness globalization for the greatest good for the greatest number, have been insensitive to workers' needs; and global trade has hemorrhaged the manufacturing sector far more than elites assumed (Autor, Dorn, & Hanson 2016). Globalization has benefited capitalist elites, while its costs have been painfully experienced by homegrown workers (Appelbaum, 2016).

Trump's frames resonated because they spoke to the powerlessness and alienation—economic, political, and racial—that so many White blue-collar workers faced in the wake of crushing economic and technological advances that eliminated jobs, causing social decay: crime, heroin addiction, pulverizing marital stress and domestic violence, and even rising mortality rates (e.g., Fausset, 2016a, 2016b). Trump was the candidate of the middle-aged worker who lost his job and had to work part-time to support his family;

> of the man who opens his morning paper to find that another of his neighbors has died of a heroin overdose; of the woman who proudly sent her son to fight in Iraq only to watch it break his body and mind . . . of a patriotic people who feel an almost apocalyptic apprehension about the future. (Trump's) great insight was to recognize and exploit that apprehension.
>
> (Vance, 2016a; see also Vance, 2016b)

As scholar Henry Olsen explained more metaphorically:

> The biggest thing that Trump offers these voters is finally somebody paying attention. Imagine that they're the wallflowers at the high school dance and they're sitting off, ignored by everybody. Suddenly, the football hero comes up and says, "Come dance with me." That's intoxicating.
>
> (Calmes, 2016, p. A10)

Trump became their blue-collar billionaire, even as he gained political capital from a canny appreciation of their malaise.

There was also a racial component, subtexts of his frames that either contained prejudiced appeals or subtly (and sometimes not so subtly) invited followers to access ethnic biases. These included his aggressive questioning of Obama's birth certificate, even after it had been proven that the first African American president had been born in the U.S.; calls to bar Muslims from entering the U.S. based on a linkage of Muslims with terrorism; and his initial refusal to disavow the support of White nationalist and former KKK member David Duke. During the early Republican primaries, those voters most likely to support Trump had a history of voting for segregationists, and in the South Carolina Republican primary 38 percent of his supporters said they wished the South had won the Civil War, while a third believed that the practice of the Islamic religion should be illegal in the U.S. (Irwin & Katz, 2016; Blow, 2016). We need to be careful here: These are correlational findings, hold only for a minority of voters, and do not show prejudiced attitudes *caused* people to vote for Trump. Some of Trump's supporters voted for Obama and Bill Clinton (Cohen, 2016), and these and other voters would deeply resent a prejudiced label. Others turned to Trump not because they were bigots, "but because they didn't know where to turn and Trump spoke to their fears" (Kristof, 2017, p. A23).

Yet theorists argue that White anxiety—steeped in economic insecurities and resentment of erosion of familiar cultural norms—formed the foundation of populist support for Trump's electoral frames (Klein, 2016; Taub, 2016). (In a similar fashion, European populism, exemplified by British voters' support of UK withdrawal from the European Union, known as Brexit, seems have been partly rooted in a cultural backlash against progressive cultural change; see Inglehart & Norris, 2016). The issues Trump raised were not new, but the manner in which he coalesced them, pulling together dark economic and cultural forces in the vernacular of the "common man" (delivered with the panache of a celebrity media pitchman), appealed to his fervently loyal base.

Clinton, Framing, and Optimism

There *was* another candidate and she used frames persuasively—she won the popular vote, after all. Clinton framed the election in terms of experience (the need to have her steady, experienced hand guiding the ship of shape in torrential times), gender issues (preserving a woman's right to choose, and protecting women from sexual aggression seemingly embraced by Trump), fixing problems "together," as she emphasized, rather than presumably divisively, and continuing Obama's record of economic success. Her focus was less on introducing new, outside-the-box frames à la Bernie Sanders than on rallying supporters around frames they already embraced and moving undecided voters toward her camp by framing the election around Trump's shortcomings.

As a candidate who had served as Secretary of State under President Obama, she stitched herself to his economic and health care accomplishments. Throughout her career, Clinton had championed change for women, children, and groups left behind. However, by dint of her long career in government and framing her campaign around her expertise, she became the agent of the status quo in a year when 3 of 5 voters said that the country was on the wrong track (Peters, Thee-Brenan, & Sussman, 2016).

On an affective level, Clinton's frames seemed to reflect an optimistic view of America's future, typically predictive of electoral success (Zullow, Oettingen, Peterson, & Seligman, 1988). and one that appealed to the more well-educated members of her base. The use of optimism and pessimism was predictably more complicated in 2016. Trump showcased optimism about America's future, promising in his convention speech to make America "strong," "proud," "safe," and "great" again. But he also infused his speeches with negative, dark images, framing America as threatened by violence perpetrated by "them," the outsiders (Healy & Haberman, 2015), a nation that he said, in different ways on many occasions, was "losing at war, losing at trade," and "losing at everything," and "losing so much" (Surowiecki, 2016, p. 42).

While one might expect voters to be wary of taking a chance, given the losses that they experienced, research suggests that people are especially prone to contemplate or pursue a gamble when feeling anxious or angry (Marcus, 2002; Marcus, Sullivan, Theiss-Morse, & Stevens, 2005; Lerner & Keltner, 2001). Classic research on framing (Kahneman, 2011) shows that people experience more pain over losses (experiencing economic hardship) than they feel joy over winning (getting a hefty raise). Sometimes people are willing to take a risk to avoid more losses and recoup what has been taken from them over the years, especially when they perceive that losses are undeserved. Trump's pessimism about the present and focus on what America and workers lost served up a powerful frame for voters. Nearly 8 in 10 voters who leaned Republican thought their side was losing politically. Individuals dissatisfied with their economic plight and convinced that "people like me don't have any say about what the government does" overwhelmingly favored Trump (Surowiecki, 2016, p. 42). For those who perceived they had lost so much, who felt the present did not measure up to a more comfortable past, Trump was the long shot worth gambling on—the candidate who, whatever their misgivings about his cringeworthy remarks (Chira, 2017), offered them a chance to recoup what they had lost.

As Trump articulated his priorities as president, questions surfaced as to whether his policies reflected his pro–working class frames. Although he kept his promise to encourage hiring American workers, he postponed a plan to create jobs by rebuilding the nation's infrastructure and cut regional organizations and job-training programs that benefited many of his economically aggrieved working class voters (Brooks, 2017). How would his voters react to these policies? Would they frame his administration's actions as inconsistent with his vaunted promises, or would they see a silver lining? Trump framed his 2016 campaign in terms of harsh populist claims, but governing required a more inclusive touch. Questions surfaced as to whether he could reframe his policies so he held onto his constituents while also building a base he needed to govern.

CONCLUSIONS

Framing is a core concept in political communication because it illuminates the "how" of politics—how political leaders promote issues, how media discuss national problems, and how voters process political information. Framing focuses on how problems are defined, the ways dots are connected to offer a thematic perspective, and the crux of a controversial political issue. Framing cuts to the core of how leaders, media, and citizens construct meaning and how power is wielded through the political meanings conveyed, distilled, and propagated through communication. In contrast to agenda-setting and priming, which focus on salience of issues, framing examines the content, interpretations, and potential solutions to gnawing political issues.

There are three broadly different frames. Equivalence frames are the most basic, keeping the information equivalent, but using different words to overlay the facts. Emphasis frames focus on different features of issues, while figurative frames highlight metaphors, hyperbole, and irony. For of all its intuitive appeal, framing lacks conceptual precision; the concept is vague and indelicately cuts across levels of analysis. Its amorphous content can frustrate efforts at academic precision, but also highlights its utility in a political world, where the ability to define the essence of problems is a key instrument of power (Schattschneider, 1960). Frames are spun by elites, promulgated by the news media, harnessed by activists, and harbored by citizens, who use them to make sense of the political world.

Research has documented framing effects, but of course, frames are not magic bullets. While they can change the language of public discourse, they are usually most likely to influence citizens when they resonate with core values and beliefs.

Politics is a battle for the frame, with different actors attempting to influence the way issues are defined, presented, highlighted, and promoted. Candidate, media, and citizen frames (as well as the host of frames promulgated by activist groups) compete to influence public opinion, a crucial force in the democratic debate to influence policy. Frame battles occur in every election, controversially in the 2016 race, where Trump called on a populist frame laced with incendiary language that resonated with White working class voters marginalized by globalization, pained by community decay, and strained by feelings of powerlessness and ethnic resentment. Clinton opted for a more conventional approach, framing herself as the candidate of experience and connecting her policies with those of a popular president.

Did frames serve democracy? In the dynamic 2016 election, outsider candidates like Trump and Sanders, along with enthusiastic coalitions of voters, pushed their frames upward, influencing recalcitrant party regulars, gaining media traction, and pushing a populist frame to the forefront of public debate. The populist frame broadened the discussion and brought new perspectives from the White working class into the discussion. But populism has always had an authoritarian, prejudiced undertone (Kazin, 1995). Veiled bigotry by Trump supporters on social media, along with reports of hateful rhetoric on the campaign trail (vandals in Minnesota scrawled "Go Back to Africa" next to the Trump campaign slogan, "Make America Great Again) served as portentous reminders that framing cannot be separated from larger moral concerns.

Yet democracy promises citizens "the freedom to choose." It does not "guarantee particular outcomes," nor that the outcomes will be framed in the most thoughtful or decorous ways (Chong & Druckman, 2007b, p. 652). As always, political communication presents us with a conflict between how candidates will frame issues to win election, and what they—Democrat, Republican, or alternative party candidates—should do to promote a deliberative discussion of the issues. The conflict is endemic in politics, whether practiced in ancient Greece, in 19th-century America, or in our country today.

REFERENCES

America and its fellow executioners. (2016, January 10). (Editorial). *The New York Times*, 10.

Appelbaum, B. (2016, October 31). Little-noticed trade fact: It's no longer rising. *The New York Times*, A1, A3.

Appelbaum, B., Cohen, P., & Healy, J. (2016, September 15). A rebounding economy remains fragile for many. *The New York Times*, A1, A19.

Autor, D.H., Dorn, D., & Hanson, G.H. (2016, January). *The China shock: Learning from labor market adjustment to large changes in trade*. NBER Working Paper No. 21906. Retrieved from www.nber.org/papers/w21906 (Accessed October 3, 2016).

Baumgartner, F.R., De Boef, S.L., & Boydstun, A.E. (2008). *The decline of the death penalty and the discovery of innocence*. New York: Cambridge University Press.

Bazelon, E. (2015, August 23). Status: Unknown. *The New York Times Magazine*, 11–13.

Blow, C.M. (2016, September 12). About the "basket of deplorables". *The New York Times*, A23.

Borah, P. (2011). Conceptual issues in framing theory: A systematic examination of a decade's literature. *Journal of Communication, 61*, 246–263.

Boyle, M.P., Schmierbach, M., Armstrong, C.L., Cho, J., McCluskey, M., McLeod, D.M., & Shah, D.V. (2006). Expressive responses to news stories about extremist groups: A framing experiment. *Journal of Communication, 56*, 271–288.

Brewer, P.R. (2001). Value words and lizard brains: Do citizens deliberate about appeals to their core values? *Political Psychology, 22*, 45–64.

Brewer, P.R., & Gross, K. (2010). Studying the effects of issue framing on public opinion about policy issues: Does what we see depend on how we look? In P. D'Angelo & J.A. Kuypers (Eds.), *Doing news framing analysis: Empirical and theoretical perspectives* (pp. 159–186). New York: Routledge.

Brooks, D. (2017, March 17). Let Bannon be Bannon! *The New York Times*, A25.

Burgers, C., Konijn, E.A., & Steen, G.J. (2016). Figurative framing: Shaping public discourse through metaphor, hyperbole, and irony. *Communication Theory, 26*, 410–430.

Bystrom, D.G., & Banwart, M.C. (2014). Reflections on the 2012 election: An agenda moving forward. In D.G. Bystrom, M.C. Banwart, & M.S. McKinney (Eds.), *Alienation: The divide & conquer election of 2012* (pp. 328–336). New York: Peter Lang.

Cacciatore, M.A., Scheufele, D.A., & Iyengar, S. (2016). The end of framing as we know it . . . and the future of media effects. *Mass Communication and Society, 19*, 7–23.

Calmes, J. (2016, August 6). As Trump rises, G.O.P. faces push on its economics. *The New York Times*, A1, A10.

Cappella, J.N., & Jamieson, K.H. (1997). *Spiral of cynicism: The press and the public good.* New York: Oxford University Press.

Chira, S. (2017, January 15). Women who voted for Donald Trump, in their own words. *The New York Times*, 12.

Chong, D., & Druckman, J.N. (2007a). A theory of framing and opinion formation in competitive elite environments. *Journal of Communication, 57*, 99–118.

Chong, D., & Druckman, J.N. (2007b). Framing public opinion in competitive democracies. *American Political Science Review, 101*, 637–655.

Chozick, A., & Alcindor, Y. (2016, February 5). Plain talk pulls younger voters to Sanders' run. *The New York Times*, A1, A15.

Cohen, R. (2016, September 11). We need "somebody spectacular". *The New York Times* (Sunday Review), 1, 6–7.

Coleman, R. (2010). Framing the pictures in our heads: Exploring the framing and agenda-setting effects of visual images. In P. D'Angelo & J.A. Kuypers (Eds.), *Doing news framing analysis: Empirical and theoretical perspectives* (pp. 233–261). New York: Routledge.

Confessore, N. (2016, March 28). How G.O.P. elites lost the party's base to Trump. *The New York Times*, A1, A12, A13.

Corrigan, L.M. (2016, September/November). Whiteness, economic precarity, and presidential politics. *Spectra, 52*(3&4), 27–31.

D'Angelo, P., & Kuypers, J.A. (Eds.) (2010). *Doing news framing analysis: Empirical and theoretical perspectives*. New York: Routledge.

de Vreese, C.H. (2010). Framing the economy: Effects of journalistic news frames. In P. D'Angelo & J.A. Kuypers (Eds.), *Doing news framing analysis: Empirical and theoretical perspectives* (pp. 187–214). New York: Routledge.

The death penalty endgame. (2016, January 17). *The New York Times* (Editorial). (Sunday Review), 10.

Druckman, J.N. (2001a). The implications of framing effects for citizen competence. *Political Behavior, 23*, 225–256.

Druckman, J.N. (2001b). On the limits of framing effects: Who can frame? *Journal of Politics, 63*, 1041–1066.

Druckman, J.N. (2004). Political preference formation: Competition, deliberation, and the (ir)relevance of framing effects. *American Political Science Review, 98*, 671–686.

Edelman, M. (1964). *The symbolic uses of politics*. Urbana: University of Illinois Press.

Edwards, D. (2015, April 19). Marco Rubio's latest global warming denial: "There has never been a moment climate is not changing". *Raw Story*. Retrieved from www.rawstory.com/2015/04/marco-rubios-latest-global-warming-denial-there-has-never-been-a-moment-climate-is-not-changing/ (Accessed January 19, 2016).

Edy, J.A., & Meirick, P.C. (2007). Wanted, dead or alive: Media frames, frame adoption, and support for the war in Afghanistan. *Journal of Communication, 57*, 119–141.

Egan, T. (2015, July 10). Not like us. *The New York Times*. Retrieved from www.nytimes. com/2015/07/10/opinion/not-like-us.html (Accessed November 2, 2016).

Ekins, E., & Haidt, J. (2016, February 5). Donald Trump supporters think about morality differently than other voters. Here's how. *Vox*. Retrieved from www.vox.com/2016/2/5/10918164/donald-trump-morality (Accessed June 14, 2016).

Entman, R.M. (2004). *Projections of power: Framing news, public opinion, and U.S. foreign policy*. Chicago: University of Chicago Press.

Entman, R.M. (2012). *Scandal and silence: Media responses to presidential misconduct*. Cambridge: Polity Press.

Fausset, R. (2016a, August 28). Trump a blue-collar hero? Ask in a blue-collar town. *The New York Times*, 11, 13.

Fausset, R. (2016b, May 26). Feeling let down and left behind, with little hope for better. *The New York Times*, A1, A14.

Feinberg, M., & Willer, R. (2015). From gulf to bridge: When do moral arguments facilitate political influence? *Personality and Social Psychology Bulletin*, *41*, 1665–1681.

Gamson, W.A., & Modigliani, A. (1987). The changing culture of affirmative action. In R.A. Braumgart (Ed.), *Research in political sociology* (Vol. 3, pp. 137–177). Greenwich, CT: JAI.

Gellman, B., & Soltani, A. (2013, December 4). NSA tracking cell phone locations worldwide, Snowden documents show. *The Washington Post*. Retrieved from www.washingtonpost. com/world/national-security/nsa-tracking-cellphone-locations (Accessed November 12, 2016).

Goodman, P.S. (2016, September 29). More jobs, but not for everyone. *The New York Times*, A1, B8, B9.

Graham, J., Haidt, J., & Nosek, B.A. (2009). Liberals and conservatives rely on different sets of moral foundations. *Journal of Personality and Social Psychology*, *96*, 1029–1046.

Haidt, J. (2012). *The righteous mind: Why good people are divided by politics and religion*. New York: Pantheon Books.

Healy, P., & Haberman, M. (2015, December 6). 95,000 words, many of them ominous, from Trump's tongue. *The New York Times*, 1, 25.

Hertog, J.K., & McLeod, D.M. (2001). A multiperspectival approach to framing analysis: A field guide. In S.D. Reese, O.H. Gandy, Jr., & A.E. Grant (Eds.), *Framing public life: Perspectives on media and our understanding of the social world* (pp. 139–161). Mahwah, NJ: Erlbaum Associates.

Hertzberg, H. (2013, April 8). Senses of entitlement. (The talk of the town). *The New Yorker*, 23–24.

Inglehart, R.F., & Norris, P. (2016, July 29). *Trump, Brexit, and the rise of populism: Economic have-nots and cultural backlash*. Paper presented to the annual meeting of the American Political Science Association convention, September, Philadelphia. Retrieved from https://research.hks.harvard.edu/publications/workingpapers/Index.aspx (Accessed November 25, 2016).

Irwin, N., & Katz, J. (2016, March 15). The geography of Trump's popularity. *The New York Times*, A3.

Iyengar, S. (1991). *Is anyone responsible? How television frames political issues*. Chicago: University of Chicago Press.

Kahneman, D. (2011). *Thinking, fast and slow*. New York: Farrar, Strauss and Giroux.

Kahneman, D., & Tversky, A. (1984). Choices, values, and frames. *American Psychologist, 39,* 341–350.

Kazin, M. (1995). *The populist persuasion: An American history.* New York: Basic Books.

Keum, H., Hillback, E.D., Rojas, H., de Zúñiga, H. G., Shah, D.V., & McLeod, D.M. (2005). Personifying the radical: How news framing polarizes security concerns and tolerance judgments. *Human Communication Research, 31,* 337–364.

Kinder, D.R. (2003). Communication and politics in the age of information. In D.O. Sears, L. Huddy, & R. Jervis (Eds.), *Oxford handbook of political psychology* (pp. 357–393). New York: Oxford University Press.

Kinder, D.R. (2007). Curmudgeonly advice. *Journal of Communication, 57,* 155–162.

Klar, S., Robison, J., & Druckman, J.N. (2013). Political dynamics of framing. In T.N. Ridout (Ed.), *New directions in media and politics* (pp. 173–192). New York: Routledge.

Klein, J. (2016, September 12–16). Don't believe the new myths about America's white working class. *Time,* 34.

Kosicki, G.M. (1993). Problems and opportunities in agenda-setting research. *Journal of Communication, 43,* 100–127.

Kristof, N. (2017, February 23). Fight Trump, not his voters. *The New York Times,* A23.

Krugman, P. (2016, October 17). Their dark fantasies. *The New York Times,* A19.

Lakoff, G. (1996). *Moral politics: What conservatives know that liberals don't.* Chicago: University of Chicago Press.

Lakoff, G. (2004). *Don't think of an elephant! Know your values and frame the debate.* White River Junction, VT: Chelsea Green.

Lakoff, G. (2016, March 2). *Why trump?* Retrieved from https://georgelakoff.com/2016/03/02/why-trump/ (Accessed October 28, 2016).

Lakoff, G., & Johnson, M. (1980). *Metaphors we live by*: Chicago: University of Chicago Press.

Laurence, J. (2003). Ross Perot's outsider challenge: New and old media in American presidential campaigns. In G. Mazzoleni, J. Stewart, & B. Horsfield (Eds.), *The media and neo-populism: A contemporary comparative analysis* (pp. 175–195). Westport, CT: Praeger.

Lecheler, S., Bos, L., & Vliegenthart, R. (2015). The mediating role of emotions: News framing effects on opinions about immigration. *Journalism & Mass Communication Quarterly, 92,* 812–838.

Lerner, J.S., & Keltner, D. (2001). Fear, anger, and risk. *Journal of Personality and Social Psychology, 81,* 146–159.

Maher, T.M. (2001). Framing: An emerging paradigm or a phase of agenda setting? In S.D. Reese, O.H. Gandy, Jr., & A.E. Grant (Eds.), *Framing public life: Perspectives on media and our understanding of the social world* (pp. 83–94). Mahwah, NJ: Erlbaum Associates.

Marcus, G.E. (2002). *The sentimental citizen: Emotion in democratic politics.* University Park: Pennsylvania State University Press.

Marcus, G.E., Sullivan, J.L., Theiss-Morse, E., & Stevens, D. (2005). The emotional foundation of political cognition: The impact of extrinsic anxiety on the formation of political tolerance judgments. *Political Psychology, 26,* 949–963.

McCombs, M., & Ghanem, S.I. (2001). The convergence of agenda setting and framing. In S.D. Reese, O.H. Gandy, Jr., & A.E. Grant (Eds.), *Framing public life: Perspectives on media and our understanding of the social world* (pp. 67–81). Mahwah, NJ: Erlbaum Associates.

McLeod, D.M., & Shah, D.V. (2015). *News frames and national security: Covering Big Brother*. New York: Cambridge University Press.

McQuail, D. (2010). *McQuail's mass communication theory* (6th ed.). Thousand Oaks, CA: Sage.

Nelson, T.E., Clawson, R.A., & Oxley, Z.M. (1997). Media framing of a civil liberties conflict and its effect on tolerance. *American Political Science Review, 91*, 567–583.

Nelson, T.E., & Oxley, Z.M. (1999). Issue framing effects on belief importance and opinion. *Journal of Politics, 61*, 1040–1067.

Nisbet, E.C., Hart, P.S., Myers, T., & Ellithorpe, M. (2013). Attitude change in competitive framing environments? Open-/closed-mindedness, framing effects, and climate change. *Journal of Communication, 63*, 766–785.

Nisbet, M.C. (2010). Knowledge into action: Framing the debates over climate change and poverty. In P. D'Angelo & J.A. Kuypers (Eds.), *Doing news framing analysis: Empirical and theoretical perspectives* (pp. 43–83). New York: Routledge.

Pan, Z., & Kosicki, G.M. (1993). Framing analysis: An approach to news discourse. *Political Communication, 10*, 55–75.

Perloff, R.M. (2013). Political persuasion. In J.P. Dillard & L. Shen (Eds.), *The Sage handbook of persuasion: Developments in theory and practice* (2nd ed., pp. 258–277). Thousand Oaks, CA: Sage.

Perloff, R.M. (2016, July 24). Needed—A 21st century populism to "keep hope alive". *Cleveland.com*. Retrieved from www.cleveland.com/opinion/index.ssf/2016/07/ enough_of_the_ dangers_of_throw.html (Accessed October 29, 2016).

Peters, J.W., Thee-Brenan, M., & Sussman, D. (2016, November 9). Exit polls confirm stark divisions along racial, gender and economic lines. *The New York Times*, P6.

Price, V., & Tewksbury, D. (1997). News values and public opinion: A theoretical account of media priming and framing. In G.A. Barnett & F.J. Boster (Eds.), *Progress in communication sciences: Advances in persuasion* (vol. 13, pp. 173–212). Greenwich, CT: Ablex.

Qin, J. (2015). Hero on Twitter, traitor on news: How social media and legacy news frame Snowden. *International Journal of Press/Politics, 20*, 66–84.

Reese, S.D. (2007). The framing project: A bridging model for media research revisited. *Journal of Communication, 57*, 148–154.

Reich, R. (2010). *Aftershock: The next economy and America's future*. New York: Knopf.

Schaffner, B.F., & Sellers, P.J. (2010). Introduction. In B.F. Schaffner & P.J. Sellers (Eds.), *Winning with words: The origins and impact of political framing* (pp. 1–7). New York: Routledge.

Schattschneider, E.E. (1960). *The semisovereign people: A realist's view of democracy in America*. New York: Holt, Rinehart & Winston.

Scheufele, D.A. (1999). Framing as a theory of media effects. *Journal of Communication, 49*, 103–122.

Scheufele, D.A. (2000). Agenda-setting, priming, and framing revisited: Another look at cognitive effects of political communication. *Mass Communication & Society, 3*, 297–316.

Scheufele, D.A., & Iyengar, S. (2014). The state of framing research: A call for new directions. In K. Kenski & K.H. Jamieson (Eds.), *The Oxford handbook of political communication theories*. New York: Oxford University Press. Retrieved from www.oxford.handbooks.com

Scheufele, D.A., & Tewskbury, D. (2007). Framing, agenda-setting, and priming: he evolution of three media effects models. *Journal of Communication, 57*, 9–20.

Sears, D. O., & Funk, C. L. (1999). The role of self-interest in social and political attitudes. In M. P. Zanna (Ed.), *Advances in experimental social psychology* (Vol. 24, pp. 1–91). San Diego: Academic Press.

Shah, D. V., McLeod, D. M., Gotlieb, M. R., & Lee, N-J. (2009). Framing and agenda-setting. In R. L. Nabi & M. B. Oliver (Eds.), *The Sage handbook of media processes and effects* (pp. 83–98). Thousand Oaks, CA: Sage.

Shah, D. V., Kwak, N., Schmierbach, M., & Zubric, J. (2004). The interplay of news frames on cognitive complexity. *Human Communication Research, 30*, 102–120.Shane, S. (2015, November 17). Debates on limits over surveillance burst open again. *The New York Times*, A1, A12.

Shen, F., & Edwards, H. H. (2005). Economic individualism, humanitarianism, and welfare reform: A value-based account of framing effects. *Journal of Communication, 55*, 795–809.

Stewart, J., Mazzoleni, G., & Horsfield, B. (2003). Conclusion: Power to the media managers. In G. Mazzoleni, J. Stewart, & B. Horsfield (Eds.), *The media and neo-populism: A contemporary comparative analysis* (pp. 217–237). Westport, CT: Praeger.

Surowiecki, J. (2016, June 6 & 13). Losers! *The New Yorker*, 42.

Takeshita, T. (2006). Current critical problems in agenda-setting research. *International Journal of Public Opinion Research, 18*, 275–296.

Taub, A. (2016, November 2). Behind the gathering turmoil, a crisis of white Identity. *The New York Times*, A6.

Tewksbury, D., & Scheufele, D. A. (2009). News framing theory and research. In J. Bryant & M. B. Oliver (Eds.), *Media effects: Advances in theory and research* (3rd ed., pp. 17–33). New York: Routledge.

Vance, J. D. (2016a, September 10). How Donald trump seduced America's white working class. *The Guardian*. Retrieved from www.theguardian.com/commentisfree/2016/sep/10/jd-vance-hillbilly-elegy-donald-trump-us-white-poor-working-class (Accessed November 3, 2016).

Vance, J. D. (2016b). *Hillbilly elegy: A memoir of a family and culture in crisis*. New York: Harper.

Wagner, M. W., & Gruszczynski, M. (2016). When framing matters: How partisan and journalistic frames affect individual opinions and party identification. *Journalism & Communication Monographs, 18*, 5–48.

Waisbord, S. (2003). Media populism: Neo-populism in Latin America. In G. Mazzoleni, J. Stewart, & B. Horsfield (Eds.), *The media and neo-populism: A contemporary comparative analysis* (pp. 197–216). Westport, CT: Praeger.

Willer, R., & Feinberg, M. (2015, November 17). The key to political persuasion. *The New York Times* (Sunday Review), 9.

Zeitz, J. (2016, July 18). How Trump is recycling Nixon's "law and order' playbook. *Politico Magazine*. Retrieved from www.politico.com/magazine/story/2016/07/donald-trump-law-and-order-richard-nixon-crime-race-214066 (Accessed October 25, 2016).

Zullow, H. M., Oettingen, G., Peterson, C., & Seligman, M. E. (1988). Pessimistic explanatory style in the historical record: CAVing LBJ, presidential candidates, and East versus West Berlin. *American Psychologist, 43*, 673–682.

PART THREE

Communication and the Presidential Election Campaign

8 Presidential Election Campaigns Past and Present

It is obvious, but important to state: Presidential election campaigns play a critical role in contemporary democracy. "Elections are arguably the single most important event in American democratic life," observed political scientist James A. Thurber. Elections, he explained, provide "an opportunity for Americans to both give their consent to be governed and to hold their representatives accountable for past performance" (Thurber, 2000, p. 1). In a similar fashion, Paolo Mancini and David Swanson (1996) noted that election campaigns

> select decision makers, shape policy, distribute power, and provide venues for debate and socially approved expressions of conflict . . . Symbolically, campaigns legitimate democratic government and political leaders, uniting voters and candidates in displays of civic piety and rituals of national renewal.
>
> (p. 1)

In short, presidential elections fulfill democracy's purpose, giving citizens the opportunity to select their leaders (Trent, Freidenberg, & Denton, 2011). Campaigns symbolically bring citizens and leaders together in quadrennial rituals of debate, discussion, and dialogue. Campaigns provide the political soil in which new movements and disenfranchised groups can flower, express their grievances, and mobilize to elect leaders who execute new policies. These are also popular myths. In reality, elections are bruising, polarizing, and can increase cynicism about politics. Losers and their supporters become embittered, and citizens feel frustrated by the lack of serious issue discussion. Presidential elections fail to engage millions of Americans: more than 4 in 10 eligible voters chose not to vote in the past two presidential elections. And yet, warts and all, elections remain the centerpiece of democracy, the best way, most theorists argue, for the demos—the populace or citizenry—to select its government.

If democracies cannot function without citizens, they certainly cannot operate without leaders—frequently maligned, impossibly human, and indispensable for democracy. Running for the presidency requires remarkable (perhaps abnormal) ambition, ego, vision, political acumen, willingness to sacrifice means to ends, and determination to make a difference in people's lives (Cramer, 1992; Stone, 2010). It also helps to be born male. The overwhelming majority of political leaders are men. Even as more women have run for office, more than 80 percent of members of Congress, 75 percent of state legislators, and 90 percent of mayors of large U.S. cities are men (Lawless & Fox, 2012).

More complexly, politics requires a unique capacity to fuse extremities: selfish and selfless, practical and principled, sincere and strategic. To be a political candidate, observed Michael Ignatieff, a Canadian academic who entered politics and became leader of Canada's Liberal Party, is to be "worldly and sinful and yet faithful and fearless at the same time. You put your own immodest ambitions in the service of others. You hope that your ambitions will be redeemed by the good you do" (Brooks, 2014). But that good requires getting one's hands soiled and impure by running for election, "a noble struggle" (Ignatieff, 2013, p. 177).

This chapter examines the communication underpinnings of this noble struggle, introducing the presidential election campaign, the focus of the next section of the book. The first portion of the chapter provides a historical overview of presidential campaign communication, beginning with American elections in the 18th century, moving through the popular (and prejudiced) politics of the 19th century, and discussing the use of message crafting in elections of the 20th and 21st centuries. It is important to appreciate historical foundations of the present era. By apprehending the past, we more keenly understand that what seems new and disturbing is not so new (and therefore perhaps less disconcerting). We also gain keener insights into exactly which facets of contemporary election campaigns are unique to the present day. The second part of the chapter, focusing on the contemporary presidential campaign, presents a political marketing perspective, examining key marketing concepts and their applications. An evaluation of technology's role in the presidential campaign follows, connecting past, present, and perhaps future.

HISTORICAL OVERVIEW

Pre-campaign America

We have come to expect that our presidential candidates will announce, with much fanfare and braggadocio, more than a year before the election, that they want to be our president. It was not always this way. As historian Gil Troy (1996) notes:

Originally, presidential candidates were supposed to "stand" for election, not "run." They did not make speeches. They did not shake hands. They did nothing to betray the slightest ambition for office. Candidates were supposed to stay on their farms in dignified silence, awaiting the people's call, as George Washington had done.

(p. 7)

The Founding Generation disdained campaigning for public office. Openly soliciting votes? Aggressively campaigning for political support? These smacked of an obnoxious ambition that the idealistic early Americans felt was unbecoming of the Enlightenment-guided citizens of the new nation. What's more, they feared that a handful of unscrupulous, ambitious campaigners would manipulate the masses, whom they held in contempt. "Popular campaigning was not only dangerous, it was improper, illegitimate, and unnecessary," leaders of America's founding generation maintained (Troy, 1996, p. 8).

This did not last long. Political acrimony and slug-it-out presidential campaigns, albeit conducted behind the veneer of finely polished doors, soon became the order of the day. An aristocratic model of presidential politics was gradually replaced by a persuasion model, in which candidates aggressively campaigned for election. But the modern campaign emerged gradually, presaged by other campaign developments.

Elite, Party, and Press Politics

During the late 18th and early 19th centuries, presidential candidates symbolically jousted through the medium of the newspaper. Politics was a rich man's game, waged not in public but in the elite but truculent pages of the political press. During the 1800 election, the candidates, President John Adams and challenger Thomas Jefferson, never left their farms. But their minions were not so meek. The two new political parties of the era—the Federalists of John Adams and Alexander Hamilton, and Thomas Jefferson's Republicans (no relation to the current Republican Party)—operated newspapers that brandished their ideology.

Pro-Jefferson newspaper editors smeared President John Adams, alleging that he plotted to create a "dynastic succession with his sons" (Troy, 1996, p. 13). Federalists called Jefferson an atheist, an anarchist, and a coward. "The engine is the press," Jefferson acknowledged. "Every man must lay his purse and his pen under contribution," he added, suggesting that if they wished to reach elite newspaper readers, candidates had to avail themselves of the power of the pen (McCormick, 1982, p. 65). And so, candidates penned harsh words lambasting their opponents, as the two political factions—the more pro-government Federalists and libertarian Republicans—diverged sharply on the issues. Yet there remained a silver lining. Despite the partisan conflicts, developments of considerable importance were occurring (Fischer, 1965). Political parties were beginning to form, and leaders began using established organs to express their ideas. Unlike the French Revolution, political leaders were not beheaded by guillotine. The opposition party did not mount a coup. Power passed from one party to the other, peaceably, amid fervent, often intense political disputes.

I would be remiss if I did not point out that that there lurked a fundamental inequity just beneath the surface. Only property owners could vote. Blacks and women could not cast ballots. By the definition of democracy advanced in Chapter 2, the U.S. was not a democracy, nowhere close to a fully democratic nation.

Popular, Prejudiced Politics

In 1828, the attacks got personal. Andrew Jackson, nationally known for his military success in the War of 1812, faced an aristocratic candidate, John Quincy Adams, the son of the second president. Jackson's newspaper editor friends concocted lies about Adams, charging that he had referred to the Dutch as "the stupid Dutch." Pro-Adams editors counterattacked, going negative to an extent that exceeds even today's highly charged campaigns, alleging that "General Jackson's mother was a common prostitute." However, Jackson, an early populist, was elected.

Jacksonian democracy, as it became known, was something of a novelty. During Jackson's time, scores of citizens followed politics more actively than they had in the past. The number of eligible voters rose dramatically as many states removed the rules restricting voting to property owners. At the time, the French writer Alexis de Tocqueville, touring America in the early 1830s, was impressed by the political tumult and the obvious pleasure Americans took in forming groups to discuss political issues. Politics was no longer the exclusive province of super-rich and educated elites; ordinary people were becoming involved. The organizing mechanism was the political party. Parties began connecting with and organizing the mass public, mobilizing citizens around party nominees (Pessen, 1985).

It came together in 1840. "Popular politics became the new American religion, as two and a half million men streamed to the polls—ten times the number enrolled in churches," Troy notes (1996, p. 20). Any strategy, no matter how goofy, that engaged the electorate was deemed acceptable. The beneficiary was William Henry Harrison, in truth a mediocre candidate, but the first to deliver a stump campaign speech on the campaign trail. Branding himself as a man of the people, in contrast to the presumably more aristocratic incumbent, President Martin Van Buren, Harrison promoted himself "as the log cabin-hard-cider candidate who, unlike the high-falutin' Martin Van Buren, was plain, simple, down-to-earth, and very much of, by, and for the people" (Boller,

2004, p. 66). The campaign was quite a spectacle, with thousands descending on Whig Party rallies, gabbing at parades that went on for miles, and brandishing campaign paraphernalia like coonskin caps, Tippecanoe badges, and Tippecanoe shaving cream, the latter named after Harrison's now controversial battle against Shawnee Indians in a place called Tippecanoe, Indiana (Jamieson, 1984).

Had this occurred today, it would all have been mocked by a cynical press as image-based campaigning or laughable political branding. But in 1840 the press was not cynical and was funded by political parties, and many party newspapers supported Harrison.

Harrison died in office, but he left an imprint on political campaign process. His campaign stimulated interest in politics, bringing more people into electoral politics than had participated before. It also signaled that popular, slogan-filled campaigns were the new normal. But there were serious downsides. Like the vast majority of 19th-century campaigns that would follow, the candidates failed miserably to place important issues on the political agenda. Candidates promoted—we can't yet say advertised—their images, and "spun" their backgrounds, eliding issues like race that they could not psychologically grasp or chose politically to avoid. Race, prejudice, and racism were the unspoken, avoided, and ultimately malignant aspects of mid-19th-century campaigns, issues destined to divide the country in the Civil War.

Even before the horrific war, with its moral and political divisions, politics had been the coin of the cultural realm. In the early decades of the 19th century, political parties became the mechanism that connected the public and its elected leaders. Parties developed structures—professional organizations, ideological platforms, conventions, and exuberant campaigns—that connected people to political leaders. During presidential campaigns, they helped organize spectacular rallies and enthusiastic marches through the streets called torchlight parades. Coordinated by political clubs composed of immigrants toiling in blue-collar jobs, the parades featured barbecues and thousands of men marching military style through streets, kerosene torches lit, a brass band leading the way. As many as 25 percent of voters participated actively in campaigns during the last half of the 19th century, and 77 percent of the electorate—primarily White men, to be sure—voted in presidential elections (Dinkin, 1989; McGerr, 1986). Although the participation was welcome, it is doubtful that the level of discourse was much higher than that of fans of two college football teams, carousing at a tailgate party in (literal) pre-game revelry.

The 1896 Transition to the 20th Century Campaign

By 1896 loud, rambunctious military-style street rallies were out of fashion. The spectacle of men marching through the streets seemed out of sync with cultural norms on the cusp of a new century (Dinkin, 1989). The Civil War–era armies of the night gave way to a business model of campaigning that revolved increasingly around national political party committees. During the 1896 campaign, Republican Party Chairman Mark Hanna employed modern bookkeeping practices, kept track of campaign developments by telephone, and raised corporate funds for the campaign, spending millions on promotion, including the first-ever campaign film. Although the campaign raised important monetary issues—the gold standard versus free silver, the latter symbolizing justice to Democrats and fiscal disaster to Republicans—Hanna ran a tightly organized campaign that reduced complex issues to clever phrases, advertising candidate William McKinley "as if he were a patent medicine," in the words of Theodore Roosevelt (Perloff, 1999, p. 35).

McKinley pursued a quiet but effective campaign strategy, delivering carefully scripted speeches to handpicked groups invited to appear at the front porch of his home in Canton, Ohio, with the remarks reprinted in local newspapers and diffused across the country (Rove, 2015). His opponent, the populist orator William Jennings Bryan, embarked on a national speech-making tour, traveling more than 18,000 miles and giving 600 speeches, nearly falling victim to exhaustion at the end of the campaign, yet foreshadowing the national presidential campaigns that would follow. Bryan could never escape the perception that he was simply a protest candidate (Kazin, 1995). His eloquent, worker-focused message represented a threat to the moneyed status quo, perhaps eliciting an early negative campaign. McKinley chieftains may have spread a rumor that if Bryan were elected, businesses would be shuttered and workers would lose their jobs (King, 2016). In fairness, Democrats supporting Bryan spread their share of false rumors as well (Rove, 2015). It was, in any case, a full-blown campaign, with Bryan crisscrossing the country, offering a heartfelt if sometimes unrealistic message on behalf of the American worker, and McKinley's men festooning homes with flags, emphasizing a theme of patriotism and unity, anticipating the image-based campaigns of the 20th century.

20th-Century Campaigns

Theodore Roosevelt took the press and presidency by storm. A big, brash, and immensely self-confident man, Roosevelt befriended, charmed, and dominated reporters in a way no president had before. He harnessed the power of the office to shape public opinion, expanding White House press rooms, modernized technology by replacing antiquated telegraphs with fancy telephones, and provided reporters White House access so long as they did not reveal the source of their stories. Despite his blatant news management, he championed transparency on a broader level, arguing that publicity could expose corporate corruption. In those days, publicity meant making information public to expose wrongdoing. But the meaning would soon change, favoring public relations and political spin (Greenberg, 2016).

The 19th-century notion that candidates should stand for election, not run, met its official obituary during Theodore Roosevelt's presidency, as he campaigned in more than 550 towns in 24 states. The persuasion genie leapt out of the political bag in the early years of the new century as even the academic Woodrow Wilson employed pithy election-year ads, and the laconic Calvin Coolidge became the first president to use radio to communicate regularly with the public.

Franklin D. Roosevelt transformed the modern presidency, seizing on the president's powers to help the working class, reform the economy, and win World War II. A canny politician and a gifted statesman, he spun political information to his desired ends. FDR expanded press conferences, engaged in spirited news management techniques, and melded his melodious voice to the new radio medium in storied "fireside chats," complemented by newsreel coverage that sculpted an image of Roosevelt as vigorous and sprightly, while ignoring the president's painful, paralyzing polio (Steele, 1985). When it came to campaigning, FDR and his successor, Harry S. Truman, whistle-stopped the country by train. National campaigns were de rigueur, and party managers developed strategies to promote candidates, organize field operations, and raise money from wealthy individuals. With television on the horizon, campaigns were set to move to the next stage.

Television and Presidential Campaigns: The Emergence of Image

John F. Kennedy placed television on the political campaign map. He exploited its focus on images to his strategic advantage, harnessing his physical attractiveness and visual acuity in the 1960 presidential debates. He turned the press conference into a political art form, calling on a comedian's talent for using nonverbal expressions to make his point and a showman's ability to deflect a question to his strategic advantage while cleverly eliding reporters' questions (see Figure 8.1). The foreign policy demands facing Kennedy were intense, and he could spin information artlessly, as during the Bay of Pigs Invasion fiasco and thoughtfully, during his finest hour, averting nuclear war during the 1962 Cuban Missile Crisis.

Beginning in the late 1950s and continuing into the '60s, concerns about elites' ability to manipulate symbols via television took on histrionic proportions. Critics speculated, in claims based more on Freudian fears than empirical evidence, that subliminal sexual images in advertising seduced the America public into buying products. Vance Packard (1957) worried, in *The Hidden Persuaders*, that "symbol manipulators" could sell politicians like soap. Daniel J. Boorstin (1964) warned of the ability of politicians to contrive artificial events (like campaign appearances at manufacturing plants, called pseudo-events that are adroitly staged for media coverage). Harking back to Plato's Allegory of the

Figure 8.1 John F. Kennedy, who recognized the ability of television to project an image, used the small screen to project an impression many Americans found congenial.

Getty Images

Cave, where prisoners believed that shadows projected on the wall of a cave were real, Boorstin challenged the widespread belief that political content on television was in some sense "real," arguing instead that political communications were frequently contrived, focused more on candidate makeup, lighting, and stagecraft, creating spectacles that an unsuspecting public perceived as authentic. Boorstin's book, aptly titled *The Image* and echoing Lippmann's (1922) concerns about the susceptibility of the mass public, had far-ranging effects on influential intellectuals (Greenberg, 2016). It presaged postmodern thinkers' concerns about a faux reality and congealed with political communication scholarship demonstrating that perceptions of media impact had strong effects, independent of any actual influences media exerted. And while Boorstin exaggerated the impact of contrived events on attitudes, he astutely highlighted the new reality of manipulating perceptions via the small television screen and the ways that politician-created pseudo-events had seamlessly become part of American political culture.

If Kennedy thrived on the image, Richard Nixon flailed with it, at first (in one sense admirably) opting to reject imagery by deciding not to wear makeup in the 1960 presidential debate, yet reluctantly embracing image-making eight years later, recognizing he needed to massage his own awkward visual appearances to win the affective hearts and susceptible minds of the American electorate. Fearing the press would disparage him, he felt his only recourse was to seize control, take matters into his own hands, and create the White House Office of Communications, which provided a centralized role for White House attempts at news management. Nixon made polling a centerpiece of his governing strategy, going so far as to manufacture supportive opinion poll findings and fabricate calls to news organizations, trying to make it appear like large numbers of ordinary citizens disapproved of what he saw as stridently negative media coverage of the presidency (Perloff, 1998). His exploitation of image metastasized into the massive public cover-up of his aides' bugging the Democratic headquarters at the Watergate Hotel in 1972, in what he viewed as a mere public relations problem that could be solved with effective PR. "Craving positive news coverage was nothing new. But Nixon was unique in allowing that desire to spill over into rampant illegality," Greenberg observed (2016, p. 400).

Mastering the Art of Media Image-Making

The detritus of Nixon's presidency included cynicism about the truthfulness of presidential communication. With the public arguably frustrated with exploitation of media imagery for unethical ends, the pendulum turned. Images weren't out—they were necessary to govern—but the "anti-image image" became the byword during Jimmy Carter's presidency, as he wore cardigan sweaters rather than suits, and projected honesty, promising "I'll never tell a lie" in the fashion of John Boy Walton (the oh-so-genuine character in the eponymous 1970s drama). But of course, presidents must massage the truth to some degree (the intent and degree to which they do this determining the ethics of their actions). Carter, beset by double-digit inflation, the seizure of hostages in Iran, and a changing global scene, did not always level with the public to the degree he promised, and events, his management of them, and questions about his leadership led to his defeat in 1980 at the hands of the first presidential candidate who had honed his pre-presidential image as an actor and TV show host in the entertainment media.

Ronald Reagan was that president. If John F. Kennedy introduced television to the presidency, Ronald Reagan consummated the marriage. Dubbed the "Great Communicator" because he understood the grammar and syntax of the medium (conveying core emotions like anger and reassurance convincingly on television with his nonverbal expressions), Reagan dismantled barriers of technology, speaking to Americans like he was a close friend, creating "the illusion of eye contact with an unseen audience" (Jamieson, 1988, p. 132; Lanzetta, Sullivan, Masters, & McHugo, 1985). Much as other presidents used the technology of their times to display leadership—Lincoln with the stump speech, FDR with radio—Reagan mastered the grammar of television, all while perpetrating the minor deception that the speechwriter's words he spoke were his own.

He spoke plainly and optimistically, using words that would come off schmaltzy when used by other communicators, accessing the national heritage of proud patriotic experiences, and telling heroic stories about ordinary Americans. A classic example is his "Morning in America" television ad that served as the symbolic cornerstone of Reagan's victorious 1984 reelection campaign.

At times indistinguishable from a sunny McDonald's commercial of the 1980s, it included images of a paperboy tossing a newspaper from a bicycle, campers hoisting an American flag, and a tractor plowing a field; it was "a star-spangled montage of Americana," words spoken to a sentimental musical score, while the narrator intoned that "it's morning again in America. Today more men and women will go to work than ever before in our country's history" (Greenberg, 2016, p. 414). A remarkable piece of advertising artistry that offered a powerful narrative of American optimism, the images displayed were nevertheless predominantly White, eliding rising inequality and high unemployment. Reagan's rhetoric, while visually evocative and rhetorically appealing, showcased his biases. Reagan perpetrated race-baited untruths about "a 'young buck' chiseling welfare and a wealthy Chicago 'welfare queen' tooling around in her Cadillac" (Baker, 2016, p. 7). Yet Reagan also used his rhetoric to unify Americans around common themes (see Figure 8.2).

Reagan's advisers honed the art of news management nearly to a science, it sometimes seemed, bringing into the popular lexicon terms like photo-op (a staged opportunity for a televised visual); sound bite (the ever-shorter summaries politicians spoke to conform to TV news constraints); and the line of the day (the major theme the White House would emphasize to the press on a given day to coalesce news coverage around one issue; Maltese, 1992). His communication strategies invited questions of whether lofty rhetoric invoked by presidents from Lincoln to Roosevelt had devolved in an age of simplified visual images—or whether the use of emotion-packed visuals exquisitely matched the communicative requirements of the times. Did Reagan deliver effective leadership, appropriately adapted to a television age, or had he substituted style for substance, offering simplified visual speechifying at the expense of thoughtful policy rhetoric?

By 1992, when Democrat Bill Clinton ran for office, it was a taken-for-granted precept that cable news had inaugurated a 24-hour-a-day news cycle and candidates needed a "war room" to craft strategy, prepare messages, and instantly respond to opposition attacks. Clinton masterfully—if not entirely honestly—navigated the storm of controversy emerging from charges of marital infidelity, appearing with his wife on *60 Minutes* to acknowledge, in the manner of the *Thirtysomething* TV show, that they did not have a perfect marriage but cared deeply for one another, denying charges, disparaging his accusers, and spinning the story to suggest these were private, not public, matters.

Figure 8.2 Ronald Reagan, with an actor's understanding of the grammar of television, conveyed compelling narratives that conjoined visuals with patriotic themes. He elevated visual image-making to an art, though the images were not always in sync with hard-fact economic realities America experienced during the 1980s (see Hertsgaard, 1988).

Getty Images

In his 1992 presidential election campaign, Clinton marketed himself as a hipper, more compassionate alternative to President George H. W. Bush. Bush was, in the eyes of Democrats, so out of touch he did not know what a supermarket scanner was and artlessly looked at his watch during a presidential debate. By contrast, Clinton played the saxophone on Arsenio Hall's late-night talk show, highlighting his familiarity with both contemporary music and media. He demonstrated his emotional sensitivity in a presidential debate by accessing his inner Oprah Winfrey, displaying empathy with a female questioner in a town hall debate, turning to her, looking her in the eye, and demonstrating sympathy for her economic plight. During his first two years in office, Clinton conducted 82 talk radio interviews and invited radio talk show hosts to the White House in 1993 to promote his health care plan (Kurtz, 1996). But a multi-million-dollar advertising campaign financed by the Health Care Insurance Association of America successfully—if deceptively—reframed his health plan as federal government–socialized health care. Lobbying groups, noting that Hillary Clinton was coordinating White House health reform, ridiculed her in spooky ads that mocked an old medical television show, *Dr. Kildare*. The narrator intoned, "She's a doctor with a prescription for disaster. She's Hillary Clinton and she's Doctor Hilldare" (Perloff, 1998, p. 251).

Clinton, like presidents who preceded and followed him, plainly stood for certain principles, notably harnessing smaller government and centrist leadership positions to help downtrodden Americans. Yet preoccupied with public image, he employed a variety of pollsters who were skilled at quantifying presidential public opinion, relying on them to test-market ideas, roll out policy initiatives, and help craft messages on a variety of issues, including his notorious *affair de coeur* with Monica Lewinsky, which cycled endlessly on television news, talk shows and the new scandal-ridden Internet websites. He trifled with truth, saying he had not had "sexual relations with that woman, Miss Lewinsky"—a truth technically since they had not engaged in intercourse, but a falsehood in the moral universe, an example of sexualized political spin.

Meanwhile, Republican legislators, outraged over Clinton's infidelity and lying under oath, sought his impeachment, keeping the story in the news, with journalists all too happy to cover the titillating tale, guaranteed to boost ratings. It was a battle of frames, Republicans hyping the sexual licentiousness of the president of the United States, Democrats emphasizing that the president's mistake was a private foible that did not bear on his public role as president. Both sides framed and spun the truth to their advantage. In the end, Congress acquitted Clinton narrowly, mirroring public opinion, which viewed Republican efforts as overreach. Public opinion, as measured by polls, constituted a democratic counterweight to the opposition party's efforts to excoriate Clinton, indicating, regardless of one's views of Clinton's behavior, that democratic processes informed policy decisions at the highest levels.

Three years later, the Clinton-Lewinsky saga, a national crisis at the time, was placed in larger perspective when the country was attacked on September 11, 2001. George W. Bush was president, having defeated Al Gore in a razor-thin electoral result finally decided by the Supreme Court. After some rhetorical success framing the war on terrorism in terms of good and evil, while being careful to separate Muslim Americans from terrorist acts committed in the name of Islam, Bush embarked on his controversial selling of a war against Iraq, arguing that Iraqi president Saddam Hussein possessed weapons of mass destruction. In a full-court press that called to mind Woodrow Wilson's propaganda-laced initiative launching American participation in World War I, the Bush administration engaged in a host of strategies, from leaking stories to public pronouncements, all spinning the false assertion that Saddam Hussein had weapons of mass destruction, necessitating, Bush claimed, an American invasion of Iraq (Rich, 2006). Saddam was ousted, but the human and international political costs were far greater than anticipated. In the 2004 election, Bush sought to access—his aides would say honorably, critics argued exploitatively—memories of the 9/11 attacks in a political ad that combined 9/11 images with the closing argument that Bush had made the country safer and stronger. It was a much darker "morning in America," sadly illustrating the grimmer reality the nation faced.

If you thought adroit image manipulation ended in 2008 with Barack Obama, who earnestly promised to end bipartisan strife in his first presidential campaign, think again. Spontaneous as it seemed at the time, his message that the country needed to transcend poll-driven "politics as usual," abetted by the 2008 mantra, "Yes We Can" (which went viral with a will.i.am hip-hop song), was pre-tested and pre-planned. Greenberg called it "the spin of no spin" (2016, p. 441). As president, Obama employed some of the same techniques as his predecessors—polling, slogans, and use of current media, now the digitally based YouTube, email blasts, Facebook, and Twitter—to promote his agenda and policy frames (see Figure 8.3). Obama recognized that political marketing does not end on Election Day, but continues throughout a president's term in office, in what is sometimes called the permanent campaign, a marketing effort steeped in persuasion, contemporary media, and that quintessential feature of modern politics: political spin (see Box 8.1). Obama aggressively employed a variety of communication platforms, even a humorous appearance on Zach Galifianakis's talk show, *Between Two Ferns*, to persuade young people to sign up for health insurance. In other areas, like gaining support for a nuclear deal with Iran or air strikes against ISIS, Obama found that even soaring rhetoric could not overcome strong partisan opposition, the public's ambivalence, and

Figure 8.3 Barack Obama harnessed the new interactive media to promote his programs, showcasing the importance of political marketing in "the permanent campaign" that extended well beyond the presidential election.

Getty Images

challenges of capturing a national audience in an era of myriad media and instantaneous platform shifting and smartphone screen swiping.

Policy was formulated by experts in the White House, but it had to be marketed and sold. Battling opponents of a U.S.–Iran nuclear weapons agreement, who spent more than $20 million on a media campaign, the Obama White House combined inter-personal persuasion with a West Wing communication-focused war room, complete with a Twitter hashtag, @The IranDeal, to galvanize support for the Iran nuclear deal (Hulse & Herszenhorn, 2015). Obama continued to harness media and an inclusive rhetoric of empathy and commonality, notable for its amity toward his foes (Hart, Childers, & Lind, 2013). He succeeded on some issues while failing on others, such as a high-stakes media campaign to persuade Republican lawmakers to let him fill a vacant seat on the Supreme Court.

Donald Trump, who seemed to be the center of every media maelstrom in his unfold-ing presidency (Manjoo, 2017), continued to harness Twitter, appealing to his base with promises to bring back jobs, borders, and dreams, but alarming many Americans with attacks on the media and false statements, such as that the illicit votes of millions of undocumented immigrants deprived him of a popular vote victory. The mercurial president dominated media—conventional, online, and social—like no other recent chief executive, eschewing the Reaganesque rule that presidents should maintain care-ful control over their image and public presentations. Following the dictates of advis-ers who preached change through disruption, he rejected the time-honored tendency of presidents to move from divisive campaign rhetoric to more inclusive governing-focused appeals that help build broad coalitions needed to push legislation through Con-gress. Instead, he continuing to lambast the media and appeal to grievances of his base. It was a much different, idiosyncratic, marketing approach.

As the preceding discussion makes clear, presidential leadership has always involved persuasion. Increasingly, in a media—correct that, a social or hybrid media—age, image-making and message-sculpting are indispensable tools in the presidential arma-mentarium. Many conceptual frameworks emphasize this, but one that is particularly germane to this book is marketing, the focus of the next section.

BOX 8.1 POLITICAL SPIN

It has been called many things: packaging, image-making, branding, marketing, news management, strategic communication. But the term that today best captures so much of contemporary political communication is spin, a "pithy, lighthearted, evocative, and . . . not necessarily derogatory" term that suggests irony, political play, and even postmodern self-awareness, as David Greenberg (2016) incisively observes (p. 7). The term has morphed into a popular meme, tweaked and adapted to describe the place where aides hype their candidate's performance in a debate (*The Spin Room*); become a humorous reference to political consultants (spin doctors, later the ironic choice of a rock group's name); and evolved to describe the oppositional segment of former Fox host Bill O'Reilly's television show ("The No-Spin Zone"), where he supposedly revealed the truth behind political events). Spin refers to a political persuasive sleight of hand.

To some degree, spin has always been part of politics, from Plato's discussion of the manipulation of appearances in his Allegory of the Cave to Aristotle's defense of political rhetoric from the multifaceted use of propaganda by the Catholic Church in the Middle Ages, through American colonists' fabrications of what we would now call media events in white-hot descriptions of the Boston Massacre, to Joe McGinnis's (1969) classic book on the marketing of Richard Nixon in 1968, *The Selling of the Presidency*, where a cigarette on the cover serves as a metaphor for selling the president. (In this sense, it was ironic that four years later Nixon presidential aide John Dean, in discussing the Watergate scandal, said there was "a cancer growing on the presidency".) Spin emerged in the mastery of presidential image-making—described by Reagan staffers' use of a "line of the day" to promote the administration's interpretation of events; continued in George W. Bush's declaration, like Tom Cruise in *Top Gun*, that the war in Iraq was over, when it actually was not; evolved with Obama's admission that presidential success involves an artful combination of public relations and politics, which Greenberg notes was also spin; and reached new levels of humor and irony with the Trump administration's insistence that appointing wealthy Wall Street financiers to Cabinet posts did not contravene his populist message. Although spin elides an exact definition because it is not a scientific term, it refers to promoting an interpretation of a political event, an attempt to shade or manage news, and place the best face on a political official's decisions.

Candidates resort to spin because they are ambitious and willing to do what it takes to get elected. They spin because they hope to escape blame for actions which, in an ethical universe, they should acknowledge. But they also spin for more defensible reasons: because they anticipate that opponents will distort their statements; in order to provide a utilitarian defense of policies that are under attack; in an effort to offer a diplomatic defense for controversial foreign

Continued

policy positions that will please one government and outrage another; and because they expect that, in a world where all is public, they have to put their best foot forward before someone steps on it electronically.

Like all political communication, spin defies easy analysis. Frequently maligned, often used to deceive and obfuscate, it is, alas, a necessary weapon in the political persuasion arsenal, pointing up the normative complexities and conundrums of politics. Greenberg takes a nuanced view, noting that as long as public opinion is sovereign, people can endure and survive spin, noting that spin can be harnessed to lead, as well as mislead, and has salutary effects when a prescient leader must massage language to persuade the public to approve a policy it does not fully understand or accept. Spin is not necessarily bad, he notes, but is problematic when employed by the wrong leaders at the wrong time for the wrong purposes (Greenberg, 2016, p. 448). But increasingly we find that so much is spun—from ads to tweets to fake news—that attempts to debunk it (like fact checks) are questioned and disparaged by opportunistic politicians, leading voters to question even honest, factual claims, in what sometimes seems to be a postmodern hall of mirrors, abetted by the endless variety of subjectivity we find on social media platforms.

In an ideal world, we want our candidates to tell the truth and offer transparent leadership, presenting clear campaign policies, adhering to consensually validated facts, telling us when they fall short, how they can do better, owning up to mistakes, and leveling with us when life's unpredictability sunders their most well-crafted plans. These are worthy goals, embraced by normative theorists of different philosophical bents. Politics, personality, and the confluence of ideals and raw ambition frequently militates against their successful execution. At the risk of sounding romantic, one thinks of the words of the poet Robert Browning and their application to the fraught world of politics. Our political leaders' reach should exceed their grasp, Browning might have observed. "Or what's a heaven for?"

POLITICAL MARKETING

Political Versus Commercial Marketing

The contemporary presidential campaign is a dogged, brutish, and image-centric exercise in political marketing. Marketing is a broad concept that describes the processes by which a society communicates and distributes products and services of value to consumers by analyzing consumers' needs, developing product modifications, and promoting products through diverse media. In commercial marketing, a seller exchanges a particular product for money from a population of consumers. In political marketing, the candidate delivers a series of promises in exchange for votes from the electorate. As political marketing scholar Bruce I. Newman (1994) notes:

> the candidate is in reality a service provider and offers a service to his consumers, the voters, much in the same way that an insurance agent offers a service to his consumers . . . Candidates operate in a dynamic environment, fast, changing, and full of obstacles that present marketing challenges that require flexibility. Like corporations around the world that alter their services to respond to a more demanding consumer in the commercial marketplace, candidates have to respond to the fast-paced changes that take place in the political marketplace.
>
> (p. 9)

Political marketing is a fascinating concept, conceptualized diversely, defined in different ways, and overlaid with different value assumptions (Butler & Harris, 2009; Cwalina, Falkowski, & Newman, 2009, 2011; O'Shaughnessy, 1999; Winchester, Hall, & Binney, 2016). Marketing now occurs in electoral campaigns across the world, in countries large and small, democratic and less democratic, attesting to the global reach of marketing communications (Rose, 2010). **Political marketing** involves the applications of marketing principles to political campaigns (both electoral and public opinion–focused), with the product a complex combination of the candidate, policy positions, and a cultivated image, communicated to voters and citizens through multiple media channels (Newman, 1999).

Wait a mass-marketed minute, you may say. Is there no difference between commercial and political marketing? Actually, marketing politics differs from marketing products in five key ways.

First, businesses are driven to make a profit; in politics, the objective is to implement a set of political goals and run a democratic government. In commercial marketing, a product's success lies along a continuum, as a company can make a profit by capturing a sizable, but not exclusive, share of the market. In elections, success is measured dichotomously: Either you win or you lose. This can make politics more vitriolic than commercial marketing—a blood sport, where candidates may be more willing to take risks to win.

Second, commercial marketing is based on hard-nosed results of marketing studies. In politics, data matter, but so does the candidate's overall philosophy and ideology. In some cases, candidates ignore marketing studies in favor of implementing a particular ideological position.

Third, political marketing operates in a more fluid and unpredictable environment than product marketing. A gaffe or insensitive candidate remark can kill a candidacy. The news media play a more important role in interpreting these and other unpredictable events than in commercial marketing. Social media also play a more volatile, time-sensitive role, altering campaign dynamics in the wake of a candidate's missteps or testy debate performance.

Fourth, the content and functions differ dramatically. While both commercial and political marketers promote and "sell" dreams, commercial marketers appeal to desires of an individual, hoping to associate the product with deep-seated or culturally cultivated values. Politics also employs symbolic appeals, but more frequently. They are directed not only to the hopes of an individual, but also to a larger cultural collective—an ethnic, religious, or political group with which the voter identifies. Politics calls more on storied national images, time-honored patriotic myths, in-group values, and prejudices, the latter evoked by coded speech.

Because politics is about governing, rather than purchase of products, it asks the individual to imagine him or herself in a grander civic project, transforming the private consumer to publicly focused citizen, a lofty identification that fills many Americans with pride, but, to others, calls up negative connotations, the way politics has been corroded by negativity and money. In politics, the product (candidate) is a service provider, and an elected official has a fiduciary relationship with voters that typically does not occur in commercial marketing.

Finally, political and commercial marketing differ in the ways branding comes into play. **Branding** is the process of creating a distinctive product image and identity, with "unique added values" in consumers' minds through the use of persuasion and marketing (Fennis & Stroebe, 2010; de Chernatony, 1998, p. xvii). Products running the gamut from Mercedes-Benz and Apple to Coca-Cola and Wrigley's have developed strong brand identities. In political marketing, branding is important, but focuses more around creating personal, people-oriented qualities—traits like honesty, empathy, courage, and compassion. The branded message also differs. Candidates develop a policy narrative that attempts to move voters emotionally as well as tangibly, offering hope that the election will bring tangible improvements in their lives. Slogans, catchphrases and even memes encapsulate the brand, serving as robust cues that access positive attitudes (Cwalina et al., 2011). Let's see how this works in contemporary presidential politics.

Political Branding: Psychological and Communication Features

Candidates strive to create a brand identity that is clear and distinguishes them from their competitors. Candidates who are the best political communicators—Reagan,

Clinton, until his sexual escapades tarnished his brand (in the language of political marketing), and Obama—have a clear, energizing brand identity. In Reagan's case, he was a charismatic champion of conservatism, a spokesperson for small government, muscular foreign policy, and a return to old-fashioned patriotic virtue. His focus, harnessing a new approach to America's economic malaise, was encapsulated by his "Are you better off now than you were four years ago?" slogan employed against President Jimmy Carter in 1980.

Clinton's brand signified that he was a new Democrat who rejected old liberalism and linked populist compassion for the ordinary worker with pragmatic, Sixties Generation openness to new solutions to time-worn problems. In 1996, he called on iconic American imagery, appealing to citizens from different walks of life (and diverse market segments), highlighting how he would "restore the American dream" and "build a bridge to the 21st century" (Newman, 2016, p. 41). He offered Americans hope by articulating policies that would help them achieve their own version of the storied American dream.

Obama's brand emphasized that he was the empathic, cool-under-pressure communicator who could articulate problems, transcend petty partisanship, and appeal to America's egalitarian ethos. Like Clinton, he had memorable slogans condensing diverse symbols in 2008—"Hope" and "Change We Can Believe In," highlighted by the iconic "Yes We Can."

Of course, reality set in, besmirching, even corroding these presidents' brands when they failed to respond effectively to national problems or their policy programs fell short. Branding promises to promote a political vision, but attempting to unify citizens around a compelling narrative does not guarantee success in the volatile world of politics.

Obama's social media-focused presidential campaigns (see next section) were intriguingly followed by Trump, who adopted a much different brand orientation. Trump's brand emphasized his brash, authentic, success-emblazoned, "tell it like it is no matter who it offends or mistreats" style. It stressed the narrative that America was headed for disaster after years of Obama-Clinton-style leadership, unless America's middle-class dreams, territorial borders, and stalwart image of yore (this could call up prejudiced imagery) were reclaimed. During the 2016 campaign, his "Make America Great Again" slogan communicated his approach with much more zest and political clarity than Clinton's more amorphous, less affect-laden, "Stronger Together." Trump was unique in an important respect: *Because of his world-famous hotels and casinos, real estate name, and television show, Trump was not just a candidate who used branded marketing. He was a brand—the first candidate in American history to ascend to the presidency with that distinction.*

Of course, political branding transcends Trump. A centerpiece is **credibility**, the time-honored construct that dates back to Aristotle and forms the foundation of persuasive effectiveness. Credibility, the receiver's perceptions of the communicator's qualities, consists of core attributes like expertise and trustworthiness. Sometimes expertise can carry the day. Let's rewind back to 1972. When President Richard Nixon competed against the dovish George McGovern in 1972, he compensated for his cold, opportunistic image with an emphasis on his intelligence and knowledge of the complex, treacherous world of foreign policy. In the view of his consultants, voters might not have liked Nixon, but they darn well respected him, and realized they needed him (Diamond & Bates, 1992), although their perceived need quickly dissipated when the Watergate scandal revealed his abuse of power.

More than 40 years later, during a much different time, Hillary Clinton emphasized her expertise: an impressive resume and leadership acumen. To many voters, her experience, particularly in foreign policy, was persuasive (Healy & Sussman, 2016). Clinton won the popular vote, after all. However, expertise was not enough. She lost the Electoral College because many voters sought change, not experience (Keeter, 2016). They were frustrated with their economic plight, or they gravitated to Trump for symbolic reasons (see Chapter 7). Others disliked Clinton, tired of what they saw as decades-long public disingenuousness, or for other reasons. They disagreed with her policy positions, secretly harbored sexist attitudes, or perceived that Clinton could not be trusted, as a result of her own public demeanor, or the way the scandal over her use of a private email server congealed with a captious media narrative stressing her penchant for secrecy.

It was intriguing and ironic. Both candidates were held in low repute by voters, but Clinton was seen as less trustworthy than Trump, even though, as the PolitiFact website documented, half of her statements were "true" or "mostly" true, in comparison to just 15 percent of Trump's, and more than four times as many of Trump's statements were judged to be "false" (Kristof, 2016). But when it comes to credibility, perceptions, honed by media, matter. Clinton could parse her words and came off guarded and strategic; Trump exuded confidence, believing what he said, even what when what he said was demonstrably false. He boisterously challenged his opponents in unguarded language that conveyed the perception that he spoke honestly, his coarseness communicating authenticity, his tweets the mirror of a brutish but seemingly authentic soul (Cillizza, 2016). He was the master of constructed credibility and "mediated authenticity" (Enli, 2015). Perceptions, media, and Trump's confidence thus combined to produce the paradox of Trump's greater trustworthiness.

There is evidence that speakers who display more confidence in their judgments exert a stronger persuasive impact on others' beliefs, even when the speakers' responses are objectively incorrect (Zarnoth & Sniezek, 1997). Trump's media persona—his "feeling of spontaneity," "the freshness of a really fine actor-artist," the electric sense "he lives in the moment"—made him seem believable and worthy of trust. However, according to one critic, if "people were really paying attention to what he says he would never, ever have been elected" (Singer, 2016, p. 65). Or perhaps his base agreed with his incendiary statements, liked the disruptive, "drain-the-swamp" positions he embraced, and excused his ethical lapses, preferring his tainted business brand to Clinton's flawed political persona, holding him to a lower moral yardstick because manipulating the means to achieve a successful end is seen as more acceptable in business than in the more publicly spirited domain of politics (Siegel, 2016).

PRESIDENTIAL CAMPAIGNS IN THE DIGITAL MARKETPLACE

Background

Digital technologies play a key role in campaign marketing. It is no longer the mass media election, as Thomas Patterson (1980) dubbed it, but the interactive media election, tweeted election, or "all media, all the time" election. Although television is still important, given its share of the market, it is no longer the only game in town. "To not have an aggressive social media strategy (today) would be the equivalent of not having an aggressive TV strategy in the 1950s," said one of Obama's senior advisers several years back. "We have to go to where the conversations are already happening" (Shear, 2015, p. A14). Campaigns use a digital cocktail of media technologies to influence voters, harnessing messages that are exquisitely targeted to particular voters' social media profiles (Stromer-Galley, 2014). The game is still power, but the techniques are refined and more personalized. As Johnson (2011) observes, campaign consultants are likely to be consumed with a variety of technology-focused questions like these:

> What are yesterday's poll numbers posted on Polling.com showing? Did you see that Twitter posting from our opponent? Are we following that potentially damaging rant on RedState.com blog site? Did you see how much traffic that YouTube posting is getting? Are we getting any traction from our pop-up ads on Google? What are they doing on our opponent's Facebook page?
>
> (p. 22)

First it was the Internet, then Web 2.0, and now a plenitude of social media on smart phone platforms have transformed campaigns (Owen, 2014; see Figure 8.4). These developments did not happen overnight. In 1996, presidential candidates created websites, and by 2000 candidate websites, with informational and biographical features, were relatively commonplace. In the early 2000s, candidate websites focused heavily on informing users of candidates' issue positions, offering biographical background and

1996	2000	2004	2006	2008	2012	2016
• Presidential candidates create websites.	• Campaign websites become commonplace.	• Democratic candidate Howard Dean becomes first presidential candidate to develop blog. • Dean changes the nature of fundraising, raising money online from many small contributors.	• YouTube videos become more powerful as a video sinks Virginia Senate candidacy of George Allen.	• Obama brings campaign into the digital age, raising record amounts of small online donations; creating a campaign social network; posting numerous YouTube videos; and harnessing social media to link campaign to volunteers.	• Social media use grows, becoming a regular part of campaigns. • Twitter becomes a major force in campaigns. • Microtargeting matures and expands.	• Twitter becomes go-to place for candidates, journalists, and citizens as Trump tweets vociferously, reaching supporters and capturing news attention. • Technological advances on social media continue apace, as Facebook Live, Twitter's Periscope app, and Snapchat live-stream videos. Live videos on small phone screens, angry partisan posts, and millions of online individual contributions to candidates characterize the animated social media presidential campaign.

Figure 8.4 Timeline of campaign changes in the digital age.

trying to forge a connection between the campaign and the site visitor (Schneider & Foot, 2006). But the sites were primitive by today's standards.

In 2004, online communications received a seismic boost when Democratic presidential candidate Howard Dean became the first presidential contender to develop a blog. Dean also innovatively brought campaign volunteers and supporters together via the Internet and raised more than $40 million online, consummating a shotgun marriage between new technologies and the time-honored constant of politics, money (Stromer-Galley & Baker, 2006). Ironically, showcasing the continued influence of conventional media, it was a bombastic but strange televised speech Dean delivered after his victory in the Iowa caucuses that torpedoed his candidacy, suggesting to leaders he might not be the most politic choice. But if he lost the battle for the nomination to John Kerry in 2004, Dean won the technological war. The strategies he pioneered have become de rigueur and have vastly expanded over the past decade.

In 2004, video files entered the political world in a big way when a JibJab video depicting John Kerry and George W. Bush in cartoon-like form singing a political variant of

"This Land Is Your Land" garnered 65 million hits. (The video was hilarious, with the animated Bush singing, "This land is your land, this land is my land. I'm a Texas tiger, you're a liberal wiener," and Kerry reprising, "This land is your land, this land is my land. I'm an intellectual, you're a stupid dumb ass!").

In 2006 political cyberspace erupted when the front-runner for the Virginia Senate race, incumbent George Allen, insulted an American student of Indian ancestry, a staff member of an opponent's campaign, who had been following Allen around the state. Frustrated by the repeated sighting of an opponent's staffer, holding a digital recorder, Allen used a little-known racial slur, calling the young man a "macaca," an arcane word defined as a female monkey. The comment, uploaded to YouTube and widely covered in conventional media, sank Allen's reelection bid. The lesson: Micro-media could diffuse messages across cyberspace, initially circumventing the mainstream media and then propelling conventional journalists to cover the story big-time.

Two years later, during the 2008 election, the Obama team harnessed online media in transformative, innovative ways. Making major financial and staff investments in digital communications, the campaign surpassed Dean's 2004 effort, raising record amounts of small online donations and even creating its own social network, MyBarackObama. com, a virtual hub that allowed the campaign to request money, enlist volunteers, and encourage people to actively partake in the campaign (Jones, 2011). Online political messaging helped Obama reach young people, who rely on the Internet for political decision-making; indeed, research suggests Obama's sophisticated digital barrage mobilized young supporters, strengthening their beliefs that they could influence politics (Owen, 2006; Tedesco, 2011; Towner & Dulio, 2011).

Described as a Mac in comparison to Clinton's PC and Republican John McCain's IBM Selectric typewriter, Obama's campaign included sophisticated online strategies to raise money and mobilize supporters, notably promotional YouTube videos that prominently featured a music video by will.i.am that set Obama's "Yes We Can" campaign mantra to music, recruiting more than 10 million hits. The campaign had its own social network and an email list of 13 million supporters, which forged connections between tech-savvy young supporters and the campaign, while also creating a digital armamentarium to reach and influence voters, many of whom did not realize the canny strategic thinking that underpinned his efforts (Friedman, 2009; Johnson, 2011; Kreiss, 2012; McKinney & Banwart, 2011). Not only did Obama's prescient campaign staff harness the Internet to recruit supporters, capitalizing on the wide diffusion of social network use among the young, they also were heavily data-driven, using technology strategically to understand voter sentiments, target key market segments, and design messages to mobilize voters in core electoral areas (Newman, 2016).

Social media became even more significant in 2012 and 2016, supplanting, if not replacing, clunk campaign websites. Twitter took off in 2012, becoming the go-to place for candidates, reporters, the campaign cognoscenti, and politically involved citizens (Hamby, 2013). In 2016, Facebook initiated Facebook Live, which allowed users to transmit live videos. Snapchat provided behind-closed-doors access to political party events and provided campaign coverage through a newly formed news division (Shear & Corasaniti, 2016). Social media also embellished its role in campaign fund-raising, as Bernie Sanders set grassroots fund-raising records by amassing millions of dollars in individual contributions (averaging $27 a pop, as he famously exclaimed), allowing him to launch a competitive presidential campaign without relying on large donations from special interest political action committees.

The next sections focus in depth on two key facets of digital political marketing: Twitter and microtargeting.

Twitter and Campaign Politics

Twitter's brevity is a communicative virtue. Its 140-character limit forced famously long-winded politicians "to quickly get to the point" (Parmelee & Bichard, 2012, p. 206). Candidates can use clever tweets to gain political traction and create interest in their campaigns (Enli & Naper, 2016). Twitter also allows candidates to circumvent the press and build a following directly through the emotional armamentarium of rapid-fire tweets, as Trump did in 2016.

Trump reached voters directly through Twitter, including disaffected Republicans who tuned out conventional media, preferring instead his trending, tempestuous tweets that titillated their smartphones, bursting through the clutter of more normal political communication and helping him develop a relationship with his supporters (Healy & Martin, 2016). With 13 million people following him, he outpaced the other candidates (Wang, 2016) in the number of followers, as well as the ways his message congealed with followers' sentiments. He employed adjectives to facilitate attacks on other candidates, used "I," "me," and his own name, retweeted the public, and had links to the news media (Pew Research Center, 2016; Tsur, Ognyanova, & Lazer, 2016). "If it wasn't for social media, I don't see Trump winning," one researcher said (Manjoo, 2016, p. B7; see Figure 8.5).

Twitter alone did not bring him success. "With 140-character bursts of id," a reporter observed, "Mr. Trump's posts are mainlined and amplified by the rest of the media; with one or two tweets, he can dominate TV, the web, newspapers and talk radio for an entire day" (Manjoo, 2016, p. B1). Trump tweeted novel, conflict-ridden, and deeply offensive comments (critiquing a candidate's facial features, implying a TV anchor was menstruating, calling out the race of a judge, charging that Hillary Clinton

Donald J. Trump ✓
@realDonaldTrump

⚙   👤 Follow

Lyin' Ted Cruz just used a picture of Melania
from a G.Q. shoot in his ad. Be careful, Lyin'
Ted, or I will spill the beans on your wife!

RETWEETS   LIKES
4,736   8,975

Figure 8.5 President Donald Trump, sometimes called the blue-collar billionaire, waged an unconventional campaign that harnessed his celebrity status and ability to connect with working class Americans at rallies and on social media. His tweets appealed to many of his followers, but could be mean-spirited and degrading.

Public Domain

belongs in jail), all of which fit journalistic routines, appealing to click-hungry media producers. This allowed him to simultaneously cultivate support among followers while engaging a ratings-hungry television media all too happy to cover his latest controversy (Rutenberg, 2016; see also Wells et al., 2016).

However, Twitter does not exert a hypodermic impact. Instead, it provides a platform for candidates to mobilize like-minded voters, gain additional brand value via supportive comments from online opinion leaders, and capture voluminous, sometimes positive, media coverage (see Chapter 10). The direct messaging between candidates and followers adds an immediacy—and real-time spontaneity—lacking in conventional news coverage, and even in large political rallies (Lee & Shin, 2014). Twitter can help candidates forge a relationship with supporters, a key aspect of branding, but it also carries risks; when online supporters dislike a candidate's tweets, they may respond with viral vitriol (Theocharis, Bárbera, Fazekas, Popa, & Parnet, 2016). What candidates gain in directly reaching supporters directly they can lose when supporters create online controversies that generate bad press. For Twitter to have an overall positive political marketing impact, candidates must consistently connect with followers, and followers must like what they read. It helps if candidates can deliver simple, palatable emotion-packed tweets, showcasing the linkage of message and medium, or the fit between message content and media format. A candidate also needs a message, or set of policy ideas, that are communicated tersely through Twitter. In 2016 it was Trump who mastered Twitter; in another year it might be a liberal Democrat with angst, attitude, and anger propelling a post-Millennial generation of voters.

Online Political Marketing

In addition to Twitter, digital marketing techniques have transformed political marketing. They have supplemented the conventional focus on demographic market segmentation with an emphasis on microtargeted campaign persuasion directed at individual users, thumbing through their smartphone apps and social media posts. In **microtargeting**, candidates target niche audiences, tailoring the appeal to match a targeted group or a particular individual's characteristics and online preferences (Issenberg. 2012; Kenski, Hardy, & Jameson, 2010). Unlike broad targeting strategies of decades past, microtargeting focuses on individual users, attempting with laser-like specificity to match messages with ever-smaller marketing segments. Consultants mine online data, gaining information on consumers' product preferences as well as offline information, such as the charities they prefer, the automobiles they buy, and their voting records. Based on this information, consultants customize appeals. An undecided voter toiling in an automobile plant might receive an email from a fellow worker on her shift, or hear from a Facebook factory worker friend who is also a campaign volunteer.

Campaign specialists buy a voter list, upload it to Facebook, and match the names to the user base. This allows them to effectively link the political—the list of registered voters—with the readily available market, Facebook users. The goal is to find matches, the database combining "the electoral information it already knows about voters with their Facebook profiles: likes, group memberships, issues or even favorites" (Willis, 2014, p. A3). Consultants use this information to tailor political advertisements to particular users, trying to reach individuals on their mobile devices using messages that cost much less to produce and distribute than commercial television advertising. "There's a level of precision that doesn't exist in any other medium," a Facebook outreach manager observed, adding that, "it's getting the right message to the right people at the right time" (Parker, 2015, p. A17; Kreiss, 2012). Consultants and staffers expend considerable time and energy not on the campaign trail or going door to door, but in high-tech "video processing rooms, using computers to rapidly produce and edit broadcast-quality video complete with sophisticated graphical overlays and animations. The completed files are transmitted digitally to the advertising agencies, who then liaise with the television companies" (Chadwick, 2013, pp. 118–119).

As impressive as the technology is, questions remain. Few empirical studies have probed the effects of microtargeting on voter attitudes. Microtargeting strategies can misclassify voters, assuming that because particular voters are aligned with unions or tune in to liberal websites, they necessarily will vote Democratic. Strategists also conflate electoral victory with the use of empirical data analytics. It is entirely possible that Obama, who aggressively used microtargeting in 2008 and 2012, won not because of his tailored online appeals, but because voters liked his demeanor and message. In 2016, Trump, who steered clear of these techniques, defeated Clinton, whose strategists embraced digitally based marketing. For all her digital mastery, she was less successful than he in turning out targeted voters in swing states (Leonhardt, 2016). Online data analytic techniques are an important marketing stratagem, but they are no panacea.

Summary

Let's take stock. Taking into account what we know about online political media, what impact have digital technologies exerted on campaign marketing? There is broad agreement that digital strategies have (1) removed barriers to communication among leaders, media, and citizens; (2) facilitated interpersonal connections among geographically separated citizens via YouTube and other platforms, enlarging our political space (Ricke, 2014; Schulz, 2014); (3) afforded candidates more opportunities to market their message (Serazio, 2014); (4) expanded the parameters of political participation, offering more opportunities for activists to challenge elites (Edgerly et al., 2013); (5) transformed formats from face-to-face to include text, tweet, and video streaming, in this way altering the language of campaign communication; (6) eviscerated norms of civility, as passionate, obscene, and prejudiced messages have become more common; (7) reduced, though by no means eliminated, the dominance of traditional news media, as candidates and citizens can more easily circumvent the press; (8) arguably increased selective political communication, where users receive primarily messages with which they agree (see Chapter 12); (9) enabled the tweet, making it a centerpiece of online campaigns; and (10) provided campaigns with new ways to study, market, and mobilize potential voters, raising classic questions of manipulation and media effects.

Perspectives

On a normative level, the politicization of digital media is a mixed bag. As noted above, there are strategic benefits, chiefly that social media offers candidates a direct, personalized way to reach voters, mirroring similar developments in commercial marketing, as Newman insightfully observes (see Conick, 2016). Just as Amazon sells books directly to customers and Uber offers one-on-one connections to people looking for rides, in this way eliminating retail businesses (book distributors and taxi companies), social media allows candidates to go directly to voters, circumventing time-honored political institutions, like parties and news media (Kerbel & Bowers, 2016). Some scholars praise this, noting that digital technologies reduce disconnection and political alienation, enhance civic engagement, treat citizens as active members of an ongoing dialogue, and provide a viable mechanism for outsider candidates to mobilize citizens via the grassroots or netroots (Campbell & Kwak, 2014; Chadwick & Stromer-Galley, 2016; Coleman, 2014; Dutton, 2014). Yet for all these benefits, social media, with their ability to arouse prejudices, in a norm-shattering way that is not acceptable on mainstream channels, have made politics more combustible and unity more difficult, in some instances enabling strident partisans to hurl hurtful epithets anonymously, in other cases giving fringe groups a mouthpiece to promote offensive and prejudiced speech.

Social media have taken a toll on the language of politics. One critic notes that online media favor "the bitty over the meaty, the cutting over the considered. It also prizes emotionalism over reason. The more visceral the message, the more quickly it circulates and the longer it holds the darting public eye" (Carr, 2015). Online political communication reifies instant communication, prioritizing instantaneous candidate responses at the expense of vision. As one writer observed:

> Technology is making campaigns dumber. BlackBerrys and iPhones mean that campaigns can respond to their opponents minute by minute and hour by hour. The campaigns get lost in tit-for-tat minutiae that nobody outside the bubble cares about. Meanwhile, use of the Internet means that Web videos overshadow candidate speeches and appearances. Video replaces verbal. Tactics eclipse vision.
> (Brooks, 2012, p. A19; see also Hart, 2013 and Merkin, 2016)

Of course, some of the same criticisms have dogged politics from the days of clichéd stump speeches to hoary political ads. Political persuasion is more immediate and interactive, certainly more entertaining, today—but not necessarily more thoughtful or dignified. Alas, no technological platform can serve up political messages optimally and without shortcomings. Many scholars, while acknowledging online media's short-comings, would agree with Chadwick (2013) that today's hybrid media system creates an environment for political communication that is "on balance, more expansive and inclusive than those that prevailed during the twentieth century" (p. 210).

CONCLUSIONS

Democracy is predicated on elections—the will of the people, vox populi, the consent or dissent of the governed. Elections are imperfect. Candidates, at their best, have noble aims, and if elected to office, can exert transformative effects on the nation. Alas, their feet are made of clay; they are tempted by their ambitions, constrained by their short-comings, and can commit egregious errors costing resources and lives.

Presidential campaigns, fundamentally an American invention, are the modality by which candidates try to persuade voters. They have changed dramatically over the years. In the late 18th century presidential candidates did not campaign for office. Fear-ful and distrustful of partisanship, leaders stood in the shadows, while their follow-ers unleashed scathing attacks in newspapers. Something good emerged from the hue and cry: Political parties evolved, offering civilized mechanisms to express political disagreements and ideally to resolve political differences. Parties connected people to leaders and mobilized voters (just White men, a stain on American government). Party-owned newspapers provided the mechanism by which parties amassed electoral support, while also bringing partisan citizens into the outskirts of an elite-dominated political process. However, dark clouds circled above, as parties nominated mediocre candidates, and neither parties nor candidates nor the bulk of newspapers worked, sin-gly or in combination, to eradicate the scourge of problems facing America, from urban squalor to slavery.

Popular, prejudiced politics gave way to party-managed, national whistle-stop cam-paigns. Party leaders orchestrated campaigns, organized field operations, raised money, and made backroom deals that secretly advanced candidates' prospects. Television brought not the onset of images (for images date back centuries to Jackson's cultivation of a populist image, and before that as well). Instead, TV ushered in the mass commu-nication and sophisticated crafting of candidate imagery. Campaign experts recognized that image—the media-cultivated, candidate-crafted, voter-constructed perception of candidates—was now a major factor in electoral politics. Image construction, a strange alchemy of candidates' policy statements, media appearances, and the art of projecting a persuasive campaign face, came of age with John F. Kennedy.

With Reagan, art and artifice became inextricably linked with a mastery of television narrative. Reagan called on an earnest commitment to political conservatism, while harnessing rhetoric, visual manipulations, and the cultivation of the new political meme—spin—to fashion himself as a "Great Communicator." He unquestionably was, but the perception itself, cultivated by reporters who equated Reagan's charm with a power to shape public opinion (Schudson, 1995), carried persuasive heft, as journalists' beliefs may themselves have subtly influenced public attitudes. As presidents continued to mold images with the media platform du jour—Clinton with the talk-show debate, Obama via YouTube, Trump with his inveterate tweets—old questions, wrapped in new digital wrapping, emerged about the intersection between artifice and authenticity, and the ways in which political leadership is inevitably a complex combination of worthy intentions, self-serving deceptions, and manufactured images, all rendered, conveyed, interpreted, and distilled through the panoply of mediated representations.

The contemporary campaign is an exercise in political marketing, the systematic application of marketing principles to politics. Political marketing differs in several ways from commercial marketing, although certain features, like branding, credibility, and targeting consumer preferences, are core components of both arenas. Technology—which has evolved with warp speed over the past decades—plays key role in candidates' efforts to influence voters. Digital technologies have transformed campaigns, removing barriers among the players; reducing (though by no means eliminating) the pervasive influences of news; expanding the forms and content by which candidates, media, and citizens communicate; and eviscerating norms of civility in venomous partisan posts. There continues to be debate about whether online media has improved the quality of campaign communications. Deliberative democracy theorists lament its short-sighted brevity and emotional animus, while defenders highlight the ways social media outlets have expanded the content and connectedness of political campaigns, giving citizen consigned to passive roles in the broadcast network era new possibilities for political participation.

Does political marketing serve democracy? Some scholars answer in the affirmative. They argue that marketing offers mechanisms by which candidates and elected officials can tap into voters' sentiments, helping politicians provide services that voters want and allowing voters to communicate their policy preferences to political service providers, electing those who deliver on promises, giving the boot to others who fail to provide what they promised. If conducted honestly and openly, scholars argue, political marketing can advance democratic aims, accurately transmitting concerns of the electorate to representatives and helping duly-elected leaders develop programs that meet voters' needs.

Others disagree. They find the marketing metaphor uneasy and disdainful of the ideals of politics: inspired leadership and thoughtful deliberation on political issues. Critics point out that voters are not customers who merely purchase a political product. They are not there to be marketed or manipulated. Instead, voters are citizens, the fundamental constituents of a democratic society, whose ideas and objectives elected leaders must represent and channel into legitimate public policy. There has been much discussion of this topic in scholarly arenas (e.g., Habermas, 1989; Rose, 2010; Scammel, 2014; Scullion, 2010). Today, one may lament that we have a non-serious, light version of politics, where people are consumers first and citizens second. Taking a more critical stand, Bennett and Manheim (2001) argue that "the very transformation of publics into exclusive target audiences is a blow to the democratic ideal of publics as inclusive deliberative bodies" (p. 280). For all his missteps, Trump steered clear of a consultant-driven political campaign, preferring to rely on his raw celebrity show–honed image-making skills, an approach that thrilled his base and incensed opponents.

There is an inherent tension between political marketing, with its focus on image manipulation and ethics. It is the time-honored conundrum that has its philosophical roots in the writings of Plato, Machiavelli, and modern philosophers. It is difficult to say that marketing is inherently moral on the grounds that it democratically appeals to voters' sentiments, because some of those sentiments are manipulated by marketers and media. Conversely, it is difficult to argue that marketing is immoral on the grounds that politicians mislead voters, because the assumption of caveat emptor applied to politics holds that voters are capable of differentiating appeals made by honest and dishonest politicians, and it is in political marketers' interest to make good on their promises. Like all persuasion, political marketing is a multifaceted combination of moral and immoral appeals, an uneasy combination of art and artifice that is endemic to democracy.

REFERENCES

Baker, K. (2016, June 19). Donald Trump's place. *The New York Times* (Sunday Review), 1, 6, 7.

Bennett, W. L., & Manheim, J. B. (2001). The big spin: Strategic communication and the transformation of pluralist democracy. In W. L. Bennett & R. M. Entman (Eds.), *Mediated politics: Communication in the future of democracy* (pp. 279–298). Cambridge: Cambridge University Press.

Boller, P. F., Jr. (2004). *Presidential campaigns: From George Washington to George W. Bush.* New York: Oxford University Press.

Boorstin, D. J. (1964). *The image: A guide to pseudo-events in America.* New York: Harper & Row.

Brooks, D. (2012, July 31). Dullest campaign ever. *The New York Times*, A19.

Brooks, D. (2014, February 14). The refiner's fire. *The New York Times.* Retrieved from www.nytimes.com/2014/02/14/opinion/brooks-the-refiners- fire.html (Accessed February 25, 2017).

Butler, P., & Harris, P. (2009). Considerations on the evolution of political marketing theory. *Marketing Theory, 9,* 149.164.

Campbell, S. W., & Kwak, N. (2014). Mobile communication and civic life: Linking patterns of use to civic and political engagement. In W. H. Dutton (Ed.), *Politics and the Internet: Critical concepts in political science* (Vol. III, *Netizens, networks and political movements*, pp. 213–234). New York: Routledge.

Carr, N. (2015, September 2). How social media is ruining politics. *Politico*. Retrieved from www.politico.com/magazine/story/2015/09/2016-election-social-media-ruining-politics-213104 (Accessed November 30, 2016).

Chadwick, A. (2013). *The hybrid media system: Politics and power*. Oxford: Oxford University Press.

Chadwick, A., & Stromer-Galley, J. (2016). Digital media, power, and democracy in parties and election campaigns: Party decline or party renewal? *The International Journal of Press/Politics, 21*, 283–293.

Cillizza, C. (2016, November 4). Why voters think Trump is a more honest candidate. *The Plain Dealer*, E4.

Coleman, S. (2014). The lonely citizen: Indirect representation in an age of networks. In W. H. Dutton (Ed.), *Politics and the Internet: Critical concepts in political science* (Vol. III, *Netizens, networks and political movements*, pp. 54–75). New York: Routledge.

Conick. H. (2016, September 26). How social media, microtargeting and big data revolutionized political marketing. *Marketing News*. Retrieved from www.ama.org/publications/marketingnews/pages/social-media . . . (Accessed November 20, 2016).

Cramer, R. B. (1992). *What it takes: The way to the White House*. New York: Random House.

Cwalina, W., Falkowski, A., & Newman, B. I. (2009). Political management and marketing. In D. W. Johnson (Ed.), *Routledge handbook of political management* (pp. 67–80). New York: Routledge.

Cwalina, W., Falkowski, A., & Newman, B. I. (2011). *Political marketing: Theoretical and strategic foundations*. Armonk, NY: M. E. Sharpe.

de Chernatony, L. (1998). Introduction. In L. de Chernatony (Ed.), *Brand management* (pp. xv–xxvi). Aldershot, England: Dartmouth.

Diamond, E., & Bates, S. (1992). *The spot: The rise of political advertising on television* (3rd ed.). Cambridge, MA: MIT Press.

Dinkin, R. J. (1989). *Campaigning in America: A history of election practices*. New York: Greenwood.

Dutton, W. H. (Ed., with the assistance of E. Dubois). (2014). *Politics and the Internet: Critical concepts in political science* (Vol. III, *Netizens, networks and political movements*). New York: Routledge.

Edgerly, S., Bode, L., Kim, Y. M., & Shah, D. V. (2013). Campaigns go social: Are Facebook, YouTube and Twitter changing elections? In T. N. Ridout (Ed.), *New directions in media and politics* (pp. 82–99). New York: Routledge.

Enli, G. (2015). *Mediated authenticity: How the media constructs reality*. New York: Peter Lang.

Enli, G., & Naper, A. A. (2016). Social media incumbency advantage: Barack Obama's and Mitt Romney's tweets in the U.S. presidential election campaign. In A. Bruns, G. Enli, E. Skogerbø, A. O. Larsson, & C. Christensen (Eds.), *The Routledge companion to social media and politics* (pp. 364–377). New York: Routledge.

Fennis, B. M., & Stroebe, W. (2010). *The psychology of advertising*. New York: Psychology Press.

Fischer, D. H. (1965). *The revolution of American conservatism: The Federalist Party in the era of Jeffersonian democracy*. New York: Harper & Row.

Friedman, M. P. (2009). Simulacrobama: The mediated election of 2008. *Journal of American Studies*, *43*(2), 341–356.

Greenberg, D. (2016). *Republic of spin: An inside history of the American presidency*. New York: W. W. Norton.

Habermas, J. (1989). *The structural transformation of the public sphere: An inquiry into a category of bourgeois society*. Cambridge, MA: MIT Press.

Hamby, P. (2013, September). *Did Twitter kill the boys on the bus? Searching for a better way to cover a campaign*. Discussion paper series, Joan Shorenstein Center on the Press, Politics and Public Policy, Harvard University. Retrieved from shorensteincenter.org/wp-content/uploads/2013/08/d80_hamby.pdf (Accessed April 28, 2016).

Hart, R. P. (2013). Politics in the digital age: A scary prospect? In T. N. Ridout (Ed.), *New directions in media and politics* (pp. 210–225). New York: Routledge.

Hart, R. P., Childers, J. P., & Lind, C. J. (2013). *Political tone: How leaders talk and why*. Chicago: University of Chicago Press.

Healy, P., & Martin, J. (2016, May 8). G.O.P. unravels as party faces Trump takeover. *The New York Times*, 1, 19.

Healy, P., & Sussman, D. (2016, September 15). Voters' view of a Donald Trump presidency: Big risks and rewards. *The New York Times*. Retrieved from www.nytimes.com/2016/09/16/us/politics/hillary-clinton-donald-trump-poll.html (Accessed October 19, 2016).

Hertsgaard, M. (1988). *On bended knee: The press and the Reagan presidency*. New York: Farrar Straus Giroux.

Hulse, C., & Herszenhorn, D. M. (2015, September 2). Coordinated strategy brings Obama victory on Iran nuclear deal. *The New York Times*. Retrieved from ww.nytimes.com/2015/09/03/world/obama-clinches-votes-to-secure-iran-nuclear-deal.html?_r=0 (Accessed November 29, 2016).

Ignatieff, M. (2013). *Fire and ashes: Success and failure in politics*. Cambridge, MA: Harvard University Press.

Issenberg, S. (2012). *The victory lab: The secret science of winning campaigns*. New York: Crown.

Jamieson, K. H. (1984). *Packaging the presidency: A history and criticism of presidential campaign advertising*. New York: Oxford University Press.

Jamieson, K. H. (1988). *Eloquence in an electronic age: The transformation of political speechmaking*. New York: Oxford University Press.

Johnson, D. W. (2011). *Campaigning in the twenty-first century: A whole new ballgame?* New York: Routledge.

Jones, C. A. (2011). Political advertising, digital fundraising and campaign finance in the 2008 election: A First Amendment normative analysis. In M. S. McKinney & M. C. Banwart (Eds.), *Communication in the 2008 U.S. election: Digital natives elect a president* (pp. 89–104). New York: Peter Lang.

Kazin, M. (1995). *The populist persuasion: An American history*. New York: Basic Books.

Keeter, S. (2016, November 18). *Election 2016: A polling postmortem*. Keynote speech, Midwest Association for Public Opinion Research Convention, Chicago.

Kenski, K., Hardy, B. W., & Jamieson, K. H. (2010). *The Obama victory: How media, money, and message shaped the 2008 election*. New York: Oxford University Press.

Kerbel, M. R., & Bowers, C. J. (2016). *Next generation Netroots: Realignment and the rise of the Internet left*. New York: Routledge.

King, S. A. (2016, February 14). An election to remember. *The New York Times Book Review* (Letter), 6.

Kreiss, D. (2012). *Taking our country back: The crafting of networked politics from Howard Dean to Barack Obama*. New York: Oxford University Press.

Kristof, N. (2016, September 15). When a crackpot seeks office. *The New York Times*, A25.

Kurtz, H. (1996). *Hot air: All talk, all the time*. New York: Times Books.

Lanzetta, J. T., Sullivan, D. G., Masters, R. D., & McHugo, G. J. (1985). Emotional and cognitive responses to televised images of political leaders. In S. Kraus & R. M. Perloff (Eds.), *Mass media and political thought: An information-processing approach* (pp. 85–116). Thousand Oaks, CA: Sage.

Lawless, J. L., & Fox, R. L. (2012). *Men rule: The continued under-representation of women in U.S. politics*. Washington, DC: Women & Politics Institute. Retrieved from www.american.edu/spa/wpi/upload/2012-Men-Rule-Report-final-web.pdf. (Accessed February 21, 2017).

Lee, E-J., & Shin, S. Y. (2014). When the medium is the message: How transportability moderates the effects of politicians' Twitter communication. *Communication Research, 41*, 1088–1110.

Leonhardt, D. (2016, November 20). The Democrats' real turnout problem. *The New York Times* (Sunday Review), 3.

Lippmann, W. (1922). *Public opinion*. New York: Free Press.

Maltese, J. A. (1992). *Spin control: The White House Office of Communications and the management of presidential news*. Chapel Hill: University of North Carolina Press.

Mancini, P., & Swanson, D. L. (1996). Politics, media, and modern democracy: Introduction. In D. L. Swanson & P. Mancini (Eds.), *Politics, media, and modern democracy: An international study of innovations in electoral campaigning and their consequences* (pp. 1–26). Westport, CT: Praeger.

Manjoo, F. (2016, November 17). Social media's globe-shaking power. *The New York Times*, B1, B7.

Manjoo, F. (2017, February 23). No relief as media obsesses on Trump. *The New York Times*, B1, B6.

McCormick, R. P. (1982). *The presidential game: The origins of American presidential politics*. New York: Oxford University Press.

McGerr, M. (1986). *The decline of popular politics: The American North, 1865–1928*. New York: Oxford University Press.

McGinniss, J. (1969). *The selling of the president*. New York: Penguin.

McKinney, M. S., & Banwart, M. C. (2011). The election of a lifetime. In M. S. McKinney & M. C. Banwart (Eds.), *Communication in the 2008 U.S. election: Digital natives elect a president* (pp. 1–9). New York: Peter Lang.

Merkin, D. (2016, August 28). Antidotes to punditry. *The New York Times Book Review*, 11.

Newman, B.I. (1994). *The marketing of the president: Political marketing as campaign strategy.* Thousand Oaks, CA: Sage.

Newman, B.I. (1999). *The mass marketing of politics: Democracy in an age of manufactured images.* Thousand Oaks, CA: Sage.

Newman, B.I. (2016). *The marketing revolution in politics: What recent U.S. presidential campaigns can teach us about effective marketing.* Toronto: University of Toronto Press.

O'Shaughnessy, N. (1999). Political marketing and political propaganda. In B.I. Newman (Ed.), *Handbook of political marketing* (pp. 725–740). Thousand Oaks, CA: Sage.

Owen, D. (2006). The Internet and youth civic engagement in the United States. In S. Oates, D. Owen, R.K. Gibson (Eds.), *The Internet and politics: Citizens, voters and activists* (pp. 20–38). London: Routledge.

Owen, D. (2014). New media and political campaigns. In K. Kenski & K.H. Jamieson (Eds.), *The Oxford handbook of political communication.* Retrieved from www.oxfordhandbooks. com. (Accessed August 3, 2016).

Packard, V. (1957). *The hidden persuaders.* New York: D. McKay.

Parker, A. (2015, July 31). Facebook expands in politics with new digital tools, and campaigns find much to like. *The New York Times,* A17.

Parmelee, J.H., & Bichard, S.L. (2012). *Politics and the Twitter revolution: How tweets influence the relationship between political leaders and the public.* Lanham, MD: Lexington Books.

Patterson, T.E. (1980). *The mass media election: How Americans choose their president.* New York: Praeger.

Perloff, R.M. (1998). *Political communication: Politics, press, and public in America.* Mahwah, NJ: Lawrence Erlbaum Associates.

Perloff, R.M. (1999). Elite, popular, and merchandised politics: Historical origins of presidential campaign marketing. In B.I. Newman (Ed.), *Handbook of political marketing* (pp. 19–40). Thousand Oaks, CA: Sage.

Pessen, E. (1985). *Jacksonian America: Society, personality, and politics* (Rev. ed.). Urbana: University of Illinois Press.

Pew Research Center. (2016, July 18). *Candidates differ in their use of social media to connect with the public.* Retrieved from www.journalism.org/2016/07/18/candidates-differ-in-their-use-o . . . (Accessed November 15, 2016).

Ricke, L.D. (2014). *The impact of YouTube on U.S. politics.* Lanham, MD: Lexington Books.

Rose, J. (2010). The branding of states: The uneasy marriage of marketing to politics. *Journal of Political Marketing, 9,* 254–275.

Rove, K. (2015). *The triumph of William McKinley: Why the election of 1896 still matters.* New York: Simon & Schuster.

Rutenberg, J. (2016, June 6). Trump show, a hit for now, faces fall test. *The New York Times,* A1, B4.

Scammell, M. (2014). *Consumer democracy: The marketing of politics.* New York: Cambridge University Press.

Schneider, S.M., & Foot, K.A. (2006). Web campaigning by U.S. presidential primary candidates in 2000 and 2004. In A.P. Williams & J.C. Tedesco (Eds.), *The Internet election: Perspectives on the Web in Campaign 2004* (pp. 21–36). Lanham, MD: Rowman & Littlefield.

Schudson, M. (1995). *The power of news*. Cambridge, MA: Harvard University Press.

Schulz, W. (2014). Mediatization and new media. In F. Esser & J. Strömbäck (Eds.), *Mediatization of politics: Understanding the transformation of western democracies* (pp. 57–73). London: Palgrave Macmillan.

Scullion, R. (2010). The emergence of the "accidental citizen": Implications for political marketing. *Journal of Political Marketing, 9*, 276–293.

Serazio, M. (2014). The new media designs of political consultants: Campaign production in a fragmented era. *Journal of Communication, 64*, 743–763.

Shear, M.D. (2015, January 20). Doing more than putting on annual address into 140 characters. *The New York Times*, A14.

Shear, M.D., & Corasaniti, N. (2016, July 25). Live videos, small screens: Campaigns hope voters like what they see. *The New York Times*, A12.

Siegel, L. (2016, September 10). The selling of Donald J. Trump. *The New York Times*, A17.

Singer, M. (2016 November 21). In character. *The New Yorker*, 64–65.

Steele, R.W. (1985). *Propaganda in an open society: The Roosevelt administration and the media, 1933–1941*. Westport, CT: Greenwood.

Stone, W.J. (2010). Activists, influence, and representation in American elections. In L.S. Maisel & J.M. Berry (Eds.), *The Oxford handbook of American political parties and interest groups* (pp. 285–302). New York: Oxford University Press.

Stromer-Galley, J. (2014). *Presidential campaigning in the Internet age*. New York: Oxford University Press.

Stromer-Galley, J., & Baker, A.B. (2006). Joy and sorrow of interactivity on the campaign trail: Blogs in the primary campaign of Howard Dean. In A.P. Williams & J.C. Tedesco (Eds.), *The Internet election: Perspectives on the Web in Campaign 2004* (pp. 111–131). Lanham, MD: Rowman & Littlefield.

Tedesco, J.C. (2011). The complex Web: Young adults' opinions about online campaign messages. In M.S. McKinney & M.C. Banwart (Eds.), *Communication in the 2008 U.S. election: Digital natives elect a president* (pp. 13–31). New York: Peter Lang.

Theocharis, Y., Bárbera, P., Fazekas, Z., Popa, S.A., & Parnet, O. (2016). A bad workman blames his tweets: The consequences of citizens' uncivil Twitter use when interacting with party candidates. *Journal of Communication, 66*, 1007–1031.

Thurber, J.A. (2000). Introduction to the study of campaign consultants. In J.A. Thurber & C.J. Nelson (Eds.), *Campaign warriors: The role of political consultants in elections* (pp. 1–9). Washington, DC: Brookings Institution Press.

Towner, T.L., & Dulio, D.A. (2011). An experiment of campaign effects during the YouTube election. *New Media & Society, 13*, 626–644.

Trent, J.S., Friedenberg, R.V., & Denton, R.E., Jr. (2011). *Political campaign communication: Principles and practices* (7th ed.). Lanham, MD: Rowman & Littlefield.

Troy, G. (1996). *See how they ran: The changing role of the presidential candidate* (Rev. ed.). Cambridge, MA: Harvard University Press.

Tsur, O., Ognyanova, K., & Lazer, D. (2016, April 29). The data behind Trump's Twitter takeover. *Politico*. Retrieved from www.politico.com/magazine/story/2016/04/donald-trump-201 (Accessed November 15, 2016).

Wang, S. (2016, October 30). Why Trump stays afloat. *The New York Times* (Sunday Review), 2.

Wells, C., Shah, D. V., Pevehouse, J. C., Yang, J., Pelled, A., Boehm, F., Lukito, J., Ghosh, S., & Schmidt, J. L. (2016). How Trump drove coverage to the nomination: Hybrid media campaigning. *Political Communication, 33,* 669–676.

Willis, D. (2014, September 11). Campaigns use Facebook tool to deliver targeted political ads. *The New York Times,* A3.

Winchester, T., Hall, J., & Binney, W. (2016). Conceptualizing usage in voting behavior for political marketing: An application of consumer behavior. *Journal of Political Marketing, 15,* 259–284.

Zarnoth, P., & Sniezek, J. A. (1997). The social influence of confidence in group decision making. *Journal of Experimental Social Psychology, 33,* 345–366.

Examining the Conundrums of Political News Bias

Acolytes of President Trump charge that the constant drumbeat of negative news about the president's performance reflects a familiar liberal media bias. Democrats, still stinging from Hillary Clinton's bruising electoral defeat, lament the ways the media showed its sexist colors by giving Clinton tough press during the 2016 campaign. Fake news continues to circulate over social media, reminiscent of 2016 bogus news reports that went viral, like the story that Obama planned to move to Canada if Trump won or the bizarre tale that a Washington, D.C., pizzeria was sheltering young children as sex slaves in a child-trafficking ring led by Hillary Clinton!

These examples illustrate the challenges of separating truth from falsehood in contemporary news, but also the time-honored, frequently misunderstood issue of bias in political news. At first blush, the American public seems to be largely of one mind on the subject, with an overwhelming number (nearly 3 in 4 Americans) claiming the news media are biased, tending to favor one side rather than covering all sides fairly. On closer analysis, though, nuances emerge, as Americans simultaneously harbor more positive beliefs about the news: Three-fourths of Americans believe that news organizations keep political leaders in line, and 82 percent trust some or a lot of the information they obtain from local news (Mitchell, Gottfried, Barthel, & Shearer, 2016). Yet in the wake of a proliferation of fake news sites, more Americans may doubt the credibility of conventional political news. What do people mean when they perceive the media are biased? Do they mean the news is too sensational or too negative, blaming the messenger for delivering the dreadful drumbeat of terrible events that occur every day? Do they confuse legitimate coverage of sordid political events with bias? Are they merely parroting back a fashionable trope ("but, of course, the media are biased. Everyone knows that.")? Are they confusing over-the-top political websites with the entirety of news media? Do they believe news favors a particular political side, and if so, is it liberal, conservative, or just positive to elites? Bias is a fascinating, multifaceted term that contains more than meets the eye (and can also be in the eye of the political beholder).

This chapter tackles these issues as it places bias under a scholarly microscope, examining the underpinnings of news bias, sorting out fact from falsehood, and reaching some conclusions about the controversial issue of political news bias. The chapter is divided into three parts. The first section introduces the modern landscape of news bias that spans cable news, websites, and Facebook. The second and third portions discuss the freighted issues of liberal and gender bias, with an eye toward appreciating critics' concerns, yet adjudicating these issues by bringing to bear scholarly research findings. The chapter offers a variety of temperate conclusions about contemporary political news, while emphasizing the important role that journalism plays in a fragmented society.

THE CONTEMPORARY NEWS LANDSCAPE

It used to be so simple. In the old days, newspapers, magazines, and broadcast media ruled the roost. They were society's gatekeepers—the keepers of society's informational gates, the institutions that chose, screened, filtered, and disseminated information from elites to citizens. For much of the 20th century, **gatekeeping** was defined as "the process by which the billions of messages that are available in the world get cut down and transformed into the hundreds of messages that reach a given person on a given day" (Shoemaker, 1991, p. 1; see also White, 1950; Bleske, 1991). The mass media were the exclusive gatekeeper, and criticisms were persistently leveled at The Media, as they were frequently lampooned. Were the news media biased? If so, what was the nature of the bias? What effect did biases, however defined, exert on politics? Were certain biases more permissible than others?

Of course, the media harbored biases, at the very least a mainstream, pro-system viewpoint that could veer left or right, depending on the issue. However, the news media claimed, at least in their public pose (arrogantly, some said), to report news from no particular perspective (Epstein, 1973), even if they actually reflected and affirmed conventional American values (Gans, 1979). The contemporary landscape is totally different, encompassing print, broadcast, and cable news; partisan websites that claim the news moniker but are flagrantly opinionated; citizen journalism, with its strengths and shortcomings; and news that is aggregated by Google and posted algorithmically via Facebook, diffusing widely. A discussion of bias and its different components requires an exploration of the modern panoply of news.

Conventional news, relayed in print, online by newspapers and magazines, and via broadcast television, continues apace, serving up investigative journalistic exposes of candidate corruption, as well as solid, sometimes insightful, other times predictable, dramatized coverage of political campaigns. Cable news shook things up, first with CNN's global coverage in the 1980s, then with Fox News. Fox interjected a conservative viewpoint, much missing in conventional news, its proponents emphasized. It was a viewpoint that, despite its "fair and balanced" slogan, was never fair and balanced, though it was marketed aggressively in this way by the company's media-savvy chairman and CEO, Roger Ailes.

Cable News With Attitude

Ailes was the modern incarnate of the media moguls of the late 19th and early 20th century, who saw their job as mobilizing the masses around their preferred candidate through the mouthpiece of the media. Orders—direct or indirect—came from the top. Ailes, long a supporter of Republican candidates and presidents, put it brazenly. "I *want* to elect the next president," he told his executives two years before the 2012 election (Sherman, 2014, p. xvi). Not only did coverage take a conservative bent (notably in the confounding of news and opinion that became common in cable programming), but Fox sought to build an agenda for conservative memes, as one journalist noted:

> Monica Lewinsky, the Swift Boat Veterans for Truth, Benghazi, "the war on Christmas." Ailes also helped weaponize the language of casual racism in the Obama era. When one of his hosts, Glenn Beck, declared on the air that the President had a "deep-seated hatred for white people," Ailes hardly reprimanded him. "I think he's right," Ailes said.
>
> (Remnick, 2016, p. 15)

And although the network got into a dust-up with Trump when Fox anchor Megyn Kelly pummeled him at the first 2016 Republican primary debate with tough questions about his mistreatment of women, research shows that Fox has had a demonstrably pro-Republican bias (Brock, Rabin-Havt, & Media Matters for America, 2012; Iyengar & Hahn, 2009). For example, during the 2012 presidential campaign, just 6 percent of Fox News's stories about Obama were positive, compared to 46 percent that trended negative (Peters, 2012).

MSNBC, formed at the same time as Fox News in 1996, has taken a liberal tilt, as anchors Keith Olbermann, Chris Matthews, and Rachel Maddow favored liberal viewpoints. This could spill over into news coverage. For example, during the 2012 general election, only 3 percent of MSBNC stories about Republican nominee Mitt Romney were positive, while 71 percent were negative (Peters, 2012). In 2016, Democratic Party officials reportedly had a direct pipeline to MSNBC, encouraging the network to give Hillary Clinton more positive press (Grynbaum, 2016). Although news on both networks is produced in concert with professional journalistic canons, their nightly interview programs, in particular, promote agendas consistent with their ideology and blur opinion with fact. They also appeal to the niche political preferences of their viewers, Fox cultivating a conservative audience, MSNBC more liberal viewers.

Ideological Websites

Fox and MSNBC are just the tip of the iceberg, as the web and social media have taken political journalism in expansive and enriching but sometimes perilous new directions. Genres like blogs and political websites are pervasive, complementing, supplementing, and for some ideologically minded users, replacing even cable news that just two decades ago transformed televised political journalism. Some blogs and opinionated commentaries are insightful, offering thoughtful opinions about politics. Other websites and blogs take reliably liberal positions (like The Huffington Post and Daily Kos) or conservative views (such as RedState, Hot Air, and TheBlaze). In other cases, online writers are ideological provocateurs, hurling invectives, revealing salacious information to discredit opponents, and combining "a relatively new form of weaponized journalism, politicking and public policy into a potent mix" (Rutenberg, 2013, p. 4).

Some of these sites seamlessly combine fact and opinion, encouraging the perception they are legitimate news sites with just a little injection of political octane when in fact they are one-sided ideological outlets that offer a skewed version of events for a cadre of sympathetic readers. These include right-wing alt-right (or alternative right) sites that endorse the preservation of White culture in the U.S. and are widely viewed as taking White supremacist, anti-Semitic positions (Rappeport, 2016). They encompass Breitbart News, which was launched more than a decade ago by a conservative provocateur. Breitbart appeals to conservative-leaning users drawn to populist, anti-elite discourse that eschews norms of diplomacy and respect. Breitbart has featured racially charged stories that condemn the Black Lives Matter movement, disparage young Muslims, and contain misleading, unsubstantiated information about Hillary Clinton (Grynbaum & Herrman, 2016). The site became widely known in 2016 when it anchored right-wing media conversations and drove the Republican agenda, in feisty ways that mobilized conservatives, but also promoted falsehoods and bizarre "paranoid logic" (Benkler et al., 2017). Its executive became the director of Trump's campaign and later a chief White House strategist until he became too colorful and controversial for even the flamboyant Trump. Other sites combine entertainment and in-your-face politics, such as a show formerly on TheBlaze, "Tomi," that featured Tomi Lahren, a bodacious, likable, 24-year-old conservative provocateur with 4.3 million followers on social media, who flaunted conventions by criticizing prominent Black celebrities like Beyoncé and Colin Kaepernick, the NFL quarterback who protested U.S. racism by kneeling when "The Star Spangled Banner" was played at football games (Bromwich, 2016).

On the left are sites like U.S. Uncut and Addicting Info that critics say are replete with fake news and sensational *National Inquirer* headlined-stories. Addicting Info included headlines like "White House Now Planting Fake Stories to Discredit Reporters Who Expose Trump's Bullsh*t," or "Former Trump Aides Admit They *Have* to Treat Trump Like a Man Baby and Control His Media Habits." At their best, ideological sites refreshingly offer alternative opinions on politics, but they don't traffic in consensually validated journalistic facts. In the worst cases, they don't check information for its reliability, don't care, and just become the political web equivalent of a supermarket tabloid.

Citizens Enter the Fray

A third component of contemporary news is citizen journalism, peopled not by professionally trained journalists but by information-consumed individuals armed with curiosity, a passion, and a high-tech smartphone (Allan & Thorsen, 2009). While a detailed discussion of citizen journalism is beyond the scope of this book, suffice it to say it is ubiquitous. It occurs when passersby with smartphones record videos of police shootings of unarmed African Americans in American cities or expose authorities' complicity with crimes in online posts. This journalism—and there is debate about whether it is—can be eye-opening, providing invaluable information that eludes traditional news organizations. However, it is also open to questions of veracity by conflating live streaming with truth. Citizen posts are influenced by the perspective of the information-gatherer, the ways the videographer shot the video, what was shot, and what was left out.

Facebook as Decider

News aggregators like Google rely on computer algorithms, or automatic decision rules, rather than human decision-making to select news for display. Google uses specific criteria, scanning major conventional news outlets like *The Washington Post*, Reuters, and BBC. Its algorithm is fundamentally based on the hyperlinks going into and leaving a particular website, and total number of visits to the website. At Reddit, an individual's page contains stories the individual likes, as well as those favored by the larger group of registered users. Facebook employs algorithms to determine which stories show up prominently in users' news feeds and will be spotlighted in the Trending section on their home pages. Its algorithm is based on users' and friends' previous engagement with websites they liked on Facebook.

Ironically, "Facebook, born of the open Internet that knocked down the traditional barriers to information, (has become) a gatekeeper itself," media critic Jim Rutenberg (2016a, p. B7) notes. Facebook, though it likes to think of itself as a technology-steeped company, is both a tech and media company that makes gatekeeping choices, sometimes favoring articles that deeply engross readers, other times prioritizing Facebook Live videos. In one instance, it took down an iconic picture of a girl running from napalm bombs during the Vietnam War because it displayed nudity. However in response to a global criticism, even civil disobedience, when people posted the image on their own Facebook pages, the company reversed itself and reinstated the photograph on its site (Scott & Isaac, 2016).

Algorithms are far from perfect criteria for deciding, in a sense, what is news. Facebook's Trending Topics, introduced in 2014, represented Facebook's first shot at curating the voluminous information posted on the social media site, in an effort to help people easily locate up-to-date information they could discuss on Facebook. The algorithms Facebook used to sift through information frequently delivered "noise," offering up an increase in words that might be popular at a time, for example, those coinciding with a celebrity event, rather than significant political news events. Recognizing this problem, Facebook hired a team of editors to figure out what constituted news (Isaac, 2016). Their criteria could be journalistically weak, since editors probably lacked background in news-gathering, choices could reflect editors' biases (liberal since they lived in pot-friendly San Francisco!), and, over the long haul, news selections were personalized, based on the content of users' friends' posts, groups users belong to, and Facebook pages they liked. Personalized news raises a host of questions, including whether citizens receive news carefully culled to reflect their biases and idiosyncratic preferences rather than information they need to make responsible decisions in a complex society. Thus, gatekeeping is far from dead; the gates and keepers have changed (and we have more control over the locks), but judgments and biases remain.

Fake News

Fake news, which became famous during the 2016 election, reflects bias—actually falsehood—at its worst. In the main, **fake news** is a fabricated story created with an intention to deceive, either to gain profitable clicks or promote a political ideology. Perhaps the most bizarre example of 2016 presidential campaign was the conspiracy-theory story that a Washington, D.C., pizza restaurant harbored young children as sex slaves as part of a child-trafficking ring led by Hillary Clinton. This led to the even more freakish (hey, this is America!) incident, where the fake news story produced real gunfire, when a man who read the story became concerned, and fired an assault rifle inside the pizzeria (Kang & Goldman, 2016). Other false news stories included the tweet shared thousands of times on Twitter and Facebook that paid protesters had been bused to rally against Trump, and that Trump had been endorsed by the pope!

Although liberals also trafficked in false news about Trump (including a fake report that Trump said Republican voters were stupid), fake stories on Trump's behalf, making allegations about his opponents, seemed to gain more traction because disseminators of fake news assumed the social media audience exposed to such stories favored Trump. They, therefore, would be more likely to believe posts that cast aspersions on Clinton. Disturbingly, some fake news was promulgated by extreme right-wing ideologues outside the U.S. who support pro-Christian nationalist, anti-immigrant causes and the policies of Russian president Vladimir Putin (McIntire, 2016). Their websites inundated American voters with false information, offering a global platform for extremists to influence the 2016 American election. However, there is no empirical evidence to indicate these fake reports influenced Americans' votes, despite embittered Democrats' beliefs that anti–Hillary Clinton stories tilted the election to Trump.

In one sense, fake news is not new. French revolutionaries threatened to punish "enemies of the people" who spread false news (Higgins, 2017). Nineteenth-century American newspapers published false reports to lure readers. There is an important difference between fake news of the past and today. Today's faux reports are circulated not by biased reporters or journalists bedazzled by power, but by non-journalists—entrepreneurs trying to make a buck, or ideological provocateurs. Given partisans' tendency to selectively perceive and tune in to information which they agree (see Chapter 12), contemporary fake news is more likely to reach those who share its ideological premises. These users then share it with like-minded others, and it takes on the imprimatur of factual truth.

Even if the reach of fake news is frequently exaggerated, the dangers are real. If news consumers begin to disregard and even dismiss truth, believing that everything is partisan and fabricated, the factual foundation of journalism is in jeopardy. The premise of classic journalism is that news outlets provide facts (not totally objective, but verified using professional standards) that citizens invoke when evaluating political issues and in deciding for whom to cast a ballot. If facts—though not objective, at least subject to consensual agreement—are falsified or distrusted, democracy is weakened. If leaders brand information that casts them in a negative light "fake news," and supporters believe them, an important foundation of democracy buckles under stress.

Summary

The contemporary political news media environment is a mélange, a potpourri, intersecting circles on a Venn diagram. On cable television it can be hard for viewers to disentangle opinions from news on MSNBC and Fox, where programs like *The Rachel Maddow Show* and *Hannity* intermingle the two or just plain ignore other viewpoints, as Hannity did with his full-throated endorsement of Trump during the '16 campaign. The intermingled news environment, where news and commentary can be close to each other, can confuse, causing readers to misidentify whether facts came from a news story or opinionated commentary on a blog, as Emily K. Vraga and her colleagues (2011) showed.

Fake news may lead to more misidentification effects. Political videos "styled as newscasts" with "newslike image memes" posted on "fly-by-night websites" contain false information that users might reasonably perceive to be true (Herrman, 2016, p. B1). The current news environment "is creating confusion, punching holes in what is true, causing a kind of fun-house effect that leaves the reader doubting everything, including real news" (Tavernise, 2016, p. A18). We aren't at the point where everyone doubts everything and takes their own version of information as truth, but there are danger signs.

This all complicates the time-honored issue of news bias. Of course, news has biases, and (in a positive development) there may actually be a more diverse range of biases available to citizens than in the days of broadcast television. In a democratic society, where news plays an important role in distilling information needed for the responsible exercise of citizenship, it is important to understand the nature of political news. The next section turns the spotlight on news: conventional, ever-changing news, as seen in newspapers, television, and online journalistic platforms. Is political news biased? Are charges of news bias supported by data? The answers may surprise you.

UNDERSTANDING POLITICAL NEWS BIAS

At the most basic philosophical level, of course, there is bias in all news. No one is objective. There is bias when a reporter picks one adjective rather than another to describe a candidate's performance in a political debate, or offers an opinionated statement in a tweet (Lawrence, Molyneux, Coddington, & Holton, 2014). Bias occurs when a photographer selects a camera angle that depicts a candidate in a more flattering pose. Bias emerges when news covers negative rather than positive aspects of public life. Everybody agrees that there are biases in mainstream news. But these are not the types of biases that animate critics. They are referring to politically motivated or ideological biases that emphasize one view of politics rather than another.

Bias is an easy label to apply, but harder to conceptualize and study. In academic circles the concept is multilayered, with "widespread disagreement about its meaning, measurement, and impact" (Lichter, 2014). Based on political media scholarship (Hofsetter, 1976; Entman, 2010), one can stipulate that **ideologically or politically based news bias** occurs when there is a consistent media pattern in presentation of an issue, in a way that reliably favors one side, or minimizes the opposing side, in a context when it can reasonably be argued that there are other perspectives on the issue that are also deserving of coverage. Let's review the components of ideological or political news bias.

First, there must be a consistent pattern in the nature of the coverage. A story that favors Democrats over Republicans does not necessarily reflect bias. For example, a story about a grassroots protest to planned Republican cuts of Obamacare, in which protesters criticized Republicans' plans to trim the Affordable Care Act, received coverage because the events were novel and dramatic, not because Republicans were criticized or Democrats were quoted positively. A series of stories that focus on a Republican president's address before Congress is not biased in favor of the Republicans, but simply reflects the attention journalists devote to the presidency. However, if most of the stories on a particular channel focused on Republicans or Democrats, regardless of whether the events merited coverage, this could reflect political bias.

Second, political bias requires abundant inclusion of content on behalf of the favored side and systematic exclusion of equivalent material from the opposing group. Tone of coverage, word choice, and even the ways that a news organization chooses to set the agenda or frame the issues could showcase political bias (e.g., Eberl, Wagner, & Boomgaarden, 2017) Again, this is complicated. Much news about President Reagan seemed to show him smiling and delivering pithy, humorous sound bites. But this did not reflect an ideological bias for Reagan (in fact, many reporters privately opposed his positions). Instead, the positive news showcased Reagan's ability to present a favorable political image and manipulate the news, or even journalists' (nonpartisan) perception that Reagan was a great communicator (Schudson, 1995).

A third requirement for ideologically based, intentional bias is that the biases emerge through reliably conducted, scientific analyses of news content. Observers from different vantage points should detect the same pattern in news coverage. Fourth, there must be other reasonable perspectives on the issue, which are minimized or excluded due to an apparent political disposition on the part of the individual journalist or media organization. Fifth, and in a related vein, the other perspectives *should* be deserving of coverage. We would not claim that news coverage of the grisly murder of an innocent person was biased because it offered sympathy for the victim. It would not make sense to charge that the story harbored bias because it failed to offer a sympathetic version of the man who had admitted stabbing the victim 50 times. The perspectives deserving of coverage must be ones that mesh with cultural values and common sense.

With a definition of bias in mind, let's move to consideration of the fractious issue of liberal bias.

UNPACKING LIBERAL NEWS BIAS

> The media are so partisan that many people are under the impression that they must take their marching orders directly from the Democratic National Committee.
>
> (Coulter, 2008, p. 19)

> The problem comes in the big social and cultural issues, where we (television journalists) often sound more like flacks for liberal causes than objective journalists. Why were we doing the work of the homeless lobby by exaggerating the number of homeless people on the streets of America? . . . Why did we give so much time on

the evening news to liberal feminist organizations, like NOW, and almost no time to conservative women who oppose abortion?

(Goldberg, 2002, p. 22)

Liberal news bias became a venomous refrain of the Trump campaign during the waning weeks of the 2016 election, as Trump charged that the news media were trying to "poison the minds" of voters with "lies, lies, lies" . . . part of a "conspiracy against you, the American people."

(Rutenberg, 2016b, p. B1)

If you watch Fox News, you have heard the charges. If you read *The Wall Street Journal*, you are familiar with the allegations: The news is left-liberal and displays a strong liberal bias. Just because intelligent people make the charge with gusto does not make it so. As students of political communication, we need to see if the allegations hold up when we examine them systematically and carefully. The focus is conventional news, news produced by reputable but diverse news organizations. There is little question, as noted earlier, that many websites are biased. But their purpose is not to offer a fair rendition of political news, but rather to push people in the direction of their biases. There may not be anything wrong with this, as opinions are the DNA of democracy. The more controversial question is whether the nation's political news, which appears in newspapers, magazines, their websites, broadcast TV, and cable TV—reflect a liberal bias.

The liberal bias thesis consists of two parts. First, critics argue that reporters and editors hold liberal, left-of-center attitudes. Second, they contend that journalists project these attitudes into news stories.

There *is* evidence that elite journalists—the national press corps that resides in Washington, D.C.—harbor liberal political attitudes (Groseclose & Milyo, 2005; Kuypers, 2014). Some of this may be a result of reporters' natural identification with the underdog, embodied in the journalistic credo that news should afflict the comfortable and comfort the afflicted. Another factor could be that reporters are more critical of authority and identify to a greater degree with society's victims than other professionals. But clearly national political reporters are more liberal politically. The top tier of national reporters tends to hold rather liberal political attitudes, with large majorities reporting that they vote for Democratic rather than Republican presidential candidates (Lichter, Rothman, & Lichter, 1986; Rivers, 1962). Even widely respected liberal commentators, such as Eric Alterman (2003), have acknowledged that there are "undeniable" instances where "a fair-minded observer might point to a pervasive liberal bias" (pp. 108–109). For example:

The Associated Press, *Washington Post, Boston Globe,* and *Time* Magazine, among others, have referred to those who oppose abortion "even in cases of rape and incest" (circumstances under which most people approve of abortion). But the media almost never refer to those who favor abortion rights "even in the final weeks of pregnancy" (circumstances under which most people oppose abortion).

(Alterman, 2003, p. 108)

Another liberal commentator, Michael Massing, provided similar testimony:

National news organizations have produced a flood of stories questioning how the death penalty is administered in this country. These accounts have documented the poor legal representation available to death-row inmates, the extra-harsh treatment minorities generally receive, and, most dramatically, the growing number of innocent people who have been condemned to death. As an opponent of capital punishment, I applaud such stories. Yet I also believe that they lean toward one side of the issue, and that the coverage would be enhanced if more attention were paid to, say, the families of murder victims and the ordeal they must endure.

(quoted in Alterman, 2003, p. 109)

Complementing these observations with empirical data, a content analysis showed that close to 6 in 10 *New York Times* stories published from 1960 to 2005 displayed a liberal, anti-death-penalty tone (Baumgartner, De Boef, & Boydstun, 2008).

Scholars have acknowledged that news coverage of a host of social issues (e.g., homelessness, gay rights, religion, and gun control) may tilt to the liberal side of the political spectrum (Entman, 2010). *The Washington Post* generated controversy with its headline shortly after conservative Supreme Court Justice Antonin Scalia died in February, 2016. The headline, "Supreme Court Conservative Dismayed Liberals," zoomed in only on aspects of Scalia's record that disappointed liberals, neglecting the preeminent conservative contributions that Scalia made to the Court. Readers criticized *The New York Times* for showing liberal bias during the 2016 election, as when an Election Day article featured the starstruck verbal and visual reflections of four photographers who covered Clinton over the years; the newspaper did not offer a similarly fawning portrait of photographers who covered Trump during his decades in the Big Apple. Although liberals profess that the news media are fair, they neglect instances where national news can favor their viewpoint.

Clearly, then, there is strong evidence that national reporters are liberal, and some indication that national media—and particularly leading elite newspapers—may tilt liberal in coverage of some issues. But, for the most part, these are anecdotal observations. How frequently does such liberal coverage occur? Does it constitute a bias? Does it hold up under scientific scrutiny?

Problems With the Liberal News Bias Thesis

As noted earlier, there are two parts of the hypothesis: (1) journalists are liberal, and (2) they project their liberal attitudes into their work, such that news contains a left-of-center bias. Let's review each contention carefully and critically.

Although, as discussed in the previous section, the Washington press corps holds liberal attitudes, mainstream reporters and editors from across the country do not. Three decades of research by David H. Weaver and his colleagues (2007) indicates that journalists from broad cross-sections of the U.S. are more conservative than national reporters in Washington, D.C. While 36 percent of journalists queried in 2002 were Democrats, 18 percent were Republican and approximately 32.5 percent regarded themselves as Independents; the remainder fell into miscellaneous categories. With more than 50 percent of respondents regarding themselves as Republican or Independent, you can hardly describe journalists as radical-liberals. What's more, reporters' bosses—media executives and owners—are business people who hold more conservative attitudes and are concerned with the economic bottom line. Their directives can push even liberal reporters to emphasize conventional viewpoints in their stories. But there is a more important factor at work. Journalists are professionals and try hard to live up to the standards of their profession. They recognize that interjecting their own biases in a news story is unprofessional and flies in the face of journalistic canons. It can turn off conservative consumers and get them fired.

Let's look at the second contention: news stories advance a liberal agenda. A problem is that much of the evidence advanced in its defense is anecdotal. Although interesting and suggestive, this does not provide compelling scientific support for the hypothesis. Ann Coulter and Bernard Goldberg, quoted at the beginning of this section, offer a litany of examples in their books, but they appear to be cherry-picked to support their argument or could be outweighed by a flurry of counterexamples. For example, in the second epigraph, Goldberg (2002) asserted that the media lavish attention on feminists but neglect conservative opponents of abortion. How do we know he is correct? He might be, but he also could have conveniently neglected all the instances in which television positively portrays pro-life opponents of partial abortion. Or his thesis might have been true at one point, but could be swamped by more recent coverage in broad sectors of the country that favored a pro-life viewpoint.

The only way to convincingly document that the volume or tone of coverage favors one political position over another is to conduct scientific content analyses, described in Chapter 3. When researchers do this, they obtain strikingly different findings than those suggested by conservative critics. In a meta-analysis, or statistical analysis of research, focused on presidential campaign news in elections from 1948 through 1996,

D'Alessio and Allen (2000) could not locate any newspaper biases that favored Democrats or Republicans. Biases for newsmagazines were negligible, although there was a slight pro-Republican bias in coverage. Television news contained a modest, though not entirely consistent, trend that favored Democratic candidates. A more recent exhaustive, innovative content analysis of political news in major news outlets found that news organizations describe issues in primarily nonpartisan terms, showing no bias toward Republicans or Democrats, except to depict both sides negatively, reflecting, if anything, a "pox on all sides" bias (Budak, Goel, & Rao, 2016; see Figure 9.1).

Cognizant that giving more favorable coverage to liberal than conservative candidates will brand them as biased in the eyes of conservative commentators, contemporary news can bend over backwards to give both sides (Puglisi & Snyder, 2011). Thus, whatever positive press *The New York Times* gave Clinton during the election was more than balanced by negative news. The newspaper broke the big story of Clinton's

Figure 9.1 The media are frequently perceived to harbor a liberal bias. Political communication scholarship debunks this notion, indicating that while there are instances of pro-liberal coverage in some elite media outlets, political news overall does not show an overall bias toward liberal positions, and in some cases quite the opposite.

Getty Images

use of a private mail server that could have breached national security information and held her feet to the fire throughout the campaign. What's more, during the months that preceded the 2016 primaries, a variety of news outlets gave Clinton, a Democrat, the most negative press of all the candidates, while providing Trump, the Republican, very positive press (Patterson, 2016).

Even if the media portray a particular individual or group in a negative light, this does not mean the coverage was *biased*. Bias involves a conscious (or unconscious) intention on the part of a communicator to slant the news in a particular way. A picture that showed Trump grimacing about a problematic meeting with a foreign leader would not reflect bias so much as a journalistic judgment that his nonverbal expression was newsworthy. In an older study, Lichter and his colleagues (1986) argued news stories that raised critical questions of nuclear power plant safety and radiation effects showcased liberal bias, reflecting liberal concern with environmental issues rather than a pro-nuclear industry slant. But this need not have telegraphed reporters' intention to discredit the nuclear issue so much as an attempt to raise awareness of a social problem, a role that journalists perform for society. Articles raising concerns about radiation effects, environmental hazards, and catastrophic accidents could have been motivated by a desire to inform the public about an issue that journalists believed had been swept under the rug by authorities, especially in the wake of a 1979 accident at the Three Mile Island nuclear power plant in Pennsylvania that led to a leak of radioactive gases into the environment.

In a similar fashion, Groseclose and Milyo (2005) presented apparent evidence for liberal bias in intriguing research that compared press citations of political groups with those of comparable elite institutions. Groseclose and Milyo compared the frequency with which news media outlets, and liberal and conservative members of Congress, cited think tanks of different ideological persuasions in a speech or communication. Think tanks or policy groups included the Brookings Institution and the NAACP on the liberal side, and the Heritage Foundation and National Right to Life Committee on the conservative side. While legislators cited liberal *and* conservative think tanks, news organizations primarily cited liberal think tanks. However, the results, while interesting, were actually more complicated. The conservative National Right to Life Committee and National Rifle Association were cited more frequently by the media than by members of Congress. The liberal American Civil Liberties Union (ACLU) was cited frequently by both legislators and the media, perhaps because a campaign finance law the ACLU opposed was a topic of national interest. This suggests that other factors besides ideological bias determine media citations. And just because the news cites a group more frequently does not tell us how positively or negatively the group or its issues were covered.

The liberal bias thesis also tends to be overstated. Conservatives are well-represented in the American media. Sean Hannity and Tucker Carlson (and for years Bill O'Reilly) offered conservative perspectives on Fox. A legion of conservative bloggers and websites are prominent on the Internet, offering plenty of news articles they perceive to reflect a liberal bias (Kuypers, 2014). The idea that the mainstream media is liberally biased is disingenuous when one considers that a core element of the media—Fox News—has garnered higher audience ratings than the other popular 24-hour news networks, CNN and MSNBC. Conservative talk radio programs and Fox News collectively recruit an audience of about 50 million (Draper, 2016). If they are outliers, not part of the mainstream media, as conservative critics sometimes allege, then they are extraordinarily potent outliers. The charge that the media showcase a liberal bias is a verbal shell game that conservatives play to make political points. Liberals can do the same.

Indeed, the interesting thing about the liberal bias thesis is that liberals have made exactly the opposite case, arguing that the news is the handmaiden of a greedy corporate establishment. In 2016 Bernie Sanders argued that "the corporate media talks about all kinds of issues except the most important issues," claiming that the profit-hungry owners of news media conglomerates develop programming that advances their bottom line, but steadfastly avoid critical problems like increasing inequality of wealth (Horowitz, 2016, p. A14). Thus, bias can often be in the eye of the beholder. And, of course, given public antipathy to The Media, politicians can always gain points by claiming media bias, as Republican Ted Cruz did in a 2016 presidential primary debate, immediately garnering audience applause. A *New Yorker* cartoon showed two armies facing off in battle, while the two kings are talking to each other in the middle of the field. One king says, "On the other hand, we could join forces and attack the media." Alas, the perception of bias and the conviction that partisan bias exists does not bias prove.

EXAMINING GENDER BIAS IN POLITICAL NEWS

Is political journalism sexist? Is coverage of female presidential contenders adequately explained by journalistic criteria? Do stereotypes of male and female politicians still occur at more subtle levels? These questions are the focus of this section, probing the intersection of yet another contemporary aspect of the news bias thesis: gender prejudices and political news.

Historical Progression

This is the way it used to be:

In 1972, the Women's Movement began to gather steam, and egalitarian supporters of women's rights emphasized that more women should run for elective office. Some dreamed of a day a woman could be elected president. But this was the 1970s, and sex-role prejudice was pervasive. Typifying the view held by many Americans, one man noted that

Women are not qualified for this high office. If one is ever elected President, she would have to depend 100% on the advice of the men she appointed to high executive positions. Heaven help us in the event of a war. She couldn't handle the awesome responsibilities.

(Falk, 2010, pp. 37–38)

Journalism contained many of the same biases. In 1984, when Democratic vice presidential candidate Geraldine Ferraro triumphantly stood before the delegates to the 1984 Democratic National Convention, NBC anchor Tom Brokaw announced: "Geraldine Ferraro . . . The first woman to be nominated for Vice President . . . Size six" (Braden, 1996, p. 15). During a time when reporters were on the constant lookout to see if a woman candidate would cry or lack the toughness to stand up to America's enemies, Ferraro was asked on the television news program, *Meet the Press*, "Do you think that in any way the Soviets might be tempted to try to take advantage of you simply because you are a woman?" (Mitchell, 2016, p. 18).

News devoted less coverage to female than male candidates running for the Senate between 1982 and 1988, and the coverage was also more negative, downplaying their chances of winning (Kahn, 1994). Women candidates running for Senate stressed their masculine traits, such as strength, over 90 percent of the time in ads, but news stories described these characteristics only about 40 percent of the time (Kahn, 1996; Beail & Longworth, 2013).

Female presidential candidates garnered less coverage than their male counterparts in 1972, 1988, 2000, and 2004. News portrayed female presidential candidates as less likely to succeed than the campaigns of comparable male candidates (Falk, 2010). News offered up stereotyped descriptions of female presidential and vice presidential candidates, describing women candidates in more emotional terms and taking note of their clothing and gender, while focusing more on men's age and appearance. A content analysis of eight metropolitan newspapers in different regions of the country from 1988 through 2008 found that news emphasized women candidates' novelty and character traits more than men's (Meeks, 2012). The coverage stemmed from gender role stereotypes reporters applied to female candidates, including **the gendered double-bind**, the sexist notion that women cannot be both professionally competent and feminine (Jamieson, 1995).

Reviewing the 2008 and 2016 Campaigns

In 2008, gender leapt to the foreground of the presidential campaign. Hillary Clinton nearly won the Democratic presidential nomination and Republicans nominated Sarah Palin for vice president. Did gender biases influence coverage?

Content analyses offer insights into this question. Although print articles offered about the same number of physical descriptions of Clinton as Obama, Clinton was described early on in more physical terms than the average for previous male presidential contenders (Falk, 2010). Some of those physical descriptions raised eyebrows. A frequently discussed *Washington Post* article remarked that "the neckline (of a black top) sat low on her chest and had a subtle V-shape. The cleavage registered after only a quick glance" (Falk, 2010, p. 158). Articles were also more likely to refer to her by her first name than they were to call Obama "Barack," or her other major competitor, John Edwards, "John."

Opinionated cable shows and websites were filled with biases, some vicious and vulgar. Radio and cable television commentaries took off the gloves. They unleashed the b-word with impunity. Conservative radio host Glenn Beck called her a "stereotypical bitch." Castration images also were invoked. Clinton was the recipient of many insulting gender-based messages. For example, Tucker Carlson, a prominent conservative TV commentator, remarked that "There's just something about her that feels castrating, overbearing and scary," and on another show noted that "I have often said, when she comes on television, I involuntarily cross my legs" (Falk, 2010, p. 165; Douglas, 2010).

It was worse on the Internet. A blogger remarked that "Hillary has awful old-lady udders, the worst boobs of any Hillary on the Internet." YouTube videos went repulsively further, with one altering images to show her with large, uncovered breasts, while two men sang "she is my cherry pie" (Falk, 2010, p. 159). Social media and websites offered a slew of degrading portrayals of Clinton, though this seems to have dissipated, if not disappeared, in 2016.

Let's be clear: Blogs, YouTube, and Facebook sites do not reflect mainstream media. They can represent fringe groups, the Wild Wild West of contemporary communications that do not profess to cover issues in a professionally journalistic fashion. They were not reporting on the news of Clinton's or Palin's campaigns. In the main, journalists did not cover Clinton or Palin this way. Indeed, some journalists were quick to criticize those who used the b-word to describe Clinton. So, how positive or negative were Clinton's and Palin's press? To answer this question, we turn to content analyses of news coverage that examine the quantity of coverage and code positivity or negativity by examining how sources quoted in the stories evaluate the candidate, adjectives reporters use to describe the candidates ("refreshing" versus "weary" or "defensive"), and the overall tone of the stories. When researchers refer to the positive or negative press candidates receive, they are describing results gleaned from content analytic studies.

Clearly, over the course of both elections Clinton received positive press, focusing on her experience, primary debate successes, how she almost shattered the glass ceiling in

2008, and how she became the first woman to gain the nomination of a major political party in the United States in 2016—an achievement that, as one article enthusiastically noted, made many women feel proud, evoking cheers and tears (Kantor, 2016). But she also received negative news coverage, garnering significantly more negative news than Obama in 2008, and more unfavorable coverage during the early 2016 campaign than any of the major candidates of both parties (Lawrence & Rose, 2010; Patterson, 2016). In 2016, there was a steady drip-drip and then an outpouring of news that focused on negative aspects of her campaign, from her emails to possible conflicts of interest with the Clinton Foundation. How can we explain her negative press? Much, though not all, can be explained by journalistic factors, the news values and routines reporters use to construct stories (see Figure 9.2).

A key factor is that Clinton was the front-runner, and reporters subject front-runners to tough questions. They believe that voters have a right to know the fallibilities of

Figure 9.2 Hillary Clinton transcended gender barriers by becoming the first American woman nominated by a major political party. During the 2016 campaign, her news coverage was frequently negative, due to the nature of political journalism routines and subtle gender biases.

Getty Images

their party's potential nominee so that they can weigh these factors when they vote (see Chapter 10). A political journalism perspective emphasizes that the negative press that Clinton received was primarily not due to gender, but represented an attempt to hold her feet to the fire as the Democratic front-runner.

In 2008, though not in 2016, Clinton received negative press, in part because her campaign committed strategic errors that were deemed newsworthy. Hillary Clinton let her husband Bill, ordinarily the consummate political strategist, meddle in her campaign, overshadowing her candidacy. He offended African Americans by ridiculing Obama's long-held opposition to the Iraq War and then dismissing the significance of his huge victory in the South Carolina primary, which had been bolstered by his ability to capture three-quarters of the Black vote. Clinton's campaign also began to unravel as a result of highly publicized interpersonal conflicts and destructive infighting among staffers (Balz & Johnson, 2009). By contrast, Obama received more positive press, partly because of his novel candidacy, his communication skills as a campaigner, and perhaps also because "Obama embodied and symbolized racial progress for many people in the United States (or at least many pundits and commentators) in a way that Clinton did not symbolize progress on sexual equality" (Lawrence & Rose, 2010, pp. 217–218, 216).

In 2016, considerable news centered on Clinton's use of a private email server that raised national security questions, while also eliciting FBI investigations of her email use, Republican outcry, and all the political implications journalists love to cover. Thirty-five percent of campaign news stories on 23 media outlets focused on Clinton's email, with many stories examining how this reflected on her character (Vavreck, 2016). There was a constant stream of negativity in Clinton's press coverage, with some of the negative press reflecting legitimate concern about her decision to use a private email server that *could* have compromised national security (O'Harrow, 2016). Other aspects of the negative news seemed rooted in the ways it congealed with the time-honored journalistic narrative that Clinton had a penchant for secrecy, as well as the press's gravitation to character attacks, rather than issues (see Chapter 10).

Over on the Republican side, in 2008, Republican vice presidential nominee Sarah Palin received negative press, but the reasons are complicated. A systematic analysis of over 2,500 newspaper articles revealed that Palin received more negative press than Democratic vice presidential candidate Joe Biden. Newspaper articles mentioned her gender six times more frequently than Biden's. They also contained significantly more references to her appearance and marital status than to Biden's, perhaps triggering stereotyped beliefs about political candidates (Miller & Peake, 2013). Some news stories were blatantly sexist, making references to her sexuality (Carlin & Winfrey, 2009), allusions reporters would not invoke for a comparable male candidate. But most of the negative press did not stem from gender biases. Instead, as Bradley and Wicks (2011) noted, "because Palin was new to the political sphere, journalists may have attempted to 'dig up the dirt' on her life and career" (p. 816). And there was plenty of "dirt" to unearth, juicy tidbits that are the fodder of political news, like her teenage daughter's pregnancy and the embarrassing revelation that the Republican National Committee had paid for Palin's expensive campaign wardrobe. But, in the main, reporters didn't dig up dirt because Palin was a woman, but, rather, because journalists feel a professional obligation to let voters know about the shortcomings of a candidate who could become vice president of the United States. There were other reasons too: news focuses on unexpected, novel issues, and on pratfalls candidates make that can entice readers to click websites or turn on the news, increasing profits for beleaguered news organizations. And, in fairness, Palin invited some of the negative press when she fumbled in an interview with *Today*'s Katie Couric, unable to name specific newspapers she read on a regular basis.

Subtle Biases About Female Candidates and Appearance

Not so fast, critics retort, suggesting that news coverage of female candidates contains subtle, but important, gender biases by focusing more on women's appearance and wardrobe than on men's.

Palin's 2008 media portrayals took on a more gendered hue than other candidates, partly due to her own self-presentation (her taste in high-priced stylish clothing was distinctive), journalistic conventions, reporters' gender stereotypes, and press focus on women's appearance and wardrobe (Finneman, 2015; Kahl & Edwards, 2009). Journalists framed Palin in a variety of ways, a function of her political complexity (Beail & Longworth, 2013). Palin took stridently stereotypically masculine issue positions, while displaying the "trappings of femininity—stiletto heels, silk shirts, and pearls," and lipstick (Lawrence & Rose, 2010, p. 221), the latter not surprising, given her famous quip that the difference between a hockey mom and a pit bull was lipstick! When she endorsed Trump in 2016, she was described in the news as wearing a "sparkly Milly beaded silk bolero jacket" that cost $695. Style experts criticized her choice of clothing, and on Twitter a marketing specialist compared her to a "disco ball hedgehog" (Baird, 2016, p. A23).

On the one hand, Palin's sartorial persona invited a flurry of feature stories. On the other hand, her coverage pointed up a continued double bind, "damned if you do and damned if you don't" aspect of news of female candidates: journalists scrutinize female candidates' appearances and criticize them when they spend money to cultivate their heavily-scrutinized wardrobe" (Finneman, 2015, p. 147).

Francis and Gregory (2015) offer a succinct statement of subtle biases that face female political candidates:

> If the rhetoric of fashion presents a more masculinized argument, she is selling out her gender by appealing to a patriarchal construction of political leadership. However, if she presents a more feminine aesthetic, she is attempting to use her sexuality to appeal to voters.
>
> (p. 215)

In 2016, when Clinton captured the Democratic nomination, a *New York Times* fashion reporter observed in an article on the fashion choices of women political leaders—Hillary Clinton, German chancellor Angela Merkel, and British prime minister Theresa May—that

> over the months until the general election . . . (Clinton) will be scrutinized in ever-more exacting detail, not just for her economic platform and her emails, but also for her body language, her eating habits, her relationships. And, yes, her clothes.
>
> (Friedman, 2016)

Hillary Clinton may have faced a dialectical conflict—or double bind—with her preference for pantsuits, and news coverage may have made the wardrobe more salient by covering Clinton's clothing over the years, as in stories about a "silk teal pantsuit" designed by Oscar de la Renta, a silver pantsuit worn to a downtown Manhattan dinner, and a tan pantsuit when she appeared on *The Late Show with David Letterman* back in 2007 (Francis & Gregory, 2015, p. 165). However, clothing could also be described in ways congenial with feminism, as in the description of Clinton's wardrobe at the third 2016 presidential debate, when she was described as "wearing a suffragette-inspired white suit" (Stockman, 2016, p. A17).

To be sure, reporters write about male candidates' clothing and their coiffure, like the changing color of Trump's hair. (When *Tonight Show* host Jimmy Fallon ran his hand through Trump's hair, Trump's critics condemned him for making nice to a candidate they disliked!) News has historically focused more on female candidates' clothing than on the apparel of their male counterparts. Some argue that focusing on women candidates' fashion appeal calls up stereotypes that emphasize physical appearance at the expense of political acumen. Others might defend the coverage, suggesting, as one fashion reporter did, that women's clothes are, after all, more interesting than men's (Friedman, 2017). Yet it was disconcerting that sexist snipes of powerful women's clothing continued after the election, with Twitter critics attacking senior White House adviser Kellyanne Conway's hair, appearance, and clothing. "Why does Kellyanne Conway always look like she's still drunk & wearing makeup from last night's bender?," one asked. Another complained that her Inauguration Day wardrobe looked like "a night terror of an android majorette" (Chira, 2017, p. A1).

When it comes to the effects of apparel-focused news, research offers suggestive but conflicting findings. On the one hand, studies find that voters do not judge male and female candidates differently when news refers positively (or negatively) to their clothing (Hayes & Lawless, 2013; see also Brooks, 2013). On the other hand, there is a large literature that women are objectified more than men—treated as objects rather than subjects or competent individuals (Fredrickson & Roberts, 1997). Media depictions that emphasize women's body or physical appearance can diminish positive evaluations of female leaders' abilities and warmth (Heflick, Goldenberg, Cooper, & Puvia, 2011), encouraging people to view women in objectified, less holistic ways. This suggests that press focus on women candidates' clothing can push voters to regress to more sex-typed evaluations of female candidates, overlooking their human qualities in favor of superficial stereotypes (see Box 9.1).

Did 2016 voters reject Hillary Clinton because news coverage of her clothing encouraged them to objectify her, viewing Clinton as less a competent candidate than a woman in a pantsuit? Or were there other more substantial reasons, such as their disenchantment with her inability to articulate a positive platform for working class Americans or her lack of candor (some would say this also called on sex-role stereotypes)? Should reporters never write about female candidates' fashion tastes, even if they are newsworthy? Are we selling Americans short, presuming they can't get beyond the occasional feature about a woman candidate's apparel? Or are reporters showing subtle sexism when they write more about female candidates' appearance than their male counterparts?

BOX 9.1 POLITICAL SEXISM

Trump's gender-laced denunciation of Hillary Clinton—"Such a nasty woman," spoken in the third presidential debate—is only one of many hostile comments that male politicians have directed at female political leaders. Others have been more vitriolic. They include: She has "the lips of Marilyn Monroe, the eyes of Caligula" (former French President François Mitterrand's insult about former British Prime Minister Margaret Thatcher); "You're more beautiful than you are intelligent" (former Italian Prime Minister Silvio Berlusconi to Rosy Bindi, an opposition member of the Italian Parliament—which could have been said of him too!); "Anyone who has chosen to remain deliberately barren, they've

Continued

got no idea about what life's about" (Australian senator Bill Heffernan about Julia Gillard, who later became the prime minister of Australia); "Did you see Nancy Pelosi on the floor? Complete disgust. If you can get through all the surgeries, there's disgust" (South Carolina Senator Lindsay Graham, making a joke about plastic surgery and former Speaker of the House Nancy Pelosi); and the familiarly condescending comment from former British Prime Minister David Cameron to Angela Eagle, a British politician, "Calm down dear" (Miller, 2016, p. A12).

These comments, as well as those more distasteful insults, point up the problem of a gender-related double bind, notably between sex-typed femininity and competence, where feminine traits are stereotypically viewed as incongruent with leadership. No "true woman" could be an effective political persuader, according to time-honored myth (Smith, 2015). Americans look for warmth and empathy from the president, but also strength and toughness. This presents a challenge for women—or actually for Americans with stereotyped views—for women are presumed, by dint of their empathy, to have difficulty projecting toughness. Herein lies the double bind: "Women who show too much strength undermine not only their ability to be 'soft' and to feel the pain of others, but also risk seeming unnaturally masculine, unwomanly, or monstrous" (Smith, 2015, p. 86). Yet we wouldn't make a comparable comment about male political leaders, charging that men who show too much compassion undermine their ability to be tough in a crisis, but also risk seeming too feminine.

"Women who attain leadership positions often are castigated as too aggressive, 'bitchy,' or worse," Vasby Anderson (2016) observes (p. 22). She suggests that Clinton has been a victim of this bind, having been characterized as a shrew and framed by the press as cold and unlikable because journalists, in essence, had difficulty accommodating her political acumen with their stereotypes about femininity. Others might disagree, countering that some of her negative press was rooted in Clinton's weakness as a candidate, her difficulty displaying a warm public persona (like, say, Massachusetts Senator Elizabeth Warren), and an inauthentic posture (Chozick & Alcindor, 2016).

Over the years, masculinity has been a core underpinning of presidential leadership in the U.S. Politics is viewed as a masculine domain, power is linked with men, and male candidates have been accorded more freedom to speak in guttural ways than female politicians. This may be changing. When a 2016 video revealed Trump bragging in profane, offensive ways about how he groped women, many media outlets called him out, framing his comments in terms of sexual power and aggressiveness rather than (in Trump's words) as "locker room talk." And with research showing that women candidates face fewer double binds concerning femininity and toughness than in years past (Brooks, 2013; Meeks & Domke, 2016), we may be approaching a new egalitarianism in politics. However, the pervasiveness of gender stereotypes suggests we have not reached this threshold yet.

CONCLUSIONS

The news media are biased.

This comment is heard so frequently today it can be considered a cliché, a cultural commonplace, even a social meme! But what does bias mean, and is the statement true? This chapter unpacked these issues, describing the contemporary panoply of political news media, where news is intertwined with entertainment, and encompasses conventional news, ideologically based cable television news and websites, citizen journalism, and information algorithmically selected and curated by social network-ing sites.

What is meant by bias? By calling news biased, people can have different things in mind, ranging from its focus on the negative to its emphasis on titillating, scurrilous events. Political observers frequently argue the news is ideologically biased. Is it? This requires the application of a clear definition of bias, and a definition was presented that emphasized political bias occurs when there is a consistent pattern in news presenta-tions that favors one side when it can be reasonably argued there are other perspectives deserving of coverage.

In one sense, political news is biased. It favors the two major party candidates (Kirch, 2013) and frames the election as a game (see Chapter 10). Beyond that, critics—usually conservative—argue that the news reflects a strong liberal political bias. The research offers a complicating picture, indicating that national reporters are liberal, and national news on some social issues can sometimes tilt liberal. However, journalists from the broad cross-sections of the U.S. are more conservative than the Washington press corps, holding a range of political views. In addition, social science studies cast doubt on the thesis that news reflects liberal bias, pointing to even-handed coverage of national elec-tions, and suggesting that factors other than an intentional intrusion of reporters' beliefs determine news coverage.

Gender bias has raised a host of other concerns about media treatment of female candidates. Historically, news coverage was horrifically sexist. This has changed dramatically, although many residues remain on websites, in social media posts, opinionated cable talk shows, and in subtle, offensive stereotypes of women candidates' appearance, as seen in depictions of Clinton and Palin in 2008 in particular. By and large, the picture has improved dramatically over the past decades. Clinton did receive substantial negative news in 2016, but much of this was rooted in journalistic factors, such as the tendency of reporters to cover (incessantly, in the view of critics) a candidate's missteps and alleged character flaws. Some of this may have interfaced with gender biases, and subtle biases in covering women's appearance and clothing remain.

The 2016 campaign showed that sex-typed and sexist issues continue apace, from the double entendre "references" between candidates Marco Rubio and Donald Trump in the primaries (Trump called Rubio "Little Marco" and Rubio responded by saying Trump had "small hands") to Trump's unseemly, disturbing boasting of sexual aggression. Appropriate focus on these issues can overshadow ways that women candidates' campaigns can also play the gender card, raising interesting issues. For example, Clinton supporters claimed that unfavorable coverage of their candidate that referred to her as "calculating," "ambitious," or "secretive" reflected unsuitable use of "coded, gender language." Yet, as *New York Times* reporter Amy Chozick, who was one of many female reporters who covered Clinton, noted,

> I don't think secretive . . . has anything to do with gender. I really don't. And I also think you can't approach every story thinking is this word going to be interpreted as sexist, you know? I mean, she's running for president. If she's being secretive by keeping a private server in her basement in Chappaqua, I don't think that has to do with gender.

Chozick lamented that, as a female reporter, she could be unfairly tarred with the "bias" label—with some people thinking "I'm in the tank 'cause I'm a woman" and others (Clinton's supporters) telling her "you're jealous, you want to take down another woman" (or) "you're a mean girl"—when, all the while, she was trying to do her job as a responsible, critical reporter (see Covering Hillary Clinton, 2016). The Clinton campaign, of course would argue that, given voters' stereotyped attitudes, reporters needed to bend over backwards to avoid gender-coded language. Journalists like Chozick would view this as an inappropriate attempt to manage the news. This, as well as the foregoing discussions, points to the complex ways that politics, gender, and continuing gender biases intersect on the campaign trail.

In closing, this chapter has discussed the many facets of bias, hopefully convincing you that there is more to bias than meets the eye, suggesting that perhaps some of your own views of media may be a little biased, and emphasizing the importance of viewing these issues with precision and care. Bias is not always bad. We applaud the "bias" of reporters who, determined to right political wrongs, dig up dirt on political corruption. The presence of diverse media biases—from classically conservative to radical-liberal—can provide a more comprehensive spectrum of views in the political marketplace, as argued by libertarian philosophers like John Stuart Mill.

Where biases become problematic is when they take morally offensive, prejudiced positions, as in racist, sexist, or anti-Semitic websites, as well as right-wing and far left-wing sites that contain inaccurate information, even fake news. These, of course, do not constitute journalism, but in the political mélange we live in, they are sometimes confused with news. The overweening perception of news bias—perpetrated by the extreme left and right—can have untoward consequences on the body politic and democracy. When extremists disdain facts, denying the responsible accumulation of evidence and derogating consensually validated methods for obtaining reliable conclusions; when critics perceive everything as "opinion," refusing to acknowledge, as various writers have noted, that everyone is entitled to their own opinions, not their own facts; when partisans label as fake news any mainstream news article with which they disagree; and when a political surrogate claims that "there's no such thing, unfortunately, anymore, of facts," journalism that serves democracy by uncovering truth and exposing lies is in jeopardy (see Truth and Lies in the Age of Trump, 2016, p. 10). It is one thing to point to news bias, areas where opinion intruded on factual reporting, and another to claim that the entire institution of news-gathering is rigged or corrupt. Political journalism is flawed, imperfect, and occasionally disturbingly biased, but in its unbridled determination to uncover truth and speak truth to political power, it remains endemic to democracy.

REFERENCES

Allan, S., & Thorsen, E. (2009). (Eds.) *Citizen journalism: Global perspectives*. New York: Peter Lang.

Alterman, E. (2003). *What liberal media? The truth about bias and the news*. New York: Basic Books.

Anderson, K. V. (2016). "Bern the witch" and "Trump that bitch": Likability/loathability on the presidential campaign trail. *Spectra, 52*(3&4), 20–26.

Baird, J. (2016, February 26). Sarah Palin's mustache. *The New York Times*, A23.

Balz, D., & Johnson, H. (2009). *The battle for America 2008: The story of an extraordinary election*. New York: Viking.

Baumgartner, F.R., De Boef, S.L., & Boydstun, A.E. (2008). *The decline of the death penalty and the discovery of innocence*. New York: Cambridge University Press.

Beail, L., & Longworth, R. K. (2013). *Framing Sarah Palin: Pit bulls, Puritans, and politics*. New York: Routledge.

Benkler, Y., Faris, R., Roberts, H., & Zuckerman, E. (2017, March 3). Study: Breitbart-led right-wing media ecosystem altered broader media agenda. *Columbia Journalism Review*.

Online: https://www.cjr.org/analysis/breitbart-media-trump-harvard- study.php. (Accessed August 21, 2017).

Bleske, G.L. (1991). Ms. Gates takes over: An updated version of a 1949 case study. *Newspaper Research Journal, 12*, 88–97.

Braden, M. (1996). *Women politicians and the media*. Lexington: University Press of Kentucky.

Bradley, A.M., & Wicks, R.H. (2011). A gendered blogosphere? Portrayal of Sarah Palin on political blogs during the 2008 presidential campaign. *Journalism & Mass Communication Quarterly, 88*, 807–820.

Brock, D., Rabin-Havt, A., & Media Matters for America. (2012). *The Fox effect: How Roger Ailes turned a network into a propaganda machine*. New York: Anchor Books.

Bromwich, J.E. (2016, December 5). The Right's new young, vocal media star. *The New York Times*, B1, B2.

Brooks, D.J. (2013). *He runs, she runs: Why gender stereotypes do not harm women candidates*. Princeton, NJ: Princeton University Press.

Budak, C., Goel, S., & Rao, J.M. (2016). Fair and balanced? Quantifying media bias through crowdsourced content analysis. *Public Opinion Quarterly, 80*, 250–271.

Carlin, D.B., & Winfrey, K.L. (2009). Have you come a long way, baby? Hillary Clinton, Sarah Palin, and sexism in 2008 campaign coverage. *Communication Studies, 60*, 326–343.

Chira, S. (2017, March 6). Another powerful woman, same sexist attacks. *The New York Times*, A1, A17.

Chozick, A., & Alcindor, Y. (2016, February 5). Plain talk pulls younger voters to Sanders's run. *The New York Times*, A1, A15.

Coulter, A. (2008). *Guilty: Liberal "victims" and their assault on America*. New York: Crown Forum.

Covering Hillary Clinton, a candidate "forged in the crucible" of conflict. *NPR Politics*. (2016, July 27). Retrieved from www.npr.org/2016/07/27/487620196/covering-hillary-clinton-a-candidate-forged-in-the-crucible of conflict (Accessed December 17, 2016).

D'Alessio, D., & Allen, M. (2000). Media bias in presidential elections: A meta- analysis. *Journal of Communication, 50*, 133–156.

Douglas, S.J. (2010). *The rise of enlightened sexism: How pop culture took us from girl power to girls gone wild*. New York: St. Martin's Griffin.

Dowd, M. (2015, August 9). Donald the disrupter. *The New York Times* (Sunday Review), 9.

Draper, R. (2016, October 2). How Donald Trump's candidacy set off a civil war within the right wing media. *The New York Times Magazine*, 36–41, 54–55.

Eberl, J-M., Wagner, M., & Boomgaarden, H.G. (2017). Are perceptions of candidate traits shaped by the media? The effects of three types of media bias. *The International Journal of Press/Politics, 22*, 111–132.

Entman, R.M. (2010). Framing media power. In P. D'Angelo & J.A. Kuypers (Eds.), *Doing news framing analysis: Empirical and theoretical perspectives* (pp. 331–355). New York: Routledge.

Epstein, E.J. (1973). *News from nowhere*. New York: Random House.

Falk, E. (2010). *Women for president: Media bias in nine campaigns* (2nd ed.). Urbana: University of Illinois Press.

Finneman, T. (2015). *Press portrayals of women politicians, 1870s-2000s: From "Lunatic" Woodhull to "Polarizing" Palin*. Lanham, MD: Lexington Books.

Francis, F.L., & Gregory, R. (2015). A sartorial tapestry: The rhetorical shifts of Hillary Rodham Clinton. In M. Lockhart & K. Mollick (Eds.), *Hillary Rodham Clinton and the 2016 election: Her political and social discourse* (pp. 141–161). Lanham, MD: Lexington Books.

Fredrickson, B.L., & Roberts, T. (1997). Objectification theory: Toward understanding women's lived experiences and mental health risks. *Psychology of Women Quarterly, 21,* 173–206.

Friedman, V. (2016, July 27). The new age in power dressing. *The New York Times.* Retrieved from www.nytimes.com/2016/07/28/fashion/hillary-clinton-theresa . . . (Accessed July 30, 2016).

Friedman, V. (2017, January 13). The woman and the brand. *The New York Times,* A18.

Gans, H.J. (1979). *Deciding what's news.* New York: Pantheon.

Goldberg, B. (2002). *Bias: A CBS insider exposes how the media distort the news.* Washington, DC: Regnery.

Groseclose, T., & Milyo, J. (2005). A measure of media bias. *The Quarterly Journal of Economics, 120,* 1191–1237.

Grynbaum, M.M. (2016, July 25). Ego clashes exposed in Democratic National Committee emails. *The New York Times,* A25.

Grynbaum, M.M., & Herrman, J. (2016, August 27). Breitbart rises from curiosity to potent voice. *The New York Times,* A1, A10.

Hayes, D., & Lawless, J.L. (2013, June 23). Voters don't care how women in politics look. *The Washington Post.* Retrieved from www.washingtonpost.com/news/wonk/wp/2013/06/23/voters-dont-care-how-women-in-politics-look/?utm_term=.e720b5989 (Accessed December 14, 2016).

Heflick, N.A., Goldenberg, J.L., Cooper, D.P., & Puvia, E. (2011). From women to objects: Appearance focus, target gender, and perceptions of warmth, morality, and competence. *Journal of Experimental Social Psychology, 47,* 572–581.

Herrman, J. (2016, November 19). The trap of exposing fake news: Eroding trust in real reporting. *The New York Times,* B1, B2.

Higgins, A. (2017, February 27). Phrase with a venomous past now rattles American politics. *The New York Times,* A1 A13.

Hofstetter, C.R. (1976). *Bias in the news: Network television coverage of the 1972 presidential campaign.* Columbus: Ohio State University Press.

Horowitz, J. (2016, February 24). News media is part of the Establishment Sanders rails against. *The New York Times,* A14.

Isaac, M. (2016, May 21). At Facebook, human backup for algorithms proved fallible. *The New York Times,* A1, B3.

Iyengar, S., & Hahn, K.S. (2009). Red media, blue media: Evidence of ideological sensitivity in media use. *Journal of Communication, 59,* 19–39.

Jamieson, K.H. (1995). *Beyond the double bind: Women and leadership.* New York: Oxford University Press.

Kahl, M.L., & Edwards, J.L. (2009). An epistolary epilogue: Learning from Sarah Palin's vice presidential campaign. In J.L. Edwards (Ed.), *Gender and political communication in America: Rhetoric, representation, and display* (pp. 267–277). Lanham, MD: Lexington Books.

Kahn, K.F. (1994). The distorted mirror: Press coverage of women candidates for statewide office. *Journal of Politics, 56,* 154–173.

Kahn, K. F. (1996). *The political consequences of being a woman: How stereotypes influence the conduct and consequences of political campaigns*. New York: Columbia University Press.

Kang, C., & Goldman, A. (2016, December 6). Fake news brought real guns in Washington pizzeria attack. *The New York Times*, A1, A17.

Kantor, J. (2016, July 28). In Hillary Clinton's nomination, women see a collective step up. *The New York Times*. Retrieved from www.nytimes.com/2016/07/29/us/politics/clinton-women-reaction.html (Accessed December 13, 2016).

Kirch, J.F. (2013). News coverage different for third-party candidates. *Newspaper Research Journal*, *34*(4), 40–53.

Kuypers, J.A. (2014). *Partisan journalism: A history of media bias in the United States*. Lanham, MD: Rowman & Littlefield.

Lawrence, R.G., Molyneux, L., Coddington, M., & Holton, A. (2014). Tweeting conventions: Political journalists' use of Twitter to cover the 2012 presidential campaign. *Journalism Studies*, *15*, 789–806.

Lichter, S.R. (2014). Theories of media bias. In K. Kenski & K.H. Jamieson (Eds.), *The Oxford handbook of political communication*. Retrieved from www.oxfordhandbooks.com. (Accessed June 7, 2016).

Lichter, S.R., & Rothman, S., & Lichter, L.S. (1986). *The media elite*. Bethesda, MD: Adler & Adler.

McIntire, M. (2016, December 18). How Putin fan peddled Trump from overseas. *The New York Times*, 1, 25.

Meeks, L. (2012). Is she "man enough"? Women candidates, executive political offices, and news coverage. *Journal of Communication*, *62*, 175–193.

Meeks, L., & Domke, D. (2016). When politics is a woman's game: Party and gender ownership in woman-versus-woman elections. *Communication Research*, *43*, 895–921.

Miller, C.C. (2016, October 22). The powerful woman: A prime target for jabs. *The New York Times*, A12.

Miller, M.K., & Peake, J.S. (2013). Press effects, public opinion, and gender: Coverage of Sarah Palin's vice-presidential campaign. *International Journal of Press/Politics*, *18*, 482–507.

Mitchell, A. (2016, June 12). For perspective on Clinton, step back 32 long years. *The New York Times*, 1, 18.

Mitchell, A., Gottfried, J., Barthel, M., & Shearer, E. (2016, July 7). *The modern news consumer: Trust and accuracy*. Pew Research Center (Journalism & Media). Retrieved from www.journalism.org/2016/07/07/trust-and-accuracy/ (Accessed December 16, 2016).

O'Harrow, R., Jr. (2016, March 27). How Clinton's email scandal took root. *The Washington Post*. Retrieved from www.washingtonpost.com/investigations/how-clintons-email-s . . . (Accessed March 28, 2016).

Patterson, T.E. (2016, June 13). *Pre-primary news coverage of the 2016 presidential race: Trump's rise, Sanders' emergence, Clinton's struggle*. Harvard Kennedy School Shorenstein Center on Media, Politics and Public Policy. Retrieved from http://shorensteincenter.org/pre-primary-news-coverage-2016-trump-c . . . (Accessed June 14, 2016).

Peters, J. (2012, November 6). Dueling bitterness on cable news. *The New York Times*, A10, A11.

Puglisi, R., & Snyder, J.M., Jr. (2011). Newspaper coverage of political scandals. *Journal of Politics*, *73*, 931–950.

Rappeport, A. (2016, August 27). Clinton denounces "alt-right" as racist, and factions embrace the spotlight. *The New York Times*, A11.

Remnick, D. (2016, August 1). Sirens in the night. *The New Yorker*, 15–16.

Rivers, W. (1962, Spring). The correspondents after 25 years. *Columbia Journalism Review*, *1*, 5.

Rogers, K. (2016, September 20). Libertarian errs again after attacks on weekend. *The New York Times*, A16.

Rutenberg, J. (2013, February 24). A conservative provocateur, using a blowtorch as his pen. *The New York Times*, 1, 4.

Rutenberg, J. (2016a, May 23). Facebook's troubling one-way mirror. *The New York Times*, B1, B7.

Rutenberg, J. (2016b, October 17). Criticism of press takes on sinister tone. *The New York Times*, B1, B4.

Sanger-Katz, M. (2016, January 20). For now, Sanders' health plan is more of a tax plan. *The New York Times*, A18.

Schudson, M. (1995). *The power of news*. Cambridge, MA: Harvard University Press.

Scott, M., & Isaac, M. (2016, September 10). The accidental gatekeeper. *The New York Times*, B1, B6.

Sherman, G. (2014). *The loudest voice in the room: How the brilliant, bombastic Roger Ailes built Fox News—and divided a country*. New York: Random House.

Shoemaker, P. J. (1991). *Gatekeeping*. Thousand Oaks, CA: Sage.

Smith, M. (2015). Authenticity, authority, and gender: *Hard Choices* as professional autobiography and transnational feminist manifesto. In M. Lockhart & K. Mollick (Eds.), *Hillary Rodham Clinton and the 2016 election: Her political and social discourse* (pp. 77–99). Lanham, MD: Lexington Books.

Stockman, F. (2016, October 21). Clinton arrives as a crusader for all women. *The New York Times*, A1, A17.

Tavernise, S. (2016, December 7). As fake news spreads lies, more readers shrug at truth. *The New York Times*, A1, A18.

Truth and lies in the age of Trump. (Editorial) (2016, December 11). *The New York Times* (Sunday Review), 10.

Vavreck, L. (2016, November 25). Candidates fed a focus on character over policy. *The New York Times*, A16.

Vraga, E. K., Edgerly, S., Wang, B. M., & Shah, D. V. (2011). Who taught me that? Repurposed news, blog structure, and source identification. *Journal of Communication*, *61*, 795–815.

Weaver, D. H., Beam, R. A., Brownlee, B. J., Voakes, P. S., & Wilhoit, G. C. (2007). *The American journalist in the 21st century: U.S. news people at the dawn of a new millennium*. Mahwah, NJ: Erlbaum Associates.

White, D. M. (1950). The "Gate Keeper": A case study in the selection of news. *Journalism Quarterly*, *27*, 383–390.

10 Political News, Polls, and the Presidential Campaign

So, how does news cover the presidential campaign? If the liberal bias thesis is overstated, which biases, routines, or factors govern press coverage? This chapter examines this question, calling on political communication research, along with journalistic examples, to describe mainstream news coverage of American presidential campaigns. The chapter first looks at venerable evidence that news focuses on the campaign as a horse race, offering recent examples. Two boxed sections describe a key accoutrement of horse race journalism: polling. In the next section, I evaluate horse race-based political journalism, examining its strengths and shortcomings. The final portion of the chapter describes key campaign news storylines, along with discussion of the logic behind much-discussed, controversial questions about 2016 news coverage of Clinton and Trump, and what this tells us about campaign news.

HORSE RACE AND STRATEGY-BASED NEWS

> The national press is entirely concerned with "horse race" and popularity . . . If thermonuclear war broke out today, the lead paragraph in tomorrow's *Washington Post* would be, "In a major defeat for (the president)."
>
> (Robinson & Sheehan, 1983, p. 140)

The news media cover presidential politics as if it were a game, a sporting event, a horse race. Journalists focus incessantly on candidates' strategies to vanquish their opponents, electoral battle plans, poll ratings, and come-from-behind tactics to overpower political rivals. Political communication scholar Thomas E. Patterson was among the first to explain and document this tendency. He was indefatigable in his criticism of media for reducing the campaign to a horse race.

The horse race metaphor dates back years, reflecting an era in which horse races were popular spectator sports. You find horse racing out of date? Fine. Replace it with the baseball pennant race, the pro football playoffs, March Madness, or the World Cup. Whatever sport you choose, the import is the same: The news media treat electoral politics as a competitive game, characterized by a battle over tactics for the prize of victory, rather than a more serious endeavor that involves a debate among different policy ideas, a contest among leaders who have articulated different visions for their country, or a critical exercise in the deliberation of ideas among citizens and leaders.

Every four years you will come across headlines like these in major news media: "Polls Show Late Surge by Kerry and Edwards; Dean Now Third" (*USA Today*, January 18, 2004); "Clinton and Obama Locked in Tight Race in Indiana" (*U.S. News & World Report*, May 2, 2008); "Shifting Tactics, Romney Attacks Surging Gingrich" (*The New York Times*, December 15, 2011); and "Winner-Take-All Contests Likely to Give Trump a Lift" (*The New York Times*, March 10, 2016). That's just during the nomination period.

During the general election campaign, the build-up of horse race news is inescapable: nearly every day a new poll and a new prognostication; when the election is projected to be close, as it was 2016, the tightness of the race is the main story (the only story, it seems), as network anchors breathlessly count down the days until the debates. Horse race news is a key part of the nominations, arguably more important during this phase because projections of who is ahead exert a more critical impact on fund-raising and a stronger influence on voters, who are less engaged in the nominations than they are in the fall campaign.

Thus, before the onset of a debate among candidates for a presidential party nomination, you will hear an adrenaline-filled, chest-stomping description of an upcoming face-off. If you were not listening closely to the names, you might be forgiven for mistaking CNN's preview of a 2012 Republican presidential primary debate, held in the fall of 2011, for one of those dramatic, storybook segments that accompanies the football playoffs, where the announcer dramatizes and romanticizes the teams and their players. The CNN montage began with scenes of cowboys, cattle, luscious streams, and mountains, befitting the western debate locale, as woodwind musical instruments chirped a musical melody. Here is what a deep-throated CNN anchor intoned before a Republican debate in Las Vegas, showcasing all the trappings of horse race, competitive drama-infused political journalism:

> From the mountain majesty of the Rockies to the deserts sands of the Mojave, the American frontier is a historic land of opportunity for Republicans. Tonight the fight for the GOP presidential nomination comes here: to a region where Barack

Obama made inroads four years ago [cut to picture of Barack Obama]; to a state that could be decisive in the primary season and the general election [camera pans to casinos and Las Vegas traffic]; for a Las Vegas event for Republican presidential contenders, on stage and in depth after a dramatic reshuffling of the pack [picture of playing cards].

During the 2016 election cycle, when the Democratic candidates held their first primary debate in Las Vegas, the optics were the same, as the news media hyped the debate, suggesting that the stakes could not be higher—are they ever lower?—while alluding to the glam image of Las Vegas.

In support of these anecdotal examples, there is abundant empirical evidence that the news media focus on the game aspect of politics, particularly in the nomination stretch of a campaign (e.g., Miller & Denham, 1994; Lavrakas & Bauman, 1995; Dimitrova, 2014; Patterson, 1993, 2016a; Sigelman & Bullock, 1991). Findings emerge from careful content analyses of election coverage, where researchers code stories to compare the proportion that focus on the horse race to those on other topics. From 1988 through 2016, more than 63 percent of news stories focused on the horse race, compared to nearly 26 percent that examined policy issues (see Table 10.1).

Stories offer the political equivalent of ringside seats to a boxing match, describing conflict between candidates with lively prose, using sports or even battlefield analogies,

Table 10.1 Horse race coverage in primary election news: 1988–2016.

*Focus of coverage (percent of stories)**

	1988	1992	1996	2000	2004	2008	2012	2016
Horse race	49	55	56	78	77	71	64	63
Policy issues	16	72	44	22	18	14	10	26

* Stories coded could include horse race and a policy focus, neither, or another category; thus the numbers do not add up to 100 percent. (An anomaly was 1992, with news media offering more policy coverage in response to candidate discussion of economic policy, and perhaps also to atone for criticism of press shortcomings in coverage of the 1988 campaign.)

Analyses for 1988–2008 based on ABC, CBS, and NBC News, with some other news supplemented, for example, Fox News in 2004 and 2008 and the PBS NewsHour in 2000. Analyses for 2012 based on analyses of print, network TV, cable, online media, and radio news.

Data and chart for 1988–2008 from Farnsworth & Lichter, The Nightly News Nightmare: Media Coverage of U.S. Presidential Elections, 1988–2008 (3rd ed.), 2011, Rowman and Littlefield. Data for 2012 from Project for Excellence in Journalism, 2012. Data for 2016 is from Patterson, 2016a.

as when reporters described how the Republican primary campaign conflict in New York between Trump and Cruz was a "fight (that) will be waged, street by street, if not stoop to stop, in places like the Bronx" (Flegenheimer & Haberman, 2016, p. A14). And earlier in the race, a reporter described the Republican Iowa caucus results with a series of sports-focused or military metaphors, noting that "powered by a surge of support from evangelical Christians," Cruz "dealt a humbling loss to Donald J. Trump," and had "fought off a barrage of attacks in the campaign's final weeks from Mr. Trump" (Martin, 2016).

Opinion polls are ceaselessly covered. Well before the Iowa caucuses, from December 21, 2015, through January 21, 2016, there were 11 polls in Iowa, 10 in New Hampshire, and 9 more national polls. Three weeks before the New Hampshire primary, there were three opinion polls in New Hampshire over the course of two days alone (Bruni, 2016). Polls taken this far before an election can be unreliable predictors of the vote, and national polls taken more than a year before the election—when the nominees have not yet been chosen—can be of little probative value. But they play a core role in contemporary campaigns, the scientific equivalent of party insiders who handicapped or helped decide convention nominees in the 19th century (see Boxes 10.1 and 10.2), and a centerpiece of contemporary horse race journalism.

Explanations

Why, you may ask, do horse race, poll-focused stories dominate news coverage, notably during the nomination period? Scholars tick off seven reasons. First, horse race stories emphasize conflict between contenders, a key aspect of news. Second, polls provide a patina of scientific respectability, cloaking the story in samples, statistics, and numbers, all of which confer credibility. They provide clear facts (although the science is more complex)—who is ahead and who is behind—rather than hazy, ambiguous, and more complex issue stories. The latter require more depth and political knowledge. They also require evaluative judgments, which could elicit accusations of reporter bias, putting journalists in the crosshairs of social media criticism. Third, horse race stories are easy to cover and make journalists the focus, allowing them to write a story or cover it on air, feeding journalists' egos. Fourth, polls offer tangible evidence of how candidates are doing, their ability to raise funds, and early evidence of their electability, reasonable criteria for journalists to cover. Fifth, horse race stories congeal with journalistic cynicism about politics, the belief that politics is a strategic power game rather than a contest among different policy directions for the country. Sixth, voters, particularly those high in political interest, follow, even prefer strategically framed, poll-dominated news (Sullivan, 2016; Trussler & Soroka, 2014), offering a market-based justification for the coverage. Finally, the election *is* perforce a horse race, with candidates strategizing, focusing on early primary victories, and incessantly following polls. After Trump clinched the Republican nomination with a decisive victory in the Indiana primary, cable TV news was filled with discussions of how he would fare against Hillary Clinton, his presidential debate strategies, and whether he could overcome her double-digit lead in the polls. Neither candidate had been nominated, but the horse race was on.

Shortcomings in Horse Race Coverage

Horse race–framed issue news is like dinner at candlelight, with a haute cuisine meal promised, suddenly laid bare, the delicacies turning out to be nothing more than dressed-up chicken nuggets and high-sodium soup. Reporters see virtually every action—a speech, policy decision, an appeal to particular voters—as driven by winning and strategizing. For example, when Hillary Clinton laid out a major energy proposal, advocating more energy production from renewable sources like the sun and wind and proposing a sevenfold increase in the installation of solar panels, reporters were quick to argue that her strategists viewed this

> as a winning issue for 2016. They believe it is a cause she can advance to win over deep-pocketed donors and liberal activists in the nominating campaign, where she is facing Democratic challengers to her left on the issue. It is also one that can be a weapon against Republicans in a general election.
>
> (Gabriel & Davenport, 2015, p. A1)

The same occurred with Donald Trump, following his call for a major expansion of the military to prevent future conflict. Although Trump provided specific numbers of proposed increases in soldiers and naval ships, reporters cast aspersions on the speech by suggesting a political motive, saying his proposal represented "the latest effort by Mr. Trump's campaign to demonstrate to voters that he can lay out detailed policy prescriptions to problems confronting the nation" and "seemed to be directed at the conservative foreign policy establishment" (Parker & Rosenberg, 2016).

The reporters may have been right. The plans could have been based in cynical election-year calculations, and by calling attention to these considerations, reporters offered voters helpful information. But academic critics argue that strategically based reporting is too cynical, ascribing the most self-interested motives to politicians. They note that public officials do articulate plans that reflect the party's platform or their constituents' needs, suggesting they are not always motivated by naked self-interest, but rather by consistency and a desire to serve constituents.

You would not know this from reading campaign news stories. Journalists frame politics negatively and through the lens of strategy. Political communication research has documented that these frames can exert substantive cognitive effects. Individuals exposed to strategy-oriented news are more likely to remember strategic information than those who receive predominately issue-framed stories (Cappella & Jamieson, 1997). The news taps into their strategy-focused schema, activating a belief (acquired from news) that politics focuses around strategy. Academic critics argue that news overstates the extent to which politics is a strategic game, in this way increasing public cynicism about politics. For example, in 2016 a large majority of Americans reported they were disillusioned with, even disgusted by, the current state of American politics (Martin, Sussman, & Thee-Brenan, 2016). How much of this is because of negative advertising, vitriolic candidate attacks, virulent social media posts, and the toxic role played by big money contributions, as opposed to frustration over ceaseless strategic game reporting? We don't know the answer, except to suggest that horse race reporting could play a role. Horse race journalism could also exert salutary effects, motivating more interest in the campaign or more serious scrutiny of campaign issues. There is not as yet evidence to support these suppositions.

BOX 10.1 SCIENCE OF ELECTION POLLS

Can you imagine an election today without a poll? Can one even conceive of a presidential campaign story that did not mention the latest tracking, trial heat, or CBS/*New York Times* poll? "Politics without polling has become as unthinkable as aviation without radar," a political writer observed (cf. Johnson, 2007, p. 87). Polls have proliferated, with a 900-fold increase in trial heat polls from 1984 to 2000 alone (Traugott, 2005). At their best, polls offer a snapshot of public opinion in a democracy, helpful in identifying voters' perceptions and concerns. Polls also have a political purpose. Presidential campaigns hire private pollsters or keep them on retainer. Candidates poll and incessantly follow polls conducted by professional polling organizations (e.g., Gallup, Pew, and Rasmussen) in the months before presidential primaries and during the primary season. Polls play a pivotal role in news media coverage and decisions by wealthy donors to finance a candidate's campaign (see Chapter 13).

Why do candidates conduct polls during the primaries and general election phases? They want to know where they stand with voters so they can adjust campaign strategies to fit the attitudes of key constituent groups. They also need to appreciate how voters evaluate the opponent, so they can engage in appropriate counter-attacks before it is too late and advertising-produced perceptions harden into convictions in voters' minds.

Continued

So . . . what exactly is a poll? A poll, note two experts, is "literally, a counting of heads" (Traugott & Lavrakas, 2008, p. 191). Of course, there is more. A **poll** is "any political sample survey of the electorate conducted by the media, politicians, or political interest groups that aims for a relatively quick and somewhat cursory tally of the public's political opinions and preferences" (Traugott & Lavrakas, 2008, p. 191). The key word here is *sample*. A sample is a scientifically selected subset of a larger population.

You might wonder why researchers sample. Why not just bite the bullet and talk to everyone? This is a virtual impossibility. Interviewing everyone in the population, what is known as a census, is expensive, time-consuming, and fraught with problems. It can be high-nigh impossible to locate certain individuals, such as those who are homeless or extremely mobile. As a result, pollsters sample. And sampling is remarkably accurate, as Traugott and Lavrakas (2008) concisely note:

> A well-drawn, scientific sample allows a pollster to conduct interviews with only a very small fraction of a population but to draw inferences with confidence from the sample's responses back to the attitudes or behavior of the entire population of interest (such as the voting eligible population). But this can be done reliably and with confidence only if the sample is drawn according to certain laws of probability. When these procedures are followed, pollsters can accurately estimate the opinions of the more than 200 million American adults who are citizens or the candidate preferences of the more than 120 million Americans who are expected to vote . . . with a sample of only a few thousand respondents. (p. 59)

These polls can accurately tap public opinion. Pseudo-polls, like online polls on sites like the Drudge Report, or phone-ins to MSNBC news, do not accurately tap voter sentiments because they do not randomly sample the population of American voters. Therefore, generalizations to the larger population of voters or citizens are inappropriate (Victor, 2016). Poll findings may simply reflect who shows up at the site at a particular time, often those with a strong ideological bent who are eager to share their pet peeves. These results can be handily manipulated by groups who want to use the poll to further their cause or candidate.

By contrast, well-executed, scientifically conducted polls can provide accurate information about the population of citizens. They advance democracy by providing a mechanism for citizens to offer feedback to leaders, connecting citizens to the exercise of power in a democracy. Polls are not foolproof and, in an age of political volatility and mobile phone technology, can misfire, as the next box describes.

BOX 10.2 POLLING IMPERFECTIONS: THE CASE OF 2016

Polling has become increasingly scientific over the past decades, offering more sophisticated and fine-tuned ways of tapping the pulse of the electorate. In 2012, pollster Nate Silver accurately predicted the electoral outcome in each of 50 states based on polls. But polls are imperfect. They can vary among themselves because pollsters use different questions, voter models, and procedures to select voters based on the likelihood they will vote. Polls always have a margin of error because elections are volatile and unexpected events occur, such as an unexpected campaign event that occurs after late-campaign polls are conducted. Polls can also fail to predict elections because their guiding assumptions do not mesh with reality. This happened in the recent 2016 election, where national polls consistently gave Clinton a several-point edge, seemingly understating Trump's support. Although national polls did a good job in forecasting Clinton's popular vote victory, polls failed to predict Trump's Electoral College victory. Why do reliable, scientific polls, like those conducted in 2016, sometimes fail? There are several reasons.

A first problem involves likely voters. Pollsters frequently focus on *likely voters*, those who are predisposed to go to vote on Election Day, figuring that focusing on them (rather than registered voters who might not vote) affords the greatest predictive bang for the buck. On some occasions, though, it can be difficult to estimate just who is likely to vote, either because turnout is much higher or lower than expected. This happened in the Michigan Democratic primary in 2016. Polls predicted Clinton would win easily, but her opponent Bernie Sanders defeated her by 1.5 percentage points. Polls, based on traditional models that did not capture the excitement a candidate like Sanders generated among young people, underestimated the number of under-30 voters who turned out for Sanders (Bialik, 2016). In the general election, polls understated Trump's support in key swing states like Wisconsin, Michigan, and Pennsylvania, in part because Trump voters turned out in greater numbers than Clinton voters. Trump recruited swing state voters who did not vote in 2012 to a much greater degree

Continued

than pollsters anticipated (Leonhardt, 2016). Pollsters' models seemed to have failed to factor in how voter anger motivated some Republicans to cast votes for Trump, or the degree to which lack of enthusiasm for Clinton reduced turnout in the traditional Democratic base.

A second reason election polls can fail to predict outcomes accurately is the classic problem of social desirability effects. Although individuals rarely lie outright to pollsters, they may prevaricate when the questions concern socially sensitive subjects, like voting for a White-supremacist candidate or voting against an African American contender (Johnson, 2007). A survey taken shortly before the 1990 Louisiana Senate primary suggested that between 22 to 28 percent of Bayou State voters favored the racist David Duke. He actually received 44 percent of the vote. Conversely, tracking polls taken late in a 1989 Virginia gubernatorial campaign indicated that African American candidate Douglas Wilder led his opponent by about 10 points. It turned out that Wilder won in a squeaker (Asher, 2012). This may have worked in the opposite way in 2016, with some Trump voters reluctant to admit to a poster they intended to vote for Trump, fearful that the admission might make them look like they supported his bigoted and misogynistic statements. Women, in particular, who liked Trump's business experience may have been uncomfortable acknowledging they intended to vote for him (Bialik & Enten, 2016). In support of this interpretation, polls taken during the spring of 2016 found that Trump fared much better in online polls than in telephone interview surveys, where voters had to publicly acknowledge to an interviewer that they supported a candidate who publicly harbored divisive issue positions (Edsall, 2016). Thus, telephone polls in swing states could have understated Trump's actual support.

A third problem with polls is non-response bias. Respondents, consumed with other tasks when the pollster calls, sometimes hang up before the interview has been completed. This creates a methodological problem. Researchers must make certain that they replace respondents who decline to be interviewed with demographically equivalent individuals. Usually, this can be accomplished, but occasionally problems creep in. This happened in 2008, when polls taken before the New Hampshire primary gave Obama a double-digit lead over Hillary Clinton. Yet Clinton won by about two percentage points, raising questions about the accuracy of pre-election polls. One reason the polls failed is that some of Clinton's stalwart supporters, union members and those low in education, were not adequately represented in the earlier interviews, partly because they were hard to reach. Rather than continuing to call these individuals, and catching them at a later point in time, some pollsters gave up. Yet these voters turned out at the polls, voting for Clinton (AAPOR, 2008). In 2016, non-response could have exerted an untoward effect if some Trump voters, feeling hostile toward mainstream media or buying Trump's claim that the election was rigged, opted not to respond to polls at all. If pollsters had trouble finding equivalent voters to replace these uncooperative respondents in their sampling interviews, this would understate actual support for Trump. In addition, state polls—which minimized Trump's support—are frequently less reliable than national polls.

Finally, polls can fail to predict accurately not because of polling limitations, but because unexpected events intervene, changing undecided voters' decision late in the campaign, after most of the polls have been conducted. FBI Director James Comey's announcement in late October 2016 that he planned to review a new trove of Clinton emails to see if they contained classified information could have revived the email issue, accessing concerns among some uncommitted voters, pushing them to reject Clinton.

It is important to note that all polls, including those that misfired in 2016, have margins of error because they are based on probability. They can't predict with absolute certainty and the best polls report their margin of error, or the degree to which the sample is likely to deviate from the population of all voters. The 2016 election polls, while accurate in the aggregate of popular vote prediction, missed the mark in predicting Trump's Electoral College victory, reminding us that experts' models can be wrong. An over-emphasis on polls, with endless news coverage of the newest blip in results, runs counter to the science of polls, which emphasizes their ability to detect broad trends, not minute changes in a volatile election.

Polls are imperfect, always in need of improvement, in view of drops in response rate, difficulty of tapping mobile phone users, and inability of Internet surveys to reach poorer, less educated voters who don't use the Internet regularly (Ornstein & Abramowitz, 2016; Zukin, 2015). Some researchers argue that social media data offers new opportunities to tap political attitudes (Schober, Pasek, Guggenheim, Lampe, & Conrad, 2016). As polls adapt (one hopes) to new technologies, it is important to remember that they provide an important mechanism to gauge citizens' attitudes and communicate their views to leaders. They are a more fine-tuned method of tapping public sentiments than other methods, like intuitive, qualitative, or "seat of the pants" guesstimates.

Continued

It is incumbent on citizens, as informed participants in the political process, to appreciate the strengths and shortcomings of pills. When you read polls, you might consider the following tips:

1.   Review the margin of error. This tells you how close the findings from the small random sample on which the poll is based are to the numbers one would obtain if the entire population had been interviewed. The smaller the margin of error, the more confidence one can have that the poll reflects the population of voters. The larger the margin of error, the less confidence one should place in the poll's findings.

2.   Examine many polls and put your trust in the average across polls. One poll could be unusual or unrepresentative.

3.   Make certain the polls are conducted by a reputable polling organization that randomly samples the population, reports the margin of error, and discusses fallibilities like the time the poll was conducted, nonresponse bias, and question wording effects.

MAJOR NEWS MEDIA STORYLINES

The press is not a conveyor belt that simply relays electoral information to the public. It does not hold up a mirror to politics, but presents particular slices and perspectives of presidential campaigns. These perspectives, less partisan than commonly assumed, are filters through which the campaign news media interpret and diffuse information about the presidential election. Commonly called **narratives** or **storylines**, they are broad frames, influenced by journalistic, professional, and economic factors, that shape campaign news reporting. The narratives are useful in distilling the panoply of political information and serve functions for politics, but also can serve as stereotypes that encourage forcing facts to fit a particular storyline or schema (Patterson, 1993). Six key narratives are: (1) **candidate schema**; (2) **the front-runner**; (3) **losing ground**; (4) **bandwagon**; (5) **electability**; and (6) **exceeding expectations storylines**.

Candidate Schema

Reporters, like all of us, develop mental frameworks or schema to organize information about candidates and gain a fix on disparate aspects of their background, style, and issue positions. Once they decide, singly and frequently in combination (responding as a collective reference group of peers), that a particular schema fits a candidate, they invoke this in news stories. During the 1980s, journalists dubbed Ronald Reagan the "Great Communicator," convinced that Reagan's charm, acting skills, and ability to use the camera to effectively persuade the public gave him "practically irresistible power to shape public opinion" (Schudson, 1995, p. 137). Although Reagan developed memorable television narratives (see Chapter 12) and his public image contributed to his popularity, he was not infallible. There were a host of reasons why he was reelected in 1984, including economic growth, his tough foreign policy positions, and the fallibilities of his Democratic opponent in 1984. Yet news stories applied the "Great Communicator" schema, creating a myth of Reagan's communicative success that may itself have influenced public opinion.

During the 2000 campaign, national journalists seemed to fix on the idea that Gore was not always truthful, fashioning this into the storyline that Gore was slippery, even a serial exaggerator (Krugman, 2016). The news media widely reported that Gore claimed to have invented the Internet, when what he actually said in a CNN interview is that he "took the initiative in creating the Internet," a statement that congealed with technology experts' belief that Gore was the first political leader to recognize the significance of the Internet (Mikkelson, 2016). Yet the news repeatedly misattributed the "I invented the Internet" comment to Gore, because it was an entertaining sound bite and reinforced the journalistic narrative view that Gore hyped and exaggerated truth for his own political benefit. When Gore made other misstatements, the news media trotted out the "dishonest, exaggerator" schema, using this as the framework to distill Gore's verbal behavior. In fairness, Gore had misstated facts on several occasions, and his nonverbal posturing invited the perception that he had a sanctimonious, holier-than-thou quality. It is unlikely he exaggerated or hyped more than other politicians, yet the Gore storyline could have contributed to low voter ratings of Gore's honesty (Johnston, Hagen, & Jamieson, 2004). This brings us to Hillary Clinton.

For years journalists viewed Clinton through the prism of a narrative emphasizing her penchant for secrecy, lack of transparency, and absence of candor. The schema emerged in the 1990s, when Clinton led a White House health reform task force that conducted its business behind closed doors in ways that frustrated legislators and the press. It continued with the 1996 discovery of missing documents from her law firm that strangely surfaced long after investigators had subpoenaed billing records from her legal work on behalf of a failed savings and loan company (Gerth, 2015). On a deeper, psychological level, the lack of transparency schema may have gained resonance from her fraught decision to stay with her husband after he engaged in widely publicized marital affairs. Of course, many Americans did not see her behavior this way, arguing that she loved her husband, despite his moral turpitude, noting that women stay with cheating spouses for a variety of understandable reasons, or stressing this was a private issue irrelevant to her public duties. Yet the lack of transparency schema served as a filter for her many achievements, such as a health reform innovator, a twice-elected senator from New York, and Secretary of State. It surfaced again like a bad penny in 2016. The penchant for secrecy seemed to emerge as a press explanation of 2016 campaign events, chiefly her freighted use of a private email server. The email story, with its many permutations, gushed and exploded across the news media, the narrative in a sense an extracting mechanism that pushed the story across the surface.

A newspaper expose revealed in March 2015 that Clinton had only used her personal email account when she was Secretary of State and did not even have a State Department email address during the time she headed that agency (Schmidt, 2015). Her decision to employ a personal account for official government business was an unorthodox decision that allowed her to decide which information would be made public, and (given her international reputation) which would be known across the world (Schmidt & Sanger, 2015). This raised questions about whether she had emailed classified information. Storing classified information in one's personal email account on a private server technically violates U.S. secrecy laws (Shane, 2015). A ceaseless stream of stories followed the initial *New York Times* stories. They examined the wisdom of her decision to use a private email server; emails she deleted, ostensibly those that concerned family matters; whether emails she sent concerned critical classified information; and subsequent FBI investigation, criticism, decision not to file criminal charges, reinvestigation late in the campaign, and exoneration once again.

While much of the press coverage of the email story was attributable to news media emphasis on conflict and possible illegal action by a presidential candidate, it is difficult not to view some of the coverage as resulting from the long-held narrative that Clinton harbored a penchant for secrecy. This narrative helped push other stories to the surface too. When Clinton was diagnosed with pneumonia during the fall campaign, reporters suggested that her tendency for privacy and fear that her opponents would exploit the story explained why she chose to initially keep her illness secret. Throughout the campaign, Clinton received consistently negative press, and this played an important role in the campaign, as discussed later in the chapter.

Other Press Storylines

Clinton also received tough press for another reason. She was the front-runner, the leader of the Democratic pack. Journalists traditionally subject front-running candidates to tough coverage. In the **front-runner storyline**, news initially gives considerable coverage to the front-running candidate who leads the pack of contenders, because she or he has high poll numbers and generates favorable comments from elite supporters. But over time, positive press is offset by negative coverage that results from reporters' desire to inform the public of chinks in the front-runner's armor and the feeling it is their professional responsibility to do so lest the candidate get a free ride to the White House (see Figure 10.1; Patterson, 1993). Reporters also subject front-runners to tough press because it is a good story: the possible fall from grace of the heir apparent, akin

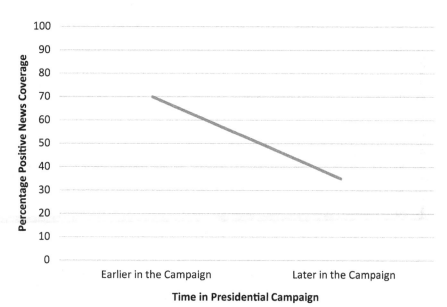

Figure 10.1 The front-runner storyline. News offers initially positive coverage to the front-runner, but over time the news becomes dramatically less positive.

to the descending fortunes of the *Sports Illustrated*–anointed, predicted winner of the American or National League Baseball pennant.

When a leading candidate's support—in polls or primary election results for the party nomination—begins to sharply decline, news reflects this and plays up the candidate's losses. Coverage becomes decidedly less favorable, as a variety of indicators—from opinions of party leaders and comments from voters—take on a negative hue. This exemplifies the **losing ground storyline**, the ways the press narrative changes to increasingly describe a candidate once seen as a contender for the party nomination as inexorably losing ground (see Figure 10.2; Patterson, 1993). The press coverage can exaggerate the decline, focusing more dramatically on political losses experienced by a leading candidate than on comparable declines of less-hyped-up rivals for the nomination. The irony is that a key reason that the candidate was lionized at the outset was because the press, based on political interviews and polls, decided he or she was a major contender.

Jeb Bush, the former Florida governor originally anointed as a front-runner, typified the losing ground scenario in 2016, with journalists focusing on his lackluster performances in primary debates, his failure to challenge Trump's aggressive comments, and, ultimately, his dismal primary election numbers. By December 2015, news coverage

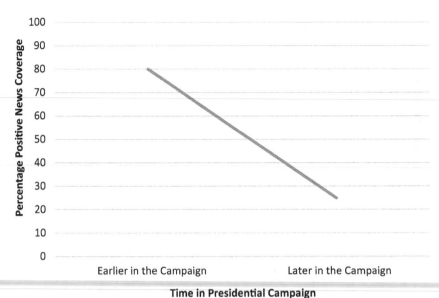

Figure 10.2 The losing ground storyline. When a candidate's ratings in opinion polls or from elites drops dramatically, news coverage becomes considerably less positive.

of Bush was 70 percent unfavorable, the most negative of any of the Republican candidates, with journalists commenting unfavorably on his demeanor, as when an article said that "Mr. Bush does not seem to be radiating much joy these days" (Patterson, 2016b). The same could have been said about other struggling Republican contenders on a dour day on the campaign trail. The negative coverage did reflect the facts on the ground. More importantly, it picked up on journalists' judgment that Bush was losing ground, in relation to what had been expected initially.

When a candidate's poll ratings or nomination contest victories increase sharply, news stories jump on the proverbial bandwagon, exemplifying the press's gaining ground, **bandwagon storyline**. News stories about the candidate increase in favorability, emphasizing that the candidate is gaining ground (see Figure 10.3; Patterson, 1993). Historically Jimmy Carter benefited from this in 1976 (see Chapter 11), as did Obama in 2008, the latter with a series of victories in state caucuses, racking up delegates, gaining support from party elites, and acquiring an air of inevitability. In 2016, as Trump began winning primaries after losing the Iowa caucuses, his coverage fit a bandwagon narrative, even though objectively he had many hurdles to cross before gaining enough delegates to clinch the nomination. Other candidates are viewed through an **electability narrative**, the frame judging candidates by their likelihood of winning the nomination, playing up particular candidates' supposedly small chances of gaining their party's nomination.

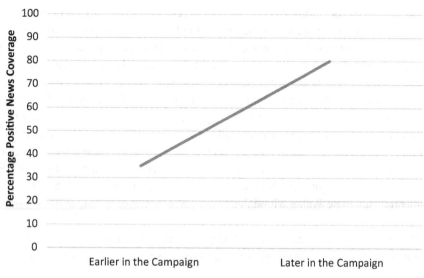

Figure 10.3 The bandwagon storyline. As a candidate's support in opinion polls rises dramatically, news coverage becomes more positive.

Candidate successes on the campaign trail and innovative policy positions can be played down because, in the view of the press (and party insiders), the candidate has a small chance of gaining the nomination. This may have afflicted Bernie Sanders in 2016, who won primaries and caucuses, but received less press coverage than Clinton (Patterson, 2016a). Given the Democratic Party's proportional distribution of delegates to candidate vote totals and her domination of superdelegates, it was very unlikely he could overcome Hillary Clinton's seemingly insurmountable lead. It was not unreasonable for journalists to perceive Sanders through an electability narrative, but it may have served as a self-fulfilling prophecy. Reverend Jesse Jackson, the charismatic outsider, Democratic candidate of 1984 and 1988, was viewed through the electability prism, resulting in criticism that the press wrote him off because he was an African American who was outside the political mainstream. The problem with the electability narrative is that by invoking horse-race criteria, based on poll and election results, the press can push voters to discount a candidate they like because they read stories saying the candidate has no realistic chance of winning.

Thus, candidates' success over the long haul of the nomination is not an objective matter fixed in stone. While there are winners and losers in particular contests, candidate performance from week to week is frequently evaluated, based on the strange, amorphous criteria of prior expectations. According to the **exceeding expectations narrative**, candidates are favorably evaluated if they performed better than expected and negatively assessed if they did worse than anticipated. Expectations are informally set by journalists, consulting polls and party leaders, with the press acting less as detached, thoughtful observers than prognosticators, oddsmakers, even handicappers in a political horse race, setting expectations that shape campaign momentum and influence candidates' decisions as to whether to campaign aggressively in certain states or drop out of the race. If they exceed expectations of victory or poll performance, they gain positive coverage. If they do not reach expectations, they are seen as potential losers and get negative press. There is a shaky, carnival-like, and self-serving aspect to all this, as humorist Russell Baker (1983) insightfully observed some years back, referring to 1984 Democratic presidential candidate Walter Mondale:

> Rotten luck . . . Mondale, we've made you the front runner . . . Without a front-runner, we'd have nobody to suffer surprising setbacks in the early stage of the campaign, and without surprising setbacks we would be stuck with a very dull story . . . It's tough, but somebody's got to make the sacrifice and be the front-runner . . . Say you get only 47 percent of that boondocks vote (in New Hampshire and Iowa). What we'll do is say, well 47 percent may not be disgraceful, but Mondale had been expected to do better, so it looks like he's all washed up . . . We of the press and TV do the expecting. You do the disappointing. That way we work together to give the country an entertaining story.
>
> (p. 12)

The expectations storyline emerged with regularity in 2016. When Republican Marco Rubio exceeded expectations by finishing just one point behind runner-up Donald Trump, he became, for a time, a darling of the political press and party establishment. His Iowa tally "gave his campaign another jolt of energy at a time when good fortune seems to be breaking his way," *The New York Times* reported (Peters, 2016, p. A1). Yet he received just 23 percent of the vote and came in third place! And when his fortunes faded and he failed to win key primaries, he was lambasted for having done worse than expected.

In all these cases, candidate viability—success in primaries, caucuses, and election polls—is the major determinant of news favorability. There is nothing sinister in journalists employing this framework. It fits professional norms and helps reporters make sense of a presidential campaign. But such an approach can lead to oversimplification and a tendency to force the facts to fit the favored storyline. What's more, it is not the only—or necessarily even the best—way to view a political campaign. As Patterson (1993) emphasizes, reporters' view of politics as a strategic game is not shared by all observers, notably voters. Unlike reporters, who see politics in terms of a game schema, voters primarily examine candidates' issue stands, leadership and performance. Voters view politics from a governing schema, looking at elections as a way to choose leaders, based on a raft of criteria, ranging from candidate likability, self-interest, agreement with candidates on key issues, and, yes, political biases, even prejudices. For better or worse, most voters do not view politics through a horse race lens.

EXPLAINING TRUMP VERSUS CLINTON CAMPAIGN COVERAGE: PRESS BIAS?

Donald Trump dominated the news during the 2016 campaign. As soon as he announced his candidacy, journalists besieged his rallies and speeches, offering live cable television (including the liberal MSNBC) coverage of trivial campaign events, covering each and every controversy he generated, discussing and writing incessantly about other candidate reactions, poll numbers, and how his candidacy would play. The coverage was totally out of proportion to his early poll numbers, low expectations he would capture the Republican nomination, and lack of credentials as a presidential contender.

Trump received substantially more television mentions than candidates from both parties during the pre-primary period (Viser, 2015). Using the number of Google News hits as an (imperfect) indicator of quantity of news coverage, he appeared in 46 percent of news coverage of the Republican candidates from mid-June to mid-July of 2015, and elicited 60 percent of Google searches about Republican contenders, substantially more than his Republican rivals (Somaiya, 2015). Patterson (2016b) reported that Trump captured the equivalent of $55 million in free advertising on major media outlets, the number based on how much it would cost to purchase this amount of advertising space or time on the equivalent print or television media outlet—1.5 times as much as his closest Republican rival received. More than a third of pre-primary news about GOP candidates focused on Trump. He dominated Republican coverage from the time he announced his candidacy in June until December 2015, and had more news media attention in the 2016 primary campaign than any another candidate. There was never a week when Republican opponents garnered more attention than Trump (Patterson, 2016a). On average, 68 percent of the news in major outlets (e.g., CBS, Fox, *USA Today*, and *The New York Times*) was positive toward Trump in 2015, prior to the nomination contests, a critical juncture that shaped voter perceptions. He ranged from a low of 63 percent in *The New York Times* to a high of 74 percent in *USA Today* (see Figure 10.4). These results are based on careful content analyses, in which trained coders, using well-defined categories, content analyze volume and tone of campaign coverage.

The press did not have to cover Trump this way (and the coverage certainly is at odds with the liberal bias thesis discussed in Chapter 9). News media covered Trump heavily—and positively, at least initially—for four reasons.

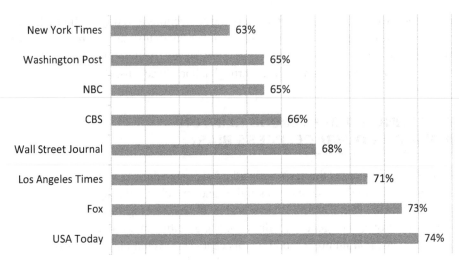

Figure 10.4 Trump's favorable press coverage in the early 2016 campaign.

(Patterson, 2016b)

First, his candidacy fit time-honored journalistic political news canons (Bennett, 2016): He was novel, dramatic, personally captivating, a celebrity known to American news viewers, attracted large crowds, and made controversial statements on current issues that generated political buzz. Second, he attracted a distinctive group of voters—working class Whites—who were very vocal about his candidacy and felt (correctly, actually) they had been marginalized, their concerns ignored by Republican elites. This was a new storyline, justifying press attention. Third, he received considerable press because he exceeded expectations of his candidacy, a classic exemplar of the bandwagon "gaining ground" candidate.

A fourth important reason for all the news about Trump is economic: His star persona—and attention from disgruntled Republican voters—brought in lots of viewers during a time when news media face declines in readership and viewership. As CBS CEO Leslie Moonves honestly observed, giving Trump lots of coverage "may not be good for America, but it's damn good for CBS" (Mazzoleni, 2016, p. 21). Hermida (2016) explained that cable television is "in the emotion business. And emotion sells" (p. 76). Newspaper and online websites provided expansive click-worthy coverage, attracting readers to iPhones, tablets, and other platforms where digital stories appear. "Trump is not just an instant ratings/circulation/clicks gold mine," one former *Today* anchor said; "he's the motherlode" (Kristof, 2016a, p. 11). Indeed he was: Thanks to Trump's braggadocio, inflammatory comments, and charismatic connections with his supporters, cable news networks attracted record-shattering numbers of viewers to primary debates and

Election Night coverage. CNN reported a 76 percent increase in prime time viewership, and the liberal MSNBC that supposedly avoided covering Trump didn't, and experienced a whopping 87 percent increase in total prime time viewers (Koblin, 2016). If ever there was a symbiotic, mutually beneficial relationship between the political press and a candidate, the connection between Trump and the press in 2016 is a quintessential example.

While much of the early coverage was positive, this changed over the course of the campaign. While nearly 7 in 10 pre-primary 2015 campaign stories were positive, just under half (49 percent) were positive during the primary and caucus campaign in 2016, as press scrutiny on the front-runner increased, party leaders increased the volume of their criticism, and journalistic exposes cast aspersions, such as a lawsuit by former students at his now defunct real estate college, Trump University, claiming Trump made misleading promises and defrauded them of tens of thousands of dollars. During the fall campaign, more negative coverage ensued as investigative stories described shady business dealings; an NBC TV *Access Hollywood* video surfaced showing Trump making lewd, aggressive comments about women; and his debate performance came under criticism, even ridicule on *Saturday Night Live*. While considerable general election coverage was unquestionably negative, Trump still continued to dominate the news.

Clinton's coverage was a study in contrast. During the pre-primary period of 2015, eight major news outlets, including CBS, Fox, USA Today, *The Los Angeles Times*, and *The Wall Street Journal*, gave Clinton the most negative press of any presidential candidates. More than 8 in 10 stories about her had a negative tone, and over the course of 2015, the tone of her coverage was more negative than positive (see Figure 10.5). If Trump's positive press attention was the equivalent of millions of dollars of favorable advertisements, "Clinton's negative coverage can be equated to millions of dollars in attack ads, with her on the receiving end" (Patterson, 2016b).

As discussed earlier, there are a number of reasons for her negative press, including the penchant for secrecy narrative and tough coverage of a front-runner, as well as Sanders' criticism of her candidacy, his supporters' disdain for her, and a drip-drip of negative stories about her role in the Clinton Foundation, raising the possibility of possible attempts by Clinton family officials to "leverage" their influence with Mrs. Clinton (Landler & Myers, 2016), charges that were more rumor than fact. In addition, the Russian hacking of the Democratic National Committee, revealed by WikiLeaks and covered by the mainstream press, provided more negative press, with stories revealing collusion of the party leadership with the Clinton campaign and party rifts. There was also gender bias directed at Clinton on virulent websites and in social media posts.

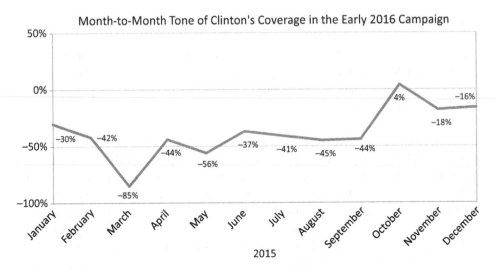

Figure 10.5 The tone of news coverage of Clinton's pre-primary campaign was consistently negative.

Source: Media Tenor, January 1—December 31, 2015 (from Patterson, 2016b)

While Clinton's coverage became more favorable over the primary campaign, and had positive moments during the Democratic Convention and her debate victories, it returned to negative press about her emails during the fall general election campaign. More than half of the news stories that mentioned candidate controversies or the economy discussed Clinton's email imbroglio (Vavreck, 2016), sometimes calling it a scandal, a journalistic construction freighted with negative connotations.

What do we make of the disparity in coverage? Clearly, partisan bias does not account for the pattern. As noted in Chapter 9, most national reporters are Democrats and probably favored Clinton. Liberal critics argue that news drew a false equivalence between Trump and Clinton's misdeeds, erring in giving Clinton more negative press, even though, by standards of fact-checking services, Trump lied nine times more often than Clinton (Kristof, 2016b). On the other hand, there was no shortage of negative information about Trump in the mainstream media and Internet. The coverage resulted from a confluence of standard journalistic factors, the power of a personality narrative, and the lure of the almighty dollar, resulting in far more coverage of Trump's rallies and grandstanding than analysis of his issue positions. On the other hand, Trump's coverage showed that an insurgent candidate can gain access to the news, providing a marginalized group (working class voters, particularly Whites) an opportunity to air their grievances, giving a candidate of their choosing a shot at the big prize. (Ironically, many of these voters felt the press was biased against their side, showcasing the power of strong attitudes.)

Patterson has argued that journalism is a miscast institution, one that was never intended by the Founding Fathers, political, leaders, or voters to play this role. However, the gatekeeping role has fallen to the media, broadly defined, and no one has yet come up with a better system. There is an unsettling imperfection in the present system. Based on news (and economic) considerations, the press opted to provide enormous coverage to a clearly popular candidate (Trump) who made many factually incorrect statements that received wide publicity and little correction, at least for a time. At the same time, news focused on the negatives—some self-inflicted, others worthy of coverage, still others less so—of a highly qualified but unpopular candidate from the other political party (Clinton). Perhaps, in some weird way, the system was fair, but the coverage certainly led one to wonder whether this was an election focused on matters of global and urgent economic concern, or a wrestling match, a food fight, or a 21st-century equivalent of Roman gladiator games staged for the masses, for the entertainment of the well-heeled elites. Sixty-two percent of general election news stories about Clinton were negative, in contrast to 56 percent unfavorable for Trump (Patterson, 2016c).

More broadly, critics have pointed to press negativity in this and other elections as part of a larger problem, where the news searches out candidate foibles, is always on the lookout for this candidate gaffe or mistake or another. In so doing, they have become part of the larger negativity culture of politics, moving from healthy skepticism to unadulterated cynicism (see the Conclusions section of this chapter for a discussion of this issue).

THE ISSUES QUANDARY

With their focus on campaign controversies, political journalists traditionally neglect issues, a classic shortcoming in presidential campaign coverage. By minimizing issue coverage, in favor of the horse race, candidate controversies, and seemingly infinite cable news discussion of what it all means for the campaign, news does little to help voters grapple with the complex problems facing the nation.

Focus on the "media campaign"—coverage of the horse race and candidate controversies—drowns out coverage of policy issues, resulting in too few analyses of candidates' positions in the larger context of problems ailing the nation. Issue coverage is frequently superficial, relegated to short sound bites with few accompanying arguments (Lowry & Shidler, 1998; Bucy & Grabe, 2007; Rinke, 2016); is dominated by journalistic commentary on cable talk shows (Jurkowitz et al., 2013); and is framed in terms of the strategic game. Much of the 2016 coverage did not analyze Clinton and Trump's issue positions (were they realistic, innovative, and how?) or their leadership attributes, but endlessly focused on how their positions were perceived by target voters, how they would play with the electorate, and what they meant for the campaign. Campaign controversies, such as Trump's sexually offensive comments and Clinton's pneumonia, dominated news. One systematic, though non-published, study found that through virtually the entire campaign, the three broadcast networks aired only 32 minutes of issues coverage, far less than in previous elections. There was preciously little coverage of climate change, poverty, the crumbling infrastructure, or details of candidates' issue positions (Tyndall Report, 2016).

As a result, voters could be ignorant of issues that bore directly on their lives. Trump supporters, who actually liked some (though by no means all) parts of Obama's Affordable Care Act, were unaware that Trump favored replacing Obamacare with health savings accounts. When informed of this after the election, these voters "expressed disbelief," calling this and related ideas "not insurance at all" (Altman, 2017, p. A23).

Of course, the "not enough coverage of issues" lament is the classic scholarly critique of presidential campaign news. It assumes that if issues were covered in more depth, voters would process the information and deliberate differently about candidates. It understates limits in time-pressed voters' motivation, as well as ability, to dig through complex issues. And it minimizes the amount of issue out there, as well as voters' knowledge of the basics of candidates' policy stands.

Indeed, news coverage of issues increased over the course of the 20th century (Sigelman & Bullock, 1991; Robinson & Sheehan, 1983). In our own age, there is ample information on issues, when you consider the volume of news articles on policy matters that appear on diverse websites. Candidate stands on trade, working class woes, immigration, and terrorism were covered prominently in 2016, and the economy was discussed frequently in news stories during the 2008 and 2012 campaigns. What's more, many voters were familiar with Clinton's email scandal, knowledgeable of Clinton's greater political experience, impressed (or depressed) by Trump's positions on immigration and Muslims, and, in the case of many of his White working class supporters, cognizant of his shortcomings, but convinced that his economic policies could improve their financial situation, as well as their symbolic status in America (Healy, 2016; Tavernise, 2016). Voters may not have been sufficiently cognizant of contextual aspects of Clinton's email scandal or nuances in global trade, and they filtered immigration and terrorism through their preexisting attitudes. However, they were, the available evidence suggests, knowledgeable about broad topics raised during the campaign.

Political journalism shies away from covering issues in depth because it puts journalists in a position of having to comment on the intellectual quality of a candidate's viewpoint, which could raise red flags of perceived bias. News producers also worry that such coverage will decrease the audience share. On the other hand, there is an abundance of coverage of policy issues in elite news outlets, with detailed stories on their mobile apps. In addition, new technologies offered a wealth of information. Snapchat delivered an array of political content directed to its 100 million users, far more than those who watch cable or broadcast news. If this content contains issues and engages young adults, that's good for the political system. The downside is that reports can be short, heavy on video, and disappear after 24 hours, providing little opportunity for depth and re-reading. The rub is that, like YouTube political videos, Snapchat is uneven and superficial; there are lots of bold colors, colloquial language, plenty of emojis, and footage of people crying or cheering on Election Night. Like much TV political news, it offers "snack food for your smartphone," issue information high in the political equivalent of trans fats and low in nutrients (Mahler, 2015).

CONCLUSIONS

The skinny on political news is the same today as it was three or four decades ago. News covers the presidential election primarily as a horse race and strategic game. Although horse race news serves a significant function—the election, after all, is a horse race; political elites and active citizens do need to know who is attracting support and why—there is more to the presidential election than strategy. News provides engaging, high-adrenaline, coverage of the strategic game for reasons rooted in the nature of contemporary journalism.

Pre-election polls are a key component of horse race news. Yet their systemic functions extend far beyond statistical estimates of likely primary election victories. With their reliable, scientific estimates of a population's political views, opinion polls provide a formal mechanism to connect citizens to leaders, allowing candidates (and elected officials) to understand the sentiments of those they represent. Polls are not perfect. Election polls in 2016 accurately forecast Clinton's popular vote victory, but fell short in predicting Trump's penultimate Electoral College win because of the unusual, volatile nature of the election, failure to adequately estimate voting patterns of enthusiastic Trump supporters, social desirability in self-reports, and perhaps last-minute campaign events. A variety of procedural problems imperil polls, such as low response rates and challenges of adequately sampling Internet users. However, technological improvements and sophisticated social media data mining offer hope that polls can continue to offer insights based on accurate reading of the body politic

Press coverage waxes and wanes, offering positive coverage to certain candidates and consistently negative coverage to others. This can seem like out-and-out-bias to observers, but as this and the previous chapter indicated, political news is better understood by prevailing journalistic storylines. In addition to the venerable horse race, political news revolves around schematic personality narratives (Gore as serial exaggerator; George W. Bush as hapless simpleton; Hillary Clinton's penchant for secrecy). These narratives can force the facts to fit journalists' preconceived schema rather than vice versa. Other storylines include tough press for the front-runner, the losing ground scenario, and the "gaining ground" bandwagon narrative. The 2016 coverage, with its heavy strategic emphasis, ups and downs for different candidates, and negative thrust (perhaps reflecting voters' dissatisfaction with the two party candidates), illustrates the ways these time-honored storylines influence news coverage.

There continues to be controversy about whether news over-covered Trump and exaggerated Clinton's foibles, with partisans from both sides viewing this issue in a predictably biased light. Although the extraordinary coverage Trump received is understandable on journalistic and economic grounds, it is difficult to square with normative criteria for how a campaign should be covered. Why Trump rather than his rivals? The coverage, which stemmed as much from its ability to capture profits for beleaguered television news networks as anything else, could have certified or legitimized Trump's candidacy, an effect cheered or jeered, depending on one's political viewpoint. It clearly was market-determined, raising at least a question as to whether news that bears on the election of a president should be based on crass market concerns. However, no one has come up with a better system—or sold it successfully to the nation's media. Clinton's negative coverage was rooted in a host of causes—the preeminence of journalistic storylines, press reporting norms, Clinton's own negative campaign style, and in the view of critics, gender bias. We don't know what impact the coverage exerted on voting behavior, although research discussed throughout this book suggests it probably exerted agenda-setting and framing effects.

A broader concern is the overwhelmingly negative tone of press coverage of the fall campaign, a trend in recent presidential campaigns. The news media focused heavily on campaign controversies (Trump's failure to release his tax returns, Clinton's you-know-what, the emails!); 90 percent of the coverage of campaign controversies was negative. "It's a version of politics that rewards a particular brand of politics," Patterson (2016c) notes, pointing out that "the real bias of the press is not that it's liberal. Its bias is a decided preference for the negative." This is complicated. On the one hand, press focus on the negative can breed cynicism, suggesting to voters that politicians are all flawed creatures, who engage in unseemly, morally questionable behavior. But some politicians who have run for president are flawed creatures who have engaged in unseemly, morally problematic behavior. It is the news media's job to bring this information to the public's attention. Moreover, as discussed in Chapter 13, negative information about candidates does not always produce unfavorable consequences; sometimes it can motivate voters to think more deeply about what they don't like or like in a political figure.

Is negative coverage of the campaign good or bad for the system? While few would disagree that some focus on the negative is helpful in exposing candidate malfeasance, scholars are of different minds on this question. Libertarian, liberal democratic–oriented scholars are likely to praise—or at least not criticize—the press for covering campaigns negatively, arguing that it is up to voters to decide how to interpret the information. Deliberative democratic and those critical of media excesses argue that journalistic negativity, pursued because it sells, lures cynical voters into the story, and, with more bashing of politicians, increases their cynicism. But this remains an empirical question. Discussing the 2016 campaign, Patterson (2016c) notes that journalists "reported all the ugly stuff they could find, and left it to the voters to decide what to make of it." Rather than distinguishing between Trump and Clinton's (very different) excesses, reporters avoided a judgment, letting voters make the choice.

Yet, as Chong and Druckman (2007) note, democracy promises citizens "the freedom to choose" (p. 652). It does not prescribe how journalists should frame the choices, nor how they should judge candidates' misdeeds. There is something to this, but it assumes that voters are equally motivated and capable of digging through claims on their own and could not benefit from just a little responsible help from journalists.

Another classic critique of the press is that it fails to provide sufficient coverage of policy issues. Although there is more issue coverage now than a century or more ago and issue news is widely available, it is in far less supply and much less prominent than news of the horse race and campaign controversies, which are of little interest to most Americans, save the pundits and game-addicted politicos. Journalists shy away from issues coverage because it is complex, might expose them to charges of bias, and seems to bore consumers (although that has not been persuasively shown).

How can issues and voter concerns receive more coverage? It is the perennial question, posed every four years after candidate and media controversy stories dominate the news yet again. A number of ideas have been proposed. One approach, adapting the public journalism of the 1990s, would ask citizens to indicate the problems they regard as most important, and organize news coverage around these issues, with a boost from social media. Another possibility is to institutionally reward news organizations for covering issues via reader clicks. Readers could click an Internet icon whenever they read an article that increased their understanding of politics. Readers' votes would be conveyed to a national journalism endowment, which could give a grant to the news outlet that produced the article (Gutmann & Thompson, 2012. This is a creative idea, but raises questions about whether readers, rather than reporters, should determine news (there are different views on this), and assumes journalism endowments have a sizable financial base.

Alternatively, it is possible that new technological platforms, like Snapchat, may offer the promise of thoroughly communicating issue information. So far, social media's performance in the issue domain has been disappointing—more superficial and visual than thoughtful and critical. But social media and new technologies offer new opportunities to reach many young people using platforms that can convey issues in ways that animate contemporary voters.

It is best not to end on a negative note. News is imperfect, but it does cover the campaign thoroughly, endlessly. It offers a democratic rendering of the candidates who would lead and the problems that dog them. Guided by storylines and journalistic values, it nonetheless manages to hold candidates' feet to the fire, forcing them to pay homage to the ritual of courting voters and giving credence to their concerns. It is far from perfect because it is frequently superficial and allows fleeting, dramatic factors to dominate the political stage. Ultimately, it reflects contradictions in political journalism between in-depth reporting and capturing a paying audience. Election news continues to evolve, becoming ever more technological, but posing the same quandaries: visual versus verbal, quality versus quantity, surface versus depth. The quest for a more comprehensive, thoughtful political news continues.

REFERENCES

AAPOR. (2008). *Report of the AAPOR Ad Hoc Committee on the 2008 presidential primary polling*. Retrieved from www.aapor.org/Report_of_the_AAPOR_Ad_Hoc_Committee_ on_the_ Presidential_Primary_Polling1.htm (Accessed December 19, 2016).

Altman, D. (2017, January 5). The health care plans voters want. *The New York Times*, A23.

Asher, H. (2012). *Polling and the public: What every citizen should know* (8th ed.) Washington, DC: CQ Press.

Azari, J.R. (2016). How the news media helped to nominate Trump. *Political Communication, 33,* 677–680.

Baker, R. (1983, February 6). Handicappers. *The New York Times Magazine*, 12.

Bennett, W.L. (2016). *News: The politics of illusion* (10th ed.). Chicago: University of Chicago Press.

Bialik, C. (2016, March 9). Why the polls missed Bernie Sanders's Michigan upset. *Five Thirty Eight*. Retrieved from http://fivethirtyeight.com/features/why-the-polls-missed-bernie-sande . . . (Accessed June 6, 2016).

Bialik, C., & Enten, H. (2016, November 9). The polls missed Trump: We asked pollsters why. *Five Thirty Eight*. Retrieved from http://fivethirtyeight.com/features/the-polls-missed-trump-we-asked-pollsters-why/ (Accessed December 19, 2016).

Bruni, F. (2016, January 24). Our insane addiction to polls. *The New York Times* (Sunday Review), 1, 3.

Bucy, E.P., & Grabe, M.E. (2007). Taking television seriously: A sound and image bite analysis of presidential campaign coverage, 1992–2004. *Journal of Communication, 57,* 652–675.

Cappella, J.N., & Jamieson, K.H. (1997). *Spiral of cynicism: The press and the public good.* New York: Oxford University Press.

Chong, D., & Druckman, J.N. (2007). Framing public opinion in competitive democracies. *American Political Science Review, 101,* 637–655.

Dimitrova, D.V. (2014). Framing the 2012 presidential election on U.S. television. In D.G. Bystrom, M.C. Banwart, & M.S. McKinney (Eds.), *Alienation: The divide & conquer election of 2012* (pp. 15–30). New York: Peter Lang.

Flegenheimer, M., & Haberman, M. (2016, April 7). Rivals assemble to hurt Trump on his home turf. *The New York Times,* A14.

Gabriel, T., & Davenport, C. (2015, July 28). Clinton lays out energy plan. *The New York Times,* A1, A17.

Gerth, J. (2015, March 13). Hillary Clinton's top five clashes over secrecy. *ProPublica.* Retrieved from www.propublica.org/article/hillary-clintons-top-five-clashes-over-secrecy (Accessed December 21, 2016).

Gutmann, A., & Thompson, D. (2012). *The spirit of compromise: Why governing demands it and campaigning undermines it.* Princeton, NJ: Princeton University Press.

Healy, P. (2016, August 13). Trump's remarks cut into support in swing states. *The New York Times,* A1, A10.

Hermida, A. (2016). Trump and the triumph of affective news when everyone is the media. In D. Lilleker, E. Thorsen, D. Jackson, & A. Veneti (Eds.), *US election analysis 2016: Media, voters and the campaign: Early reflections from leading academics* (p. 76). Poole, England: Centre for the Study of Journalism, Culture and Community.

Johnson, D.W. (2007). *No place for amateurs: How political consultants are reshaping American democracy* (2nd ed.). New York: Routledge.

Johnston, R., Hagen, M.G., & Jamieson, K.H. (2004). *The 2000 presidential election and the foundation of party politics.* New York: Cambridge University Press.

Jurkowitz, M., Hitlin, P., Mitchell, A., Santhanam, L., Adams, S., Anderson, M., & Vogt, N. (2013). *The state of the news media 2013: The changing TV news landscape.* Pew Research Center's Project for Excellence in Journalism. Retrieved from www.stateofthemedia.org/2013/special-reports-landing-page/the . . . (Accessed March 17, 2016).

Kirch, J.F. (2013). News coverage different for third-party candidates. *Newspaper Research Journal, 34*(4), 40–53.

Koblin, J. (2016 December 29). Cable news networks report a banner year in 2016. *The New York Times,* B2.

Kristof, N. (2016a, March 27). My shared shame: The media made Trump. *The New York Times* (Sunday Review), 11.

Kristof, N. (2016b, August 7). Clinton's fibs vs. Trump's huge lies. *The New York Times* (Sunday Review), 9.

Krugman, P. (2016, September 5). Clinton gets gored. *The New York Times,* A19.

Landler, M., & Myers, S.L. (2016, August 23). More questions about email use shadow Clinton. *The New York Times,* A1, A10.

Lavrakas, P.J., & Bauman, S.L. (1995). Page One use of presidential pre-election polls: 1980–1992. In P.J. Lavrakas, M.W. Traugott, & P.V. Miller (Eds.), *Presidential polls and the news media* (pp. 35–49). Boulder, CO: Westview Press.

Leonhardt, D. (2016, November 20). The Democrats' real turnout problem. *The New York Times* (Sunday Review), 3.

Lowry, D. T., & Shidler, J. A. (1998). The sound bites, the biters, and the bitten: A two-campaign test of the anti-incumbent bias hypothesis in network TV news. *Journalism & Mass Communication Quarterly, 75*, 719–729.

Mahler, J. (2015, May 3). Campaign coverage via Snapchat could shake up the 2016 elections. *The New York Times*. Retrieved from www.nytimes.com/2015/05/04/business/media/campaign-coverage-via-snapchat-could-shake-up-the-2016-elections.html (Accessed January 4, 2017).

Martin, J. (2016, February 1). Ted Cruz wins Republican caucuses in Iowa. *The New York Times*. Retrieved from www.nytimes.com/2016/02/02/us/ted-cruz-wins-republicans-cau . . . (Accessed May 23, 2016).

Martin, J., Sussman, D., & Thee-Brenan, M. (2016, November 4). In poll, voters express disgust in U.S. politics. *The New York Times*, A1, A16.

Mazzoleni, G. (2016). Did the media create Trump? In D. Lilleker, E. Thorsen, D. Jackson, & A. Veneti (Eds.), *US election analysis 2016: Media, voters and the campaign: Early reflections from leading academics* (p. 21). Poole, England: Centre for the Study of Journalism, Culture and Community.

Mikkelson, D. (2016, September 5). *Web of lies. Snopes.com*. Retrieved from www.snopes.com/quotes/internet.asp (Accessed December 22, 2016).

Miller, M. M., & Denham, B. (1994). Horserace, issue coverage in prestige newspapers during 1988, 1992 elections. *Newspaper Research Journal, 15*, 20–28.

Ornstein, N. J., & Abramowitz, A. I. (2016, May 20). Stop the polling insanity. *The New York Times*. Retrieved from www.nytimes.com/2016/05/20/opinion/stop-the-polling-insanity.html (Accessed December 19, 2016).

Parker, A., & Rosenberg, M. (2016, September 7). Donald Trump vows to bolster nation's military capacities. *The New York Times*. Retrieved from www.nytimes.com/2016/09/08/us/politics/donald-trump-speech.html (Accessed December 20, 2016).

Parker, A., & Rosenberg, M. (2016, September 8). Trump proposes vast expansion of U.S. military. *The New York Times*, A1, A16.

Patterson, T. E. (1993). *Out of order*. New York: Knopf.

Patterson, T. E. (2016a, July 11). *News coverage of the 2016 presidential primaries: Horse race reporting has consequences*. Harvard Kennedy School Shorenstein Center on Media, Politics and Public Policy. Retrieved from http://shorensteincenter.org/news-coverage-2016-presidential-primarie . . . (Accessed July 12, 2016).

Patterson, T. E. (2016b, June 13). *Pre-primary news coverage of the 2016 presidential race: Trump's rise, Sanders' emergence, Clinton's struggle*. Harvard Kennedy School Shorenstein Center on Media, Politics and Public Policy. Retrieved from http://shorensteincenter.org/pre-primary-news-coverage-2016-trump-c . . . (Accessed June 14, 2016).

Patterson, T. E. (2016c, December 7). *News coverage of the 2016 general election: How the press failed the voters*. Harvard Kennedy School Shorenstein Center on Media, Politics and Public Policy. Retrieved from https://shorensteincenter.org/news-coverage-2016-general-election/ (Accessed April 26, 2017).

Peters, J. W. (2016, February 3). Rubio campaign dispatches its army and new lines of attack. *The New York Times*, A1, A15.

Rinke, E. M. (2016). The impact of sound-bite journalism on public argument. *Journal of Communication, 66*, 625–645.

Robinson, M. J., & Sheehan, M. A. (1983). *Over the wire and on TV: CBS and UPI in Campaign '80*. New York: Russell Sage Foundation.

Schmidt, M. S. (2015, March 2). Hillary Clinton used personal email account at State Dept., possibly breaking rules. *The New York Times*. Retrieved from www.nytimes.com/2015/03/03/us/politics/hillary-clintons-use-of-private-email-at-state-department-raises-flags.html (Accessed December 22, 2016).

Schmidt, M. S., & Sanger, D. E. (2015, August 15). F.B.I. is tracking path of classified email from the State Dept. to Clinton. *The New York Times*, A14.

Schober, M. F., Pasek, J., Guggenheim, L., Lampe, C., & Conrad, F. G. (2016). Social media analyses for social measurement. *Public Opinion Quarterly, 80*, 180–211.

Schudson, M. (1995). *The power of news*. Cambridge, MA: Harvard University Press.

Shane, S. (2015, March 12). A claim of no classified emails in a place that classifies routinely. *The New York Times*, A19.

Sigelman, L., & Bullock, D. (1991). Candidates, issues, horse races, and hoopla: Presidential campaign coverage, 1888–1988. *American Politics Quarterly, 19*, 5–32.

Somaiya, R. (2015, July 25). Trump's wealth and early poll numbers complicate news media's coverage decisions. *The New York Times*, A14.

Sullivan, M. (2016, March 6). Waiter, where's our (political) spinach? *The New York Times* (Sunday Review), 10.

Tavernise, S. (2016, November 13). Amid years of decay, Ohioans flipped votes, seeking change. *The New York Times*, 1, 14.

Traugott, M. W. (2005). The accuracy of the national pre-election polls in the 2004 presidential election. *Public Opinion Quarterly, 65*, 642–654.

Traugott, M. W., & Lavrakas, P. J. (2008). *The voter's guide to election polls* (4th ed.). Lanham, MD: Rowman & Littlefield.

Trussler, M., & Soroka, S. (2014). Consumer demand for cynical and negative news frames. *The International Journal of Press/Politics, 19*, 360–379.

Tyndall Report (2016). *Comments: Issues? What issues?* Retrieved from http://tyndallreport.com/comment/20/5778/ (Accessed December 21, 2016).

Vavreck, L. (2016, November 25). Candidates fed a focus on character over policy. *The New York Times*, A16.

Victor, D. (2016, September 28). Why you shouldn't trust "polls" conducted online. *The New York Times*. Retrieved from www.nytimes.com/2016/09/29/us/politics/why-you-shouldnt-believe-most-online-polls.html?_r=0 (Accessed December 28, 2016).

Viser, M. (2015, October 16). Trump machine whirring on endless media exposure. *The Boston Globe*, A1, A4.

Zukin, C. (2015, June 21). What's the matter with polling? *The New York Times* (Sunday Review), 1, 9.

Presidential Nominations in the Media Age

"It seems a remote prospect," a reporter penned when Donald Trump announced his candidacy in June, 2016, "that Republicans, stung in 2012 by the caricature of their nominee, Mitt Romney, as a pampered and politically tone-deaf financier, would rebound by nominating a real estate magnate who has published books with titles such as, 'Think Like a Billionaire' and 'Midas Touch: Why Some Entrepreneurs Get Rich—and Why Most Don't.'"

(Burns, 2015)

"All his life," columnist Joe Nocera (2015) confidently observed, "Trump has had a deep need to be perceived as a 'winner.' He always has to be perceived coming out on top. That's why, ultimately," Nocera predicted, "I don't think he'll ever put himself at the mercy of actual voters in a primary. To do so is to risk losing. And everyone will know it. He'll be out before Iowa. You read it here first."

Well, it didn't quite turn out that way. Several expert prognosticators who predicted Trump's demise had political egg on their face. Even pollster Nate Silver, who correctly predicted the electoral outcome of each state in 2012, got it wrong. After Trump became the presumptive nominee in May 2011, Silver (2016) acknowledged that "if you'd told me a year ago that Trump would be the nominee, I'd have thought you were nuts."

In 2015, the common wisdom was that Jeb Bush, empowered by a large fund-raising chest and an established political name, would easily gain the Republican nomination. It didn't turn out that way.

On the Democratic side, there was a humdrum consensus that Clinton would sail to the nomination. When Bernie Sanders entered the race ("Bernie, who?," experts chortled), few expected him to present a serious challenge to Hillary Clinton. Yet he upended her plans as he won scores of primaries and caucuses, and changed the ideological tenor of the race.

Events also upended predictions in 2008. In that year, the venerable Clinton and iconic former New York City mayor Rudy Giuliani were odds-on favorites to win their parties' nominations (Popkin, 2012). But Giuliani faded, a victim of poor strategic choices, a message that never caught on, and the drip-drip of negative news about his personal life. Clinton found herself out-organized by the tech-savvy Obama campaign, a once-in-a-generation candidate whose speeches moved millions. At the time, though, Clinton seemed invincible and Giuliani a front-runner.

Campaigns are unpredictable. Social science models offer insights, but the confluence of factors that intersect—candidate messaging, an amalgam of strategic state-by-state choices, and the political psychology of voters—can imperil the most successful of prognostications. As with sports, if we knew who would win at the outset, there would be no need to play the game. At the outset, it seems obvious who will capture the party's nomination. Then reality sets in, and it becomes equally obvious when a candidate withdraws that he or she did not really have a lick of a chance at the get-go, and it was predestined that the eventual nominee would gain his or her party's nod. Such is the beauty of 20/20 hindsight.

Communication plays a key role in the nomination process. News media influence voters' beliefs about who is a serious candidate, while also shaping fund-raisers' perceptions of candidate viability. Social media can help mobilize support for insurgent campaigns. Opinion polls and primary debates alter the trajectory of a campaign in ways that would have been unheard of in the political party–dominated nomination process of yore. The distinctive process by which America selects its nominees for president has shortcomings but also strengths, and has evolved into something far different than the country's founders would have anticipated.

This chapter describes the presidential nomination process, offering an explanation (though not a justification) of a sometimes arcane, sometimes volatile series of events, with a focus on political communication. The first section provides a short overview, describing the basic terminology of presidential nominations. The next sections explore the four phases of the campaign: (1) pre-primaries; (2) first critical caucuses and primaries; (3) subsequent state primaries, and (4) summer nominating conventions. The chapter tracks these campaign phases, with evaluations of the nominating process, its potential remedies, a discussion of the fraught role played by elite delegates, and the communicative features of the nominating conventions.

You have probably followed presidential nominations in the media, a lot or a little, depending on your interest. Perhaps you have been curious or even puzzled about the legion of primaries that candidates contest, the ways they trudge through small states in quest of votes, and the seemingly endless horse race coverage, tweets, and online chatter on the part of political leaders, partisans, and reporters. This chapter will help you make sense of it all, develop a critical understanding, appreciate methods behind the madness, and perhaps suggest some ideas for how to improve an imperfect process.

OVERVIEW

The primaries are a fixture in presidential politics. Candidates must win primaries—and caucuses—if they want to gain the nomination of the Republican and Democratic parties. A **presidential primary** is a statewide election that gives voters the opportunity to select the party's presidential nominee. Voters cast votes in a secret ballot, just as they do in a general election. Caucuses are different. As the name suggests, a caucus involves people talking and discussing issues. A **caucus** is a local, public gathering where party members publicly deliberate about candidates, decide which presidential candidate they will support, and choose delegates to the nominating convention. A caucus is a public event, where party members try to persuade one another to support one or another candidate. There is a complication. Technically, when voters cast ballots or indicate caucus preferences, they are not voting for a candidate, but a delegate. A **delegate** is a typically a member of a political party, an individual who attends the nominating convention and formally casts a vote for a candidate. Delegates tend to be political activists and hold more extreme views of issues than both rank-and-file party members and voters (Polsby, Wildavsky, Schier, & Hopkins, 2012). (This may not be bad: Strong positions on issues propel people to become involved in presidential elections, and that's a good thing.)

You might wonder why we still have delegates. The practice seems arcane and old-fashioned. The tradition harks back to the 19th century when party leaders dominated nominating conventions and delegated certain individuals to perform the nitty-gritty tasks of running the convention and selecting nominees (Wayne, 2008). In the 1800s, party leaders selected delegates; today, they are perforce chosen by voters in primaries and caucuses. But in politics, as in other walks of life, traditions have staying power, remaining long after the original impetus for the decision is gone. Delegates are the formal linkage between voters and the political party, providing a mechanism by which votes cast by citizens translate into the political party's choice for president.

Although the process is exponentially more democratic than two centuries ago, when party bosses chose the nominees, it is not purely or entirely democratic. Only a minority of eligible voters, often less than 1 in 5 and just about 1 in 3 in 2016, actually vote in the political primaries (DeSilver, 2016). As noted earlier, when voters cast their ballots, they technically are not just voting for candidates, but for delegates (Buchanan & Parlapiano, 2016). The process by which votes translate into delegates is intricate, arcane, governed by rules that can change and, as you might expect, highly political. We will get to the technical aspects of this issue when the chapter turns to conventions. For now, let's delve into communication and the nomination process. The focus is explaining how a demanding, dynamic, and crazy-quilt process works, and the roles media and campaigning play in the presidential nominations.

PRE-PRIMARIES

Background

The nomination season begins early—really early, long before the presidential election is on the minds of American voters. With no incumbent running in 2008, the race was wide open, and candidates were exploring a potential dash for the White House two years before the November election. Ten Republicans and eight Democrats campaigned energetically for their party's nomination as early as April 2007. During the 2012 campaign, well before the crucial Iowa caucuses began, nine Republican horsemen and one Republican horsewoman, fearing an Obama apocalypse, grabbed their reins in hopes of capturing their party's presidential nomination. In 2016, a record 17 Republicans contested for the nomination, while five Democrats wrestled for the nomination of their party, with four candidates actively challenging Hillary Clinton, entering the race well more than a year before the election. By contrast, the duration of national election campaigns in Europe is much shorter—weeks or months, depending on the country.

Why does the American presidential election campaign last so long? Why does it start so early? Running for president costs a lot of money, and candidates need time to raise the cash to pay for television advertisements and campaign staff. They need to develop a viable organization, with competent consultants, pollsters, lawyers, speechwriters, and rank-and-file volunteers. They must build a reservoir of voter support in early caucus and primary states like Iowa and New Hampshire. To be successful, candidates must also gain national visibility through news coverage, tweets, and prominence on social media. Increasingly, in media-saturated America, success is about gaining attention and appearing viable across a variety of platforms, and viability takes time to establish.

The pre-primary portion of the campaign has been called the "invisible primary." The name bespeaks an appreciation that the primary (and caucus) period begins months before the first votes are counted, as candidates sponsor fund-raisers, try to increase voter recognition, and strive to gain credibility with the news media in ways that can elude the recognition of ordinary voters (Polsby et al., 2012). On a broader, deliberative democratic level, the pre-primaries can be viewed as a series of national political conversations among politicians, media, and the public, although typically directed at the more partisan members of the electorate who follow campaigns (Cohen, Karol, Noel, & Zaller, 2008).

The pre-primary period starts in the winter or spring of the year before the election, beginning when candidates announce their intention to run for president. It lasts until the Iowa caucuses in January or February of the presidential election year. The pre-primary phase is a relatively recent addition to the campaign, having exerting a significant impact only over the last decade or so. But what an impact it has exerted! It has arguably become the most decisive feature of the nominating campaign, critically influencing voters' opinions and winnowing down candidates for the later phases of the nominating contest.

The keys to success during this pivotal period are *(1) obtaining visibility from multiple media, particularly coverage from conventional media like cable TV (they still matter, actually a great deal); (2) gaining high numbers in the countless opinion polls taken in the early caucus state of Iowa and across the nation; and (3) typically creating a perception of ascendance by attracting money from leading party donors.* "Visibility," Nelson Polsby and his colleagues note, "is important because news media coverage introduces candidates to the voters and shapes popular perceptions of the various contenders" (2012, p. 100). National news coverage also serves a heuristic function: It conveys key information to party leaders, fund-raisers, and voters, suggesting that the candidate is a viable contender for the race. It is a funny, self-fulfilling process that bespeaks the power of media coverage. A candidate gains coverage in the media because he or she is deemed a serious contender—and media attention causes the candidate to be an ever more viable candidate for office. There is a downside. As Patterson (2016) notes, "the nominating campaigns of candidates who are ignored by the media are almost certainly futile, while the campaigns of those who receive close attention get a boost."

The Internet and social media have provided a helping hand for insurgent, outsider, sometimes populist, candidates, giving them broad platforms to reach and influence voters (Cohen et al., 2008). While outsider candidates used media before the Internet—from prejudiced populist candidates like George Wallace in 1968 to the quirky but thoughtful Ross Perot in 1992—new media offer ways to reach voters more quickly than before, as well as ways to mobilize activist constituents. Obama harnessed social media in 2008, and Trump ran much of his campaign around Twitter in 2016. Social media enhanced the breadth of both campaigns, bringing new voters into the process, perhaps working via modern twists on the classic two-step flow (see Chapter 3). Social media opinion leaders can influence less active followers, gaining the attention of reporters who write widely shared stories, and diverse fund-raisers who contribute money to promising candidates, like Sanders in 2016.

Twitter played a key role in Trump's rise. A relentless, regular user of Twitter—far more than the other candidates—he exploited Twitter to bolster his brand, relying on a social medium that bypasses traditional news media. With Twitter a centerpiece of his political armamentarium, he sent out controversial tweets that sharply defined his issue positions and targeted his competitors ("Would anyone vote for that?" he cruelly tweeted above an image of Carly Fiorina's face). These then were retweeted or mentioned in millions of online social media conversations, as many as 6.3 million—eight times as many as several key Republican competitors—during the pre-primary period (Barbaro, 2015). Trump dominated online political conversations, and this made news, delivering a double whammy of political publicity. "With 140-character bursts of id," a reporter observed, "Mr. Trump's posts are mainlined and amplified by the rest of the media; with one or two tweets, he can dominate TV, the web, newspapers and talk radio for an entire day" (Manjoo, 2016, p. B1).

Although Trump eviscerated time-honored rules for success, he also exploited one of the most important maxims to his advantage: Gain media coverage and plenty of it. From the beginning, Trump dominated news media, appealing to news values like novelty and prominence, a result of his outsized celebrity presence, crowds he attracted, and colorful, inflammatory tweets. Trump attracted online and mainstream news attention for another reason. He had a message that appealed to marginalized White working class voters, framed persuasively (see Chapter 7).

In the Democratic Party, Bernie Sanders's liberal message and alternative vision for the party captivated many young people, attracting waves of supporters, generating widespread news coverage (Leland, 2016). Sanders's denunciations of capitalistic profits and raging inequality, with his "crusty, to-the-barricades" exhortations, resonated, connecting with the idealism of his youthful audience (Healy & Berenstein, 2015). In the same fashion, eight years earlier, Barack Obama recruited popular support and significant news attention during the early nomination period because of his charismatic appeal, his distinctive message that emphasized his opposition to the Iraq War, and his branded political marketing strategy laced with a popular slogan ("Yes, We Can").

Trump, Sanders, and Obama ascended because they captured press attention, developed a message that captivated their base, and exploited online media. Remember that a small minority of voters participate in the primaries and caucuses. Thus, candidates must develop and market messages that appeal to an active, politically involved base.

Pre-primary Polls, Debates, and the New Winnowing Effect

Pre-primary candidate debates have increased in prominence over the past several election cycles, with more debates held during the invisible primaries than in years past. The first Republican debate, with all eyes on Trump and all ears on how the other candidates would respond to his attacks, attracted 23.9 million viewers, the most viewed presidential primary debate in history (Koblin, 2015).

Debates exert a host of minor, subtle, and major effects on voters, as will be discussed in Chapter 14. For now, the point is that debates, which occur well before the first votes have been cast, showcase the role that forces outside the institutional political system exert on nominations. The news media and polls have come to exert a preternatural impact on the pre-primaries, as seen in their impact on candidate selection in debates. Their influence challenges and in some cases supplants the time-honored role played by political parties, a favorite focus of political scientists (Cohen et al., 2008).

In 2016, with 17 Republicans running for president, cable network executives believed it would be unwieldy (and bad for ratings) if all 17 candidates shared the stage. Each candidate would get very little time to articulate his or her views, discussion among candidates could get chaotic, and it wouldn't be good television. At least that was a logic that seemed to govern the decision-making at networks like Fox and CNN. Setting a standard for debates that followed, Fox announced that it would use poll data to select the 10 candidates to participate in a major debate in primetime, allowing the remainder to partake in the "undercard" or "kids' table debates," as they were humorously called (see Figure 11.1).

From a political perspective, this is a stunning, jaw-dropping change. In years past, the key events that winnowed down the list of potential contenders were early caucuses and primaries. While reliance on these early contests is not without problems, as will be discussed in the next section, the decisions were based at least on votes, the behavioral brick and mortar of democracy. But with Fox's first debate in August 2015 and debates that followed, a profit-making news organization with preciously little grounding in traditional democratic politics—a business that is not accountable to voters or the political process—arrogated to itself the right to decide which candidates should gain the greatest access to citizens and which should be relegated to the secondary, non-prime time undercard debate.

The decision was made by polls. Fox announced that candidates who placed in the top 10 in an average of the five most recent national opinion polls recognized by Fox News and conducted by scientifically reputable polling organizations would participate in the main debate. Why just five polls? Why not more? Polls vary in their acceptable margin of error, sample sizes, and predictive ability. It also was not clear that the difference

Figure 11.1 In a key development attesting to the critical role news media play in presidential campaigns, in 2016 cable television networks decided which candidates should participate in the prime-time Republican pre-primary debates based on their standing in opinion polls. For better or worse, profit-making news organizations with no formal grounding in traditional democratic politics arrogated to themselves the choice of which candidates should partake in the main debates. Fox News chose 10 of 17 Republican candidates to participate in the first Republican pre-primary debate, held in Cleveland in August 2015.

Getty Images

between the 10th candidate, who got chosen, and the 11th, who was relegated to the undercard debate, was statistically meaningful. The choice of 10 candidates is arbitrary, based on neither normative nor sound methodological criteria, but, instead, on media logic. Ten is a simple number to wrap one's head around and probably about the most that can be accommodated on a stage, visible to a national audience.

Complicating matters, other cable networks used different rules for inclusion, such as CNN's rule in its December 15, 2015, Las Vegas debate: an average of 3.5 percent in national polls, *or* at least a 4 percent average in Iowa polls, *or* at least 4 percent average in New Hampshire polls (Bradner, 2015). The Fox Business Network used different criteria to qualify in its January debate: placing in the top six in an average of recent national polls, or in the top five in an average of recent New Hampshire or Iowa polls. The process was arbitrary and vague. It was not clear how networks averaged polls or why certain polls were used rather than others. To some degree, a lower-tier candidate's chances of reaching fellow citizens depended on the particular polling criteria a network happened to select.

In the networks' defense, it *could* be unwieldy to have 17 candidates on stage, some criteria had to be selected, and polls were at least based roughly on democratic preferences. But polls can be unreliable indicators of voter preferences at this early juncture of the campaign. They also can reflect temporary swings in public attitudes or a trivial public gaffe. For good or ill, the news media now play a critical role, never legally sanctioned or popularly vetted, in the nomination process. *Candidate viability is no longer decided exclusively by party elites or directly by voters, but by decisions media gatekeepers make, based on polls (which are themselves influenced by horse race news) long before any voter casts a ballot.*

It is not that media arrogates certain candidates to the top based on arbitrary criteria, partisan bias, or their likability. (If it was likability, neither Clinton nor Trump, both disliked by many voters, would have risen to the top of the debate cards!) Instead, for better or worse, television news decided which candidates would participate in pre-primary party debates based on journalistically based criteria. Candidates who did not fare well in early polls (and theoretically, though not necessarily, could have been outstanding candidates) did not get to participate in prime-time debates, mortally wounding their candidacies.

While the number of voters watching pre-primary debates is typically small, news and social media buzz can amplify effects. Years ago, there were no pre-primary televised debate encounters between candidates, and the only debate effects that occurred were in the general election campaign. Now, with the number and media spectacle of debates greatly enhanced, debates can strengthen, reinforce, weaken, and occasionally decimate candidacies.

In 2012, Texas Governor Rick Perry committed a deadly stumble in a November 2011 debate in Michigan. Stating that as president he would get rid of three federal agencies, he could remember only two. For the life of him he could not articulate the third department he sought to eliminate. After a painful 53 seconds of hemming and hawing, all he could offer was "Sorry, Oops." With a media outlet describing his performance with a paraphrase of the Britney Spears song, "Oops, he did it again," and scores of ensuing stories that questioned his political expertise (and intelligence), Perry never regained his footing, quitting the race in January. (In a note of high irony, the department that he planned to dismantle but could not remember—the Department of Energy—was the one Trump tapped him to lead in his administration.)

Debates can legitimize candidates, as they did for Donald Trump, a never-elected real estate billionaire who showed he could fend off criticism and appear, if not always presidential, tough and credible with Republican audiences. Debates seemed to have done the same for Bernie Sanders, a never-before presidential candidate who showed, through his relentless though civil attacks on Wall Street and Hillary Clinton's elite ties with the financial sector, that he appealed to the liberal, progressive Democratic base. Republicans George Pataki, Rick Perry, and Scott Walker—all governors with national panache—dropped out as a result of lackluster performance in early debates. On the Democratic side, Jim Webb and Lincoln Chafee withdrew after failing to excite supporters in the first Democratic debate or to significantly raise their poll numbers. Although debates can focus on issues—Sanders's emphasis on inequality and free college tuition are examples—they frequently are about nonverbal jockeying for position, appeals to the base, and delivering a memorable quip that can be artfully promoted, and shared by a candidate's supporters on social media. Debates in and of themselves do not determine who advances in the nomination process. Compared with general election debates, they attract relatively few viewers, and mostly those with strong preexisting partisan preferences. However, they can polish a candidate's image, solidify support with the base, and in rare but consequential cases, torpedo a candidate's chances for the nomination.

Summary

There is method to the apparent madness of who emerges from the volatile, unpredictable pre-primary process. Candidates are more likely to succeed in the early phase if they (a) attract news attention; (b) have solid poll numbers that place them in the now consequential debates; (c) perform well in debates (or at least do not embarrass themselves), and (d) have a coherent message that captivates activist voters who participate in the primaries and caucuses. These criteria are not undemocratic, nor are they necessarily unreasonable ways to winnow down a wide race of contenders. In fact, they make good sense. At the same, for better or worse, they privilege media, making media attention—both conventional and social media—a dominant factor that influences the early nomination process.

IOWA, NEW HAMPSHIRE, AND THE EARLY NOMINATION PROCESS

Suppose we started from scratch and wanted to devise the best way to structure the nomination system. We might use the general election as a model and hold a national primary election for each party, giving each candidate a fair chance to gain a majority of votes. Or we might propose a series of regional primaries. There could be primary elections in the North, South, East, and West, perhaps staggered to keep political energy levels high. Alternatively, if we felt that it was important for each state to hold a primary, we might emphasize the big representative states in each region, letting them hold their primaries (or caucuses) first. What we probably would not want to do is to pick two small, totally unrepresentative states, arrange that they hold their elections first, and then suggest that candidates who did not fare well in these state contests should withdraw from the race.

But that is exactly how the process works!

The first and pivotal electoral contests take place in Iowa and New Hampshire. These states have many strengths: low crime, pleasant lifestyle, bucolic scenery (for example, New Hampshire's breathtaking White Mountains and Iowa's verdant farmland). But they hardly represent the country as a whole. The states are both more rural than urban. Iowa, dubbed the "Hawkeye State," is in the heart of the Corn Belt; New Hampshire, the "Granite State," is filled with quarries. Iowa has the 30th highest population and New Hampshire is ranked 42nd. They are overwhelmingly White (Iowa, 92 percent; New Hampshire, 94 percent). Their demographics, economics, climate, and some of their politics (New Hampshire's libertarian state motto is "Live Free or Die") do not mirror the rest of the country.

Iowa, bucolic and picturesque like a Grant Wood painting, is particularly unrepresentative. Iowa voters caucus in public, in preference groups categorized by candidates, with group decisions influenced by arguments and interpersonal persuasion. This is a far cry from the private voting booth and secret ballot that characterize primary elections. What's more, the caucuses do not accurately represent Iowa's demographics. Caucuses are held in early evening and do not permit absentee votes; as a result, they leave out key clusters of voters, such as medical personnel who must stay with their patients, restaurant employees, gas station workers on the night shift, and parents who can't afford a babysitter.

And yet as sure as farmers harvest Iowa corn every October and syrup lovers produce maple sugar in New Hampshire every February, the presidential campaigns expend enormous amounts of time and resources in the Hawkeye and Granite States every four years.

Iowa and New Hampshire traditionally capture the lion's share of media attention during the primary campaign period. This attention is far out of proportion to what one would expect, based on their population and the number of electoral votes the two states command. Some years back, when researchers first content analyzed news coverage of Iowa and New Hampshire, they discovered that the contests in these two states—which accounted for just 3 percent of the U.S. population and 10 of the 270 Electoral College votes needed for election to the presidency—received 34 percent of television network news coverage of the primaries (Lichter, Amundson, & Noyes, 1988). The news coverage that the two states receive dwarfs the amount given to primaries in larger states, like California, New York, and Texas (see also Buell, 2000). You might think of this visually by imagining two maps of the United States, the first the states in proportion to news about nominating contests, the second the states in proportion to their electoral votes. In the first map, Iowa and New Hampshire loom large, big or bigger than New York, California, and Florida. In the second, they are puny, reflecting the relatively small number of electoral votes the two states contribute to the Electoral College (Adams, 1987).

Why Iowa? Why New Hampshire? There are historical reasons. New Hampshire has held the nation's first primary since 1920. Iowa held caucuses since the mid-1800s, although they did not become politically consequential until 1976 when they made considerable hay (so to speak) about Jimmy Carter's surprisingly strong showing. (There are actually several successive Iowa caucuses—precinct, county, and state; hence the use of the plural, caucuses).

These two contests assume outsized importance because they are the first tests of strength in the electorate, and the media love firsts. "Iowa is not first because it is important; it is important because it is first," Winebrenner and Goldford (2010) note (p. 340). They also appeal to journalistic emphasis on the horse race, excitement, and drama. That they take place in very different areas of the country lends a sense of representativeness, although it is a false sense of representatives when it comes to the nation as a whole.

It is not just the news media that focus heavily on these early nomination contests. The candidates themselves devote extensive resources to winning or placing in Iowa and New Hampshire. Party leaders closely monitor candidate performances. Fund-raisers look to see which candidates led the pack and are therefore deserving of their support. Active, committed voters from both parties use the results to make judgments about which candidates they will support in their own state primaries. Are these two contests politically consequential because the media lavish coverage on them, or do the media lavish coverage because they are politically consequential? It is a little bit of both, as media coverage has established in the eyes of voters and political elites that the outcomes preordain success in the fight for the nomination (Mayer, 2010). "Were it not for the media," two scholars note, "the Iowa caucus and New Hampshire primary results would be about as relevant to the presidential nomination as opening-day baseball scores are to a pennant race" (Paletz & Entman, 1981, p. 36).

Politics, Communication, and the Perceptual Campaign

Unlike larger states, where it is high-nigh impossible to travel from city to city to meet voters, candidates talk with Iowa and New Hampshire voters one-on-one, in folksy hangouts, restaurants, and bars. Advertising and big media buys are less important than talking directly with voters, in what is known as retail politics. A positive aspect of both contests is that candidates try to blend with voters, reaching out to understand their concerns using old-fashioned, homey techniques. Richard Gephardt, a long-time Missouri congressman, moved his mother to Iowa to cultivate the senior citizen crowd during the 1988 campaign. Twenty years later, Connecticut Senator Christopher Dodd moved his family to a three-bedroom house in Des Moines, even reenrolling a 6-year-old daughter from a Washington, D.C., kindergarten in an Iowa school. Hoping to win the New Hampshire primary, Connecticut Senator Joseph Lieberman moved his family to a small Manchester apartment.

In Iowa, candidates with a passionate message that connects with committed voters and an impeccably organized campaign frequently win. In 2008. Obama relied on his college student minions, the children's crusade of 2008, to thoroughly canvass the Hawkeye State. In 2016, Republican Ted Cruz recognized that a key to winning Hawkeye State voters is a ferociously dedicated, strategically organized ground game, coordinated by volunteers on the ground who can canvass door-to-door, run phone banks, traffic in social media, and set up events that attract crowds and capture coverage on television or on stories streamed through the Internet. Focusing strategically on Iowa's evangelical Christian voters, who constitute close to two-thirds of Republican caucus participants, Cruz won the 2016 Iowa caucuses.

An early victory in Iowa spells instant success in the media horse race sweepstakes. The classic example occurred in 1976 when a little-known former Georgia governor, Jimmy Carter, recognizing the political import of a strong performance in Iowa, devoted considerable energy and resources to the state. Carter came in first, but here's the thing: He garnered just 28 percent of the vote, besting his Democratic rivals (though falling substantially short of the 37 percent who said they were uncommitted to any candidate). Nonetheless, the news media saw a story—or perhaps created one. The legendary *New York Times* reporter R. W. Apple pronounced that Carter had "burst from the pack," and had "scored an impressive victory in yesterday's Iowa Democratic precinct caucuses" (Perloff, 2016, p. E1; Winebrenner & Goldford, 2010, p. 68). This, along with other elite media coverage, ushered in a bonanza of positive press attention for Carter, gifting him with five times as much post-Iowa coverage as any other candidate, vaulting him above his rivals and delivering the momentum needed to cruise to victory in New Hampshire, and become the unassailable frontrunner and ultimately the Democratic nominee.

As Mayer (1987) observed, the victorious candidate in Iowa or New Hampshire is portrayed in the press as popular, exciting, confident, in control: in short, a leader. His poll ratings are increasing; his organization is growing; his message is catching on; his crowds are large and enthusiastic. His opponents, by contrast, are dead, dying, or in disarray.

(p. 14)

Candidates can also gain positive press by doing better than expected, in line with the exceeding expectations storyline discussed in Chapter 10. In 1992, Bill Clinton, on the political ropes because of allegations about his past (that he'd had an extramarital affair and avoided the draft), convinced New Hampshire voters he cared deeply about their economic plight, emphasizing that he would be with them "till the last dog dies." When he came in second place (with just 26 percent of the vote), he called himself the "Comeback Kid." Playing on storied sports metaphors, he declared victory and rode the momentum to a score of primary victories (see Figure 11.2).

Figure 11.2 Bill Clinton campaigned aggressively for the 1992 Democratic presidential nomination, particularly in Iowa and New Hampshire. When he came in second in New Hampshire, after news coverage of a sexual liaison threatened to derail his candidacy, he spun the runner-up outcome as a victory.

Getty Images

Figure 11.2 *(Continued)*

Losses in Iowa and New Hampshire can be devastating. Losers no longer receive the mother's milk of political press: news coverage. They are saddled with a "losing ground" storyline. The political cognoscenti—the elite cadre of reporters, consultants, party leaders, and campaign donors—conclude that the candidate is not a viable contender. It's not done conspiratorially, but through the realm of perceptions, increasingly communicated via social media posts. Candidates who fail to come in first, second, or third are not perceived as winners, and perceptions translate to reality when it comes to news, politicians' endorsements, and dollars donated to campaigns. Wealthy people and, to a much lesser extent, ordinary voters do not want to donate their money to a candidate who is seen as likely to lose. *In every election since 1976, no candidate has won the Republican or Democratic nominations without winning either the Iowa or New Hampshire contests (except Bill Clinton, who was unopposed in 1996 and came in second in New Hampshire in 1992, but claimed he won!).*

Evaluation of Iowa and New Hampshire

In the decades-long, never-ending debate about Iowa and New Hampshire, there are communication pros as well as the standard cons. Defenders note that in an age of mass political advertising and YouTube videos, it is refreshing to have nomination contests in states sufficiently small that candidates can talk to voters one-on-one, engage in grassroots campaigns, listen to their problems, look them in the eye, and explain their policy proposals in ordinary language at the local diner. The two state contests also provide an early test of candidates' moxie, one that doesn't exclusively require big media buys, in this way providing an element of surprise, giving outside-the-pack candidates with innovative ideas the chance to break out. Finally, precisely because of their small size, the states can galvanize supporters, energizing activists and voters in an era when this is the exception rather than the rule. With same-day registration policies in place through the 2016 election, both states encourage people to participate in a political party event (Redlawsk, Tolbert, & Donovan, 2011). The robust discussions that precede the contests—particularly in Iowa, where candidate speeches can precede the actual vote—highlight the policy-based thinking and deliberation that are the shining lights of democracy.

There are definitely positive aspects to the news media's enshrining these two early contests as critical to the nomination. These are balanced by various negatives. The first is the states' stunning lack of representativeness of the national party electorate. A second downside is that horse race coverage advances winners with coverage disproportionate to their margin of victory. In addition to examples described previously, one thinks back to 2012. In that year, Republican candidate Mitt Romney captured the lion's share of news coverage about the Iowa caucuses, although he defeated opponent Rick Santorum by just eight votes. Yet a little over two weeks later, a reanalysis of certified vote totals revealed that Santorum actually won, by 34 votes. But it was too late: Romney had won the beauty contest coverage, gaining needed momentum for the New Hampshire primary. A third shortcoming is the early contests' tendency to (occasionally) push less well-known yet promising candidates out of contention. Back in 1992, Larry Agran, a little-known Democratic mayor from Irvine, California, who had proposed an interesting plan to revive American cities, was ignored by journalists, who viewed him as a likely loser with little chance to win the New Hampshire primary. Yet voters were intrigued, and he fared well in a January opinion poll. However, the news did not report his strong position in the poll, skipping over Agran to focus on the poll standing of other major political candidates, calling on a standard press storyline, perforce denying Agran the attention needed to propel his candidacy forward (Meyrowitz, 1992; Schudson, 2011).

The Contests That Follow

Although victories in Iowa and New Hampshire are critical, they are not sufficient to propel a candidate to become the Republican or Democratic nominee. Candidates rarely win both Iowa and New Hampshire, so the momentum of Iowa can be cancelled by a loss in New Hampshire. Well-heeled candidates are apt to stay in the race longer than they used to. Even as the list of viable candidates is winnowed down, the race for delegates continues into the critical winter and spring nomination contests. Candidates face off on a succession of Tuesdays and Saturdays, notably on Super Tuesday, the series of elections in delegate-rich states held in early March. Big-money politics that relies on advertisements funded by political action committees works in concert with rallies directed at a candidate's base, geared to gaining news coverage and social media buzz. This can include blatantly prejudiced appeals, highlighting the role that ethnic prejudice continues to play in American campaigns. South Carolina has been a flashpoint, illustrated by the Republican primary campaign of 2000.

In 2000, George W. Bush needed to derail his competitor, Arizona Senator John McCain, after McCain thrashed Bush in New Hampshire. Bush's minions unloaded a searing underground campaign that tarnished McCain with a series of distorted, racist messages. An email message claimed "McCain chose to sire children without marriage," and flyers said he had a "Negro child." The information was false, derived from the fact that the McCains had lovingly adopted a dark-skinned child from Bangladesh years before. Messages falsely claimed McCain's wife was a drug addict and that McCain, who had served in Vietnam and acted courageously as a prisoner of war, committed treason as a POW (Gooding, 2004). The attacks were never tied to Bush, though political observers suspected Bush consultant Karl Rove, who had a reputation for unleashing dark, deceptive tactics. The campaign was widely believed to have influenced South Carolina Republican voters, resulting in a big Bush win that propelled him to victories in subsequent primary states, ethically tainted by the stain of South Carolina.

Politics ain't bean bag, as the expression goes. It is a contact sport, characterized by unethical, scurrilous attacks that show no signs of going away. It is important to understand the reality of campaigns, however, and it is becoming increasingly apparent that the old rules for success may not apply today.

In a frequently cited book, aptly titled *The Party Decides*, Cohen and his colleagues ((2008) concluded that party leaders are key opinion leaders, who influence party stalwarts and the party's base of voters to align with the candidate they believe has the best chance of winning election. "Supporting the candidate with the most insider endorsements, who is also likely to be widely viewed as the most viable candidate, may be taken by these voters as a low-cost and reasonable course of action," they observed (p. 297). However, as noted in Chapter 8, political marketing is increasingly eliding the "middlemen," like party leaders who used to symbolically intercede between candidates and voters. With social media, candidates like Trump have gone directly to voters, harnessing a message that appealed to many Republicans who felt marginalized by party elites. Sanders did some of the same, winning primaries despite the silently orchestrated opposition of pro-Clinton party leaders. To the extent that direct candidate-to-voter marketing enhances democratic decision-making, it is a good thing.

On the other hand, certain verities remain. After the early retail political contests, candidates need money to consummate expensive media buys. They also need a compelling message, ideally a vision that appeals to their core supporters, and an effective strategy to market this message so that supporters provide candidates with the currency needed for victory: votes.

Evaluating the Media-Based Nomination System

Now that I have discussed strategic foundations of the nominating system, it is instructive to turn to normative issues. Does the media-focused nomination process advance democratic aims or adversely affect the body politic? There is broad consensus that, for all the shortcomings in the present system, it is far and away better than the old-style method, in which party leaders chose candidates in closed-door sessions, trading their support for political favors. The current system happens out in the open, exposing candidate, party, and media foibles to the sunlight of democracy. The lengthy campaign tests candidates, weeding out those who do not have the political savvy or psychological stamina to withstand the slings and arrows of a presidential nomination. It forces candidates to build a cohesive organization in a multitude of states. To the extent that these skills are required in the nation's chief executive, perhaps the current system does a pretty good job separating out the presidential wheat from the chaff. But this does not mean that the contemporary nominating system is free of problems.

Critics emphasize that the nomination process is too long, beginning more than a year and a half before the general election. The long campaign can dispirit voters and expends millions of dollars that could be spent on more important political issues. Second, the disproportionate emphasis on Iowa and New Hampshire can disenfranchise, or minimize the impact of, nomination contests in other more representative states that happen to occur later. In some instances, the presumptive nominee has already been chosen before citizens in later primary states vote, giving them far less input than individuals who happen to live in states that hold their contests earlier. Even those who defend the current system recognize that it has serious flaws. A number of ideas have been suggested.

One proposal is a national primary election that would be held one day in late spring during the presidential election year. The direct primary would eliminate the hegemonic influence of early contests in small states, give voters in all states an equal chance to affect the outcome, and tame the tide of media momentum that can propel candidates toward the nomination based on fleeting, whimsical campaign events. However, a national primary has shortcomings. It would hardly eliminate media effects. In fact, it would accentuate their impact. Without the corrective mechanism afforded by sequential primaries, wherein a candidate's gaffe that loomed large in one contest is forgotten by the time another primary rolls around, a dramatic, but trivial, ill-timed campaign misstep could doom a candidate's chances of winning a national primary.

Another alternative is regional primaries. Primaries and caucuses could be grouped geographically, so that all the states in a certain geographical sphere hold primaries on the same day. Regional primaries would be scheduled sequentially from March to July (Polsby et al., 2012). This plan represents a compromise between the current state-by-state method and a national primary. However, the disproportionate influence of early contests would continue, as one region would have to go first, and this outcome would winnow out candidates for the later contests. Regional primaries would also work to the advantage of candidates who had political clout in the geographical area of the first regional contest. This could be minimized to some degree by rotating the order of geographical primaries every four years. Political advertising would assume a central role in regional primaries, as it would in a national primary, advantaging already known or independently wealthy candidates.

A third idea is to continue the present system because it gives each state a role and affirms the importance of public discussions in caucus states. However, to prevent the stranglehold Iowa and New Hampshire have over the system, the order of state contests would be varied each presidential election year, so that a different state went first, second, third, and so forth. Some years the first primary or caucus could be in Michigan or Illinois; other years, Texas or Colorado. This way the road to the nomination might be as likely to begin in Detroit, Decatur, Dallas, or Denver as in Des Moines (Perloff, 2016). However, this plan would not reduce the length of the nominations, nor would it eliminate the impact that early contests exert on the outcome.

Although each of these ideas have shortcomings, they call attention to the limitations in the present system and the need for reform.

NOMINATING CONVENTIONS

Historical Background

The path from primaries and caucuses to the convention is both simple and complex. Candidates who win the most, or the most delegate-rich, primaries and caucuses become their party's nominee. That's the simple part. The process of translating victories to convention delegates is complex. There is not a one-to-one relationship between victories in the nominating contests and convention. Instead, the delegate math is complicated, varying as a function of a particular state, political party, and party rules at a given time. It is far removed from the way many people presume candidates are nominated—more stupefying, intricate, and political.

In early America, representatives of Congress chose the party nominees for president. Then, as political parties began to dominate politics, power diffused from elite leaders to a cadre of party leaders. Parties held nominating conventions that were filled with drama. A candidate might not be nominated the first time—on the first ballot—but on a second or third ballot. Party leaders called the shots, selecting nominees, bartering and horse-trading in smoke-filled back rooms (no one knew about tobacco-causing carcinogens in those days). Contested, brokered, multi-ballot conventions were the norm. Abraham Lincoln captured the 1860 nomination on the third ballot. This continued through much of the 20th century, with Woodrow Wilson gaining the Democratic nomination on the 46th ballot and the obscure John W. Davis gaining the Democratic nomination in 1924 on the 103rd ballot, only to lose to Republican Calvin Coolidge (Goist, 2016). The public knew virtually none of what happened behind closed doors.

Reforms began in the early 20th century. Frustrated by boss control over parties and committed to democratic processes, a group of political reformers, the Progressives, helped initiate primaries to give voters an opportunity to select presidential nominees. Primaries took off slowly. About 12 states held primaries in 1912. The number of state primaries fluctuated over the next five decades; on the average, about 15 states held presidential primaries, and no more than 40 percent of the convention delegates at the nominating conventions came from primary states (Wayne, 2008). Party leaders still wielded considerable influence over the nomination process. John F. Kennedy entered primaries in 1960 to demonstrate to party leaders that voters would accept his presidential candidacy, even though they knew he was a Roman Catholic. He did not contest primaries to amass delegates based on raw primary victories. Instead, he entered to impress the party honchos. Even as conventions became seemingly more transparent, with television covering them gavel-to-gavel and journalists reveling in the grandiosity, tacitly giving their imprimatur to the process, appearances deceived. The electorate was left out of the picture; party leaders could control what was brought to the floor, and dissident perspectives were not tolerated.

The process was headed for a collision, as 1960s-style democracy and the power of television collided with the old guard at the Democratic National Convention in Chicago in 1968. Violence ran rampant on the city streets when police viciously beat youthful protesters who had gathered in Chicago, in graphic scenes shown live on national television. The police violence cast a shadow on the proceedings inside and, in liberal Democrats' minds, was connected with undemocratic procedures party leaders employed to nominate Hubert H. Humphrey. In the wake of the violence and recognition that the nomination process was controlled by the party brass, who could strong-arm dissenters, a blue-ribbon panel, the McGovern-Fraser Commission, called for a fairer, more open process of choosing delegates, one that was less beholden to the dictates of party elites. The commission recommended that popular elections—primaries, held during the year of the general presidential election—serve as the major mechanism by which convention delegates would be selected. The Democratic Party adopted the report, and state legislatures subsequently passed laws that made the changes binding for both Democrats and Republicans. As a result, the overwhelming majority of delegates to the nominating conventions are indirectly selected by voters in primary elections and caucuses. "Politicians chosen by membership-based mass parties" were "replaced by politicians . . . sold by advertising to voters," Lind observed (2016, p. 6), an improvement, but not without its share of drawbacks, as we have seen.

The Ins, Outs, and Shortcomings of Delegate Selection

Delegates date back to the 19th century, a historical vestige awkwardly merged with the more democratic processes in caucuses and primaries. Political parties had to fashion a way to connect popular democratic outcomes in nomination contests with formal votes cast at nominating conventions. A candidate needs a bare majority of delegates to win the party's nomination: In 2016, a candidate needed to capture 1,237 of the some 2,472 Republican delegates, and 2,383 of the 4,765 Democratic National Convention delegates. The bulk of Democratic Party delegates are allocated proportionately according to the percentage of votes captured in a state nomination contest. To gain delegates, a Democratic candidate must win at least 15 percent of the votes cast in a state primary or caucus. This ensures that a candidate have at least a modicum of popularity in order to claim delegates. The Republican procedure is more variable, giving more freedom to states; some states use proportional representation, others winner-take-all, and still others a hybrid of the two (Sides, 2016).

There is a substantial but inexact relationship between primary and caucus votes won and number of delegates awarded. Candidates who have won more primaries and caucuses, particularly in populous states, have a greater number of delegates than candidates who lost caucuses and primaries. But there is far from a one-to-one relationship between votes and delegates, making the process less than perfectly democratic. A Democratic Party candidate could fall short of the 15 percent requirement, receiving 14 percent of the votes in a primary, and receive no delegates. And then there are superdelegates, as the Democrats call them, or automatic delegates in the Republicans' parlance.

Superdelegates or automatic delegates are elite members of the party, such as elected officials, national committee members, and well-known party leaders. These delegates are not bound by the outcome in their state and are free to vote for whomever they want. Party officials came up with this gambit to ensure that they could still influence the nomination process, especially if voters chose an ideologically palatable, but unelectable, candidate. However, superdelegates (the more popular term) cast an anti-democratic pall on the process. A candidate could win a majority of delegates in nomination contests, but fail to gain enough delegates to clinch the nomination because unelected superdelegates preferred the opponent. For example, in New Hampshire in 2016, Sanders won big, defeating Clinton by a large margin and gaining 15 delegates. Because of proportional representation, Clinton netted nine delegates. And because six New Hampshire superdelegates supported her, she was in effect tied with Sanders, even though he bested her by a sizable margin in the primary (Peters, 2016a).

The delegate selection process is a mongrel, reflecting an odd combination of history, desire to accord respect to party leaders, and modern democracy. It is not purely democratic. Critics (like Sanders and Trump supporters in 2016) lamented that candidates could win many nomination contests but be frozen out because either superdelegates, in the case of Sanders, favored their opponent or because they faced a brokered convention where delegates are no longer bound to respect voters' will after the first and second ballots. Defenders of the delegate system argue that parties should maintain control of their conventions, adding that the procedure provides a safeguard against the nomination of a demagogic candidate by voters, in line with the Founding Fathers' sometimes justifiable suspicion of the masses. Critics of superdelegates and automatic delegates disagree, pointing out that in the case of presidential nominations, one of the world's oldest democracies is not perfectly democratic.

The Promotional Communication Convention

Caucuses and primaries select the party nominee, however imperfectly. Conventions ratify the choice and promote the ticket before a national audience, functioning primarily as a weeklong advertisement for the candidates and the party, "effectively a four-night miniseries before an audience of 20 million people or more" (Zeleny & Rutenberg, 2008). Party leaders hire media production experts who script the convention down to the wire. What looks spontaneous to a television audience has been scheduled, organized, orchestrated, pre-planned, revised, and then readied for final production well in advance. Conventions are designed as a send-off to present the party and its nominees in the best possible political light, animated by theatrics, featuring a cast of thousands of delegates, centering on the candidates and their beautiful families, and ideally, revolving around a coherent storyline that the candidates can take into the fall campaign. Recognizing that the conventions offer one of the few times when voters are motivated to tune in to partisan speeches, parties do their best to entice viewers, hoping the speeches, party ideology, and miscellaneous hoopla will influence opinions and behavior. But things don't always work out that way: Conventions can be unpredictable, and intra-party conflict can spill onto the media stage.

It has become an increasingly theatrical, technological show. As early as the 1996 Democratic convention, President Bill Clinton addressed the convention delegates from a giant TV screen as he traveled across the Midwest. "From time to time," a columnist sarcastically observed, "he beams down at the convention . . . a loving apolitical presence who has paused along his route of march to extend a warm, electronic hug to those who await him" (Feagler, 1996, p. 2A). A dozen years later, in 2008, both party conventions used theatrics—props, lighting, and special effects. Obama accepted his party's nomination at an outdoor stadium, with fireworks, video screens, and rock star entertainment. "On the 50-yard line of the football field, at a reported cost of $6 million, they erected a plywood Parthenon, its fake Grecian columns suggesting the White House," columnist William Safire (2008) observed. Parodying Obama's book, *The Audacity of Hope*, Safire derided the convention as "the audacity of hype."

In 2012, Republican Party leaders called on producers and designers who had worked on Broadway and NBC, as well as on studios that built television sets for Oprah Winfrey. Their mission? To create a set, milieu, and trimmings that would change perceptions of nominee Mitt Romney, who came off stiff, formal, and not particularly warm. To do this, they constructed a $2.5 million Frank Lloyd Wright–style stage. "From its dark-wood finish to the brightly glowing high-resolution screens in the rafters that look like skylights, every aspect of the stage has been designed to convey warmth, approachability and openness," a reporter wrote (Peters, 2012, p. A1). With broadcast networks showing just about an hour of the convention in prime time, party leaders recognized that they had to efficiently communicate just the right political image. The irony was not lost: They worked intensively to display Romney's nonchalance, although it was far from clear whether their efforts had succeeded.

"A battle of the network stars," *The New York Times* headlined in 2016, calling the Republican and Democratic conventions a colossal media battle between two television series stars the nation had viewed for decades: a choice of getting provoked by an improv (Trump) or becalmed by a script (Clinton); World Wide Wrestling (the Donald) versus staid CBS (Hillary) (Poniewozik, 2016). News viewed the important political platform and party-building issues that occur at conventions through the prism of entertainment television.

In sum, conventions are scripted, patriotic events, filled with feel-good moments, heartfelt spousal endorsements of the nominee, inspirational movies, bands, and an endless supply of red, white, and blue balloons. At some basic philosophical level, a convention, as columnist Frank Bruni (2012) observed, "is a communal lie, during which speakers and members of the audience project an excitement 10 times greater than what they really feel and a confidence about the candidate that they only wish they could muster" (p. A21). But televised feel-good moments don't always emerge. There is a limit to the degree to which consultants can gin up spontaneity and replace reality with a bonanza of good cheer. Republicans struggled to put a good face on the 2016 convention. Many regulars and party stalwarts stayed away from the convention because they opposed Trump. Others were reluctant to endorse him enthusiastically, and a rump group of rebellious delegates staged a floor fight over convention rules, trying to embarrass Trump and failing, but showcasing some of the divisions that roiled the party.

Partisanship and Rhetoric

Inside the convention, serious business does occur. Conventions are gatherings of the party faithful, who—though they do disagree among themselves on issues, some years more than others—collectively espouse a particular philosophy of politics. As Shafer notes, "national party conventions are the major, purely partisan, formal institutions of American politics" (2010, p. 264). Articulating a trenchant ideology that guides the party and serves as the focus for the upcoming campaign is a strength of party conventions, even as candidates take positions at variance with party theology, and the two parties typically offer a fairly conventional perspective on politics with a paucity of outside-the-political-box ideas. The party's ideology is summarized in its platform, a document few voters read, but one that offers a succinct statement of where the party stands on the issues. Platforms can reflect general agreement on issues, as well as divisions, as occurred in 2016 when the Republican Party adopted strong social conservative positions on homosexuality and the traditional family—conventional Republican staples—while bowing to Trump's distinctive focus on building a wall along the nation's southern border (Peters, 2016b).

Political speeches play a key role in rallying the troops, particularly keynote addresses. In 2004 a young Barack Obama energized Democrats, using poise, eloquent content, and adroit turns of phrase as he intoned that "there's not a liberal America and a conservative America; there's the United States of America."

Vice presidential candidates and presidential contenders who are relatively new to the national stage use speeches accepting the party's nomination to introduce themselves to the voting public. In 2008, Sarah Palin portrayed herself as an ordinary American, reared with good, small-town values, unimpressed by media elites, a modern-day Harry Truman, a 21st-century female incarnate of Jimmy Stewart's title character in *Mr. Smith Goes to Washington*. Four years later the Republican vice presidential nominee, Wisconsin Congressman Paul Ryan, embellished the small-town biographical narrative, describing how he lived on the same block in Janesville, Wisconsin where he grew up and still belongs to "the same parish where I was baptized." He embraced the conservative ethos of small government, pledging to place "hard limits on the size of government," thrilling conservative convention delegates.

Presidential contenders use their acceptance speeches to offer a touching biographical story and narrative designed to propel them into the fall campaign. In an age of personalized politics, relating raw emotion sensitively—and with apparent sincerity—is a valued attribute in nominees who aspire to the presidency. In 1992 Bill Clinton told his audience that he never met his father, who was killed in a car wreck, but that he was raised by a dedicated mother who taught him about family values, sacrifice, hard work, and the courage she displayed fighting breast cancer. The self-disclosure may have been sincere, but it was exquisitely scripted to the "Oprah-style" "tell-all" ethos of entertainment television.

Scripted and hokey as convention speeches can sometimes be, they can also inspire. In 1992, Mary Fisher, a mother of two who had improbably contracted HIV, moved the Republican national convention to tears when she said, "I am one with a black infant struggling with tubes in a Philadelphia hospital. I am one with the lonely gay man sheltering a flickering candle from the cold wind of his family's rejection." Senator Ted Kennedy, after mounting an unsuccessful challenge to President Carter in 1980, delivered a bombastic rhetorical masterpiece, as he called up images of shuttered factories and assembly lines of Indiana, as well as a grandmother in East Oakland who relinquished the phone she used to call her grandchildren in order to pay her rent. In their name and on their behalf, he issued the now legendary dramatic summation: "For all those whose cares have been our concern, the work goes on, the cause endures, the hope still lives, and the dream shall never die." Inspirational rhetoric, a time-honored political tradition, continues to move audiences.

In the main, conventions, as exemplars of campaign persuasion, are designed to shore up the base and warm the lukewarm. Nominees strive to gain a political bounce in the polls, a momentum-building increase that emerges from audience exposure to the litany of persuasive speeches, partisan rhetoric, and repetitive onslaughts against the opposition party. Conventions usually produce a bounce or upsurge in the nominee's popularity, but it is only a short-term gain that can quickly dissipate (Wayne, 2008). With declining interest in the conventions and fewer swing voters likely to be impacted by what they see, the boost conventions provide nominees is smaller and of more limited political consequence (Silver, 2012).

For example, in 2016, the Democrats produced a better, savvier, more expertly produced televised convention than the Republicans. The Democrats had A-list celebrity entertainers like Katy Perry and Alicia Keys, more compelling speakers, and an organized political message. The Republicans (oddly, given their penchant for organization) produced a more disorganized show, with can-you-believe-they-did-that? mistakes, such as minor plagiarism in the speech of Melania Trump, along with intra-party divisions, from a convention floor fight to Republican rival Ted Cruz's embarrassing refusal to endorse Trump in a prime-time speech. Yet in continued evidence of his supporter's devotion to his brand, Trump got a bounce from his convention, enough to keep him competitive in the explosive fall campaign (Rutenberg, 2016).

Looking beyond 2016 and polling bounces, it is helpful to view conventions in a larger symbolic framework. There is a small silver lining. For all the candidate platitudes, they provide a ceremonial public space for journalists, political figures, and citizens, at least vicariously, to interact. They "help to symbolically organize democratic politics and provide key ritual moments . . . that legitimate the transfer of civic power" (Kreiss, Meadows, & Remensperger, 2015, p. 593). Although citizens necessarily play a small role, they can critique and participate through the increasingly vocal outlets of social media.

CONCLUSIONS

Primaries and caucuses are the arteries and veins of the presidential nomination process. They are open, transparent, and media-driven. Although the process is substantially more democratic than in the 19th century, when nominees were chosen by party leaders in much-mythologized smoke-filled rooms, the contemporary system has its own set of rituals, idiosyncrasies, and drawbacks.

There are four phases of the nominating process: (1) pre-primaries or invisible primaries; (2) the Iowa caucuses and New Hampshire primary; (3) the long series of state primaries; and (4) the late summer conventions. Pre-primaries lay the groundwork. Candidates who recruit substantial funds, perform well in candidate debates, gain respectable poll numbers, and are viewed as serious contenders by the news media advance to the early primaries, bolstered by the double-edged storyline sword of high expectations. The news media and polls play a critical winnowing role, nowhere more visible than the ways that television news networks use polls (making statistical oversimplifications) to decide which candidates should participate in the major pre-primary political debates. Pre-primary and primary campaign debates, which can be remarkably superficial when it comes to discussing policy issues, offer candidates an opportunity to gain access to party faithful.

Critics lament that the system affords too much power to an institution—the press—that is not accountable to voters and has no formal grounding in the electoral process. On the other hand, the system is transparent and, in the main, allows candidates to make their best case to voters in highly public settings, increasingly by mobilizing a base through social media.

Through historical quirks, the Iowa caucuses and New Hampshire primary assumed a role in nomination politics that is far out of proportion to their size or electoral representativeness. These early contests winnow down the candidate field, with losers in Iowa and New Hampshire forced to drop out as a result of a reduced fund-raising base and perceptions that their candidacies are not viable. Given the role media play in transmitting and generating expectations, perceptions quickly become synonymous with reality. As discussed in Chapter 10, news promotes storylines—the front-runner scenario, the losing ground storyline, and bandwagon narrative—that can influence electoral outcomes. Favorable news coverage of winners in Iowa and New Hampshire, and diminished focus on losers, can advance victors' fortunes while pushing losers out of the race. As the primaries move into delegate-rich, larger states, advertising and modern political marketing become more important, showcasing the role money plays in the nomination process.

Nominating conventions certify and promote nominees selected in the primaries and contests. Conventions have evolved over the years, becoming more public and democratic, but the procedures for choosing a nominee are not fully democratic. Allocation of delegate seats to automatic delegates or superdelegates lends an elitism to the process, which has rankled some voters, as well as candidates who fear they might not gain the support of the party leadership. The main purpose of conventions is promotion, with conventions functioning as a weeklong miniseries designed to rally the party faithful around candidates and a platform that has been hammered out, sometimes rancorously, in the weeks before the convention. A party's leadership naturally prefers conventions that are seamless and well-choreographed, and that give the nominees a bounce into the fall campaign, even though that bounce is transient and less politically consequential than frequently assumed. On a larger, symbolic level, conventions offer a ceremonial space for politicians, journalists, and citizens to come together, although, truth be told, the grand opportunity can be squandered by feel-good, made-for-TV moments and rhetoric.

The normative aspects of the nomination system have been long debated. Critics argue that the nomination process is too long, gives disproportionate attention to two unrepresentative states, and assigns undue weight to peripheral increases in media momentum. It also engages only a small minority of eligible voters. Defenders emphasize that the system lets voters know who is best able to survive a grueling test for the presidency, presents substantial news coverage of an intensely competitive race, and is transparent to the point that just about any statement or action a candidate performs will be publicized by somebody on some television show or social media post. For all their faults, primary campaigns offer an opportunity for insurgent candidates to present outside-the-box proposals to voters, as Sanders and Trump did in 2016. Whatever one may think of Trump's and Sanders's messages, they seemed to set the agenda, bringing new issues like trade, immigration, and, more generally, populism to the electoral fore. The purpose of elections is not to provide moral evaluation of political programs, some of which may be interesting, others inflammatory, but to give people the chance to adjudicate among them by choosing candidates whose proposals they find most congenial. These are all benefits of the contemporary nomination process. Yet there is little doubt that the system can be improved, and a number of remedies have been proposed, from regional primaries to varying the two states that lead off the nomination contests so that the process is more representative.

Yet, despite a plethora of post-election proposals, little changes. Recommendations to change the nomination system and provide life to political conventions are routinely offered, but the status quo rumbles on. There is always a feeling of déjà vu—many ideas are put forth and never see the light of day once the election is over. The nominations and conventions continue to bear the tired trademark of two-party sameness. The status quo, alas, continues to disenfranchise third parties. Third (and fourth) parties are disadvantaged by the American system's time-honored two-party tradition and absence of proportional representation in legislative elections that could jump-start alternative political groups (Amy, 1993).

REFERENCES

Adams, W. C. (1987). As New Hampshire goes . . . In G. Orren & N. W. Polsby (Eds.), *Media and momentum: The New Hampshire primary and nomination politics* (pp. 42–59). Chatham, NJ: Chatham House.

Amy, D. J. (1993). *Real choices/new voices: The case for proportional representation elections in the United States*. New York: Columbia University Press.

Barbaro, M. (2015, October 5). Pithy, mean and powerful: How Donald Trump mastered Twitter for 2016. *The New York Times*. Retrieved from www.nytimes.com/2015/10/06/us/politics/donald-trump-twitter-. . . . (Accessed May 18, 2016).

Bradner, E. (2015, December 10). CNN Republican presidential debate criteria announced. *CNN Politics*. Retrieved from www.cnn.com/2015/11/20/politics/republican-presidential-deb . . . (Accessed May 19, 2016).

Bruni, F. (2012, August 28). Huggability and helium. *The New York Times*, A21.

Buchanan, L., & Parlapiano, A. (2016, April 3). How votes for Trump could become delegates for someone else. *The New York Times*, 20.

Buell, E. H., Jr. (2000). The changing face of the New Hampshire primary. In W. Mayer (Ed.), *In pursuit of the White House 2000: How we choose our presidential nominees* (pp. 87–144). Chatham, NJ: Chatham House.

Burns, A. (2015, June 16). Donald Trump, pushing someone rich, offers himself. *The New York Times*. Retrieved from www.nytimes.com/2015/06/17/us/politics/donald-trump-runs-fo. . . (Accessed August 12, 2016).

Busch, A. E., & Mayer, W. G. (2004). The front-loading problem. In W. G. Mayer (Ed.), *The making of the presidential candidates* (pp. 1–43). Lanham, MD: Rowman & Littlefield.

Cohen, M., Karol, D., Noel, H., & Zaller, J. (2008). *The party decides: Presidential nominations before and after reform*. Chicago: University of Chicago Press.

DeSilver, D. (2016, June 10). *Turnout was high in the 2016 primary season, but just short of 2008 record*. Pew Research Center. Retrieved from www.pewresearch.org/fact-tank/2016/06/10/turnout-was-high-in-the-2016-primary-season-but-just-short-of-2008-record/ (Accessed March 14, 2017).

Fausset, R. (2017, August 12). Conservatives revel in "fury" in Trump's talk. *The New York Times*, A1, A10.

Feagler, D. (1996, August 28). Act one: Night of miracles raises curtain on big show. *The Plain Dealer*, 2A.

Goist, R. (2016, April 3). Contested conventions through decades and film. *The Plain Dealer*, A15.

Gooding, R. (2004, November). The trashing of John McCain. *Vanity Fair*. Retrieved from www.vanityfair.com/politics/features/2004/11/mccain200411 (Accessed January 5, 2017).

Healy, P., & Berenstein, E. (2015, October 12). How Bernie Sanders connects with his audience. *The New York Times*. Retrieved from www.nytimes.com/interactive/2015/10/12/us/politics/bernie-sanders-campaign-video-analysis.html (Accessed May 18, 2016).

Koblin, J. (2015, August 8). Republicans set record, outdrawing elite sports. *The New York Times*, A13.

Kreiss, D., Meadows, L., & Remensperger, J. (2015). Political performance, boundary spaces, and active spectatorship: Media production at the 2012 Democratic National Convention. *Journalism*, *16*, 577–595.

Leland, J. (2016, January 31). They're mad and sure their guy is the one to lead the fight. *The New York Times*, 1, 21.

Lichter, S. R., Amundson, D., & Noyes, R. (1988). *The video campaign: Network coverage of the 1988 primaries*. Washington, DC: American Enterprise Institute for Public Policy Research.

Lind, M. (2016, May 15). Is there too much democracy in America or too little? *The New York Times* (Sunday Review), 6.

Manjoo, F. (2016, May 19). The trouble with Twitter. *The New York Times*, B1, B7.

Mayer, W. G. (1987). The New Hampshire primary: A historical overview. In G. R. Orren & N. W. Polsby (Eds.), *Media and momentum: The New Hampshire primary and nomination politics* (pp. 9–41). Chatham, NJ: Chatham House.

Mayer, W. G. (2010). How parties nominate presidents. In L. S. Maisel & J. M Berry (Eds.), *The Oxford handbook of American political parties and interest groups* (pp. 185–203). New York: Oxford University Press.

Meyrowitz, J. (1992, March–April). The press rejects a candidate. *Columbia Journalism Review*, 46–47.

Nocera, J. (2015, September 29). Is Donald Trump serious? *The New York Times*. Retrieved from www.nytimes.com/2015/09/29/opinion/joe-nocera-is-donald-tr . . . (Accessed May 15, 2016).

Paletz, D.L., & Entman, R.M. (1981). *Media power politics*. New York: Free Press.

Patterson, T.E. (2016, June 13). *Pre-primary news coverage of the 2016 presidential race: Trump's rise, Sanders' emergence, Clinton's struggle*. Harvard Kennedy School Shorenstein Center on Media, Politics and Public Policy. Retrieved from http://shorensteincenter.org/pre-primary-news-coverage-2016-trump-c . . . (Accessed June 14, 2016).

Perloff, R.M. (2016, January 31). Letting Iowa pick first is not fair to the rest of us. *The (Cleveland) Plain Dealer*, E6.

Peters, J.W. (2012, August 20). A careful effort seeks to reveal a real Romney. *The New York Times*, A1, A12.

Peters, J.W. (2016a, April 10). Primary process has many voters feeling sidelined. *The New York Times*, 1, 15

Peters, J.W. (2016b, July 19). "Traditional" marriage, border wall and coal on tap. *The New York Times*, A13.

Polsby, N.W., Wildavsky, A., Schier, S.E., & Hopkins, D.A. (2012). *Presidential elections: Strategies and structures of American politics* (13th ed.). Lanham, MD: Rowman & Littlefield.

Poniewozik, J. (2016, July 17). Battle of the network stars. *The New York Times* (Arts & Leisure), 1, 13.

Popkin, S.L. (2012). *The candidate: What it takes to win—and hold—the White House*. New York: Oxford University Press.

Redlawsk, D.P., Tolbert, C.J., & Donovan, T. (2011). *Why Iowa? How caucuses and sequential elections improve the presidential nominating process*. Chicago: University of Chicago Press.

Rutenberg, J. (2016, July 29). Clinton's convention was made for TV. Trump's was made for Twitter. *The New York Times*, B1, B7.

Safire, W. (2008, August 31). The audacity of hype. *The New York Times*. Retrieved from www.nytimes.com/2008/08/31/opinion/31safire.html (Accessed March 14, 2017).

Schudson, M. (2011). *The sociology of news* (2nd ed.). New York: Norton.

Shafer, B.E. (2010). The pure partisan institution: National party conventions as research sites. In L.S. Maisel & J.M. Berry (Eds.), *The Oxford handbook of American political parties and interest groups* (pp. 264–284). New York: Oxford University Press.

Sides, J. (2016, February 16). Everything you need to know about delegate math in the presidential primary. *The Washington Post*. Retrieved from www.washingtonpost.com/news/monkey-cage/wp/2016/02/16 . . . (Accessed May 14, 2016).

Silver, N. (2012, August 29). Measuring a convention bounce. *International New York Times*. Retrieved from http://fivethirtyeight.blogs.nytimes.com/2012/08/29/measuring-a-con . . . (Accessed July 26, 2016).

Silver, N. (2016, May 4). Why Republican voters decided on Trump. *Five Thirty Eight*. Retrieved from fivethirtyeight.com/features/why-republican-voters-decided-on-trump/ (Accessed May 16, 2016).

Wayne, S.J. (2008). *The road to the White House 2008: The politics of presidential elections* (8th ed.). Boston: Thomson Wadsworth.

Winebrenner, H., & Goldford, D.J. (2010). *The Iowa precinct caucuses: The making of a media event* (3rd ed.). Iowa City: University of Iowa Press.

Zeleny, J., & Rutenberg, J. (2008, August 17). For convention, Obama's image is all-American. *The New York Times*. Retrieved from www.nytimes.com/2008/08/ 18/us/politics/18convention.html (Accessed January 6, 2017).

PART FOUR

Political Persuasion

12 Persuasion in the Presidential Campaign and the White House

You can view presidential campaigns through a variety of lenses. Campaigns are the essence of democracy, a pathway by which candidates reach citizens in the democratic mainstay of elections. Campaigns provide venues for deliberation and opportunities to debate alternative solutions to the nation's problems. They are quadrennial rituals that pump up the nation's political circulation, energizing the body politic with the oxygen of ideas and the adrenaline of hope. On the negative side, they are superficial, deceptive, elite-controlled events that pull the wool over the eyes of voters. In either case, to candidates and consultants, elections are one thing and one thing only: exercises in persuasion. They are strategic battles to convince Americans to cast their votes in favor of a particular candidate. The armamentarium consists of arguments and appeals, delivered interpersonally, on television, in videos streamed across the Internet, and arrayed across social media pages.

From a normative perspective, political persuasion showcases the trade-offs that necessarily accompany the democratic benefits communication provides. Political persuasion prizes the freedom to deliver unbridled message on behalf of a cause, giving candidates the opportunity to campaign for public office and citizens the ability to discuss, question, and argue with what they say. These come with trade-offs and dysfunctions—anger, animus, vitriolic posts, and disillusionment—complicating, but also illuminating, the dynamics of political communication. The next three chapters provide a formal examination of the roles persuasion plays in elections and governing. This chapter introduces classic perspectives on persuasion, applies these models to contemporary electoral politics, and describes the role that persuasive—or, more precisely, rhetorical—messages play in presidential policymaking. Chapter 13 examines presidential campaign advertising. Chapter 14 explores the persuasive aspects of presidential debates, while also examining the policy issues that drive debates.

The first section of the present chapter provides an overview of traditional political science perspectives to campaigns, calling attention to macro factors, as well as the importance of understanding persuasive campaign dynamics. The second portion reviews a classic persuasion model, discussing its implications for presidential campaigns. The third section extends this discussion by exploring the power of strong attitude, selective exposure, and normative implications. The final section adopts a broader approach, examining the ways presidents have harnessed messages and rhetoric in the service of persuasion.

CAMPAIGN EFFECTS: A VIEW FROM POLITICAL SCIENCE

Political scientists traditionally approach campaigns from the perspective of macro indicators, events that shape voting behavior. Economic conditions (the general state of the economy, economic growth, and the unemployment level) are important determinants of electoral outcomes (Rosenstone, 1983; Bartels, 2006). Favorable or improving economic conditions benefited Ronald Reagan in 1984 and Bill Clinton in 1996. Dismal economic straits helped unseat Jimmy Carter in 1980 and led to the defeat of George W. Bush's Republican Party in 2008. Other macro factors influencing the election outcome include the popularity of the president (notably, when he/she is up for reelection) and how the presidential nominees fared in their respective presidential primaries. In addition, when voters are satisfied with the current economic and political climate, they are likely to vote for the candidate of the incumbent's party. When dissatisfied, they are apt to cast votes for the candidate of the other political party (Holbrook, 1996).

Viewing the election from the perch of macro indicators, the 2016 election was more complicated than it initially appeared. The nation experienced sustained economic growth under Obama's Democratic administration, and unemployment rates dropped sharply, especially when compared to levels experienced during the 2009 downturn that followed the 2008 financial crisis. According to some models, this gave Clinton, the heir apparent to fellow Democrat Obama, an edge. However, the economy was recovering slowly, and was certainly not booming, as in 1964, 1972, and 2000, when economic strength forecast the success of the incumbent (Lyndon Johnson and Richard Nixon in 1964 and 1972), or the candidate from the president's party (Vice President Al Gore in 2000). With an average of only a 1.2 percent growth in personal income during 2012–2016 (Gelman, 2016), substantial declines in manufacturing jobs, and the unemployment rate twice as high for high school than college graduates, economic indicators foretold a close election.

A political science view emphasis on macro factors is instructive because it calls attention to the ways that media, political marketing, and online communication work within larger parameters that shape the contours of electoral campaigns. But the campaign is critical. Campaigns communicate information about economic growth, unemployment, and presidential popularity to voters. It is through the media that voters obtain the information that they use to assess the candidates' economic policies. There are so many different ways that macroeconomic trends can be framed—the gross domestic product can be described as better or worse than expected; the economy can be said to be generating or retarding growth; and employment can be discussed in regional terms, with a focus on different parts of the country. The ways candidates frame the economy can influence voters, priming them and convincing them to view factually based or ambiguous economic trends in positive or negative lights. News can emphasize certain frames to the exclusion of others. During the 2000 election, which arguably favored the Democrats because the economy fared well during Clinton's second term, news focused on candidate integrity in light of the Clinton impeachment scandal. This worked to the disadvantage of Gore, as news frames questioned his honesty, in light of the Clinton impeachment scandal, focusing more on this issue than the economy (see Chapter 10 and Johnston, Hagen, & Jamieson, 2004).

When a candidate makes a particular aspect of economic issues a centerpiece of the campaign—as Trump did in 2016—and builds a constituency around economic (and related symbolic) issues, voters can more easily connect broad economic indicators to their own situation. Had Trump ignored blue-collar woes or Clinton campaigned more with working class voters, the election might have turned out differently. There are also a truckload of unpredictable campaign features that broad macroeconomic factors exclude, ranging from candidate gaffes to global crises that enter into the voting equation. Research shows that campaigns are important; conventions, debates, and momentum shape voting behavior (Holbrook, 1996). To be sure, economic and political parameters set limits on campaign effects. But we cannot understand the underpinnings of electoral outcomes without taking into account the processes and effects of persuasive campaign messages.

ELABORATION LIKELIHOOD MODEL

You probably know people who are not interested in politics or don't care about the complexities of political issues. You also know people who are passionate about politics and have strong ideological perspective on political issues. The Elaboration Likelihood Model (ELM) emphasizes that these two groups—the apathetic and the passionate—process messages in very different ways. In a similar fashion, the ELM emphasizes that same person will process campaign persuasive messages differently, depending on whether the election concerns issues of importance to the individual, and whether he or she has sufficient knowledge and ability to understand issues at stake in the election.

The ELM is a preeminent model of attitude change. It emphasizes that voters process messages differently under different conditions, based on the likelihood they will elaborate on, or think carefully about, their arguments. The ELM also places a premium on process, arguing that the ways that voters process messages is of critical importance in understanding strategies that will influence their political attitudes (Petty, Briñol, & Priester, 2009).

A key factor is **involvement**, or the perception that an election is personally relevant or impinges directly on the self. When voters are low in involvement, they do not perceive the campaign is relevant to their pocketbooks or principles, and don't care much about the outcome of the election. When voters are high in involvement, they care a lot about the election, perceiving that it bears on their economic livelihood, political concerns, or deep-seated values. Involvement in turn has implications for political processing. The ELM stipulates that there are two routes by which people process messages: the **peripheral** and **central** routes (see Figure 12.1). The peripheral route is characterized by the use of simple, routinized, easy-to-process modes of thinking. The central route involves systematic processing of messages, as well as deeper, even ideologically based (and politically biased) examination of campaign messages. Under low involvement, individuals process information peripherally; under high involvement they elaborate centrally.

Low Involvement

When people are relatively uninterested in a campaign, lack motivation to follow it closely, and do not perceive the campaign bears on their own lives or values, they don't pay careful attention to campaign messages. The campaign is not a big deal to them and they don't expend much intellectual effort on what candidates say. When people lack motivation (or the ability to understand campaign issues), they process campaign information peripherally, relying on mental shortcuts, or heuristics, and simple affective cues. To influence these voters, campaigns must meet them where they are, designing simple messages that do not require extensive mental processing (see Figure 12.1a). Candidates need to match the message with voters' preference for heuristics and peripheral political decision-making. If you are a candidate appealing to voters with little interest in the campaign, you (sadly, perhaps) do not want to engage them in much serious thought. You don't want to develop a complex, abstract message that requires cognitive scrutiny. Instead, the ELM suggests, you should devise simple appeals with credible, feel-good cues. You want messages that swiftly connect with voters' low-interest, short-circuited ways of making up their political minds.

Low involvement can occur at the level of the election or the voter. Certain elections are low in involvement for most voters. These include state legislative races, judicial

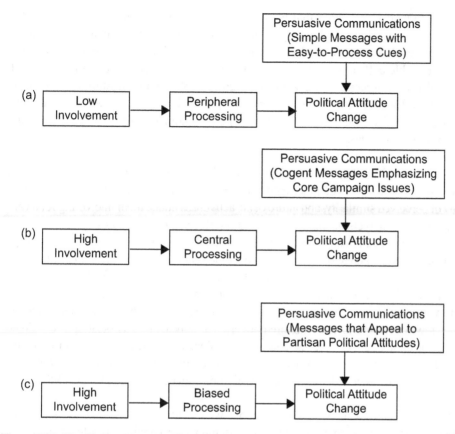

Figure 12.1 The Elaboration Likelihood Model, applied to political persuasion.

elections, and even contests for the U.S. Congress. The presidential campaign is more involving for most Americans for historical and symbolic reasons—and because the media make it a big deal. However, voters vary in their level of involvement in the presidential election campaign. (Interestingly, state and local elections can be of greater significance than the presidential race because they directly influence such tangible matters as college education, property taxes, and children's schools.) As noted earlier, the ELM stipulates that that when voters are low in involvement in a particular election, messages are more likely to succeed if they link up with their relatively effortless, lackadaisical preference for processing political information. What types of messages are most persuasive under low involvement?

The ELM offers specific predictions. First, low-involved voters are likely to be influenced by messages from highly credible communicators, who can be relied on to offer intelligent political advice. Thus Hillary Clinton depended heavily on former

President Obama, reasoning that low-involved Democratic voters might support her simply because Obama, who they respected, embraced her candidacy. On a more everyday level, a low-involved voter could go along with the advice of a politically knowledgeable colleague or a Facebook friend, who is perceived to be familiar with political issues. Accepting the views of high-credible communicators requires little cognitive effort but offers relative certainty, giving low-involved voters confidence that their vote decision is based on the opinions of someone who knows the ins and outs of political issues.

Second, likable, similar, and physically attractive candidates can carry the day with low-involved voters, as voters let their affect guide them, allowing the halo of a smile, glow of perceived similarity, and allure of attractiveness nudge them into voting for a candidate (Bailenson, Iyengar, Yee, & Collins, 2008; Rosenberg, 1987). Low-involved voters also may support candidates who look and sound presidential, a simple decision-making rule that disadvantaged female candidates over the years because women didn't fit the stereotype of the tall, seemingly strong male figure. For some low-involved voters, Trump, with his confidence and business panache, could have seemed presidential, providing them with a quick way to make their voting decision. Other strategies are also effective under low involvement. Time-honored advertising appeals like associating a candidate with pleasant images (family, rustic hometown tableau, Americana settings, or multicultural diversity) can produce positive evaluations, simply via the psychological power of association and higher-order classical conditioning (Stuart, Shimp, & Engle, 1987).

Repeated exposure to new candidates about whom little is known enhances positive affect. When voters encounter many advertisements for candidates in lower-involved elections, the mere exposure to candidates produces positive attitudes, by increasing their likability or activating the heuristic that candidates who advertise a lot are competent political figures (Grush, McKeough, & Ahlering, 1978). Just watching a lot of ads won't cause people to vote for the advertised candidates when voters are highly involved, as they bring more substantive considerations to bear in these cases. However, under low involvement, candidates with a large advertising budget who frequently beam their names to voters benefit from the simple psychology by which repetition increases positive affect. It is the same process that benefits companies that advertise soap and toothpaste, raising normative questions.

Finally, party affiliation can serve as a peripheral cue, propelling voters to vote for the candidate from their preferred political party. Voters invoke the heuristic that a candidate from their party is more likely to execute policies they support than the candidate from the opposing party. When an issue is low in salience or perceived importance, people rely on political party cues, as when Democrats prefer the Democratic candidate and Republicans their party's standard-bearer, seemingly reflexively, in the absence of knowledge of the candidate's position on specific issues (Ciuk & Yost, 2016).

Low-involved voters make decisions quickly, with little thought, invoking what Cialdini (2009) calls a "click-whirr," an automatic, machine-like decision-making strategy. They could use a party heuristic, voting for the Republican candidate because they grew up in a Republican household; employ an ethnic heuristic, casting their ballot for the Irish candidate because they link the Irish with politics; or utilize a gender cue, supporting a woman candidate because their opinion leaders say we need more women in politics, without any knowledge of whether the particular female candidate shares the voter's values or issue positions. Of course, votes based on political party, ethnicity, and gender can also reflect thoughtful, ideological-based assumptions that the candidate embraces values that will advance America, or that voting for candidates from a particular ethnicity or gender will enrich the nation by prizing diversity. This latter strategy exemplifies central processing, to be discussed below, as voters systematically process political information. Thus, identical voting behavior can reflect different psychological considerations, a tenet of the ELM and an important reason to study the psychology of political campaigns.

Normative Concerns

The psychology of low involvement raises normative issues. Some scholars praise the use of heuristics, the informational shortcuts described earlier, noting that people have neither time nor ability nor motivation to master all aspects of the political universe, but they do their best, relying on what Popkin (1991) calls "gut rationality." People reasonably turn to dependable rules of thumb, using a variety of proxies for more complicated or abstract decision-making criteria. Critics disagree, noting that reliance on heuristics can lead to misinformed decisions. Voters, particularly those low in political sophistication, can make short-circuited voting decisions that do not accurately reflect their actual political preferences (Lau & Redlawsk, 2001). Consider a steelworker who supported Trump because he liked his patriotic swagger, epitomized by Trump's "America First" slogan. If the worker also relies on subsidies or Medicaid to pay for his health insurance, he might regret his decision if Republicans approved a plan that cut subsidies and reduced Medicaid assistance. A manufacturing worker who voted for Obama in 2012 based on Democratic Party cues ("I always support the Democrat") could have been disappointed when she discovered Obama favored expanded free trade policies that cost the voter her job in the steel mills. Informational shortcuts are just that, shortcuts, and sometimes a shortcut, like judging a candidate's honesty from sensational media reports, can lead one astray. Trusting "gut checks" can led to prejudiced voting when one's "gut" is steeped in racial stereotypes.

Additional limitations in low-involvement voting emerged from an Illinois state primary election of some years back. Voters relied on a questionable heuristic—the candidate's name. Lacking involvement and motivation to follow the race, they followed their gut and feelings, preferring candidates with smooth-sounding names (Fairchild and Hart) over those with less pleasant-sounding names (Sangmeister and Pucinski). Perhaps they assumed that Fairchild and Hart, with their roll-off-the-tongue names and pro-Americana associations, were more appealing and more in sync with their interests. Perhaps they were prejudiced toward the candidates with ethnic names. It turned out that Mark Fairchild and Janice Hart were followers of the extremist and unconventional political candidate Lyndon LaRouche, a possible conspiracy theorist with unorthodox views, such as constructing a tunnel under the Bering Strait, in contrast to other candidates' more conventional views (O'Sullivan et al., 1988). Such is the danger of following peripheral cues when one is low in involvement—a relatively unusual situation, to be sure, but a cautionary tale about contemporary democracy.

High Involvement

Normative quandaries like these are less relevant when voters are highly involved in the election and capable of appreciating the political issues at stake. When the election is highly involving or personally relevant, voters think very differently about political messages than under low involvement. Concerned about how the electoral outcome could affect their pocketbooks, their employment prospects, children's economic security and their political values, they are motivated to attend closely to campaign messages. The ELM says that when voters are high in involvement and recognize the election can affect issues that bear on their own lives, they process campaign messages centrally and systematically (see Figure 12.1b). They examine whether presidential candidates have proposals that will advance voters' self-interest and personal needs. They evaluate whether candidates favor policies that, in voters' views, are good for their families and even the country as a whole. Messages are most likely to influence high-involved voters if they persuasively address voters' economic and social concerns, contain compelling policy arguments, and offer hopeful solutions to vexing issues of national concern (e.g., Ladd, 2007). Independent voters, whose lack of commitment to candidates can motivate systematic consideration of issues, can be influenced by early campaign messages, although the effects can dissipate over time (Vavreck, 2009). Contrary to popular opinion, voters are not empty vessels and campaigns aren't just circuses. Policy messages matter, but only when voters are high in involvement, concerned about the economic or symbolic issues in the campaign.

In 2008, Independent voters, who ordinarily leaned Republican, were primarily concerned with economic issues, in view of the financial crisis that befell the country. John Butler, who owned a floral shop near Youngstown, Ohio, exemplified these voters.

Living in a part of the country hit hard by the economic downturn, Butler related that he had no choice but to lay off 25 of his 26 employees and drop his health insurance policy. "I looked at my situation and realized I couldn't afford to vote for McCain. I was as shocked as anyone," he said (Belkin, 2008, p. A5). Obama won many of these Independent voters in 2008, as he blamed the Republicans for the financial crisis, offered up his plan to cure economic ills, and presented cogent appeals that resonated with highly involved, economically insecure voters.

Eight years later, self-interest came to the fore again. Highly involved working class voters, feeling ignored and marginalized by trade policies that bled manufacturing jobs, found Donald Trump's policies on trade enticing. Stark County, Ohio, an old manufacturing community south of Cleveland where voters chose Democrats in the past three presidential elections, switched to Trump in 2016. "His points really hit home for us," said Jacob Hawk, a 23-year-old electrician who voted for Obama in 2012. "A huge portion of it was just bringing jobs back to Ohio" (Tavernise, 2016, p. 14). Disgruntled with Democrats for not bringing promised jobs, viewing Clinton as pro-trade and therefore anti-manufacturing (a reasonable, but contestable, assessment), and dismayed by Clinton's lack of credibility, voters in this region of Ohio turned overwhelmingly to Trump.

Involvement is complex. When voters are high in involvement, they perceive the election is personally relevant. This can tap into other considerations besides economic, such as the degree to which candidates' positions match voters' issue stands, reflect their deeper ideologies, or even tap into deep-seated prejudices (Killian, Schoen, & Dusso, 2008; Sears, Lau, Tyler, & Allen, 1980). Thus, some highly involved Democratic voters processed campaign communications systematically, supporting Clinton for *both* economic and symbolic political reasons. They perceived that her policies advanced their economic self-interest, but liked her on a symbolic, value-based level, agreeing with her pro-choice position on abortion, and believing she would be an excellent role model as the first female U.S. president. On the other hand, some White working class voters, like Ohio's Jacob Hawk, preferred Trump because he offered a more compelling economic message than Clinton, while others favored him for symbolic reasons, such as his evocation of cultural nostalgia for a halcyon American past, or old-fashioned patriotism.

As these examples show, high-involvement central processing can call on strong political values. Few people are neutral when it comes to politics. As the ELM notes, individuals process information in biased ways when they are high in involvement. **Biased processing** occurs when voters interpret messages through the filtering lens of their own attitudes, favoring what is consistent with their viewpoint and rejecting ideas advocated by the other side (see Figure 12.1c). In some cases candidates design partisan messages on hot-button, "wedge" issues, like abortion, immigration, and gay marriage (Hillygus & Shields, 2008). These emotional messages call up voters' strong attitudes, propelling them to the polls. Such messages are controversial, even ethically question-able when they are deliberately designed to access religious or racial prejudice.

STRONG ATTITUDES, SELECTIVITY, AND SOCIAL JUDGMENTS

Attitudes on such issues as affirmative action, abortion, immigration, and gun control can be fiercely held. Voters can also display fervent loyalty to their preferred political party. Animated by a well-developed ideological worldview, voters evaluate candidates through the prisms of their political viewpoints. Strong attitudes are characterized by symbolic attachments, linkage to core social values, certainty (people are convinced their attitude is correct), and extremity (their attitudes are on the extreme ends of the political distribution). Entrenched attitudes are likely to persist over time and prove impervious to influence (Krosnick & Petty, 1995).

Strong attitudes are a blessing and a curse: They embolden people to become involved in politics and work for change, but they also can blind individuals to alternative posi-tions on the issue. When people have a strong position on an issue, they invariably see everything related to the topic through the lens of their attitude. Armed with a strong attitude, people are hardly objective, but deeply subjective and frequently unwilling to consider alternative points of view, lauding supporters and scorning opponents with a viral pen on social media. Strong partisans can be fiercely loyal to their political party, to the point of putting aside their intellectual beliefs and giving credence to the position advocated by their cherished group. Party loyalties—rooted in issue positions, but also symbolic attachments and identifications with socially significant groups that run the gamut from evangelical Christians to the NAACP—continue to exert a powerful impact on attitudes and voting behavior (Saunders & Abramowitz, 2007). Let's see how this works by examining an intriguing study.

Selective Perception

Liberals and conservatives harbor different attitudes about social welfare that flow from their values. Liberals, emphasizing a value of compassion, favor government aid to the poor, while conservatives, stressing individual responsibility, support stricter govern-ment policies toward welfare. Cohen (2003) explored how these psychological biases played out in a study of liberals' and conservatives' attitudes toward welfare. Not sur-prisingly, he found that liberal, pro-Democratic college students endorsed generous government welfare benefits for the poor, if they were told most congressional Dem-ocrats favored it. Similarly, conservative, pro-Republican college students supported a more stringent government welfare policy when informed that most congressional Republicans favored it. Here's the kicker, the intriguing finding: When liberal students were told that most congressional Democrats favored a stricter, *conservative* welfare policy, they supported it; and when conservative students learned that most congressional Republicans supported the *liberal* welfare policy, they favored it. That's right. Partisans altered their views to conform to what those on *their* side endorsed. When we hear that *our* side endorses a policy, even one we don't initially agree with, we may even be willing to change our beliefs because now it seems like it's the right policy, the one the good guys embrace. This occurs all the time in politics.

A classic example is attitudes toward health care. Conservatives once embraced the idea of an individual mandate, the notion that every American should be required to purchase insurance (provided he or she does have insurance at a workplace) or pay a financial penalty. The notion was rooted in the conservative principle that others should not be forced to bear the costs of a problem caused by a particular individual. According to conservatives, uninsured individuals who got sick and, by law, were entitled to treatment by a physician, should not be able to pass the bill for their treatment on to others with insurance (Cooper, 2012). The idea that everyone should be required to buy insurance was championed by Republican thinkers—until Obama placed it at the heart of the Affordable Care Act. Once Democrats endorsed it, the idea was anathema, another example of government overreach. Republicans now opposed an individual mandate, a notion they had championed when it had been endorsed by their side.

On the other side of the political ledger, liberals long decried the U.S. government intelligence apparatus, pointing to the willful distortion of evidence and poor quality of intelligence during the run-up to the 2003 Iraq War. They lambasted the Bush administration and CIA for errantly claiming Iraq had weapons of mass destruction, a primary reason the U.S. invaded Iraq. Yet they were more than happy to accept the views of the same intelligence apparatus when it claimed that Russia hacked email files at the Democratic National Committee to help elect Donald Trump. When CIA intelligence was touted by a Republican president, they opposed it. When it was used to suggest that a Republican president wasn't entirely legitimate because a U.S. adversary helped put him in office, they embraced it.

This illustrates **selective perception**, the psychological tendency to perceive messages so they are consistent with a strong preexisting viewpoint. Political messages—blogs, speeches, debate performances, and ads—run up against the blockage of psychological selectivity. Voters with strong partisan sentiments quickly reject positions that are at odds with their attitudes. They assimilate supportive, slightly ambiguous positions to their side, and contrast opposing views, assuming they are more different from their viewpoint than they actually are. Voters with strong partisan attitudes come to the election campaign with their minds made up, ready to pounce on weaknesses from the opposing candidate, affirm positions that support a preexisting viewpoint, and lambast Facebook friends who dare to disagree, to the point of defriending them.

A classic example of selective perception occurred on Election Night 2000, when Democratic presidential candidate Al Gore and Republican George W. Bush were locked in a tight race. However, Bush had a 1,784-vote lead in Florida. If Bush held onto his lead, he would gain enough electoral votes to win the presidential election. Gore, of course, challenged the outcome, arguing that when an election is in doubt, it is best to meticulously count the votes by hand. (He also thought this strategy could work to his advantage.) Bush's team filed a lawsuit, arguing the opposite position—that manual recounts are enormously subjective. When an automatic voting machine–conducted recount still showed Bush the winner in Florida, both sides diverged in their perceptions of the outcome. Eighty-nine percent of Bush voters believed the results that declared Bush the winner were a fair and accurate count. Democratic backers of Gore had a different view: 83 percent of Gore voters perceived that the results were neither a fair nor an accurate rendering of the vote (Berke & Elder, 2000). Thus, when people have strong attitudes, they interpret factual evidence in line with their preexisting sentiments. The same evidence could be seen in diametrically opposing ways, depending on whether it favors your side or your opponent's, or confirms what you believe or disputes your preexisting viewpoint.

SELECTIVE EXPOSURE

At the Branding Iron Roadhouse, a popular bar in Lime Ridge, Wisconsin (population 165), residents are happy to discuss the Green Bay Packers (and their dexterous quarterback, Aaron Rodgers), the unpredictable weather, and the most nutritious food for Black Angus cattle. But don't get them started on politics, because, in this town that split about 50–50 for Trump and Clinton in 2016, people are careful who they talk to and what they say, for fear of alienating a fellow beer-guzzling customer. "I try to hang around with the people that I'm used to hanging around with, people that I know share my beliefs," said Larry Mundth, a 61-year-old dairy farmer, suggesting he was a Democrat and preferred to talk with Democrats who adopted a positive outlook and were "optimistic," unlike the presumably more pessimistic Republicans (Bosman, 2017, p. 11).

Mundth, the Wisconsin resident, unwittingly exemplified a classic political communication concept, selective exposure, a cousin of selective perception described earlier. **Selective exposure** is the tendency of individuals to tune in to and prefer information that supports their existing political beliefs. It occurs when liberals flip on MSNBC's Rachel Maddow's liberal evening program or click to Facebook posts that lambast Republicans. Selective exposure operates when conservatives gravitate to Rush Limbaugh, Fox

News, and conservative news apps. It happens when you find yourself reading more posts that agree with your position on an issue, like immigration or gun control.

The concept dates back more than half a century, when early political communication researchers found that political partisans were more likely to come across material that was consistent with their preexisting attitude than disputed their viewpoint (Lazarsfeld, Berelson, & Gaudet, 1944). According to classic psychological theory, people tune in to politically congenial information because it is mentally comforting to read articles that confirm their attitudes. Reading articles on the opposite side of the issue provokes cognitive dissonance, an uncomfortable feeling that occurs when we come across information that conflicts with our attitudes. Dissonance is an unpleasant psychological state—it's not fun to hear someone disagree with a strong perspective we hold. One way to reduce dissonance that occurs when we learn others dispute our position is to locate articles and posts that affirm our preexisting viewpoint. Selective exposure offers the warm cocoon of social approval from others. Tuning in to supportive materials also occurs because it is easier to process consistent than inconsistent information (Stroud, 2014).

Selective exposure is a feature of everyday life. We live in social worlds peopled by individuals like us. Americans tend to live near and talk to others who share their points of view (Bishop, 2008). Voters are more inclined to communicate with people who share their political attitudes than with their counterparts from the other side (Mutz, 2006). People are more apt to turn to blogs, talk radio, and television news programs that support their political views than platforms that oppose their attitudes (Johnson, Bichard, & Zhang, 2009; Wicks, Wicks, & Morimoto, 2014; see Skovsgaard, Shehata, & Strömbäck, 2016 for evidence in a Swedish context).

Survey research shows that conservative Republicans are more likely to listen to conservative talk radio programs, watch Fox News, and access politically conservative websites. Liberal Democrats, by contrast, are more inclined to gravitate to liberal radio programs, watch CNN and MSNBC, and access politically liberal websites (Stroud, 2008). Although not all voters seek out congenial political information from media, partisans do. Sixty-four percent of conservative Republicans utilize at least one politically conservative media outlet, in comparison to only 26 percent of liberal Democrats. Seventy-six percent of liberal Democrats consume at least one liberal media genre, in comparison to 43 percent of conservative Republicans (Stroud, 2008). Conservative talk show host Rush Limbaugh attracts primarily like-minded Republicans. In research conducted some years back, but likely to hold today, 70 percent of Limbaugh's listeners reported they were conservative, and less than 10 percent of Democrats reported that they ever listened to Limbaugh's program (Jamieson & Cappella, 2008). Partisans' political predispositions seem to predict their selection of diverse political media (Stroud, 2008).

This does not prove selective exposure. Perhaps Republicans listen to Limbaugh because the businesses that advertise on his program sell products that Republican entrepreneurs need to purchase. Maybe Democrats are drawn to NPR because NPR news stories furnish information about government that Democratic listeners, who are public sector employees, need to perform their jobs effectively. We need evidence from controlled experiments that show partisan political attitudes, rather than extraneous factors, cause people to prefer supportive information. Two studies provide this evidence.

In an experimental study, Iyengar and Hahn (2009) developed a series of identical news stories that were attributed to Fox News, CNN, National Public Radio, or the BBC. Research participants read a series of headlines that were attributed to one of the four news outlets. Individuals were asked to indicate which of the four news reports they would like to read. As selective exposure predicted, conservatives and Republicans preferred news reports from Fox. They avoided stories from the more liberal NPR and CNN. Liberals opted to read stories from CNN and NPR. They avoided Fox.

In another controlled study with real-world overtones, Stroud (2011) gave research participants the opportunity to browse political magazines in a waiting room. To thank them for participation in the study, participants were told they could choose a free magazine subscription. True to selective exposure, conservatives and Republicans were more inclined to select subscriptions to politically conservative magazines, while liberals and Democrats were more likely to select subscriptions to liberal magazines.

Living in echo chambers that reverberate with their political positions, partisans can feel even more strongly about their worldviews when they obtain information from congenial political media sources (Jamieson & Cappella, 2008; Stroud, 2010, 2011). As discussed in Chapter 9, the media don't consistently bend left or right. Although the news does contain biases, and some are ideologically based, a simple characterization of the news as liberal or conservative is factually incorrect. No matter, political leaders frequently accuse the media of favoring a particular bias, and this in turn can cause partisans to attribute **hostile media bias** to news outlets. This occurs when people with strong political views presume media coverage is biased against their side and in favor of their opponents (Vallone, Ross, & Lepper, 1985; Perloff, 2015). Hostile media bias can intensify efforts to tune in to articles, posts, and media outlets that favor "my" side over my adversaries. If I am a conservative and believe mainstream media is hopelessly biased against my side, I derogate articles that appear in conventional media, ridiculing the media itself by calling it "lamestream media," and tune in more aggressively to Fox News, Breitbart, and conservative websites. If I'm a liberal and perceive that only a handful of news organizations are politically aware or "woke," maintaining that most news media display right-of-center biases, I will make sure I watch MSNBC and read *The Huffington Post* or Daily Kos online.

The problem with hostile media biases, from a normative perspective, is that individuals, particularly those with strong political attitudes, can end up distrusting and doubting all news. While it is, without question, good to be skeptical about information you receive from news reports, one can take this (like any extreme view) too far. If people think the news is biased against their side, they can reject any presentation of factual information, even when a report is accurate and provides evidence disconfirming their belief. Hostile media biases prevent them from gaining useful information they need as citizens to make important political choices. To the extent that they selectively gravitate to like-minded media outlets that reaffirm their point of view, they are, as the philosopher John Stuart Mill (1859/2009) famously said, "deprived of the opportunity of exchanging error for truth" (p. 20).

"Seek and You Will Find"

In cases such as those described above, a series of politically reinforcing spirals can ensue. People tune in to like-minded political content, and the content propels them to feel even more strongly that their side is right (Slater, 2007; Knobloch-Westerwick et al., 2015). Media exposure leads to strengthening of partisan beliefs, which leads to a preference for congenial media, and renewed exposure in turn produces even stronger attitudes on the topic. It all resembles a spiraling curve that winds around the attitude, tightening the grip, producing a more polarized, less tolerant position on the issue.

Consider the contentious issue of global warming. Conservative news channels like Fox News tend to question evidence for global warming, while liberal news outlets like MSNBC and mainstream channels like CNN (along with most environmental scientists) treat it as a reality caused by human beings. Lauren Feldman and her colleagues (2014) looked at media use and beliefs about global warming at two points in time: the fall of 2008 and the spring of 2011. In 2008, as selective exposure would predict, use of conservative media channels, such as Fox News and Rush Limbaugh's radio program, was associated with skepticism about global warming and lack of support for government policies to reduce global warming effects. Also, in line with selective exposure, use of more liberal media in 2008, like MSNBC, CNN, and National Public Radio, was related to belief in global warming and favoring government taking steps to reduce it. The researchers then reinterviewed survey respondents some three years later, asking them about their media use and global warming beliefs. Here is where the process gets interesting.

Use of conservative media in 2008 enhanced use of conservative media channels in 2011. Similarly, tuning in to more liberal media in 2008 strengthened use of liberal media channels in 2011. Reliance on conservative and liberal media in turn contributed to stronger global warming beliefs in 2011, in line with partisan biases. Conservatives were more critical of global warming, liberals more convinced of its severity. It is a cyclical process: Use of like-minded media strengthens beliefs and causes you to gravitate to partisan media channels; consumption of the media then produces even stronger partisan beliefs. It is a closed system. A biblical "Ask and it will be given to you; seek and you will find" phenomenon seems to be occurring. But this creates a chamber of echoes, where people hear only their side and "may become more and more isolated on their own ideological islands in which certain facts are accepted while others are questioned and discarded." It therefore hampers "much-needed progress toward policy solutions to important problems such as global warming," Feldman and her colleagues observed (2014, p. 607).

Selectivity in the Social Media World

How pervasive is selective exposure today? Are there conditions under which it is less likely to occur? These issues have sparked debate (Garrett, 2009a; Garrett et al., 2014; Holbert, Garrett, & Gleason, 2010). While partisans can display preferences for opinion-congruent information (Stroud, 2014; Camaj, 2014), there is scant evidence that they *selectively avoid* opposing perspectives (Jang, 2014), and in some instances people seek out ideas from the other side (Garrett, 2009b; Garrett, Carnahan, & Lynch, 2013; Johnson & Kaye, 2013; Weeks, Ksiazek, & Holbert, 2016), particularly if they don't have strong political views (see Camaj, 2014 and Edgerly, 2015). In many instances, people remain interested in a variety of perspectives, tuning in to general-interest political media outlets for news (Weeks et al., 2016).

When it comes to social media, the picture is more complicated than frequently assumed. On the one hand, an intensive analysis of Facebook showed that selective exposure is the main determinant of information diffusion, promoting the development of politically homogeneous, polarized online communities (Del Vicario et al., 2016). So, selective exposure lives on social media. But there is evidence on the other side as well. People come across plenty of non-supportive political ideas on Facebook's News Feed (Manjoo, 2015). Facebook, a primary source of news for at least 30 percent of Americans, can provide people with diverse sources of information, making it difficult to ignore information with which one disagrees (Messing & Westwood, 2014). In a study of more than 10 million partisan Facebook users, researchers found that almost 29 percent of the news stories that appear on Facebook's News Feed seemed to present viewpoints that conflicted with their political beliefs. About 23 percent of individuals' online friends harbor opposing political views (Manjoo, 2015; see also Liang, 2014 and Webster, 2014). Intriguingly (and complexly), social media channels that promote political homogeneity also offer considerable exposure to opposing points of view (Flaxman, Goel, & Rao, 2016).

Thus, selective exposure is a psychological force to be reckoned with. It is facilitated by social media algorithms that put people in touch with content they have viewed in the past. Yet it seems most likely to emerge when people have strong political attitudes and are certain their attitudes are correct (Stroud, 2014). Like political polarization, which is driven by partisans, who increasingly dislike their counterparts from the other side (Lelkes, 2016), selective exposure to like-minded information is most frequently found among those with strong, passionate attitudes.

Selectively tuning in to platforms that reinforce their viewpoints, partisans can live in different "fact universes" (Fallows, 2016, p. 13), gaining access to social media that showcase "facts" they support (free trade has destroyed manufacturing) and rarely coming across evidence that disputes their preferred position (i.e., automation has hurt manufacturing as much, if not more, than most trade). Armed with their version of the facts (sometimes from politically congenial fake news sites they trust; see Weeks & Garrett, 2014) and discrediting more reliable information, people can become ensconced in their political silos. As a result of use of biased news sites, they hold inaccurate political beliefs (Garrett, Weeks, & Neo, 2016) and adhere to them tenaciously, exacerbating polarization (see Figure 12.2).

Efforts to correct these political misperceptions can be remarkably unsuccessful. What's more, almost paradoxically, the attempt to correct these mistaken beliefs can strengthen them, a result of what Nyhan and Reifler (2010) call a "backfire effect." "Corrective information in news reports may fail to reduce misperceptions and can sometimes increase them for the ideological group most likely to hold those misperceptions," the researchers concluded (p. 323; see also Wojcieszak & Price, 2010; Skurnik, Yoon, Park, & Schwarz, 2005; Thorson, 2016). As a result of selective perception and the tenacious motivation to confirm biases that come under question, efforts to aggressively counteract such misperceptions may only strengthen their impact (Ignatius, 2016). These backfire effects are most likely to occur among extreme partisans. Those with more moderate views (most voters) may not encounter false news, or if they do, are less motivated to remember their content.

It is important to keep this in perspective. Fake news does not have demonstrably large effects. Selective exposure to ideologically congruent facts or avoidance of evidence that challenges a preexisting viewpoint is most pervasive among committed partisans, those with strong political beliefs. Alas, partisans, with loud viral voices, can dominate conversations on social media, increasing animus and exacerbating polarization.

Normative Evaluation

Scholars frequently paint selective exposure in dark colors, focusing on its negative effects. It turns out that there is a silver lining. Tuning in to media outlets that reinforce

Figure 12.2 Political polarization, where more voters are on the extreme ends of the political distribution and are hostile to their opponents from the other side, has been increasing in recent years. Driven by partisans, it can be exacerbated by selective exposure to social media sites that support voters' preexisting sentiments. Selective exposure has its positive features too, as it can propel participation in political activities.

Getty Images

your point of view has positive influences as well. It energizes you, strengthens your core beliefs, and propels you to get involved in political campaigns. In an engaging analysis, Natalie Jomini Stroud (2011) found that conservatives and Republicans who use conservative media genres, and liberals and Democrats who rely on liberal news programs, are particularly likely to participate in politics. "Partisans using likeminded media are simply more active in politics. They seem to be motivated and energized by partisan media," she notes, adding that "partisan media have a place in a democracy. They can unite likeminded individuals, help them to organize their political thinking,

Figure 12.2 *(Continued)*

and motivate them to participate" (pp. 176, 183). Other research also finds that exposure to pro-attitudinal news enhances political participation, suggesting that selective exposure to congenial cable shows and social media posts can exert salutary effects (Wojcieszak, Bimber, Feldman, & Stroud, 2016; Hasell & Weeks, 2016).

Turning to media outlets that reinforce your point of view has positive effects. It helps you identify differences between the two parties (Arceneaux & Johnson, 2013), access your beliefs, and translate a passionate attitude into political action.

There are many downsides, though. As discussed throughout this book, democracy, particularly the deliberative type, emphasizes an open-minded exploration of different perspectives through communication. Ideally, this involves a give-and-take persuasion, in which citizens listen to different points of view. Unfortunately, political persuasion has become about talking points, preaching to the already converted. As Miller (2005) noted, "marshaling a cause to persuade those who start from a different perspective is a lost art. Honoring what's right in the other side's argument seems a superfluous thing that can only cause trouble, like an appendix." This kind of persuasion—which honors what is right in our adversary's arguments—sadly eludes us. As Mutz (2002) puts it, "if people are surrounded by people who think much like they do, they will be less aware of the legitimate arguments on the other side of contemporary political controversies" (p. 122).

Social media has exacerbated the problem. News aggregators readily customizes content to fit individuals' preferences, and social media algorithmically amplifies "ideological segregation by automatically recommending content an individual is likely to agree with" (Flaxman et al., 2016, p. 299). People then share these posts with similar others, creating "filter bubbles" (Pariser, 2011) or environments that are politically congenial, segregated, and oh-so-reinforcing of what they already believe. This deprives citizens of alternative viewpoints and even discordant facts, which can help them develop habits of the heart that encourage questioning, not blind acceptance, of government orthodoxy.

Exposure to politically congenial media content reinforces partisan biases, increasing people's certainty that their extreme attitudes are correct; it bolsters political polarization, inducing biased perceptions of public opinion, further reducing partisans' willingness to compromise their positions (Levendusky 2013; Stroud, 2010, 2011; Tsfati, Stroud, & Chotiner, 2014; Tsfati & Chotiner, 2016). "Today, in a world of a twenty-four-hour news cycle, stories can reverberate more rapidly through the information environment in a way that was not possible before," Matthew Levendusky observes (2013, p. 157). Exposed primarily to information from their side, attending to articles that disparage the other political party, partisans may see more polarization than there is, perceiving opponents on the other side as more extreme than they actually are (Levendusky & Malhotra, 2016). Partisan animus, encouraged by selective exposure and perception, can intensify elite polarization, encouraging politicians to take extreme positions to reach their base.

Vexing questions arise. How does one balance the need for dedicated political activism, emboldened by passionate belief in the correctness of one's own side, with an appreciation of different points of view? How does one reconcile the realization that people who see different viewpoints are more tolerant and less angry, but less likely to roll up their shirtsleeves to partake in politics? (Mason, 2016; Mutz, 2006). How do you achieve a balance between communications that reinforce partisans' perspectives, thus encouraging political participation, with those that challenge their viewpoints, spurring political reflection? (Lee, Hwak, & Campbell, 2015). These are classic conundrums in political communication, layered over with the instantaneity, ubiquity, and animus of social media.

Social Judgment Theory and Political Persuasion

All this is interesting, from an academic perspective. From a political perspective, the question involves persuasion: how to harness knowledge of strong attitudes in the service of influence and winning election. This returns us to the focus of the chapter—political persuasion—and brings up a classic theory of social judgments and attitudes.

Persuasion theorists emphasize that the best way to influence a strongly held attitude is to appreciate its dynamics and understand its underlying structure. Nearly half a century ago, psychologists Muzafer and Carolyn Sherif (1967) developed a social judgment theory approach to study persuasion and social attitudes. **Social judgment theory** emphasizes that people do not objectively evaluate a communication based on the merits of the arguments. Instead, they compare the advocated position with their own viewpoint. If the communicator is generally in sync with what they believe, they accept the message and may even feel stronger about the issue. If the speaker takes a position that seems to diverge from their opinion, they distance or contrast the speaker's position from their own and reject the communicator's arguments. The lesson for political candidates is clear: Don't try to change voters' attitude about an issue, particularly a hot-button topic like abortion or guns. Instead, try to convince voters that you share their attitude on the topic. Be careful what you say, lest voters interpret your statement as indicating general disagreement with their position, leading them to reject your candidacy. Appeal to voters in your base with strong, strident ("red-meat," though why not "green-veggie"?) appeals. Employ a battery of message strategies to influence the undecided.

According to social judgment theory, attitudes consist of a spectrum of evaluations—a range of acceptable and unacceptable positions, as well as positions toward which the individual has no strong commitment, is ambivalent, or is undecided. The *latitude of rejection* contains those positions that the individual finds objectionable, including the most objectionable position. The *latitude of acceptance* includes of all those positions on an issue that an individual finds acceptable, including the most acceptable position. Lurking between these two regions is the *latitude of noncommitment*, which consists of those positions on which the individual has preferred to remain noncommittal. This is the arena of the "don't know," "not sure," and "haven't made up my mind"—the classic undecided voter.

Latitude of Rejection

Candidates know they have failed when a message falls into the latitude of rejection, becoming the political kiss of death, causing voters to reject their candidacy. This is one reason candidates equivocate and avoid taking strong positions they believe, but which alienate key constituencies. Embracing these views can get them into hot viral water, their comments shared endlessly on YouTube. One can lament politicians' reluctance to speak their mind and admire outsider leaders like Bernie Sanders. However concern about political landmines remains a fact of public life. For example, as a candidate and president, Obama walked a delicate line on the issue of race, mindful that if he mentioned the issue too fervently he would be rejected by some White voters who ambivalently supported him in 2008. However, if he failed to speak out on racial prejudice, African Americans would view his presidency as a lost opportunity.

Obama struggled with the racial quandary throughout his presidency. He expressed empathy with the parents of Trayvon Martin, when their son was tragically killed in Florida for reasons that many thought were rooted in racial prejudice. "If I had a son, he'd look like Trayvon," Obama said, with much compassion. But, acting on the advice of media staffers, he declined to appear on Black Entertainment Television during his first six months of office. "I'm not the president of Black America. I'm the president of the United States of America," he emphasized (Kantor, 2012).

In these ways, Obama was following the precepts of social judgment theory, which warns of the perils of taking a position that is politically objectionable to key voting blocs. Selective perception complicates matters. Even a nuanced appeal that nonetheless contains an untoward word, the drop of ambiguity, or an expression seen as hostile to in-group members can be viewed as unequivocally negative by staunch partisan supporters, leading to rejection of a candidacy. Thus, candidates spend more energies, in social judgment theory terms, focusing on voting blocs that fall into the latitudes of acceptance and non-commitment.

Latitude of Acceptance

For supportive, latitude of acceptance voters, candidates develop messages to reinforce these voters' positive attitudes, encouraging them to translate a favorable attitude into voting behavior. In political terms, these persuasive appeals are known as **mobilization, or getting out the base.**

Communication plays an important part in voter mobilization. A particularly effective method to mobilize voters in many elections is simply "contact from an enthusiastic human being" (Lizza, 2012, p. 66). Research shows that voters who have been interpersonally contacted by campaign volunteers are often more likely to vote than those who have not been contacted. Re-contacting people who indicated an intention to vote increases the likelihood they will turn out at the polls (Green & Gerber, 2008). By reminding voters of their commitment to vote for a particular candidate, campaigns can put the idea at the top of their awareness, activate democratic norms, and help people translate attitude into action. Even having a presidential campaign field office in a community can increase a candidate's vote share, although the overall impact is relatively small (Masket, Sides, & Vavreck, 2016).

Social media is quickly complementing or replacing these old strategies. In an intriguing field experiment, researchers randomly assigned individuals 18 years and older in the U.S. who clicked onto Facebook on November 2, 2010—the day of U.S. midterm congressional elections—to one of three groups (Bond et al., 2012). Those assigned to the social message group saw a message at the top of their news feeds that encouraged them to vote, offered a link to nearby polling places, displayed a counter indicating the number of Facebook users who reported they previously voted, and showed profile pictures of users' Facebook friends who had clicked a "I Voted" button. Those in the informational group viewed the message, polling place information, the counter showing the number of Facebook users reported previously voted, but no pictures of faces of friends. The control group did not receive a message.

Individuals in the social message group were more likely than informational message users to click the polling place link and the "I Voted" button. This could reflect social desirability effects—a desire to say one did the socially correct thing—rather than actual voting. After reviewing actual public voting records, the researchers found that users who received the social message were significantly more likely to vote than those who received the informational message or no message at all. A social contagion effect, fueled by similarity between friends and users, seems to have occurred, helping explain why pictures of friends increased perceived and actual voting. The social friendship cues activated civic duty or a social norm (through either central or peripheral processes), or exerted an impact via conformity pressures. To be sure, the study was conducted during the early years of the political Facebook era, when its novelty might have contributed to the effect. Encouragement to vote from Facebook friends might not have the same impact in a hotly contested presidential or highly involved election, where partisan ties could be more consequential. However, the findings indicate that social media mobilization can work, suggesting that contemporary technologies could encourage participation in various elections (Jones et al., 2017). From a political persuasion perspective, they suggest that political mobilization can be an effective tool to persuade supportive voters to turn out at the polls (though it remains possible—and troubling—that targeted voters may be responding peripherally to a conformist appeal).

These types of communication effects have not been lost on political campaigns. During the 2012 general election campaign, campaigns relentlessly mined voters' personal information, hoping to tailor persuasive messages that fit them like a political glove. With the aid of demographic data campaign specialists had purchased, consultants had access to swing voters' age, race, party affiliation, and even shopping preferences. Campaign workers also asked supporters to grant them access to their Facebook profiles to offer a glimpse of their interpersonal networks. Armed with this information, a union supporter in Ohio who visited a Big Labor website was asked to contact a colleague from work who presumably might be susceptible to a pro-Obama appeal from a trustworthy, politically similar source (Duhigg, 2012). Of course, in 2016, Trump eschewed these strategies, preferring straightforward political marketing techniques that relied on emotive tweets to mobilize supporters and capitalized on favorable television news coverage to broaden his political base. By contrast, Democratic, pro-Clinton consultants, who preferred microtargeting strategies, witnessed firsthand that sometimes the snazziest, most high-tech strategy can fail if it does not link up with voters' needs.

Latitude of Noncommitment

The most complicated persuasive appeals are directed at undecided, ambivalent voters whose political attitudes are in the latitude of noncommitment. These can be highly involved voters who centrally process campaign appeals, filtering messages through their preexisting political attitudes.

With 4 in 10 voters having trouble making up their minds because they believed neither Trump nor Clinton would be a good president, many Americans weighed the pros of Clinton, Trump, and none of the above (Williamson, 2016). There was more cognitive complexity—amid recognition of each candidate's foibles—than partisan commentators frequently assumed. Some voters thought Trump lacked the temperament to be president, leaned toward Clinton, but perhaps turned against her when the FBI director raised the specter in late October that new emails might contain classified information.

(They didn't.) After the election, some Clinton supporters groused that the late-campaign FBI scare pushed undecided voters into Trump's camp—a plausible but as yet unproven assertion. On the other hand, there is evidence suggesting that some people actually believed Russian-spread fake news critical of Clinton, a belief that could have hurt Clinton toward the end of the campaign, though this too remains interesting, but unproven (Osnos, Remnick, & Yaffa, 2017).

Exemplifying ambivalence, other undecided voters liked the prospect that Clinton would become the first female president, but worried that her pro-trade policies would hurt their families. Others, like Jacob Hawk, the 23-year-old Ohio electrician who voted for Obama in 2012 because "he inspired people to be better," flipped to Trump because he liked his economic program to bring jobs back to Ohio (Tavernise, 2016, p. 14). Still other voters, particularly in the reliably blue states, stuck with Clinton, because they were offended by Trump's statements or found her long record of experience persuasive. To influence undecided and latitude of noncommitment voters, candidates employ a rich potpourri of frames that call on ELM, political marketing, and persuasion approaches emphasizing matching a message to an uncertain voter's needs.

Throughout the campaign, politicians must balance principle with pragmatics, becoming "shape-shifting" communicators who showcase, as Machiavelli extolled, "a flexible disposition, varying as fortune and circumstances dictate" (Saward, 2014, p. 723). It is the classic conundrum of politics, adapted to the social media age. Politicians must adapt their messages to their audiences, but if they do this too glibly, they become unctuous, the epitome of what people hate in politics. If they do it too little, they do not appeal to broad constituencies and fail to win election.

Persuasion continues after the election, extending into the White House—part of what has been called the never-ending persuasion campaign that characterizes contemporary politics. The next section explores the content and effects of presidential communication, viewed through a different perspective—the time-honored frameworks of rhetoric and presidential speech.

AFTER THE ELECTION: PERSUASION AND THE PRESIDENCY

Historical Foundations

Politics is largely a word game. Politicians rise to power because they can talk persuasively to voters and political elites. Once in power, their daily activities are largely verbal—commands, dialogues, debates, formulation of proposals, laws, orders, decisions, and legal opinions.

(Graber, 1981, p. 195)

Political language occupies a prominent spot in the modern presidency. It is through words that candidates campaign for election, presidents try to gain support for policy initiatives, and citizens reflect on the nation's storied and stained historical past. Although the focus of this chapter and section has been on the persuasive influences of electoral communications, it is helpful to examine a related, if broader, issue—the ways that presidents harness rhetoric, or political language, to persuade the public to adopt policy initiatives.

The study of political language is one of the oldest areas of academic study, calling on classical and contemporary rhetoric, as articulated by Aristotle, Burke, and contemporary political communication scholars (Jamieson, 1988; Coe, 2014). **Political rhetoric** focuses on the verbal content, argumentation, symbolic components, and stylistic features of public communication designed to persuade. Although the term "rhetoric" has a bad name, conjuring equivocal, platitude-filled, consultant-driven speeches, it has a grand history, if one reflects on the eloquence of Lincoln, Franklin Delano Roosevelt, John F. Kennedy, and Ronald Reagan. Rhetoric is also a field of classical academic study, expanded and extended to fit the present day.

During the late 18th and early 19th centuries, presidents rarely gave speeches, accustomed to post-Enlightenment written communication and fearing that persuasive speeches might incite mob violence. In these early days, leaders conveyed their opinions through newspapers written and distributed by political parties. As stump speeches became an accepted method of presidential campaigning, candidate addresses became more common, though, with the eloquent exception of Lincoln, they were not employed to influence public opinion or policy. This changed in the 20th century, with the development of a more expansive view of the presidency, new electronic technologies, and the recognition that presidential success required mobilizing public opinion.

Following in the rhetorical footsteps of his distant cousin, the early 20th-century president Theodore Roosevelt, Franklin Delano Roosevelt harnessed the dominant medium of his times, radio, to build unity and an agenda for his programs. Blessed with a melodious voice, FDR had the ability to inspire confidence and trust, his voice like an intimate friend, capable of inspiring faith and moving people to tears when he spoke of poverty and the suffering experienced by families whose sons died during the Second World War (Euchner, 1990).

In the media age that followed, Kennedy adapted the presidency to the new visual medium, harnessing television to deliver important speeches and displaying a 1960s late-night talk show host's comfort before the cameras in his televised press conferences.

If Kennedy fundamentally introduced television to the presidency, Reagan consummated the marriage. Reagan appreciated the grammar and syntax of the small screen, leading Jamieson (1988) to observe that "Reagan is to television what corned beef is to rye" (p. 119; see Figure 12.3). Unlike his predecessor, Jimmy Carter, who spoke in complex, often convoluted language, Reagan spoke in short sentences not weighted down by modifying structures, his speeches scoring high in verbal activity, momentum, and optimism (Hart, 1984). He was the first president to systematically adapt his speech to fit the narrative requirements of the small screen, an easy transition for him given his early career as an actor and host of a 1950s TV show. When people say Reagan was a "great communicator" (the term became a cliché in the 1980s), they have in mind his use of four rhetorical attributes that are now commonly employed by presidents, as Jamieson (1988) explained.

Figure 12.3 Ronald Reagan was the first president to systematically adapt his televised speeches to the narrative requirements of the small screen, speaking in short, optimistic sentences, personifying themes, and activating common visual experiences. Critics lamented that he created an illusion of intimacy, offering up a speechwriter's words as if they were his own.

Getty Images

First, Reagan called on *televisual props*, showing as well as telling. Rather than activating people's imaginations by quoting the words of Washington and Jefferson, Reagan instructed the television medium to do people's cognitive work for them; images of the Washington Monument and Jefferson Memorial appeared as Reagan spoke of the city's history. Second, Reagan *personified themes*, using ordinary Americans to illustrate the major themes of televised addresses. When discussing American heroes, he made the abstract concrete by describing citizens like Lenny Skutnik, who dove into the Potomac River to rescue a woman who survived an airplane crash. Third, he accessed *common visual experiences*, building a case based on collective memories common to the culture, drawing on popular novels, movies, and TV dramas. Fourth, rather than reciting facts or policy arguments, Reagan relied on *dramatic narrative*, connecting his plans with American mythology, retelling stories of self-reliance, harnessing time-honored optimism, and placing the American people, rather than himself, at the center of his political narrative. His approach fit television to a tee, congealing with the medium's preference for simple stories and human drama. He spoke simply, with concrete imagery. "We have every right to dream heroic dreams," Reagan said, in one poignant speech.

> Those who say that we're in a time when there are no heroes, they just don't know where to look. You can see heroes every day going in and out of factory gates . . . Their patriotism is deep. Their values sustain our national life.
>
> (Hart, 1984, p. 228)

Appealing as it was, Reagan's rhetoric raised political communication quandaries. Critics pointed to his failure to employ conventional argumentation, a preference for television-style visual exemplars, and reliance on patriotic schmaltz. They argued that he pulled the wool over the eyes of the public, inducing Americans to believe that all was good when pressing problems, like economic inequality, remained. Reagan's admirers demurred, viewing the criticism as snobbish and elitist. They countered that critics failed to appreciate how Reagan's majestic words and pictures they called up congealed with the medium. They objected to the charge that he manipulated the public, arguing that this castigated the preferences of millions of his supporters, and it was insulting to suggest that the public is putty in the hands of a presidential communicator.

The debate about Reagan raises interesting issues about presidential leadership that remain relevant today. To the extent that presidential communication in a media age involves mastering the media, Reagan experienced great success. He communicated emotions gracefully and his speeches—poignant, eloquently tailored to the occasion—helped frame his policies. Yet on another level, one feels unsettled, recognizing that Reagan never wrote his speeches, relied on speechwriters to craft his messages, and excelled at delivering messages others wrote. He cultivated "an ability both to create the illusion of eye contact with an unseen audience and to converse with a camera," offering up a speechwriter's words as if they were his own, creating an "illusion of spontaneity"—a small, but not unsubstantial, political deception (Jamieson, 1988, p. 132).

A Public, Rhetorical Presidency

From the 1960s on, presidents increasingly recognized that presidential power rested on persuasion and social influence—in the ability to break bread, transact bargains, even threaten and coerce, as Lyndon Johnson famously did in the 1960s to gain congressional approval of Great Society legislation. But presidential power has declined since Johnson's time. The number of political layers—ideological groups, business lobbies, and activist organizations, all cultivating supporters on social media—has expanded. Reverence for the presidency has declined. As Whicker noted back in 1993, "American government is so complex and divided, and society is so pluralistic, presidents have only limited power. Their major power stems as much from opportunities to persuade key audiences as from formal powers" (p. 114).

A foundation of this power is rhetoric—verbal, symbolic persuasion. Scholars have noted that we have a rhetorical presidency (Tulis, 1987), a strategic presidency (Edwards, 2009), and a public presidency (Edwards, 1983), where presidents must "go public" (Kernell, 1993), making their case to the people, marketing their policies to different constituencies, and hoping to use public opinion as a cudgel to influence Congress. Scholars have studied these issues, examining how presidents (a) broadly use rhetoric in ritualistic speech at events ranging from national holidays to grief-laden eulogies (Hart, 1987); (b) call on specific forms of political language (for example, optimistic words, spoken with the ringing rhetoric of freedom, as well as religiously focused rhetoric; Coe, 2007; Hart, 1984; Domke & Coe, 2008); and (c) employ different rhetorical genres, depending on the generic occasion or context (e.g., inaugural addresses, State of the Union speeches, war rhetoric, and farewell addresses; see Coe & Neumann, 2011).

The inaugural address is one of the most significant occasions of presidential address. During inaugurals, presidents hone rhetoric to achieve tangible and symbolic purposes. They seek to unify the citizenry, constituting the audience as "the people." They reaffirm time-honored national values and articulate the major principles that will guide their administration, linking values to particular policies. More broadly, they call on the past, focus on the present, and stretch toward the future (Campbell & Jamieson, 2008). Inaugurals have famously articulated visions, with moving aphorisms, spanning FDR's "the only thing we have to fear is fear itself," Kennedy's rhythmic "ask not what your country can do for you, ask what you can do for your country," and Reagan's "government is not the solution to our problem; government is the problem."

Inaugurals set the tone of presidential policymaking. In his first inaugural, Obama spoke of "a new era of responsibility" that built on the decades-old liberal democratic order that presumed America would transcend its own interests to uplift its allies and countries in need. By contrast, Donald Trump, in a forthright speech with simple plain language—and light on flowery speech and metaphors—emphasized economic nationalism, unabashedly putting patriotism and "America first." He eschewed humility in the wake of a bruising electoral campaign, departing from his predecessors, and chose not to extend an olive branch to his electoral foes, preferring instead to offer an "I alone can fix it" braggadocio that appealed to his many marginalized followers, while alienating his foes (Bruni, 2017, p. 5). Obama's and Trump's different rhetorical messages shaped their divergent foreign and economic policies, even as events overtook their plans.

When presidential speeches succeed (and they don't always exert their intended impact), presidential words do, as well as say (Campbell & Jamieson, 2008). Official and ceremonial speeches can "constitute" or create the symbolic framework for a president's term in office, set the terms of political discourse, and, even more broadly, define the actual institution of the presidency, as Coe (2014) helpfully notes. In short, words are not just objects hurled into the air; they matter, framing presidential policy in ways that advance democracy or, alternatively, serve as Orwellian obfuscators that enable leaders to strategically avoid pressing problems and maintain their grip on the levers of power.

Presidents vary in their style of speech. Some (to their detriment) favor complex phrases (Jimmy Carter), others enjoy simple words (Reagan) or plain upbeat speech (George W. Bush) while still others, like Obama, emphasize empathy and commonality (Hart, Childers, & Lind, 2013). The most recent, Trump, has favored plain language and short emotive Twitter bursts.

Limits and Effects of Presidential Rhetoric

The foregoing discussion assumes that presidential communication exerts substantive influences on public opinion. Social judgment theory and selective biases remind us of the limits of political rhetoric, a theme developed by Edwards (2009), who emphasizes that, for all the pomp and circumstance, presidential speeches (or YouTube videos or tweets) are frequently unable to change strongly held political attitudes. Divided government, where members of the opposition party dominate Congress, blocking presidential initiatives, has impeded the effectiveness of White House rhetorically based campaigns (Edwards, 2003). The multiplicity of media platforms makes it difficult for the president to reach, let alone influence the public.

But if we look at more subtle effects, we glimpse a different picture. First, presidential speeches can draw people together, helping cement a national identity by invoking time-honored values. Speeches on the occasion of national tragedies, like George W. Bush's national address after 9/11, can transform a multiplicity of private individuals into a committed citizenry, bound by grief, determined take steps to preserve and protect the nation. Obama's speeches after the Newtown and Charleston massacres may not have changed attitudes toward gun violence, but they reconstituted individuals as public citizens, accessing a common American identity (although their unifying, constitutive effects were stronger on pro-gun control Democrats than pro-gun rights Republicans). Especially today, during a time of multiple niche media, where individuals gravitate to their own media platforms—cable entertainment television, social media posts, and live-streaming interactive apps—a presidential speech that can transform privately consumed individuals into publicly focused citizens, if only for a time, has exerted an important political impact. Of course, the positive effects are frequently diluted by selective perceptions, where partisan supporters post only portions that congeal with their values and reject the rest.

A second effect of presidential communication is on agenda-building and framing. Obama's speeches about health reform in 2009 helped shape and build an agenda that led to policy reform. George W. Bush's speeches in the immediate aftermath of 9/11 persuasively framed the attacks as an assault on freedom, while taking pains to emphasize that the U.S. was not at war with Muslims, but with those who committed terrorist acts in the name of Allah. While a president cannot change long-held values or partisan attitudes with a single message, the chief executive can influence public opinion. Presidents can demonstrate that the White House embraces a position consistent with American values. They can harness partisan cues that bring voters from their party into the fold and counter frames articulated by leaders from the political opposition or foreign leaders, helping reframe the debate in ways congenial with White House goals. When presidents promote policy proposals that the public likes, they increase the odds that a recalcitrant Congress will approve the legislation (Canes-Wrone, 2006).

Rhetorical Challenges Today

Presidents have more difficulty reaching a mass audience than they did when three broadcast television networks and a handful of elite newspapers ruled the roost (e.g., Young & Perkins, 2005). Citizens may not hear their speeches in their entirety, but only in snippets, and, as noted earlier, they may only hear snippets that support their preexisting sentiments. Presidents, inevitably molding rhetoric to the technology of the times, run the risk that ever more entertaining marketing attempts, such as Obama's promotion of his health care plan on Zach Galifianakis's bawdy Internet program,

"Between Two Ferns," diminish the majesty of the office. On the other hand, in an era dominated by social media, presidents have no choice but to adapt their messages to online media platforms.

We now enter a new chapter with a president who uses modern technology, Twitter, eliding the mainstream media, giving him control of the message, allowing him to reach Americans directly. Twitter is also a platform that is remarkably superficial, raising questions about making policy with "Twitter bursts and offhand remarks" (Shear & Glanz, 2016, p. A1). For example, when, as president-elect in December 2016, Trump tweeted that "the United States must greatly strengthen and expand its nuclear capability," condensing to 140 characters a range of complex interpretations and policy options, there were many questions. By "greatly strengthen" did he mean to modernize U.S. nuclear weapons, expand them qualitatively, or deploy them in closer proximity to Eastern European adversaries? By "expand" did he mean move nuclear warheads from stockpiles in reserve to active deployment, or build and deploy new nuclear weapons? (Fisher, 2016, p. A17). His language, what he meant, and how it was interpreted in the U.S., Russia, and China carried enormous implications for U.S. policy and whether it would trigger an arms race, or push Russia and China to the bargaining table.

Trump's frequent use of assurances like "totally," as well as "jumpy inserts and repetition—speech as montage"—showcased his adoption of a verbal style in sync with the short, snappy, staccato utterances of social media, notably Twitter (McWhorter, 2017, p. 6). He eschewed the formal, even metaphorical, language presidents have classically invoked, emphasizing casual talk rather than speech with the classicisms of written language. In a sense, he was a political leader exquisitely attuned to reaching people (for better or worse), through the technology of the times (Arthur, 2014).

While some feared his impulsive tweets devalued the Oval Office, others praised his ability to communicate in a language that Americans understood and enjoyed, illustrated by the way that his mode of ending tweets, "Sad!," was frequently imitated, even by his detractors. Trump's tweets and plainspoken language, a reflection of the increasing informality of political speech, have been simple, direct, and devoid of the circumlocutions and equivocations that cause Americans to hate politics. His short messages also brought ordinary people into the fold, as people tweeted back their reactions to his tweets. But Trump's casual, careless use of language carried risks. He seemed to fail to appreciate that a president's statements "are more signals than statements, vehicles meant to convey larger messages" (McWhorter, 2017, p. 6); his utterances could simplify when more nuanced messages were appropriate. They could defy diplomacy, destabilizing global relations as when he irritated the British by insisting, in the absence of facts, that Britain's spy agency had wiretapped him at the request of President Obama.

His truculent, unabashedly emotive tweets in the wake of a North Korean nuclear threat unnerved foreign leaders who preferred more carefully-calibrated language to calm a volatile situation. But they thrilled his supporters, long frustrated by Obama's cautious, effete utterances that had failed to stem North Korean aggression (Fausset, 2017). Thus, his speech, exquisitely adapted to the digital age, stoked the hopes of supporters, but pushed opponents further into the latitude of rejection, seemingly dividing more than they unified the citizenry, and rarely rising to the level of rhetoric, as practiced by previous presidents of both parties.

More than a century after Theodore Roosevelt, with his flamboyant personality, revolutionized presidential communication (Brands, 2002), rhetoric—or, let's say, symbolic verbal argumentation—remains an important component of the presidential persona, a way for presidents to circumvent Congress and influence public opinion directly. It is no magic bullet, but can exert a host of effects, both positive (framing issues and building constituencies for important policies) and negative (misleading the public and equivocating about pressing problems). But to the degree that presidential rhetoric serves salutary purposes, one can appreciate its effects by engaging in a quick thought experiment. Imagine for a moment the vacuum that would be left were presidents not to give inaugural addresses, State of the Union speeches, eulogies, or celebratory speeches on the occasions of great individual, community, or national accomplishments. The public spaces that words did not fill would be gaping and noticeable to all. Presidents' optimistic, unifying messages, rare, yet so necessary in a fragmented, fractious age, would never be heard.

CONCLUSIONS

Presidential campaigns are full-throated efforts to persuade voters. They provide aspiring representatives of the people with an opportunity to make a cogent case that their programs will serve the citizenry, while giving voters the chance to decide if candidates' plans serve their needs. Persuasion is primarily a positive force. It is not coercive, but a largely civilizing influence that embraces logic, verbal arguments, evidence, and emotional appeals. Persuasion becomes problematic when it is strident and mean-spirited, and encourages stubbornly biased consideration of issues rather than tolerance, although even this is complex as attack messages have their defenders (see Chapter 13).

Electoral persuasion occurs in campaigns, a primarily American contribution to the electoral process. Conventional political science approaches emphasize that macroeconomic and broad political factors set the parameters in which campaigns occur. Yet campaigns are critical, for they communicate the frames by which these macro factors are understood and interpreted. Campaigns also provide a mechanism by which voters can hold public officials accountable for their promises. Campaigns involve so many volatile, unpredictable aspects that you cannot appreciate electoral persuasion without considering their impact.

The Elaboration Likelihood Model provides a framework with which to view campaigns. It emphasizes the influence of voter motivations on processing of persuasive messages, as well as the role that processing strategy (peripheral or central) plays in the design of persuasive messages. Its main mantra is that you cannot understand or develop persuasive political messages without appreciating the motivation, ability, and cognitive processes voters bring to bear to the electoral context. Under low involvement, voters process messages peripherally, and simple appeals, based on endorsements, likability, and party-based heuristics, are typically effective. Normative concerns can arise when voters employ superficial decision shortcuts to make up their minds, ignoring information that would have helped them make a more self-serving or wiser decision. When voters are involved in an election, they care about the outcome and think carefully about the issues. Appeals to voters' self-interest and carefully framed economic arguments can carry the day, as seen in recent presidential elections.

Yet we should not underestimate the role that voters' own attitudes play in elections. Voters evaluate candidate messages through the prisms of their political attitudes, leading to biased processing of candidate messages. When people have strong attitudes, they perceive messages selectively, not always fairly or even rationally. They assimilate supportive information, reject credible evidence that is inconsistent with their worldviews, filter policy positions through their preferred political party, and mightily try to interpret messages so they confirm what they already think about politics. They are hardly open-minded, engaging instead in selective perception and selective exposure.

Selective exposure has generated considerable interest in our hyper-partisan era. There is considerable evidence that people are more likely to tune in to information that supports their preexisting viewpoint, preferring ideologically congruent programs and websites. However, there are important exceptions and complicating evidence, indicating that people are exposed to opposing political information, probably much more than they were during the three-broadcast-network era of yore. And yet, fueled by digital algorithms that recommend supportive information, hostile media bias, and "seek-and-you-shall-find" politically reinforcing spirals, social media can promote ideological segregation, where people live in political worlds that reinforce what they already believe rather than challenging them with alternative viewpoints. This can be exacerbated by (a) exposure to occasional fake news that confirms existing biases; (b) the difficulty of correcting mistaken beliefs induced by false information conveyed by political leaders;

and (c) lack of exposure to authentic information that challenges these false or misleading reports. Unsettling as these issues are, it is important not to magnify the problem. Selective exposure in ideologically segregated groups occurs primarily among strong partisans, and the mainstream media, to which social media users have access, routinely debunk false news reports. Normatively, partisan selective exposure has trade-offs: It encourages vigorous participation in politics, but promotes polarization and fuels intolerance, a classic conundrum of democracy.

Candidates, of course, are interested in persuasion, not normative ideals. A classic persuasion approach, social judgment theory, calls attention to the importance of matching message to the nature of voters' political attitudes. Stipulating that political issues can fall into voters' latitude of rejection, acceptance, and noncommitment, it offers broad suggestions of how candidates can influence voters. In particular, when a candidate's message falls into core voters' latitude of acceptance, mobilization of the base can be effective, usually, though not always, when it capitalizes on digital microtargeting techniques.

Persuasion continues to play a role in the next part of what has been called the permanent campaign—the strategic wielding of influence in the White House. Influence is exercised by the use of rhetoric and political language, classic features of political persuaders' armamentarium. Ronald Reagan was a master in adapting rhetoric to the contemporary age, calling on personification, televisual props, and dramatic narrative persuasively and in ways people could understand. His rhetorical strategies helped him wield influence in the White House, as much by his ability to influence perceptions that he was a "great communicator," which in turn shaped public opinion. Although critics continue to lament that he persuaded more by anecdote than argument, his ability to mold his speech to the narrative of the medium and offer dignified appeals to the national spirit have gained adherents in the years since his presidency.

In an age when presidents must "go public" to persuade the citizenry and elites, presidential communication is an important element of policy. It can set agendas, frame issues, and mobilize supporters, while also obfuscating, misleading, and dispiriting when it is superficial or factually untrue. In an age of social media, where presidential messages are not given the play of prime-time addresses, presidents can have difficulty reaching the public, let alone influencing citizens. Twitter has become the go-to modality for political leaders and presidents, but what it offers in reach is offset by its terse lack of explanatory detail and tendency to promote outbursts rather than arguments.

Campaigns remain an artful and important aspect of democracy, but a highly imperfect one. They can be negative and superficial, eliding key issues because discussing these issues will annoy or turn off key constituents. They are not designed to get the public thinking about complex policy problems or help voters appreciate that solving the nation's political conundrums requires an appreciation of diverse points of view. They are designed to elect one candidate at the expense of the others—a worthy goal, integral to democracy, but one that does not value deliberation or the cultivation of tolerance. In a social media age, where animus and exposure to supportive information can frequently hijack attempts to see both sides, this is becoming an increasingly troubling liability.

REFERENCES

Arceneaux, K., & Johnson, M. (2013). *Changing minds or changing channels? Partisan news in an age of choice*. Chicago: University of Chicago Press.

Arthur, C.D. (2014). *Economic actors, economic behaviors, and presidential leadership: The constrained effects of rhetoric*. Lanham, MD: Lexington Books.

Bailenson, J.N., Iyengar, S., Yee, N., & Collins, N.A. (2008). Facial similarity between voters and candidates causes influence. *Public Opinion Quarterly*, *72*, 935–961.

Bartels, L.M. (2006). Priming and persuasion in presidential campaigns. In H.E. Brady & R. Johnston (Eds.), *Capturing campaign effects* (pp. 78–112). Ann Arbor: University of Michigan Press.

Belkin, D. (2008, November 1). In Ohio, downturn upends old loyalties. *The Wall Street Journal*, A5.

Berke, R.L., & Elder, J. (2000, November 30). Public splits on party lines over vote and long delay. *The New York Times*, 1, A30.

Bishop, B., & Cushing, R.G. (2008). *The big sort: Why the clustering of likeminded America is tearing us apart*. Boston: Houghton-Mifflin.

Bond, R.M., Fariss, C.J., Jones, J.J., Kramer, A.D.I., Marlow, C., Settle, J.E., & Fowler, J.H. (2012). A 61-million-person experiment in social influence and political mobilization. *Nature*, *489*, 295–298.

Bosman, J. (2017, January 29). In divided Wisconsin county, Packers talk is O.K. But politics are off limits. *The New York Times*, 11, 20.

Brands, H.W. (2002). Politics as performance art: The body English of Theodore Roosevelt. In L.G. Dorsey (Ed.), *The presidency and rhetorical leadership* (pp. 115–128). College Station: Texas A&M University Press.

Bruni, F. (2017, January 22). The Commander in Chief who buried humility. *The New York Times* (Sunday Review), 1, 5

Camaj, L. (2014). Need for orientation, selective exposure, and attribute agenda-setting effects. *Mass Communication & Society*, *17*, 689–712.

Campbell, K.K., & Jamieson, K.H. (2008). *Presidents creating the presidency: Deeds done in words*. Chicago: University of Chicago Press.

Canes-Wrone, B. (2006). *Who leads whom? Presidents, policy, and the public*. Chicago: University of Chicago Press.

Cialdini, R.B. (2009). *Influence: Science and practice* (5th ed.). Boston: Pearson Education.

Ciuk, D.J., & Yost, B.A. (2016). The effects of issue salience, elite influence, and policy content on public opinion. *Political Communication*, *33*, 328–345.

Coe, K. (2007). The language of freedom in the American presidency, 1933–2006. *Presidential Studies Quarterly*, *37*, 375–398.

Coe, K. (2014). Presidential address. In K. Kenski & K.H. Jamieson (Eds.), *The Oxford handbook of political communication*. Retrieved from www.oxford.handbooks.com. (Accessed July 1, 2016).

Coe, K., & Neumann, R. (2011). The major addresses of modern presidents: Parameters of a data set. *Presidential Studies Quarterly, 41*, 727–751.

Cohen, G.L. (2003). Party over policy: The dominating impact of group influence on political beliefs. *Journal of Personality and Social Psychology, 85*, 808–822.

Cooper, M. (2012, February 14). Conservatives sowed idea of health care mandate, only to spurn it later. *The New York Times*. Retrieved from www.nytimes.com/2012/02/15/health/policy/health-care-mandate-was-first-backed-by-conservatives.html (Accessed April 28, 2017).

Del Vicario, M., Bessi, A., Zollo, F., Petroni, F., Scala, A., Caldarelli, G., Stanley, H.E., & Quattrociocchi, W. (2016). The spreading of misinformation online. *Proceedings of the National Academy of Sciences, 113*(3), 554–559.

Domke, D., & Coe, K. (2008). *The God strategy: How religion became a political weapon in America*. New York: Oxford University Press.

Duhigg, C. (2012, October 14). Campaigns mine personal lives to get out vote. *The New York Times*, 1, 14.

Edgerly, S. (2015). Red media, blue media, and purple media: News repertoires in the colorful media landscape. *Journal of Broadcasting & Electronic Media, 59*, 1–21.

Edwards, G.C., III. (1983). *The public presidency: The pursuit of popular support*. New York: St. Martin's Press.

Edwards, G.C., III. (2003). *On deaf ears: The limits of the bully pulpit*. New Haven, CT: Yale University Press.

Edwards, G.C., III. (2009). *The strategic president: Persuasion and opportunity in presidential leadership*. Princeton, NJ: Princeton University Press.

Euchner, C.C. (1990). Presidential appearances. In *The presidents and the public* (pp. 109–129). Washington, DC: Congressional Quarterly.

Fallows, J. (2016, September 11). Watch your rhetoric. *The New York Times* (Book Review), 13.

Feldman, L., Myers, T.A., Hmielowski, J.D., & Leiserowitz, A. (2014). The mutual reinforcement of media selectivity and effects: Testing the reinforcing spirals framework in the context of global warming. *Journal of Communication, 64*, 590–611.

Fisher, M. (2016, December 23). 140 characters and a wide range of meanings. *The New York Times*, A17.

Flaxman, S., Goel, S., & Rao, J.M. (2016). Filter bubbles, echo chambers, and online news consumption. *Public Opinion Quarterly, 80*, 298–320.

Garrett, R.K. (2009a). Politically motivated reinforcement seeking: Reframing the selective exposure debate. *Journal of Communication, 59*, 676–699.

Garrett, R.K. (2009b). Echo chambers online? Politically motivated selective exposure among Internet news users. *Journal of Computer-Mediated Communication, 14*, 265–285.

Garrett, R.K., Carnahan, D., & Lynch, E.K. (2013). A turn toward avoidance? Selective exposure to online political information, 2004–2008. *Political Behavior, 35*, 113–134.

Garrett, R.K., Gvirsman, S.D., Johnson, B.K., Tsfati, Y., Neo, R., & Dal, A. (2014). Implications of pro- and counterattitudinal information exposure for affective polarization. *Human Communication Research, 40*, 309–332.

Garrett, R.K., Weeks, B.E., & Neo, R.L. (2016). Driving a wedge between evidence and beliefs: How online ideological news exposure promotes political misperceptions. *Journal of Computer-Mediated Communication, 21*, 331–348.

Gelman, A. (2016). Trump-Clinton was expected to be close: The economy said so. In D. Lilleker, E. Thorsen, D. Jackson, & A. Veneti (Eds.), *US election analysis 2016: Media, voters and the campaign: Early reflections from leading academics* (p. 41). Poole, England: Centre for the Study of Journalism, Culture and Community.

Graber, D.A. (1981). Political language. In D. Nimmo & K.R. Sanders (Eds.), *Handbook of political communication* (pp. 195–223). Newbury Park, CA: Sage.

Green, D.P., & Gerber, A.S. (2008). *Get out the vote. How to increase voter turnout* (2nd ed.). Washington, DC: Brookings Institution Press.

Greenhouse, S. (2016, July 5). Trump's Rust Belt allure. *The New York Times* (Sunday Review), 6.

Grush, J.E., McKeough, K.L., & Ahlering, R.F. (1978). Extrapolating laboratory exposure research to actual political elections. *Journal of Personality and Social Psychology, 36*, 257–270.

Hart, R.P. (1984). *Verbal style and the presidency: A computer-based analysis.* Orlando, FL: Academic Press.

Hart, R.P. (1987). *The sound of leadership: Presidential communication in the modern age.* Chicago: University of Chicago Press.

Hart, R.P., Childers, J.P., & Lind, C.J. (2013). *Political tone: How leaders talk and why.* Chicago: University of Chicago Press.

Hasell, A., & Weeks, B.E. (2016). Partisan provocation: The role of partisan news use and emotional responses in political information-sharing in social media. *Human Communication Research, 42*, 641–661.

Hillygus, D.S., & Shields, T.G. (2008). *The persuadable voter: Wedge issues in presidential campaigns.* Princeton, NJ: Princeton University Press.

Holbert, R.L., Garrett, R.K., & Gleason, L.S. (2010). A new era of minimal effects? A response to Bennett and Iyengar. *Journal of Communication, 60*, 15–34.

Holbrook, T.M. (1996). *Do campaigns matter?* Thousand Oaks, CA: Sage.

Ignatius, D. (2016, August 4). Why facts don't matter to Trump's supporters. *The Washington Post.* Retrieved from www.washingtonpost.com/opinions/why-facts-don't-matter-to . . . (Accessed August 6, 2016).

Iyengar, S., & Hahn, K.S. (2009). Red media, blue media: Evidence of ideological sensitivity in media use. *Journal of Communication, 59*, 19–39.

Jamieson, K.H. (1988). *Eloquence in an electronic age: The transformation of political speechmaking.* New York: Oxford University Press.

Jamieson, K.H., & Cappella, J.N. (2008). *Echo chamber: Rush Limbaugh and the conservative media establishment.* New York: Oxford University Press.

Jang, S.M. (2014). Challenges to selective exposure: Selective seeking and avoidance in a multitasking media environment. *Mass Communication & Society, 17*, 665–688.

Johnson, T.J., Bichard, S.L., & Zhang, W. (2009). Communication communities or "cyberghettos?" A path analysis model examining factors that explain selective exposure to blogs. *Journal of Computer-Mediated Communication, 15*, 60–82.

Johnson, T.J., & Kaye, B.K. (2013). The dark side of the boon? Credibility, selective exposure and the proliferation of online sources of political information. *Computers in Human Behavior, 29*, 1862–1871.

Johnston, R., Hagen, M.G., & Jamieson, K.H. (2004). *The 2000 presidential election and the foundation of party politics.* New York: Cambridge University Press.

Jones, J.J., Bond, R.M., Bakshy, E., Eckles, D., & Fowler, J.H. (2017). Social influence and political mobilization: Further evidence from a randomized experiment in the 2012 U.S. presidential election. *PLoS ONE, 12*(4), e0173851. Retrieved from https://doi.org/10.1371/journal.pone.0173851. (Accessed April 30, 2017).

Kantor, J. (2012, October 21). For president, a complex calculus of race and politics. *The New York Times*, 1, 22.

Kernell, S. (1993). *Going public: New strategies of presidential leadership* (2nd ed.). Washington, DC: Congressional Quarterly Press.

Killian, M., Schoen, R., & Dusso, A. (2008). Keeping up with the Joneses: The interplay of personal and collective evaluations in voter turnout. *Political Behavior, 30*, 323–340.

Knobloch-Westerwick, S., Mothes, C., Johnson, B.K., Westerwick, A., & Donsbach, W. (2015). Political online information searching in Germany and the United States: Confirmation bias, source credibility, and attitude impacts. *Journal of Communication, 65*, 489–511.

Krosnick, J.A., & Petty, R.E. (1995). Attitude strength: An overview. In R.E. Petty & J.A. Krosnick (Eds.), *Attitude strength: Antecedents and consequences* (pp. 1–24). Hillsdale, NJ: Lawrence Erlbaum Associates.

Ladd, J.M. (2007). Predispositions and public support for the president during the war on terrorism. *Public Opinion Quarterly, 71*, 511–538.

Lau, R.R., & Redlawsk, D.P. (2001). Advantages and disadvantages of cognitive heuristics in political decision making. *American Journal of Political Science, 45*, 951–971.

Lazarsfeld, P.F., Berelson, B., & Gaudet, H. (1944). *The people's choice: How the voter makes up his mind in a presidential campaign.* New York: Columbia University Press.

Lee, H., Kwak, N., & Campbell, S.W. (2015). Hearing the other side revisited: The joint workings of cross-cutting discussion and strong tie homogeneity in facilitating deliberative *and* participatory democracy. *Communication Research, 42*, 569–596.

Lelkes, Y. (2016). Mass polarization: Manifestations and measurements. *Public Opinion Quarterly, 80*, 392–410.

Levendusky, M.S. (2013). *How partisan media polarize America.* Chicago: University of Chicago Press.

Levendusky, M.S., & Malhotra, N. (2016). (Mis)perceptions of partisan polarization in the American public. *Public Opinion Quarterly, 80*, 378–391.

Liang, H. (2014). The organizational principles of online political discussion: A relational event stream model for analysis of Web Forum deliberation. *Human Communication Research, 40*, 483–507.

Lizza, R. (2012, October 29 & November 5). The final push: The Obama team's high-risk strategy. *The New Yorker*, 62–63, 66–69.

Lord, C.G., Ross, L., & Lepper, M.R. (1979). Biased assimilation and attitude polarization: The effects of prior theories on subsequently considered evidence. *Journal of Personality and Social Psychology, 37*, 2098–2109.

Manjoo, F. (2015, May 8). Facebook finds opposing views trickle through. *The New York Times*, A1, B7.

Masket, S., Sides, J., & Vavreck, L. (2016). The ground game in the 2012 presidential election. *Political Communication, 33,* 169–187.

Mason, L. (2016). A cross-cutting calm: How social sorting drives affective polarization. *Public Opinion Quarterly, 80,* 351–377.

McWhorter, J. (2017, January 22). How to listen to Donald Trump every day for years. *The New York Times* (Sunday Review), 1, 6.

Messing, S., & Westwood, S. J. (2014). Selective exposure in the age of social media: Endorsements trump partisan source affiliation when selecting news online. *Communication Research, 41,* 1042–1063.

Mill, J. S. (1859/2009). *On liberty and other essays.* New York: Kaplan.

Miller, M. (2005, June 4). Is persuasion dead? *The New York Times.* Retrieved from www.nytimes.com/2005/06/04/opinion/04miller_oped.html (Accessed January 14, 2017).

Mutz, D. C. (2002). Cross-cutting social networks: Testing democratic theory in practice. *American Political Science Review, 96,* 111–126.

Mutz, D. C. (2006). *Hearing the other side: Deliberative versus participatory democracy.* Cambridge: Cambridge University Press.

Nyhan, B., & Reifler, J. (2010). When corrections fail: The persistence of political misperceptions. *Political Behavior, 32,* 303–330.

O'Sullivan, C. S., Chen, A., Mohapatra, S., Sigelman, L., & Lewis, E. (1988). Voting in ignorance: The politics of smooth-sounding names. *Journal of Applied Social Psychology, 18,* 1094–1106.

Osnos, E., Remnick, D., & Yaffa, J. (2017, March 6). Active measures: What lay behind Russia's interference in the 2016 election—and what lies ahead? *The New Yorker,* 40–55.

Pariser, E. (2011). *The filter bubble: What the Internet is hiding from you.* New York: Penguin Press.

Perloff, R. M. (2015). A three-decade retrospective on the hostile media effect. *Mass Communication and Society, 18,* 701–729.

Petty, R. E., Briñol, P., & Priester, J. R. (2009). Mass media attitude change: Implications of the elaboration likelihood model of persuasion. In J. Bryant & M. B. Oliver (Eds.), *Media effects: Advances in theory and research* (3rd ed., pp. 125–164). New York: Routledge.

Popkin, S. L. (1991). *The reasoning voter: Communication and persuasion in presidential campaigns.* Chicago: University of Chicago Press.

Rosenberg, S. W., & McAfferty, P. (1987). The image and the vote: Manipulating voters' preferences. *Public Opinion Quarterly, 57,* 31–47.

Rosenstone, S. J. (1983). *Forecasting presidential elections.* New Haven, CT: Yale University Press.

Saunders, K. L., & Abramowitz, A. I. (2007). The rise of the ideological voter: The changing bases of partisanship in the American electorate. In J. C. Green & D. J. Coffeey (Eds.), *The state of the parties: The changing role of contemporary politics* (pp. 299–315). Lanham, MD: Rowman & Littlefield.

Saward, M. (2014). Shape-shifting representation. *American Political Science Review, 108,* 723–736.

Sears, D.O., Lau, R.R., Tyler, T.R., & Allen, H.M., Jr. (1980). The self-interest vs. symbolic politics in policy attitudes and presidential voting. *American Political Science Review, 74,* 670–684.

Shear, M.D., & Glanz, J. (2016, December 23). Trump says U.S. should "expand" nuclear ability. *The New York Times,* A1, A17.

Sherif, M., & Sherif, C.W. (1967). Attitude as the individual's own categories: The social judgment-involvement approach to attitude and attitude change. In C.W. Sherif & M. Sherif (Eds.), *Attitude, ego-involvement, and change* (pp. 105–139). New York: Wiley-Blackwell.

Skovsgaard, M., Shehata, A., & Strömbäck, J. (2016). Opportunity structures for selective exposure: Investigating selective exposure and learning in Swedish election campaigns using panel survey data. *The International Journal of Press/Politics, 21,* 527–546.

Skurnik, I., Yoon, C., Park, D.C., & Schwarz, N. (2005). How warnings about false claims become recommendations. *Journal of Consumer Research, 31,* 713–724.

Slater, M.D. (2007). Reinforcing spirals: The mutual influence of media selectivity and media effects and their impact on individual behavior and social identity. *Communication Theory, 17,* 281–303.

Stroud, N.J. (2008). Media use and political predispositions: Revisiting the concept of selective exposure. *Political Behavior, 30,* 341–366.

Stroud, N.J. (2010). Polarization and partisan selective exposure. *Journal of Communication, 60,* 556–576.

Stroud, N.J. (2011). *Niche news: The politics of news choice.* New York: Oxford University Press.

Stroud, N.J. (2014). Selective exposure theories. In K. Kenski & K.H. Jamieson (Eds.), *The Oxford handbook of political communication.* New York: Oxford. Retrieved from www.oxfordhandbooks.com

Stuart, E.W., Shimp, T.A., & Engle, R.W. (1987). Classical conditioning of consumer attitudes: Four experiments in an advertising context. *Journal of Consumer Research, 14,* 334–349.

Tavernise, S. (2016, November 13). Amid years of decay, Ohioans flipped votes, seeking change. *The New York Times,* 1, 14.

Thorson, E. (2016). Belief echoes: The persistent effects of corrected misinformation. *Political Communication, 33,* 460–480.

Tsfati, Y., & Chotiner, A. (2016). Testing the selective exposure-polarization hypothesis in Israel using three indicators of ideological news exposure and testing for mediating mechanisms. *International Journal of Public Opinion Research, 28,* 1–24.

Tsfati, Y., Stroud, N.J., & Chotiner, A. (2014). Exposure to ideological news and perceived opinion climate: Testing the media effects component of spiral-of-silence in a fragmented media landscape. *The International Journal of Press/Politics, 19,* 3–23.

Tulis, J.K. (1987). *The rhetorical presidency.* Princeton, NJ: Princeton University Press.

Vallone, R.P., Ross, L., & Lepper, M.R. (1985). The hostile media phenomenon: Biased perception and perceptions of media bias in coverage of the Beirut massacre. *Journal of Personality and Social Psychology, 49,* 577–585.

Vavreck, L. (2009). *The message matters: The economy and presidential campaigns.* Princeton, NJ: Princeton University Press.

Webster, J. G. (2014). *The marketplace of attention: How audiences take shape in a digital age.* Cambridge, MA: MIT Press.

Weeks, B. E., & Garrett, R. K. (2014). Electoral consequences of political rumors: Motivated reasoning, candidate rumors, and vote choice during the 2008 U.S. presidential election. *International Journal of Public Opinion Research, 26,* 401–422.

Weeks, B. E., Ksiazek, T. B., & Holbert, R. L. (2016). Partisan enclaves or shared media experiences? A network approach to understanding citizens' political news environments. *Journal of Broadcasting & Electronic Media, 60,* 248–268.

Whicker, M. L. (1993). The case against the war. In M. L. Whicker, J. B. Pfiffner, & R. A. Moore (Eds.), *The presidency and the Persian Gulf war* (pp. 111–129). Westport, CT: Praeger.

Wicks, R. H., Wicks, J. L., & Morimoto, S. A. (2014). Partisan selective exposure during the 2012 presidential election. *American Behavioral Scientist, 58,* 1131–1143.

Williamson, E. (2016, July 10). Mrs. Clinton, Mr. Trump, or none of the above. *The New York Times* (Sunday Review), 8.

Wojcieszak, M., Bimber, B., Feldman, L., & Stroud, N. J. (2016). Partisan news and political participation: Exploring mediated relationships. *Political Communication, 33,* 241–260.

Wojcieszak, M., & Price, V. (2010). Bridging the divide or intensifying the conflict? How disagreement affects strong predilections about sexual minorities. *Political Psychology, 31,* 315–339. Young, G., & Perkins, W. B. (2005). Presidential rhetoric, the public agenda, and the end of presidential television's "golden age". *Journal of Politics, 67,* 1190–1205.

13 Political Advertising in Presidential Campaigns

They are the Darth Vader, the Voldemort of contemporary politics—the online-streamed equivalent of the Black Death. These, albeit with a little dramatic embellishment, are apt metaphors for the public's perception of political advertising. Few aspects of modern politics generate as much criticism as political commercials, particularly negative spots. What comes to mind when you think of political ads? Probably unfavorable images. Political commercials are blood sport for the news media, which thrive on lamenting their effects, but then focus endlessly on their strategic implications, replaying controversial ads, exacerbating their impact. Political ads are a mythologized, misunderstood aspect of political communication, much in need of debunking and clarification. This chapter addresses these issues, focusing on presidential campaign advertising and covering a wide range of issues. The first section of the chapter places political ads in their contemporary campaign context, discussing finances and strategy. The second portion explicates different categories of political ads. The third section, calling on research and examples, describes political advertising effects, focusing on negative advertising. The fourth portion examines the normative features of political ads—how they serve and hinder democracy. The final section extends this discussion with an in-depth examination of the legal issues surrounding negative ads and the broader issue of money in politics.

STRATEGIC FEATURES OF POLITICAL ADVERTISING

As discussed in Chapter 12, advocacy plays a central role in political campaigns. In a democracy, candidates must make their best case to voters, explaining their stand on the issues, and why they will serve voters more effectively than their adversaries (Fridkin & Kenney, 2011). A central component of campaign advocacy is political advertising, paid political speech, and it has several strategic features.

Political Advertising Is an Expensive Proposition

Billions of dollars are spent on televised political advertising nationwide. In Nevada, where ads blanketed the evening news, the general manager of a Las Vegas television station said, "We have a joke around here. Pretty soon, we're going to have such long commercial breaks that people are going to tune in and all they'll hear is: 'Hello, welcome to News 3. And goodbye'" (Peters, 2012, p. A16).

During the 2015–2016 election cycle, approximately $2.83 billion was expended on televised political advertising for different elections. An estimated $845 million was spent on more than a million presidential election ads (Fowler, Ridout, & Franz, 2016). That's a lot of advertising! As Erika Franklin Fowler, Travis N. Ridout, and Michael M. Franz, who have conducted comprehensive research on political campaign advertising, explain, "if every one of these ads aired back-to-back, they would be broadcast for nearly 1500 straight days without stop" (p. 447).

Although both presidential candidates spent a great deal of money on campaign marketing, 2016 was an aberration in that they spent less than in the previous election—$845 million in 2016, compared to the $1.2 billion that Obama, Romney, and their supporters doled out in 2012 (Peters & Shorey, 2016). Presidential candidate expenditures dropped in 2016 because both candidates were so well-known that advertising was less important in shaping an image. In addition, Trump, relying on news and social media, spent much less than Clinton (Motta, 2016), and considerably less than his Republican counterpart in 2012.

Political Ads Are Increasingly Funded by Outside Political Groups

Political commercials are sponsored by candidates, political parties, and interest groups, the latter under the rubric of super political action committees or super PACs. While candidates still sponsor numerous political ads in congressional and presidential races (Fowler, Franz, & Ridout, 2016; Fowler et al., 2016), an increasing number of prominent campaign ads are purchased by super PACs, which have expanded their influence since the Supreme Court's Citizens United decision paved the way for unlimited spending in elections.

Super PACs now pay for numerous political ads that are bankrolled by corporations, unions, lobbying groups, or billionaires who have doled out tens of millions of dollars in a presidential election cycle. Super PACs, sometimes operating secretly and independently of campaigns, can underwrite nasty attack ads. It's a game: Candidates can condemn the attack spots, saying they are shocked at how negative the ads have become. At the same time, they benefit from PAC-sponsored attacks on their opponents. Many ads targeting Trump during the Republican primaries were produced by super PACs that supported, but were not formally linked, with his rivals for the nomination. This allowed his rivals to benefit from attack ads they embraced, but could not be held accountable for producing.

Political Advertising Has Become More Negative

In 1952, 25 percent of political ads were negative. In 1960, when John F. Kennedy faced Richard Nixon, only 12 percent of major political ads were negative (West, 2010). Then came President Lyndon Johnson's iconic "Daisy" ad in 1964, where a girl picked petals off a daisy as a nuclear bomb exploded into a mushroom cloud. The ad never mentioned Johnson's opponent by name, but suggested (rather unsubtly) what he might do if elected president. (The ad provoked so much protest it was yanked after one showing. How times have changed! The spot, mild by current standards, would now be endlessly viewed on YouTube.) In 1964, 59 percent of major ads were negative. Influenced by the apparent success of the "Daisy" spot and responding to the turbulence of the late 1960s, both candidates expanded the use of attack ads in 1968.

Negative ads declined in the 1970s, in the wake of the national soul-searching that occurred after the end of the Vietnam War and Watergate. But they increased dramatically over the course of the 1980s. The 1988 election remains the most negative on record, with the incendiary attacks by George H. W. Bush on Democrat Michael Dukakis, including ads that controversially suggested that a Dukakis prison policy had led to brutal Black-on-White crime. Negative, highly changed ads continued apace, dropping and rising in particular years, but still accounting for a majority of prominent political ads in the general election (see Figure 13.1).

Who devises negative ads? They are created, poll-tested, and executed by a cadre of political consultants, pollsters, and advertising gurus who are typically allied with one political party rather than another, love the exhilarating, cutthroat world of politics and are motivated by one thing only: winning (Strother, 2003). A controversial aspect of negative advertising is **opposition research**, labor-intensive investigations designed to uncover liabilities in an opponent's record, like toxic previous statements and politically problematic alliances, as well as personality quirks and sexual skeletons in the closet. Opposition research is used in local election campaigns and prodigiously in presidential races, exemplified by Democratic supporters of Hillary Clinton in 2016, who hired a political consulting firm to dig up dirt on Trump's previous scandals and shortcomings (Shane, Confessore, & Rosenberg, 2017). Defenders of "oppo research," as it is affectionately (if warily) called, point out that it can help unearth facts the public has a right to know. These include discovering that a

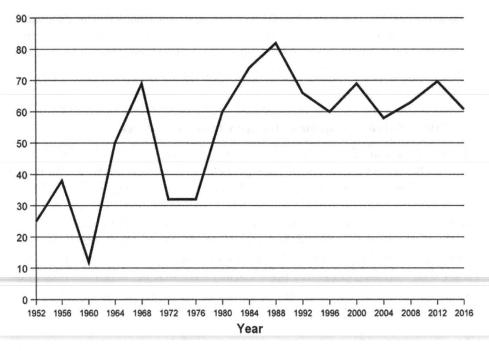

Figure 13.1 Negative advertising as a proportion of total ads in presidential elections.

seemingly pure-as-the-driven-snow candidate is actually a liar, thief, drunk, or sexual pervert—facts that, if not disclosed until after the election, could be cast aside by the now victorious elected official (Huffman & Rejebian, 2012). Critics of opposition research counter-argue that the business of secretly looking for skeletons in a candidate's closet is seamy, demeans politics, and discourages capable, if mildly flawed, candidates from pursuing elected office. Nowadays, when electronic snooping—hacking—can reliably reveal a candidate's skeletons, the ethics of opposition research are even more relevant, and the implications more disturbing.

Political Advertising Is Intensely Strategic

Negative ads begin long before the general election, launched even before the first vote is cast in a primary or caucus. For example, in just a five-day period in early January 2016, more than three weeks before the Iowa caucuses, candidates and their supporters in both parties doled out some $5.9 million in TV ads, a large amount compared to monies spent in 2012 (Corasaniti, 2012). Candidates and political action committees continued the onslaught throughout the primaries, thrusting and parrying with negative TV and YouTube spots.

During the general election campaign, advertising becomes more strategic, as consultants direct some ads toward the partisan base and target other spots at undecided (latitude of noncommitment) voters in battleground states. Rather than spending money on advertising purchases in all 50 states (or campaigning in each state, as Nixon foolishly did in 1960, expending valuable resources), consultants argue that they get a bigger bang for the buck by making ad buys in key swing states. Arguing that it is not cost-effective to spend money in states that are locked up by one candidate, strategists emphasize targeted purchases in states where the outcome is in doubt. In 2008 and 2012, battleground states widely viewed as critical to the electoral outcome received the lion's share of ads. Voters in Nevada, Virginia, Florida, and Ohio received large numbers of ads. In 2016, Trump focused his attention on three must-win states—Florida, Pennsylvania, and Ohio—devoting resources to these states, minimizing attention to other states that he either had in the bag or was not likely to win (Burns & Haberman, 2016). Pro-Clinton groups directed negative advertising to battleground states of Ohio and Florida (Vavreck, 2016a), while other pro-Democrat super PACs directed a Spanish-language ad campaign at Latino voters in Florida and Nevada (Corasaniti & Shorey, 2016).

The big advertising story of 2016 is that Clinton outspent Trump, airing nearly more than 400,000 ads at a cost of $258 million in the 2015–2016 election cycle, compared with Trump's 121,000 ads, costing $91 million (Fowler et al., 2016). Yet even though Clinton spent more on advertising than Trump—the expenditure gap between the two candidates unusually large—she lost the election, perhaps because she failed to advertise as strategically as she might have. As it turned out, the Clinton campaign erred by not directing more of its advertising dollars at White working class voters in key states like Michigan, Pennsylvania, and Wisconsin, underestimating Trump's support, mistakenly relying on flawed state polls, and presuming that negative rather than positive appeals would be effective. In Michigan and Wisconsin, Trump was a more dominant force in local television advertising for much of the fall campaign, and Clinton failed to broadcast ads in these states until the last week of the election. This may have been consequential, although, as discussed later in the chapter, political advertising, while effective, is nothing if not complex.

Campaigns deploy multiple strategies, devising online as well as television spots, and developing "press ads," commercials not necessarily designed to be aired on TV but shown directly to reporters in hopes of creating a stir, gaining free coverage on national cable or local television news (Chadwick, 2013). Candidates strategize by directing promotional messages to YouTube and Twitter, where costs are typically cheaper and Millennial voters can be reached, though not necessarily voters who lack the economic resources to regularly tap into the social web (Edgerly, Bode, Kim, & Shah, 2013)

POLITICAL ADVERTISING CONTENT AND EFFECTS

Studying Political Advertising

What appeals do political ads employ? How can we be sure they have become more negative over time? To answer these and other questions about the nature of political ads, researchers conduct content analyses, as described in Chapter 3. In his content analytic research on political advertising, Benoit (2014) has found that candidates can acclaim, taking a positive approach by highlighting their virtues; go negative, by attacking the other candidate; or defend themselves from the opponent's attack, refuting or denying the opponent's charges. The content of claims, attacks, and defenses can concern policy issues or image, that is, a candidate's character or personal attributes. Although issues and image differ conceptually, they also overlap.

When a candidate stakes out a strong position on terrorism, he or she projects a strong foreign policy *image*. In some cases, a candidate's perceived dishonesty—Gore in 2000 and Clinton in 2016—can become a key *issue* for voters, a consideration that news coverage can prime justifiably or out of proportion to its electoral importance. In addition, an issue position, typically believed to be a centrally processed argument, can serve as a peripheral cue, as when a low-involved voter responded to a slogan (Bill Clinton's "It's the economy, stupid") rather than his comprehensive economic plan. Complicating matters, an appeal to *image* can be an argument, the main *issue* the candidate wants voters to appreciate (e.g., Michael Dukakis's admonition that the 1988 election was not about ideology, but competence, specifically his, and the perceived lack of competence of his opponent George H. W. Bush). Thus, the familiar dichotomy between issue and image is more blurred than commonly assumed.

The content of ads depends on electoral context, such as primary versus general election campaign; if the election is for state or federal office; and whether an incumbent faces reelection or the race features two challengers for public office. Interestingly, across primary and general election campaigns, candidate ads focus on policy more than character. Fifty-seven percent of ads across elections focus on policy and 43 percent on character (Benoit, 2014). As we will see, Hillary Clinton in 2016 became a prominent exception to this adage.

Content of Negative Ads

What is a negative commercial, or even more broadly, a negative campaign advocacy message? This is not as simple as it seems, as there are different components of negative messages that have different political implications (Fallis, 2014).

First, as noted above, negative ads differ in whether they criticize the opposing candidate's issue positions, image, or both. In 2016, Clinton's many negative ads focused on Trump's personality attributes and qualifications for the presidency. Less than 1 in 10 of Clinton's attack ads criticized Trump's policies, while about 9 in 10 emphasized his personality attributes, such as his temperament or inflammatory statements that seemed to cast doubt on his fitness as a role model (Fowler et al., 2016). Clinton focused far less on policy issues than have other presidential candidates. By contrast, Trump emphasized policy more, regularly contrasting his vision of America from Clinton's. This strategy that may have helped him frame his candidacy more substantively in the minds of undecided voters, tipping the scales for these more centrally processing citizens.

A second aspect of negative ads involves the content of the attack. Negative ads can (1) criticize the opponent directly with a frontal attack on character or motives; (2) mention both the candidate sponsoring the ad and the opponent (a contrast or comparative ad); or (3) use an indirect approach, with an implication or even innuendo about the targeted candidate (Johnson-Cartee & Copeland, 1991; Fowler et al., 2016).

A third attribute of a negative campaign messages is tone. Advertisements can be civil, criticizing the opponent or her issue position in a courteous, polite, respectful manner, or uncivil, employing, aggressive, brutish attacks, with all sorts of televisual features to enhance the effect. Uncivil ads are commonplace, part of what Berry and Sobieraj (2014) broadly call "the outrage industry" and what Mutz (2015) might describe as "in your face" media politics. Uncivil campaigning is hardly new, dating back centuries (see Box 13.1).

Defining exactly what constitutes incivility is difficult, partly due to cultural and temporal parameters (Jamieson, Volinsky, Weitz, & Kenski, 2014). What is viewed as civil discourse in one era can be deemed uncivil in another and vice versa. Racist political language that would have been seen as acceptable in the 1850s and even much later would today be deemed as uncivil at the very least. Use of mild obscenities, which would have raised eyebrows in the 1950s would not elicit a flinch today. Complicating matters, incivility has different components, and individual differ in how they view uncivil ads, as well as their tolerance for attack ads (Stryker, Conway, & Danielson, 2016; Fridkin & Kenney, 2011). However, few would disagree that that certain comments—Trump's calling women "fat" or "ugly," and bragging about sexual assault in a video, saying "I moved on her like a bitch"—are unquestionably uncivil. In addition, Clinton's comment that half of Trump's supporters could be placed into "the basket of deplorables" is certainly an uncivil way of describing his voters. During the 2016 campaign, there was considerable incivility in negative political ads and persuasion.

Nonetheless, it is important to remember that negative ads need not be uncivil or mean. They can make legitimate criticism of an opposing candidate in a civil fashion.

A fourth characteristic of negative ads is their use of dramatic production techniques, such as compelling camera angles, dark colors, foreboding music, grainy realistic images, the narrator's use of a menacing tone, and letting the targeted candidate speak his own words, as Clinton did in 2016.

Finally, negative messages can vary in accuracy, deceptiveness, and the extent to which they invite viewers to draw false inferences. Consultants are careful to design ads that are largely accurate because opponents can easily pounce on factual mistakes, using these to launch negative ads of their own. Political spots can also be accurate—literally true—but misleading, inviting viewers to make false inferences.

BOX 13.1 STORIED HISTORY OF UNCIVIL NEGATIVE CAMPAIGNS

Uncivil negative campaigning has a long history in political discourse. In ancient Rome, the orator Cicero labeled his opponent a butcher, a monster, and a scoundrel (Jamieson et al., 2014). Uncivil political campaigns in the U.S. date back to the earliest elections. Long before critics lambasted the Clintons and Bushes for trying to install an elite dynasty in the White House, Thomas Jefferson's allies accused President John Adams of plotting to create a dynasty with his sons. Jefferson's opponents called him the anti-Christ and a demagogue. One can go on and on; it becomes almost intoxicating (or depressing) to track the animus that courses through American politics.

In 1800, John Adams's supporters claimed Jefferson was "mean-spirited" and the "son of a half-breed Indian squaw, sired by a Virginia mulatto father." Another message claimed that Jefferson's victory over Adams would result in the practice of "murder, robbery, rape, adultery, and incest" (Baumgartner & Francia, 2016, p. 115). During the 1800 election, an interesting incident occurred that typified the negative politics of the era. A Federalist woman from a small Connecticut town was so afraid of what might happen to the family Bible if Jefferson became president that she gave her Bible to the only Jefferson supporter she knew and asked him to keep it for her. He tried to convince her that her fears about Jefferson had no merit, but she was not persuaded. "My good woman," he finally, said, "if all the Bibles are to be destroyed, what is the use of bringing yours to me? That will not save it when it is found." "I'm sure it will," responded the woman. "It will be perfectly safe with you. They'll never think of looking in the house of a Democrat for a Bible!" (Boller, 2004, pp. 17–18).

Even Lincoln, who was called "the ugliest man in the Union," was frequently criticized and he responded humorously. In one of his debates with Stephen Douglas in 1858, he responded to the charge that he was two-faced, saying, "I leave it to my audience. If I had another face, do you think I'd wear this one?" (Jamieson, 1986, p. 10).

Negative campaigns, though not attacks ads (as advertising was not part of the political landscape) continued apace, famously seen in 1884 when Republicans made hay out of the fact that Democrat Grover Cleveland had a child out of wedlock. "Ma! Ma! Where's my Pa?," Republicans chanted, raising an issue that would not merit a full-throated negative campaign today. After Cleveland won, his supporters cried out, "Ma! Ma! Where's my Pa? Gone to the White House— Ha! Ha! Ha!" (Johnson-Cartee & Copeland, 1991, pp. 6–7). (If political ridicule is a constant, one can only hope the quality of rhyming has improved over the years.)

Negative campaigns, the precursor to today's negative advertising, have always characterized American elections for several reasons: the psychology of partisanship involves strong, vitriolic feelings, the promise of power tempts candidates to use these strategies all the more frequently, and they are legal. When we think that uncivil campaigning is a recent invention, it is helpful to remember that the path of politics has always been littered with vicious attacks, for good or ill.

NEGATIVE ADVERTISING EFFECTS

Limits of Negative Ads

It is widely assumed that negative ads exert massive effects. Television journalists spend hours dissecting their impact. Political action committees spend millions on targeted ads. Notorious spots, like the "Willie Horton" ad of 1988 (see Box 13.2) and the anti– John Kerry "Swift Boat" ads, are assumed to have changed the minds of millions of voters. But sometimes the obvious is not true, and in other instances, common assumptions are proven false. Such is the case with negative commercials.

Wait, how can that be, you ask? Why would consultants counsel spending millions? Why would political groups expend their resources if they are ineffective? It's a complex matter, and social science is the study of precisely this: complex phenomena. From a scientific perspective, just because people believe something to be true does not mean it is empirically true. People thought gender stereotypes were true, but research, too numerous to mention here, showed they are wildly false. Researchers test hypotheses with data to examine popular claims. In the case of political advertising, and negative ads in particular, research provides a more nuanced picture of campaign media effects. As Lau, who has conducted considerable research on this topic over the years, concluded after a meta-analytic statistical study of more than 100 studies, "there is no consistent evidence in the research literature that negative political campaigning 'works' in achieving the electoral results that attackers desire" (Lau, Sigelman, & Rovner, 2007, p. 1185).

There is not a one-to-one relationship between money spent on advertising and electoral success. Candidates can spend millions on advertising and lose the election. Clinton dominated Trump on the airwaves, outnumbering Trump in ads by about a 3 to 1 margin (Motta, 2016) and outspending him in political advertising dollars, but she lost the Electoral College. During the primaries, Trump's Republican rivals directed considerable advertising firepower against him, only to lose the nomination. How can this be? Why doesn't advertising have the powerful effects it is alleged to exert? There are a number of reasons.

First, Political Ads May Not Reach Their Target Audience

With the plethora of media outlets today, it is more difficult to presume that televised or Internet ads will be seen (let alone influence) targeted voters.

Second, Negative Ads Do Not Change Partisans' Attitudes

People who strongly support a candidate will not alter their opinion after watching a series of negative ads directed against their candidate. Strong attitudes, steeped in values, are hard to change (Krosnick & Petty, 1995). As discussed in Chapter 12, selective psychological processes and social judgment latitudes are filters through which people perceive candidates.

Third, Negative Ads Won't Influence Voters if They Fail to Address Salient Political Concerns

Consider the visceral anti-Trump spots that used Trump's own voice against him, such as those where he called a woman "a slob" who "ate like a pig," as teenage girls depicted in the ads nervously stroked their hair or straightened their clothes before a mirror. These ads were intended to persuade undecided women voters to vote against Trump and may have had this impact on some voters. Yet they were singularly ineffective with many women living in battleground states, who were familiar with Trump's comments and allegations of sexual aggression and voted for him nonetheless. They downgraded his comments ("he kind of reminds me of my ex-husband," a Kentucky woman said), questioned whether his remarks captured his true sex-role attitudes, citing his daughter Ivanka as a role model for girls, or, centrally processing the election, accepted his warts as the price to pay for a candidate whose business background served as a persuasive argument that he would bring back jobs and improve the economy (Chira, 2017, p. 12). While the ads were hard-hitting and memorable, they did not address the central, salient factors propelling undecided voters to cast their vote for Trump. For example, the ads may have been ineffective because they focused on Trump's personal characteristics rather than outlining policy-based reasons why he was not suitable for office. (Alternatively, voters could have resisted anti-Trump ads because they approved of Trump's sexism.)

Fourth, Negative Ads Will Not Work if the Hit (Mafia Language is Sometimes Used to Describe Negative Campaigning) Is Too Strong, Below the Belt, Unbelievable, Socially Inappropriate, or Deeply Offensive

For example, consider an emotional ad that attacked Republican opposition to abortion even in the case of rape by showing a young woman calling her father on the phone, only to be interrupted by a police lieutenant telling him his daughter has been raped. The ad was so intensely emotional that it shocked and saddened focus group respondents more than it changed their attitudes (Kern, 1989).

Influences of Negative Advertising

Let's complicate the picture a little here. Political advertising effects are not an all-or-none proposition. That they don't have massive effects doesn't mean we should throw up our hands, give up, and assume they have no influences. As the chapters on agenda-setting and framing indicated, political media can have particular types of effects, under particular conditions—and the effects can be interesting, even politically significant. Neither science (research on political media impact) or practice (the wisdom of political consultants acquired from years of experience) would suggest that political advertising has massive, election-changing influences. There is not a one-to-one (or even close to that) relationship between number of political ads (or campaign finance expenditures) and victory in high-involved, presidential elections.

Consider also that people say they hate negative ads—one media consultant compared them to birth pains. Critics assume this means that, therefore, political ads don't work. However, people can be somewhat influenced by negative messages they don't like if the messages contain compelling information. Moreover, there is a semantic confound. Voters react negatively to "negative ads," but this is partly due to the unfavorable connotation that the words "negative campaigning" evoke in voters (Mattes & Redlawsk, 2014). "Negative campaigning" or "negative advertising" call up images of vivid, vicious ads, as well as constellations of beliefs, acquired from news exposure, that negative ads are bad, unfair, or uncivil. Not all negative ads fit into these categories. When researchers examine particular negative ads, without the loaded words, they find evidence of advertising impact.

What effects do negative political spots have on voters? Before offering an answer, it is instructive to examine the challenges facing researchers trying to document negative advertising impacts. An investigator may find a correlation between self-reported exposure to an ad and changes in attitude toward the targeted candidate. However, this assumes that respondents can accurately recall their exposure, and that the ad—as opposed to a news report on the ad or a social media post regarding the ad—exerted the impact. In addition, the fact that exposure is correlated with exposure does not prove the ad causes the impact. The direction of causation could go the other way, with prior attitude leading voters to seek out a politically congenial ad. Even if an effect can be reliably determined, it is not clear that the impact will last for long or influence vote intention, let alone actual voting behavior (e.g., Fallis, 2014).

For these and other reasons, research shows a mixed record of negative advertising, and negative campaign, effects. In a meta-analysis, Lau and his colleagues (2007) found that negative campaigns can reduce support for targeted candidates, but also boomerang, undermining positive attitudes toward the candidate who launched the attack. The ambiguity stems from methodological issues like unreliability of measurement, as well as the likelihood that negative ad success in decreasing support for the targeted candidate is neutralized by reducing liking of the attacker. With this in mind, let's examine what we know about the subtle effects of negative ads.

Recall

One reliable effect is on memory. There is empirical evidence that people remember negative ads better than positive spots, and recognize negative ads more accurately and quickly than positive ads (Lau et al., 2007; Newhagen & Reeves, 1991; Shapiro & Rieger, 1992; see also Soroka & McAdams, 2015). There are several reasons for this. Humans may be neurologically wired to respond more strongly to negative than to positive stimuli (Soroka, 2014). Psychologically, negative information captures our attention, exerting a stronger impact on impressions. Perhaps because people hope or expect that events will be positive, they are captivated by the negative. Consider this example: You go to a party. Four friends say kind, nice things about your outfit, your sense of humor, the quality of your work, even your pet cat. One friend calls your recent Facebook post "obnoxious." Which comment do you remember? Which one causes you to ruminate on your drive home? Research suggests it is the sarcastic crack. In the same fashion, negative political information can be more memorable than positive statements.

Another reason negative ads are more memorable than positive ads is because they garner more press attention. News replays visceral negative ads because they are good television, are perceived to bring in viewers, are a cheap way to fill up airtime, and fit the journalistic news value of the election as a conflict-filled strategic game. Negative ads also can generate clicks on YouTube and light up social media pages.

Visceral negative ads gain an almost surreal credibility because they congeal with voters' beliefs and typically sour political mood. Many Americans distrust positive information about candidates, figuring it is all puff and fabricated. Perceiving that is politics is, after all, a combat sport, negative ads resonate because they conform to voters' view of the political world, an attitude negative ads simultaneously shape. During the tremulous 2016 election, most voters were dissatisfied with the candidates, and close to 60 percent of voters said they were "frustrated" and "disgusted" with the campaign (Kludt, 2016). In this environment, negative ads fit the prevailing voter mood. The linkage between sour political mood and negative advertising can confer credibility on these ads, or prime the negative ad, making it more accessible in memory.

Learning and Reinforcement

Negative ads have other cognitive influences. We know that political advertising facilitates learning, enhancing knowledge of candidates' issue positions and personal qualities (Freedman, Franz, & Goldstein, 2004; Kaid, 2004, 2006; Fowler et al., 2016). Given that negative ads are short and condense issue positions to a snippet, knowledge is relatively superficial.

Negative ads, like political ads more generally, can bolster partisan attachments, strengthening attitudes, even increasing political participation and mobilizing the base in close elections (Ansolabehere & Iyengar, 1995; Kim, Wang, Gotlieb, Gabay, & Edgerly, 2013; Matthes & Marquart, 2015). Voters filter political ads through their attitudes, interpreting them in light of partisan attachments and feelings about the candidates (West, 2014). Negative spots that resonate with preexisting attitudes can strengthen commitment to a preferred candidate.

Conditional Effects

Negative ads do not work in a vacuum and are moderated by a host of contextual factors. Contextual variables that can influence negative advertising effects include (1) the competitiveness of the race; (2) the degree to which information environment is polarized (with ads primarily coming from one political party; Kim et al., 2013); (3) whether the attacks are funded by a super PAC rather than a candidate (Dowling & Wichowsky, 2015); (4) the emotions the ad arouses, such as anger, anxiety, or hope (e.g., Cho, 2013); and (5) the level of incivility of the negative message (Fridkin & Kenny, 2011).

Defining the Meaningful Issues

"Campaigns," as Kinder (2003) observed, "are not so much debates over a common set of issues as they are struggles to define what the election is about" (p. 365). This statement captures the essence of what candidates strive to achieve in political advertisements. Candidates use ads to set the agenda, prime issues, negatively frame the opponent, and wrap the campaign around their own issues and strengths. As discussed in detail in Chapters 6 and 7, candidates strive mightily to achieve these goals, focusing on particular agendas (e.g., the economy, trade, immigration, or inequality), hoping to prime these issues so they come quickly to mind when voters cast their ballots. Candidates invoke a host of frames emphasizing those that appeal to the ideology of the base or will connect with undecided voters.

Ads that resonate with voter concerns, priming agendas and framing issues persuasively, can influence voters. There is evidence that advertising exposure is associated with increased poll support for candidates (Fowler et al., 2016). This doesn't prove advertising effects, but in conjunction with research and concepts reviewed above, it suggests that political spots can lead to short-term, sometimes consequential, strategic advantages. Clinton's margin over Trump increased by more than 2.5 points in locales where she ran more advertisements than he did. Clinton lost support to Trump in battleground states, like Wisconsin, where he out-advertised her (Vavreck, 2016b). We cannot pinpoint precisely the quantitative role advertising played in Clinton's popular vote success; nor do we know exactly the impact that advertising seems to have played in Trump's Electoral College victory, pivoted on close, but decisive, victory margins in battleground states.

The academic literature finds that political advertising can exert effects, but the influences are more circumscribed and specific than popular media discussions of negative advertising suggest. This could partly be methodological: It can be difficult to empirically document causal influences of political media. It is challenging to tease out advertising impact from other campaign events. It is possible that political ads exert grand effects. However, the available evidence—and in social science, that is all you have to go with—offers a more nuanced picture. Scholars believe that negative ads influence voters, but their assessment of effects is more conditional, a reminder that popular presumptions of political media effects are not always borne out by data.

When discussing negative ads, political consultants refer to viscerally negative advertisements, like Willie Horton (1988) or Swift Boats (2004) or pro-Obama ads in 2012 that incorrectly blamed Romney for a steelworker's plight (see Box 13.2). However, these are not representative of the totality of negative ads, some of which fail or never get seen. We also don't know exactly how effective these classic ads were, although there is some reason to believe they influenced attitudes. Despite the ambiguity, candidates and consultants stick with negative ads, presuming they are effective, and afraid if they don't go negative, they will lose in a close race to an opponent who has no qualms with attack ads.

NORMATIVE EVALUATION OF NEGATIVE ADVERTISING

What is the normative verdict on negative ads? Do they exert salutary or penurious effects on politics? Now that you appreciate the scientific evidence, let's examine the issue more philosophically.

In Defense of Negative Ads

Critics frequently charge that negative campaign ads turn off voters, reducing interest in politics. But there is little evidence that negative campaigns depress voter turnout in the aggregate (Arceneaux & Nickerson, 2010; Lau & Pomper, 2004; Lau et al., 2007). In fact, negative ads have several positive features.

First, negative ads tend to focus more on issues than positive spots (Fowler et al., 2016; Geer, 2006). A positive ad may not trash the opponent, but it can contain lots of puffed-up, Pollyannaish descriptions of the candidate. Negative ads frequently criticize the opponent's position on an economic, health, social, or foreign policy issue. The ad may put the opponent down, but it bases its argument on something more substantial than puff. It can offer a policy-based criticism or evidence, which constitutes a cogent argument against voting for a candidate. And unlike positive ads, which just tell you about the position of the candidate who sponsors the ad, negative ads impart information about both the sponsor and the target (Geer & Vavreck, 2014). In this way, negative spots can perform a valuable political function—helping candidates differentiate themselves from their opponents (Benoit, 2014). Ads that make civil criticisms of the opposing candidate, offering arguments rather than verbal aggression (Rancer & Avtgis, 2014), can be a legitimate way to promote a campaign.

Second, negative ads get people thinking, arguing, and actively processing politics. They engage voters' minds in a way that blander positive ads do not (see Brader, 2006; Kam, 2006). Spots that highlight relevant campaign content in a civil manner may actually increase interest and electoral participation (Fridkin & Kenney, 2011).

Third, negative campaign messages can encourage activists to work harder for their candidate and knock on more doors, with arguments against the opposing candidate at the ready (Brooks & Geer, 2007). After all, it is the partisans, not the ambivalent, who participate in electoral causes (Mutz, 2006). They are the ones who live in campaign offices during the campaign, making phone calls day in and day out. Partisans are the foot soldiers of democracy. If negative ads activate and persuade them to go out and work harder for their side, that can't be an entirely bad thing. It is undoubtedly good for politics.

Fourth, negative advertising provides a check on the system, offering useful correctives to politicians' puffed-up, sometimes-deceptive-positive claims. As critic Bradley Smith points out, "Without attention-grabbing, cogent, memorable, negative campaigning, almost no challenger can hope to win unless an incumbent has just been found guilty of a heinous crime (1996, p. A22). Negative ads provide candidates with a legitimate rhetorical mechanism to challenge incumbent presidents. They give challengers a way to lay out shortcomings in incumbents' records. As political scientist John C. Geer notes, "If the public wants to have accountability, someone has to do the accounting and that accounting is not done through positive feel-good appeals, but through harsh political attack where voters are made aware of the problems of the incumbent" (2006, p. 110). Absent negative commercials, Ronald Reagan might not have convinced the electorate to unseat Jimmy Carter, who presided over a sagging economy with double-digit inflation. Without negative ads, Bill Clinton could not have called out George H. W. Bush for his lackluster stewardship of America's economic ship of state.

Negative ads offer a check on incumbents. They give people political fodder they can call on when casting their votes. They force incumbents to stay accountable to voters. They also give newcomers a mechanism by which they can challenge the old guard and, theoretically, inject change into the system. More generally, they provide all candidates with a way of challenging and contesting an adversary's statements that are offensive, immoral, or prejudiced.

Criticisms of Negative Ads

The preceding arguments present a forceful defense of negative advertising. There is another side too, one that calls attention to shortcomings in negative spots.

First, for all their presentation of policy positions, negative ads (like their positive counterparts) frequently provide a superficial rendition of candidate positions on issues. They offer little by way of thoughtful political arguments, other than a 15- or 30-second denunciation.

Second, although negative ads do not depress turnout, they can, under some conditions, dispirit voters (Krupnikov, 2011), diminishing both trust in government and political efficacy, the belief that people can make a difference in politics (Ansolabehere & Iyengar, 1995; Lau & Pomper, 2004; Lau et al., 2007). Indeed, there is evidence that watching candidates disagree about politics up close, advancing arguments in a mean-spirited way, exacerbates negative feelings about the opposition, reducing the legitimacy of opposing viewpoints and diminishing political trust (Mutz, 2007; Mutz & Reeves, 2005; see also Moy & Pfau, 2000, and Gervais, 2014).

Third, negative ads reward opposition research, a tawdry type of political consulting in which strategists dig for dirt and try to uncover skeletons in the opponent's closet. Advertising specialists take these juicy, occasionally seamy tidbits and place them front and center in negative spots. This is a mean-spirited way to knock off a candidate who may otherwise have a fine record of public service. It can take candidates' statements out of context and imply that one misstatement, inept policy decision, or foolish personal behavior is a fair representation of a candidate's personality or time-honored record of attainments. Negative advertising abuses persuasion, exploiting storytelling to present a narrative, illustrated with evocative cinematic techniques, that slams, cuts down, and ridicules another human being for one unctuous purpose: Unseating the candidate and yanking away his or her power.

Fourth, negative ads can trifle with truth in ways that can be ethically problematic. To be sure, positive spots do the same. And negative spots do offer issue-based criticisms of incumbents' records and can raise reasonable questions about the opponent's positions on policy questions or qualifications for office. But here is the rub: Negative ads that contain factual distortions about the opponent can leave an imprint on memory, more so, research suggests, than inaccuracies communicated in positive spots. Research indicates that individuals can remember information they hear, while forgetting the source of the information. They retain "'facts' that are not factual," forgetting that they were conveyed by a biased, self-interested source (Zacks, 2015, p. 12). Attack ads that are factually inaccurate or invite false inferences trifle with truth, undermining ethical communication (see Box 13.2).

To be sure, negative ads can present cogent arguments against the opponent, provide a check on incumbents, and advance democratic aims. The problem lies in the negative spots that emphasize verbal aggression rather than argumentation. They take the low road, present uncivil attacks, and offer brazen condemnations of the opponent, guided, perhaps inevitably, given humans' political nature, by the proviso that in politics "winning is everything" (Strother, 2003, p. 1).

Thus, the normative balance sheet on negative ads is complex and quite interesting. Negative ads are not uniformly bad for the system, or good. Much depends on the way the negative attack is framed, and its tone. Negative ads can reduce turnout, but they may also animate strong partisans, propelling them to cast a vote when they view ads attacking their preferred candidate. After reviewing the literature, Lau and Rovner (2009) suggest that malicious mudslinging can turn voters off, but legitimate arguments against the opposing candidate might mobilize partisans, particularly Independents and those who centrally process campaign messages. Unfortunately, it is the uncivil ads that get the most attention on news and the greatest social media traffic, and these are the spots that can have deleterious effects on the citizenry.

BOX 13.2 CLASSIC DECEPTIONS

When critics talk about negative advertising deceptions, they frequently have several ads in mind. President Johnson's 1964 "Daisy" commercial, mentioned earlier, implied that opponent Barry Goldwater would start a nuclear war. Its indirect appeal is mild, by today's standards. Three exemplars of deceptive advertising are the anti-Dukakis "Willie Horton" ads of 1988, the Swift Boat Veterans' spots of 2004, and the anti-Romney advertisements a pro-Obama group produced in 2012. Let's begin with 1988, the most negative presidential advertising campaign in modern history.

In 1988 Vice President George H.W. Bush faced Democratic nominee Michael Dukakis, a former governor of Massachusetts. In the summer, Dukakis led George H.W. Bush by 17 points. Bush's consultants figured if they wanted to win they could not just emphasize Bush's experience as vice president or economic growth in the Reagan-Bush '80s. They had to go negative. Focus group participants said they were uncomfortable with Dukakis's support of a Massachusetts prison furlough program that permitted prisoners to receive weekend passes from jail. The intent of furloughs is to help reintegrate prisoners into society, so they are less likely to commit crimes when they are ultimately released. Massachusetts allowed one prisoner, Willie Horton, to receive as many as 10 weekend passes from jail. Horton was significant in several respects. He was a convicted murderer. On one of his prison leaves, he fled to Maryland, where he kidnapped a young couple and repeatedly raped the woman. Horton was Black, the woman White.

And so a series of infamous ads was developed, televised, and repeatedly shown, one memorably called "Revolving Door." This spot used the image of a revolving door to highlight Dukakis's policy of permitting prisoners to go in and out of prison, presumably forever. In the ad, the announcer stated that: "As governor, Michael Dukakis vetoed mandatory sentences for drug dealers. He vetoed the death penalty. His revolving door prison policy gave weekend furloughs to first-degree murderers not eligible for parole." The visual track reinforced the message by showed a revolving door containing bars that rotate back and forth as a long line of men in prison uniforms walk in and out the door (West, 2014).

The words "*268 escaped*" were then superimposed on the screen, cueing the announcer to dramatically intone: "While out, many committed other crimes, like kidnapping and rape." The ad invited the incorrect inference that 268 first-degree murderers had jumped furlough to rape and kidnap innocent people (Jamieson, 1992). But of the 268 prisoners who skipped furlough during Dukakis's first two terms as governor, only four were first-degree murderers not eligible for parole, and only one of these went on to kidnap and rape. That man was Willie Horton. Obviously, if four prisoners jump furlough, it is bad, and if one kidnaps and rapes, it is terrible. But the ad implied more, and the implication distorted the truth.

There was another, more serious problem with the anti-Dukakis advertising campaign. Another ad running at the same time starkly portrayed Horton, a "scowling Black man with a disheveled Afro" (Mayer, 2012, p. 42; see Figure 13.2). While on furlough, the ad said, he raped a White woman and stabbed her fiancé. The ads—*268 escaped* and the Horton spots—worked together, encouraging voters to see a Black man—a murderer and rapist—as the personification of Dukakis's revolving door prison policy. The ads deliberately invoked a racist archetype and linked it with Dukakis, priming voters and perhaps triggering fears and hostility among some Whites (Mendelberg, 2001). The man who developed the ads, Larry McCarthy, defended them, noting that people take crime seriously, the ads evoked suburban mothers' biggest fear, and he just wanted to find a way to move voters (Mayer, 2012). But that begs the question of why the ad chose to deliberately prime a racist myth.

Sixteen years later, in 2004, Bush's son, George W. Bush, faced a tough opponent, Democrat John Kerry, in a bruising campaign that focused on the tragedy of 9/11, the Iraq War, and improbably on the Vietnam War, long a focus of controversy for Baby Boom political leaders like Bush and Kerry. Kerry served in Vietnam during the late 1960s, expertly commandeering military patrol boats,

Continued

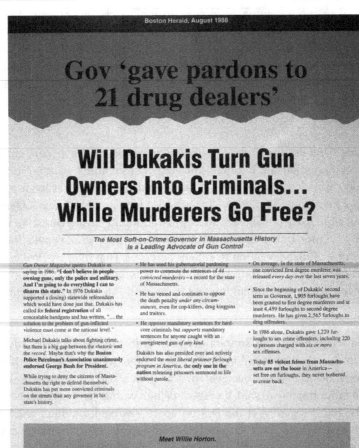

Figure 13.2 A controversial 1988 negative ad campaign deliberately linked Democratic nominee Michael Dukakis's anti-crime programs with a Black prisoner (shown below), inviting false inferences and promoting racist associations.

called swift boats, that came under enemy fire. He demonstrated exemplary leadership, while getting wounded himself. Kerry received several medals for his bravery. After his tour of duty, Kerry became a celebrated anti-war activist, condemning the war, even throwing away his medals in a public protest. It was the latter denunciations that got him in trouble with other veterans who served in Vietnam, some of whom understandably resented what they viewed as his stunning lack of patriotism. When Kerry ran for president in 2004, these Swift Boat Veterans developed a widely viewed series of negative ads that sought to discredit Kerry by claiming he had fabricated his military heroics and lied about a wound for which he received a Purple Heart. The veterans' charges were riddled with contradictions and inaccuracies, belying their claims and undermining their motives (Zernike & Rutenberg, 2004). However, their advertising campaign, which Kerry mistakenly failed to contest, may have reduced Kerry's credibility with some voters. In any case, it led to the creation of a new word. "Swiftboating," synonymous with smearing a candidate with personal attacks.

Eight years later came the "Soptic" ads, developed by a pro-Obama PAC, which were also effective, but misleading and staggeringly false. The ads, aired in the spring of 2012, were directed against the presumptive Republican nominee, Mitt Romney. They starred Joe Soptic, a steelworker who spoke dryly and sadly about how he and his family lost their health care when Mitt Romney and Bain Capital closed his steel plant in Kansas. "And a short time after that my wife became ill," he said, as the visual showed a shuttered plant with empty buildings, strewn with barbed wire. Speaking slowly and sadly, Soptic intoned that, "I don't know how long she was sick and I think maybe she didn't say anything because she knew we couldn't afford the insurance." When she became ill, he took her to the hospital. "That's when they found the cancer and by then it was Stage 4 . . . There was nothing they could do for her. And she passed away in 22 days." He added, with biting understatement, "I do not think Mitt Romney realizes what he's done to anyone. And, furthermore, I do not think Mitt Romney is concerned."

The negative ad laid the blame for Soptic's wife's death on Bain Capital and, by implication, at Mitt Romney, the president of the private equity firm. The ad contained a string of falsehoods. Romney was no longer coordinating day-to-day issues at Bain Capital when the steel plant closed its doors. It was not clear that Bain was directly responsible for the plant's closing. Although Soptic suggested that his wife lost her health care because he lost his job at the steel plant, this

Continued

was not true. Soptic's wife had insurance of her own even after he was laid off, and she did not pass away immediately after his layoff, but five years later. The ad cruelly blamed Romney for a woman's death, when the truth was much different. *The Washington Post* rated the ad as highly inaccurate, giving it four Pinocchios. Nonetheless, the Soptic ads may have created the impression that Romney was an insensitive plutocrat, an image that may have stuck in the minds of undecided voters at a time when they were just learning about the campaign.

The Federal Trade Commission (FTC), which regulates advertising in the U.S., stipulates that deceptive selling practices are unlawful. The problem is determining what constitutes a deceptive ad. The FTC allows advertisers considerable freedom in making claims that can border on the deceptive, both to protect freedom of speech and avoid standing in the way of marketers' freedom to sell products as they wish. It is difficult to define exactly what is legally deceptive. The FTC has been reluctant to regulate political ads because, for better or worse, this would involve government restrictions on political speech, endemic to democracy. The price of this freedom is ads like Horton that invite false inferences, and spots like Swift Boats and Soptic that make questionable, arguably incorrect factual statements. While respect for honesty might argue for restricting the ads, the FTC would be hard-pressed to win in court, where the bar is set high for restrictions on free speech. Making questionable claims or those that invite false inferences does not usually rise to the level of illegal deception. Restricting political ads would also set a precedent for government interference with political speech. Thus, most critics of these negative ads prefer other solutions, such as those discussed below.

CORRECTING MISPERCEPTIONS

How can misleading ads be controlled, countered, or checked? Ironically, one practical way to counter untruthful or misleading speech is more speech. Candidates who have been unfairly attacked can respond by rebutting the attacks in an advertisement of their own. It is commonly believed that Michael Dukakis and John Kerry ceded key political ground to their Republican opponents by failing to counter claims perpetrated in negative ads. Most experts believe that silently, politely ignoring opponents' attacks increases their credibility, inviting the perception that targeted candidates lack the courage of facts to challenge the negative claims. The challenge is how candidates can respond without burnishing their own reputation. Research suggests that candidates targeted by attack ads should hit back, reframing the criticism, and counterattacking.

But counterattacking can also produce a backlash among voters who dislike negative campaigns (Craig, Rippere, & Grayson, 2014). Although appropriate counterattacks can neutralize criticism, from a broader democratic view, it is not clear whether attacks followed by counterattacks clarify or crystallize voters' cognitions, or improve the quality of political information voters hold.

Thus, fact-checking by news media and specialized organizations has been advanced as a method to publicize and refute inaccurate claims. FactCheck.org and PolitiFact.com offer non-partisan checks on deceptive ads. Non-partisan fact-checkers scrutinize candidate ads, comparing claims candidates make about opponents with verifiable facts, looking to see if the claims are factually accurate. Journalists frequently turn to these groups when preparing articles that discuss negative ads. Fact-checks that challenge the accuracy of an ad can correct misimpressions, causing voters to perceive the misleading ad as less accurate and less fair (Fridkin, Kenney, & Wintersieck, 2015; Cappella & Jamieson, 1994). Effects can be stronger for individuals with low tolerance for negative campaigns (Fridkin et al., 2015). The mere presence of ad watches can discourage candidates from spewing lies. Unfortunately, they have shortcomings.

First, fact-checking news reports run the risk of magnifying the effects of the misleading spot (Ansolabehere & Iyengar, 1995). In their zeal to describe the juicy, misleading tidbits of a particular ad, journalists rebroadcast, or in websites attach, the ad, giving it free publicity and a double whammy of promotion. News viewers may see or hear the deceptive ad and ignore the journalistic criticism, much to the delight of strategists who developed the spot.

Second, technical problems can minimize fact-check effects. The printed information that identifies the sponsor of the ad—or corrects the misinformation—may not be on the screen long enough to allow viewers to process and remember the information (West, 2010). This is less true of web-based services, which print a litany of corrections that can be perused.

The third problem is viewer selectivity. In an era of niche media, people can tune in to cable news programs, blogs, and posts that reinforce their view of the political world, while blissfully ignoring programming with which they disagree. As a result of selective exposure, viewers may not see fact checks that correct false claims made by their candidate. This is unfortunate, as it means that partisan voters may never gain exposure to facts that challenge a deceptive claim. What's more, partisans share fact-checking messages in a highly selective manner, only retweeting messages that cast their party's candidate in a positive light and filtering fact-checking messages that support the candidate from the opposing party (Shin & Thorson, 2017).

Making matters worse, campaign consultants play to these trends. They sometimes derogate fact-checkers, adopting a self-serving, strangely postmodern critique. Back in 2012, after PolitiFact gave one prominent Romney ad a "Pants on Fire" rating, its most deceptive designation, the Romney campaign chose to dig in its heels. Rather than acknowledging the inaccuracy and trying to correct it, a Romney aide maligned fact-checking services, suggesting that fact checkers have their own biased beliefs, and the campaign was not going to let itself be guided by fact-checkers (that is, by facts). At different points of a presidential campaign, both sides have repeated claims that were false (Cooper, 2012). By trying to suggest that "hey, it's all relative, and fact-checkers are biased too," campaign consultants derogate legitimate fact-checking services. Willing to sell out truth for power, they denigrate the need for accurate information that is essential for responsible voting—and governing.

THE BROADER PERSPECTIVE OF CAMPAIGN FINANCE

Political advertising is economically situated in the larger domain of campaign finance, a controversial, legally fraught arena that shapes the parameters of paid political speech. Although opinions differ on the ethics and jurisprudence, there is no disagreement that money plays a major role in politics. "Bigly," as President Donald Trump would say— and as a billionaire who has doled out money to many campaigns, including his own, he knows.

There is nothing wrong with people spending money on political commercials. The problem is equality of access to the political elites. During campaigns and in the years between elections, people with deep financial pockets give more to public officials than those with less money. Well-heeled political lobbies can vastly outspend their less financially well-endowed counterparts. As Scholzman, Verba, and Brady (2012) point out:

> Organizations representing those with deep pockets vastly outnumber advocates for the middle class and the poor. And of the billions of dollars spent annually on lobbying in Washington, 72 percent comes from organizations representing business interests, and no more than 2 percent from organizations representing the vast majority below the very top.
>
> (p. 2)

This is legal, but not entirely ethical, because money buys access. The rich have more access to candidates and more ability to influence policies once candidates are elected than do the poor and middle class.

Let's focus on elections. During the first portion of the 2016 presidential campaign, just 158 families and their businesses contributed more than $175 million to Democratic and Republican candidates, more than half of the money expended at this juncture of the presidential race. The overwhelming number of the big donors were older, rich White men. Many live near one another in the richest neighborhoods in the country, are business partners and occasionally "poker buddies," who patronize the same symphonies and museums (Confessore, Cohen, & Yourish, 2015). In 2012, Sheldon Adelson, a billionaire casino mogul, shelled out $16 million to a PAC that supported Newt Gingrich's 2012 candidacy for the Republican presidential nomination (Confessore, 2012a). The brothers Koch—Charles and David—both billionaire conservative businessmen raised an estimated $200 million for independent political groups opposing Barack Obama's reelection. Over on the Democratic side, well-heeled liberal donors, like billionaire financier George Soros, pumped some $100 million into independent liberal organizations that supported Democratic candidates in the 2012 election (Confessore, 2012b). Unions and other Democratic groups were on board, presumably spending hundreds of millions of dollars on national, state, and municipal elections. And on both sides of the political aisle, huge donations given to independent liberal and conservative groups now can be kept secret, passed through organizations that hide the names of the donors who wrote the checks.

All this is legal, a result of the 2010 Supreme Court **Citizens United** decision that stipulated the government could not ban independent political spending by corporations and unions in elections. Critics condemned the 5–4 decision, arguing that it would allow big corporations to "flood the political marketplace" and "drown out" the views of ordinary Americans (Liptak, 2010). Defenders praised the decision, calling it a victory for free speech. As a result of the Court decision, independent political groups have more freedom to run ads to support candidates they favor and to take down candidates they oppose. Many the political advertisements you saw on TV or online in 2016 were developed by super political action committees, or super PACs.

Campaigns need money. They use it to pay for political ads, but also to send out old-fashioned political mailings. They need bucks to hire consultants and pollsters, but also to field grassroots campaign offices across the country, where staff members must be hired to train volunteers, make telephone pitches to undecided voters, and register sympathetic voters in swing states. Campaigns are expensive, and during each electoral cycle, costs seem to rise to a new, unprecedented level.

What role should money play in politics? Should government restrict the ability of rich donors—aka fat cats (or big dogs, if you prefer a canine metaphor)—to make lavish donations to political campaigns? It is a time-honored question, one that goes back to previous eras, where corruption was the coin (literally) of the realm. One thing is clear: You cannot understand contemporary presidential politics without appreciating the role that money and campaign finance play in the process.

The battle lines have been sharply drawn. Conservatives argue that government does not have the right to bar corporations from trying to influence electoral outcomes, emphasizing that corporations have legal rights, like people. Liberals respond that corporate money corrupts the political marketplace, exerting an undue impact on elections and elected officials. In order to understand the current era, a brief historical review is helpful.

Watergate

Jaw-dropping ethical abuses occurred in the wake of the Watergate scandal, which unfolded after a team of burglars, their actions sanctioned by President Nixon's attorney general, broke into the Democratic National Committee headquarters at the Watergate Hotel in Washington, D.C., in June 1972. Incredibly, Nixon's presidential reelection campaign earmarked money to pay the burglars and paid them hush money to keep quiet. Thus, secret campaign funds helped finance the Watergate burglary and cover-up. During this period, in the early 1970s, other abuses occurred. The dairy industry donated $2 million to Nixon's campaign and was awarded with an increase in price supports for milk, allowing executives to make more money off dairy products. The telephone conglomerate, known then as International Telephone and Telegraph (ITT), promised $400,000 to fund the 1972 Republican convention in San Francisco. In exchange, the Justice Department settled an antitrust case in a manner favoring ITT; Nixon personally went to bat for ITT (Wertheimer, 2012).

Post-Watergate Reforms

It takes a lot for the two houses of Congress to pull together and pass sweeping campaign reform. Watergate served as a massive impetus. In 1974, Congress implemented major changes to campaign finance laws in an effort to curtail the parties' dependence on wealthy donors, discourage secret campaign contributions, and reduce the high cost of presidential campaigns. The new legislation placed limits on how much money an individual donor could give to a candidate and stipulated that contributions above a certain amount had to be publicly identified. It established an independent government agency, the Federal Election Commission, to enforce election law, and required substantial disclosure of campaign spending.

But opponents, arguing that campaign reforms threatened free speech, objected, and took their case to the Supreme Court. In the 1976 *Buckley v. Valeo* decision, the Court took a libertarian turn, arguing that Congress could *not* limit **campaign expenditures**.

"Money is speech," they declared, and candidates "can spend as much as they want of their own money on their campaigns; it would be unconstitutional to limit their expenditures" (Toobin, 2012, p. 43–44). But it was okay for Congress to limit **campaign contributions** since this was only a component of candidate support and would not imperil free speech. Thus, Congress could restrict how much money a particular individual gave to a campaign. It was a dizzyingly complicated distinction, but the upshot was that candidates could spend their own fortunes on their campaigns, if they wanted to. To forbid this was to violate the First Amendment, the Court ruled. Conservatives generally liked aspects of the decision because it preserved the right of individuals to spend as much as they wanted to get elected. Liberals were ambivalent, disputing the notion that money equals speech. In their view, this worked to the advantage of well-heeled, millionaire candidates.

McCain-Feingold

The Watergate reforms failed to stop the diffusion of big money into political campaigns. Moneyed interests found new ways to circumvent the law. The 2002 Bipartisan Campaign Reform Act, sponsored by Senators John McCain and Russell Feingold, sought to eliminate the loopholes. First, it barred political parties from raising unlimited "soft money" campaign contributions, which are technically made outside federal political campaign laws. In effect, this meant that corporations, unions, and millionaires could not make unlimited donations to parties. Second, the law banned corporate or union funding of broadcast or cable media advertisements that mentioned a candidate within a specified period. A union- or corporate-funded broadcast ad that mentioned a candidate constituted "electioneering." It could not appear within 30 days of a primary or within 60 days of a general election. The logic was that these ads could have a major impact during the key periods when many voters made up their minds. Big donations could exert an extraordinary impact, giving rich organizations the ability to exert undue sway over electoral outcomes. The law was not perfect, but it imposed limits.

The Supreme Court Expands Free Speech and Opens the Floodgates

Conservatives were furious. Believing that the First Amendment was sacrosanct and brooked no exceptions, they could not, for the life of them, see why there should be any limits on advertising whatsoever. This was America, after all. Liberals responded that yes, this is America, and the "m" in America stands for money! Big money talks, drowning out smaller voices. But money has a right to talk, conservatives said; it is speech. *Buckley* said it was. Liberals responded that the decision was flawed and unfair. So the argument went.

On the lookout for an opportunity to challenge the McCain-Feingold law, conservatives found one, and an odd case it was. In the run-up to the 2008 election, a conservative nonprofit corporation called Citizens United produced a documentary, *Hillary: The Movie*, that used news, interviews, and creepy music to undermine the candidacy of Hillary Clinton. Now remember the McCain-Feingold law? It said that any communication that mentioned a candidate and ran it a month before a primary was "electioneering" and illegal. The Federal Election Commission said this was true of *Hillary: The Movie*. Thus, it could not be broadcast. Arguing this was unconstitutional, conservatives took the case to the Supreme Court.

Conservatives argued that "corporations had the right under the First Amendment to spend unlimited amounts on election advertising" (Lewis, 2014, p. 6). They implicitly argued that corporations are no different than individuals, imbued with the same right as "natural persons" to spend unlimited money on behalf of their preferred candidate. Liberals contested the idea that corporations are in any way equivalent to persons. "Whatever else corporations may be, they are not the sum of their people," Lewis argued (2014), adding that "the modern corporation is a brilliant invention of 19th century capitalism" (p. 6).

Arguing that that money is equivalent to speech, conservative libertarians argued forcefully before the Supreme Court. This time, conservatives won. In a 5–4 decision, the Court held that that *the government could not prohibit spending by corporations and unions in elections*. Corporations, unions, and rich individuals—the Court said there was no difference among these three entities—could give as much money as they wanted to develop an ad that mentions a candidate and could run the ad up to Election Day. They could sponsor the ad themselves or funnel the money to an independent political group, which could develop the advertisement. Citizens United permitted the establishment of a new political group, the super PAC, that could explicitly speak in favor of a candidate's campaign, criticize opponents, and raise as much money as it saw fit, so long as it did not contribute to the candidate's war chest (Franklin, Franz, & Ridout, 2016). The ban on corporate and union contributions to parties and candidates remained. But Citizens United shattered post-Watergate era restraints on campaign spending and key aspects of the 2002 McCain-Feingold law. It was a victory for unrestrained free speech.

Defenders made a strong case for the decision. "Speech is an essential mechanism of democracy," Supreme Court Justice Anthony Kennedy wrote in defense of the decision, adding that "the First Amendment protects speech and speaker" (Toobin, 2012, pp. 45–46). "Speech is . . . constitutionally protected," noted conservative law professor Michael W. McConnell, "not because we doubt the speech inflicts harm, but because we fear the censorship more" (2012, p. 14). For conservatives, money is speech and free speech is sacrosanct.

Liberals thundered back, arguing that the Supreme Court decision would unleash "a torrent of money from businesses and the multimillionaires who run them, and as a result (would lead to) "the corporate takeover of American politics" (Bai, 2012, p. 14). Contesting conservatives' claim that money is equivalent to speech, they noted that money is not evenly distributed across different economic groups. They acknowledged that individual freedom to spend money in a campaign is important, but argued that Congress has a more substantial interest in ensuring the integrity of elections. They argued, as Justice Stephen Breyer observed in a subsequent decision, that "where enough money calls the tune, the general public will not be heard" (Liptak, 2014, p. A16).

Critics and defenders of Citizens United generally agree that the decision has had three, largely unintended, problematic consequences.

First, spending by outside groups has increased astronomically since the Supreme Court's decision. Independent non-political party spending on campaigns has risen in recent years, with the growth of super PACs. As a result of Citizens United, established political parties—flawed organizations, but at least with ties to elected officials—have been sidelined, playing a much less influential role than they did in years past. Because parties cannot legally receive unlimited amounts of money, but independent political groups can, the spout through which money passes is controlled by the rich players in American politics (Rutenberg, 2014). There are rich players on the Right, and rich players on the Left. Either way, the wealthy underwrite American campaigns.

Complementing this trend, in a landmark 2014 decision, the Supreme Court narrowly struck down a time-honored cap on the total amount of money an individual donor could contribute to federal candidates in the biennial electoral cycle. While conservatives emphasized that financial caps placed an unnecessary burden on individuals' right to participate in elections, liberals stressed government's interest in preventing the corroding influence of money. That more money has been spent, primarily by rich individuals and special interest super PACs, makes it more likely winning candidates will feel beholden to do the bidding of these groups after the election.

Defenders of Citizens United counter that the amount of money political groups spend on advertising every four years is a pittance compared with the dollars doled out by businesses for commercial ads every day, particularly for events like the Super Bowl, where a 30-second spot costs $5 million. And that's just one ad. Few criticize excesses in corporate spending. Conservatives argue that, given the essential role that election play in a democracy, we should encourage groups to exercise their constitutional right to free speech. It's a fair point, but it begs the question of whether money is speech, and access is evenly distributed across income lines.

A second problem with Citizens United is that many donations given to super PACs are kept secret. A $250,000 contribution to a super PAC supporting Romney in 2012 came from a group that had a post office box for a headquarters, but no apparent employees (Confessore & Luo, 2012). Technically, super PACs have to disclose donors by law. But to skirt this, donations are frequently passed through tax-exempt advocacy organizations that can legally hide the names of the donors who wrote the checks. Because they are technically not political organizations, these "dark money" groups, as they are appropriately called (Mayer, 2016), are not required to reveal the names of their donors to the Federal Election Commission (McIntire & Confessore, 2012). This runs counter to the ethos of transparency that guided post-Watergate campaign finance reforms. As a result of abuses committed in the wake of Citizens United, voters do not know who is donating to campaigns, the groups behind an advertisement, and the sponsors of political ads.

The secrecy—or, if you prefer, dishonesty—problem seems to get worse with every election. During the 2014 election, a particularly expensive midterm campaign, hidden financial donors with obscure names like B-PAC or patriotic-sounding ones like Alliance for a Free Society, unloaded tens of millions of dollars late in the campaign (Confessore & Willis, 2014). The sources of the money were hard to locate. Groups frequently do not disclose donors and could be nothing but shell companies for the special interests that developed the ads. In some state congressional races, the political action committees raise nearly all their funds from out-of-state. (In one case, a group that called itself Kansans Support Problem Solvers did not include anyone from Kansas.) Yet the groups claim to be fervently concerned with problems facing state residents. The hidden wealthy donors—with ideological or selfish agendas—poured their money into negative, frequently vitriolic ads. Because of the loose rules that resulted from Citizens United, voters have no way of connecting a paid political message with the people who fund it, in violation of the transparency so critical to electoral democracy.

Third, candidates can collude with special interest super PACs, violating the spirit, if not the letter, of Citizens United. The Supreme Court said super PACs could raise as much money as they wanted to support or oppose a candidate. However, in order to prevent money from corrupting a candidate's campaign, whereby the candidate would curry favor with the super PAC in exchange for future favors, super PACs were not allowed to contribute directly to a candidate's campaign war chest. So, they contribute indirectly.

Attack ads are funded by political action committees that operate independently of candidates' campaigns, but they have the candidate's tacit, wink-and-a-nod acceptance. This allows candidates to benefit from nasty, sometimes deceptive, advertisements without having to take responsibility. Although candidates cannot directly coordinate their campaigns with super PACs, they can coexist within a shrouded gray area that allows candidates and super PACs to coordinate their tasks if plans are shared in public, in plain view of everyone (Corasaniti, 2015). Thus, candidates like 2016 Republican presidential contender Carly Fiorina developed a totally public Google calendar of events, allowing a super PAC access to this so it could promote Fiorina's activities. For example, knowing that Fiorina was scheduled to appear at a campaign event, members of a supportive super PAC showed up before she came to set up tables, with placards and posters they had paid for. Increasingly, PACs are financing activities, such as organizing campaign volunteers, that candidates used to fund, in this way circumventing the letter of the law, sometimes with candidates' blessing, hoping for payback later. There is evidence that this works. Candidates benefit when an outside group "does their dirty work" (Dowling & Wichowsky, 2015, p. 19). They gain when an outside group sponsors a negative ad because voters do not link the candidate to the attack spot. But these procedures run afoul of the spirit of the law, reducing transparency, and thwarting democratic tenets.

What to Do?

These problems may raise red flags in your mind, causing you to wonder about the state of American democracy. Or you may retort that these are hypothetical problems: We do not know for sure that big donors have actually influenced elected officials' policy decisions, that the overlapping roles between super PACs and candidates have caused any harmful effects, or that the hundreds of millions of dollars spent on political ads converted any voters. After all, the Clinton campaign, along with pro-Clinton super PACs, outspent Trump and his supporters, but she lost.

One may approve of Citizens United because it enshrines free speech. That's a legitimate argument, and the majority of the Supreme Court agrees. What's more, as the Bernie Sanders campaign demonstrated in 2016, a popular candidate with a message and missive can run a campaign—at least in the primaries—without reliance on corporate super PACs. The Sanders campaign raised $230 million during the primary campaign; about $216 million was raised online, with each supporter donating an average of just $27.

The problem with Citizens United is less the consequences, which are debatable, than the processes for inequitable electioneering it has encouraged. Critics are troubled by the ways that Citizens United reduces transparency, encourages secretive political activities, and increases the ability of the rich to bankroll political campaigns (see Bai, 2012; Lessig, 2011). With super-rich oligarchs funding the bulk of political ads, campaigns have become battles between billionaire moguls from the Left and the Right. One can accept this as an inevitable consequence of First Amendment freedom, or suggest alternative ways to finance campaigns (Ackerman & Ayres, 2002; Lessig, 2011). These alternative proposals are not without problems, but they represent thoughtful solutions to campaign finance ills.

Lessig, focusing on public funding of congressional elections, suggests that the first $50 of the tax revenue each American pays the U.S. Treasury each year be converted into a "democracy voucher." Each voter could decide to allocate the voucher in whatever way he or she wanted, giving the entire $50 to a particular candidate, or dividing it among different candidates. Candidates could accept the money, so long as they agreed the only funds they would use to finance their campaigns would be democracy vouchers or small citizen contributions. They could not accept money from PACs. Lessig calculates that if every registered voter participated in the system, it would yield millions of dollars in campaign funds for each electoral cycle. This could remove the taint of corporate contributions, ensure that campaigns are funded by citizens, not the richest 1 percent, and restore trust to the political process.

It's a worthy idea, but not without drawbacks. Notably, it does not solve the problem of inequality. Candidates with fewer resources would be hard-pressed to pay for the advertising needed to persuade voters to contribute democracy voucher to their campaigns. Wealthier, politically connected, and arguably more status quo–situated candidates could easily bankroll the advertising that could persuade voters to allocate democracy dollars to their already well-heeled campaigns. To proponents of Lessig's plan, this is better than what we have now, because it at least puts campaign finance decisions in the hands of citizens, not super PACs. But it remains unclear if enough people would actually pony up their money to democracy vouchers, whether unsavory characters might find ways to persuade gullible voters to use their vouchers for candidates these persuaders favored, and if the proposal would survive constitutional challenges.

Imperfect as it may be, Lessig's plan reflects popular discontent with campaign finance-as usual and a belief that the rich have gamed the political system. If political writer E. J. Dionne (1991) is correct that "a nation that hates politics will not long survive as a democracy" (p. 355), then we need to consider ways of changing the system so it continues to respect the First Amendment but takes into account the corrosive influences of money on politics. Requiring full disclosure of donors to political ads and reducing the influence of dark money in politics is a start. This would not impinge on the First Amendment (a problem with some proposals to counter Citizens United). However, it could bring needed transparency to campaign finance.

Overhaul of the system is another possibility, with modifications of Lessig's with proposals that are politically palatable and feasible. As campaign reformer Zephyr Teachout (2015) argued:

We need to provide enough public funding for campaigns so that anyone with a broad base of support can run for office, and respond effectively to attacks, without becoming dependent on private patrons. Running for office shouldn't be a job defined by permanent begging at the feet of the wealthiest donors in the country.

(p. A21)

CONCLUSIONS

Frequently criticized, constantly lamented, political advertising is the bête noire, the grand object of dislike, in the presidential campaign. Political ads, particularly negative spots, are presumed to have no redeeming democratic features and perceived to be all-powerful. Neither assumption holds up under social scientific study. Ads do have salutary democratic features and frequently fail to achieve their political objectives.

Political ads play an important strategic role in presidential campaigns. They are expensive, targeted at must-win states, and increasingly financed by outside political groups, many of which have little accountability. Political ads have become more negative over the years, with negative spots increasingly directed online to YouTube and other venues. There is a science, as well as an art, to political advertising. Content analyses document that ads differ in terms of whether they focus on issues or images—and contrary to popular assumptions, these categories are not dichotomous, but can overlap. Negative ads have different components, differing in whether attacks are direct or comparative, their level of civility, and their accuracy. While negative campaigning dates back to antiquity and to scores of colorful, vitriolic American electoral elections, paid negative commercials are a mid-20th-century phenomena, increasing in their production savvy in recent decades.

Contrary to popular myth, negative ads are not all-powerful; far from it. Like all political communications, they can succeed or fail, their effects limited by voters' preexisting attitudes, appropriateness of content, and the degree to which the ad resonates with voter concerns. Like all political communications, negative advertising influences are influenced by context and conditions. They can be memorable, reinforce strong attitudes, and define the issues in the campaign through agenda-setting, priming, and framing. There is evidence suggesting they can move the polls, sometimes consequentially, but we lack precision in specifying the strength of these effects. Despite their conditional and sometimes limited impact, ads continue to be a staple in campaigns, because consultants believe they work, they *can* influence candidate attitudes, and candidates don't want to risk losing the election because they failed to advertise. Thus, the perception that ads work is as important an influence on strategic advertising choices as their actual effects.

Even more interesting is the normative balance sheet on political ads, particularly negative spots. Ads exert salutary effects, providing issue information and serving as a check on automatic reelection of incumbents. Negative spots that are civil and emphasize argumentation, rather than aggression, can advance democratic aims. Ads *can* be negative, but not nasty. But these virtues of negative spots are neutralized by drawbacks, including brute incivility in so many prominent ads, reductions in political efficacy, and communication of inaccurate, misleading information that may be reinforced by partisan selective exposure. Political advertising deception is a complicated construct and can be difficult to demonstrate convincingly in court. Because government agencies are loath to regulate political spots, for political and legal (First Amendment) reasons, efforts to promote truth rest on increasing voters' critical awareness and systematic fact-checks. The latter can be effective, but given selective exposure in today's media environment, the correct information may never reach voters, thereby failing to correct the misimpression the negative ad instilled.

Political ads are situated in the broader domain of campaign finance, and there are reasonable differences of opinion on the merits of campaign finance reform. The 2010 Supreme Court Citizens United decision, which followed several decades of jurisprudence, stipulated that the federal government cannot ban independent spending by corporations and unions in elections. This opened the floodgates to unprecedented corporate spending, pleasing First Amendment advocates, but distressing critics who worry about the possibility that well-heeled outside groups can control the direction of American politics. It is hard to tie increases in spending in politics to Citizens United because we do not have a control group that would permit examination of how groups would have advertised in the absence of the ruling. And there are cogent arguments on behalf of allowing groups to advocate as freely as they wish, on the assumption that money is equivalent to speech. But is it? If the rich have more ability to engage in paid speech than everyone else and greater access to elected officials, is campaign finance truly democratic? At the very least, Citizens United has produced a palpable increase in the number of ads that do not disclose donors, more possibilities of collusion between super PACs and candidates, and less transparency—in short, more dark money and less electoral sunshine.

Political advertising, particularly negative campaigning, is a messy, complex business, fraught with systemic benefits and democratic costs. In the end, presidential elections are about persuasion, and persuasion is not equivalent to truth. As Geer (2006, p. 158) notes, "politics is about disagreement," and disagreement is bound to lead its protagonists to cannily frame, slant, and even distort. Lau and Pomper (2004) emphasize that "elections are about choices, not courtesy" (p. 93). On the other hand, when candidates use words deceptively, they reduce the quality of voter choice. When they resort to uncivil attack ads, they denigrate democratic discourse. When super PACS spend millions on ads, they affirm the value of speech—but *their* speech, not that of less afflu-ent citizens, who cannot pay for political spots. Alas, political advertising, in Schud-son's (1986) words, remains an "uneasy persuasion."

REFERENCES

Ackerman, B., & Ayres, I. (2002). *Voting with dollars: A new paradigm for campaign finance.* New Haven, CT: Yale University Press.

Ansolabehere, S., & Iyengar, S. (1995). *Going negative: How attack ads shrink and polarize the electorate.* New York: Free Press.

Arceneaux, K., & Nickerson, D. W. (2010). Comparing negative and positive campaign mes-sages: Evidence from two field experiments. *American Politics Research, 38,* 54–83.

Bai, M. (2012, July 22). How did political money get this loud? *The New York Times Magazine,* 14, 16, 18.

Baumgartner, J. C., & Francia, P. L. (2016). *Conventional wisdom and American elections: Exploding myths, exploring misconceptions* (3rd ed.). Lanham, MD: Rowman & Littlefield.

Benoit, W. L. (2014). *A functional analysis of political television advertisements.* Lanham, MD: Lexington Books.

Berry, J. M., & Sobieraj, S. (2014). *The outrage industry: Public opinion media and the new incivility.* New York: Oxford University Press.

Boller, P. F., Jr. (2004). *Presidential campaigns: From George Washington to George W. Bush.* New York: Oxford University Press.

Brader, T. (2006). *Campaigning for hearts and minds: How emotional appeals in political ads work.* Chicago: University of Chicago Press.

Brooks, D. J., & Geer, J. G. (2007). Beyond negativity: The effects of incivility on the electorate. *American Journal of Political Science, 51,* 1–16.

Burns, A., & Haberman, M. (2016, July 31). 3 states seen as "must wins" for Trump bid. *The New York Times,* 1, 17.

Cappella, J. N., & Jamieson, K. H. (1994). Broadcast adwatch effects: A field experiment. *Com-munication Research, 21,* 342–365.

Chadwick, A. (2013). *The hybrid media system: Politics and power.* New York: Oxford Univer-sity Press.

Chira, S. (2017, January 15). Women who voted for Donald Trump, in their own words. *The New York Times,* 12.

Cho, J. (2013). Campaign tone, political affect, and communicative engagement. *Journal of Communication, 63,* 1130–1152.

Confessore, N. (2012a, April 13). Campaigns plan maximum push to raise money. *The New York Times,* A1, A15.

Confessore, N. (2012b, May 8). Liberal donors will spend big on grass roots. *The New York Times,* A1, A16.

Confessore, N., Cohen, S., & Yourish, K. (2015, October 10). The families funding the 2016 election. *The New York Times.* Retrieved from www.nytimes.com/interactive/2015/10/11/us/politics/2016-presidential-election-super-pac-donors.html (Accessed January 21, 2017).

Confessore, N., & Luo, M. (2012, February 2). Secrecy shrouds "Super PAC" funds in latest filings. *The New York Times*, A1, A16.

Confessore, N., & Willis, D. (2014, November 3). Hidden donors spend heavily on attack ads. *The New York Times*, A1, A16.

Cooper, M. (2012, September 1). Fact-checkers howl, but both sides seem attached to dishonest ads. *The New York Times*, A12.

Corasaniti, N. (2015, October 1). Fiorina's "Super PAC" gives help in plain sight. *The New York Times*, A20.

Corasaniti, N. (2016, January 8). Advertising wars of 2016 campaign erupt in a changing television arena. *The New York Times*, A14.

Corasaniti, N., & Shorey, R. (2016, October 23). Outside money favors Clinton at a 2-to-1 rate over her rival. *The New York Times*, 1, 18.

Craig, S.C., Rippere, P.S., & Grayson, M.S. (2014). Attack and response in political campaigns: An experimental study in two parts. *Political Communication, 31*, 647–674.

Dionne, E.J., Jr. (1991). *Why Americans hate politics*. New York: Simon & Schuster.

Dowling, C.M., & Wichowsky, A. (2015). Attacks without consequence? Candidates, parties, groups, and the changing face of negative advertising. *American Journal of Political Science, 59*, 19–36.

Edgerly, S., Bode, L., Kim, Y.M., & Shah, D.V. (2013). Campaigns go social: Are Facebook, YouTube and Twitter changing elections? In T.D. Ridout (Ed.), *New directions in media and politics* (pp. 82–99). New York: Routledge.

Fallis, T.W. (2014). Political advertising. In K. Kenski & K.H. Jamieson (Eds.), *The Oxford handbook of political communication*. Retrieved from www.oxfordhandbooks.com. (Accessed July 17, 2016).

Fowler, E.F., Franz, M.M., & Ridout, T.N. (2016). *Political advertising in the United States*. Boulder, CO: Westview Press.

Fowler, E.F., Ridout, T.N., & Franz, M.M. (2016). Political advertising in 2016: The presidential race as outlier? *The Forum: A Journal of Applied Research in Contemporary Politics, 14*, 445–469.

Freedman, P., Franz, M., & Goldstein, K. (2004). Campaign advertising and democratic citizenship. *American Journal of Political Science, 48*, 723–741.

Fridkin, K.L., & Kenney, P.J. (2011). Variability in citizens' reactions to different types of negative campaigns. *American Journal of Political Science, 55*, 307–325.

Fridkin, K.L., Kenney, P.J., & Wintersieck, A. (2015). Liar, liar, pants on fire: How fact-checking influences citizens' reactions to negative advertising. *Political Communication, 32*, 127–151.

Geer, J.G. (2006). *In defense of negativity: Attack ads in presidential campaigns*. Chicago: University of Chicago Press.

Geer, J.G., & Vavreck, L. (2014). Negativity, information, and candidate position-taking. *Political Communication, 31*, 218–236.

Gervais, B.T. (2014). Following the news? Reception of uncivil partisan media and the use of incivility in political expression. *Political Communication, 31*, 564–583.

Huffman, A., & Rejebian, M. (2012). *We're with nobody: Two insiders reveal the dark side of American politics*. New York: Morrow.

Jamieson, K.H. (1986). The evolution of political advertising in America. In L.L. Kaid, D. Nimmo, & K.R. Sanders (Eds.), *New perspectives on political advertising* (pp. 1–20). Carbondale, IL: Southern Illinois Press.

Jamieson, K.H. (1992). *Dirty politics: Deception, distraction, and democracy.* New York: Oxford University Press.

Jamieson, K.H., Volinsky, A., Weitz, I., & Kenski, K. (2014). The political uses and abuses of civility and incivility. In K. Kenski & K.H. Jamieson (Eds.), *The Oxford handbook of political communication.* Retrieved from www.oxfordhandbooks.com. (Accessed July 17, 2016).

Johnson-Cartee, K.S., & Copeland, G.A. (1991). *Negative political advertising: Coming of age.* Hillsdale, NJ: Lawrence Erlbaum Associates.

Kaid, L.L. (2004). Political advertising. In L.L. Kaid (Ed.), *Handbook of political communication research* (pp. 155–202). Mahwah, NJ: Lawrence Erlbaum Associates.

Kaid, L.L. (2006). Political advertising. In S.C. Craig (Ed.), *The electoral challenge: Theory meets practice* (pp. 79–96). Washington, DC: CQ Press.

Kam, C.D. (2006). Political campaigns and open-minded thinking. *Journal of Politics, 68,* 931–945.

Kern, M. (1989). *30-second politics: Political advertising in the eighties.* New York: Praeger.

Kim, Y.M., Wang, M., Gotlieb, M.R., Gabay, I., & Edgerly, S. (2013). Ambivalence reduction and polarization in the campaign information environment: The interaction between individual- and contextual-level influences. *Communication Research, 40,* 388–416.

Kinder, D.R. (2003). Communication and politics in the age of information. In D.O. Sears, L. Huddy, & R. Jervis (Eds.), *Oxford handbook of political psychology* (pp. 357–393). New York: Oxford University Press.

Kludt, T. (2016, September 21). *Pew poll: Most voters "frustrated," "disgusted" with 2016 election.* Retrieved from www.cnn.com/2016/09/21/politics/pew-poll-hillary-clinton-donald-trump/ (Accessed September 22, 2016).

Krosnick, J.A., & Petty, R.E. (1995). Attitude strength: An overview. In R.E. Petty & J.A. Krosnick (Eds.), *Attitude strength: Antecedents and consequences* (pp. 1–24). Hillsdale, NJ: Lawrence Erlbaum Associates.

Krupnikov, Y. (2011). When does negativity demobilize? Tracing the conditional effect of negative campaigning on voter turnout. *American Journal of Political Science, 55,* 796–812.

Lau, R.R., & Pomper, G.M. (2004). *Negative campaigning: An analysis of U.S. Senate elections.* New York & Lanham, MD: Rowman and Littlefield.

Lau, R.R., & Rovner, I.B. (2009). Negative campaigning. *Annual Review of Political Science, 12,* 285–306.

Lau, R.R., Sigelman, L., & Rovner, I.B. (2007). The effects of negative political campaigns: A meta-analytic reassessment. *Journal of Politics, 69,* 1176–1209.

Lessig, L. (2011). *Republic, lost: How money corrupts Congress—and a plan to stop it.* New York: Twelve.

Lewis, E.L. (2014, October 5). Who are "We the People"? *The New York Times* (Sunday Review), 1, 6.

Liptak, A. (2010, January 21). Justices, 5–4, reject corporate spending limit. *The New York Times,* Retrieved from www.nytimes.com/2010/01/22/us/politics/22scotus.html?_r=1 (Accessed January 22, 2017).

Liptak, A. (2014, April 3). Justices, 5–4, kill key spending cap in political races. *The New York Times*, A1, A16.

Mattes, K., & Redlawsk, D.P. (2014). *The positive case for negative campaigning*. Chicago: University of Chicago Press.

Matthes, J., & Marquart, F. (2015). A new look at campaign advertising and political engagement: Exploring the effects of opinion-congruent and-incongruent political advertisements. *Communication Research, 42*, 134–155.

Mayer, J. (2012, February 13 & 20). Attack dog. *The New Yorker*, 40–44, 47–49.

Mayer, J. (2016). *Dark money: The hidden history of the billionaires behind the rise of the radical right*. New York: Doubleday.

McConnell, M.W. (2012, June 24). You can't say that. *The New York Times Book Review*, 14.

McIntire, M., & Confessore, N. (2012, July 8). Groups shield political gifts of businesses. *The New York Times*, 1, 15.

Mendelberg, T. (2001). *The race card: Campaign strategy, implicit messages, and the norm of equality*. Princeton, NJ: Princeton University Press.

Motta, M. (2016). Air war? Campaign advertising in the 2016 presidential election. In D. Lilleker, E. Thorsen, D. Jackson, & A. Veneti (Eds.), *US election analysis 2016: Media, voters and the campaign: Early reflections from leading academics* (p. 34). Poole, England: Centre for the Study of Journalism, Culture and Community.

Moy, P., & Pfau, M. (2000). *With malice toward all? The media and public confidence in democratic institutions*. Westport, CT: Praeger.

Mutz, D.C. (2006). *Hearing the other side: Deliberative versus participatory democracy*. Cambridge: Cambridge University Press.

Mutz, D.C. (2007). Effects of "in your face" television discourse on perceptions of a legitimate opposition. *American Political Science Review, 101*, 621–635.

Mutz, D.C. (2015). *In-your-face politics: The consequences of uncivil media*. Princeton, NJ: Princeton University Press.

Mutz, D.C., & Reeves, B. (2005). The new videomalaise: Effects of televised incivility on political trust. *American Political Science Review, 99*, 1–15.

Newhagen, J.E., & Reeves, B. (1991). Emotion and memory responses for negative political advertising: A study of television commercials used in the 1988 presidential election. In F. Biocca (Ed.), *Television and political advertising, Volume 1: Psychological processes* (pp. 197–220). Hillsdale, NJ: Lawrence Erlbaum Associates.

Peters, J.W. (2012, October 16). 73,000 political ads test even a city of excess. *The New York Times*, A1, A16.

Peters, J.W., & Shorey, R. (2016, December 10). Trump spent far less than Clinton, but he still reimbursed his companies well. *The New York Times*, A12.

Rancer, A.S., & Avtgis, T.A. (2014). *Argumentative and aggressive communication: Theory, research, and application* (2nd ed.). New York: Peter Lang.

Rutenberg, J. (2014, October 19). Money talks. *The New York Times Magazine*, 26–33, 51, 53.

Schlozman, K.L., Verba, S., & Brady, H.E. (2012, November 11). Sunday dialogue: Giving all citizens a voice. *The New York Times* (Sunday Review), 2.

Schudson, M. (1986). *Advertising, the uneasy persuasion*. New York: Basic Books.

Shane, S., Confessore, N., & Rosenberg, M. (2017, January 12). How a political crisis spilled out of a lurid, unverified dossier. *The New York Times*, A1, A21.

Shapiro, M.A., & Rieger, R.H. (1992). Comparing positive and negative political advertising on radio. *Journalism Quarterly*, *69*, 135–145.

Shin, J., & Thorson, K. (2017). Partisan selective sharing: The biased diffusion of fact-checking messages on social media. *Journal of Communication*, *67*, 233–255.

Smith, B.A. (1996, October 8). Time to go negative. *The Wall Street Journal*, A22.

Soroka, S., & McAdams, S. (2015). News, politics, and negativity. *Political Communication*, *32*, 1–22.

Soroka, S.N. (2014). *Negativity in democratic politics: Causes and consequences*. New York: Cambridge University Press.

Strother, R.D. (2003). *Falling up: How a redneck helped invent political consulting*. Baton Rouge: Louisiana State University Press.

Stryker, R., Conway, B.A., & Danielson, J.T. (2016). What is political incivility? *Communication Monographs*, *83*, 535–556.

Teachout, Z. (2015, January 26). Legalized bribery. *The New York Times*, A21.

Toobin, J. (2012, May 21). Money unlimited. *The New Yorker*, 36–47.

Vavreck, L. (2016a, October 29). In potent attack ads, rivals let each other do the talking. *The New York Times*, A14.

Vavreck, L. (2016b, October 20). Do TV campaign ads matter? Trump gives rare chance to find out. *The New York Times*, A17.

Wertheimer, F. (2012, June 14). Citizens United: Watergate redux. *Politico*. Retrieved from www.politico.com/news/stories/0612/77436.html (Accessed January 17, 2017).

Wesleyan Media Project. (2016, October 18). *Presidential ad volumes less than half of 2012*. Retrieved from mediaproject.wesleyan.edu/releases/oct-2016/ (Accessed March 23, 2017).

West, D.M. (2010). *Air wars: Television advertising in election campaigns, 1952–2008* (5th ed.) Washington, DC: CQ Press.

West, D.M. (2014). *Air wars: Television advertising and social media in election campaigns 1952–2012* (6th ed.). Washington, DC: CQ Press.

Zacks, J.M. (2015, February 15). Why movie "facts" prevail. *The New York Times* (Sunday Review), 12.

Zernike, K., & Rutenberg, J. (2004, August 20). The 2004 campaign; Advertising; Friendly fire: The birth of an attack on Kerry. *The New York Times*. Retrieved from www.nytimes.com/2004/08/20/us/the-2004-campaign-advertising-friendly-fire-the-birth-of-an-attack-on-kerry.html?_r=0 (Accessed July 19, 2017).

CHAPTER

14 Presidential Debates and Postscript

The Super Bowl, Wimbledon Tennis Championship, NBA Finals, and World Soccer Cup all rolled into one. The 21st-century equivalent of the final episodes of *The Fugitive*, *M*A*S*H**, and *Seinfeld*, with the 2013 finale of *Breaking Bad* thrown in for good measure. Presidential debates are the high holidays of American presidential politics (Dayan & Katz, 1992)—the day the mediated earth stands still, if only briefly and with breathless anticipation, as the heavyweights of presidential politics battle like latter-day Roman gladiators or unsparing verbal pugilists on a televised stage fashioned for the occasion. In the view of media commentators, they are centerpieces of the electoral feast, the main events of the general election campaign that draw massive audiences, so much so that restaurants and bars plan entertainment extravaganzas, like the Alamo Drafthouse in Dallas that featured a themed menu, including a "Donald Trump Build A Wall Around It Taco Salad" and "Hillary's Leak Pizza."

Presidential debates epitomize the ways entertainment and politics merge seamlessly in American politics: the exaggerated, hyped impact news media attribute to debates, while aggrandizing journalists' role; the challenges candidates face, struggling with the incongruity of discussing policy issues in a format that militates against serious discussion; and the manner in which voters respond, listen, critique, tweet, praise, and process the only campaign events that allow for dialogue between the major political contenders for the U.S. presidency.

Debates have a long history in American politics. "The American political system grew up with debate," Kathleen Hall Jamieson and David S. Birdsell (1988) remind us. "Colonial assemblies debated revolution, the Constitutional Convention debated the Constitution, and Congress debated the law" (p. 17).

The most famous debates—the ones that leap to mind when political debates are discussed—were the Lincoln-Douglas debates of 1858. Abraham Lincoln, who had served in Congress and acquired a reputation as a spellbinding orator, ran against the incumbent, Stephen Douglas, for a U.S. Senate seat in Illinois. They debated seven times in as many Illinois cities. The debates were amazing, rhetorical tours de force that harnessed legal argumentation, historical appeals to the Founding Fathers, and stirring moral oratory. The issue was slavery. Douglas embraced popular sovereignty. He adopted the relativist position that questions of morality must be decided by the people themselves. Thus, each state had the right to decide to continue slavery or abolish the institution. Lincoln adopted an absolutist natural rights perspective, forcefully arguing that slavery was morally wrong (Zarefsky, 1990). The Lincoln-Douglas debates have been justly celebrated as masterful exemplars of political rhetoric. Let's not mythologize them.

First, they took place in a senatorial—not, as often assumed, presidential—campaign. Arguments may have been lofty, but they were also weapons of electoral persuasion. Both debaters crafted arguments to appeal to voters. Douglas won the election, in part because his debate and campaign arguments persuaded Illinois's undecided swing voters that Lincoln was a radical abolitionist.

Second, contrary to legend, audiences probably were not enraptured and mesmerized by the debaters' eloquence. Many of the thousands who attended the debates were picnicking, their attention focused on the food and not the candidates; others attended not to hear the arguments but to partake in the drama of the moment (Zarefsky, 1990). Theatrics captivated the crowd. People interrupted one of Douglas's opening speeches by shouting, "Hit him again" (Mutz, 2015, p. 208). In this way, audience members were not unlike today's political junkies who tune in to CNN or Fox to follow the horse race or hope their candidate draws first blood.

A third myth of Lincoln-Douglas involves the premise of the debates. The very assumption that slavery should be debated nowadays strikes us as preposterous, offensive to our moral sensibilities. It seems so patently obvious that slavery has no defense that any formal debate on the topic seems inappropriate, and certainly unworthy of celebration. At the time, sadly, the issue was a matter of debate, reminding us that political communication is a function of a particular time and place.

This brings us to today. With presidential debates a central part of the presidential campaign landscape, it is important to appreciate debate content and effects, as well as the larger policy complexities. This chapter examines debates from a variety of vantage points, demythologizing them, describing their attributes, and discussing their political and broader normative impacts. The chapter is divided into six sections. The first portion of the chapter sets the stage by discussing major functions of debates and defining a presidential debate. The second section examines the strategic features of debates, along with pros and cons of different debate formats.

The third section reviews the modern history of presidential debates, focusing on iconic moments in an effort to provide students with an appreciation of legacy issues that underpin contemporary media discussions of debates. The fourth and fifth portions describe social science research on general election and primary debates, as well as normative issues. The final portion of the chapter provides a postscript on the presidential election, offering a final bookend to the text.

DEBATE FUNCTIONS AND DEFINITIONS

Presidential debates serve different functions for the political communication system (Benoit, 2007, 2014a). For candidates they are, first and foremost, *political* events. From the perspective of presidential candidates, debates offer key opportunities "to win over undecided voters, to reinforce voters who have already made a decision concerning whom to vote for," and to change the minds of more open-minded voters (Hinck, 1993, p. 2). Candidates do not want to educate the electorate. They want to exploit debates to achieve concrete political objectives (Kraus, 1988).

Debates play a different role for voters. They help voters decide which candidate best serves their interest, who shares their values, and how the candidates might perform as president. For partisan activists, debates are key opportunities to shore up the base and articulate strategies to appeal to swing voters. For less involved voters, they are like stock car races, where you cheer for your driver and secretly hope an exciting minor accident will occur, in the form of a gaffe or goof committed by the opposing candidate. Partisan tweets are frequently hostile, humorous jabs at the opposing candidate, as when Trump's opponents remarked on his weirdly creeping behind Clinton in the second debate of 2016.

For news media, debates are a premier event in the horse race, the championship laps between the horses, the penultimate boxing match between two prize fighters. The news covers them this way, focusing endlessly on candidates' debate preparations, pre- and post-debate polls, what a candidate has to do in order to avoid a knockout punch, and hours-long analysis following the debate about dramatic candidate statements, controversies, gaffes, and how their performance played with the base or undecided voters. To be sure, the news covers candidates' policy statements and provides useful fact-checks. It is a complicated picture. But focus on issues, not surprisingly, pales in comparison to journalists' focus on the strategic game, as well as character and attack messages, the latter overrepresented in news media coverage (Benoit, 2014b).

Presidential debates also perform symbolic functions for the political system as a whole. They represent the only live, real-time forum in which candidates stand, side by side, discussing policy issues. They put potential leaders before citizens in a relatively unmediated forum. Unlike political commercials or microtargeted Internet messages, they are not packaged by consultants prior to being seen by voters. Unlike news, they are not screened and edited by journalistic gatekeepers. They are exercises in civic education that help citizens acquire new information, approach issues more complexly, and broach new perspectives to vexing problems. At least that is the hope.

These functions can conflict. A debate that advances a candidate's political needs may not serve voters if it evades the issues. A feisty, contentious encounter that drives news media interest can be short on issues. And a debate that discusses policy issues complexly and thoughtfully can drive away partisans looking for blood. Chalk these complexities up to the continued conundrums of political communication that serves diverse functions for a democratic society. More broadly, though, presidential debates have exerted a functional impact on the political system. Over the past several decades, candidate debates have become institutionalized aspects of a host of elections: gubernatorial, congressional, and even local mayoral races (Birdsell, 2014). And while debates have shortcomings, they focus on issues facing a community and affirm the importance of citizen participation in democratic elections. Those, at least, are the lofty goals, achieved in varying degrees, sometimes a great deal, other times not so much.

Definition

Let's cut to the chase. Presidential debates are not authentic debates. A **debate**, as Auer (1962) notes, is "(1) a confrontation, (2) in equal and adequate time, (3) of matched contestants, (4) on a stated proposition, (5) to gain an audience decision" (p. 146). Classical or trained debaters research a topic, present detailed arguments, and prepare persuasive rebuttals on a specific issue. One side defends the proposition and the other refutes it. A judge determines who wins, based on carefully honed criteria. A well-respected genre of debate, derived from the classic 1858 debates, is called Lincoln-Douglas.

Although candidates in the presidential debates compete for the most powerful position on the planet, they do not debate in the true sense of the word. They do not debate a stated proposition, like "Public colleges should offer free tuition," or "Young adults should not be required to buy health insurance," or "There should be a 10 percent tax on imports." Instead, debates revolve around generic domestic policies or foreign affairs. Questions can focus on image, like a candidate's likability or experience. Debaters are not forced to address specific issues or rebut opponents. They can elide issues and ignore opponents' arguments. A judge does not adjudicate the decision, based on a reasoned analysis of arguments and rebuttals. A poll is taken after the debate, and Americans use a host of criteria, including the candidate's nonverbal skills and demeanor, to decide who won. Many observers, including supporters of Donald J. Trump, felt that a debate was not won on issues, but on who came across as more authentic and bolder. In short, debates are about image and appearances, to a large degree the antithesis of genuine advocacy-centered, argument-focused debate.

Better to view a debate as a joint appearance or face-to-face encounter. A **presidential debate** is defined as "the joint appearance by two or more opposing candidates, who expound on their positions, with explicit and equitable provisions for refutation without interruption" (Martel, 1983, p. 2). Even so, debates can feature considerable clash on the issues (McKinney & Carlin, 2004). Candidates formulate arguments on policy matters, proclaiming accomplishments, attacking the opponent, and offering spirited defenses of their own positions (Benoit & Harthcock, 1999), although the quality of their arguments can be open to question.

DEBATE POLITICS AND FORMATS

Nomination Campaign Debates

In recent years, pre-primary and primary campaign debates have come to exert more important strategic influences on the nomination process. They too have become media events, as dramatically illustrated by the first Republican debate in August 2015 that featured Trump's first appearance in a debate and attracted 23.9 million viewers, the most viewed presidential primary debate in history (Koblin, 2015).

Pre-primary and primary campaign debates are usually sponsored by media, like Fox and CNN, as well as Facebook. As discussed in Chapter 11, primary debates can build and influence candidacies, as well as destroy them. Republican presidential candidate Rick Perry discovered this in 2012 when he could not remember the name of a Cabinet department he intended to dismantle. Republican Senator Marco Rubio experienced a drop in support in 2016 when Chris Christie, a pugilistic New Jersey governor, mocked him for reciting well-rehearsed canned debate lines attacking President Obama. After Christie instructed the audience to be ready to hear Rubio's scripted speech, Rubio unfathomably recited the canned lines again, fulfilling Christie's prediction and inflicting a deadly wound on his credibility. Primary debates can exert these effects because they are viewed by an unusually attentive audience of involved voters, and gaffes like these are repeated in the conventional and social media so frequently they influence voters directly, or indirectly via the comments of party opinion leaders.

Nomination campaigns debates are also important because they can legitimize candidacies, providing insurgent candidates with the imprimatur of television network–conferred legitimacy. Debates seemed to propel the candidacies of outsider contenders, like Trump and Bernie Sanders. Debates can focus heavily on images and silly attacks (as in Trump's calling Rubio "Little Marco," with its phallic connotations, or Bush "low energy," an appellation that, coupled with Bush's mediocre debate performances, doomed his candidacy). Pre-primary and primary debates perform a winnowing function, helping select candidates, reducing the pool to the most viable contenders and significantly influencing voters' attitudes (Baumgartner & Francia, 2016). Debates can focus on policy concerns, as seen in the Sanders-Clinton debates, with their focus on issues spanning free trade, gun control, and inequality in America. Because candidates debate to polish their images, issue concerns blend seamlessly with images, as candidates emphasize policies that will advance their cause and derail an opponent, another example of how issues and images are not opposites, but blend into one another.

Presidential Debate Preparations

Modern presidential debates began in 1960, with the Kennedy-Nixon debates, the first televised debates between presidential candidates. After a 16-year hiatus, which probably occurred as a result of the aftershocks of the Kennedy assassination, '60s protests, and Watergate, presidential debates began in earnest in 1976. Debates have been held in every presidential election since then. They are now ritualized, institutionalized features of the American presidential election. Presidential debates are sponsored by the Commission on Presidential Debates, an organization that chooses formats and moderators.

Long before the actual debates occur, candidates' consultants engage in a series of strategic debates about the debates themselves. Considerations include length of time for answers to questions, whether candidates should sit or stand, if candidates should be able to take notes with pencil and paper, and even the proper height of the podium. In Elaboration Likelihood Model terms, these may be peripheral cues, but they can influence audience impressions.

Consider the height factor. Consultants do not want their candidate to be at a disadvantage. In 1976, Jimmy Carter, who was shorter than President Gerald Ford, reportedly inserted lifts in his shoes and wore them during the debates (Jamieson & Birdsell, 1988). Prior to the 1984 vice presidential debate, Democratic consultants did not want their candidate—the 5'4" Geraldine Ferraro—to be looking up at the more than 6-foot-tall Republican candidate, George H. W. Bush. Overruling Republicans' objections, they constructed a ramp that resembled the floor covering so Ferraro could be closer to Bush's height without having to visibly step up on any object.

Political adviser Myles Martel aptly noted:

> It would be no exaggeration to compare the . . . presidential debate process with an advanced game of chess. Nearly every move regarding the decisions to debate,

formats, strategies and tactics, and the execution of the debate(s) themselves, [is] fraught with political implications.

(Kraus, 1988, p. 33)

Not surprisingly, candidates extensively prepare, trying to rebut anticipated arguments from the opponent. They stage mock debates, with fellow politicians role-playing their opponent. In 2012, Senator John Kerry, the Democratic nominee in 2004, played Mitt Romney in Obama's debate preparations. Republican Senator Rob Portman, an experienced presidential debate role-player, took on the Obama role for Romney. He was so good at parroting probable Obama attacks he actually got under Romney's skin.

In 2016, Hillary Clinton spent hours in pre-debate preparation, trying to figure out how best to psyche out Trump, looking for insights into his psychological insecurities, seeking ways to undermine and even needle him, even consulting experts in psychology to learn how Trump would react to harsh verbal attacks from a female adversary on the debate stage. By contrast, Trump eschewed preparation, sensing you could think too much, disdaining scripted rehearsals, arguing that debates are won not on policy wonk arguments, but on television-style authenticity and display of bold leadership (Healy & Flegenheimer, 2016). "It was Tony Soprano vs. [his psychiatrist] Dr. Melfi, TV's biggest antihero blustering against the woman who had gotten inside his head" (Poniewozik, 2016).

Each candidate's weaknesses were the other's strengths. Trump faced the challenge of showing voters that a man who never held elected office and had a habit of mouthing off rancorous remarks could sound presidential. Clinton, the ever-prepared expert who struck voters as insincere, needed to show voters she was a genuine, likable person, who could parry Trump's insulting remarks with grace and verve. Clinton approached debates as a feisty doctoral student cramming for exams, Trump as an improvisational actor confident in his experience on the celebrity stage.

Strategists play the expectations game, tamping down expectations for their candidate. Back in 1996, when President Bill Clinton ran against Republican Bob Dole, Dole's campaign managers deliberately poor-mouthed their candidate as the debate approached. "Surely everybody in America knows Bill Clinton is the greatest debater since Benjamin Disraeli," a Dole aide said, comparing Clinton to the storied British prime minister in an effort to reduce expectations for Dole (Perloff, 1998, p. 388). Sixteen years later, in 2012, a senior Romney adviser engaged in an even bigger hype, saying that Obama "is widely regarded as one of the most talented political communicators in modern history" (Bruni, 2012, p. 27). Obama, for his part, pooh-poohed his debating skill, saying "Governor Romney, he's a good debater. I'm just O.K."

Formats

There are usually three 90-minute presidential debates that are frequently held strategically at universities located in battleground states. The structure of the debate varies, depending on the format and negotiations between rival candidates in a particular election. The amount of time candidates get to respond to questions, number of minutes allocated for rebuttals, and whether there is time for general discussion of debate questions depends on the particular debate (Tuman, 2008). Opening and closing statements are standard features of presidential debates.

There are three debate formats: (1) **press conference**, where a group of pre-selected reporters ask candidates questions; (2) **single moderator,** where the moderator, typically a television news anchor or political correspondent, asks questions and serves as umpire; (3) **town hall meeting**, featuring questions from the audience, frequently undecided voters, typically moderated by a well-known journalist.

Each format has strengths and weaknesses. The press conference ensures that panelists are experienced and will ask knowledgeable questions that bear on policy. Its weakness is that reporters can be oblivious to the real-world problems that afflict voters, or can pose queries designed solely to entrap candidates (Hellweg, Pfau, & Brydon, 1992). Reporters, who view candidates in a staunchly adversarial role, can ask snarky "Gotcha" questions designed to pin the candidate down, sometimes on a trivial or unimportant aspect of the campaign. In 2015, John Harwood of CNBC asked Trump if he was running a "comic book version of a presidential campaign," a question that was unnecessarily provocative and unlikely to yield anything but a crisp denial or counter-attack from the candidate. On the other hand, candidates frequently evade questions, so it serves voters when reporters try to pin candidates down on policy matters.

The single moderator format reduces the chaos of having a team of journalists hurl questions at candidates. Much depends on the skill of the moderator in making sure candidates stick by the rules. There are different perspectives on how moderators can most effectively coordinate debates. One view is they should take a laissez-faire, passive role, opting not to intervene or possibly bias the debate with their perspectives, in this way giving the public an unvarnished look at the candidates without a journalistic filter. The downside is that moderators can lose control of the debate, as occurred in 2012 when Jim Lehrer of PBS permitted Romney and Obama to talk beyond their allotted limits, opting not to press them when they made misleading statements. In other cases, moderators can unwittingly show bias. When Matt Lauer of NBC hosted a candidate forum in 2016, he subjected Hillary Clinton to scrutiny about her use of a private email server while failing to challenge Trump's false claim that he had opposed the 2003 Iraq War from the outset.

A second view is moderators should take an active stance, making certain that factual mistakes candidates make (and there are many of them) do not go unchallenged, taking pains to ensure that sometimes deliberate misstatements are not viewed as facts. Candy Crowley of CNN did just this during the second 2012 presidential debate, correcting Romney on a factually incorrect statement he made about the attack on U.S. diplomats in Libya. While providing accurate information in debates is a virtue, the problem is that hosts can do this selectively, correcting one candidate and not the other, or providing a more dramatic correction for one candidate at a critical juncture in the debate than for his or her adversary.

The main benefit of town meeting debates is they bring ordinary people into the electoral process, allowing voters to question candidates directly. By giving citizens the opportunity to communicate directly with candidates for the highest office in the land, the town hall meeting privileges democratic values. Candidates adopt a more voter-centered style, focusing on issues that are on voters' minds (McKinney, 2005). People can zero in on issues that elude the elite media, but are on voters' radar screens. For example, in 2012, a woman asked the candidates to explain their positions on gun control, in the wake of a recent school shooting.

On the other hand, the town hall format has shortcomings. Sometimes voters don't ask good questions. Town hall meetings also do not always provide opportunities for follow-up questions, which can push candidates to articulate ideas or clarify misleading remarks. The 2016 town hall debate showed what can happen when moderators steal the thunder from the audience. The moderators—consumed by Trump's and Clinton's reactions to new revelations of Trump's comments about groping women—dominated portions of the debate, forcing the debate to focus more on character issues journalists enjoy than on bread-and-butter concerns that occupy voters (Vernon & Spike, 2016).

There is no perfect format, and there continues to be discussion about how each format can function optimally. A lesson from 2016 is that moderators should ask tough questions without grilling candidates, and town hall debates should not be hijacked by the moderators.

MODERN HISTORY OF KEY PRESIDENTIAL DEBATES

1960: Visuals Matter

If there is one debate that defined the presidential debates of the 20th century, it was this one. If you had to select the debate that generated the most famous empirical study, it would be this one. If scholars were asked to name the debate that exerted the largest impact on the election—or was widely *perceived* to have had the greatest effect on the election—it would be the first debate between John F. Kennedy and Richard M. Nixon during the heat of the fall 1960 presidential election (see Figure 14.1).

Kennedy immediately took the offensive in the debate, using his opening statement to lay out a vision (the need to get America moving again), and to create a favorable

Figure 14.1 The iconic Kennedy-Nixon debate of 1960. During the first presidential debate, Kennedy's personal appearance—his elegance and handsome features— contrasted sharply with Nixon's unseemly jowls and five o'clock shadow. The debate produced a sea change in attitudes toward political media, leading observers to conclude that on TV the visual dwarfs the verbal. Frequently overlooked is that during the campaign and the fourth debate, Kennedy articulated misleading claims about a U.S.-Soviet missile gap that he knew were false or at least questionable, but likely perpetrated them to win votes.

Getty Images

impression of himself as a bold, energetic leader. As the debate wore on, Nixon regained his stride, developing compelling arguments. But even when he articulated compelling arguments, Nixon looked fatigued and ill, "his eyes exaggerated hollows of blackness, his jaws, jowls, and face drooping with strain" (White, 1962, p. 289). In fact, Nixon was recovering from a knee injury sustained a month before. He refused to use TV makeup, his light skin did not project well before the camera, and his notorious "five o'clock shadow" coarsened his face. His physical maladies registered with voters. The next day, a now famous research study was conducted. The survey found that people who watched the debate on television believed Kennedy had won. But those who listened to the debate on radio came to the opposite conclusion: They thought Nixon had won (Kraus, 1996).

The study has been endlessly discussed, the findings ceaselessly dissected. Did candidate looks eclipse what they said? Did the television medium favor appearance over verbal substance? Alternatively, did Kennedy's nasal New England twang sound worse over radio, reducing his credibility with radio listeners? How reliable or scientifically valid were the findings? We don't know the answers to these questions. The common assumption that "Kennedy won on television and Nixon on radio" is undercut by methodological questions, such as these. The best scholarship on the subject suggests that appearance did count for a great deal in the first of the four Kennedy-Nixon debates. Kennedy's visual presence, coupled with Nixon's unseemly appearance, probably led TV viewers to pronounce him the winner (Kraus, 1996).

The debate produced a sea change in attitudes toward political media. A generation of consultants and candidates concluded that on television the visual dwarfs the verbal, and physical appearance outperforms substantive issues. Nixon ruefully concluded that

> what hurt me the most in the first debate was not the substance of the encounter between Kennedy and me, but the disadvantageous contrast in our physical appearances . . . The fact remains one bad camera angle on television can have far more effect on the election outcome than a major mistake in writing a speech.
>
> (Kraus, 1996, pp. 83–84)

Resonating to Nixon's message and the received wisdom on this issue, presidential candidates in the years that followed paid close attention to the role visual image could play in debates, maintaining eye contact with the camera, smiling at appropriate moments to convey likability, and installing an inclining ramp near the podium so a shorter candidate could appear taller, in this way gaining the imprimatur of credibility.

But the popular consensus simplifies political reality. On the one hand, visual impressions do play a critical role in presidential debates. Appearance does count. Peripheral cues can overwhelm substantive arguments. But Kennedy complemented his attractive image with persuasive arguments and compelling words. Absent verbal substance, appearance counts for little in debates, even on TV. Second, the first 1960 debate enhanced Kennedy's image and probably contributed to his razor-thin victory (White, 1962). But contrary to myth, it was not the sole reason he defeated Nixon. Kennedy also benefited from a heartfelt, but politically strategic, phone call to the wife of Rev. Martin Luther King Jr., expressing sympathy upon learning that her husband faced a six-month jail term for courageously protesting segregation in Atlanta. The phone call may have won the support of many Black voters.

Another important aspect of the 1960 debates deserve mention, one that is rarely discussed in the media-centric focus. For all his charisma and detailed discussion of issues, Kennedy misspoke on a critical foreign policy issue, errantly charging, without credible evidence, that there was a missile gap between the U.S. and Soviet Union. He alleged in the fourth debate and throughout the campaign that the Soviets would surpass the U.S. in its development of armed missiles, a claim that was bogus. Kennedy knew there was no missile gap, having been informed of this by the CIA during the campaign; or at least he knew that intelligence estimates of a missile gap were open to question (Reeves, 2009; Preble, 2004). Nonetheless, he perpetuated the myth so he could appear tough on Communism (Donaldson, 2007). Another lesson of the 1960 debates was that good looks, charm, and cleverly packaged distortions of truth could carry the day in the new television-dominated politics.

Narrative and Argumentation Win Debates

When Ronald Reagan debated President Jimmy Carter in 1980, there were conflicting expectations about Reagan's performance. He was an experienced political figure, a former California governor, and movie actor whose communication skills were well-respected. But some voters harbored concerns that he was a political extremist and perhaps, when it came to military interventions, a little "trigger-happy." He needed to turn in a strong debate performance, and he did (see Figure 14.2). Reagan articulated a persuasive vision, brimming with ideas and optimism. In his closing statement, speaking confidently and looking intently into the camera, he invited voters to consider whether they were "better off than [they] were four years ago," following up with a series of rhetorical questions that invited the conclusion that his opponent had left the country in an economic malaise. In all likelihood, the lines had been scripted long in advance. No matter. They were delivered with dramatic force, humor and an understatement that bolstered their impact. They also hit home with Americans

Figure 14.2 Ronald Reagan overcame the doubts of skeptics in a 1980 presidential debate. In a performance peppered with humorous one-liners and unified by an optimistic narrative, he outperformed his opponent, President Jimmy Carter. The debate showed that narrative and cogent argumentation, especially when delivered by an experienced TV hand, can be pivotal in presidential debates.

Getty Images

who were frustrated by a poor economy, double-digit inflation, and Carter's apparent inability to change economic course.

There was more to Reagan's debate performance than the famous one-liners. He presented an optimistic message, bolstered by strong arguments, and steeped in a narrative that paid homage to the aspirations of the electorate (Ritter & Henry, 1994). He promised to lead a crusade "to take government off the backs of the great people of this country and turn you loose again to do those things that I know you can do so well." He presented a thematic approach, infused with symbols, in contrast to Carter's more lackluster performance.

Argumentation plays an important part in debates. Candidates who advance coherent arguments, harness evidence, forcefully rebut the opponent's claims, connect ideas with time-honored symbols, and embed their statements in a compelling narrative win debates.

1992, 2012, and 2016: Nonverbal Political Communication Effects

In a media age, the ability to project a credible image on television and images streamed across the Internet counts for a lot. To be sure, televisual mastery of the medium, in the absence of cogent, or at least politically savvy arguments, will not carry the day in presidential debates. Yet while one can debate—that's the word—whether visual cues *should* count so heavily (there are arguments for and against), there is little question that candidates who accommodate their message to the formal properties of the small screen fare well in televised debates.

In a 1992 presidential debate, Bill Clinton showcased one of the core components of credibility: goodwill. With voters concerned that President George H. W. Bush had lost touch with ordinary Americans, Clinton decided to play the empathy card in a town hall debate. A woman, Marissa Hall, boldly came up to ask, "How has the national debt personally affected each of your lives?" It was a strange question because the debt is a macro entity that has indirect and very complex effects on individuals, but the woman wanted to see how the candidates related to the economic plight of ordinary people. Bush, taking the question literally, understandably stumbled, even asking the woman to rephrase her question. "I'm not sure I get it. Help me with the question and I'll try to answer it," he said. Clinton, recognizing that an intellectual answer was less important than conveying empathy, turned, Oprah-Style, to Ms. Hall, walked toward her, looked her in the eye and asked her ever so gently to explain "how it affected you again. You know people who've lost their jobs and lost their homes?" He conveyed goodwill, explaining that in his state when people lost their jobs, "there's a good chance I'll know them by their names." Candidates emphasized empathy long before television. However, Clinton's nonverbal pivot to the voter (with its shameless emotional manipulation) demonstrated an appreciation of the subtle cues of the television medium.

During the first 2012 presidential debate between Obama and Romney, Obama seemed listless and detached, and occasionally disdainful during the debate, eyeing his notes, looking down or gulping when Romney criticized his stewardship of the economy. Romney was lithe, alert, looking intently at the camera during his closing remarks, in contrast to the nonverbally inert Obama. Romney was full of energy, the boxer always on his feet, jabbing the opponent with punch after punch, hardly the wooden figure of months before. He seemed to exude confidence, whereas Obama appeared tentative at times. Polls showed Romney won the debate, in no small part because of his sensitivity to communicator cues and TV optics. Obama later acknowledged that his nonverbal and other communicative behavior worked to his disadvantage (Nagourney, Parker, Rutenberg, & Zeleny, 2012, p. 14). More generally, there is evidence that a political leader's display of situationally inappropriate facial expressions prompts visual attention and leads to unfavorable evaluations (Gong & Bucy, 2016).

A more graphic example of inappropriate nonverbal communication occurred at the 2016 second presidential debate when Trump, trying to showcase alpha-male dominance, aggressively prowled around the stage, showing how he "bullies with his body language," (with) "arms outstretched, arms pointing downwards, palms forward, characteristically signaling his connection with the common man through the distinctive, demonstrative gestures of New York" (Beattie, 2016, p. 30; see Figure 14.3).

Figure 14.3 During the second debate of the 2016 presidential campaign, Donald Trump aggressively prowled around the stage, establishing a situationally inappropriate alpha-male presence. However, his performance played well with his base. For all the media discussion of Trump's body language, on a more substantive level, the debate fell short of normative expectations in its lack of give-and-take between the candidates on specific policy issues.

Getty Images

His use of particular nonverbal metaphoric gestures—the arms raised, palms stretched outward—communicated danger. As he attacked Clinton in the debate, "he chopped, he pointed, he sliced. Trump was now fully armed. He heckled, he interrupted, he glowered as Clinton talked, issuing a nonverbal running commentary on what she was saying" (Beattie, 2016, p. 30). Although some of his supporters liked what they saw, polls showed Clinton won the debate. The split screen, and his inappropriate nonverbal displays, probably enhanced negative evaluations of Trump, at least among those critical of his demeanor (see Seiter, Weger, Kinzer, & Jensen, 2009).

SOCIAL SCIENCE RESEARCH ON PRESIDENTIAL DEBATES

The debates discussed earlier in this chapter are interesting and historically significant. They offer clues about debate effects. But to gain a more comprehensive understanding of candidate debate content and effects, we need to look at content analyses and studies of debate effects across a variety of elections, examining different electoral contexts.

Content

William L. Benoit has argued that candidates must strategically differentiate themselves from opponents in debates by acclaiming, touting their virtues or the benefits of their policies; attacking their opponents' policies or character; and defending themselves against opponents' actual or expected attacks. In a comprehensive content analysis of presidential primary and presidential election debates across different decades, debates in congressional, gubernatorial, and mayoral elections, and in 10 countries, including France, the Ukraine, and South Korea, Benoit (2014b) found that candidates harness acclaims most often, followed by attacks and defenses. Candidates also focus on policy issues more than character, presuming voters find policy acclaims more compelling. Incumbent candidates use more acclaims, defending their records, while challengers sensibly attack more frequently.

Primary election debates focus more on character appeals than do general election debates. Presumably, candidates find personal qualities a useful way to differentiate themselves from their competitors in the primaries. In the general election, where many voters centrally process candidates' claims, an emphasis on issues represents a more strategic choice. Debates stand out from other political communication formats in their appeal to positive, rather than negative, candidate messages. However, debates in particular elections (such as those characterized by voter anger and insurgent candidates, as in 2016) may feature more candidate attacks than acclaims.

Methodological Issues

This brings us to the important question of whether debates influence election outcomes. It's the quintessential question, posed by candidates, consultants, and pundits. You need to appreciate that it is challenging to assess the effects of debates on electoral outcomes. It is empirically difficult to tease out debates from other media events occurring at the same time of the campaign. Just because opinions about candidates change after a debate does not mean the debate caused the impact. Effects could have resulted from the debate, news commentary following the debate, a combination of the debate and news commentaries, social media comments, or from unrelated messages, like negative ads that replay candidate debate gaffes. Second, it is hard to quantify the contribution of exposure to debates on the outcome of the election. Measurements can be unreliable, and it is difficult to parcel out debate effects from other campaign influences. Nonetheless, social scientists have tried to determine the impact of presidential debates on voter attitudes and behaviors.

Debate Effects on Voters

The first effects are obvious, but important to state. Presidential debates influence exposure and gratifications. First, debates attract huge national audiences, motivating voters to seek particular gratifications, in keeping with the uses and gratifications approach discussed in Chapter 3 (Katz, Blumler, & Gurevitch, 1974) The first presidential debate between Clinton and Trump was the most viewed presidential debate in history, with 84 million viewers, edging out Carter-Reagan with 81 million Americans watching in 1980 (Koblin, 2016). Vice presidential debates attract large audiences too, though not usually as large as presidential debates. The much-anticipated 2008 Biden-Palin vice presidential debate was the most watched VP debate with some 70 million viewers. Viewers watch debates for many reasons, including good-citizen purposes, like information-seeking and trying to reduce uncertainty about a vote decision, as well as for partisan reasons, cheering one's candidate on or reaffirming dissatisfaction with the opposing candidate. Much like people showed up at the 1858 Lincoln-Douglas debates to regale in the circus atmosphere, today's debate viewers tune in for the drama, the hoopla, and the possibility that a candidate will deliver a zinger or commit a gaffe. The humorist Molly Ivins joked, with tongue not entirely in cheek, that "political debates are sort of like stock-car races—no one really cares who wins, they just want to see the crashes" (Hahn, 1994, p. 208).

Millions watch debates, which is a good thing. But it's not like viewers are glued to the TV or smartphone screen, taking in every word or policy position. Attention is sporadic. Few individuals watch a debate from start to finish, and only the political junkies watch all of the presidential and vice presidential debates (Sears & Chaffee, 1979). What's more, watching a debate does not mean that people buy into everything that candidates say. Exposure does not equal effects. Debates are increasingly social media shows, with viewers tweeting and posting, multitasking at a furious pace, showcasing how the audience has become an active spectator-participant in political debates. And while tweets are hardly representative of the reactions of the entire viewing audience, they provide an early nonscientific indication of who is besting whom, which candidate's comments leave a visceral impact, or whose partisans are most engaged.

Second, congealing with the hopes of deliberative democratic theorists, presidential debates expand understanding of political issues. They increase knowledge, expand the number of campaign issues voters use to assess candidates, help solidify cognition and affect, and bond together favorable sentiments toward a preferred candidate (Benoit, Hansen, & Verser, 2003; Carlin & McKinney, 1994; Holbrook, 1999; Miller & Mac-Kuen, 1979; Sears & Chaffee, 1979). In a contemporary wrinkle, issue-based tweeting facilitates knowledge acquisition (Jennings, Coker, McKinney, & Warner, 2017). More generally, debate viewing bolsters political information efficacy, or voters' beliefs that they have the information necessary to meaningfully partake in politics. Information efficacy in turn can enhance political interest, discussion, and voting. As Benjamin R. Warner and Mitchell S. McKinney (2016) note, the increased political information efficacy generated by debates "represents a significant social benefit" (p. 37). The converse is also true: Those who do not view debates, who are generally lower in education, income, and efficacy, become comparatively less knowledgeable, increasing knowledge gaps and alienation.

A third impact of debates is reinforcement and affirmation of voters' preexisting candidate attitudes. As we know from Klapper's (1960) old but classic book, as well as contemporary research on voter selectivity (see Chapter 12), voters filter debates through their preexisting biases. Even when the opponent outperforms their candidate, partisans do not necessarily develop a favorable image of the competitor. In 2004 Democrat John Kerry bested Bush in the debates, but no matter. Republican viewers did not change their attitudes toward Bush or develop a favorable image of Kerry (Cho & Ha, 2012). Partisan viewers also point fingers, emphasizing the misstatements and "lies" told by the other side, while glossing over mistakes committed by their candidate. Tweets and other animated posts during debates are typically partisan communiques.

During the second presidential debate of 2012, Romney offered an impassioned defense of his commitment to equality in the workplace, explaining that as governor of Massachusetts he made a "concerted effort" to find women who had the qualifications to become members of his Cabinet. But when he mentioned that women's groups (who he approached to help him) brought back "whole binders full of women," his peculiar word choice created a feeding frenzy on the Internet, stimulating a Facebook fan page called "Binders Full of Women," which recruited numerous satirical likes. Liberals read in Romney's phrase an insincere support for women's rights, conveniently ignoring his statements that he sought to bring qualified women into his Cabinet and a willingness to offer them flexible working hours.

Similarly during the tumultuous debates of 2016, partisan tweets were in strong supply, particularly among Clinton supporters. Tweets in the first debate played up Hillary's entrance in a red pantsuit; in the second debate, many focused on the lack of a handshake and Trump's prowling around Clinton on stage, as the post from a college professor who wrote, "I'm a Muslim, and I would like to report a crazy man threatening a woman on a stage in Missouri!" During the third debate, shortly after Trump muttered that Clinton was "such a nasty woman," the phrase #NastyWoman rapidly began trending on Twitter. These tweets can humorously animate partisans and showcase active involvement in a debate. However, academic as this may sound, they aren't exactly exemplars of thoughtful political discourse.

Similarly, vice presidential debates (where the adage to candidates is "first do no harm") tend to reinforce partisan preferences, conveyed through polls and social media. In the *Saturday Night Live*–satirized 2008 Palin-Biden debate, both candidates performed well, enhancing ratings of their image and issue expertise (McKinney, Rill, & Watson, 2011). Biden seemed to have won on debating points, answering the moderator's questions and rebutting Palin's arguments more effectively. Palin, for her part, displayed issue knowledge and projected confidence. Her litany included "Joe Six-Pack," "you betcha," "doggone it," and lots of dropped g's. She smiled, winked and conveyed folksy vitality. Many Republicans felt energized, their doubts about her competence reduced, if not totally eliminated. Her performance seemed to have solidified the base.

The first three presidential debate effects—exposure, expanded knowledge, and partisan reinforcement—derive exclusively from the debates. The fourth influence concerns news coverage of debate outcomes. Debates, of course, occur in the context of a voracious press. The news media do not just cover the debate live, but analyze it afterwards, focusing, of course, on the politics, not primarily on the substance of what was said. News media verdicts on who won the debates, delivered by anchors and decided by polls, can function as heuristics, peripheral cues that affect voters' evaluations. Thus, news coverage of debates—as well as post-debate satire (Baumgartner, Morris, & Walth, 2012)—can influence public opinion. While news effects can provide the winning candidate with a temporary poll bump, they usually are not consequential. However, the elections of 1976 and 2000 offer an interesting counterpoint suggestive of electoral effects.

The classic example of news media effects occurred in the wake of the second 1976 debate between President Gerald Ford and his Democratic challenger, Jimmy Carter. A panelist asked Ford a question about U.S.–Soviet relations, suggesting that the Soviet Union might be getting the better of the U.S. After initially arguing that his administration had been pursuing negotiations with the Soviet Union from the vantage point of strength, Ford seemed to accept the premise of the question, responding defensively in a devastating blunder. "There is no Soviet domination of Eastern Europe, and there never will be under a Ford administration," he said, seemingly failing to appreciate the obvious fact that in 1976 the Soviet Union dominated and even occupied Eastern European countries.

The gaffe was not immediately apparent to most Americans. Polls conducted after the debate revealed a razor-thin outcome, with 44 percent saying Ford won, 43 percent giving the nod to Carter, and the rest undecided. But, oh what a difference a day makes! As the networks played and replayed Ford's statement, and comments that he had blundered, voters took notice. Polls conducted between 5 p.m. and midnight the day after the debate showed how much difference a day can make in politics. The verdict now? Sixty-two percent thought Carter won, while 17 percent called Ford the winner.

Polls thus demonstrated the impact news exerts on perceptions of debate winners (Berquist, 1994; Lemert, Elliott, Bernstein, Rosenberg, & Nestvold, 1991; Patterson, 1980). Here's the rub: Although Ford's statement was inaccurate and misleading, it was not the profound error of judgment that journalists suggested at the time. When you go back and read the debate transcript, you discover that what Ford meant when he said that "there is no Soviet domination of Eastern Europe" was that *the citizens* of Eastern European nations—for example, Poland, Romania, and Yugoslavia—did not regard themselves as in any way dominated by the Soviet state, and each country had its own autonomy, freedom, and pride (Perloff, 2016). As it turned out, Ford got it right. About a dozen years later, in the late 1980s, the people of Eastern Europe, impelled by the irrepressible nationalistic spirit to which Ford alluded, pushed for freedom from the chains of Soviet domination in the human rights movements that propelled the liberation of Eastern Europe in 1989. During the debate, Ford got carried away by his own rhetoric and made a statement that was factually incorrect.

And he got hammered for it. You can argue that when someone is running for president, or is president, he or she should be held to a higher standard. If candidates make a mistake in a high-profile presidential debate, they should be held accountable in news media reports. Or you can argue that the news blew this story totally out of proportion, stuck in a feeding frenzy that fit the professional conventions of contemporary journalism. In any case, the news coverage—along with Ford's ineptness in stubbornly sticking to his statement—caused opinions of Ford's debate performance to plummet. Ford lost ground at a key moment in the campaign, Carter gained momentum, and public perceptions shifted in Carter's favor. The news media's verdict on the second Ford-Carter debates may have played a small role in Carter's narrow defeat of Gerald Ford.

During the heated 2000 presidential campaign, journalists subtly and sometimes humorously advanced different narratives of candidates Al Gore and George W. Bush. Bush was viewed as not especially bright and a mediocre student—in short, an "inexperienced dolt" (Jamieson & Waldman, 2003, p. 60). News features described Gore as prone to embellishing the truth and hyping his professional biography, so much so that Gore as "serial exaggerator" became a news meme. (Although the news claimed Gore said he invented the Internet, that was never so. Gore famously said that he "took the initiative in creating the Internet." Gore seemed to be suggesting that he deserved credit because, as a senator, he had taken a leadership role in Congress approving funding that transformed a small computer network into a computerized global system. However, the claim seemed farfetched.)

The journalistic narrative took on importance in the wake of the first presidential debate. During the debate, in an effort to emphasize his leadership experience, Gore claimed that he accompanied the director of the Federal Emergency Management Agency to visit the site of forest fires in Texas. It turned out that, although Gore had toured disaster sites as vice president, he had not accompanied the director to the Texas forest fires. Gore also slightly misspoke about Florida school overcrowding, although the substance of his remarks was accurate (Jamieson & Waldman, 2003). Post-debate press coverage emphasized the inaccurate and "suspect" nature of Gore's statements. One may regard this as legitimate focus on a candidate's tendency to misstate facts or over-coverage of a peripheral issue. In either case, post-debate news coverage influenced voter perceptions of the debate. Opinions of Gore's honesty declined over the course of the following week. A survey found that as each day passed, more respondents believed Bush won the debate (Jamieson & Waldman, 2003).

Do Debates Influence Electoral Outcomes?

The scholarly consensus is that debates can change the outcome of a presidential election, but they rarely do. By the time that debates occur, in September and October of the fall campaign, most voters have their minds made up (Holbrook, 1996). Despite the media hoopla, debates are more likely to attract partisans, who have their minds made up and view debates primarily to cheer on their candidate (Stimson, 2004). Many undecided but likely voters have already developed perceptions of candidates that are not easy to shake with a debate performance, even if a candidate seems less than likable. Some low-involvement voters who are still undecided may not tune in to the debate. Thus, a debate victory by a come-from-behind candidate may not influence judgments. In addition, debates rarely feature knockout punches or provide new information about either candidate's issue positions or images that have not been glimpsed before.

In many cases, debates solidify the position of the front-runner. Or there is a cancellation effect, whereby a candidate does poorly in one debate and then overwhelms the opponent in the next. Debates can move the polls, but usually don't alter the outcome of the election (Sides & Vavreck, 2013). In 2016, reputable polls showed Clinton won all three debates, but what good did it do her? For a complex of reasons discussed earlier in the book—such as Trump's unexpected performance in battleground states, abetted by political ads, as well as lower-than-expected turnout among Democratic voters—Trump won the election.

In a handful of cases, debates seemed to have been consequential. I say "seemed to be" because we do not have iron-clad empirical proof because of the difficulties of establishing cause and effect in empirical research. There is some reason to believe the 1960 Kennedy-Nixon debates turned the tide for Kennedy. The first Kennedy-Nixon debate of 1960 elevated Kennedy's image, and Kennedy's poll ratings increased from neck-in-neck with Nixon to four percentage points after the last debate (e.g., Harwood, 2012). Reagan's stunning defeat of Carter in the 1980 debate may have worked to Reagan's electoral advantage by quieting fears about Reagan's riskiness, elevating his credibility, and turning out Reagan voters. Egged on by a feeding frenzy of news coverage, the key 1976 Carter-Ford debate and the 2000 Bush-Gore debates may have contributed to Carter and Bush's victories (Hillygus & Jackman, 2003).

Even if they don't change the electoral outcome, debates influence campaign dynamics. Challengers typically gain stature by holding their own and keeping their cool when appearing in the same public forum as the president (Polsby, Wildavsky, Schier, & Hopkins, 2012). Debates, both presidential and vice presidential, drive news coverage and influence online buzz. They can also solidify a campaign narrative. This occurred when Bill Clinton portrayed George H. W. Bush, who glanced at his watch at the town hall debate of 1992, as out of touch with the problems of ordinary Americans (Baumgartner & Francia, 2016). His glance at his watch may have signaled deep boredom or a nervous tic that had little bearing on Bush's competence or motivation. If the latter, whatever emphasis it received in the campaign was out of proportion to its substantive relevance to Bush's candidacy for a second term. Although we don't know the impact it had on voting (and it was probably small), its continued emphasis in media discussions showcases the news media's narcissistic preoccupation with television's impact on presidential campaigns.

BALANCE SHEET ON PRESIDENTIAL DEBATES

With the previous discussions of strategy, content, and effects as backdrop, we can now explore three broad issues surrounding presidential debates: style and substance, issues, and third party candidates.

Style Versus Substance

Critics argue that candidates' nonverbal behaviors swamp the content of what they say. Candidates are evaluated on their television communication skills rather than on the arguments they speak. A sneer or discomfited look can speak louder than a carefully honed rhetorical argument. For example, in the first 2012 debate, Obama offered a cogent defense of his health care policy and lamented the lack of specificity in Romney's plans. But he was widely criticized because he looked down at his notes, grimaced, and seemed less animated than Romney. Does style overwhelm substance in debates?

The question has long generated controversy. You can find inklings of it in ancient Greece, when Plato criticized the Sophists, teachers who traveled from city to city, offering courses on oratory and speaking style. To Plato, truth was the highest value. He lamented that the Sophists sacrificed painstaking arguments for "the quick, neat, and stylish argument that wins immediate approval—even if this argument has some hidden flaw" (Chappell, 1998, p. 516). The style versus substance conundrum arises regularly in American politics, famously in the presidential debates of 1988, when Democrat Michael Dukakis gave a direct, logical, and truthful answer to a question on the death penalty, but was savaged for his lack of emotion (see Box 14.1).

The issue is complex. It is true that television debates do place visual, nonverbal, and TV communication skills front and center. But one can argue that it is eminently reasonable to focus on a candidate's personal qualities when deciding how to cast a vote. Leadership in a media age consists of manipulating images. One can argue that part of the substance of a debate is the style in which candidates present their answers. As Martel (1983) aptly observes:

> To put this issue in perspective, it might be helpful to ask this question: When a person seeking a job wears his best suit for the interview, attends more meticulously than usual to grooming needs, and demonstrates more poise, better listening habits and closer attention to what he says than usual, is he being unduly manipulative? Of course not. Job interviews are imbued with image-oriented rituals rooted in the applicant's needs for survival and success. Campaign debates

too, are forms of job interviews imbued with image-oriented rituals which we need to understand before passing judgment.

(p. 3)

BOX 14.1 TRUTH VERSUS TRICKERY IN A CLASSIC DEBATE

A classic moment in the 1988 presidential campaign came early in the second presidential debate. The Democratic nominee, Massachusetts Governor Michael Dukakis, faced Republican Vice President George H.W. Bush. It had been a hard-fought campaign, with Republicans pummeling Dukakis for his "icy" demeanor and lack of emotion. Commentators hoped Dukakis would show some affect, offering viewers a visual made-for-television moment.

Hoping to elicit an emotional response, CNN anchor Bernard Shaw began the debate by asking Democratic nominee Michael Dukakis a freighted question: "Governor, if Kitty Dukakis were raped and murdered, would you favor an irrevocable death penalty for the killer?"

Dukakis answered without hesitating. "No, I don't Bernard," he replied. "And I think you know that I've opposed the death penalty during all of my life."

Post-debate reaction to Dukakis's reply was swift and harsh. He had shown no emotion, critics charged. Couldn't he have at least evinced some raw affect when asked what he would do if his wife were raped and killed? He had flubbed the "warm and fuzzy test," pundits declared. However, journalist Roger Simon offered a different perspective:

> People across the country would express outrage over Dukakis' calm and cool answer. Yet was Dukakis' position that outrageous? . . . Dukakis believed that people of principle make principled decisions. And they stick to them. That is what integrity is about. O.K., the critics said, but even if Dukakis didn't favor the death penalty, couldn't he have shown a little emotion in answering the question?

After all, Dukakis' handlers had said before the debate that they were preparing him for a "Willie Horton type" question. And they had written

Continued

an "emotional" answer for Dukakis. It was one in which he talked about his father, a doctor for fifty-two years, who at age seventy-seven, had been beaten, bound and gagged by an intruder looking for drugs . . . And then he would talk about his elder brother, Stelian, who had been killed by a hit-and-run driver in 1973. It was an answer in which Dukakis said he knew what it was like to be a victim of crime. But when the time came to give the answer, Dukakis did not. Instead, he told the truth. Dispassionately, he expressed his true feelings. And he was savaged for it. He was savaged for giving a sincere and unemotional answer instead of giving an insincere and emotional one.

But if he had given the prepared answer, would that really have made him any more warm? Or would it have just made him a better performer, a better actor? If he had given his prepared response, the people, press included, would have praised him. He would have been congratulated for delivering his lines as written, just as George Bush did.

By the final presidential debate, we were demanding the road show. Fool us, we were saying. Trick us. Fake a little sincerity for us. (Simon, 1990, pp. 292–293)

Debate About Issues

Contrary to what critics argue, issues are discussed in debates, far more than other formats. In the final presidential debate of 2016, Clinton offered a staunch defense of women's right to maintain control over their bodies without interference from government, including a defense of the controversial procedure known by its critics as late-term, partial-birth abortion (Stockman, 2016). Trump disagreed, forcefully denouncing late-term abortion. The candidates presented sharply different positions on a host of other issues, including gun control, immigration, and race relations.

But there are downsides. Issues are discussed vaguely, questions are elided, and important problems are ignored. Although the Earth reached its highest temperature ever in 2016, and global warming is increasingly posing cataclysmic threats to the planet, the candidates were not asked one question about how they would come to grips with climate change (Leonhardt, 2016).

From the perspective of deliberative democracy, which prizes thoughtful debate, issue discussions in debates are embarrassingly superficial, frequently focused around jabbing the opponent and rallying the base than on offering cogent argumentation. Jabs mobilize partisans; cogent arguments serve laudatory philosophical goals. It is easy to understand which choice candidates make. Adding philosophical insult to injury, candidates make numerous misleading or false statements that fact checks correct, but few voters see. And debates rarely focus on issues on the horizon that will likely occupy the chief executive. The 1988 debates did not focus on the consequences of the end of Communist rule in Eastern Europe. The debates of 2000 sadly did not focus on terrorism that was around the corner. The 2012 presidential debates did not concentrate on trade and the working class, two key issues during the 2016 campaign. And although Hinck (1993) argues that debates showcase a precious democratic virtue—"choice through rational dialogue" (p. 7)—argumentation can be less than civil, full of insults and injuries that can reduce political trust and tolerance for an opposing viewpoint (Mutz, 2015).

Third Party Participation

Should third or fourth party candidates participate in presidential debates? There is more to this freighted issue than meets the eye. Third party candidates have participated in debates just twice. Independent candidate John B. Anderson debated Ronald Reagan in 1980 (President Carter, fearing it would reduce his political support, refused to debate Anderson). Independent candidate Ross Perot, a popular populist candidate and early opponent of free trade that outsourced jobs, participated in the 1992 presidential debates.

The Commission on Presidential Debates stipulates that third party candidates must garner an average of 15 percent of support in five major opinion polls to qualify for debates. However, excluding third party candidates gives the debates a status quo, Establishment focus. More radical issues and controversies that the two parties would rather not handle are left out of debates.

On the other hand, there is a reason for limiting debates to the major two parties and insisting that third parties have a modest 15 percent public support before they can partake. Do you know how many alternative political parties and groups there are in the U.S.? Where would you draw the line? Defenders of the present structure argue that by opening the floodgates, debate planners would render debates absurd or meaningless, seriously reducing their utility for candidates trying to rebut their major party opponent and voters trying to decide which of the two major party candidates for whom to vote. But the argument is problematic; it presumes voters would find a third party candidate disruptive rather than useful. To a large degree, it is the two major parties who manage to bridge their differences (amazing how they can do that when electoral consequences are at stake!), uniting in their opposition to third party candidates' participation. They fear participation by a third party candidate could hurt their candidate's chances, adding nettlesome unpredictability to the debate encounter. There is historical basis for skepticism about third parties. Third parties have fared poorly in American elections, and there are structural advantages that favor the major two parties. At the same time, the 15 percent rule guarantees that debate arguments will be framed around familiar issues, with candidates reluctant to go outside the partisan box to stake out innovative, status quo-challenging proposals.

CONCLUSIONS

Presidential debates are media events that bestride the fall campaign like a colossus. However, as research indicates, they are more media spin and hype than contests that significantly shape campaign outcomes. One of the myths, prominently and predictably highlighted by the news, is that debate are of monumental significance for the campaign. Although debates do have benefits and can exert broad, sometimes positive effects on voters, they do not ordinarily turn the tide for one candidate rather than another.

Debates serve different, sometimes conflicting functions for candidates, voters, and the political system. For the larger system, debates are ideally exercises in civic education that help the nation come to grips with complex, contested issues, while also exerting a civilizing effect on a contentious election. Although presidential debates are not debates in the classic sense of the term, they offer a joint appearance of two or more candidates discussing issues, and rebutting one another's claims, with minimal filtering from the press.

Debates represent high-stakes encounters for presidential candidates. Candidates usually prepare extensively and focus endlessly on optics and appearances. Consultants play the expectations game, trying to tamp down expectations for their candidate, such that a less-than-stellar performance can be declared a success. It is all a part of strategic spin. The three major debate formats—press conference, single moderator, and town hall meeting—have benefits and shortcomings, with debates now occurring in the pre-primary, primary, and general election campaigns, so much so that by the end of the primaries, voters are exhausted by the panoply of predictable, frequently uncivil candidate clashes.

More than a half century of research on presidential debates, from Kennedy-Nixon to Clinton-Trump, has yielded a host of conclusions that speak to the important roles played by image projection (so accepted it is a debate meme), narrative, argumentation, nonverbal appropriateness, and news media verdicts, although the latter probably have less impact today than in the broadcast news era of a couple decades ago. Although debates rarely change the outcome of an election, they can be consequential, influencing momentum and swaying undecided voters when the race is particularly close.

Presidential debates expand voters' understanding of political issues, influence image assessments, and reinforce preexisting sentiments, expressed in partisans' frequently sarcastic, negative tweets about the opposing candidate. To the extent that debates increase interest in the campaign and encourage supporters to translate attitude into political participation, they exert positive effects on the system.

What is the balance sheet on debates? Are they good for democracy? Or are they a media circus that hype entertaining style over political substance? Both are true. Presidential debates provide voters with exposure to candidates' issue positions and the clash of divergent ideas. They facilitate learning, interpersonal discussion, and political efficacy. Although debates prize likability and can overemphasize nonverbal cues, they offer a glimpse of how a candidate might lead through communication in a media age. And although many lament the showbiz, hyped-up atmosphere of debates, the drama can attract less politically involved voters to the campaign, at least for a time.

Debates have flaws as well. Candidates duck questions, offer sound-bite answers, tell untruths, and avoid discussion of big issues that could advance democracy, for fear their answers could alienate swing voters. And yet debates can help civilize hard-fought campaigns (not always and probably not in 2016), in this way advancing one of democracy's core values: choice through discussion.

A major virtue of debates is they give voters an opportunity to hear candidates explain what they would do as president and their positions on issues, in a format that requires give-and-take and candidate clash. And yet debates frequently disappoint those who hope that a thoughtful, deliberative discussion of issues will emerge. The scope of issues discussed is narrow and candidate positions rarely go outside a predictable range.

Scholars have suggested revitalizing debates with new approaches, like focusing a debate on a narrow topic; featuring a 45-minute candidate debate followed by a British parliamentary-style discussion, with congressional leaders asking feisty questions; or even holding a national contest in which young people compete to ask the most non-standard but thoughtful questions. One of the perennial conundrums of presidential debates is whether third party candidates should participate. One has to balance the benefits of introducing new ideas into a tired format with the drawback of including candidates who could distract voters from the task of deciding which of the two major party contenders is best suited to be president. The obvious appeal of third party contenders is that they could force the debate to focus on outside-the-two-party-box ideas, perhaps bringing disenchanted voters into the electoral process.

Debates, alas, involve trade-offs, hardly surprising since they are both argumentative encounters and political events that occur in a polarized electoral environment. Given their potential, it behooves scholars to dream up ways to improve debate formats so they can be as effective in educating as they are in electioneering—as helpful in offering novel solutions as trotting out the tried-and-true.

POSTSCRIPT

After the lacerating 2016 campaign ended, there were the usual cries for reform. Some critics, concerned about voter ignorance about issues (reinforced by selective exposure to supportive social media), recommended an epistocracy, or government by the knowledgeable (Brennan, 2016; Crain, 2016). Others, lamenting the bracing incivility and rampant negativity, wondered how campaigns got this bad.

But, of course, they always have been "bad," if by that is meant negative, shrill, and caustic. Campaigns are about persuasion, and persuasion is not always—or usually— pretty. At the same time, campaigns provide a systemic mechanism to bring citizens into the political process, mandating communication between elites (a word that now has overwhelmingly negative connotations) and the public. Campaign communication is fraught, complex, good, bad, and everything in between, with interpretation depending on your point of view and sometimes clarified by scholarly theories. To their credit, campaigns can place new issues at the top of the public and policy agendas. To some degree, the 2016 campaign succeeded on this score. It brought the excesses of trade, hardship suffered by marginalized working class Americans, gnawing income inequality, and immigration to the zenith of the campaign agenda at different junctures, thanks to Trump and Sanders. During a time when politicians tune their ears most closely to their active supporters or those who contribute the most to their campaigns (Aldrich, 2013), we watched candidates listen to the needs of voters angry at political elites and fed up with indifference to their concerns. Voter anger, though hyped by the news media, became an agenda-building factor in the campaign, allowing citizens to vent, enabling them to influence the political tableau of the 2016 election. Voter anger and incivility became so pressing that one could easily ignore one of the most significant aspects of the campaign—the nomination of the first woman as a major party candidate, her representation of issues important to many women, and her popular vote victory.

Although Trump raised issues that had been pushed to the background, capturing the respect and affection of millions, he did so in ways that were tawdry, uncivil, disrespectful of the truth (to put it decorously), and undemocratic, as when he charged that the election was rigged, in the absence of evidence, made statements that were false, and threatened to lock up a candidate of the opposition party. Clinton, for her part, could never shake widespread perceptions—some self-inflicted, others media effects, some rooted in gender biases—that she was untrustworthy. She failed to convince battle-ground state voters that she had their interests at heart.

For all the focus on issues salient to voters, important issues were neglected, receiving scant mention by candidates or the media, such as climate change and enduring poverty. Nor was there serious discussion of either the threat posed by North Korea, particularly urgent in view of its successful atomic weapon test in September 2016, or specific ways to solve the conflict in Syria, also important given the region's instability and failure of previous policies to end the slaughter.

Choices are inevitable, trade-offs inescapable, and the focus of a campaign is inevitably (and properly) political. Campaigns are not primarily educational endeavors. They are attempts at persuasion, with deliberation and electioneering always at cross-purposes. Perhaps a more temperate view is appropriate, one that respects the tension between winning a campaign and civic enlightenment. As Ahn, Huckfeldt, and Ryan (2014) note, "In a democratic society, enlightenment is always a work in progress, with inter-mediate outcomes that are always less than perfect." Democratic politics, they soberly but wisely note, always look bad in comparison to utopian, idealistic alternatives, but these alternatives "have thus far proven to be either impossible to realize or dangerous to embrace" (p. 257).

And yet, the recent election, with its verbal savagery, unremitting horse race news of trivial pursuits, and appalling derision of facts, offers a counterpoint to Churchill's time-worn observation that democracy is justified because its ills are less severe than all other forms of government. Democracy is fraying at the edges and showing signs of deterioration. An overwhelming majority of American voters expressed displea-sure at their choices in 2016. In a similar fashion, many French voters, frustrated by their leaders' failure to keep previous promises and dissatisfied with the policies of two starkly different candidates (one favoring strident law and order, the other global capitalism as usual), were thinking of abstaining from voting in the May 2017 pres-idential election runoff (Blaise & Rubin, 2017). Voters across Western democracies have less trust in political institutions, an indication of what Norris (2011) has called "democratic deficits." Even democratic precepts are at risk: A recent study reported that the proportion of young Americans who believe it is absolutely important to live in a democratic nation has dropped from 91 percent in the 1930s to 57 percent today (Brooks, 2017).

To be sure, the online environment, with the ability to engage in instant, two-way com-munication with politicians, news organizations, and fellow citizens, injects the adrena-line of efficacy into the process. People encounter non-supportive political information on Facebook, with as many as 1 in 3 news stories shown on Facebook's News Feed offering viewpoints that conflict with users' own beliefs, far more than they probably came across on TV in the broadcast-news-bestrides-the-earth days (Manjoo, 2015), although it is not clear how often users read or peruse these posts. Partisan selective exposure, particularly by activists who play an influential role in politics, is on the upswing, contributing to polarization and intolerance (Levendusky, 2013). Access to broadband Internet increases exposure to partisan programming, exacerbating political polarization (Lelkes, Sood, & Iyengar, 2017).

The emergence of fake news intensifies the problem. Not only are people more apt to believe fake news that reinforces their viewpoint, but they may be increasingly willing to assimilate ideas that are based on falsehoods, not facts. Democracy requires an acceptance of viewpoints that collide with established views and recognition of the role that empirical facts play in adjudicating policy debates. And while fake news is not yet sufficiently pervasive nor impactful to represent a threat to democratic values, it signals looming dark clouds. When political leaders deride empirical truths, ranging from climate change to the size of the inauguration, insisting on "alternative facts," as the Trump administration did (though they are not the only ones), or argue that the media is "the opposition party" (Grynbaum, 2017), foundational assumptions of democracy become unglued.

A 2016 *New Yorker* cartoon captured the problem. The cartoon showed a game show with contestants at a lectern, separated from the moderator by a screen with the words in capitals: FACTS DON'T MATTER, and the caption: "I'm sorry, Jeannie, your answer was correct, but Kevin shouted his incorrect answer over yours, so he gets the points" (*The New Yorker*, 2016).

It would be funny if the problem were not so serious. Still, humor is a salve, pointing out that all is not lost, reminding us that democracy has always been imperiled; the public, media, and leaders have a long history of flaws; and, with appreciation of its contemporary limitations and attention to thoughtful improvements, democracy can be strengthened. The question is how this can be accomplished and how anger can be translated to activism in a timely fashion, as economic, environmental, and global terrorist threats loom large.

REFERENCES

Ahn, T.K., Huckfeldt, R., & Ryan, J.B. (2014). *Experts, activists, and democratic politics: Are electorates self-educating?* New York: Cambridge University Press.

Aldrich, J.H. (2013). Partisan polarization and satisfaction with democracy. In D.M. Shea & M.P. Fiorina (Ed.), *Can we talk? The rise of rude, nasty, stubborn politics* (pp. 121–141). New York: Pearson.

Auer, J.J. (1962). The counterfeit debates. In S. Kraus (Ed.), *The great debates: Kennedy vs. Nixon, 1960* (pp. 142–150). Bloomington: Indiana University Press.

Baumgartner, J.C., & Francia, P.L. (2016). *Conventional wisdom and American elections: Exploding myths, exploring misconceptions* (3rd ed.). Lanham, MD: Rowman & Littlefield.

Baumgartner, J.C., Morris, J.S., & Walth, N.L. (2012). The Fey effect: Young adults, political humor, and perceptions of Sarah Palin in the 2008 presidential election campaign. *Public Opinion Quarterly, 76*, 95–104.

Beattie, G. (2016). How Donald Trump bullies with his body language. In D. Lilleker, E. Thorsen, D. Jackson, & A. Veneti (Eds.), *US election analysis 2016: Media, voters and the campaign: Early reflections from leading academics* (p. 30). Poole, England: Centre for the Study of Journalism, Culture and the Community.

Benoit, W.L. (2007). *Communication in political campaigns*. New York: Peter Lang.

Benoit, W.L. (2014a). The functional theory of political campaign communication. In K. Kenski & K.H. Jamieson (Eds.), *The Oxford handbook of political communication*. New York: Oxford University Press.

Benoit, W.L. (2014b). *Political election debates: Informing voters about policy and character*. Lanham, MD: Lexington Books.

Benoit, W.L., Hansen, G.J., & Verser, R.M. (2003). A meta-analysis of the effects of viewing U.S. presidential debates. *Communication Monographs, 70*, 335–350.

Benoit, W.L., & Harthcock, A. (1999). Functions of the great debates: Acclaims, attacks, and defenses in the 1960 presidential debates. *Communication Monographs, 66*, 341–357.

Berquist, G. (1994). The 1976 Carter-Ford presidential debates. In R.V. Friedenberg (Ed.), *Rhetorical studies of national political debates, 1960- 1992* (2nd ed., pp. 29–44). Westport, CT: Praeger.

Birdsell, D.S. (2014). Political campaign debates. In K. Kenski & K.H. Jamieson (Eds.), *The Oxford handbook of political communication*. Retrieved from www.oxfordhandbooks.com. (Accessed July 30, 2016).

Blaise, L., & Rubin, A.J. (2017, May 1). France's poor and disillusioned may skip vote, helping Le Pen. *The New York Times*, A1, A10.

Brennan, J. (2016). *Against democracy*. Princeton, NJ: Princeton University Press.

Brooks, D. (2017, April 21). The crisis of western civ. *The New York Times*, A25.

Bruni, F. (2012, October 2), Trembling before Mitt. *The New York Times*, A27.

Carlin, D.B., & McKinney, M.S. (1994). *The 1992 presidential debates in focus*. Westport, CT: Praeger.

Chappell, T. (1998). Platonism. In R. Chadwick (Ed.), *Encyclopedia of applied ethics* (Vol. 3, pp. 511–523). San Diego: Academic Press.

Cho, J., & Ha, Y. (2012). On the communicative underpinnings of campaign effects: Presidential debates, citizen communication, and polarization in evaluations of candidates. *Political Communication, 29*, 184–204.

Crain, C. (2016, November 7). None of the above. *The New Yorker*, 67–71.

Dayan, D., & Katz, E. (1992). *Media events: The live broadcasting of history*. Cambridge, MA: Harvard University Press.

Donaldson, G. (2007). *The first modern campaign: Kennedy, Nixon, and the election of 1960*. Lanham, MD: Rowman & Littlefield.

Gong, Z.H., & Bucy, E.P. (2016). When style obscures substance: Visual attention to display appropriateness in the 2012 presidential debates. *Communication Monographs, 83*, 349–372.

Grynbaum, M.M. (2017, January 27). Media bashed again, as chief strategist piles on. *The New York Times*, A1, A16.

Hahn, D.F. (1994). The 1992 Clinton-Bush-Perot presidential debates. In R.V. Friedenberg (Ed.), *Rhetorical studies of national political debates, 1960–1992* (2nd ed., pp. 187–210). Westport, CT: Praeger.

Harwood, J. (2012, October 1). Using debates to turn electoral tide is difficult but not impossible. *The New York Times*, A12.

Healy, P., & Flegenheimer, M. (2016, August 30). Clinton piles up research in bid to needle Trump. *The New York Times*, A1, A15.

Hellweg, S.A., Pfau, M., & Brydon, S.R. (1992). *Televised presidential debates: Advocacy in contemporary America.* New York: Praeger.

Hillygus, D.S., & Jackman, S. (2003). Voter decision making in Election 2000: Campaign effects, partisan activation, and the Clinton legacy. *American Journal of Political Science, 47*, 583–596.

Hinck, E.A. (1993). *Enacting the presidency: Political argument, presidential debates, and presidential character.* Westport, CT: Praeger.

Holbrook, T.M. (1999). Political learning from presidential debates. *Political Behavior, 21*, 67–89.

Jamieson, K.H., & Birdsell, D.S. (1988). *Presidential debates: The challenge of creating an informed electorate.* New York: Oxford University Press.

Jamieson, K.H., & Waldman, P. (2003). *The press effect: Politicians, journalists, and the stories that shape the political world.* New York: Oxford University Press.

Jennings, F., Coker, C., McKinney, M., & Warner, B. (2017). Tweeting presidential primary debates: Debate processing through motivated Twitter instruction. *American Behavioral Scientist*. doi:10.1177/0002764217704867. Retrieved from journals.sagepub.com/home/abs (Accessed April 9, 2017).

Katz, E., Blumler, J.G., & Gurevitch, M. (1974). Preliminary overview—Utilization of mass communication by the individual. In J.G. Blumler & E. Katz (Eds.), *The uses of mass communications: Current perspectives on gratifications research* (pp. 19–32). Beverly Hills, CA: Sage.

Klapper, J.T. (1960). *The effects of mass communication.* New York: Free Press.

Koblin, J. (2015, August 8). Republicans set record, outdrawing elite sports. *The New York Times*, A13.

Koblin, J. (2016, October 21). Final debate is watched by 71 million. *The New York Times*, A15.

Kraus, S. (1988). *Televised presidential debates and public policy.* Hillsdale, NJ: Lawrence Erlbaum Associates.

Kraus, S. (1996). Winners of the first 1960 televised presidential debate between Kennedy and Nixon. *Journal of Communication, 46*(4), 78–96.

Lelkes, Y., Sood, G., & Iyengar, S. (2017). The hostile audience: The effect of access to broadband Internet on partisan affect. *American Journal of Political Science, 61*, 5–20.

Lemert, J.B., Elliott, W.R., Bernstein, J.M., Rosenberg, W.L., & Nestvold, K.J. (1991). *News verdicts, the debates, and presidential campaigns.* New York: Praeger.

Leonhardt, D. (2016, October 20). The debates were a failure of journalism. *The New York Times.* Retrieved from www.nytimes.com/2016/10/20/opinion/campaign-stops/the-debates-were-a-failure-of-journalism.html? (Accessed January 26, 2017).

Levendusky, M. (2013). *How partisan media polarize America.* Chicago: University of Chicago Press.

Manjoo, F. (2015, May 8). Facebook finds opposing views trickle through. *The New York Times,* A1, B7.

Martel, M. (1983). *Political campaign debates: Images, strategies, and tactics.* New York: Longman.

McKinney, M. S. (2005). Engaging citizens through presidential debates: Does the format matter? In M. S. McKinney, L. L. Kaid, D. G. Bystrom, & D. B. Carlin (Eds.), *Communicating politics: Engaging the public in democratic life* (pp. 209–221). New York: Peter Lang.

McKinney, M. S., & Carlin, D. B. (2004). Political campaign debates. In L. L. Kaid (Ed.), *Handbook of political communication research* (pp. 203–234). Mahwah, NJ: Lawrence Erlbaum Associates.

McKinney, M. S., Rill, L. A., & Watson, R. G. (2011). Who framed Sarah Palin? Viewer reactions to the 2008 vice presidential debate. *American Behavioral Scientist, 55,* 212–231.

Miller, A. H., & MacKuen, M. (1979). Informing the electorate: A national study. In S. Kraus (Ed.), *The great debates: Carter vs. Ford, 1976* (pp. 269–297). Bloomington: Indiana University Press.

Mutz, D. C. (2015). *In-your-face politics: The consequences of uncivil media.* Princeton, NJ: Princeton University Press.

Nagourney, A., Parker, A., Rutenberg J., & Zeleny, J. (2012, November 8). How a race in the balance went to Obama. *The New York Times,* P1, P14.

The New Yorker. (2016, December 5), 59.

Norris, P. (2011). *Democratic deficit: Critical citizens revisited.* New York: Cambridge University Press.

Patterson, T. E. (1980). *The mass media election: How Americans choose their president.* New York: Praeger.

Perloff, R. M. (1998). *Political communication: Politics, press, and public in America.* Mahwah, NJ: Lawrence Erlbaum Associates.

Perloff, R. M. (2016, September 23). How a debate turning point allowed circus to come to town. *The Plain Dealer,* E2.

Polsby, N. W., Wildavsky, A., Schier, S. E., & Hopkins, D. A. (2012). *Presidential elections: Strategies and structures of American politics* (13th ed.). Lanham, MD: Rowman & Littlefield.

Poniewozik, J. (2016, September 27). How the split screen framed Trump and Clinton. *The New York Times.* Retrieved from www.nytimes.com/2016/09/28/arts/television/presidential-debate-donald-trump-hillary-clinton.html?_r=08module . . . (Accessed January 24, 2017).

Preble, C. A. (2004). *John F. Kennedy and the missile gap.* DeKalb: Northern Illinois University Press.

Reeves, R. (2009, February 10). Missile gaps and other broken promises. *The New York Times.* Retrieved from https://100days.blogs.nytimes.com/2009/02/10/missile-gaps-and-other-broken-promises/?_r=0 (Accessed April 1, 2017).

Ritter, K., & Henry, D. (1994). The 1980 Reagan-Carter presidential debate. In R. V. Friedenberg (Ed.), *Rhetorical studies of national political debates, 1960–1992* (2nd ed., pp. 69–93). Westport, CT: Praeger.

Sears, D. O., & Chaffee, S. H. (1979). Uses and effects of the 1976 debates: An overview of empirical studies. In S. Kraus (Ed.), *The great debates: Carter vs. Ford, 1976* (pp. 223–261). Bloomington: Indiana University Press.

Seiter, J. S., Weger, H., Jr., Kinzer, H. J., & Jensen, A. S. (2009). Impression management in televised debates: The effect of background nonverbal behavior on audience perceptions of debaters' likeability. *Communication Research Reports, 26*, 1–11.

Sides, J., & Vavreck, L. (2013). *The gamble: Choice and chance in the 2012 presidential election*. Princeton, NJ: Princeton University Press.

Simon, R. (1990). *Road show*. New York: Farrar, Straus, Giroux.

Stimson, J. A. (2004). *Tides of consent: How public opinion shapes American politics*. Cambridge: Cambridge University Press.

Stockman, F. (2016, October 21). Clinton arrives as a crusader for all women. *The New York Times*, A1, A17.

Tuman, J. S. (2008). *Political communication in American campaigns*. Thousand Oaks, CA: Sage.

Vernon, P., & Spike, C. (2016). Analysing debate questions: Is it time to rethink the town hall? In D. Lilleker, E. Thorsen, D. Jackson, & A. Veneti (Eds.), *US election analysis 2016: Media, voters and the campaign: Early reflections from leading academics* (p. 31). Poole, England: Centre for the Study of Journalism, Culture and the Community.

Warner, B. R., & McKinney, M. S. (2016, September/November). Debating the presidency. *Spectra, 52*(3&4), 34–39.

White, T. H. (1962). *The making of the president 1960*. New York: Athenaeum.

Zarefsky, D. (1990). *Lincoln Douglas and slavery: In the crucible of public debate*. Chicago: University of Chicago Press.

Glossary

Agenda: issue or event that is perceived at a particular point in time as high in importance. The public agenda consists of the issues that the public views as most important, while the policy agenda concerns issues that top the priority list of political leaders.

Agenda-building: the process through which policy agendas, or the political priorities of political elites, develop and are influenced by factors such as the media agenda and public opinion.

Agenda-setting: the process through which media communicate the importance or salience of issues to the public, influencing public perceptions of the most important issues facing the nation or a community.

Bandwagon storyline: tendency of the press to provide more favorable coverage to a candidate who is gaining ground.

Biased processing: processing strategy by which individuals interpret messages through the filtering lens of their own attitudes, evaluating messages in ways that confirm their preexisting biases.

Branding: process of creating a distinctive product image, in this case a unique, cultivated political image created and constructed through persuasion and marketing.

Campaign contributions: money others give to a candidate's campaign that, according to a 1976 Supreme Court decision, could be limited.

Campaign expenditures: money candidates spend on campaigns that, according to a 1976 Supreme Court decision, could not be limited.

Candidate schema: see **schema**.

Caucus: a local public gathering where party members publicly deliberate about candidates, decide which presidential candidate they will support, and choose delegates to the nominating convention.

Central processing route: pathway to persuasion by which individuals carefully, systematically, or deeply process a persuasive message.

Checks and balances: the classic notion, derived from the framing of the U.S. Constitution, that different branches of government check each other to protect one group from gaining too much power, theoretically balancing one another out. While checks and balances help prevent one government branch from dominating, they also promote gridlock and lack of legislative action in Congress.

Citizens United: 2010 Supreme Court decision that ruled the government cannot prohibit spending by corporations and unions in elections. The decision expanded free speech, a clearly positive outcome. However, it also increased the likelihood that special interest money could corrupt the political process.

Classical Greek direct democracy: as expounded in ancient Athens, this philosophical approach emphasizes direct citizen participation in politics, equality in theory (though not in practice), and citizens' obligation to contribute to the common good of the community. It also emphasizes the role played by rhetorical debate and formulation of reasoned arguments about justice.

Comparative political communication: the study of political media processes and effects as they occur in different countries, with a focus on a nation's distinctive media and political systems, as well as how the economic and political structure of a country's media structure influences political media content.

Constructionism: an approach to political media effects, combining psychological and mass communication approaches, that examines how people actively construct meaning from media messages.

Content analysis: a systematic method to quantitatively examine the characteristics, themes, and symbols in a communication.

Cultivation: classic mass communication theory of how media convey a culture's dominant narratives, instilling these beliefs in citizens through a broad process of political socialization.

Debate: a confrontation between matched adversaries on a particular proposition to gain the decision of an audience, typically a judge evaluating debate arguments according to specific criteria.

Delegate: an individual who attends the nominating convention and formally casts a vote for a candidate. Most delegates are chosen through the primaries and caucuses; elite superdelegates are elected officials and influential members of parties.

Deliberation: a process where citizens engage in the expression of reasoned opinions to find solutions to common problems and assess those solutions.

Deliberative democracy: a contemporary perspective on democratic theory that emphasizes the importance of organized deliberation on issues; citizens' articulation of cogent arguments that can be publicly justified and exert an impact on policy; and communications that promote reflection and collective dialogue on politics.

Democracy: a form of government that, in its bare-bones form, emphasizes rule of the people. Numerous, more complex perspectives on democracy have been formulated over the years. They stipulate, in the main, that democracy mandates the right of all citizens to vote, free and fair elections that involve more than one political party, freedom of expression, including freedom for those who oppose the party in power, and protection of human rights, notably those of minorities.

Elaboration Likelihood Model: social psychological model of persuasion that emphasizes cognitive processes. Applied to politics, the model suggests that political persuasion strategies flow from the ways that voters process messages, with voters processing messages peripherally, centrally, and via biased evaluations.

Electability narrative: news media frame that evaluates and interprets candidate performance in presidential primaries in terms of their electability or chances of capturing the nomination.

Elite democratic theory: a perspective asserting that democracy involves a competition among elite groups or influential political parties. Elite democracy emphasizes that citizens can fulfill their democratic function simply by exercising their obligation to vote for or against different elites.

Elites: leaders; influential individuals who wield power, as a function of income, status, or political connections.

Emphasis frame: a frame frequently employed in political communication that highlights message features that do not contain equivalent information and vary in the way the problem is defined and evaluated.

Equivalence frame: a type of frame in which identical information is presented differently through adroit use of logically equivalent, but differently phrased, information.

Exceeding expectations narrative: news media storyline that focuses on whether candidates have done better than expected, an amorphous criteria by which candidates who exceed expectations gain positive press.

Experiment: a controlled study that provides evidence of causation through random assignment of individuals to a treatment or control group.

Fake news: a fabricated story created with an intention to deceive, either to gain profitable clicks or promote a political ideology. Fake news has become an increasing problem in the era of online political news, though it its impact is less consequential than sometimes assumed.

Family communication patterns: ways in which parents communicate politics to children, primarily by emphasizing harmony or encouraging concept exploration.

Figurative frame: a type of frame that emphasizes conceptual metaphors, hyperbole, and irony.

Frame: the central organizing theme of a narrative on a political issue, harnessed by leaders, media, and public to explain events.

Framing: selecting particular aspects of an issue and making connections in ways that emphasize a particular political definition, evaluation, or remedy.

Front-runner storyline: tendency of news media to provide more coverage of the front-runner in a presidential election, as well as more critical press.

Gatekeeping: process by which media filter and screen information, using diverse criteria, determining the news that will reach citizens of a democracy.

Gendered double-bind: sexist notion that women political candidates cannot be both professionally competent and feminine.

Heuristic: mental shortcut used to help an individual make a political decision, such as voting.

Horse race news: press coverage that emphasizes who is ahead, polls, and the strategic game, in the manner of a classic horse race.

Hostile media bias: psychological perception that occurs when people with strong political attitudes presume media coverage is biased against their side and in favor of their antagonists.

Hypothesis: a specific prediction, ideally derived from a theory, that can be tested through empirical study.

Hyperreality: postmodern concept of political reality emphasizing murky, seamless combination of false and actual content, and the central role mediated representations play in communicating politics.

Intermedia agenda-setting: the impact that news coverage from particular, traditionally elite media outlets exerts on coverage by other media in a community, state, or country.

Involvement: personal relevance of an election or issue.

Irony: a complex comedic device that uses language to suggest an incongruity between the surface and deeper meanings of an event.

Knowledge gap: a philosophically problematic situation in which media exacerbate existing differences in knowledge between the "haves," or individuals high in socioeconomic status, and the "have-nots," or those lower in education and status.

Liberal democracy: the classical libertarian approach that emphasizes the importance of preserving individual liberties and politics as a marketplace of ideas, in which truth emerges, as Mill put it, through its collision with falsehood.

Limited effects model: a model of mass communication effects stipulating that political media have minimal impact, with reinforcement of existing attitudes their primary influence. A controversial view, it has been discredited, yet revitalized recently, viewed as offering insights into contemporary political media effects.

Losing ground storyline: the ways the press narrative changes to increasingly describe a candidate once seen as a contender for the party nomination as inexorably losing ground.

Mainstreaming: cultivation theory concept suggesting that exposure to mediated, typically televised portrayals of politics overrides diverse orientations viewers bring to the experience, accentuating similarities among different viewers, cultivating a belief in the dominant cultural viewpoint.

Microtargeting: analytic and marketing strategy whereby candidates target niche audiences, tailoring appeals to match a particular group or specific individuals, mining online information to direct appeals to ever-smaller marketing segments.

Mobilization: political strategy whereby candidates try to persuade their base of core supporters to vote, using social judgment and other persuasion theory appeals.

Narrative: see **storyline**.

Normative theory: a theory that prescribes or suggests how life ought to be lived; in the present case, a guiding political philosophy that offers prescriptive guidelines for democracy and political communication.

Observational learning: process of political socialization by which children and adolescents acquire political attitudes and behaviors by vicarious observation of political role models.

Opinion leader: influence agent that can shape audience attitudes, via interpersonal communication or online technologies, like social media.

Opposition research: intensive research conducted by political consultants to locate liabilities, inconsistencies, and sexual skeletons in the opponent's record. It is practically useful but ethically questionable.

Peripheral processing route: pathway to persuasion by which individuals process information quickly, superficially, and via heuristics or simple decision rules.

Political communication: a complex, communicative activity in which language and symbols, employed by leaders, media, citizens, and citizen groups, exert a multitude of effects on individuals and society, as well as on outcomes that bear on the public policy of a nation, state, or community.

Political marketing: application of marketing principles to politics, with the political product a complex combination of the candidate, policy positions, and (strategically) branded image, communicated to voters and citizens through multiple media channels.

Political news bias: a consistent media pattern in presentation of an issue, in a way that reliably favors one side, or minimizes the opposing side, in a context where it can reasonably be argued that there are other perspectives on the issue that are also deserving of coverage.

Political rhetoric: verbal content, argumentation, symbolic components, and stylistic features of public communication intended to persuade, spanning rhetoric in ancient Greece to political speeches today.

Political socialization: the manner in which a society transmits knowledge, norms, attitudes, and values about politics, from generation to generation, preserving continuity and ideally facilitating change.

Politics: the public clash and debate among groups (who have different degrees of power) regarding resources, visions, and policies, with the goal of reaching broad-based decisions that are binding on and may benefit the larger collective.

Poll: a sample survey of the electorate or citizenry that can convey valuable information about public sentiments to leaders.

Populism: a time-honored political movement that champions the needs of working people, derogates elites, and emphasizes nativist, nationalistic sentiments over global, classically liberal viewpoints,

Presidential debate: the joint appearance by at least two competing presidential candidates, who articulate their positions, with formal rules for refutation of opposing arguments.

Pre-primaries: the first stage of the presidential nomination process, whereby candidates use mass and social media to build a strong base of support, and convince the press (and party elites) they are serious contenders for the presidency.

Press conference debate: presidential debate format where a group of pre-selected reporters asks candidates questions; the questions can be analytical, but can elide issues of interest to voters.

Primary: a state-wide election that gives voters the opportunity to select the party's presidential nominee, using a secret ballot.

Priming: the impact of the media agenda on the criteria voters employ to evaluate candidates for public office.

Propaganda: a form of communication in which the leaders of government have near or total control over the transmission of information, typically relying on mass media deception to influence masses of people.

Public sphere: interpersonal or virtual domain concerned with societal and political topics that transcend private, individual issues. There is debate about whether the public sphere stimulates reasoned debate or rancorous arguments.

Republic: representative democracy; a democratic form of government that derives its legitimacy from citizens' election of other citizens to represent them in policy-making decisions.

Salience: perceived importance of an issue.

Satire: a form of humor that employs ridicule to expose leaders' foibles.

Schema: a mental structure that includes systematic knowledge about situations and people that has been extracted from previous experiences. Schema can be employed by citizens to understand politics and by reporters to make sense of and simplify elections.

Selective exposure: psychological tendency of individuals to tune in to and prefer information that supports their existing political beliefs.

Selective perception: psychological tendency to perceive messages so they are consistent with a preexisting political attitude.

Separation of powers: power is constitutionally shared by three branches of government: the executive (e.g., president), legislative (Congress) and judicial (Supreme Court). This involves a series of checks and balances among the three branches.

Single moderator debate: presidential debate format where one moderator asks questions and serves as umpire; it can reduce chaos, but can break down if order and equity are not maintained.

Social judgment theory: classic psychological theory of attitudes and persuasion that emphasizes the role that preexisting attitudes play in judgments of persuasive messages. Messages are persuasive to the degree they are perceived as congenial with an existing attitude, ineffective if they contradict a core attitude, and capable of influence if they fall into voters' latitude of noncommitment.

Social science: a scientific approach to understanding human cognition and behavior that tests hypotheses derived from theories, using different research methods, to build a body of knowledge.

Spin: promotional, mischievously playful, and ironic contemporary political communication describing political consultants' willful attempts to package a candidate's performance in the best light and, more broadly, the deceptive uses of political persuasion designed to put the best face on a candidate or issue, at the expense of truth.

Storyline: broad framework by which the news interprets and evaluates candidates, offering an interpretive story about a particular presidential candidate or election.

Survey: a questionnaire or interview-based study that seeks to document a correlation or relationship between two or more variables in a real-world setting, identifying factors that can best predict a particular outcome.

Theory: a large, sweeping conceptualization that offers a wide-ranging explanation of a phenomenon and generates concrete hypotheses about when and why specific events will occur.

Town hall debate: presidential debate format that features questions from an audience of voters; it puts citizen questions front and center, but this can be a problem if questions are frivolous or unclear.

Two-step flow: Classic model of communication effects stipulating that media influence opinion leaders, who in turn influence the public via interpersonal or online communication.

Subject Index

Page numbers in italic indicate a figure and page numbers in bold indicate a table.

Author Index